BUILDING STRATEGIES FOR COLLEGE READING

A TEXT WITH THEMATIC READER

— FOURTH EDITION —

Jane L. McGrath

Professor Emerita

Paradise Valley Community College

PEARSON

Prentice Hall

UPPER SADDLE RIVER, NEW JERSEY 07458

Library of Congress Cataloging-in-Publication Data

McGrath, Jane L.
    Building strategies for college reading : a text with thematic reader / Jane L. Mcgrath.—4th ed.
        p. cm.
    Includes bibliographical references (p.) and index.
    ISBN 0-13-184889-5
    1. College readers.   2. Reading (Higher education)   I. Title.
    PE1122.M268 2004
        808'.0427--dc22

                                                                            2004006020

Editorial director: Leah Jewell
Senior acquisitions editor: Craig Campanella
Editorial assistant: Joan Polk
Project liaison: Fran Russello
Permission specialist: Connie Golden
Director of marketing Beth Mejia
Prepress and manufacturing manager: Nick Sklitsis
Prepress and manufacturing buyer: Ben Smith
Creative design director: Leslie Osher
Art director: Carmen DiBartolomeo
Cover/interior design: PreMediaONE, A Black Dot Group Company
Cover art: The Image Bank
Photo researcher: Kathy Ringrose
Image permission coordinator: Debbie Hewitson
Composition/full-service project management: Pine Tree Composition, Inc.
Printer/binder: Von Hoffman Press, Inc
Cover printer: The Lehigh Press, Inc.

Credits and acknowledgments borrowed from other sources and reproduced, with permission, in this textbook appear on pages xi-xii.

Pearson Education LTD. London
Pearson Education Singapore, Pte. Ltd
Pearson Education Canada, Ltd
Pearson Education—Japan
Pearson Education Australia PTY, Limited

Pearson Education North Asia Ltd
Pearson Educación de Mexico, S.A. de C.V.
Pearson Education Malaysia, Pte. Ltd
Pearson Education, Upper Saddle River, New Jersey

10 9 8 7 6

Student Edition:
ISBN 0-13-184889-5

Instructor's Edition:
ISBN 0-13-184894-1

CONTENTS

CHAPTER 5

READING MULTIPARAGRAPH SELECTIONS   120

CHAPTER 6

READING GRAPHICS   154

CHAPTER 7

UNDERSTANDING THE AUTHOR'S POINT OF VIEW   191

CHAPTER 8

ORGANIZING THE INFORMATION YOU NEED   222

PREFACE

If we are going to talk about teaching reading comprehension, then we are going to have to look for methods of teaching that create active rather than passive readers. . . . Learners must be provided with materials that motivate them to become actively involved in constructing meaning, strategic guidance and support when their own repertoire of strategies is not adequate, a connection to writing as a similar meaning-making activity, questions and discussion that help them focus on both the content being created and the strategy being used, and meaningful interactions with other readers so that meanings and strategies can be shared.

(Irwin, J. W. *Teaching Reading Comprehension Processes*,
2nd ed. 1991. Upper Saddle River, NJ: Prentice Hall.)

The revisions in this fourth edition of *Building Strategies for College Reading* evolved from answering the question, What changes will better prepare students to succeed in American history, biology, business, sociology, and every other course of study?

I am convinced that adopting the skills, strategies, attitudes, and habits associated with effective reading are vital for success in college and in life and that those skills, strategies, attitudes, and habits can be developed and improved through relevant and applicable instruction and guided practice. This text provides the foundation for that instruction and practice.

Firmly focused on helping students develop strategies for reading college-level expository prose, this is a "textbook" reading text: it mirrors typical content-area texts in form and structure, and it includes a wealth of authentic text excerpts and four complete textbook chapters. In addition, its thematic approach promotes a meaningful, connected understanding of topics that allows students to profit from more sophisticated material than is possible with isolated readings.

This text, like the introductory text *Basic Skills and Strategies for College Reading*, second edition, and the next-level text *Strategies for Critical Reading*, encourages students to see themselves as active participants in the reading process—readers who can set and accomplish reading and study goals and objectives. Therefore, *Building Strategies for College Reading*, fourth edition,

- presents detailed instruction in and examples of the reading skills students must master to be successful in college;
- encourages students to develop a repertoire of reading and study strategies and provides guided activities as they learn to select and use different strategies for different tasks;
- provides abundant *authentic* practice with complete articles, essays, text pages, and textbook chapters;
- stresses the importance of transferring skills and strategies to other readings and other classes;

- encourages students to realize that expanding their vocabulary is fundamental to college success;
- provides extensive practice opportunities in four topical thematic units so that as students broaden their conceptual background knowledge, they see themselves as successful readers; and
- persuades students to plan, monitor, and evaluate their own learning.

This explanation of a *skill* and a *strategy* by Alexander and Jetton clarifies how I use the terms in this text: "During the 1970s, when it first dotted the reading landscape, the term strategies signified a form of mental processing that deviated from traditional skills-based reading. However, any distinctions between skill and strategies that seemed apparent then have begun to fade, leaving many to wonder where skills end and strategies begin. As a way to unearth those contrasts, we propose two differences between skillful and strategic processing, relevant to text-based learning: automaticity and intentionality. . . . Skills are, in essence, essential academic habits. They are routinized, automatic procedures we employ when we engage in any nontrivial task. Thus, skilled readers, like skilled cooks or skilled accountants, have honed essential domain procedures to a level of automaticity. . . . The same procedures (e.g., finding main ideas) can fit under both the skill and strategy categories. The appropriate label rests on whether the reader consciously evokes the procedure or is simply functioning in a typical, automatic way." (Alexander, P. A., and T. L. Jetton, "Learning from Text: A Multidimensional and Developmental Perspective." In M. L. Kamil, P. B. Mosenthal, P. D. Pearson, and R. Barr (Eds.), *Handbook of Reading Research*, Vol. III, 2000, Mahwah, NJ: Lawrence Erlbaum, pp. 295–96.)

ORGANIZATION OF THE TEXT

The basic organization remains the same in this edition: nine instructional chapters and four thematic reading units, plus the appendices, glossary and topic index. The text continues to provide an array of authentic reading tasks to prepare students to meet the demands of the texts and tasks they will encounter in future classes.

CHAPTERS

The nine chapters provide instruction in reading skills necessary for effective reading and study. Students practice adapting and using a variety of strategies to help them fulfill their purpose.

Each chapter now begins with an "Idea to Think About" to help students place the topic and the skill in an understandable context before they begin to work. The "At a Glance" chapter outline and the new "Chapter Focus" ask students to look at the chapter as a whole—its main purpose—before they begin to work on the parts.

The paragraphs and multiparagraph expository pieces come from texts, magazines, newspapers, and government publications. Text excerpts include

American government	biology
American history	business

art	business communications
career exploration	the Internet
computers	interpersonal communications
criminal justice	meteorology
earth science	music
economics	personal development
English	personal finance
environmental science	psychology
geography	social problems
health	sociology
health occupations	speech
history	stress management
human relations	

Each chapter ends with a series of "Chapter Review Questions" and the opportunity for more practice and skill assessment in the "Use Your Strategies" sections. A variety of questions and activities to extend thinking are available in "Reflect and Connect" and "Log On to the Web." The Web exercises direct students to Internet sites appropriate to specific tasks. Although all sites were operational at the time this edition went to press, some may be outdated or changed when you are ready to use them.

Themes

The four thematic reading units each include a full textbook chapter—Theme 1, Chapter 16 from *Government by the People,* twentieth edition; Theme 2, Chapter 8 from *Business,* seventh edition; Theme 3, Chapter 5 from *Social Problems,* eleventh edition; Theme 4, Chapter 14 from *Biology: Science for Life*—plus related readings and editorial cartoons on the unifying topic. The book provides an abundant collection of authentic material—more readings than are needed for a quarter or semester—so instructors may select topics and readings to best meet the needs of students.

Each theme begins with an introduction to the topic and the readings. Each selection in the theme begins with information about the author, definitions for unusual vocabulary, and a concept or idea for students to think about as they read. Each selection is followed by vocabulary, comprehension, and reflect and connect questions. Some questions require recall of specific information, while others are more process-oriented. Each theme ends with a "Log On to the Web" activity, "Reflect and Connect" questions, and suggestions for "Further Reading" to encourage students to continue reading and thinking about the topic.

Because the thematic approach supplies multiple exposures to a topic, it provides a scaffolding of knowledge that allows students to handle more sophisticated material than isolated readings might allow. This approach also encourages a more meaningful and connected understanding of a topic and promotes thinking as students view a topic from several perspectives.

NEW TO THE FOURTH EDITION

Instructors who used the third edition will find a variety of small modifications and several major changes in the fourth edition. Included in the major changes are the following:

A new format and look. This edition has a more inviting and text-like appearance. The use of color throughout the book and reprinting the theme's text chapters in full-color should make students more comfortable with transferring skills to other texts and assignments.

Inside the covers. I have added information inside the covers for two reasons: First, it is important information students can use immediately, and Second, since most college textbooks now include important, general information inside the front cover, this feature helps prepare students for other texts.

New chapter elements. Each chapter opens with "An Idea to Think About" to help students place the topic and the skill in an understandable context before they begin to work. In addition, I'm hopeful that this element will help students realize that the chapter-opening features in their other texts—case studies, theoretical scenarios, narratives, anecdotes—are useful. The "Chapter Focus" provides basic research about why the topic is important. To mirror most content texts, heads and subheads are no longer phrased as questions. Please encourage students to rephrase them as part of their preview activity.

Expanded practice on most topics with special emphasis on understanding main ideas and implied main ideas. Although it may be impossible to ever provide "enough" main idea exercises, I have expanded both the discussion and practice of this important skill. In addition, students work on the underlying skill of making inferences before asking them to infer a main idea.

Chapter readings. More than half of the examples and exercises are new to this edition. There is additional emphasis on reading authentic text materials. In each chapter, new practice and "Use Your Strategies" exercises are picked up directly from content area texts. Factors such as student interests, current affairs, readability level, and writing style influence my selection of readings.

Themes. Theme 1, "First Amendment Freedoms," and Theme 4, "Biodiversity," are totally new to this edition and were developed with our students' needs and interests in mind. In Theme 2, "Today's Workplace," and Theme 3, "Violence and Crime," more than half of the readings are new or revised. In addition, all the themes include an editorial cartoon.

IN APPRECIATION

Although my name appears on the cover, many wonderful people contributed to the development and production of this fourth edition. First, I am very grateful to my students. Their enthusiasm and perseverance have always been vital to our classroom successes. My thanks to my colleagues across the Maricopa Community Colleges and across the United States for sharing their ideas and expertise to make this text more useful for students.

For their invaluable reviews of the third edition as I prepared my revision plan for this fourth edition, I am indebted to Pamela C. Leggat, Northern Virginia Community College; Barbara Nixon, Salem Community College; Joan Mauldin, San Jacinto College; and JoAnn Forrest, Prairie State College.

I am thankful for the cadre of dedicated professionals at Prentice Hall and Pine Tree Composition, especially Craig Campanella, senior editor English, Joan Polk, editorial assistant, and John Shannon, production editor, who provided unfailing optimism and support for this three-book revision extravaganza. And, my sincere thanks to Larry McGrath, my partner in all of life's adventures. Without his wisdom, good humor, technical expertise, and encouragement this book would not exist.

And, thank *you* for inviting me into your classroom. I welcome your suggestions and will be delighted to hear your comments at *Jellenjay@aol.com*.

Jane L. McGrath

ABOUT THE AUTHOR

Jane L. McGrath earned her undergraduate degree and M.A. in education and mass communications and her Ed.D. in reading education from Arizona State University. During her more than twenty-five years with the Maricopa Colleges, McGrath taught a variety of reading, English, journalism, and computer applications courses. She was named Innovator of the Year by the Maricopa Colleges and the League for Innovation in Community Colleges for Project Read-Aloud, a college-community service program, and has received Outstanding Citizen awards from the cities of Tempe and Phoenix, Arizona, for her community service activities. McGrath's other books include *Basic Skills and Strategies for College Reading: A Text with Thematic Reader, second edition,* and *Strategies for Critical Reading.* In addition to her work in reading education, McGrath and her husband Larry write for the high-performance automotive industry. Their work has appeared in magazines such as *Drag Racing Today* and *Circle Track,* and their monthly column appears in *Performance Racing Industry.*

CREDITS LIST

"The Scope & Method of Economics"; "Excess Supply" Case, Karl E.; Fair, Ray C., Principles of Economics, Updated Edition, 6th Edition, © 2003. Reprinted by permission of Pearson Education, Inc., Upper Saddle River, NJ.

"How To Read Faster" by Bill Cosby source Power of Printed Word Series Reprinted with permission of International Paper Company.

Excerpt: "Industry and the North, 1790s-1840s" pp206-208 Faragher, John Mack; Buhle, Mari Jo; Czitrom, Daniel; Armitage, Susan H., Out of Many, Brief Edition, Combined, 3rd Edition, © 2001. Reprinted by permission of Pearson Education, Inc., Upper Saddle River, JN.

"Groups and Organizations pp163-165 by Macionis, John J., Sociology, 9th Edition, © 2003. Reprinted by permission of Pearson Education, Inc., Upper Saddle River, NJ.

Dictionary definitions Webster's New World Dictionary, 3rd College Ed.

"Applying: The Sociology of Sport" pp18-20 by Macionis, John J., Sociology, 9th Edition, © 2003. Reprinted by permission of Pearson Education, Inc., Upper Saddle River, NJ.

"Hummingbirds: Jewels on Wings" 1988 by Robert L. McGrath as appeared in FEDCO Reporter.

"Earth-Sun Relationships" p28 Lutgens, Frederick K.; Tarbuck, Edward J., Atmosphere, The: An Introduction to Meteorology, 8th Edition, © 2001. Reprinted by permission of Pearson Education, Inc., Upper Saddle River, NJ.

"Structural Changes in the U.S. Economy" p309. Macionis, John J., Social Problems (Hardcover), 1st Edition, ©2002. Reprinted by permission of Pearson Education, Inc., Upper Saddle River, NJ.

"Have a Good Night" by Robert L. McGrath, source A Better Life for You.

"Nonverbal Communication" p150 DuBrin, Andrew J., Human Relations for Career and Personal Success, 5th Edition, © 1999. Reprinted by permission of Pearson Education, Inc., Upper Saddle River, JN.

"Debate and Compromise" p48 Berman, Larry; Murphy, Bruce Allen, Approaching Democracy (Electronic Reprint), 3rd Edition, © 2001. Reprinted by permission of Pearson Education, Inc., Upper Saddle River, NJ.

"Running the Small Business: Reasons for Successes & Failures" pp185-191by Griffin, Ricky W.; Ebert, Ronald J., Business, 5th Edition, © 1999. Reprinted by permission of Pearson Education, Inc., Upper Saddle River, NJ.

Excerpt: "The Early Romantics" p191 text only (permissions does not include illustrations that may be original to another source) Meyer, Donald C., Perspectives On Music, 1st Edition, ©2003s. Reprinted by permission of Pearson Education, Inc., Upper Saddle River NJ.

"Common Types of Interview Questions" p248-249 Bienvenu, Sherron; Timm, Paul R., Business Communication: Discovering Strategy, Developing Skills, 1st Edition, ©2002. Reprinted by permission of Pearson Education, Inc., Upper Saddle River, NJ.

"Making the Grade in College" by Jana Lynn.

"Special Nutritional Needs of Athletes and Active Individuals" by Greenberg and Dintiman with permission of Prentice Hall.

"Happiness is First Things First" by Linda Weltner The Boston Globe 8/21/98.

"How to Punctuate" by Russell Baker, The Power of Printed Word.

"Why Preserve Biodiversity?" p15 by Audesirk, Teresa; Audesirk, Gerald; Byers, Bruce E., Biology: Life On Earth, 6th Edition, © 2002. Reprinted by permission of Pearson Education, Inc., Upper Saddle River, JN.

"Prest-o! Change-o!" by Jimmy Tomlin, Sky Magazine.

"Glittering Alice; Sad Eleanor" by Richard Cohen ©1980 The Washington Post, The Washington Post Writers Group Reprinted with Permission.

"Alcohol and Other Drugs" pp228-229 Social Problems (Hardcover), by Macionis, John J., 1st Edition © 2003, Reprinted by permission of Pearson Education, Inc., Upper Saddle River, NJ.

"Excess Supply" Case, Karl E.; Fair, Ray C., Principles of Economics, Updated Edition, 6th Edition, © 2003. Reprinted by permission of Pearson Education, Inc., Upper Saddle River, NJ.

Excerpt & Figure 6.5 © 1991 Business 2/e by Griffin & Ebert.

Excerpt & Figure 2-1 © 1991, Introduction to Geography by Bergman and McKnight.

Excerpt & Figure 19-2 ©1991, Business 2/e by Griffin & Ebert.

Excerpt & Figure 20-3 © 1991, Business 2/e by Griffin & Ebert.

Figure 2.17 pp 39. Rice, Laura Williams; Rice, Robert P., Practical Horticulture, 5th Edition, © 2003. Reprinted by permission of Pearson Education, Inc., Upper Saddle River, NJ.

Excerpt and 2 Illustrations p360 ©1991 Discovering Philosophy by White.

"Seven Steps to Safer Sunning" by Paula Kurtzweil, FDA Consumer.

Excerpt & Figure 9-27 by Bergman and McKnight, Introduction to Geography.

Excerpt & Figure 7-7 by Winger & Frasca, Personal Finance.

Excerpt & Figure 5-1 by Griffin & Ebert, Business.

Excerpt and Figure 7-1 pp153-154, © 2003, Rice, Laura Williams; Rice, Robert P., Practical Horticulture, 5th Edition, © 2003. Reprinted by permission of Pearson Education, Inc., Upper Saddle River, NJ.

Figure 30.14; Excerpt pp588-589. Freeman, Scott, Biological Science, 1st Edition, © 2002. Reprinted by permission of Pearson Education, Inc., Upper Saddle River, NJ.

Excerpt and Figure 5.8 pp111. Burns, James MacGregor; Peltason, J.W.; Cronin, Thomas E.; Magleby, David B.; O'Brien, David M., Government by The People, National, State, and Local Version, 2001-2002 Edition, 19th Edition, © 2002. Reprinted by permission of Pearson Education, Inc., Upper Saddle River, NJ.

"The Health-Illness Continuum", by Greenberg and Dintiman, Exploring Health.

"The Fear of Crime" pp60. Schmalleger, Frank, Criminal Justice Today, 6th Edition, © 2001. Reprinted by permission of Pearson Education, Inc., Upper Saddle River, NJ.

"Execution Has Benefit Doesn't It?", by E.J. Montini. Reprinted by permission Phoenix Newspapers, Inc.

"Computers Can't Teach Awareness", by Liz Caile, The Mountain Ear, May, 1992.

Excerpt from Computers & Information Processing 3/e ©1991, by Fuori and Gioia.

"Why I Don't Compute" by Roger Rosenblatt, Modern Maturity.

"How to Write With Style" by Kurt Vonnegut.

The Big Picture: Approaching Reading as a Process

Map out your future, but do it in pencil.

—Jon Bon Jovi

AN IDEA TO THINK ABOUT

Jake has been trying to shed a few pounds of extra weight and get in shape. He has talked to his doctor, a fitness trainer, and a nutritionist about strategies he can use to help him reach his goals. He's given their advice a lot of thought and enjoys talking to his friends about his plans for changing his behavior. He's reading a book on cooking healthy, low-fat meals. He even made some sacrifices in his budget and bought a top-of-the-line exercise bike.

Unfortunately, Jake hasn't lost any flab.

Why? Although he has learned several reliable strategies and has good intentions, he still spends his evenings eating cheese curls and chips in front of the television. Until Jake starts using some of the strategies regularly, like eating right and riding the bike, he won't make much progress toward his goals.

Don't be like Jake. When you discover new reading and study strategies, adapt them to fit your needs, and use them in your classes and at work.

CHAPTER FOCUS

Reading is often defined as the ability to draw meaning from the printed page and interpret this information accurately and appropriately.

While that single-sentence definition is true, it tends to make reading sound easy. It does not convey the active, multidimensional nature of what you do while you are reading. As Grabe and Stoller (2002) point out, a simple definition of reading

- does not express the many skills, strategies, and knowledge bases you must use in combination, and often in parallel, to create the overall comprehension abilities we call reading; and

- does not convey the idea that you have several possible purposes for reading, and each purpose requires you to use a somewhat different combination of skills and strategies.

Your purposes for reading may include the following:

- Reading to search—when you read to get specific information for a particular purpose;

- Reading for pleasure—when you read material to be entertained;

- Reading for general comprehension—when you read to gain a good understanding of the main ideas, not to remember specific details;

- Reading to learn—when you read to gain a thorough understanding of the main ideas and the significant details that support and develop them in order to increase your knowledge base;

- Reading to integrate information—when you read to synthesize information from multiple sources, identify points of comparison and opposition, assess the relative importance of the information, and compare it with what you know in order to incorporate new information into your knowledge base.

As an example, consider the complex nature of what you do to successfully "read to learn" from one text chapter. Research by Anderson and Armbruster (1984) shows that a single text page can have as many as fifty separate but connected ideas. As a result, to read that one text chapter, you must sort, understand, integrate, and assimilate hundreds of ideas.

But don't be discouraged. It is not an impossible task. You can build a repertoire, or inventory, of reading and study strategies to help you identify, understand, organize, and remember the information you need. Although the distinction between skills and strategies is not always clear, I think of a skill as something you perform automatically and a **strategy** as a technique you consciously select to complete a task accurately and efficiently.

Just as the skilled carpenter must equip a toolbox with a large assortment of specialized tools to be able to select just the right ones to do each job, you need a toolbox jam-packed with reading and study strategies so you can select the ones appropriate to each task.

This chapter introduces a collection of strategies you can add to your reading toolbox. As you read about these strategies, compare and contrast them with the strategies you use. The more aware you are of your current reading process, the easier it is to add new strategies. And, the more strategies you have to select from, the more likely you can match the appropriate ones to your reading tasks.

APPROACHING READING AS A PROCESS

When you sit down to write a multiparagraph essay or report, you don't expect the first words you type, from the opening word of the introduction to the final word of the conclusion, to be your finished product. Because writing is a process, you expect to use a variety of prewriting, writing, rethinking, revising, and editing strategies before you have a final document that meets your purpose.

Reading is also a process. Therefore, you cannot expect to read straight through from the first word of an assignment to the last word and understand everything the author says and means. Depending on your purpose and the difficulty level of the material, you should expect to use a variety of prereading, reading, and reviewing strategies to accomplish your purpose.

For example, when you pick up a newspaper, you are usually reading for general comprehension. You probably want to finish the newspaper fairly rapidly, since few people try to read every line or even every article in a newspaper. That means you typically read a page with some combination of searching and general reading, letting the headlines act as cues. When one catches your interest, you probably check the length of the article, consider what you already know about the subject, and then read through a number of paragraphs to understand the information. When you decide you have enough information, you stop reading the article. If you want to remember the information to be able to tell a friend, you probably review important ideas or significant details before you put the paper away.

Anytime you read, you make important decisions about what you want to know and what combination of strategies will help you successfully gather that information. In fact, researchers have found that a primary characteristic of skilled readers is that they flexibly apply multiple reading strategies in a purposeful manner. These include **planning strategies** such as setting a purpose and goals for reading and making predictions about what the author will say; reading strategies such as varying reading style according the difficulty and purpose; and reviewing strategies such as paraphrasing summarizing (Pressley & Afflerbach, 1995; Pressley, Brown, El-Dinary, & Afflerbach, 1995; Wyatt et al., 1993).

In this chapter I have organized a variety of prereading, reading, and reviewing strategies under three major categories: plan, do, and review.

WHY PLAN → DO → REVIEW?

Everyone looks for ways to be successful. American executives strive to compete with aggressive competitors, teachers seek ways to enrich student learning, and students like you look for ways to improve academic performance.

I believe that one key to improving performance—on a widget production line or on a sociology chapter—is viewing the task as a cycle of activity:

- You plan what you need to do.
- You implement your plan.
- You review how well you did.
- Based on what you accomplished and what still needs to be done, you revise your plan and continue the cycle.

Plan→Do→Review Cycle

Plan to Read
    Preview the selection.
    Clarify your specific purpose for reading.
    Activate prior knowledge.
    Estimate how difficult the material is for you.

Do the Reading
    Monitor your comprehension as you read.
        Restate ideas in your own words.
        Compare what you are reading to what you know.
        Answer questions.
    If you don't understand, stop and clarify.
        Define unfamiliar words.
        Review graphics.
        Read surrounding paragraphs.
        Seek help.

Review What You Read
    Answer questions.
    Determine what else you need to know and repeat cycle.
    Test yourself.
    Participate in a study group.
    Consolidate and integrate information.

For example, let's say you develop a plan to read a section in your psychology text chapter to be able to list and explain the three psychological dimensions of our visual world. When you finish reading, you can recall and explain only two: hue and brightness. So, you develop and implement a plan to find and reread the portion of the chapter on the third element. When you finish rereading, you review the information you gained on saturation as well as the previous information on hue and brightness. Then, depending on what you must do with the information, you construct a schedule to regularly review all the information.

The next pages outline specific strategies of the **Plan → Do → Review cycle** and how to use them.

Plan to Read

When you get a writing assignment, you probably take time to consider what you know about the topic, think about the different approaches you could use, and speculate about what kind of information you might need to gather *before* you ever begin to write. Now, compare that with how you typically begin a reading assignment. If you're like many students, you simply begin reading. You wait for the author's message to unfold.

This is because we typically view writing as active but reading as passive. That is, we think of writers as actively producing something, while we think of readers as passive consumers of information. However, reading is *not* a passive activity. Reading is an active, thinking process of understanding an author's ideas, connecting those ideas to what you already know, and then organizing all the ideas so you can remember and use them.

Planning strategies like previewing, clarifying your purpose, activating your prior knowledge, and estimating the difficulty level of the material help you become an active reader and give you a head start on good comprehension; they set you up to be successful. To get an idea of why planning strategies are important, read this paragraph from a stockbroker's newsletter.

> Writing or selling Options against stock you already own is a strategy that is conservative and usually works well in a trading market. An Option is either a call (a right to buy 100 shares of stock at a specified price in the future) or a put (a right to sell 100 shares of stock at a specified price in the future). Thus an Option buyer or seller who owns no stock (called uncovered or naked) is a speculator who is looking at making large percentage returns on a small amount of invested capital in a short time. This individual would be paying the Option premium to us, the covered writer. (Schneider, Kirk's Quotes)

How successfully did you read the paragraph? How do you know if you were successful?

If you're like many students, you may not be very confident of your success. Although you can say all the words, unless you have a working knowledge of the stock market, the content of the paragraph is difficult. In addition, since you didn't have a specific purpose for reading, it was probably difficult to know if you understood what was expected.

Now, read the paragraph to answer the question, Is writing Options against your own stock considered a risky or a conservative strategy?

> Writing or selling Options against stock you already own is a strategy that is conservative and usually works well in a trading market. An Option is either a call (a right to buy 100 shares of stock at a specified price in the future) or a put (a right to sell 100 shares of stock at a specified price in

the future). Thus an Option buyer or seller who owns no stock (called uncovered or naked) is a speculator who is looking at making large percentage returns on a small amount of invested capital in a short time. This individual would be paying the Option premium to us, the covered writer. (Schneider, Kirk's Quotes)

How successful were you this time? How do you know if you were successful?

I suspect you evaluated yourself very successful. This is because you found the information you were looking for—that writing Options against your own stock is a conservative strategy—in the first sentence. You clearly knew you had achieved your goal and you stopped reading before you got into content that called for a more advanced understanding of the stock market.

As you can see, even with the same paragraph, the reading requirements can be very different. Begin every reading assignment with activities that will help assure your success. Strategies you can use include the following:

- **Preview** the selection.
- **Clarify** your specific purpose for reading.
- Activate your **prior knowledge** .
- Estimate how difficult the material is for you.

Planning Strategies

Preview the Selection

Previewing is like looking at a completed jigsaw puzzle before you try to put individual pieces together. But previewing a reading selection is not a random activity; it is a systematic survey of key structural organizers, like headings and subheadings. Although specific organizers vary among types of reading material, all such features highlight and emphasize important information and are keys to understanding the content.

Previewing a Textbook　You preview a text before you read the first chapter to understand who wrote it, how it's organized, and the topics to be covered. During preview, you read elements at the front of the book such as the

- title page
- preface
- table of contents
- about the author

You also look at the various styles of type and design that are used. These devices aren't just decorations to make it visually appealing, they are selected to give the reader clues about the relative importance of the ideas. For more information about how to use these clues can help you accurately and efficiently gather information see *Using Textbook Clues* in the Appendix.

In addition, you locate any aids such as the following that will help you as you complete class assignments:

- glossary
- index

- appendices
- suggested answers

The more comprehensive your understanding of the book and the author, the more insight you will have for understanding the content.

Previewing a Text Chapter   When you preview a chapter, you read any element that helps give you a general understanding of the core ideas and their organization, such as

- chapter objectives
- headings and subheadings
- introductory and concluding paragraphs
- boldface, underlined, and italic words and phrases
- graphics
- margin annotations
- end-of-chapter summaries and questions

Once you become familiar with how to preview, you will be able to preview a thirty-page text chapter with clear structural elements in about ten minutes.

Previewing Other Material   Organizing structures for newspaper, magazine, and journal articles vary among publications; however, they almost all run the author's byline and often a short biography of the author. Journal articles often include a paragraph at the beginning that summarizes content and boldface or italic type to highlight key terms or concepts.

Clarify Your Specific Purpose for Reading

Identify what you want to have learned when you finish reading. Often, your instructor gives you a purpose such as, "Read this chapter to prepare for tomorrow's lecture." Unfortunately, general purposes like that are not much help because they don't help you identify what you need to know when you finish reading. Without a specific **purpose for reading**, you have no way of knowing if you understand the information you need.

When you are reading for learning, you have a greater chance for success if you have clearly identified reasons for reading, such as, "I want to be able to answer the end-of-chapter questions," or "I need to understand the formula so I can complete the experiment in lab tomorrow." When you don't have any other reasons for reading, try turning the chapter's headings and subheadings into questions—your purpose then becomes to read to answer the questions.

Activate Your Prior Knowledge

Research confirms what most of us have figured out by trial and error: the more we know about the subject we're reading, the easier it is to understand. So, just as you take time to think about a subject before you begin to write about it, you should take time to think about a subject before you begin to read about it. For example, as you preview, jot down what you know about the topics in the chapter's headings and subheadings. If you have turned the headings and subheadings into questions, try answering them based on your current knowledge. Then, as you read, you can modify and add to your answers.

Estimate How Difficult the Material Is for You

Based on your purpose and what you have learned by previewing, such as how difficult the vocabulary is and your knowledge about the topic, predict how difficult the assignment will be for you. For example, if you are reading a chapter called "How Do We Use Computers?" just to identify and list ten general-usage categories, and you are familiar with computers, you can predict the assignment will be relatively easy and you'll cover the material quickly. On the other hand, if you are reading to understand all the facets of each of the categories to prepare a speech on computer usage, and you've never read much about computers, you can predict the assignment will take you some time.

Taking time to plan *before* you begin to read makes it more likely you will understand what you need and less likely you will waste time.

Exercise 1 **Practice the Planning Strategies**

It's the first Monday of the semester and your economics professor has just assigned Chapter 1, "The Scope and Method of Economics," in your text (*Principles of Economics*, sixth edition, by Case & Fair). On Wednesday she's going to lecture on "Why Study Economics?" Use this three-page excerpt from the chapter to practice your planning strategies.

PREVIEW THE SELECTION

Read the following elements:

- chapter title
- chapter outline (on right side of first excerpt page)
- introduction (10 paragraphs on excerpt pages 1–2)
- headings (1) and sentence explanation (excerpt page 2)
- first-level subheadings (1) and paragraph (excerpt page 2)
- second-level subheadings (3) (excerpt pages 2–3)
- vocabulary definitions in margin

THE SCOPE AND METHOD OF ECONOMICS

Karl E. Case & Ray C. Fair

Dr. Case is the Katherine Coman and A. Barton Hepburn Professor of Economics at Wellesley College and is a Visiting Scholar at the Federal Reserve Bank of Boston. Dr. Fair is Professor of Economics at Yale University. This excerpt is from their text Principles of Economics *sixth edition.*

THE SCOPE AND METHOD OF ECONOMICS

Why Study Economics?
To Learn a Way of Thinking
To Understand Society
To Understand Global Affairs
To Be an Informed Voter

The Scope of Economics
Microeconomics and
    Macroeconomics
The Diverse Fields of Economics

The Method of Economics
Theories and Models
Economic Policy

An Invitation

***Appendix: How to Read
    and Understand Graphs***

The study of economics should begin with a sense of wonder. Pause for a moment and consider a typical day in your life. For breakfast you might have bread made in a local bakery with flour produced in Minnesota from wheat grown in Kansas and bacon from pigs raised in Ohio packaged in plastic made in New Jersey. You spill coffee from Colombia on your shirt made in Texas from textiles shipped from South Carolina.

After class you drive with a friend in a Japanese car on an interstate highway that is part of a system that took 20 years and billions of dollars to build. You stop for gasoline refined in Louisiana from Saudi Arabian crude oil brought to the United States on a supertanker that took 3 years to build at a shipyard in Maine.

Later you log onto the Web with a laptop computer assembled in Indonesia from parts made in China and send e-mail to your brother in Mexico City, and you call a buddy on a cell phone made by a company in Finland. It is picked up by a microwave dish hiding in a church steeple rented from the church by a cellular company that was just bought by a European conglomerate.

You use or consume tens of thousands of things, both tangible and intangible, every day: buildings, rock music, compact discs (CDs), telephone services, staples, paper, toothpaste, tweezers, soap, digital watches, fire protection, antacid tablets, banks, electricity, eggs, insurance, football fields, computers, buses, rugs, subways, health services, sidewalks, and so forth. Somebody made all these things. Somebody decided to organize men and women and materials to produce them and distribute them. Thousands of decisions went into their completion. Somehow they got to you.

In the United States 135 million people — almost half the total population — work at hundreds of thousands of different jobs producing over $9 trillion worth of goods and services every year. Some cannot find work; some choose not to work. Some are rich; others are poor.

The United States imports over $170 billion worth of automobiles and parts and about $70 billion worth of petroleum and petroleum products each year; it exports around $55 billion worth of agricultural products, including food. High-rise office buildings go up in central cities. Condominiums and homes are built in the suburbs. In other places homes are abandoned and boarded up.

Some countries are wealthy. Others are impoverished. Some are growing. Some are stagnating. Some businesses are doing well. Others are going bankrupt.

At any moment in time every society faces constraints imposed by nature and by previous generations. Some societies are handsomely endowed by nature with fertile land, water, sunshine, and natural resources. Others have deserts and few mineral resources. Some societies receive much from previous generations—art, music, technical knowledge, beautiful buildings, and productive factories. Others are left with overgrazed, eroded land, cities leveled by war, or polluted natural environments. *All* societies face limits.

> **economics**   The study of how individuals and societies choose to use the scarce resources that nature and previous generations have provided.

> **Economics** is the study of how individuals and societies choose to use the scarce resources that nature and previous generations have provided. The key word in this definition is *choose*. Economics is a behavioral, or social, science. In large measure it is the study of how people make choices. The choices that people make, when added up, translate into societal choices.

The purpose of this chapter and the next is to elaborate on this definition and to introduce the subject matter of economics. What is produced? How is it produced? Who gets it? Why? Is the result good or bad? Can it be improved?

WHY STUDY ECONOMICS?

There are four main reasons to study economics: to learn a way of thinking, to understand society, to understand global affairs, and to be an informed voter.

TO LEARN A WAY OF THINKING

Probably the most important reason for studying economics is to learn a way of thinking. A good way to introduce economics is to review three of its most fundamental concepts: *opportunity cost, marginalism,* and *efficient markets.* If your study of economics is successful, you will use these concepts every day in making decisions.

Opportunity Cost   What happens in an economy is the outcome of thousands of individual decisions. Households must decide how to divide their incomes among all the goods and services available in the marketplace. People must decide whether to work or not to work, whether to go to school, and how much to save. Businesses must decide what to produce, how much to produce, how much to charge, and where to locate. It is not surprising that economic analysis focuses on the process of decision making.

Nearly all decisions involve trade-offs. A key concept that recurs in analyzing the decision-making process is the notion of *opportunity cost.* The full "cost" of making a specific choice includes what we give up by not making the alternative choice. The best alternative that we forgo, or give up, when we make a choice or a decision is called the **opportunity cost** of that decision.

> **opportunity cost**   The best alternative that we forgo, or give up, when we make a choice or a decision.

This concept applies to individuals, businesses, and entire societies. The opportunity cost of going to a movie is the value of the other things you could have done with the same money and time. If you decide to take time off from work, the opportunity cost of your leisure is the pay that you would have earned had you worked. Part of the cost of a college education is the income you could have earned by working full time instead of going to school. If a firm purchases a new piece of equipment for $3,000, it does so because it expects that equipment to generate more profit. There is an opportunity cost, however, because that $3,000 could have been deposited in an interest-earning account. To a society, the opportunity cost of using resources to put astronauts on the moon is the value of the private/civilian goods that could have been produced with the same resources.

Opportunity costs arise because resources are scarce. *Scarce* simply means "limited." Consider one of our most important resources—time. There are only 24 hours in a day, and we must live our lives under this constraint. A farmer in rural Brazil must decide whether it is better to continue to farm or to go to the city and look for a job. A hockey player at the University of Vermont must decide whether she will play on the varsity team or spend more time improving her academic work.

Marginalism and Sunk Costs   A second key concept used in analyzing choices is the notion of *marginalism.* In weighing the costs and benefits of a decision, it is important to weigh only the costs and benefits that arise from the decision. Suppose, for example, that you live in New Orleans and that you are weighing the costs and benefits of visiting your mother in Iowa. If business required that you travel to Kansas City, the cost of visiting Mom would be only the additional, or *marginal,* time and money cost of getting to Iowa from Kansas City.

Consider the cost of producing this book. Assume that 10,000 copies are produced. The total cost of producing the copies includes the cost of the authors' time in writing the book, the cost of editing, the cost of making the plates for printing, and the cost of the paper and ink. If the total cost were $600,000, then the average cost of one copy would be $60, which is simply $600,000 divided by 10,000.

Although average cost is an important concept, a book publisher must know more than simply the average cost of a book. For example, suppose a second printing is being debated. That is, should another 10,000 copies be produced? In deciding whether to proceed, the costs of writing, editing, making plates, and so forth are irrelevant, because they have already been incurred—they are *sunk costs.* **Sunk costs** are costs that cannot be avoided, regardless of what is done in the future, because they have already been incurred. All that matters are the costs associated with the additional, or marginal, books to be printed. Technically, *marginal cost* is the cost of producing one more unit of output.

There are numerous examples in which the concept of marginal cost is useful. For an airplane that is about to take off with empty seats, the marginal cost of an extra passenger is essentially zero; the total cost of the trip is essentially unchanged by the addition of an extra passenger. Thus, setting aside a few seats to be sold at big discounts can be profitable even if the fare for those seats is far below the average cost per seat of making the trip. As long as the airline succeeds in filling seats that would otherwise have been empty, doing so is profitable.

> **sunk costs**   Costs that cannot be avoided, regardless of what is done in the future, because they have already been incurred.

Efficient Markets—No Free Lunch   Suppose you are ready to check out of a busy grocery store on the day before a storm, and seven checkout registers are open with several people in each line. Which line should you choose? It is usually the case that the waiting time is approximately the same no matter which register you choose (assuming you have more than 12 items). If one line is much shorter than the others, people will quickly move into it until the lines are equalized again.

As you will see later, the term *profit* in economics has a very precise meaning. Economists, however, often loosely refer to "good deals" or risk-free ventures as *profit opportunities.* Using the term loosely, a profit opportunity exists at the toll booths if one line is shorter than the others. In general, such profit opportunities are rare. At any one time there are many people searching for them, and, as a consequence, few exist. Markets like this, where any profit opportunities are eliminated almost instantaneously, are said to be **efficient markets.** (We discuss *markets,* the institutions through which buyers and sellers interact and engage in exchange, in detail in Chapter 2.)

> **efficient market**   A market in which profit opportunities are eliminated almost instantaneously.

The common way of expressing the efficient markets concept is "there's no such thing as a free lunch." How should you react when a stockbroker calls up with a hot tip on the stock market? With skepticism. There are thousands of individuals each day looking for hot tips in the market. If a particular tip about a stock is valid, there will be an immediate rush to buy the stock, which will quickly drive its price up.

This economists' view that very few profit opportunities exist can, of course, be carried too far. There is a story about two people walking along, one an economist and one not. The noneconomist sees a $20 bill on the sidewalk and says, "There's a $20 bill on the sidewalk." The economist replies, "That is not possible. If there were, somebody would already have picked it up."

There are clearly times when profit opportunities exist. Someone has to be first to get the news, and some people have quicker insights than others. Nevertheless, news travels fast, and there are thousands of people with quick insights. The general view that profit opportunities are rare is close to the mark.

Exercise 1   **Questions**

WAS YOUR PREVIEW SUCCESSFUL?

1. What is the title of the chapter?
2. What is the purpose of the chapter?
3. What is economics?
4. How many main reasons for studying economics are Case and Fair going to discuss?

BASED ON YOUR PREVIEW

1. Clarify your specific purpose for reading. Your professor gave you a general purpose: prepare for Wednesday's lecture on "Why Study Economics?" Since this is too general to guide your reading, turn the subheadings and boldface terms into questions you want to answer. For example, the first boldface term becomes "What is economics?" As you read, you answer the questions.
2. Activate your prior knowledge. Think about some of the things you know about economics. For example, what are some of the elements that influence what you spend?
3. Estimate how difficult the material is for you. Based on the vocabulary, the authors' writing style, and how much you know about the topics, estimate how difficult you think this chapter will be for you to understand.

Do the Reading

Did you ever fall asleep while you were playing a game or watching your favorite television comedy? Probably not. Did you ever fall asleep while you were reading an assignment for class? Probably. What makes the difference? Your active involvement in the task.

Unfortunately, students often view reading as a passive task—something that doesn't require attention or action. For example, passive readers are content to sit back and let the words pass by their eyes as their minds slip into neutral or consider what to have for lunch. They "wake up" a few pages later and wonder if they've missed anything important. Anytime you become passive, you rapidly lose interest and drift away.

Successful readers, like successful athletes, stay actively involved. Active physical and mental involvement keeps you interested and committed. Strategies you can use include the following:

Reading Strategies

Monitor Your Comprehension

Consider what would happen if you were putting a bicycle together but you were missing a gear chain or handlebars. If a critical element were missing, you'd stop and try to solve the problem. If you didn't, you'd wind up investing hours of your time in a bike that didn't work.

For similar reasons, active readers don't wade through twenty pages of text and then stop and say, "I missed something on page four," or "I didn't understand pages five through fifteen."

By continuously monitoring, or checking, your comprehension, you can keep track of your progress. Use **comprehension monitoring strategies** like these to make certain you understand what you read:

Restate Ideas in Your Own Words. At the end of a sentence or paragraph, rephrase the idea in your own words.

Compare What You Are Reading to What You Know. Ask yourself how this new information fits with what you know. Does it reinforce your previous knowledge? Does it contradict what you previously thought? Does it add new information?

Answer Questions. Connect what you are reading to questions you need to answer.

If You Don't Understand, Stop and Clarify

If you discover that you do not understand what you are reading, use one of these fix-up strategies to get yourself back on track:

Define Unfamiliar Words. Make certain you understand the words the author uses. If an unfamiliar word isn't defined in the context or the text's glossary, check your lecture notes or a dictionary, or ask someone.

Review Graphics. Review all associated graphics and their explanations to see if they clarify the text information.

Read Surrounding Paragraphs. Starting a paragraph or two before the problem text, reread with the specific goal of clarifying your question. Try rereading the objectives, headings, and subheadings to see if they contain ideas or concepts that help you to understand the material. Or, try reading the paragraphs that follow the problem text to see if they help your understanding.

Seek Help. When you have clarified the vocabulary, reread appropriate passages, and reviewed other text aids, and the information is still unclear, look for help outside the text. For example, read about the topic or idea in your notes or in another book to see if a different approach helps your understanding. Or, ask someone. Potential resources include your professor, a teaching assistant, a tutor, or a classmate.

Exercise 2 ▶ Practice the Reading Strategies

Use the previous three-page excerpt from Chapter 1, "The Scope and Method of Economics," (*Principles of Economics,* sixth edition, by Case and Fair) on pages 9–11 to practice your reading strategies. Remember, your purpose for reading is to answer the questions you created from the heading, subheadings, and boldface terms. Anytime you don't understand what you are reading, stop and fix the problem.

REVIEW WHAT YOU READ

Think about when you first learned to do something like drive a car, type, or play the guitar. If you practiced daily, you found yourself doing a little better each day. If, however, you didn't practice for two or three weeks, you probably forgot so much that you needed to start with some of the basics again.

It doesn't matter how old we are; without review, we forget information very quickly. In fact, without good review at regular intervals, we forget as much as 80 percent of what we have read. In addition, reviewing helps us to integrate new information with what we already know. It helps us put information into perspective.

To be most effective, review sessions should be spaced out over time. You should arrange your first review session within 24 hours of reading and continue to review the information on a regular schedule. Reviewing periodically helps you commit information to your long-term memory. Other review strategies you can use include the following:

REVIEWING STRATEGIES

Answer Questions.   Write out or talk through the answers to the questions you identified in your plan.

Determine What Else You Need to Know.   Occasionally, on small assignments or familiar material, you will achieve your reading comprehension goals at the end of one Plan → Do → Review cycle. However, don't be surprised to discover gaps in your knowledge. When you do, just develop and use a new plan to help you fill in the information you need.

Test Yourself.   Make up a test or have a classmate make one up to test you on the material. Make a set of question-and-answer flash cards for a convenient carry-along review tool by writing a question on one side of a 3″ × 5″ card and the answer on the reverse side.

Participate in a Study Group.   Join a group of classmates to review concepts, share notes, and take practice tests.

Consolidate and Integrate Information.   Combine your knowledge, your lecture notes, and what you've gained from reading to form one coherent picture.

Exercise 3   Practice the Review Strategies

WAS YOUR READING SUCCESSFUL?

1. What is economics?
2. Why should you study economics?
3. Why is it important to learn economics as a way of thinking?
4. What is opportunity cost?
5. What is marginalism?
6. What are sunk costs?
7. What are efficient markets?

If you were able to fulfill your purpose for reading—to answer the questions you created by turning the subheadings into questions—you do not need to develop a plan to reread portions of the text.

As for reviewing, you know you will be using the information you gathered from Chapter 1, "The Scope and Method of Economics," as you listen to Wednesday's lecture. After the lecture, take time to integrate the lecture and text information and to develop a schedule to systematically review the information.

Exercise 4 **Plan → Do → Review**

1. Adapt strategies from the plan → do → review cycle to complete an assignment in a textbook for another class.

2. Turn in a list that describes (a) the planning strategies you used, (b) the reading, monitoring, and/or fix-up strategies you used, (c) how you knew you had fulfilled your purpose for reading, and (d) what review strategies you will use.

CHAPTER 1 REVIEW QUESTIONS

1. Why should you view reading as a process?
2. Describe why the planning stage of the cycle is important and list three specific strategies.
3. Explain why it's important to be an active reader.
4. What are two strategies you can use to monitor your comprehension?
5. What are two fix-up strategies you can try when you don't understand what you are reading?
6. Explain why review is necessary, and list two review strategies.

Use Your Strategies 1

For this exercise, assume your instructor has asked you to read this selection to prepare for tomorrow's introductory lecture on good reading habits. (1) Develop your plan, (2) do the reading, and (3) answer the questions that follow the selection. If this were a real assignment, you would also need to plan a review strategy.

BILL COSBY

International Paper Company asked Bill Cosby—who earned his doctorate in education and has been involved in projects that help people learn to read faster—to share what he's learned about reading more in less time.

HOW TO READ FASTER

Bill Cosby

[1]When I was a kid in Philadelphia, I must have read every comic book ever published. (There were fewer of them then than there are now.)

[2]I zipped through all of them in a couple of days, then reread the good ones until the next issues arrived.

[3]Yes indeed, when I was a kid, the reading game was a snap.

[4]But as I got older, my eyeballs must have slowed down or something! I mean, comic books started to pile up faster than my brother Russell and I could read them!

[5]It wasn't until much later, when I was getting my doctorate, I realized it wasn't my eyeballs that were to blame. Thank goodness. They're still moving as well as ever.

[6]The problem is, there's too much to read these days, and too little time to read every word of it.

[7]Now, mind you, I still read comic books. In addition to contracts, novels, and newspapers. Screenplays, tax returns, and correspondence. Even textbooks about how people read. And which techniques help people read more in less time.

[8]I'll let you in on a little secret. There are hundreds of techniques you could learn to help you read faster. But I know of three that are especially good.

[9]And if I can learn them, so can you—and you can put them to use *immediately*.

[10]They are commonsense, practical ways to get the meaning from printed words quickly and efficiently. So you'll have time to enjoy your comic books, have a good laugh with Mark Twain or a good cry with *War and Peace*. Ready?

[11]Okay. The first two ways can help you get through tons of reading material—fast—*without reading every word*.

[12]They'll give you the *overall meaning* of what you're reading. And let you cut out an awful lot of *unnecessary* reading.

1. PREVIEW—IF IT'S LONG AND HARD

[13]Previewing is especially useful for getting a general idea of heavy reading like long magazine or newspaper articles, business reports, and nonfiction books.

[14]It can give you as much as half the comprehension in as little as one-tenth the time. For example, you should be able to preview eight or ten 100-page reports in an hour. After previewing, you'll be able to decide which reports (or which *parts* of which reports) are worth a closer look.

[15]*Here's how to preview:* Read the entire first two paragraphs of whatever you've chosen. Next read only the *first sentence* of each successive paragraph. Then read the entire last two paragraphs.

[16]Previewing doesn't give you all the details. But it does keep you from spending time on things you don't really want—or need—to read.

[17]Notice that previewing gives you a quick, overall view *of long, unfamiliar* material. For short, light reading, there's a better technique.

2. SKIM—IF IT'S SHORT AND SIMPLE

[18]Skimming is a good way to get a general idea of light reading—like popular magazines or the sports and entertainment sections of the paper.

[19]You should be able to skim a weekly popular magazine or the second section of your daily paper in less than half the time it takes you to read it now.

[20]Skimming is also a great way to review material you've read before.

[21]*Here's how to skim:* Think of your eyes as magnets. Force them to move fast. Sweep them across each and every line of type. Pick up *only a few key words in each line.*

[22]Everybody skims differently.

[23]You and I may not pick up exactly the same words when we skim the same piece, but we'll both get a pretty similar idea of what it's all about.

[24]To show you how it works, I circled the words I picked out when I skimmed the following story. Try it. It shouldn't take you more than 10 seconds.

My brother Russell thinks monsters live in our bedroom closet at night. But I told him he is crazy.

"Go and check then," he said.

I didn't want to. Russell said I was chicken.

"Am not," I said.

"Are so," he said.

So I told him the monsters were going to eat him at midnight. He started to cry. My Dad came in and told the monsters to beat it. Then he told us to go to sleep.

"If I hear any more about monsters," he said, "I'll spank you."

We went to sleep fast. And you know something? They never did come back.

[25]Skimming can give you a very good *idea* of this story in about half the words—and in less than half the time it'd take to read every word.

[26]So far, you've seen that previewing and skimming can give you a *general idea* about content—fast. But neither technique can promise more than 50 percent comprehension, because you aren't reading all the words. (Nobody gets something for nothing in the reading game.)

[27]*To read faster and understand most*—if not all—of what you read, you need to know a third technique.

3. CLUSTER—TO INCREASE SPEED *AND* COMPREHENSION

[28]Most of us learned to read by looking at each word in a sentence—*one at a time.*

[29]Like this:

My—brother—Russell—thinks—monsters. . . .

[30]You probably still read this way sometimes, especially when the words are difficult. Or when the words have an extra-special meaning—as in a poem, a Shakespearean play, or a contract. And that's O.K.

[31]But word-by-word reading is a rotten way to read faster. It actually *cuts down* on your speed.

[32]*Clustering* trains you to look at *groups* of words instead of one at a time—to increase your speed enormously. For most of us, clustering is a *totally different way of seeing what we read.*

[33]*Here's how to cluster:* Train your eyes to see *all* the words in clusters of up to three or four words at a glance.

[34]Here's how I'd cluster the story we just skimmed:

My brother Russell thinks monsters live in our bedroom closet at night. But I told him he is crazy.

"Go and check then," he said.

I didn't want to. Russell said I was chicken.

"Am not," I said.

"Are so," he said.

So I told him the monsters were going to eat him at midnight. He started to cry. My Dad came in and told the monsters to beat it. Then he told us to go to sleep.

"If I hear any more about monsters," he said, "I'll spank you."

We went to sleep fast. And you know something? They never did come back.

[35]Learning to read clusters is not something your eyes do naturally. It takes constant practice.

[36]Here's how to go about it: Pick something light to read. Read it as fast as you can. Concentrate on seeing three to four words at once rather than one word at a time. Then reread the piece at your normal speed to see what you missed the first time.

[37]Try a second piece. First cluster, then reread to see what you missed in this one.

[38]When you can read in clusters without missing much the first time, your speed has increased. Practice 15 minutes every day and you might pick up the technique in a week or so. (But don't be disappointed if it takes longer. Clustering *everything* takes time and practice.)

[39]So now you have three ways to help you read faster. *Preview* to cut down on unnecessary heavy reading. *Skim* to get a quick, general idea of light reading. And *cluster* to increase your speed and comprehension.

[40]With enough practice, you'll be able to handle *more* reading at school or work—and at home—in *less time*. You should even have enough time to read your favorite comic books—and *War and Peace!*

Use Your Strategies 1 Questions

1. Describe your plan.
2. List Cosby's three main techniques about how to read faster. (If you didn't find the three techniques, or cannot remember them, reread the appropriate sections.)

Use Your Strategies 2

For this exercise, assume your professor has instructed you to read this chapter to answer two questions. Develop your plan and do the reading to answer these two questions: 1) At the beginning of the nineteenth century, what percent of Americans lived on farms? 2) The market revolution, the most fundamental change American communities ever experienced, was the outcome of three interrelated developments. List them.

Preindustrial Ways of Working

JOHN MACK FARAGHER, MARI JO BUHLE, DANIEL CZITROM & SUSAN H. ARMITAGE

Dr. Faragher is the Arthur Unobskey Professor of American History at Yale University. Dr. Buhle is Professor of American Civilization and History at Brown University. Dr. Czitrom is Professor and Chair of History at Mount Holyoke College. Dr. Armitage is Professor of History at Washington State University. This three-page excerpt is from Chapter 12, "Industry and the North, 1790s–1840s" in the third edition of Out of Many: A History of the American People.

KEY TOPICS

■ Preindustrial ways of working and living

■ The nature of the market revolution

■ The effects of industrialization on workers in early factories

■ Ways the market revolution changed the lives of ordinary people

■ The emergence of the middle classs

PREINDUSTRIAL WAYS OF WORKING

The Lowell mill was a dramatic example of the ways factories changed traditional ways of working and living. When Lowell began operation, 97 percent of all Americans still lived on farms, and most work was done in or near the home. There was a community network of barter and mutual obligation. Work was slow, unscheduled, and task oriented. A rural artisan worked when he had orders, responding to demand, not to the clock. "Home" and "work" were not separate locations or activities, but intermixed.

Urban Artisans and Workers

In urban areas, skilled craftsmen had controlled preindustrial production since the early colonial period. Trades were perpetuated through a formal system of apprenticeship in which a boy went to work in the shop of a master, usually at the age of twelve or fourteen. Over the next three to seven years the young apprentice learned all aspects of the craft, gaining increasing responsibility and status as the day approached when he could strike out on his own. During that time, the master not only taught the apprentice his trade but housed, fed, and clothed him. Usually the apprentice lived with the master craftsman and was treated more like a member of the family than an employee. Thus, the family-learning model used on farms was formalized in the urban apprenticeship system. At the end of the contract period, the apprentice became a journeyman craftsman. Journeymen worked for wages in the shop of a master craftsman until they had enough capital to set up shop for themselves.

Although women as well as men did task-oriented skilled work, the formal apprenticeship system was exclusively for men. Because it was assumed that women would marry, most people thought that all girls needed to learn were domestic skills. Women who needed or wanted work, however, found a small niche of respectable occupations as domestic servants, laundresses, or seamstresses, often in the homes of the wealthy, or as cooks in small restaurants or as food vendors on the street. Some owned and managed boardinghouses. Prostitution, another common female occupation (especially in seaport cities), was not respectable.

Patriarchy in Family, Work, and Society

Like the farm family, an entire urban household was commonly organized around one kind of work. Usually the family lived at the shop or store, and all family members worked with the craftsman at his trade. A printer's wife, for example, would be capable of keeping most of the shop's functions going in the printer's absence and of supervising the work of apprentices and her children. Some artisans, like blacksmiths, needed shops separate from their homes but probably relied on their children to fetch and carry and to help with some of the work. Others, like bakers, who generally had to get up in the middle of the night to perform their work, relied on their wives to sell their products during the day.

In both rural and urban settings, working families were organized along strictly patriarchal lines. The man had unquestioned authority to direct the lives and work of family members and apprentices and to decide on occupations for his sons and marriages for his daughters. His wife had many crucial responsibilities—feeding, clothing, child rearing, taking care of apprentices, and all the other domestic affairs of the household—but in all these duties she was subject to the direction of her husband. Men were heads of families and bosses of artisanal shops; although entire families were engaged in the enterprise, the husband and father was the trained craftsman, and assistance by the family was informal and generally unrecognized.

222   Chapter 12   Industry and the North 1790s–1840s

The patriarchal organization of the family was reflected in society as a whole. Legally, men had all the power: neither women nor children had property or legal rights. For example, a married woman's property belonged to her husband, a woman could not testify on her own behalf in court, and in the rare cases of divorce the husband kept the children, for they were considered his property. When a man died, his son or sons inherited his property. The basic principle was that the man, as head of the household, represented the common interests of everyone for whom he was responsible—women, children, servants, apprentices. He thus controlled everything of value, and he alone could vote for political office.

The Social Order

In this preindustrial society everyone, from the smallest yeoman farmer to the largest urban merchant, had a fixed place in the social order. The social status of artisans was below that of wealthy merchants but decidedly above that of common laborers. Yeoman farmers, less grand than large landowners, ranked above tenant farmers and farm laborers. Although men of all social ranks mingled in their daily work, they did not mingle as equals, for great importance was placed on rank and status, which were distinguished by dress and manner. Although by the 1790s many artisans who owned property were voters and vocal participants in urban politics, few directly challenged the traditional authority of the rich and powerful to run civic affairs. The rapid spread of universal white manhood suffrage after 1800 democratized politics (see Chapter 10). At the same time, economic changes undermined the preindustrial social order. New York cabinetmaker Duncan Phyfe and sailmaker Stephen Allen amassed fortunes from their operations. Allen when he retired, was elected mayor of New York, customarily a position reserved for gentlemen. These artisans owed much of their success to the ever-expanding effects of the economic upheaval known as the market revolution.

THE MARKET REVOLUTION

The market revolution, the most fundamental change American communities ever experienced, was the outcome of three interrelated developments: rapid improvements in transportation (see Chapter 10), commercialization, and industrialization. Improved transportation allowed both people and goods to move with new ease and speed. Commercialization involved the replacement of household self-sufficiency and barter with the production of goods for a cash market. And industrialization involved the use of power-driven machinery to produce goods once made by hand.

The Accumulation of Capital

In the northern states, the business community was composed largely of merchants in the seaboard cities: Boston, Providence, New York, Philadelphia, and Baltimore. Many had made substantial profits in the international shipping boom of the period 1790–1807 (as discussed in Chapter 9). Such extraordinary opportunities attracted enterprising people. John Jacob Astor, who had arrived penniless from Germany in 1784, made his first fortune in the Pacific Northwest fur trade with China and eventually dominated the fur trade in the United States through his American Fur Company. Astor made a second fortune in New York real estate, and when he retired in 1834 with $25 million he was reputed to be the wealthiest man in America. Many similar stories of success, though not so fabulous as Astor's, demonstrated that risk-takers might reap rich rewards in international trade.

When the early years of the nineteenth century posed difficulties for international trade, some of the nation's wealthiest men turned to local investments. In Providence, Rhode Island, Moses Brown and his son-in-law William Almy began to invest some of the profits the Brown family had reaped from a worldwide trade in iron, candles, rum, and African slaves in the new manufacture of cotton textiles. Cincinnati merchants banded together to finance the building of the first steamboats to operate on the Ohio River.

Much of the capital for the new investments came from banks, both those in seaport cities that had been established for the international trade. But an astonishing amount of capital was raised through family

WEALTH IN BOSTON, 1687–1848				
Percent of the Population	**Percent of Wealth Held**			
	1687	**1771**	**1833**	**1848**
Top 1 percent	10%	16%	33%	37%
Top 10 percent	42	65	75	82
Lowest 80 percent	39	29	14	4

This table tracing the distribution of wealth in Boston reflects the gains made by merchants during the international shipping boom of 1790–1807 and the way in which intermarriage between wealthy families consolidated these gains.

connections. In the late eighteenth century, members of the business communities in the seaboard cities had begun to consolidate their position and property by intermarriage. In Boston, such a strong community developed that when Francis Cabot Lowell needed $300,000 in 1813 to build the world's first automated cotton mill in Waltham, Massachusetts (the prototype of the Lowell mills), he had only to turn to his family network.

Southern cotton provided the capital for continuing development. Because Northerners built the nation's ships, controlled the shipping trade, and provided the nation's banking, insurance, and financial services, the astounding growth in southern cotton exports enriched northern merchants almost as much as southern planters. In 1825, for example, of the 204,000 bales of cotton shipped from New Orleans, about one-third (69,000) were transshipped through the northern ports of New York, Philadelphia, and Boston. Although imperfectly understood at the time, the development of northern industry was paid for by enslaved African American labor. The fact is that the surprising wealth that cotton brought to southern planters fostered the market revolution.

The Putting-Out System

Initially, the American business community invested not in machinery and factories but in the "putting-out system" of home manufacture, thereby expanding and transforming it. In this significant departure from preindustrial work, people still produced goods at home but under the direction of a merchant, who "put out" the raw materials to them, paid them a certain sum per finished piece, and sold the completed item to a distant market. A look at the shoe industry in Lynn, Massachusetts, shows how the putting-out system transformed American manufacturing.

Long a major center of the shoe industry, Lynn, in 1800, produced 400,000 pairs of shoes—enough for every fifth person in the country. The town's 200 master artisans and their families, including journeymen and apprentices, worked together in hundreds of small home workshops called "ten-footers" (from their size, about ten feet square). The artisans and journeymen cut the leather, the artisans' wives and daughters did the binding of the upper parts of the shoe, the men stitched the shoe together, and children and apprentices helped where needed. In the early days, the artisan commonly bartered his shoes for needed products. Sometimes an artisan sold his shoes to a larger retailer in Boston or Salem. Although production of shoes in Lynn increased yearly from 1780 to 1810 as markets widened, shoes continued to be manufactured in traditional artisanal ways.

The investment of merchant capital in the shoe business changed everything. In Lynn, a small group of Quaker shopkeepers and merchants, connected by family, religious, and business ties, took the lead in reorganizing the trade. Financed by the bank they founded in 1814, Lynn capitalists like Micajah Pratt built large, two-story central workshops to replace the scattered ten-footers. Pratt employed a few skilled craftsmen to cut leather for shoes, but he put out the rest of the shoemaking to less-skilled workers who were no longer connected by family ties. Individual farm women and children sewed the uppers, which, when completed, were soled by farm men and boys. Putting-out workers were paid on a piecework basis; the men and boys earned more than the women and children but much less than a master craftsman or a journeyman. This arrangement allowed the capitalist to employ much more labor for the same investment than with the traditional artisan workshop. Shoe production increased enormously: the largest central shop in 1832 turned out ten times more shoes than the largest shopkeeper had sold in 1789. Gradually the putting-out system and central workshops replaced artisan's shops. Some artisans became wealthy owners of workshops, but most became wage earners, and the apprenticeship system eventually disappeared.

The putting-out system moved the control of production from the individual artisan households to the merchant capitalists, who could now control labor costs, production goals, and shoe styles to fit certain markets. For example, the Lynn trade quickly monopolized the market for cheap boots for southern slaves and western farmers, leaving workshops in other cities to produce shoes for wealthier customers. This specialization of the national market—indeed, even thinking in terms of a national market—was new. Additionally, and most important from the capitalist's point of view, the owner of the business controlled the workers and could cut back or expand the labor force as economic and marketplace conditions warranted. The unaccustomed severity of economic slumps like the Panics of 1819 and 1837 made this flexibility especially desirable.

While the central workshop system prevailed in Lynn and in urban centers like New York City, the putting-out system also fostered a more dispersed form of home production. By 1810 there were an estimated 2,500 so-called outwork weavers in New England, operating handlooms in their own homes. Other crafts that rapidly became organized according to the putting-out system were flax and wool spinning, straw braiding, glove making, and the knitting of stockings. For example, the palm-leaf hat industry that supplied farm laborers and slaves in the South and West relied

Use Your Strategies 2 Questions

1. Describe your plan.
2. At the beginning of the nineteenth century, what percentage of Americans lived on farms?
3. The market revolution, the most fundamental change American communities ever experienced, was the outcome of three interrelated developments. List them.
4. Describe any information you still need to find and/or understand and your plan to accomplish it.
5. Explain how you would review.

Use Your Strategies 3

For this exercise, assume the assignment to read this chapter is simply listed in your course syllabus. You have not been given any specific reasons for reading. Develop your plan and do the reading.

Groups and Organizations

JOHN MACIONIS

Dr. Macionis is professor of sociology at Kenyon College, Gambier, Ohio. In addition to his teaching, he is known for his twenty years of work as a popular textbook author. This three-page excerpt is from Chapter 7, "Groups and Organizations" in his introductory text Sociology, *ninth edition.*

GROUPS AND ORGANIZATIONS

Back in 1948, people in Pasadena, California, paid little attention to the opening of a new restaurant. Yet one small business—owned by brothers Maurice and Richard McDonald—would not only transform the restaurant industry but also introduce a new organizational model copied by countless businesses of all kinds.

The McDonald brothers' basic concept, which we now call "fast food," was to serve meals quickly and cheaply to large numbers of people. The brothers trained employees to perform highly specialized jobs, so that one person grilled hamburgers while others "dressed" them, made French fries, whipped up milkshakes, and presented the food to the customers in assembly-line fashion.

As the years went by, the McDonald brothers prospered, and they decided to move their single restaurant from Pasadena to San Bernardino. It was there, in 1954, that Ray Kroc, a traveling blender and mixer merchant, paid them a visit.

Kroc was fascinated by the efficiency of the brothers' system and saw the potential for a whole chain of fast-food restaurants. The three launched the plan as partners. Soon, however, Kroc bought out the McDonalds, and he went on to become one of the greatest success stories of all time. Today, about 28,000 McDonald's restaurants have served more than 150 billion hamburgers to people throughout the United States and in 120 other nations around the world.

The success of McDonald's is evidence of more than just the popularity of hamburgers. The larger importance of McDonald's lies in the extent to which the principles that guide this company are coming to dominate social life in the United States and elsewhere (Ritzer, 1993, 1998, 2000).

We begin with an examination of *social groups*, the clusters of people with whom we interact in much of our daily lives. As we shall see, the scope of group life expanded greatly during the course of the twentieth century. Having evolved from a close-knit world of families, local neighborhoods, and small businesses, our society now turns on the operation of huge businesses and other bureaucracies that sociologists describe as *formal organizations*. Understanding how this expanding scale of life came to be—and what it means for us as individuals—are this chapter's main objectives.

SOCIAL GROUPS

Almost everyone seeks a sense of belonging, which is the experience of group life. A **social group** is made up of *two or more people who identify and interact with one another.* Human beings come together in couples, families, circles of friends, churches, clubs, businesses, neighborhoods, and large organizations. Whatever its form, a group is made up of people with shared experiences, loyalties, and interests. In short, while keeping their individuality, members of social groups also think of themselves as a special "we."

Not every collection of individuals can be called a group. People with a status in common, such as women, homeowners, gay men, soldiers, millionaires, and Roman Catholics, are not a group but a *category*. Although they know others who hold the same status, most are strangers to one another.

163

SUPPLEMENTS: An outline and supplementary lecture material for Chapter 7 are included in the *Data File.*
RESOURCE: An excerpt of Cooley's analysis of primary groups appears in the Macionis and Benokraitis companion reader, *Seeing Ourselves.*
NOTE: "Primary" is derived from the Latin word *prime*, meaning "first"; "secondary" is from the Latin *secund(us)*, meaning "following."

NOTE: Cooley used only the term "primary group"; others introduced the term "secondary group" into sociological terminology, inferring the concept from Cooley's writings. Cooley did his first research for the U.S. Census, collecting statistics on street railways.
GLOBAL: The importance of traditional solidarities—of race, ethnicity, religion, or clan—typically surprises the U.S. traveler in less economically developed countries.

As human beings, we live our lives as members of groups. Such groups may be large or small, temporary or long-lasting. The United States is regarded as a country where people are especially likely to form groups based on kinship, heritage, or some shared interest.

What about students sitting together in a lecture hall or bathers enjoying a hot day at the beach? Some people in such settings may interact, but only with a few others. These temporary, loosely formed collections of people are better termed a *crowd.* In general, crowds are too anonymous and transitory to qualify as groups.

The right circumstances, however, can turn a crowd into a group. People riding in an elevator that stalls between floors generally recognize their common plight and turn to each other for help. Sometimes out of accidents and disasters, people form lasting relationships.

PRIMARY AND SECONDARY GROUPS

Acquaintances commonly greet one another with a smile and a "Hi! How are you?" The response is usually, "Just fine, thanks. How about you?" This answer is often more scripted than truthful. In most cases, providing a detailed account of how you are *really* doing would make most people feel so awkward they would beat a hasty retreat.

Sociologists designate two types of social groups, depending on the degree of genuine personal concern that members show for one another. According to Charles Horton Cooley (1864–1929), a **primary group** is *a small social group whose members share personal and enduring relationships.* Bound by *primary relationships*, people typically spend a great deal of time together, engage in a wide range of activities, and feel that they know one another well. Although not without conflict from time to time, members of primary groups display real concern for each other's welfare. The family is every society's most important primary group.

 For a biographical sketch of Charles Horton Cooley, see the Gallery of Sociologists at http://www.TheSociologyPage.com

Cooley called these personal and tightly integrated groups *primary* because they are among the first groups we experience in life. In addition, the family and early play groups hold primary importance in the socialization process, shaping attitudes, behavior, and social identity.

Primary relationships give people a comforting sense of security. In the familiar social circle of family or friends, people feel they can "be themselves" without worrying about the impression they are making.

Members of primary groups help one another in many ways, but they generally think of their ties as ends in themselves rather than as means to some other end. In other words, we prefer to think that kinship and friendship link people who belong together. Moreover, members of a primary group tend to view each other as unique and irreplaceable. Especially in the family, we are bound to others by emotion and loyalty. Brothers and sisters may not always get along, but they always remain siblings.

In contrast to the primary group, the **secondary group** is *a large and impersonal social group whose members pursue a specific goal or activity.* In most respects, secondary groups have precisely the opposite characteristics of primary groups. *Secondary relationships* involve weak emotional ties and little personal knowledge of one another. Most secondary groups are short term, beginning and ending without particular significance. Students in a college sociology course, for instance, who probably will not see many of the others again after the semester ends, exemplify the secondary group.

Secondary groups include many more people than primary groups. For example, dozens or even hundreds of people may work together in the same office, yet most of them pay only passing attention to one another. In some cases, time may transform a group from

NOTE: Primary groups involve bonds of affection but not necessarily of intimacy. Parents generally strive to treat children in an evenhanded and equal, if therefore impersonal, fashion. The adjectival form of "family"—*familiar*—also implies something less than intimacy. See the marriage box in Chapter 18 ("Family").

NOTE: Some categories of groups—peer groups, for example—cut across the primary-secondary continuum.

DISCUSS: Under what circumstances does somebody feel "used" by a friend? What does this feeling tell us about the character of ideal friendship?

NOTE: Emphasizing the expressive component while discounting the instrumental element of primary relationships is an example of Goffman's concept of idealization.

Q: "Blood is thicker than water." Old saying

secondary to primary, as with co-workers who share an office for many years. But, generally, members of a secondary group do not think of themselves as "we."

Whereas members of primary groups display a *personal orientation,* people in secondary groups have a *goal orientation.* Secondary ties need not be hostile or cold, of course. Interaction between students, co-workers, and business associates often is pleasant even if it is impersonal. But whereas primary group members define themselves according to *who* they are in terms of kinship or personal qualities, people in secondary groups look to one another for *what* they are or what they can do for each other. Put simply, people in secondary groups tend to "keep score," mindful of what they give others and what they receive in return. This goal orientation means that secondary group members usually remain formal and polite. In a secondary relationship, therefore, we ask the question "How are you?" without expecting a truthful answer.

Table 7–1 summarizes the characteristics that distinguish primary and secondary groups. Keep in mind that these traits define two types of groups in ideal terms; many real groups contain elements of both. But putting these concepts at opposite ends of a continuum helps us describe and analyze group life.

Many people think that small towns and rural areas have mostly primary relationships and that large cities are characterized by more secondary ties. This generalization holds much truth, but some urban neighborhoods—especially those populated by people of a single ethnic or religious category—are very tightly knit.

GROUP LEADERSHIP

How do groups operate? One important element of group dynamics is leadership. Many small friendship groups have no leader at all, but most large secondary groups have a formal chain of command.

Two Leadership Roles

Groups typically benefit from two kinds of leadership. **Instrumental leadership** is *group leadership that emphasizes the completion of tasks.* Members look to instrumental leaders to get things done. **Expressive leadership,** on the other hand, is *group leadership that focuses on collective well-being.* Expressive leaders take less of an interest in achieving goals than in raising group morale and minimizing tension and conflict between members.

Because they concentrate on performance, instrumental leaders usually have formal, secondary relationships with other group members. Instrumental

TABLE 7–1 Primary Groups and Secondary Groups: A Summary		
	Primary Group ←→	**Secondary Group**
Quality of Relationships	Personal orientation	Goal orientation
Duration of Relationships	Usually long term	Variable; often short term
Breadth of Relationships	Broad; usually involving many activities	Narrow; usually involving few activities
Subjective Perception of Relationships	As ends in themselves	As means to an end
Typical Examples	Families; circles of friends	Co-workers; political organizations

leaders give orders and reward or punish members according to their contribution to the group's efforts. Expressive leaders build more personal, primary ties. They offer sympathy to a member going through a tough time, keep the group united, and lighten a tense moment with humor. Whereas successful instrumental leaders enjoy more *respect* from members, expressive leaders generally receive more personal *affection.*

In the traditional North American family, the two types of leadership are linked to gender. Historically, cultural norms bestowed instrumental leadership on men, who, as fathers and husbands, assumed primary responsibility for earning income and making major family decisions. Expressive leadership traditionally belonged to women: Mothers and wives encouraged supportive and peaceful relationships between family members. One result of this division of labor was that many children had greater respect for their fathers but closer personal ties with their mothers (Parsons & Bales, 1955; Macionis, 1978a).

Greater equality between men and women has blurred this gender-based distinction between instrumental and expressive leadership. In most group settings, women and men now assume both leadership roles.

Three Leadership Styles

Sociologists also characterize leadership in terms of decision-making style. *Authoritarian leadership* focuses

Use Your Strategies 3 Questions

AFTER YOU READ

1. Describe your plan.

2. Explain and verify how you know your reading was successful. For example, during the planning stage, did you set questions for yourself? Did you answer them correctly after reading?

3. Describe any information you still need to find and/or understand and your plan to accomplish it.

4. Explain your review strategy.

REFLECT AND CONNECT

A. The specific strategies you need to be successful in your biology class are different than those you need in your English class, which are different than those you need in your psychology class. In fact, what you must do to be successful in your psychology class with Professor Smith is different than what your friend must do to be successful in his psychology class with Professor Jones. To develop a plan to be successful in each of your classes, talk with each of your instructors. Ask for advice on taking notes, reading the text, and preparing for her exams. Gather information about requirements and assignments. Make a list of the specific actions you must do to be successful in each class.

B. One of the fix-up strategies you can use when you have difficulty understanding what you are reading is to ask someone for help. For each of your classes, identify two people you can call on for help. After you have checked with your sources, list when and where they are available and how to contact them.

C. Where do you normally do your reading and studying? Do you think that environment helps or hurts your comprehension? What are some ways you could improve your environment?

LOG ON TO THE WEB

These Web sites contain study skills information or links to reading and study skills information.

Log on to one of these sites or use a search engine to locate another academic help site.

http://www.rio.maricopa.edu/ci/riointernet/ss/study/main.shtml

http://studyweb.chemek.cc.or.us

http://www.dartmouth.edu/~acskills/success/index.html

http://www.ucc.vt.edu/stdysk/stdyhlp.html

Read at least two sections of information on the site. Write down one strategy you discovered that you are adding to your toolbox and turn it in to your professor.

REFERENCES

Anderson, T. H., & B. B. Armbruster. (1984). "Studying." In P. D. Pearson (Ed.), *Handbook of Reading Research*. New York: Longman, 657–79.

Grabe, W. & F. Stoller. (2002). *Teaching and Researching Reading*. Great Britain: Pearson Education, 9.

Pressley, M., & P. Afflerbach. (1995). *Verbal Protocols of Reading: The Nature of Constructively Responsive Reading*. Hillsdale, NJ: Erlbaum.

Pressley, M., R. Brown, P. B. El-Dinary, & P. Afflerbach. (1995). "The comprehension instruction that students need: Instruction fostering constructively responsive reading." *Learning Disabilities Research and Practice*, 10, 215–224.

Wyatt, D., M. Pressley, P. El-Dinary, S. Stein, P. Evans, & R. Brown. (1993). "Comprehension strategies, worth and credibility monitoring, and evaluations: Cold and hot cognition when experts read professional articles that are important to them." *Learning and Individual Differences*, 5, 49–72.

read-ing (red´in) *adj.* **1** inclined ... ad or study **2** ma...
reading n. **1** the act or practic... ...person who read...
of books **2** a public entertainm... ...which literary ...
aloud **3** the extent to which a ... ...n has read **4** ma...
meant to be read **5** the amoun... ...asured as by a ba...
thermometer **6** the form of a specified word, sentenc...

Building Vocabulary

English is such a deliciously complex and undisciplined language, we can bend, fuse, distort words to all our purposes. We give old words new meanings, and we borrow new words from any language that intrudes into our intellectual environment.

—Willard Gaylin

AN IDEA TO THINK ABOUT

English truly is a living language. We invent new words, transform words from other languages, and create new definitions for existing words. We even stop using words that no long work for us. And now, Netlingo and IM (instant messaging) are adding a whole new dimension of acronyms, abbreviations, and emoticons—keyboard characters used to create pictures—into our language.

That's a very good thing for writers because it means they can use whatever combination of words they think will best communicate their thoughts and ideas. However, it's not necessarily a positive thing for readers because it means we often run into words we don't understand. This is unfortunate because studies have shown that when students come across an unknown word in a text, they spend little time searching the text for context cues or looking up the word's meaning in a dictionary (Nist & Olejnik, 1995).

What do you do when you come across a word you don't know? Perhaps you ask someone what it means or you look it up in the dictionary. What else could you try?

CHAPTER FOCUS

Vocabulary knowledge increases reading comprehension (Anderson & Freebody, 1981; Bauman & Kameenui, 1991; Beck & McKeown, 1991). That means the more words you understand, the more likely you are to accurately comprehend what you read.

One way to increase the number of words you know is to work through a text- or computer-based program designed to add words to your vocabulary. The goal of many of these programs is for you to learn 500 to 1,000 new words and their common dictionary definitions.

Another way to improve your vocabulary, and your comprehension, is to become actively involved with the words you read. To accomplish this, you must use a variety of strategies, including using context clues, applying your knowledge of word parts, and checking the dictionary, because "what an expert reader does when encountering an unknown . . . word in one text situation may differ from what is done when an unknown . . . word is met in another textual situation" (Duffy, Roehler, & Herrmann, 1988).

As you preview this chapter, turn the main headings into questions. For example, change the next heading, "Using Context Clues to Define Words and Phrases," to "How can I use context clues to define words and phrases?" and jot down your preliminary answers. Then, as you read and gain new information, revise your answers.

USING CONTEXT CLUES TO DEFINE WORDS AND PHRASES

Define these five words: *call, put, covered, uncovered,* and *naked.*

That was easy, wasn't it? Yet in this paragraph from the stockbroker's newsletter you read in Chapter 1, your definitions for the words probably didn't help you understand the paragraph.

Writing or selling Options against stock you already own is a strategy that is conservative and usually works well in a trading market. An Option is either a *call* (a right to buy 100 shares of stock at a specified price in the future) or a *put* (a right to sell 100 shares of stock at a specified price in the future). Thus an Option buyer or seller who owns no stock (called *uncovered* or *naked*) is a speculator who is looking at making large percentage returns on a small amount of invested capital in a short time. This individual would be paying the Option premium to us, the *covered* writer. (Schneider, Kirk's Quotes)

This is because words do not have just one isolated meaning. Words take on meaning from their **context**, that is, they are used in conjunction with other words in the sentence and surrounding sentences.

Active readers—readers thinking about and looking for related information—can often use the context to help them understand the meaning of an unfamiliar word. For example, I just gave you a **context clue**: I defined what I meant by "active reader" and set it off with dashes (—).

For more examples, look back in the stockbroker's paragraph. For four of the words—*call, put, uncovered, naked*—the writer gives specific definitions for the words. To help you define the word *covered,* he gives the definition for its opposite—*uncovered.*

Word meanings you construct using context clues are not wild guesses; they are reasoned **inferences** drawn from the author's information. To infer a definition, you combine all the information an author provides and figure out the meaning the word has in this context. Unless the passage is extremely difficult and contains too many unfamiliar words, using context clues can save you time and assure that you have the best definition for the context.

Types of Context Clues

Authors use a variety of context clues. These passages from Macionis's *Sociology* illustrate several of the most common clues.

An author often directly states a *definition* for a word.

A DEFINITION CONTEXT CLUE   A distinctive perspective is central to the discipline of *sociology,* which is defined as the scientific study of human social activity. As an academic discipline, sociology is continually learning more about how human beings as social creatures think and act.

Explanation   Macionis gives a specific definition for *sociology:* "the scientific study of human social activity."

Sometimes authors help you understand a word or phrase by giving an *example* or an *explanation.*

AN EXAMPLE CONTEXT CLUE   When describing cultural diversity, sociologists often use the term *subculture.* Teenagers, Polish-Americans, homeless people, and "southerners" are all examples of subcultures within American societies. Occupations also foster subculture differences, including specialized ways of speaking, as anyone who has ever spent time with race car drivers, jazz musicians, or even sociologists can attest.

Explanation   Macionis helps us understand the term *subculture* by giving examples: teenagers, Polish-Americans, homeless people, and southerners, race car drivers, jazz musicians, and sociologists.

AN EXPLANATION CONTEXT CLUE   One way to limit distortion caused by personal values is through the *replication* of research. When the same results are obtained by subsequent studies, there is increased confidence that the original research was conducted objectively.

Explanation   Macionis explains what he means by *replication:* subsequent studies.

Occasionally, authors use the *opposite* of the word as a clue.

USING AN OPPOSITE TERM AS A CONTEXT CLUE   Each of the methods of conducting sociological investigation described so far involves researchers personally collecting their own data. Doing so is not always possible, however, and it is often not necessary. In many cases, sociologists engage in *secondary analysis.*

Explanation   In this paragraph Macionis gives a clue to what *secondary analysis* means by talking about its opposite: ". . . investigation described so far involves researchers personally collecting their own data," and "Doing so is not always possible. . . ."

As we have seen, authors also use *punctuation marks,* such as dashes, colons, parentheses, or commas, to call attention to their word clues.

PUNCTUATION AS A CONTEXT CLUE   The logic of science is clearly expressed in the *experiment*—a research method that investigates cause-and-effect relationships under highly controlled conditions. Experimental research tends to be explanatory, meaning that it is concerned not with just what happens but with why. Experiments are typically devised to test a specific *hypothesis*—an unverified statement of a relationship between any facts or variables. In everyday language, a hypothesis is simply a hunch or educated guess about what the research will show.

Explanation   Macionis uses a dash (—) to indicate he is giving a definition for *experiment* and *hypothesis.*

EXAMPLE   Assume you are reading your astronomy text and come to the unfamiliar words *perihelion* and *aphelion.* See how you can use the context clues the author provides to determine their meanings.

> *Perihelion* is the point in the earth's orbit when the distance between the earth and the sun is at its minimum, as opposed to *aphelion.*

Explanation   The author defined *perihelion* directly (the point in the earth's orbit when the distance between the earth and the sun is at its minimum) and clued you to the definition of *aphelion* by stating it is the opposite (therefore, *aphelion* must be the point in the earth's orbit when the distance between the earth and the sun is at its maximum).

Exercise 1   **Defining Words Using Context Clues**

Use the author's context clues to unlock the meaning of the italicized words and phrases in these passages. Write the meaning of the word or phrase and describe the context clues you used.

1. The World Wide Web (WWW or Web) is a collection of standards and protocols used to access information available on the Internet. This information is in the form of documents linked together in what is called a *hypermedia* system. Hypermedia is combined-use multimedia (text, images, video, and sound) in a Web presentation page. (Leshin, *Student Resource Guide to the Internet*)

2. *Like terms* are terms that have the same variables with the same exponents. (Angel, *Elementary Algebra for College Students*)

3. Another distinctive feature of social psychology is that it is an experimentally based science. As experimental scientists, we test our assumptions, guesses, and ideas about human social behavior *empirically* and systematically rather than by relying on folk wisdom, common sense, or the opinions and insights of philosophers, novelists, political pundits, grandmothers, and others wise in the ways of human beings. (Aronson, Wilson, & Akert, *Social Psychology*)

4. A composer often provides a marking for *tempo*, or overall speed, to help convey the character of a composition. (Politoske, *Music*)

5. *Computerphobia*, the fear of computers, is apparently affecting more and more people as microcomputers continue to be plugged into more and more homes, schools, and offices throughout the land. This relatively recent phenomenon, also known as *cyberphobia*, occurs in a large proportion of students and professionals. (Fuori & Gioia, *Computers and Information Processing*)

6. In general, people *emigrate* from countries where they have limited prospects for earning a living, and they *migrate* to countries where they believe that economic opportunities await them. (Rubenstein, *Introduction to Human Geography*)

7. The American Psychological Association (APA) code calls on psychological scientists to respect the dignity and welfare of human subjects. People must participate voluntarily and must know enough about the study to make an intelligent decision about participating, a doctrine known as *informed consent*. (Wade & Tavris, *Psychology*)

8. Despite extensive media attention since the summer of 1988, global climate change remains a challenge to *lay comprehension*. One study found that 12 of 14 ordinary citizens surveyed had heard of global warming, but all held fundamental misconceptions about the process (Kempton, 1990). (Wilson & Henson, *Learning about Global Warming: A Study of Students and Journalists*)

9. At any time in history, there has been widespread agreement that some things are desirable and worth fighting for. . . . All of them, however, depend on power, for the distribution of power determines who can and cannot impose his or her will on others. In one sense, there is no single cause of war, but a *myriad*. (Kagan, Ozment, & Turner, *The Western Heritage*)

10. While *finer soil particles* (clay and silt) are carried on to finally settle out in lakes and bays, *coarser materials* (sand, stones, and rocks) eroded from gullies below poorly placed storm drains and stream bank are deposited in the bottom of the stream channel itself. (Nebel & Wright, *Environmental Science*)

USING PARTS OF A WORD TO HELP DEFINE IT

Another strategy you can use to understand a word is to analyze the parts of the word. For example, some words, such as *headache, overqualified,* and *childlike,* are combinations of two individual words. You can usually define these compound words by defining each individual word.

You can also look for a **root word** and any prefixes and/or suffixes as clues to the meaning of the entire word. The root is the basic part of a word. Adding a **prefix** at the beginning of a root word and/or a **suffix** at the end of a root word makes additional words. Prefixes and suffixes change the meaning of the root word. A suffix can also change the way a word can be used in a sentence and its part of speech. Combining the meanings of the word parts can help you understand the whole word.

For example, look at these words: *thermometer, thermal, thermostat, hypothermia, hyperthermia,* and *geothermal.* Each one contains a form of the root word *therm.* When you know that *therm* means heat, you have a key to understanding each of the words.

The more word parts you have in your knowledge base, the more words you will understand. For example, knowing that the prefix *geo* means earth, you understand that geothermal has to do with the earth's temperature. Plus, you have a key to understanding *geography, geocentric, geode, geodynamics, geology,* and *geomagnetic.*

Now, let's assume you are reading an astronomy text and you come to the words *perihelion* and *aphelion,* but the text does not provide any context clues. If you know, or can easily discover, the meanings of the word parts, you can define the words as easily as with context clues:

> *perihelion: peri* from the Greek meaning *near* + *helios* from the Greek meaning *the sun* = near the sun
>
> *aphelion: apo* from the Greek meaning *away from* + *helios* from the Greek meaning *the sun* = away from the sun

These meanings for *perihelion* and *aphelion* are very similar to the definitions we got from the context clues. We just used a different strategy.

Continuing the example, if you know that *apolune* means the point in the path of a body orbiting the moon that is farthest from the center of the moon, what does *perilune* mean? By combining what you already knew about *peri* (near) with the new information (*lune* means moon), you know that *perilune* means the point in the path of a body orbiting the moon that is nearest the center of the moon.

Linguists estimate that about half of the words in the English language are derived from Greek and Latin roots. So, the more word parts you know, the more words in that word "family" you can understand. In fact, researchers estimate that for every word part you know, you have the key to unlock the meaning of about seven more words.

Be aware, however, that because many of our roots, prefixes, and suffixes come from the ancient Latin, Greek, and Anglo-Saxon languages, the spelling and meanings may have changed over the years. Those changes can make using this strategy a challenge.

The following table lists some common word parts, their definitions, and an example word.

WORD PART	DEFINITION	EXAMPLE WORD
a, an	without, not	amoral, anarchy
able, ible	able to	visible
aminus, halare	breath	animate, exhale
ance, acy, ency	action, quality, state of	privacy
annu, anni	year	annual
ante, pre	before	antechamber, prepared
anthrop	humankind	anthropology
anti, contra	against	antidote, contradict
aqua	water	aquarium
archi	chief, first	archbishop
aster, astro	star	astronomy
audi, aur	hear	auditorium
auto	self	autobiography
bene	good	beneficial
bi, di	two, both	biannual, dichotomy
bio	living organisms	biology
carcin	cancer	carcinogen
cardio	heart	cardiology
cent, hecto	hundred	century
chrono	time	chronograph
circum, peri	around	circumvent, perimeter
con, com, co	with, together	congregate
crede	belief	credibility
de	down or away	depose
deca	ten	decade
demo	the people	democracy
derm	skin	dermatologist
dict	speak	diction
dis	not or away	dislike
divers	different	diverse
duc, duct	lead, make, shape	reproduce
ec, eco	habitat	ecology
ence, ency	action, quality of	competency

WORD PART	DEFINITION	EXAMPLE WORD
er, or, st	one who, thing which	actor
ex	out	exhale
flect, flex	bend	reflect, flexible
fy, ify, ize	make, form into	magnify
ful, ose	full of	careful, verbose
gene, gen	origin, type	genetics
geo	earth	geography
geron, geras	aging, old age	gerontology
grad, gress	to go, take steps	graduate, regress
graph, graphy	writing, record	autobiography
halare, aminus	breath	exhale, animate
helio	sun	heliotrope
hemi	half	hemisphere
hemo	blood	hemoglobin
hetro	different	heterosexual
homo	same	homosexual
hyper	excessive, more than normal	hyperthermia
hypo	low, less than	hypothermic
il, in, im, ir	in/into or not	illogical, inactive
inter	among, between	intermural
intra	within, inside	intramural
ism	quality or doctrine of	conservatism
kilo	thousand	kilometer
less	without	homeless
lingua	language	bilingual
literate, literatus	able to read/write	illiterate
locu, loqu, log	speak	loquacious
logy	study of	anthropology
macro	large	macroeconomics
mal	bad	malfunction
manu	by hand	manual
mega	large	megastore
meter	to measure	thermometer
micro	small	microeconomics
milli	thousand	millimeter
miss, mitt	send	transmit

WORD PART	DEFINITION	EXAMPLE WORD
mono, uni	one, single	monotone, unity
mor, mort	die	mortician
morph	form	amorphous
multi	many	multifaceted
neo	new	neophyte
nomen, nym	name	synonym
non	not	noncooperation
ology	study of	biology
omni	all, everywhere	omnipresent
para	beside, beyond	paranormal
pathy	feeling	empathy
ped, pod	foot	pedestrian
peri, circum	around	perimeter, circumvent
phobia	fear	claustrophobia
phono	sound	phonograph
poly	many	polygamy
port	carry	portable
post	after, behind	postmortem
pre, ante	before, in front of	prepared, antechamber
pro	in favor of, ahead of	progress
proto	original; chief	prototype
pseudo	false	pseudonym
psych	mind, soul	psychology
quad, tetra	four	quadruplets, tetrad
quint, penta	five	quintuplet, pentagram
re	again	reproduce
retro	backward	retrospective
scribe, script	write	prescription
sect, seg	cut	dissect
semi	half	semicircle
soph	wise	philosophy
spect	look at, see	inspect
sub	under, below	subway
super, supra	above	supervisor
tact, tang	touch	tactile, tangible
tele, trans	across, over a distance	telegraph, transport
therm	heat	thermometer

WORD PART	DEFINITION	EXAMPLE WORD
ultra	beyond, excessive	ultraism
un, non	not	uncooperative
uni, mono	one	unity, monotone
vid, vis	see	video, visible

Exercise 2 ▸ Defining Words Using Word Parts

Use the table and your understanding of word parts to discover the meaning of the italicized words in these passages. Write the meaning of the word or phrase.

1. It is the loss of this *biodiversity* and the loss of *irreplaceable* ancient forests that most concern environmentalists about the issue of logging in national forests. (Scott, "Hoots to Blame?")

2. In the industrialized countries, 3.3 percent of the adult population is *illiterate.* For the developing countries as a whole, the figure is 35 percent and rises as high as 60 percent in the 47 least developed countries. (Bequette, *UNESCO Courier*)

3. In *telecommunications* we are moving to a single worldwide information network, just as economically we are becoming one global marketplace. (Naisbitt & Aburdene, *Megatrends 2000*)

4. Baca recalls her role in the beginning of the Chicano Mural Movement when she was searching for a way to express her own experience as a Hispanic American artist. Greatly influenced by the Mexican muralists, Baca discovered a means of community *empowerment.* (Estrada, "Judy Baca's Art for Peace")

5. Moving from our analysis of the term communication, we now examine the process of communication. We begin by studying a communication model and the three types of communication important to our study in this text: *intrapersonal, interpersonal,* and mass communication. (Bittner, *Each Other*)

6. The compost pile is really a teeming *microbial* farm. (Office of Environmental Affairs, *Backyard Composting*)

7. We hold these truths to be self-evident, that all men are created equal, that they are endowed by their creator with certain *unalienable* rights, that among these are life, liberty, and the pursuit of happiness. (Declaration of Independence)

8. Erathosthenes, the first person of record to use the word *geography,* accepted that Earth was round, as few did in his day; he also calculated its *circumference* within an amazing 0.5 percent accuracy. (Rubenstein, *Introduction to Human Geography*)

9. *Democracy* has evolved over time in America—and is still evolving. To illustrate, consider how many of your classmates have the power to vote and participate in politics. Virtually all of you do now. On the other hand, how many of your classmates are free white males over the age of twenty-one who also own land? This small handful of people in your

class would have been the only ones entrusted with the vote at the time of the framing of the Constitution. (Berman & Murphy, *Approaching Democracy*)

10. Moving air, like moving water, is turbulent and able to pick up loose debris and *transport* it to other locations. (Lutgens & Tarbuck, *Foundations of Earth Science*)

USING A DICTIONARY TO DEFINE WORDS AND PHRASES

There will be times when you can't piece together any helpful information from the context or the structure of the word. When this happens, take the time to look the word up in the book's glossary or a dictionary.

A glossary is a quick, easy-to-use resource because it lists only the specific meaning of the word as it is used in the book. Not all books provide a glossary (and even those that do sometimes won't provide enough information—such as how to pronounce the word), so sometimes you must consult a dictionary.

A dictionary is a reliable source of all the definitions for a word. In addition, the dictionary lists the correct spelling variations, pronunciations, parts of speech, and derivations.

EXAMPLE   The meaning of the word *rudimentary* in this passage is not clear. Does it mean low or high?

> The increasing power of the personal computer is making it possible to develop applications that are smarter and more responsive to the user. . . . Anyone who has used a spelling or grammar checker has experienced this type of application at a very *rudimentary* level.

If *rudimentary* is an unfamiliar word, your best resource is the dictionary.

> **ru·di·men·ta·ry** (rōō′də men′tər ē, -men′trē) *adj.* of, or having the nature of, a rudiment or rudiments; specif., *a)* elementary *b)* incompletely or imperfectly developed *c)* vestigial Also **ru′di·men′tal** — **ru·di·men·tari·ly** (rōō′də men ter′ə lē, -men′tər ə lē) *adv.* —**ru′di·men′ta·ri·ness** *n.*

Explanation   Since the word means elementary, in this passage the author means that anyone who has used a spelling or grammar checker has experienced this type of application at a very *basic* or *low* level.

Assume that this time when you come across *perihelion* and *aphelion* in your astronomy text, you don't have any context clues and you don't know the meaning of the word parts. Looking up the words in a dictionary gives you literal meanings similar to those you determined by using context clues or word parts.

> **peri·he·li·on** (per′i hē′lē ən, -hēl′yən) *n., pl.* **-li·ons** or **-li·a** (-ə) ⟦ModL < Gr *peri-*, around + *hēlios*, the SUN¹⟧ the point nearest the sun in the orbit of a planet, comet, or man-made satellite: see APHELION, illus.

a|phe|li·on (ə fēʹlē ən, -fēlʹyən) ***n.***, *pl.* **-li·ons** or **-li|a** (-ə) ⟦ModL, altered (as if Gr) by Johannes KEPLER < earlier *aphelium* < Gr *apo-*, from + *hēlios*, SUN¹; modeled on L *apogaeum*, APOGEE⟧ the point farthest from the sun in the orbit of a planet or comet, or of a man-made satellite in orbit around the sun: opposed to PERIHELI-ON

Unfortunately, finding the correct meaning of a word in the dictionary is not always this clear-cut. Many words have more than one meaning and can be used as more than one part of speech. Each time you look up a word in the dictionary, your job is to sort through the many definitions, select the one definition you think best fits the context, and fit that meaning back into the original context to be certain it makes sense.

EXAMPLE If you look up the word *base* in a dictionary, you find a variety of definitions.

base¹ (bās) ***n.***, *pl.* **basʹes** (-iz) ⟦ME < OFr *bas* < L *basis*, BASIS⟧ **1** the thing or part on which something rests; lowest part or bottom; foundation **2** the fundamental or main part, as of a plan, organization, system, theory, etc. **3** the principal or essential ingredient, or the one serving as a vehicle *[paint with an oil base]* **4** anything from which a start is made; basis **5** *Baseball* any of the three sand-filled bags *(first base, second base, or third base)* that must be reached safely one after the other to score a run **6** the point of attachment of a part of the body *[the base of the thumb]* **7** a center of operations or source of supply; headquarters, as of a military operation or exploring expedition **8** *a)* the bottommost layer or coat, as of paint *b)* a makeup cream to give a desired color to the skin, esp. in the theater **9** *Archit.* the lower part, as of a column, pier, or wall, regarded as a separate unit **10** *Chem.* any compound that can react with an acid to form a salt, the hydroxyl of the base being replaced by a negative ion: in modern theory, any substance that produces a negative ion and donates electrons to an acid to form covalent bonds: in water solution a base tastes bitter, turns red litmus paper blue, and, in dissociation theory, produces free hydroxyl ions: see pH **11** *Dyeing* a substance used for fixing colors **12** *Geom.* the line or plane upon which a figure is thought of as resting *[the base of a triangle]* **13** *Heraldry* the lower portion of a shield **14** *Linguis.* any morpheme to which prefixes, suffixes, etc. are or can be added; stem or root **15** *Math. a)* a whole number, esp. 10 or 2, made the fundamental number, and raised to various powers to produce the major counting units, of a number system; radix *b)* any number raised to a power by an exponent (see LOGARITHM) *c)* in business, etc., a starting or reference figure or sum upon which certain calculations are made —***adj.*** forming a base —***vt.*** **based, basʹing 1** to make or

Select the best dictionary definition of *base* for each of the following sentences.

1. In the expression 4^2, the 4 is called the *base,* and the 2 is called the exponent.

2. The Ionic order's most striking feature is the column, which rests on an ornately profiled *base* of its own.

3. The closing of the military *base* in the region prompted a quick economic decline.

4. Today's experiment will show whether the compound is *base* or acid.

5. Both investigation teams were working from the same *base* information.

Exercise 3 Selecting the Best Dictionary Definition

Each of the italicized words or phrases has multiple dictionary definitions.
Write the definition that best fits the context.

1. Your career depends not only on your efforts, but also on the efforts of
   many other people. You cannot be successful by yourself. You can only
   be successful as part of a joint effort by many different people, by acting in *harmony* with other people. All through your career, you will find
   yourself interdependent with other people. (Johnson, *Human Relations and
   Your Career*)

   > **har·mo·ny** (här′mə nē) *n.*, *pl.* **-nies** ⟦ME *armony* < OFr *harmonie* <
   > L *harmonia* < Gr < *harmos*, a fitting < IE base *ar- > ART, ARM¹⟧ **1**
   > a combination of parts into a pleasing or orderly whole; congruity **2**
   > agreement in feeling, action, ideas, interests, etc.; peaceable or
   > friendly relations **3** a state of agreement or orderly arrangement
   > according to color, size, shape, etc. **4** an arrangement of parallel
   > passages of different authors, esp. of the Scriptures, so as to bring
   > out corresponding ideas, qualities, etc. **5** agreeable sounds; music **6**
   > *Music a*) the simultaneous sounding of two or more tones, esp. when
   > satisfying to the ear *b*) structure in terms of the arrangement,
   > modulation, etc. of chords (distinguished from MELODY, RHYTHM) *c*)
   > the study of this structure —***SYN.*** SYMMETRY

2. The growth of the Sun Belt and the decline of the Snow Belt were tied
   to new resource problems facing the United States in the 1970s. For the
   first time in its history the country faced an *acute* energy crisis. (Unger,
   These United States)

   > **a·cute** (ə kyo͞ot′) *adj.* ⟦L *acutus*, pp. of *acuere*, sharpen: see ACUMEN⟧
   > **1** having a sharp point **2** keen or quick of mind; shrewd **3** sensitive
   > to impressions *[acute* hearing] **4** severe and sharp, as pain, jeal-
   > ousy, etc. **5** severe but of short duration; not chronic: said of some
   > diseases **6** very serious; critical; crucial *[an acute* shortage of work-
   > ers] **7** shrill; high in pitch **8** of less than 90 degrees *[an acute*
   > angle]: see ANGLE¹, illus. **9** INTENSIVE (sense 3) —**a·cute′ly** *adv.* —
   > **a·cute′ness** *n.*
   > **SYN.**—**acute** suggests severe intensification of an event, condition, etc.
   > that is sharply approaching a climax *[an acute* shortage]; **critical** is
   > applied to a turning point which will decisively determine an outcome *[the
   > critical* battle of a war]; **crucial** comes into contrast with **critical** where a
   > trial determining a line of action rather than a decisive turning point is
   > involved *[a crucial* debate on foreign policy] See also SHARP

3. Science is an important foundation of all sociological research and,
   more broadly, helps us to *critically* evaluate information we encounter
   every day. (Macionis, *Sociology*)

   > **crit·i·cal** (krit′i kəl) *adj.* **1** tending to find fault; censorious **2** char-
   > acterized by careful analysis and judgment *[a sound critical* esti-
   > mate of the problem] **3** of critics or criticism **4** of or forming a
   > crisis or turning point; decisive **5** dangerous or risky; causing anxi-
   > ety *[a critical* situation in international relations] **6** of the crisis of
   > a disease **7** designating or of important products or raw materials
   > subject to increased production and restricted distribution under
   > strict control, as in wartime **8** *a*) designating or of a point at which
   > a change in character, property, or condition is effected *b*)
   > designating or of the point at which a nuclear chain reaction
   > becomes self-sustaining —**crit′i·cal·ly** *adv.* —**crit′i·cal·i·ty** (-kal′ə tē)
   > or **crit′i·cal·ness** *n.*

4. A *front* usually is in constant motion, shifting the position of the boundary between the air masses but maintaining its function as a barrier between them. Usually one air mass is actively displacing the other; thus
   the *front* advances in the direction dictated by the movement of the
   more active air mass. (Bergman & McKnight, *Introduction to Geography*)

front (frunt) *n.* ⟦ME < OFr < L *frons* (gen. *frontis*), forehead, front < IE *bhren-*, to project > OE *brant*, steep, high⟧ **1** *a)* the forehead *b)* the face; countenance **2** *a)* attitude or appearance, as of the face, indicating state of mind; external behavior when facing a problem, etc. *[to put on a bold front] b)* [Colloq.] an appearance, usually pretended or assumed, of social standing, wealth, etc. **3** [Rare] impudence; effrontery **4** the part of something that faces forward or is regarded as facing forward; most important side **5** the first part; beginning *[toward the front of the book]* **6** the place or position directly before a person or thing **7** a forward or leading position or situation ☆**8** the first available bellhop or page, as in a hotel: generally used as a call **9** the land bordering a lake, ocean, street, etc. **10** [Brit.] a promenade along a body of water **11** the advanced line, or the whole area, of contact between opposing sides in warfare; combat zone **12** a specified area of activity *[the home front, the political front]* **13** a broad movement in which different groups are united for the achievement of certain common political or social aims ☆**14** a person who serves as a public representative of a business, group, etc., usually because of his or her prestige ☆**15** a person or group used to cover or obscure the activity or objectives of another, controlling person or group **16** a stiff bosom, worn with formal clothes **17** *Archit.* a face of a building; esp., the face with the principal entrance **18** *Meteorol.* the boundary between two air masses of different density and temperature —*adj.* **1** at, to, in, on, or of the front **2** *Phonet.* articulated with the tongue toward the front of the mouth: said of certain vowels, as (i) in *bid* —*vt.* **1** to face; be opposite to **2** to be before in place **3** to meet; confront **4** to defy; oppose **5** to supply or serve as a front, or facing, of —*vi.* **1** to face in a certain direction *[a castle fronting on the sea]* ☆**2** to act as a FRONT (senses 14 & 15): with *for* —**in front of** before; in a position ahead of

5. The effects created by different intensities of sound, or dynamics, are basic to all musical expression. In traditional music, we often first become aware of the impact of dynamic effects upon hearing very sudden changes from soft to loud, or vice versa. For some of us, the first awareness of musical dynamics is very obvious, as in the so-called "Surprise" Symphony of Franz Joseph Haydn (1732–1809). Here, the surprise is a *radical* change in volume, a very loud chord coming on the heels of a gentle melody. (Politoske, *Music*)

rad·i·cal (rad'i kəl) *adj.* ⟦ME < LL *radicalis* < L *radix* (gen. *radicis*), ROOT[1]⟧ **1** *a)* of or from the root or roots; going to the foundation or source of something; fundamental; basic *[a radical principle] b)* extreme; thorough *[a radical change in one's life]* **2** *a)* favoring fundamental or extreme change; specif., favoring basic change in the social or economic structure *b)* [R-] designating or of any of various modern political parties, esp. in Europe, ranging from moderate to conservative in program **3** *Bot.* of or coming from the root **4** *Math.* having to do with the root or roots of a number or quantity —*n.* **1** *a)* a basic or root part of something *b)* a fundamental **2** *a)* a person holding radical views, esp. one favoring fundamental social or economic change *b)* [R-] a member or adherent of a Radical party **3** *Chem.* a group of two or more atoms that acts as a single atom and goes through a reaction unchanged, or is replaced by a single atom: it is normally incapable of separate existence **4** *Math. a)* the indicated root of a quantity or quantities, shown by an expression written under the radical sign *b)* RADICAL SIGN —*SYN.* LIBERAL —**rad'i·cal·ness** *n.*

6. Of special concern to anyone seeking to enact justice are criminal justice and civil justice—both of which are aspects of a wider form of equity termed social justice. Social justice is a concept that *embraces* all aspects of civilized life. (Schmalleger, *Criminal Justice Today*)

em·brace[1] (em brās', im-) *vt.* **-braced', -brac'ing** ⟦ME *embracen* < OFr *embracier* < VL *imbrachiare* < L *im-*, in + *brachium*, an arm: see BRACE[1]⟧ **1** to clasp in the arms, usually as an expression of affection or desire; hug **2** to accept readily; avail oneself of *[to embrace an opportunity]* **3** to take up or adopt, esp. eagerly or seriously *[to embrace a new profession]* **4** to encircle; surround; enclose *[an isle embraced by the sea]* **5** to include; contain *[biology embraces botany and zoology]* **6** to take in mentally; perceive *[his glance embraced the scene]* —*vi.* to clasp or hug each other in the arms —*SYN.* INCLUDE —**em·brace'a·ble** *adj.* —**em·brace'ment** *n.* —**em·brac'er** *n.*

7. Democracy as a political system has become increasingly popular. Freedom House recently reported that "in 1900, 70 countries had governments elected on the principal of universal adult *suffrage*. Today, there are 119 such countries, or 62 percent of all the countries in the world." (Berman & Murphy, *Approaching Democracy*)

> **suf·frage** (suf′rij) *n.* ⟦ME < MFr < ML(Ec) < L *suffragium*, decision, vote, suffrage < *sub-* (see SUB-) + *fragor*, loud applause, orig., din, a crashing < IE base *bhreĝ-*, to crash, BREAK⟧ **1** a prayer or act of intercession or supplication **2** a vote or voting; esp., a vote in favor of some candidate or issue ☆**3** the right to vote, esp. in political elections; franchise

8. Until the nineteenth century, psychology was not a formal *discipline*. Of course, most of the great thinkers of history, from Aristotle to Zoroaster, raised questions that today would be called psychological. (Wade & Tavris, *Psychology*)

> **dis·ci·pline** (dis′ə plin′, -plən) *n.* ⟦ME < OFr *descepline* < L *disciplina* < *discipulus*: see DISCIPLE⟧ **1** a branch of knowledge or learning **2** *a)* training that develops self-control, character, or orderliness and efficiency *b)* strict control to enforce obedience **3** the result of such training or control; specif., *a)* self-control or orderly conduct *b)* acceptance of or submission to authority and control **4** a system of rules, as for a church or monastic order **5** treatment that corrects or punishes —*vt.* **-plined′, -plin′ing 1** to subject to discipline; train; control **2** to punish —*SYN.* PUNISH — **dis′ci·plin′a|ble** *adj.* —**dis′ci·plin|al** *adj.* —**dis′ci·plin|er** *n.*

9. The objective of nuclear power technology is to control nuclear reactions so that energy is released gradually as heat energy. As with *plants* powered by fossil fuels, the heat energy is used to boil water and produce steam, which then drives conventional turbogenerators. (Nebel and Wright, *Environmental Science*)

> **plant** (plant, plänt) *n.* ⟦ME *plante* < OE < L *planta*, sprout, twig, prob. back-form. < *plantare*, to smooth the soil for planting < *planta*, sole of the foot < IE *plat-*, var. of base *pla-*, broad, flat > PLAIN¹⟧ **1** any of a kingdom (Plantae) of eukaryotes generally characterized by the ability to carry on photosynthesis in its cells which contain chloroplasts and have cellulose in the cell wall, including all thallophytes and embryophytes **2** a young tree, shrub, or herb, ready to put into other soil for growth to maturity; a slip, cutting, or set **3** an herb, as distinguished from a tree or shrub **4** the tools, machinery, buildings, grounds, etc. of a factory or business **5** the equipment, buildings, etc. of any institution, as a hospital, school, etc. **6** the apparatus or equipment for some particular mechanical operation or process *[the power plant of a ship]* **7** [Slang] a person placed, or thing planned or used, to trick, mislead, or trap —*vt.* ⟦ME *planten* < OE *plantian* & OFr *planter*, both < L *plantare* < the *n.*⟧ **1** *a)* to put into soil, esp. into the ground, to grow *b)* to set plants in (a piece of ground) **2** to set firmly as into the ground; fix in position **3** to fix in the mind; implant (an idea, etc.) **4** to settle (a colony, colonists, etc.); found; establish **5** to furnish or stock with animals ☆**6** to put a stock of (oysters, young fish, etc.) in a body of water **7** [Slang] to deliver (a punch, blow, etc.) with force **8** [Slang] *a)* to place (a person or thing) in such a way as to trick, trap, etc. *b)* to place (an ostensible news item) in a newspaper, etc. with some ulterior motive, as in order to mold public opinion **9** [Slang] *a)* to hide or conceal *b)* to place (something) surreptitiously where it is certain to be found or discovered —**plant′like′** *adj.*

10. Sumerian and Babylonian schools emphasized language and literature, accounting, legal practice, and mathematics, especially geometry, along with memorization of much *abstract* knowledge that had no relevance to everyday life. (Kagan, Ozment, & Turner, *The Western Heritage*)

ab·stract (*for adj.*, ab strakt′, ab′strakt′; *for n. 1 & vt. 4*, ab′strakt′; *for n. 2*, ab′strakt′, ab strakt′; *for vt. 1, 2, & 3*, ab strakt′) **adj.** [[< L *abstractus*, pp. of *abstrahere*, to draw from, separate < *ab(s)*-, from + *trahere*, to DRAW]] **1** thought of apart from any particular instances or material objects; not concrete **2** expressing a quality thought of apart from any particular or material object /beauty is an *abstract* word/ **3** not easy to understand; abstruse **4** theoretical; not practical or applied **5** designating or of art abstracted from reality, in which designs or forms may be definite and geometric or fluid and amorphous: a generic term that encompasses various non-realistic contemporary schools —**n. 1** a brief statement of the essential content of a book, article, speech, court record, etc.; summary **2** an abstract thing, condition, idea, etc. —**vt. 1** to take away; remove **2** to take dishonestly; steal **3** to think of (a quality) apart from any particular instance or material object that has it; also, to form (a general idea) from particular instances **4** to summarize; make an abstract of —**SYN.** ABRIDGMENT —**in the abstract** in theory as apart from practice —**ab·stract′er** *n.* —**ab·stract′ly** *adv.* —**ab·stract′ness** *n.*

CONNOTATIVE MEANINGS

Up to this point we've concentrated on finding a <mark>literal meaning</mark>, or <mark>denotative meaning</mark>, for a word. But words often mean more than their dictionary definitions. That is, words can suggest meanings that trigger an assortment of feelings and emotions. These associated meanings are called <mark>connotations</mark>—what the word makes the reader think about and feel. Because of these meanings beyond the literal, authors can subtly influence readers with the words they select.

For example, which of these descriptions do you think I prefer?

Dr. McGrath is petite, has reddish-brown hair, and has a good sense of humor.

Dr. McGrath is a runt, has reddish-brown hair, and has a good sense of humor.

Yes, even though I have a good sense of humor, I do prefer being called petite. Why? Because even though both petite and runt mean "short" in the dictionary, they make me feel differently because of their connotations. For me, the connotation of petite is positive: small and delicate. The connotation of runt is negative: unnaturally short.

Consider the differences between the denotative and connotative meanings of the italicized words in each pair of passages.

A. Jeff was very *confident* about getting the job because he scored well on the written exam.

B. Jeff was very *cocky* about getting the job because he scored well on the written exam.

A. Because they felt so strongly about the issue, Karen and Bill took part in a *rally* at the capital.

B. Because they felt so strongly about the issue, Karen and Bill took part in a *demonstration* at the capital.

In everyday reading, however, you don't have two versions of the same passage to compare. Therefore, once you have determined the literal meaning, ask yourself if the word or phrase makes you feel or react—positively or negatively—beyond its meaning.

For example, does the word seem to soften the impact of the message (*antipersonnel weapon* instead of *bomb*) or intensify your reaction to the message (*guerrilla fighters* instead of *freedom fighters*)?

Authors choose words for their maximum impact—including their connotative meaning. You must understand both the denotative and connotative meaning of the words to fully understand the author's message. We'll take another look at how authors influence us by their choice of words in Chapter 7.

Exercise 4   **Consider Both the Connotative and Denotative Meanings**

Read each pair of words. List their literal definitions and then describe their connotations.

1. a. jock   b. athlete
2. a. reserved   b. inhibited
3. a. collect   b. hoard
4. a. impertinent   b. bold
5. a. nerd   b. techie
6. a. elderly gentleman   b. old man

Read each passage with special attention to the italicized phrases. Why do you think the author selected those words? What message does the author want to convey? What other words or phrases could be used that would be more neutral?

7. After *unsuccessfully peddling his idea* to every monarch of Western Europe, Columbus finally interested the rulers of Spain. (Unger, *These United States*)

8. By *crushing black leaders*, while *inflating the images of Uncle Toms* and celebrities from the world of *sport and play*, the mass media were able to *channel and control the aspirations and goals of the black masses.* (Cleaver, *Soul On Ice*)

9. To many minds, Hillary Clinton is the *quintessential yuppie mother* of the 1990s, juggling career and family with remarkable skill. (Editorial, *The Arizona Republic*)

10. Exemptions from ESA (the Endangered Species Act) can be granted by the *so-called God Squad,* which is convened at the request of the U.S. Secretary of the Interior. (Berke, "The Audubon View," *Audubon*)

FIGURATIVE LANGUAGE

From my drifting hot air balloon, the Hawaiian Islands looked like breadcrumbs floating in a bowl of soup.

Enthusiasm bubbled out of the petite 22-year-old Chrissy Oliver with the effervescence of a just-opened split of champagne.

Homelessness is a rusty blade ripping through the soul of humanity.

Each of these statements is an example of **figurative language**: using words in an imaginative way to help the reader comprehend the message more clearly. Certainly, I could have written the statements literally: "The Hawaiian Islands look small," "Chrissy Oliver was happy to win the race," or "Homelessness causes untold problems," but I would have taken the risk that you could not picture exactly what I wanted you to understand.

Although figurative language may not make sense literally, it does help you form a mental image, or picture, of what an author is talking about. Figurative expressions often compare something the author thinks you already know about to what he or she wants you to understand. The most basic of these comparisons are called **similes** (direct comparisons using the words *like* or *as*) and **metaphors** (implied comparisons).

For example, "the Hawaiian Islands looked like bread crumbs floating in a bowl of soup" is a direct comparison, because I say directly that the Islands look *like* floating breadcrumbs. I am comparing something I think you can picture (how bread crumbs look floating in a bowl of soup) to what I want you to be able to picture (how the Hawaiian Islands looked as I saw them from the hot air balloon—small pieces of land floating in the ocean").

"Homelessness is a rusty blade ripping through the soul of humanity" is an example of an implied comparison because I do not directly state what I am comparing. I just expect you to understand the comparison: like the many problems that result from a rusty knife ripping through flesh, many problems result from homelessness. I use this language because I think you can picture the problems a rusty knife ripping a wound in flesh would cause and I want you to use that picture to imagine the problems homelessness causes.

EXAMPLE   Consider this paragraph by historian John Lukacs. What comparison does he make? What does he want you to picture and understand from the figurative expressions in this passage?

> As the great French thinker Georges Beranos once wrote: "The worst, the most corrupting lies are problems wrongly stated." To put this in biological terms: without an honest diagnosis there can be no therapy, only further decay and perhaps even death. So I must sum up seven deadly sins of misdiagnosis: seven deadly problems that now face this country because of their intellectual misstatements. (Lukacs, *Our Seven Deadly Sins of Misdiagnosis*)

Explanation   Lukacs wants you to picture the nation as a sick person to whom the doctor has given the wrong diagnosis. Before the person (the nation) can be cured, the illness (the problem) has to be correctly identified.

EXAMPLE   In this paragraph, training and development specialist Ron Zemke employs two comparisons. What does he want you to picture and understand from the figurative expressions?

> The auditorium lights grow dim. A diffusion of sunrise hues washes languidly across a sweep of rear-projection screens. From beneath stage level, rising in single file like a septet of hunter's moons, come the seven letters of the sacred rite: Q-U-A-L-I-T-Y. (Zemke, *"Faith, Hope and TQM," Training*)

Explanation In the second sentence Zemke compares the slides coming on the screen to a slow, colorful sunrise. Then, he compares the appearance of the seven (septet) letters of the word *quality* to the wondrous appearance of large, bright (hunter's) moons.

When a passage doesn't make sense to you at the literal level, check to see if the author is using figurative language. However, if you have difficulty understanding a part of the figurative comparison, like "hunter's moons," you may need to ask someone about the literal meaning of the expression. You must understand the literal before you can use the author's words to create a mental picture.

Exercise 5 **Understanding Figurative Language**

Describe what the author is comparing and what you should picture and understand from the figurative language in each of these passages.

1. This is our hope. This is the faith that I go back to the South with. With this faith we will be able to hew out of the mountain of despair a stone of hope. With this faith we will be able to transform the jangling discords of our nation into a beautiful symphony of brotherhood. (King, "I Have A Dream," speech delivered in Washington, DC, August 28, 1963)

2. The performance improvement efforts of many companies have as much impact on operational and financial results as a ceremonial rain dance has on the weather. (Schaffer & Thompson, "Successful Change Begins with Program Results," *Harvard Business Review*)

3. "Whatever women do—even just wiggling their thumbs—their neuron activity is more greatly distributed throughout the brain," says Dr. Mark George, a psychiatrist and neurologist at the Medical University of South Carolina.
    When a man puts his mind to work, neurons turn on in highly specific areas of the brain. When a woman does, her brain cells light up such a patchwork that the scans look like a night view of Las Vegas. (Hales, "If You Think We Think Alike, Think Again," *Ladies' Home Journal*)

4. Literacy came more slowly to the lower social classes, as authorities feared too much knowledge in the hands of the uneducated or poorly educated would only fan the fires of discontent. (Kagan, Ozment, & Turner, *The Western Heritage*)

5. The flowering of Etruscan civilization coincides with the Archaic age in Greece. During this period, especially near the end of the sixth and early in the fifth century B.C., Etruscan art showed its greatest vigor. (Janson & Janson, *A Basic History of Art*)

6. But time has proven that R. E. "Ted" Turner—Captain Outrageous to the press—is crazy like a fox. (Griffin & Ebert, *Business*)

7. If Tina Brown's *New Yorker* [magazine] was a chocolate bar, Mr. Remnick's is a compacted stick of low-fat granola. (Varadarajan, *Wall Street Journal*)

8. "Plodding" is not the word to describe the article by David Remnick in the *New Yorker* for that is not an apt way to relate to readers an experience akin to bathing in cold glue. (Varadarajan, *Wall Street Journal*)

9. While conservative sentiments very much influence today's public policy, it is important to recognize that national feelings, however strong,

have historically been somewhat akin to the swings of a pendulum. (Schmalleger, *Criminal Justice Today*)

10. Their great love, in which she lived completely immersed, seemed to be ebbing away, like the water of a river that was sinking into its own bed; and she saw the mud at the bottom. (Flaubert, *Madame Bovary*)

DEFINING WORDS AND PHRASES WHILE READING

Unfortunately, real reading tasks are not as obvious as the excerpts used in the examples and practice exercises. Even in texts where authors highlight important definitions in the text's margins, it's still up to you to understand the surrounding material. To be successful every time you read, you must use a variety of strategies.

When you encounter a word or phrase that hinders your understanding, you may check to see if there are any context clues you can use. Or, if you recognize the parts of the word, perhaps that is all the clue you need. You work smarter, not harder. But you also realize that if context clues, word analysis, and your experience don't yield a probable meaning for the word, you must take time to consult an outside resource, like the dictionary.

Exercise 6 ▶ Defining Words While Reading

For this exercise, assume your professor has instructed you to read this part of the chapter to gain a general understanding of how sociology looks at sports and to define 14 words and phrases: *insights, manifest functions, latent functions, dysfunctional consequences, accessible, exclusion, stamina, social prestige, taints, astronomical salaries, micro-level, spontaneous, unpredictable,* and *rookie.*

JOHN MACIONIS

Dr. Macionis is professor of sociology at Kenyon College, Gambier, Ohio. This excerpt is from Chapter 1, "The Sociological Perspective," in Macionis's Sociology, *eighth edition.*

APPLYING THE PERSPECTIVES: THE SOCIOLOGY OF SPORT

John Macionis

[1]People in the United States love sports. Soccer moms (and dads) drive their eight-year-olds to practice, and teens play pick-up basketball after school. Weekend television is filled with sporting events. A large share of the daily news covers recent games and the latest on sports stars like Mark McGuire (baseball), Shaquille O'Neal (basketball), and Mia Hamm (soccer). Overall, sports in the United States are a multibillion-dollar industry.

What sociological insights can the three theoretical paradigms give us about this familiar part of everyday life?

THE FUNCTIONS OF SPORTS

[2]A structural-functional approach directs attention to the ways sports help society to operate. Their manifest functions include providing recreation, physical conditioning, and a relatively harmless way to "let off steam." Sports have important latent functions as well, from fostering social relationships to generating tens of thousands of jobs. Perhaps most important, sports encourage competition and the pursuit of success, both of which are central to our way of life.

[3]Sports also have dysfunctional consequences. For example, colleges and universities intent on fielding winning teams sometimes recruit students for their athletic ability rather than their academic aptitude. Not only does this practice pull down the academic standards of a school, it shortchanges athletes who devote little time to academic work.

SPORTS AND CONFLICT

[4]A social-conflict analysis begins by pointing out that sports are closely linked to social inequality. Some sports—including tennis, swimming, golf, and skiing—are expensive, so participation is largely limited to the well-to-do. Football, baseball, and basketball, however, are accessible to people of all income levels. In short, the games people play are not simply a matter of choice but also reflect social standing.

[5]Throughout history, sports have been oriented primarily toward males. For example, the first modern Olympic Games, held in 1896, barred women from competition; in the United States, until recently even Little League teams in most parts of the country did not let girls play. Such exclusion has been defended by unfounded notions that girls and women lack the strength and stamina to play sports or that women lose their femininity when they do. Thus, our society encourages men to be athletes while expecting women to be attentive observers and cheerleaders. Today, more women play professional sports than ever before, yet they continue to take a back seat to men, particularly in sports with the most earnings and social prestige.

[6]Although our society long excluded people of color from big league sports, the opportunity to earn high incomes in professional sports has expanded in recent decades. Major League Baseball first admitted African American players when Jackie Robinson broke the color line and joined the Brooklyn Dodgers in 1947. Fifty years later, in 1997, when professional baseball retired the legendary Robinson's number 42 on all teams, African Americans (13 percent of the U.S. population) accounted for 15 percent of Major League Baseball players, 65 percent of National Football League (NFL) players, and 77 percent of National Basketball Association (NBA) players (Center for the Study of Sport in Society, 2000).

[7]One reason for the increasing proportion of people of African descent in professional sports is that athletic performance—in terms of batting average or number of points scored per game—can be precisely measured, regardless of any white prejudice. It is also true that some people of color make a particular effort to excel in athletics, where they

perceive greater opportunity than in other careers (Steele, 1990; Hoberman, 1997, 1998). In recent years, in fact, African American athletes have earned higher salaries, on average, than white players.

[8]But racial discrimination still taints professional sports in the United States. For one thing, race is linked to the positions athletes play on the field in a pattern called "stacking." . . . More broadly, African Americans figure prominently in only five sports: football, basketball, baseball, boxing, and track. Across all of professional sports, the vast majority of managers, head coaches, and owners of sports teams are white (Gnida, 1995; Smith & Leonard, 1997).

[9]We might ask who benefits the most from professional sports. Although individual players may get astronomical salaries, and millions of fans enjoy following their teams, at bottom, sports are big business—generating property for a small number of people (predominantly white men). In sum, sports in the United States are bound up with inequalities based on gender, race, and economic power.

SPORTS AS INTERACTION

[10]At a micro-level, a sporting event is a complex drama of face-to-face interaction. In part, play is guided by the players' assigned positions and the rules of the game. But players are also spontaneous and unpredictable. Informed by the symbolic-interaction paradigm, then, we see sports less as a system than as an ongoing process.

[11]From this point of view, too, we expect each player to understand the game a little differently. Some thrive in a setting of stiff competition, whereas for others, love of the game may be greater than the need to win. (The ancient Romans recognized this fact, evident in our word "amateur," literally, "lover," which designates someone who engages in some activity for the sheer love of it.)

[12]Beyond different attitudes toward competition, team members also shape their particular realities according to the various prejudices, jealousies, and ambitions they bring to the game. Then, too, the behavior of any single player also changes over time. A rookie in professional baseball, for example, may feel self-conscious during the first few games in the big leagues. In time, however, most players fit in comfortably with the team. Coming to feel at home on the field was slow and painful for Jackie Robinson—the first African American to play in the major leagues, beginning in 1947—who knew that many white players, and millions of white fans, resented his presence. In time, however, his outstanding ability and his confident and cooperative manner won him the respect of the entire nation.

Exercise 6 Questions

Write the meaning of these words and phrases.

1. insights
2. manifest functions
3. latent functions

4. dysfunctional consequences

5. accessible

6. exclusion

7. stamina

8. social prestige

9. taints

10. astronomical salaries

11. micro-level

12. spontaneous

13. unpredictable

14. rookie

REMEMBERING WORDS

You must "get," or understand, something before you can "forget" it. That is, how effectively you remember something usually depends on how completely you learned it in the first place. Sometimes when we say, "I forgot," what we mean is, "I didn't understand it."

In addition, unless you actively work at remembering new words, you will likely have to rediscover the meaning each time you see the word. It's been estimated that you must use a new word at least ten times before it's really "yours." Although there is not one best method for remembering everything, using several of your senses will help: see it, say it, hear it, write it.

One Strategy for Learning the Meanings of Words and Phrases

One strategy for learning—understanding and remembering—new words and phrases is to use flashcards. Write the word and sentence (context) on the front of a 3″ × 5″ index card. Also note the class and/or text page number.

Unger/History, p. 495

nuances

Henry James was acutely aware of the <u>nuances</u> in human relationships, and wrote about men and women in comfortable circumstances whose lives revolved about the subtleties of taste, class, and nationality, and crises of personal integrity.

On the back of the card write the definition (the one that most closely fits the way the word was used in your original sentence). You can also write a sentence with a personally meaningful context.

slight variations, subtle differences

During negotiations, the diplomat was aware of the nuance of every word and gesture.

Use the cards during spare moments to review and test yourself. Sometimes, look at the word and try to recall the definition. At other times, look at the definition and try to recall the word.

CHAPTER 2 REVIEW QUESTIONS

1. Explain the term *context*. List two types of context clues authors use.

2. Explain what it means to use the parts of a word to help define it. Give one example.

3. List one advantage and one disadvantage of using the dictionary to define an unfamiliar word.

4. Explain the difference between the denotative meaning and connotative meaning of a word. Give one example of a word that can have connotative as well as denotative meanings.

5. Explain why it's important to understand both the denotative and connotative meanings of words and phrases.

6. Explain the purpose of figurative language. Give one example.

Use Your Strategies 1

For this exercise, assume your professor has instructed you to read this essay for general comprehension, not to remember specific details. To accomplish your purpose, you will need to understand the figurative language McGrath uses in addition to the definitions of words and phrases such as *hover, diminutive, hibernation, territorial-minded, fledglings,* and *aerial antics.*

ROBERT L. MCGRATH

Robert McGrath is a freelance writer. His work appears in numerous national publications. This selection was first published in FEDCO Reporter.

HUMMINGBIRDS: JEWELS ON WINGS

Robert L. McGrath

[1]You've probably enjoyed watching those tiny rainbow-pinioned helicopters hover at the feeder in your backyard—or perhaps at your neighbor's. But how much do you really know about these jewels on wings?

[2]Hummingbirds come in a variety of colors, though mostly in the same diminutive size that makes them stand out as among nature's most remarkable creatures.

[3]There are more than 300 kinds, but amazingly, only the ruby-throated hummingbird is found east of the Mississippi River. Western states are home to as many as 18 different types, with the bulk of the others in the family inhabiting Central and South America. None are found outside the Western Hemisphere.

[4]Their kaleidoscopic plumage has no solid color. Instead, there are tiny barbs on each feather, placed so they break and refract light, just as a mirror or a diamond will do. While the male hummingbird is more colorful than his mate, underparts of both male and female are usually gray or a variety of other shades, while head and back are often a glowing green.

[5]The birds sport so many patches of different tints, they're often named after precious jewels—ruby, topaz, emerald, amethyst-throated.

[6]Those whirring wing-beats are made possible by special hinges within their bone structure that permit helicopter-like rapid vibrating and feathering. Suspended or backward flight requires about 54 wing-beats per second, while normal dodging, darting flight reaching 50 miles per hour takes up to 75 beats of its narrow wings.

[7]Because it uses so much energy in flight, a hummingbird goes into a state resembling hibernation at night when it rests from a constant labor of gathering food. When awake, its normal temperature is over 100 degrees; it falls to as low as 64 degrees when it's asleep. The hummingbird's heartbeat, however, is super fast. While human beings average 72 beats a minute, the hummer's regular rate is 615 beats a minute when in flight.

[8]The territorial-minded male hummingbird vigorously defends his space against other birds, cats, or even snakes. Yet, once he has selected his mate and courtship is complete, the male leaves everything else to his partner. She alone builds the solid little nest—so small a quarter placed on top of it would stick out over the edges—using plant fibers, lichens, and bark, then cementing this miniature cup with saliva glue and spider webs.

[9]It takes 21 days for the female to hatch her two pea-sized pearly eggs. She then begins the endless duty of feeding the helpless, ever-hungry chicks by herself, a task lasting three weeks, when the fledglings are ready to fly.

[10]Anyone with a hummingbird feeder can enjoy a thrill a minute watching these winged wonders display their aerial antics—the most exciting in the world of birds.

Use Your Strategies 1 Questions

1. Write the meanings of these words and phrases:
   A. hover (¶1)
   B. diminutive size (¶2)
   C. state resembling hibernation (¶7)
   D. territorial-minded (¶8)
   E. fledglings (¶9)
   F. aerial antics (¶10)

2. Identify and explain
   A. two figurative phrases in paragraph 1
   B. two figurative phrases in paragraph 4
   C. one figurative phrase in paragraph 9

Use Your Strategies 2

For this exercise, assume your professor has instructed you to read this chapter to gain a general understanding of the relationship between Earth and the sun and to define seven terms: *manifestations, phenomenon, essence, rotation, revolution, perihelion,* and *aphelion.*

FREDERICK K. LUTGENS AND EDWARD J. TARBUCK

Dr. Lutgens and Dr. Tarbuck are both professors emeritus at Illinois Central College. This excerpt is from Chapter 2, "Heating Earth's Surface and Atmosphere," in the eighth edition of their introductory meteorology text The Atmosphere.

EARTH-SUN RELATIONSHIPS

Frederick K. Lutgens and Edward J. Tarbuck

¹From our experiences, we know that the Sun's rays feel hotter on a clear day than on an overcast day. After taking a barefoot walk on a sunny day, we realize that city pavement becomes much hotter than a grassy boulevard. A picture of a snow-capped mountain reminds us that temperature decreases with altitude. And we know that the fury of winter is always replaced by the newness of spring. You may not know, however, that these occurrences are manifestations of the same phenomenon that causes the blue color of the sky and the red color of a brilliant sunset. All such common occurrences are a result of the interaction of solar energy with Earth's atmosphere and its land–sea surface. That is the essence of this chapter.

EARTH–SUN RELATIONSHIPS

²Earth intercepts only a minute percentage of the energy given off by the Sun—less than one two-billionth. This may seem an insignificant amount until we realize that it is several hundred thousand times the electrical

generating capacity of the United States. Solar radiation, in fact, represents more than 99.9 percent of the energy that heats our planet.

[3]Solar energy is not distributed equally over Earth's land–sea surface. The amount of energy received varies with latitude, time of day, and season of the year. Contrasting images of polar bears on ice rafts and palm trees along a remote tropical beach serve to illustrate the extremes. It is the unequal heating of Earth that creates winds and drives the ocean's currents. These movements, in turn, transport heat from the tropics toward the poles in an unending attempt to balance energy inequalities. The consequences of these processes are the phenomena we call weather. If the Sun were "turned off," global winds and ocean currents would quickly cease. Yet as long as the Sun shines, the winds *will* blow and weather *will* persist. So to understand how the atmosphere's dynamic weather machine works, we must first know why different latitudes receive varying quantities of solar energy and why the amount of solar energy changes to produce the seasons. As we shall see, the variations in solar heating are caused by the motions of Earth relative to the Sun and by variations in Earth's land–sea surface.

Earth's Motions

[4]Earth has two principal motions—rotation and revolution. **Rotation** is the spinning of Earth about its axis that produces the daily cycle of daylight and darkness. In the following chapter, we will examine the effects that this daily variation in solar heating has on the atmosphere.

[5]The other motion of Earth, **revolution,** refers to its movement in orbit around the Sun. Hundreds of years ago, most people believed that Earth was stationary in space. The reasoning was that, if Earth were moving, people would feel the movement of the wind rushing past them. Today we know that Earth is traveling at nearly 113,000 kilometers (70,000 miles) per hour in an elliptical orbit about the Sun. Why don't we feel the air rushing past us? The answer is that the atmosphere, bound by gravity to Earth, is carried along at the same speed as Earth.

[6]The distance between Earth and Sun averages about 150 million kilometers (93 million miles). Because Earth's orbit is not perfectly circular, however, the distance varies during the course of a year. Each year, on about January 3, our planet is about 147 million kilometers (91 million miles) from the Sun, closer than at any other time. This position is called the **perihelion.** About six months later, on July 4, Earth is about 152 million kilometers (94 million miles) from the Sun, farther away than at any other time. This position is called the **aphelion.** Although Earth is closest to the Sun and thus receives more energy in January than in July, this difference plays only a minor role in producing seasonal temperature variations. As proof, consider that Earth is closest to the Sun during the cold Northern Hemisphere winter.

The Seasons

[7]We know that it is colder in winter than in summer, but if variations in solar distance do not cause this seasonal temperature change, what does? We adjust to the continuous change in the duration of daylight that occurs throughout the year by planning our outdoor activities accordingly. The gradual but significant *change in day length* certainly accounts for some of

the difference we notice between summer and winter. Furthermore, a gradual change in the angle of the noon Sun above the horizon is quite noticeable (Figure 2–1). . . .

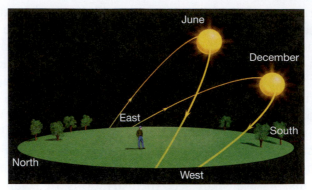

Figure 2–1 Daily paths of the sun for June and December for an observer in the middle latitudes in the Northern Hemisphere. Notice that the angle of the Sun above the horizon is much greater in the summer than in the winter.

Use Your Strategies 2 Questions

Write the meanings of these words and phrases.

1. manifestations (¶1)
2. phenomenon (¶1)
3. essence (¶1)
4. rotation (¶4)
5. revolution (¶5)
6. perihelion (¶6)
7. aphelion (¶6)

Use Your Strategies 3

Directions: For this exercise, assume your professor has instructed you to read this chapter to identify the two major structural changes that have taken place in the American economy and to define these words and concepts: *migration, immigration, Great Depression, primary sector of the economy,* and s*econdary sector of the economy.*

JOHN MACIONIS

Dr. Macionis is professor of sociology at Kenyon College, Gambier, Ohio. In addition to his teaching, he is known for his twenty years of work as a popular textbook author. This excerpt is from Chapter 12, "Work and the Workplace" in his book Social Problems.

STRUCTURAL CHANGES IN THE U. S. ECONOMY

John Macionis

STRUCTURAL CHANGES IN THE U.S. ECONOMY

[1]Many of the problems related to work in the United States have been brought on by changes in the economy itself. Over the history of the country, there have been two major, structural changes to the economy. The first change, which began about 200 years ago, was the Industrial Revolution; the second change, which started in the 1950s, is the Information Revolution. As we shall see, both revolutions transformed not only the economy but people's entire way of life.

The Industrial Revolution

[2]The first transformation was taking place by the beginning of the nineteenth century, when most people lived in rural areas and small towns. Back then, most people worked in the *primary sector* of the economy, producing raw materials by farming, fishing, ranching, mining, or clearing forests. But, gradually, the nature of work changed, as factories sprang up from New England to the new and rapidly growing cities of the Midwest. The Industrial Revolution pushed workers into the *secondary sector* of the economy, in which most people transformed raw materials into finished products: Factory workers, for example, turned wood into furniture and steel into rail-road tracks and, later, into automobiles.

[3]Figure 12–1 shows that, by 1900, the greatest share of jobs were industrial. This meant that millions of workers had left the farm to live in or near large cities, where factories were located. Many people—especially

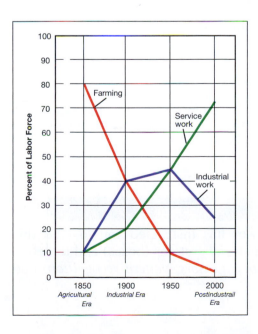

Figure 12–1 The Changing Nature of Work in the United States, 1850–2000

Sources: Author estimates based on U.S. Census Bureau (2000) and U.S. Department of Labor (2000).

those who stayed behind in rural areas—saw this migration as a serious problem, because it drained the population of small rural communities, many of which became nothing but "ghost towns." Thus, from this point of view, the Industrial Revolution threatened a traditional way of life that had existed in this country since the colonial period.

[4]But the Industrial Revolution changed the United States in another important way: by encouraging high levels of immigration. The new factories and rapidly growing cities attracted tens of millions of people from abroad—mostly from Europe, but from many other parts of the world as well. These men and women came to the United States in search of work and a better life. But they were not always welcomed. As explained in Chapter 3 ("Racial and Ethnic Inequality"), many people were critical of what they saw as a tide of foreign immigrants threatening this country's established way of life.

[5]Most of those who came to the United States to pursue their dreams found that life was far from easy. Living in the new industrial cities often meant settling for poor housing, sometimes with little heat and no sanitation. Factories offered jobs, but the pay was low, the hours were long, and the work was back-breaking and often dangerous. Many jobs involved rigid and monotonous routines amid smoke and deafening noise; moreover, supervisors closely monitored their workers and tolerated no complaint. In short, companies treated workers—especially immigrants, who spoke little English—as little more than muscle power. Because they needed wages to live, and because they were not organized to demand better working conditions, workers had little choice but to take whatever work they could find.

[6]The early decades of the last century were a difficult time for all working people in the United States. The struggle became worse by the 1930s, when the Great Depression—a major economic collapse—put more than one-quarter of the labor force out of work. . . .

Use Your Strategies 3 Questions

Write the meanings of these words and phrases.

1. primary sector of the economy (¶2)
2. secondary sector of the economy (¶2)
3. migration (¶3)
4. immigration (¶4)
5. Great Depression (¶6)

Use Your Strategies 4

For this exercise, assume your professor has instructed you to read this chapter to identify the three separate memory systems (boxes) and to define these five terms: *consistent, peer, sensory memory, pattern recognition,* and *short-term memory.*

CAROLE WADE AND CAROL TAVRIS

Dr. Wade began her academic career at the University of New Mexico, where she taught courses in psycholinguistics and developed the first course at the university on the psychology of gender. She has taught at San Diego Mesa College, College of Marin, and is now affiliated with Dominican University of California. Dr. Tavris is a noted writer and lecturer on the importance of critical and scientific thinking in psychology. She has taught in the psychology department at UCLA and the Human Relations Center for the New School for Social Research in New York. This one-page excerpt is from Chapter 7, "Memory," in their text Invitation to Psychology, *second edition.*

THE THREE-BOX MODEL OF MEMORY

Carole Wade and Carol Tavris

THE THREE-BOX MODEL OF MEMORY

[1]The information-processing model of three separate memory systems—sensory, short-term, and long-term—remains a leading approach because it offers a convenient way to organize the major findings on memory, does a good job of accounting for these findings, and is consistent with the biological facts about memory described in Chapter 4. Let us now peer into each of the "boxes."

Sensory Memory: Fleeting Impressions

[2]In the three-box model, all incoming sensory information must make a brief stop in **sensory memory,** the entryway of memory. Sensory memory includes a number of separate memory subsystems, as many as there are senses. Visual images remain in a visual subsystem for a maximum of half a second. Auditory images remain in an auditory subsystem for a slightly longer time, by most estimates up to two seconds or so.

[3]Sensory memory acts as a holding bin, retaining information in a highly accurate form until we can select items for attention from the stream of stimuli bombarding our senses. It gives us a brief time to decide whether information is extraneous or important; not everything detected by our senses warrants our attention. **Pattern recognition,** the identification of a stimulus on the basis of information already contained in long-term memory, occurs during the transfer of information from sensory memory to short-term memory.

[4]Information that does not quickly go on to short-term memory vanishes forever, like a message written in disappearing ink. That is why people who see an array of 12 letters for just a fraction of a second can report only 4 or 5 of them; by the time they answer, their sensory memories are already fading (Sperling, 1960). The fleeting nature of sensory memory is actually beneficial; it prevents multiple sensory images—"double exposures"—that might interfere with the accurate perception and encoding of information.

Short-term Memory: Memory's Scratch Pad

[5]Like sensory memory, **short-term memory (STM)** retains information only temporarily—for up to about 30 seconds by most estimates, although some researchers think that the maximum interval may extend to a few minutes. In short-term memory, the material is no longer an exact sensory image but is an encoding of one, such as a word or a phrase. This material either transfers into long-term memory or decays and is lost forever.

[6]Individuals with brain injury, such as H. M., demonstrate the importance of transferring new information from short-term memory into long-term memory. H. M., you will recall, can store information on a short-term basis; he can hold a conversation and he appears to be fine when you first meet him. He also retains implicit memories. However, for the most part, H. M. cannot retain explicit information about new facts and events for longer than a few minutes. His terrible memory deficits involve a problem in transferring explicit memories from short-term storage into long-term storage. With a great deal of repetition and drill, H. M. can learn some new visual information, retain it in long-term memory, and recall it normally (McKee & Squire, 1992). But usually information does not get into long-term memory in the first place.

[7]Besides retaining new information for brief periods while we are learning it, short-term memory holds information that has been retrieved from long-term memory for temporary use, providing the mental equivalent of a scratch pad. Thus short-term memory functions in part as a *working memory*. When you do an arithmetic problem, your working memory contains the numbers and the instructions for doing the necessary operations, plus the intermediate results from each step. The ability to bring information from long-term memory into working memory is not disrupted in patients like H. M. They can do arithmetic, converse, relate events that predate their injury, and do anything else that requires retrieval of information from long-term into short-term memory. . . .

Use Your Strategies 4 Questions

Write the meanings of these words and phrases.

1. consistent (¶1)
2. peer (¶1)
3. sensory memory (¶2)
4. pattern recognition (¶3)
5. short-term memory (¶5)

REFLECT AND CONNECT

A. As times and technology change, so do the words we use to describe them. We invent new words, like *extreme sports* and *e-commerce*. We change the meaning of "old" words. For example, to *surf* now means spending time online looking for information, and *uninstall* can mean being fired or laid off from a job. What are some other words that have come into English or changed in meaning during the last two years? How do you think the changes happen?

B. Describe a time when you used a particular word, in writing or speaking, because of its connotation. What was your purpose? Were you successful? Has anyone successfully convinced you to do or not do something by his or her choice of words?

LOG ON TO THE WEB

The Web has a wealth of information to assist in building your vocabulary. There are general dictionary sites like these:

> *http://www.m-w.com/netdict.htm*
> *http://www.dictionary.com/*
> *http://www.yourdictionary.com/*

There are also specialized dictionary sites:

> *http://whatis.techtarget.com/* (definitions and explanations of Internet terms)
> *http://www.getty.edu/research/tools/vocabulary/* (fine art and architecture)

There are also sites with information about language. At sites like these you'll find the meanings of idioms from *at the eleventh hour* to *zip your lip:*

> *http://www.eslcafe.com/idioms/*
> *http://home.t-online.de/home/toni.goeller/idiom_wm/*

To find the meaning of acronyms from IBM to NPOESS, log on to *http://www.Acronymfinder.com*

Log onto one of these sites or use a search engine to locate another "vocabulary" site. Write down (1) the complete Web address of the site you visited, (2) the name of the person or company who sponsors and maintains the site, (3) a sentence describing what you did or read, (4) the most important thing you learned from the activity, and (5) when and why you might use the site again.

REFERENCES

Anderson, R. C., & P. Freebody. (1981). "Vocabulary Knowledge." In J. T. Guthrie (Ed.), *Comprehension and Teaching*, Newark: International Reading Association, 77–117.

Bauman, J. F., & E. J. Kameenui. (1991). "Research on Vocabulary Instruction: Ode to Voltaire." In J. Flood (Ed.), *Handbook of Research on Teaching the English Language Arts*, New York: Macmillan, 604–631.

Beck, I., & M. McKeown. (1991). "Conditions of Vocabulary Acquisition." In P. D. Pearson (Ed.), *Handbook of Reading Research,* Vol. 2, New York: Longman, 789–814.

Duffy, G. G., L. R. Roehler, & B. A. Herrmann. (1988). "Modeling Mental Processes Helps Poor Readers Become Strategic Learners." *The Reading Teacher,* 41, 762–767.

Nist, S. L., & S. Olejnik. (1995). "The Role of Context and Dictionary Definitions on Varying Levels of Word Knowledge. *Reading Research Quarterly,* 30, 172–189.

read-ing (red´in) *adj.* **1** inclined ... ...d or study **2** mad...
reading n. **1** the act or practic... ...person who reads
of books **2** a public entertainm... ...which literary m...
aloud **3** the extent to which a ... ...has read **4** mat...
meant to be read **5** the amoun... ...asured as by a ba...
thermometer **6** the form of a specified word, sentenc...

Understanding Main Ideas

Iron rusts from disuse; stagnant water loses its purity and in cold weather becomes frozen; even so does inaction sap the vigor of the mind.

—Leonardo da Vinci

AN IDEA TO THINK ABOUT

Your English professor posts an assignment for your class: Write a paragraph on the topic "college grading systems." How likely is it that each of the twenty-five or so paragraphs you and your classmates write gives your professor the same information about college grading systems? Realistically, it is very unlikely.

Although you would all write on the same topic, you would each concentrate on a distinct thought about the topic. For example, one of you might concentrate on how college grading systems have changed over the years and another on the differences between high school and college grading systems. Another student might concentrate on the unfairness or worthiness of grades while someone else might focus on the differences among college grading systems. The focus, or main idea, would be the most important information in the paragraph. All of the other information would develop and support that main idea.

Just as it would be important for your professor to understand your main idea, it is important for you to understand the authors' main ideas when you read. Think back to an assignment in which your instructor asked you to read for the main ideas of the chapter. How did you begin your search? What did you look for? How did you know when you had found a main idea? When you found what you thought was a main idea, did you stop reading?

CHAPTER FOCUS

Understanding individual vocabulary words is important, but reading is more than saying and understanding words. As discussed in Chapter 1, reading is an active, multidimensional process that requires you to use many skills, strategies, and knowledge bases in combination, and often in parallel, to create the overall comprehension abilities we call reading.

Comprehension abilities are those that enable you to understand what you read. And, as you would expect, research shows that skilled readers are excellent comprehenders (National Reading Panel, 2000; Snow, Burns, & Griffin, 1998).

To achieve their comprehension goals, skilled readers combine multiple strategies to improve their understanding and memory of text passages (Pressley & Afflerbach, 1995). For example, when college students acquire and apply comprehension strategies—such as looking for the main idea—their academic performance improves (Taraban, Rynearson, & Kerr, 2000).

In this chapter you will practice strategies for identifying the main idea of an **expository** paragraph whether it is directly stated or implied. An expository paragraph is written specifically to report or explain facts, events, or ideas, rather than narrate a story or describe a scene.

WHAT IS A MAIN IDEA?

A **main idea** is the general idea that unifies, or ties together, all the ideas and sentences in a paragraph. A main idea is often called an "umbrella idea" because it "covers" all the other information in the paragraph. A well-written paragraph has a main idea that is either directly stated or implied. For example, if you wrote a paragraph about how college grading systems have changed over the last twenty-five years, all the sentences would fit together to support and explain that one idea.

When you read to learn, identifying and understanding the main idea of a paragraph are essential to good comprehension because you need the primary idea to connect all the information.

A main idea has two components: the topic—the who or what the author is writing about, and the controlling thought—what the author wants you to know or understand about that topic.

Identifying the Topic

The first step in identifying the main idea of a paragraph is to discover the **topic**.

The topic of a paragraph is a word or short phrase that answers the question, Who or what is the author writing about?

EXAMPLE   Find the topic in this paragraph.

> ¹Conflict within and among workplace teams can arise for any number of reasons. ²For example, teams and individuals may become angry because they believe they are competing for scarce or declining resources, such as money, information, and supplies. ³Team members may disagree about who is responsible for a specific task (usually the result of poorly defined boundaries). ⁴Poor communication among the team can lead to misunderstandings and misperceptions about other team members, causing conflict. ⁵Basic differences in values, attitudes, and personalities may lead to arguments. ⁶Conflict can also arise in teams because individuals or teams are pursuing different goals. (adapted from Bovée, Thill, & Schatzman, *Business Communication Today*)

Explanation   The topic of this paragraph is "conflict within and among workplace teams." This phrase answers the question, Who or what is the author writing about?

In addition, the phrase, or a synonymous phrase, appears in every sentence: (1) conflict within and among workplace teams, (2) teams and individuals may become angry, (3) disagree, (4) conflict, (5) arguments, (6) conflict. Authors often use repetition to clue readers to the topic.

Exercise 1   **Identifying the Topic of a Paragraph**

Read the paragraph and then write the word or phrase that best expresses the topic. In other words, answer the question, Who or what is the author writing about?

1. Aggressive communicators tend to employ an angry, confrontational manner in their interactions with others. For example, aggressive communicators are usually loud and verbally abusive. They often yell at others when things don't go their way. Someone who constantly uses "you" messages, causing the receiver of the information to feel on the defensive immediately, is usually an aggressive communicator. (Adapted from Donatelle & Davis, *Access to Health*)

2. The winter of 1779 was the worst winter in a century. For example, in the hollow of land tucked between Long Hill and the Watchung Mountains called Jockey Hollow, it snowed twenty-eight times that winter, and the drifts were so high that they covered the fences. The storm that

raged for three days in January was "one of the most tremendous snowstorms ever remembered; no man could endure its violence many minutes without danger of his life," Dr. James Thatcher reported. (Adapted from Boydston, Cullather, Lewis, McGerr, & Oakes, *Making a Nation*)

3. Although recent crime trends in the United States are downward, by world standards, the U.S. crime rate is high. There were 15,517 murders in the United States in 2000, about one every half-hour around the clock. In large cities such as New York, rarely does a day pass with no murder; in fact, more New Yorkers are hit with stray bullets than people deliberately gunned down in most large cities elsewhere in the world. Overall, the U.S. violent crime rate is about five times greater than Europe's; the U.S. property crime rate is twice as high. The contrast is even greater between our society and the nations of Asia, including India and Japan, where rates of violence and property crime are among the lowest in the world. (Macionis, *Sociology*)

4. Flowering plants, or angiosperms, consist of two major regions, the root system and the shoot system. The root system consists of all the roots of a plant. Roots are branched portions of the plant body that are embedded in the soil. The shoot system consists of leaves, buds, and (in season) flowers and fruits. The shoot system is usually located above the ground. (Adapted from Audesirk, Audesirk, & Byers, *Biology: Life on Earth*)

5. Demography is the subfield of sociology that studies how social conditions are distributed in human populations and how those populations are changing. When we ask how many people are affected by a particular condition or problem—for example, when we want to know how many people are affected by crime or unemployment—we are asking a demographic question. The answers to demographic questions consist of numerical data about people affected compared to those who are not affected. (Kornblum & Julian, *Social Problems*)

6. In the United States, a firm that attempts to monopolize an industry or conspires with other firms to reduce competition risks serious penalties. The most famous recent antitrust case was brought by the Justice department against Microsoft in the late 1990s. Microsoft was accused of attempting to monopolize the Internet browser market and other anticompetitive practices. In June 2000, the court agreed that Microsoft violated U.S. antitrust laws and ordered that Microsoft be broken up into two separate companies. (Case & Fair, *Economics*)

Identifying the Controlling Idea

While the topic of a paragraph is important, remember that it is only one part of the main idea. In addition to the topic, the main idea includes the **controlling thought**—what the author wants you to know or understand about the topic.

To avoid mistaking the topic for the main idea, always clarify the author's focus, or controlling thought, by answering the question, What does the author want me to know or understand about the topic?

EXAMPLE   What do the authors want you to know or understand about "conflict within and among workplace teams" in this paragraph?

[1]Conflict within and among workplace teams can arise for any number of reasons. [2]For example, teams and individuals may become angry because they believe they are competing for scarce or declining resources, such as money, information, and supplies. [3]Team members may disagree about who is responsible for a specific task (usually the result of poorly defined boundaries). [4]Poor communication among the team can lead to misunderstandings and misperceptions about other team members, causing conflict. [5]Basic differences in values, attitudes, and personalities may lead to arguments. [6]Conflict can also arise in teams because individuals or teams are pursuing different goals. (Adapted from Bovée, Thill, & Schatzman *Business Communication Today*)

Explanation   In this paragraph the authors want you to understand that conflict within and among workplace teams "can arise for any number of reasons."

Exercise 2   Identifying the Controlling Idea of a Paragraph

In Exercise 1, you identified the topic in each of these paragraphs. Now, for each paragraph, write the word or phrase that best expresses the controlling idea. In other words, answer the question, What does the author want me to know or understand about the topic?

1. Aggressive communicators tend to employ an angry, confrontational manner in their interactions with others. For example, aggressive communicators are usually loud and verbally abusive. They often yell at others when things don't go their way. Someone who constantly uses "you" messages, causing the receiver of the information to feel on the defensive immediately, is usually an aggressive communicator. (Adapted from Donatelle & Davis, *Access to Health*)

2. The winter of 1779 was the worst winter in a century. For example, in the hollow of land tucked between Long Hill and the Watchung Mountains called Jockey Hollow, it snowed twenty-eight times, and the drifts were so high that they covered the fences. The storm that raged for three days in January was "one of the most tremendous snowstorms ever remembered; no man could endure its violence many minutes without danger of his life," Dr. James Thatcher reported. (Adapted from Boydston, Cullather, Lewis, McGerr, & Oakes, *Making a Nation*)

3. Although recent crime trends in the United States are downward, by world standards, the U.S. crime rate is high. There were 15,517 murders in the United States in 2000, about one every half-hour around the clock. In large cities such as New York, rarely does a day pass with no murder; in fact, more New Yorkers are hit with stray bullets than people deliberately gunned down in most large cities elsewhere in the world. Overall, the U.S. violent crime rate is about five times greater than Europe's; the U.S. property crime rate is twice as high. The contrast is even greater between our society and the nations of Asia, including India and Japan, where rates of violence and property crime are among the lowest in the world. (Macionis, *Sociology*)

4. Flowering plants, or angiosperms, consist of two major regions, the root system and the shoot system. The root system consists of all the

roots of a plant. Roots are branched portions of the plant body that are embedded in the soil. The rest of the plant is the shoot system, usually located above the ground. The shoot system consists of leaves, buds, and (in season) flowers and fruits. (Adapted from Audesirk, Audesirk, & Byers, *Biology: Life on Earth*)

5. Demography is the subfield of sociology that studies how social conditions are distributed in human populations and how those populations are changing. When we ask how many people are affected by a particular condition or problem—for example, when we want to know how many people are affected by crime or unemployment—we are asking a demographic question. The answers to demographic questions consist of numerical data about people affected compared to those who are not affected. (Kornblum & Julian, *Social Problems*)

6. In the United States, a firm that attempts to monopolize an industry or conspires with other firms to reduce competition risks serious penalties. The most famous recent antitrust case was brought by the Justice department against Microsoft in the late 1990s. Microsoft was accused of attempting to monopolize the Internet browser market and other anticompetitive practices. In June 2000, the court agreed that Microsoft violated U.S. antitrust laws and ordered that Microsoft be broken up into two separate companies. (Case & Fair, *Economics*)

UNDERSTANDING STATED MAIN IDEAS

Authors often directly state the main idea of a paragraph in a sentence. In fact, some researchers have found that as many as 75 percent of the paragraphs in textbooks contain a **directly stated main idea** (Smith & Chase, 1991).

The main idea sentence, also called the topic sentence, states the topic and controlling thought and clearly focuses the reader's attention on the author's message.

The topic sentence is often the first sentence in a paragraph. However, the topic sentence can appear anywhere in a paragraph. It can be in the middle of the paragraph, tying the beginning and ending together; at the end of the paragraph, as a summary; or even split between two sentences in the paragraph.

No matter where the topic sentence is located, your strategy for finding and understanding the main idea is the same:

1. Identify the topic by answering the question, Who or what is the author writing about?
2. Identify the controlling thought by answering the question, What does the author want me to know or understand about the topic?
3. Combine the topic and controlling thought, and locate the topic sentence.
4. Rephrase the sentence in your own words.

EXAMPLE Identify the topic, the controlling thought, and then the main idea sentence in this excerpt from Barker and Barker's *Communication*.

[1]In a class where a professor used the sound "uh" some 20 times during the first five minutes of class, students could hardly help keeping count. [2]The problem was that the professor didn't test the class on his "uhs," and many students didn't pass the test on the lecture. [3]Of course it's easy to blame speakers for their sins. [4]As effective listeners, however, we can't afford to let such mannerisms keep us from getting important points from the message. [5]Focusing on the important elements in the communication setting rather than on the speaker's mannerisms is a much more profitable expenditure of listening energy.

Explanation   Who or what are Barker and Barker writing about? *Listening.* What do they want you to understand about listening? *Focusing on the important elements in the communication setting rather than on the speaker's mannerisms is a better use of listening energy.* Therefore, in this paragraph, the main idea is directly stated in sentence 5.

One way to rephrase sentence 5 is, "To be an effective listener, you should pay attention to what a speaker says and not how he or she says it."

EXAMPLE   Identify the topic, the controlling thought, and then the main idea sentence in this excerpt from *Moral Reasoning* by Grassian.

[1]Aristotle's sexist view is still shared by many people. [2]For example, it is not uncommon to hear people say, "No woman should ever be President of the United States; women are too emotional for such responsibilities." [3]Such a claim reflects the still common belief that the sex of an individual is highly correlated with psychological characteristics and, as such, may be used as an indicator of an individual's capacity to perform certain tasks. [4]As a result of this belief, women are often treated unequally in our society.

Explanation   Who or what is Grassian writing about? *People with sexist views.* What does he want you to understand about people with sexist views? *They often cause women to be treated unequally.* Therefore, in this paragraph, the main idea is split between sentence 1 and sentence 4.

Exercise 3   **Identifying Stated Main Ideas**

In this exercise combine the topic (which you identified in Exercise 1) and the controlling idea (which you identified in Exercise 2), and identify the main idea sentence in each paragraph.

1. [1]Aggressive communicators tend to employ an angry, confrontational manner in their interactions with others. [2]For example, aggressive communicators are usually loud and verbally abusive. [3]They often yell at others when things don't go their way. [4]People who constantly use "you" messages, causing the receiver of the information to feel on the defensive immediately, are usually aggressive communicators. (Adapted from Donatelle & Davis, *Access to Health*)

2. [1]The winter of 1779 was the worst winter in a century. [2]For example, in the hollow of land tucked between Long Hill and the Watchung

Mountains called Jockey Hollow, it snowed twenty-eight times, and the drifts were so high that they covered the fences. [3]The storm that raged for three days in January was "one of the most tremendous snowstorms ever remembered; no man could endure its violence many minutes without danger of his life," Dr. James Thatcher reported. (Adapted from Boydston, Cullather, Lewis, McGerr, & Oakes, *Making a Nation*)

3. [1]Although recent crime trends in the United States are downward, by world standards the U.S. crime rate is high. [2]There were 15,517 murders in the United States in 2000, about one every half-hour around the clock. [3]In large cities such as New York, rarely does a day pass with no murder; in fact, more New Yorkers are hit with stray bullets than people deliberately gunned down in most large cities elsewhere in the world. [4]Overall, the U.S. violent crime rate is about five times greater than Europe's; the U.S. property crime rate is twice as high. [5]The contrast is even greater between our society and the nations of Asia, including India and Japan, where rates of violence and property crime are among the lowest in the world. (Macionis, *Sociology*)

4. [1]Flowering plants, or angiosperms, consist of two major regions, the root system and the shoot system. [2]The root system consists of all the roots of a plant. [3]Roots are branched portions of the plant body that are embedded in the soil. [4]The rest of the plant is the shoot system, usually located above the ground. [5]The shoot system consists of leaves, buds, and (in season) flowers and fruits. (Adapted from Audesirk, Audesirk, & Byers, *Biology: Life on Earth*)

5. [1]Demography is the subfield of sociology that studies how social conditions are distributed in human populations and how those populations are changing. [2]When we ask how many people are affected by a particular condition or problem—for example, when we want to know how many people are affected by crime or unemployment—we are asking a demographic question. [3]The answers to demographic questions consist of numerical data about people affected compared to those who are not affected. (Kornblum & Julian, *Social Problems*)

6. [1]In the United States, a firm that attempts to monopolize an industry or conspires with other firms to reduce competition risks serious penalties. [2]The most famous recent antitrust case was brought by the Justice department against Microsoft in the late 1990s. [3]Microsoft was accused of attempting to monopolize the Internet browser market and other anticompetitive practices. [4]In June 2000, the court agreed that Microsoft violated U.S. antitrust laws and ordered that Microsoft be broken up into two separate companies. (Case & Fair, *Economics*)

Exercise 4   Identifying Stated Main Ideas

Identify the main idea sentence(s) in each paragraph. Remember, it is a good idea to rephrase the sentence using your words to make sure you understand what the author means.

1. [1]Glaciers, despite their barren, stationary appearance, support many kinds of life. [2]Fish thrive in the rivers of ice melt that flow underneath. [3]Ice worms tunnel through the surface and eat pollen that blows in

from nearby forests. [4]Flowers sometimes bloom in the dust that collects on the edges. [5]Some of these ice flowers grow as high as four feet. (Lapp, Flood, & Farnan, *Content Area Reading and Learning*)

2. [1]Research has revealed that the attitude you have at the beginning of a task determines the outcome of that task more than any other single factor. [2]For example, if you believe you will be able to succeed at a particular undertaking and you approach the endeavor with a sense of excitement and joyful expectation, your chances of achieving success are much higher than if you face the task with dread and apprehension. [3]In other words, self-fulfilling prophesies can yield positive or negative results depending on your expectations. (Adapted from Abascal, Brucato, & Brucato, *Stress Mastery*)

3. [1]Spectacular, powerful, and sometimes deadly, lightning is one of the most common weather phenomena. [2]It has been estimated that lightning strikes the earth about 100 times every second. [3]Yet despite its frequent occurrence, lightning is still not completely understood. (National Center for Atmospheric Research, *Lightning*)

4. [1]In spite of the good intentions of many writers, fictional characters are predominantly white and do not accurately portray reality. [2]The population of the United States consists of about 12 percent blacks, 8.2 percent Hispanics, 2.1 percent Asians, and 2 percent Native Americans, and 20 percent of all people have a disabling condition—but most fiction portrays quite a different reality. (Seger, *Creating Unforgettable Characters*)

5. [1]Carbon monoxide is a by-product of combustion, present whenever fuel is burned. [2]It is produced by common home appliances, such as gas or oil furnaces, gas refrigerators, gas clothes dryers, gas ranges, gas water heaters or space heaters, fireplaces, charcoal grills and wood burning stoves. [3]Fumes from automobiles and gas-powered lawn mowers also contain carbon monoxide and can enter a home through walls or doorways if an engine is left running in an attached garage. (BRK Brands, *What You Need to Know about the Leading Cause of Poisoning*)

6. [1]Regardless of how motivated and committed you are, sometimes you must take a number of small steps to reach your goal. [2]For example, suppose that you have not exercised for a while. [3]You decide that you want to get into shape and your goal is to be able to jog 3 to 4 miles every other day. [4]You realize that you'd face a near-death experience if you tried to run even just a few blocks in your current condition. [5]So you decide to start slowly and build up to your desired fitness level gradually. [6]During week 1, you will walk for one hour every other day at a slow, relaxed pace. [7]During week 2, you will walk the same amount of time but will speed up your pace and cover slightly more ground. [8]During week 3, you will speed up even more and will try to go even farther. [9]You continue taking such steps until you reach your goal. (Adapted from Donatelle & Davis, *Access to Health*)

7. [1]A few people living in very remote regions of the world may be able to provide all of their daily necessities. [2]The crop grown or product manufactured in a particular place may be influenced by the distinctive features and assets of the place. [3]But most economic activities undertaken in one region are influenced by interaction with decision-makers

located elsewhere. [4]The choice of crop is influenced by demand and prices set in markets elsewhere. [5]The factory is located to facilitate bringing in raw materials and shipping out products to the markets. (Rubenstein, *An Introduction to Human Geography*)

8. [1]In the second half of the last century there was a communications revolution. [2]The advent of television after World War II made far more news more immediately available to people in advanced industrial nations than had ever been possible before. [3]In subsequent decades we saw the advent of cable television, TV magazine shows like *60 Minutes*, the Internet, and specialized magazines catering to a wide variety of interests. [4]This communications revolution has had a lasting impact on our perspective of social problems. (Kornblum & Julian, *Social Problems*)

9. Most hospitality organizations target a defined group of customers. A targeted group of customers is part of what is commonly referred to as one's niche market. Quick-food service operators tend to target a different mix of customers than full-service restaurants. A resort hotel focuses on a distinct clientele compared with a downtown business hotel and so forth. (Martin, *Providing Quality Service*)

10. [1]Lyndon B. Johnson was in many ways the antithesis of his predecessor. [2]Middle-aged, rugged, earthy, and self-made rather than young, elegant, and patrician, Johnson lacked the glamour of Kennedy. [3]Yet he was incomparable as a legislative leader. [4]His long years as Senate leader had honed his talent for getting laws enacted. [5]Few politicians could hold out against the "Johnson treatment" for very long, and in the course of his five years as president, Johnson initiated more significant legislation than any chief executive since Franklin D. Roosevelt. (Unger, *These United States*)

MAKING INFERENCES WHILE READING

First, let's sort out the meanings of two often-confused words: imply and infer. To imply means to express indirectly—to hint at, to suggest. To infer means to arrive at a conclusion from information—to arrive at a logical conclusion, to make an educated guess. Therefore, the author implies; the reader infers.

You make several types of inferences when you read. For example, you discovered in Chapter 2 that you often use the information an author provides to figure out the meaning of an unfamiliar word. In the sentence, *"Perihelion* is the point in the earth's orbit when the distance between the earth and the sun is at its minimum, as opposed to *aphelion,"* you used the author's direct definition of *perihelion* (the point in the earth's orbit when the distance between the earth and the sun is at its minimum) to define its opposite, *aphelion* (the point in the earth's orbit when the distance between the earth and the sun is at its maximum).

Using a similar strategy, you can infer an author's main idea by using what the author does say to arrive at a logical inference about the main idea. As semanticist S. I. Hayakawa says in *Language in Thought and Action,* an inference is "a statement about the unknown made on the basis of the known."

But You Must Be Careful

An inference is a *reasonable* conclusion—a logical guess based on what the author says. To increase your chances of making valid, appropriate inferences,

1. Be sure you understand what is stated. It's almost impossible to make a statement about what *is not known* if you are unclear about what *is known*.
2. Make certain your inferences are based on and supported by the information the author does give.
3. Check that your inferences are not contradicted by any of the author's stated information.

UNDERSTANDING IMPLIED MAIN IDEAS

Although every paragraph has a main idea, it is not always stated in one sentence; in some paragraphs an author only implies the main idea. That is, you cannot find one sentence or combine two sentences to accurately state the main idea.

Without a topic sentence, you must add together all the information in the paragraph and infer the main idea. However, your basic strategy for finding and understanding the **implied main idea** is almost the same as when there is a topic sentence:

1. Identify the topic by answering the question, Who or what is the author writing about?
2. Identify the controlling thought by answering the question, What does the author want me to know or understand about the topic?
3. Combine the topic and controlling thought and
4. Write a main idea sentence in your own words.

EXAMPLE   The following paragraph does not have a topic sentence. However, when you add together what is stated, you can infer the main idea.

> "Never do today what you can put off until tomorrow." That is the motto of the procrastinator. We all procrastinate to one degree or another. It becomes a major problem in your work life when important tasks or responsibilities are left undone or are completed in a slipshod manner because inadequate time was left to complete the task properly. Procrastination lowers anxiety in the short run due to the relief we feel from task avoidance. But it greatly increases our stress in the long run as tasks pile up or time runs short. (Abascal, Brucato, & Brucato, *Stress Mastery: The Art of Coping Gracefully*)

Explanation   What is the topic? *Procrastination*. What do the authors want you to understand about procrastination? *It can cause problems and increase stress*. Thus, we can infer the main idea is that continually procrastinating will create problems and increase stress.

EXAMPLE   Identify the main idea of this paragraph by the President's Committee on Employment of the Handicapped.

> [1]In 1943 Public Law 16 significantly advanced vocational rehabilitation services for veterans. [2]A year later, the G. I. Bill of Rights provided veterans with allowances for educational training, loans for the purchase and construction of homes, farms, and business property, and compensation for periods of unemployment. [3]Benefits were continued and enlarged in subsequent years in response to the Korean and Vietnam wars.

Explanation   Who or what is the Committee writing about? *Government benefits for veterans.* What do they want you to understand about government services for veterans? *An increasing array has been offered since 1943.* Thus, we can infer the main idea is that since 1943, the government has provided an increasing array of benefits for veterans.

Exercise 5   Identifying Implied Main Ideas

The main idea in these paragraphs may be implied. Write the main idea of each paragraph.

1. In the Dick and Jane readers some of us remember from our childhoods, a family consisted of a married couple, two or three well-behaved children, and a dog and a cat. Father wore suits and went out to work; mother wore aprons and baked cupcakes. Little girls sat demurely watching little boys climb trees. Home meant a single-family house in a middle-class suburban neighborhood. Color the lawn green. Color the people white. Family life in the textbook world was idyllic; parents did not quarrel, children did not disobey, and babies did not throw up on the dog. (Delfattore, *What Johnny Shouldn't Read—Textbook Censorship in America*) ·

2. On the job you will periodically face challenges not directly related to the work you do. Prejudice and discrimination based on factors such as age, sex, race, ethnicity, and disability are common problems. Sexual harassment—any uninvited verbal or physical behavior related to sexuality—is of concern in today's work environment. Knowing what to do if you are confronted and then making wise choices can lessen the trauma. Being sensitive to others in the work environment so that you don't unwittingly create problems is most advisable. Refraining from sexist or racist comments and language may require effort, but it is the fair and decent way to behave. Challenging your own stereotypes and eliminating personal prejudice will make this easier. Acceptance and equal treatment of others are keystones of positive human relations. (Hanna, *Person to Person: Positive Relationships Don't Just Happen*)

3. What do lawn mowers, cellular phones, roller blades, Viagra pills, fat substitutes, nicotine patches, pornography, banks, breast implants, cable TV, animal cloning, baby food, and workers' wages have in common? They are all regulated in some way by the government. Because virtually every activity in the United States is supervised by government in one form or another, regulation is a vast enterprise. Not surprisingly, any activity as pervasive as this generates controversy. From small busi-

ness owners who have to spend several days each year filling out dozens of forms and complying with federal regulations to Microsoft's Bill Gates, there is constant criticism of government's regulatory intrusiveness. (Burns, Peltason, Cronin, Magleby, & O'Brien, *Government by the People*)

4. In studying magazine and newspaper ads, Erving Goffman (1979) documented the pattern by which men usually appear taller than women, implying male superiority. Women, he found, were more frequently presented lying down (on sofas and beds) or, like children, seated on the floor. Men's facial expressions exuded competence and authority, whereas women often appeared childlike. While men focused on the products being advertised, women focused on the men, playing a supportive and submissive role. (Macionis, *Sociology*)

5. Although the exact determinants of personality are impossible to define, researchers do know that our personalities are not static. Rather, they change as we move through the stages of our lives. Our temperaments also change as we grow, as illustrated by the extreme emotions experienced by many people in early adolescence. Most of us learn to control our emotions as we advance toward adulthood. (Donatelle & Davis, *Access to Health*)

6. Does it matter whether a message is well organized as long as its point is eventually made? Why not just let your ideas flow naturally and trust your audience to grasp your meaning? For one thing, misinterpreted messages lead to wasted time reading and rereading, poor decision making, and shattered business relationships. When you consider such costs, you begin to realize the value of clear writing and good organization. (Bovée, Thill, & Schatzman, *Business Communication Today*)

7. The Department of Agriculture recommends that if you drink alcoholic beverages, do so in moderation. Alcoholic beverages are high in calories and low in nutrients. Heavy drinkers, especially those who also smoke, frequently develop nutritional deficiencies. They also develop more serious diseases such as cirrhosis of the liver and certain types of cancer. This is partly true because of the loss of appetite, poor food intake, and impaired absorption of nutrients. One or two standard-sized drinks per day appear to cause no harm in normal, healthy, nonpregnant adults. Some medical specialists believe that moderate doses of alcohol help prevent heart disease by preventing arteries from becoming clogged with fatty deposits. (DuBrin, *Human Relations*)

8. Police departments across the country make regular reports to the Federal Bureau of Investigation (FBI), which puts together an annual book of crime statistics titled *Crime in the United States: The Uniform Crime Report* (or, simply, *UCR*). This book includes data on felonies—serious crimes—of two kinds. First is crime against property, which is crime that involves theft or destruction of property belonging to others. Crimes against property include burglary, larceny-theft, motor-vehicle theft, and arson. Second is crime against persons, which is crime that involves violence or the threat of violence against others. Crimes against persons include murder and manslaughter, aggravated assault, forcible rape, and robbery. (Macionis, *Social Problems*)

9. Erosion is the movement of soil particles from one place to another and is a process that is detrimental to the fertility of the soil. Water or wind

are usually the agents of movement with the soil being washed away by heavy rain or improper irrigation or blown away by wind. (Rice & Rice, *Practical Horticulture*)

10. Our memories are not exact replicas of experience. Sensory information is summarized and encoded—for example, as words or images—almost as soon as it is detected. When you hear a lecture, for example, you may hang on to every word (we hope you do), but you do not memorize those words verbatim. You extract the main points and encode them. (Wade & Tavris, *Invitation to Psychology*)

Exercise 6   Identifying the Main Idea of a Paragraph

The main idea in these paragraphs may be stated or implied. Write the main idea of each paragraph.

1. Business education has undergone more change in the last ten years than it has in the last century. The education reform movement, recent technological innovations, increasing cultural diversity in the workforce, and the emergence of the global marketplace have all had a dramatic impact on the office support curriculum. Businesspersons and educators alike are trying to cope with what Tom Peters calls "a world turned upside down." What was appropriate just a few years ago must be continually evaluated and updated to keep pace with the rapidly changing workplace. (Jaderstrom, White, & Ellison, "The Changing Office Support Curriculum: Preparing Students for the Future," *The Balance Sheet*)

2. Since all of my recommendations call upon you to prepare for speaking by writing out, in some form, what you wish to say, it is, first of all, of great importance to recognize that what is written to be read has a radically different character from what is written to be heard. The remarkable difference between listening and reading—the one requiring you to keep moving forward irreversibly with the flow of speech, the other allowing you to proceed at your own pace and to go forward or backward at will by simply turning the pages—demands that you accommodate what you write for listening, as contrasted with what you must do for readers. (Adler "Preparing and Delivering a Speech," *How to Speak, How to Listen*)

3. To know how much it costs to produce a good or service, I need to know something about the production techniques that are available and about the prices of the inputs required. To estimate how much it will cost me to operate a gas station, for instance, I need to know what equipment I need, how many workers, what kind of building, and so forth. I also need to know the going wage rates for mechanics and unskilled laborers, the cost of gas pumps, interest rates, the rents per square foot of land on high traffic corners, and the wholesale price of gasoline. Of course, I also need to know how much I can sell gasoline and repair services for. (Case & Fair, *Economics*)

4. Health care presents a variety of social problems to all of the world's societies. In more affluent regions like Western Europe, North America, and Australia, the problems associated with physical health often involve reducing inequalities in access to high-quality health care. In impoverished regions of the world, where high-quality medical care is

often lacking, the social problems associated with physical health are even more profound. These problems include the spread of infectious diseases, high rates of infant and maternal death, low life expectancies, scarcities of medical personnel and equipment, and inadequate sewage and water systems. (Kornblum & Julian, *Social Problems*)

5. Of all the traditional presentation media, 35mm slides promise to make the best impression on an audience. There is something attention grabbing and impressive about seeing well-executed color slides on a big screen. At the same time, slides are the greatest challenge to produce from the desktop (computer). Creating 35mm slides is not a solo activity like running the company newsletter off a laser printer. Making slides requires additional hardware in the form of a slide recorder, and maybe even another computer. (Thompson, "Sliding Home," *PC Publishing and Presentations*)

6. There exists a long-standing fiction that tools and technologies have no inherent value built into them, but only reflect the values of the people who use them. In fact, that's never been the case. There has never been a neutral technology. All technologies are power. A lance gives us more projectile power than our throwing arm. An automobile gives us more locomotive power than our legs and feet. The Internet provides us with more communication power than is possible through face-to-face interaction. (Rifkin, "A Radically Different World," *Forbes ASAP*)

7. In the final decades of the twentieth century, increasingly sophisticated computers quickly became a basic element of our lives. We now find microprocessors at work in the vast majority of U.S. households and businesses, and in cars and trucks as well. Surveys show that in 2001, almost 55 percent of U.S. households had at least one personal computer, and almost 45 percent of U.S. households were connected to the Internet (U.S. Census Bureau, 2001). As computers become more numerous—as well as more powerful, smaller, and more portable—they will rewrite the rules of social life in the twenty-first century. (Macionis, *Sociology*)

8. The founders of England's New World colonies hoped to replicate the social order that they had known at home. For that reason, as early as 1619, the Virginia Company began to pay for the transportation of single women to the colony. These women were forbidden to marry servants. Instead, they were supposed to become brides for the unmarried planters who were beginning to make fortunes in the tobacco boom. As in England, it was expected that men would perform all the "outside" labor, including planting, farming, and taking care of the large farm animals. Women would do all the "inside" work, including preserving and preparing food, spinning thread and weaving cloth, making and repairing clothing, and tending the garden. In English society, a farmer's wife thus was not simply a man's sexual partner and companion, she was also the mistress of the household economy, performing work vital to success. "In a new plantation," the Virginia Assembly noted in 1619, "it is not known whether a man or woman be more necessary." Both men and women were vital to the social and economic order that the English wanted to create in the Chesapeake. (Boydston, Cullather, Lewis, McGerr, & Oakes, *Making a Nation*)

9. Although each person's body has individual requirements for sleep and rest, sleep requirements tend to decrease with age. For example, newborns typically average 20 hours of sleep per day, while elderly persons may require only 5–6 hours per day. Infants and children sleep more soundly and have a harder time waking up than older adults. (Wolgin, *Being a Nursing Assistant*)

10. The relationship between stress and your health is neither simple nor straightforward. Stress will not automatically cause you to become physically ill. The impact of stress on your health is mediated by a variety of personality variables, as well as your genetic makeup and environment. But physically, it is clear that when you are under prolonged stress your immune system can be weakened, creating vulnerability to illness and bodily system breakdown. Furthermore, stress can create a wide assortment of psychosomatic problems in which the weakest link in your system of organs, muscles, and glands is affected. (Abascal, Brucato, & Brucato, *Stress Mastery*)

THE NEED TO BE FLEXIBLE

Although skilled readers look for a stated or implied main idea in every paragraph, they realize that there may not be one. In real reading, unlike these selected examples and exercises, authors do not always use a consistent pattern of one main idea per paragraph. For example, an author might have one paragraph with an inferred main idea and then state a main idea in the next paragraph to cover two or three paragraphs. For this reason, you must always read actively and be willing to apply strategies flexibly.

CHAPTER 3 REVIEW QUESTIONS

1. What is a main idea?
2. What is your strategy for identifying the main idea of a paragraph?
3. Why is it important to restate the main idea in your own words?
4. Define the two words *imply* and *infer*.
5. What are some steps you can take to increase your chances of making valid, appropriate inferences?

Use Your Strategies 1

Define the italicized word in each paragraph, then write the main idea of each paragraph in your own words.

1. Couples seeking a divorce will not always find it easy to reach agreement on issues that affect their children, but they should attempt to do so before telling their children about the *impending* separation. Children, even very young children, need to be prepared for the divorce. They need information about where they will live, who will take care of

them, where they will go to school, and whatever other issues are of major concern to them. (NIMH, *Caring About Kids: When Parents Divorce*)

2. At times we half-heartedly make efforts to remember facts that stand out, and completely miss the speaker's main points. This habit has also been referred to as "majoring in minors." Unless we listen with an intent to understand the *essence* of the message, we may fall into the habit of picking and choosing only selected tidbits to process and remember. When we put these bits together at the end of the presentation or conversation, we may find that we have a totally incorrect perception of what the speaker was trying to get across. (Barker & Barker, *Communication*)

3. A glance at a globe or a view of Earth from space reveals a planet *dominated* by the ocean. It is for this reason that Earth is often referred to as the blue planet. The area of Earth is about 510 million square kilometers (197 million square miles). Of this total, approximately 360 million square kilometers (140 million square miles), or 71 percent, is represented by oceans and marginal seas (meaning seas around the ocean's margin, like the Mediterranean Sea and Caribbean Sea). Continents and islands comprise the remaining 29 percent, or 150 million square kilometers (58 million square miles). (Lutgens & Tarbuck, *Foundations of Earth Science*)

4. We know little about the details of timekeeping in prehistoric eras, but wherever we turn up records and artifacts, we usually discover that in every culture, some people were *preoccupied* with measuring and recording the passage of time. Ice-age hunters in Europe over 20,000 years ago scratched lines and gouged holes in sticks and bones, possibly counting days between phases of the moon. Five thousand years ago, Sumerians in the Tigris-Euphrates valley in today's Iraq had a calendar that divided the year into 30-day months, divided the day into 12 periods (each corresponding to 2 of our hours), and divided these periods into 30 parts (each like 4 of our minutes). We have no written records of Stonehenge, built over 4000 years ago in England, but its alignments show its purposes apparently included the determination of seasonal or celestial events, such as lunar eclipses, solstices and so on. (National Institute of Standards and Technology, *A Walk Through Time*)

5. Overweight is a hefty problem in the United States. It's estimated that 24 percent of men and 27 percent of women in this country—about 34 million Americans—are obese. And sometimes it seems that there are 34 million different diets or diet products promoted to combat the problem. The latest to win the nation's *fervent* attention is a revival of a sort—a return to very low calorie diets, generally 400 to 800 calories per day. (*FDA Consumer*)

6. In countries where two or more languages *coexist*, confusion often arises. In Belgium, many towns have two quite separate names, one recognized by French speakers, one by Dutch speakers, so that the French Tournai is the Dutch Doornik, while the Dutch Luik is the French Liège. The French Mons is the Dutch Bergen, the Dutch Kortrijk is the French Courtrai, and the city that to all French-speaking people (and indeed most English-speaking people) is known as Bruges (and pronounced "broozsh") is to the locals called Brugge and pro-

nounced "broo-guh." Although Brussels is officially bilingual, it is in fact a French-speaking island in a Flemish Lake. (Bryson, *Mother Tongue*)

7. Writers who read only their own words are like chefs who eat only their own cooking. How can you tell if your marinara has enough garlic if you've never tried another's? Similarly, how can you judge if your *protagonist* is sympathetic enough if you don't study how other writers create their characters? (Bonnie, "How To Read A Short Story," *Writer's Digest*)

8. Despite the rich variety of *indigenous* local cultures around the globe, the world is increasingly coming to look like one place. In consumer goods, architecture, industrial technology, education, and housing, the European model is pervasive. (Bergman & McKnight, *Introduction to Geography*)

9. Opening a checking and a savings account is the first step in establishing your credit worthiness. Credit can be a useful tool for managing your expenses and your household budget. There are, however, unfortunate examples of those who have let credit work against them rather than for them. With some care, credit can become a useful instrument in financial planning. Borrowing to purchase assets, such as a home, which are likely to increase in value, can be a wise investment strategy. On the other hand, borrowing to increase present *consumption*, or to purchase assets that will decrease in value, places a burden on our future ability to consume. Too much, and it can result in a vicious cycle, with an ever-increasing burden of obligations as we attempt to repay old debts with new loans. (Winger & Frasca, *Personal Finance*)

10. A current reference book for criminal trial lawyers says, "Alibi is different from all of the other defenses . . . because . . . it is based upon the premise that the defendant is truly innocent." The defense alibi denies that the defendant committed the act in question. All of the other defenses we are about to discuss grant that the defendant committed the act, but they deny that he or she should be held criminally responsible. While *justifications* and excuses may produce findings of "not guilty," the defense of alibi claims outright innocence. (Schmalleger, *Criminal Justice Today*)

Use Your Strategies 2

For this exercise, assume your professor has instructed you to read this essay to define these words and concepts: *altered, consequent decrease, latter,* and *underpinning;* and to identify the main ideas of paragraphs 3, 8, 9, and 11.

ROBERT L. MCGRATH

Robert McGrath is a freelance writer based in Irvine, California. This selection is from the National Research Bureau's A Better Life for You.

HAVE A GOOD NIGHT

Robert L. McGrath

[1]Sleep. Everyone does it, yet no one understands it. You can even do without it for limited periods with no serious effects, provided you get back to normal within a reasonable time. You spend, on average, one third of your life asleep—time that's a fundamental part of who you are, how you feel, what you do. And that makes it worth thinking about.

[2]Sleep is an altered state of consciousness, a recurring state of inactivity, with consequent decrease in responsiveness to events in one's environment. Like eating and breathing, it's a natural mind-body function, the foundation of your health, fitness and well being.

[3]The long-held belief that you need at least eight hours of sleep per night has been proved incorrect. Actual requirements vary with each individual. Some people need nine hours of sleep; others get by nicely on six. The average for most people is about seven-and-a-half hours.

[4]There are two distinct types of rest: active and quiet. Researchers identify active sleep as REM, rapid eye movement, wherein movements of the eyeballs beneath closed lids accompany more intense activity in the brain than during quiet sleep. The latter consists of several stages, all categorized as non-REM or NREM sleep.

[5]Say you sleep eight hours. Two will be spent in REM sleep, the remaining six in NREM, shifting from one stage of depth to another. You sleep in cycles, drifting from NREM sleep to REM sleep and back again in 90 to 100 minute intervals.

[6]It is believed that dreams generally occur during periods of REM sleep, and that the shallower the sleep, the greater number of dreams you will have. Your desires, worries, and other tensions may have direct bearing on what you dream about.

[7]Don't let these details bother you. They're not as important as the knowledge that a good night's sleep is the basis for your feeling good—a mirror of your days past and an underpinning for better days ahead.

[8]Know, too, that as your life progresses, your sleeping habits will probably change. As you grow older, you'll need less total sleep-time, much less deep NREM sleep, a little less REM sleep, and you'll experience more waking periods during the night. Because the sleep mechanism is totally integrated with every other function and activity of body and mind, such changes are to be expected; they should not be a source of worry.

[9]What about that old bugaboo, insomnia? There is seldom a single identifiable cause. It may be physical—pain from heart disease, arthritis, backache, diabetes, or hypertension. It may be psychological—emotional stress, anxiety, depression. And it may be behavioral—poor lifestyle habits such as overeating, faulty nutrition, failure to exercise, irregular times for going to bed and arising. Or there may be overlapping of any or all of these elements.

[10]So what do you do about it? Regular exercise is one answer. A tired body is a basic requirement for sleep at deeper levels. Healthful eating habits can help. Try to achieve a relaxed body and an easy mind—let go of your day and welcome the night. And forget those sleeping pills—they will not produce natural sleep, but rather a state of minor anesthesia, artificial and distorted.

[11]Remember Goldilocks, and choose your bed carefully, aware that some are too big, some too hard, some too small, some too soft. Make sure your bed is just right for you. Since you spend more time in your bedroom than any other room in your house, take time to plan it for peace, privacy, and comfort.

[12]Then relax. Be glad a good night's sleep restores you to your energetic self, ready to face a new day primed for come-what-may.

[13]Sleep well! Sweet dreams!

Use Your Strategies 2 Questions

1. Define these words and phrases:

   a. altered ([2])   c. latter ([4])

   b. consequent decrease ([2])   d. underpinning ([7])

2. Write the main idea of paragraphs 3, 8, 9, and 11.

Use Your Strategies 3

For this exercise, assume your professor has instructed you to read this page to define these words and concepts: *nonverbal communication, reliable indicators, convey,* and *cultural differences;* and to identify the main idea in each of the five paragraphs.

ANDREW J. DuBRIN

An accomplished author, Dr. DuBrin brings to his work years of research experience in business psychology. An active speaker, Dr. DuBrin currently teaches leadership and organizational behavior at the Rochester Institute of Technology. This one-page excerpt is from Chapter 6, "Communicating With People," in his Human Relations *text.*

NONVERBAL COMMUNICATION

Andrew J. DuBrin

NONVERBAL COMMUNICATION (SENDING AND RECEIVING SILENT MESSAGES)

[1]So far we have been talking mostly about spoken communication. However, much of the communication among people includes nonspoken and nonwritten messages. These nonverbal signals are a critical part of everyday communication. As a case in point, *how* you say "Thank you" makes a big difference in the extent to which your sense of appreciation registers. In **nonverbal communication** we use our body, voice, or environment in numerous ways to help put a message across. Sometimes we are not aware how much our true feelings color our spoken message.

[2]One problem of paying attention to nonverbal signals is that they can be taken too seriously. Just because some nonverbal signals (such as yawning or looking away from a person) might reflect a person's real feelings, not every signal can be reliably connected with a particular attitude. Jason may put his hand over his mouth because he is shocked. Lucille may put her hand over her mouth because she is trying to control her laughter about the message, and Ken may put his hand over his mouth as a signal that he is pondering the consequences of the message. Here we look at seven categories of nonverbal communication that are generally reliable indicators of a person's attitude and feelings.

Environment or Setting

[3]Where you choose to deliver your message indicates what you think of its importance. Assume that a neighbor invites you over for dinner to discuss something with you. You will think it is a more important topic under these circumstances than if it were brought up when the two of you met in the supermarket. Other important environmental cues include room color, temperature, lighting, and furniture arrangement. A person who sits behind an uncluttered large desk, for example, appears more powerful than a person who sits behind a small, cluttered desk.

Distance from the Other Person

[4]How close you place your body relative to another person's also conveys meaning when you send a message. If, for instance, you want to convey a positive attitude toward another person, get physically close to him or her. Putting your arm around someone to express interest and warmth is another obvious nonverbal signal. However, many people in a work setting abstain from all forms of touching (except for handshakes) because of concern that touching might be interpreted as sexual harassment.

[5]Cultural differences must be kept in mind in interpreting nonverbal cues. To illustrate, a French male is likely to stand closer to you than a British male, even if they had equally positive attitudes toward you. A set of useful guidelines has been developed for estimating how close to stand to another person (at least in many cultures). . . .

Use Your Strategies 3 Questions

1. Define these words and phrases:

   a. nonverbal communication (¶1)   **c.** convey (¶4)

   b. reliable indicators (¶2)   **d.** cultural differences (¶5)

2. Write the main idea of each paragraph.

Use Your Strategies 4

For this exercise, assume your professor has instructed you to read this excerpt on the turning point of the Constitutional Convention to define these words and concepts: *unicameral, bicameral, proportional representation, narrowly averted, exemplary record,* and *preordained;* and to identify the main idea in each of the five paragraphs.

LARRY BERMAN AND BRUCE ALLEN MURPHY

Dr. Berman is the founding director of the University of California, Washington Center, and the author or co-author of nine books and numerous articles. Dr. Murphy is a nationally recognized scholar on the American Supreme Court, civil rights and liberties, judicial behavior, and judicial biography. He is currently the Fred Morgan Kirby Professor of Civil Rights in the Department of Government and Law at Lafayette College. This excerpt about the Constitutional Convention is from Chapter 2, "The Founding and The Constitution," in their text Approaching Democracy.

DEBATE AND COMPROMISE

Larry Berman and Bruce Allen Murphy

DEBATE AND COMPROMISE: THE TURNING POINT OF THE CONVENTION

[1]The Articles of Confederation failed because the prospect of a veto by each state over the actions of the central government had resulted in a powerless Confederation Congress. Thus, the composition of the new Congress and its means of selection were critical issues at the Convention. Would it be one house (unicameral), as before, or two houses (bicameral), as some delegates now preferred? Would the members be apportioned by the population of each state (proportional representation), as in the Virginia Plan; or would each state have the same number of representatives (one-state, one-vote), as in the New Jersey Plan? By the middle of June the Convention had split into two opposing groups: the "big states" composed of Massachusetts, Pennsylvania, Virginia, New York, the Carolinas, and Georgia (the southern states sided with the big states, believing that given

their large size, proportional representation would eventually be in their interest), against the rest of the states, whose only hope for influence lay in the equal representation scheme.

[2]Repeatedly in the early debates the small states failed to pass the New Jersey Plan, partly because Maryland's Luther Martin had alienated his colleagues by giving a virulent, two-day speech against proportional representation. Martin's effort backfired when the delegates quickly approved proportional representation for the legislature. However, when the delegates also voted to establish a bicameral legislative branch to provide some sort of balance of power, the issue now became how the upper house of Congress, known as the Senate, would be apportioned.

[3]During this debate, Georgia delegate Abraham Baldwin later recalled, "The convention was more than once upon the point of dissolving without agreeing upon any system." At this turning point in the debate, it was the selfless action of Baldwin and several other delegates that narrowly averted the complete failure of the Convention. The large-state delegates sought proportional representation in both the Senate and in the House of Representatives, as the lower house was called, giving them total control over the Congress, while the small-state delegates pressed for the old Articles of Confederation system of equality of votes in the legislature. Because of their numbers, the large states expected to win the issue by a narrow margin. But well-timed absences and changes of heart ended the big states' chances for dominance in the Senate and in the process saved the Convention from failure.

[4]When the vote was taken on the question of Senate representation, Maryland's Daniel of St. Thomas Jenifer, who otherwise had an exemplary record of attendance for the Convention, deliberately stayed away, keeping Maryland allied with the small states. Then, the three Georgia delegates conspired to switch their state's vote from the big-state position to the small-state position. Two of them suddenly left the Convention, and the third delegate, Abraham Baldwin, voted for the small-state position. Thus, proportional representation in the Senate failed.

[5]With compromise now possible, a committee consisting of one member from each state was formed to prepare suggestions for resolving the question of representation in the Senate. When the selection process for the committee was finished, it turned out that every member favored the small states' position, so the result was preordained. What would emerge was a plan acceptable to the small states but capable of being passed by the large states as well.

Use Your Strategies 4 Questions

1. Define these words and phrases:

   a. unicameral (¶1)
   b. bicameral (¶1)
   c. proportional representation (¶1)
   d. narrowly averted (¶3)
   e. exemplary record (¶4)
   f. preordained (¶5)

2. Write the main idea of each paragraph.

REFLECT AND CONNECT

A. Select three paragraphs in a current reading assignment from another class. Identify the main idea in each paragraph.

B. Assume that you need to write a paragraph on the topic "health care costs in America." Decide what your controlling thought will be and write a topic sentence (main idea) for your paragraph. Now, select a second (different) controlling idea and write a second topic sentence. Discuss how the controlling ideas would influence the kind of information you put in each paragraph.

LOG ON TO THE WEB

These sites contain information on major authors or links to author information. Log on to one of these sites or use a search engine to locate information on your favorite author.

http://lang.nagoya-u.ac.jp/~matsuoka/AmeLit.html
http://andromeda.rutgers.edu/~jlynch/Lit/
http://www.cnn.com/books/dialogue/

Write down (1) one main idea about the author; (2) basic information about the author such as age, birthplace, and current status; and (3) titles of two works. Turn it in to your professor.

REFERENCES

National Reading Panel. (2000). "Teaching Children to Read: An Evidence-based Assessment of the Scientific Research Literature on Reading and Its Implications for Reading Instruction." Washington, DC: U.S. Department of Health and Human Services.

Pressley, M., & P. Afflerbach. (1995). *Verbal Protocols of Reading: The Nature of Constructively Responsive Reading.* Hillsdale, NJ: Erlbaum.

Smith, B. D., & N. D. Chase. (1991). "The Frequency and Placement of Main Idea Topic Sentences in Psychology Textbooks." *Journal of College Reading,* 24(1), 31–41.

Snow, C. E., M. S. Burns, & P. Griffin (Eds.). (1998). *Preventing Reading Difficulties in Young Children.* Washington, DC: National Academy Press.

Taraban, R., K. Rynearson, & M. S. Kerr. (2000). "Metacognition and Freshman Academic Performance." *Journal of Developmental Education,* 24(1).

Identifying Supporting Details and Using Relationships Among Ideas

It's not that I'm so smart, it's just that I stay with problems longer.

—Albert Einstein

AN IDEA TO THINK ABOUT

If stating an idea were enough to make it understood, there would be no books or essays. Each piece of writing would consist of only a topic sentence. Of course more is needed. Writers must explain, expand, and support their ideas. Sometimes facts or logic are called for, sometimes narration of events, and sometimes examples, illustrations, and reasons. A mathematics textbook calls for clear, step-by-step reasoning, with many examples and exercises to reinforce each lesson. New interpretations of historical events call for background information, direct evidence, and support from authoritative sources. The way that an author chooses to develop a main idea depends on the work's purpose and its intended audience (Veit, Gould, & Clifford, 1990).

As you prepare to read this chapter, think about how you decide what is important when you're reading. Do you try to remember everything? Do you try to remember more details in some subjects than in others? Do you vary the amount of detail you try to remember depending on what you plan to do with the information?

CHAPTER FOCUS

As you know from Chapter 3, skilled readers have excellent comprehension. They use many skills, strategies, and knowledge bases in combination, and often in parallel, to understand what they read.

On the other hand, unsuccessful readers have poor comprehension. This is often because they

- fail to maintain interest or concentration;
- fail to understand key words;
- fail to understand key sentences;
- fail to understand how sentences relate to one another;
- fail to understand how the information fits together in a meaningful way—how it is organized (Parker, Hasbrouck, & Denton, 2002).

Chapters 1 through 3 illustrated strategies you can use to minimize or eliminate the first three problems on the list. This chapter presents strategies for reducing or eliminating problems four and five.

This chapter has two major, interconnected sections. The first is understanding how the ideas and sentences in a paragraph relate to one another—in other words, differentiating among the main idea, **major supporting details**, and **minor supporting details**. The second is understanding how those ideas and details fit together—that is, identifying how the paragraph is organized or structured.

UNDERSTANDING HOW IDEAS AND SENTENCES IN A PARAGRAPH RELATE TO ONE ANOTHER

As discussed in the previous chapter, a well-written expository paragraph has one main idea that is either directly stated or implied. The main idea is the general idea that unifies, or ties together, all the ideas and sentences in a **paragraph**. To understand a paragraph, you must understand the main idea.

However, understanding the main idea is not enough. To fully comprehend a paragraph, you also need to know how each of the other ideas and sentences relate to the main idea and/or to the other ideas and sentences.

There are no rules about how many sentences can be in a paragraph or about how many details should be in a paragraph. This means each paragraph is unique and can have any combination of these types of sentences:

1. A topic sentence that states the main idea. A paragraph can have only one topic sentence.

2. A major detail sentence with one or more specific details that directly develop and support the main idea. A paragraph can have any number of major details.

3. A minor detail sentence with one or more very specific details that develop and support the previous major detail. A paragraph can have any number of minor details supporting a major detail.

4. A sentence that includes a major detail that develops and supports the main idea and one or more minor details to develop and support that major detail. A paragraph can have any number of sentences that include a major detail along with its supporting minor detail (or details).

5. A **transitional sentence** that links one idea to another. A transitional sentence can link two ideas within a paragraph or can appear at the end of a paragraph to connect what you have just read with what you are about to read in the next paragraph.

In addition, you will occasionally find an irrelevant sentence. An irrelevant sentence is one that does not support and develop the main idea or any of the major details or provide a bridge to the next idea.

EXAMPLE In Chapter 3 you identified the first sentence of this paragraph as the main idea. Now, consider the other four sentences in the paragraph. For each sentence, answer the question, How does this sentence relate to the main idea and the other sentences?

> [1]Glaciers, despite their barren, stationary appearance, support many kinds of life. [2]Fish thrive in the rivers of ice melt that flow underneath. [3]Ice worms tunnel through the surface and eat pollen that blows in from nearby forests. [4]Flowers sometimes bloom in the dust that collects on the edges. [5]Some of these ice flowers grow as high as four feet. (Lapp, Flood, & Farnan, *Content Area Reading and Learning*)

Explanation

Sentence 1 contains the main idea—"glaciers support many kinds of life"—therefore, it is the *topic sentence*.

Sentence 2 contains a specific detail that directly supports and explains the main idea—fish are one of the "many kinds of life"—therefore, it is a *major detail*.

Sentence 3 contains a specific detail that directly supports and explains the main idea—ice worms are one of the "many kinds of life" —therefore, it is a *major detail*.

Sentence 4 contains a specific detail that directly supports and explains the main idea—flowers are one of the "many kinds of life" —therefore, it is a *major detail*.

Sentence 5 contains a very specific detail that supports and explains the previous major detail about flowers—how tall "flowers" grow—therefore, it is a *minor detail*.

Visually, the relationships among the ideas and sentences in the paragraph appear like this:

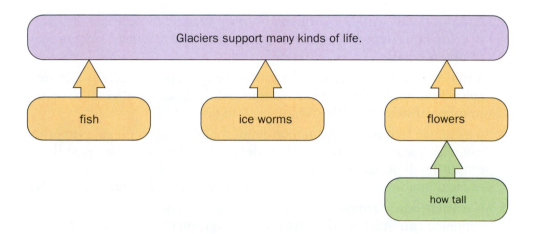

EXAMPLE   In this paragraph you identified the first sentence as the main idea. Now, consider how the other four sentences in the paragraph relate to the main idea and the other sentences.

> [1]Flowering plants, or angiosperms, consist of two major regions, the root system and the shoot system. [2]The root system consists of all the roots of a plant. [3]Roots are branched portions of the plant body that are embedded in the soil. [4] The shoot system consists of leaves, buds, and (in season) flowers and fruits. [5] The shoot system is usually located above the ground. (Adapted from Audesirk, Audesirk, & Byers, *Biology: Life on Earth*)

Explanation

Sentence 1 contains the main idea—"flowering plants consist of two major regions, the root system and the shoot system"—therefore, it is the *topic sentence*.

Sentence 2 contains a specific detail that directly supports and explains the main idea—one of the "two major regions," the root system consists of all the roots of a plant—therefore, it is a *major detail*.

Sentence 3 contains a very specific detail that supports and explains the previous major detail—roots are branched portions of the plant body that are in the soil—therefore, it is a *minor detail*.

Sentence 4 contains a specific detail that directly supports and explains the main idea—one of the "two major regions," the shoot system consists of leaves, buds, and (in season) flowers and fruits—therefore, it is a *major detail*.

Sentence 5 contains a very specific detail that supports and explains the previous major detail—the shoot system is usually located above the ground—therefore, it is a *minor detail*.

Visually, the relationships among the ideas and sentences in the paragraph appear like this:

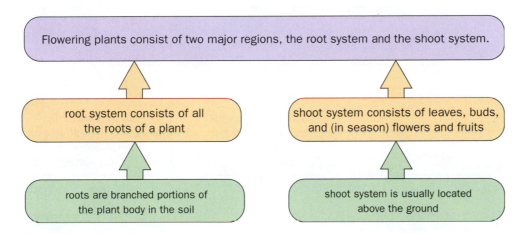

Often, however, details are not so clearly separated. Authors sometimes combine major and minor details in the same sentence.

EXAMPLE   Identify the topic sentence and then decide how the various levels of information included in the sentences relate to the main idea and the other details.

> [1]A survey is a widely used research method in which subjects respond to a series of items or questions in a questionnaire or an interview. [2]Surveys are particularly suited to studying what cannot be observed directly, such as political attitudes, religious beliefs, or the private lives of couples. [3]Like experiments, surveys can be used to investigate the relationship among variables. [4]They are also useful for descriptive research, in which subject responses help a sociologist to describe a social setting, such as an urban neighborhood or gambling casino. (Macionis *Sociology*)

Explanation

Sentence 1 is a *topic sentence* because it contains the main idea: A survey is a widely used research method in which subjects respond to a series of items or questions in a questionnaire or an interview.

Sentence 2 includes both a major and minor detail:

> *Major*—suited to studying what can't be observed
>
> *Minor*—examples of what can't be observed: political attitudes, religious beliefs, private lives

Sentence 3 contains a major detail—used to investigate relationships among variables (like experiments)

Sentence 4 includes both a major and minor detail:

> *Major*—useful for descriptive research in which subject helps describe social setting

Minor—examples of social setting: urban neighborhood or gambling casino

Visually, the relationships among the ideas and sentences in the paragraph appear like this:

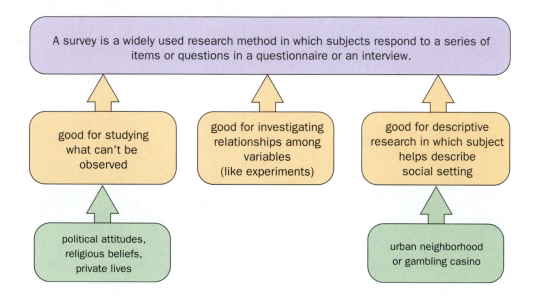

Keep Your Purpose in Mind

Although you must understand the relationships among all the ideas and sentences in a paragraph, the number of major and minor details you need to remember depends on your purpose for reading. Even when you are reading to learn—to have a thorough understanding of the main ideas and the significant details that support and develop them—the number of major and minor details you need to remember varies with the specific assignment.

Exercise 1   **Identifying How Ideas and Sentences Relate to One Another**

Read the paragraph and then label the primary role each sentence has in the paragraph: main idea, major detail, minor detail, major detail with minor detail, transition, or irrelevant.

1. [1]Many cancers can be directly or indirectly attributed to environmental factors called carcinogens (kar-SIN-O-jens). [2]Carcinogens stimulate the conversion of a normal cell to a cancer cell. [3]Common classes of carcinogens include chemicals, radiation, and viruses. [4]Some carcinogens are mutagens (MO-ta-jens)—that is, they damage DNA strands and may cause chromosomal breakage. [5]Radiation is a mutagen that has carcinogenic effects. (Martini, Bartholomew, & Welch, *The Human Body*)

2. [1]Gestures help members of a culture clarify confusing messages, but differences in body language can be a major source of misunderstanding during intercultural communication. [2]For example, people in the United States and Canada say no by shaking their heads back and forth, people in Bulgaria nod up and down, people in Japan move their right

hand, and people in Sicily raise their chin. [3]Similarly, U.S. business-people assume that a person who won't meet their gaze is evasive and dishonest. [4]However, in many parts of Asia, keeping one's eyes lowered is a sign of respect. (Bovée, Thill, & Schatzman, *Business Communication Today*)

3. [1]At the end of the sixteenth century the Spanish and the French were the only European powers directly involved in North America. [2]The Spanish had built a series of forts along the Florida coast to protect the Gulf Stream sea lanes used by the convoys carrying wealth from their New World colonies. [3]The French were deeply involved in the fur trade of the St. Lawrence River. (Faragher, Buhle, Czitrom, & Armitage, *Out of Many*)

4. [1]Nearly 4000 minerals have been named and about 40 to 50 new ones are identified each year. [2]However, no more than a few dozen minerals make up most of the rocks of Earth's crust and as such are classified as the rock-forming minerals. [3]Silicon and oxygen combine to form the framework of the most common mineral group, the silicates. [4]Perhaps the next most common mineral group is the carbonates—carbon plus oxygen plus other elements. [5]Other common rock-forming minerals include gypsum and halite. (Adapted from Lutgens & Tarbuck, *Foundations of Earth Science*)

5. [1]Sculpture is categorized according to whether it is carved or modeled and whether it is a relief or freestanding. [2]Relief remains tied to the background, from which it only partially emerges, in contrast to free-standing sculpture, which is fully liberated from it. [3]A further distinction is made between low relief and high relief, depending on how much the carving projects. (Janson & Janson, *A Basic History of Art*)

6. [1]The great economic expansion of the middle and late 1920s was in part stimulated by readily available credit. [2]Interest rates remained low through the decade. [3]Thousands of citizens could and did borrow money to invest in factories and productive machinery, buy houses, and acquire expensive goods "on the installment plan." [4]Foreigners borrowed extensively from American bankers, and the borrowed dollars soon came back to pay for imported American automobiles, electrical equipment, petroleum, wheat, and corn. (Unger, *These United States*)

7. [1]All sound is produced through three stages: energy source, vibrating element, and resonating chamber. [2]Most instruments can be identified by how they operate in these three stages. [3]The flute, for example, uses the human breath as an energy source; the air then vibrates as it is blown across the opening; and the tubular body of the flute serves as the resonating chamber. [4]The clarinet is similar to the flute, but differs in its second stage; instead of the air blowing across an opening, the clarinet's vibrating element is a little strip of wood called a reed. [5]The trumpet, on the other hand, uses the vibration of the player's lips against a metal cup called the mouthpiece to start the vibration. (Meyer, *Perspectives on Music*)

8. [1]Many different kinds of theories have been advanced to explain all sorts of rule-violating behavior. [2]Some observers of the contemporary scene, for example, find explanations for modern-day violence and seemingly increased rates of criminal victimization in the now widespread and commonplace episodes of violence in the American media—especially on television, in music, and in film. [3]Experts who

study the media estimate that the average American child watches 8,000 murders and 100,000 acts of violence while growing up. [4]At a recent international conference, Suzanne Stutman, President of the Institute for Mental Health Initiatives in Washington, reported that studies consistently show that the extent of exposure to television violence in childhood is a good predictor of future criminal behavior. (Schmalleger, *Criminal Justice Today*)

9. [1]Earth has two principal motions—rotation and revolution. [2]Rotation is the spinning of Earth about its axis. [3]Revolution refers to the movement of Earth in its orbit around the Sun. (Lutgens & Tarbuck, *The Atmosphere*)

10. [1]Even in the first weeks after birth, infants differ in activity level, mood, responsiveness, soothability, and attention span (Belsky, Hsieh, & Crnic, 1996; Kagan, 1994). [2]Some are irritable and cranky; others are calm and sweet-natured. [3]Some will cuddle up in an adult's arms and snuggle; others squirm and fidget, as if they dislike being held. [4]Some smile easily; others fuss and cry. (Wade & Tavris, *Invitation to Psychology*)

UNDERSTANDING HOW IDEAS AND SENTENCES ARE ORGANIZED

There is no doubt that understanding the relationships among the ideas and sentences in a paragraph improves your comprehension. To help you identify those important relationships, an author usually organizes or structures his or her writing in the way that most clearly demonstrates those connections.

It is useful to determine an author's organization or structure because it provides a clue to locating and sorting out the relationships among details you need. When you spot one of the common development structures, such as comparison and contrast, you think and read actively because you know to look for the similarities and differences the author is providing to support and explain the main idea.

Unfortunately, many readers are unfamiliar with the different types of text structures that authors use, and this unfamiliarity hinders their comprehension (Bakken, Mastropieri, & Scruggs, 1997; Cook, 1983). In fact, research has shown that readers can profit from learning strategies that help them identify and apply appropriate structure-specific strategies (Downing, Bakken, & Whedon, 2002).

Six common structures, or **rhetorical patterns**, used in expository text are examples, **comparison** and/or **contrast**, classification, **cause and effect**, process or sequence, and definition. In addition, authors often combine two patterns.

To help you identify the structure and thus understand the relationships among the ideas and sentences, an author may use common words, phrases, or punctuation marks as clues. Called **signal words**, directional words, and sometimes **transition words**, they serve to point out a particular type of information or move you in a specific direction of thought.

For example, when you see phrases such as *in summary, in conclusion,* or *to sum up,* you know that the next information will be a recap or summary of the previous information. Or, when you see words such as *central, principal, chief, major, main, key, primary,* or *significant,* you know to look for an important point.

Please remember, however, that experienced readers use their knowledge of **text structures** to locate main ideas and distinguish them from supporting details so that comprehending and recalling the text is easier (Conlin, 1992). That means discovering the author's organizational pattern or structure is not your reason for reading; you are just using what you can discover about the way information is organized to help you understand the relationships among the ideas and sentences.

Text Structure: Examples

Listing relevant examples, explanations, or illustrations to support and develop the main idea is one of the most common structures in academic material. In this pattern the author typically states the main idea in the first sentence. The second sentence is a major detail that usually begins with a word or phrase designed to alert you to the example. Topic sentences such as the following alert you to watch for examples:

■ The best strategy for staying warm is to rely on an old mountaineering technique known as layering, a method that helps the body maintain a comfortable balance between heat generated and heat lost. For example, the first layer. . . .

Watch for details that give examples of layering.

■ A magazine is custom-designed for its special audience. For instance, *Redbook* and *Cosmopolitan*. . . .

Watch for details that give examples of magazines that are custom-designed for an audience.

Words that can signal examples include *for example, to illustrate, for instance, such as, specifically, namely,* the abbreviations *i.e.* and *e.g.,* and numbered elements.

Words that suggest a continuation of the same type of thought include *and, too, in addition, moreover, or, also, furthermore, as well as, besides, furthermore, in other words,* and *another.*

EXAMPLE Determine the main idea of this paragraph. Then, identify the relationships among the other ideas. In other words, determine how Donatelle and Davis structure the information.

> [1]We can prevent or reduce the risks for cardiovascular diseases by taking steps to change certain behaviors. [2]For example, controlling high blood pressure and adjusting our diets are two things we can do to reduce the risk for heart attacks. [3]By maintaining our weight, lowering our intake of sodium, and changing our lifestyles to reduce stress, we can lower blood pressure. [4] To prevent clogging of arteries we can adjust our diets by reducing our intake of saturated fats and cholesterol. (Adapted from Donatelle & Davis, *Access to Health*)

Explanation Donatelle and Davis state their main idea in the first sentence. They develop and support their main idea with a major detail in sentence 2 and minor details in sentences 3 and 4 that give specific examples.

Text Structure: Compare and Contrast

To compare means to tell how two or more objects, places, events, people, or ideas are alike. To contrast means to tell how two or more objects, places, events, people, or ideas are different.

Authors can develop and support their main idea by giving the likenesses, the differences, or the likenesses and differences between or among things using one of two common structures. The block style first describes one thing in its entirety and then describes the other thing in its entirety. The alternating style switches back and forth, comparing and/or contrasting the things trait by trait.

Topic sentences such as the following alert you to watch for likenesses and/or differences:

- Running for the local school board is similar to running for a major political office in many ways, but there are also important differences.

  Watch for details that tell how running for the school board and a major office are alike and how they are different.

- Despite the diversity of ecosystems, they are alike in some ways.

  Watch for details that tell how various ecosystems are alike.

- Although there may be some similarities between the lighting techniques of studio and outdoor photographers, their differences are critical.

  Watch for details that tell how the lighting techniques are different.

Words that may indicate comparison include *similarly, like, the same as, compared to, in the same way, likewise, so too, also, the same is true for, both, parallels, resembles, equally,* and *just as.*

Words that may indicate contrast include *but, yet, on the other hand, however, then again, instead, nevertheless, on the contrary, unlike, in contrast to, whereas, in spite of, although, conversely, different from, rather than,* and *just the opposite.*

EXAMPLE   Determine Long's main idea and how he develops the details to support that idea.

> [1]A computer system can be likened to the biological system of the human body. [2]Your brain is the processing component. [3]Your eyes and ears are input components that send signals to the brain. [4]If you see someone approaching, your brain matches the visual image of this person with others in your memory (storage component). [5]If the visual image matches that of a friend, your brain sends signals to your vocal cords and right arm (output components) to greet your friend with a hello and a handshake. [6]Computer system components interact in a similar way. (Long, *Introduction to Computers and Information Processing*)

Explanation   Long supports his main idea (a computer system is like a human biological system) by describing how the two systems are alike (*brain* *is like processing component; eyes and ears are like input components; memory is like storage component; vocal cords and arm are like output components).*

EXAMPLE   In this paragraph determine the author's main idea and how the details support that idea.

> [1]For diversity, Canyonlands National Park gives even the Grand Canyon a run for its money. [2]Its 337,570 acres range in elevation from 3,700 feet at the head of Lake Powell to more than 7,000 feet at the highest point on the south boundary above Salt Creek. [3]Like the Grand Canyon, Canyonlands protects a great inner gorge carved by the Colorado River, with a rim high above that offers awesome views. [4]But here, too, are flats studded with slickrock needles and spires, an intricate system of side canyons decorated with massive stone arches, and rich archeological resources famous for fine rock art. (The Sierra Club Guides to the National Parks)

Explanation   The author of this paragraph develops the main idea (*Canyonlands National Park is at least as diverse as the Grand Canyon*) by describing how they are alike (*they both have an inner gorge carved by the Colorado River and a high rim with an awesome view*) and how they are different (*Canyonlands has flats studded with slickrock needles and spires, an intricate system of side canyons decorated with massive stone arches, and rich archeological resources famous for fine rock art*).

Text Structure: Classification

Authors commonly use classification when they want to break a large subject into parts to examine how each part contributes to the whole. Additionally, when an author needs to bring order to a group of ideas, activities, or things, he or she often organizes information according to parts, characteristics, functions, or types. An author can also use classification to divide things into categories, or groups, with several individual units within each group.

The main idea usually identifies what will be classified and often tells how many groups will be considered. Topic sentences such as these point to classification of information:

- To understand the importance of growth and dormancy in the life of a plant, let us first classify plants into four botanical groups according to the length of time they live.

  Watch for the label of each group and the length of time each group lives.

- There are four basic ways to accomplish the purchase of mutual fund shares at that day's net asset value. These ways are to transfer from a money fund, with a wire transfer from your bank, through a telephone purchase, or by opening a new account by wire.

  The author itemizes ways to buy mutual funds at a specific value; watch for details that tell how each way works.

Words that can signal the author has itemized or classified the information include *categories, classifications, groups, classes, ways, elements, features, methods, kinds, types, parts, factors, issues, reasons, sorts,* and numbered elements.

EXAMPLE   Determine Bittner's main idea. How does it appear he will develop the details of Eric Berne's approach to understanding human interaction?

> [1]The psychiatrist and proponent of transactional analysis, Eric Berne, developed an interesting approach to understanding human interaction. [2]At the core of his approach is what he called the ego state. [3]In the simplest terms, there are three types of ego states which are, according to Berne, present in every individual (adult state, parent state, child state). [4]To better understand these three types in relation to what we have already been discussing about self-concept, think of them as different self-concepts which we possess and relate to at any given time. (Bittner, *Understanding Self-Concept*)

Explanation   Bittner develops his main idea (*the concept of the ego state is at the center of Berne's theory of human interaction*) by dividing it into three types (*adult state, parent state, child state*). In the original text the paragraphs that follow this one contain an in-depth look at each of the three states.

Text Structure: Cause and Effect

Authors use cause and effect—reasons and results—to explain why or how something happened and the result of the action. Using a cause-and-effect structure, an author can examine the reasons for events or situations and their consequences, look at the known benefits or outcomes of a set of conditions, or predict the possible consequences of a given situation.

An author can begin with the cause and give the result, or can begin with the result and give the cause. There can be a single cause with a single effect, a single cause with multiple effects, multiple causes with a single effect, or multiple causes with multiple effects.

Furthermore, cause-effect can be a causal chain in which, like falling dominoes, an action results in an effect, which causes something else, which causes something else, and so on.

Topic sentences such as the following alert you to look for a cause-and-effect relationship:

■ Many factors contributed to the increase in college enrollments in the 1980s.

  The author gives the effect—increased college enrollment; watch for details that give the causes.

■ Although it is difficult to predict all of the long-term effects of air pollution, a few are already known.

  The author gives the cause—air pollution; watch for details that give the effects.

  Words that signal cause include *because, for this reason, due to, cause, on account of,* and the phrase *if [this], then [this].*

Words that signal a result or effect include *as a result, since, consequently, so, therefore, thereby, thus, in effect, resulting,* and *the outcome is.*

EXAMPLE   Determine Strongman's main idea and how he develops and supports the main idea.

[1]Within psychology, there has been a long-standing link between personality and abnormal behavior, an understanding of the former often being regarded as important to the study of the latter. [2]Perhaps one reason for this is the impact of the early psychoanalysts on both fields. [3]A very brief comment therefore might be useful on some of the links between emotion and personality.
(Strongman, *The Psychology of Emotion*)

Explanation   Strongman develops his main idea—the effect (*there has been a long-standing link between personality and abnormal behavior*) by looking at one cause (*the impact of the early psychoanalysts on both fields*).

Text Structure: Sequence or Process

Sequence and process are similar structures that use many of the same signal words. However, the kind of information presented is different.

In sequence, the author presents information such as directions, instructions, or historical events according to chronological, or time, order. For example, authors of history texts often use sequence to help the readers understand when events happened.

In process, the author typically wants you to understand how a complex system works, functions, or develops. For example, authors of anatomy and physiology texts often use process to explain body functions.

Topic sentences such as the following point to a sequence:

■ The interview, like any research, is a time-consuming process that involves a number of steps.

  Watch for details that give the steps.

■ Now, let us consider the key events in American history between 1620 and 1786.

  Watch for the dates and the events.

■ Topic sentences such as the following point to a process:
■ Regardless of how long a plant lives, it will usually pass through four stages of maturation: germination, juvenility, maturity, and senescence.

  Watch for details that describe and explain each stage of the process.

■ Let us look at the passage of air from the external environment (oxygen in air) to the lungs.

  Watch for details that explain how the respiratory system works.

Words and punctuation that may indicate time sequence or process include items numbered *first, second, third,* and so on, *previously, earlier, before, meanwhile, at the same time, simultaneously, while, during, last, later, next, after, afterward, eventually, in the past, in the future, at present, next, then, finally, eventually, following this, steps, at the start, to begin, initially, during the next hour, day,* or *year,* and specific times or dates

EXAMPLE   In this paragraph determine Tocquet's main idea and how he develops it.

[1]For the extraction of a square root the mental calculation broadly follows the normal method: first, you divide the number into groups of two figures, you look for the largest square contained in the first group, you carry the root as the first result and subtract this square from the first group. [2]Next, you mentally add on to the remainder the first figure of the second group and divide the number thus obtained by twice the first figure carried; you retain this quotient as the second figure of the root required. [3]As can be seen, the process is rather complicated and lengthy. (Robert Tocquet, *The Magic of Numbers*)

Explanation   Tocquet supports his main idea (*to mentally calculate a square root you use about the same procedure as when you calculate with pencil and paper*) by giving the sequence of steps needed to complete the process. He uses two signal words—*first* and *next*—and a series of punctuation marks to help you follow the process.

Text Structure: Definition

In academic material, authors often need to restrict and clarify a definition or explain their personal interpretation of the meaning of a term or concept. This is done in a variety of ways. Common methods of providing definitions include giving one or more dictionary definitions or one or more connotative meanings, tracing the etymology, comparing and/or contrasting the word with other terms, providing examples, and by negation—telling what it doesn't mean.

Topic sentences such as the following alert you to watch for definitions:

■ The word *politician* has many meanings.

  Watch for details that give various meanings.

■ Psychologists are wary when asked to write about aggression; it is a definitional minefield.

  Watch for details that give various definitions.

Words that may signal definition include *defined as, is, known, the term means, is stated as,* and *is used to mean.*

EXAMPLE   Determine Grassian's main idea and how he develops the details to support his idea.

[1]The concept of euthanasia is used today with varying meanings. [2]In its original Greek meaning, "euthanasia" meant no more than an easy and painless death (eu = well; thanatos = death) and was later extended to refer to the work of a physician in alleviating as far as possible the suffering of dying. [3]Today, however, "euthanasia" is often used synonymously with that of "mercy killing" and as such entails the bringing about of death. [4]The *American Heritage Dictionary* (1975) defines "euthanasia" as "the action of inducing the painless death of a person for reasons assumed to be merciful." [5]As this definition demonstrates, central to our current concept of euthanasia is the idea that such an action be motivated by a desire to be merciful to or to do good to the recipient. [6]As such, when most people are asked to think of a case of euthanasia they imagine a person who is dying of a painful terminal illness, such as cancer, and is given some lethal drug or injection that is meant to "put him out of his misery." (Grassian, *Moral Reasoning*)

Explanation Grassian develops and supports his main idea (*"euthanasia" has different meanings*) by giving five definitions of the word. He begins with the original Greek meaning and traces the meaning to today's usage.

Combination of Text Structures

Up to this point, you have been working with paragraphs selected because they showed one primary structure. But don't be misled. In real reading situations many of the structures are not this precise or obvious. Authors often combine structures to develop their paragraphs. And, as you'll see in the next chapter, they almost always use a combination of structures to develop **multi-paragraph selections** such as a chapter.

EXAMPLE Determine Donatelle and Davis's main idea. What details do they provide to help you understand their idea? How do they develop the details?

[1]Endogenous and exogenous depression are sometimes called unipolar depression because their victims suffer depression only. [2]Conversely, victims of manic-depressive mood disorder suffer from violent mood swings. [3]Manic depressives may be energetic, creative, vivacious, and "happy" for a time and then become severely depressed. [4]Thus the characteristic mania of happiness followed by the melancholy of depression classifies the disorder as a bipolar affliction. [5]Between 10 and 15 percent of the total American population is afflicted with manic-depressive mood disorders. (Donatelle and Davis, *Access to Health*)

Explanation Donatelle and Davis mainly want you to understand that manic depression is a bipolar affliction because it causes significant highs and lows. They first contrast victims of manic depression with victims of endogenous and exogenous depression (termed unipolar depression) by telling how their moods are different from each other—unipolar depressives suffer only depression; manic depressives suffer great mood swings. Then they give an effect of this mood swing—it's classified as bipolar.

A Caution

Remember, discovering the author's organization or structure is not your reason for reading. You are just using what you discover about the structure as a clue to understanding the relationships among the ideas and sentences so that comprehending and recalling the text is easier.

> **Exercise 2** ▶ **Determining Relationships Among Ideas**

Read each paragraph and then answer the questions.

1. [1]Many [of the North American Indian] tribes were skilled in handicrafts, making beautiful pottery, light and swift birchbark canoes, and implements of copper. [2]Some wove a kind of cloth from the inner bark of trees. [3]Others, however, lived very simply, with few artifacts. [4]The numerous peoples of California, for example, blessed with a mild climate and abundant food, made do with simple clothing and crude houses. [5]Only their beautiful basketwork revealed their skills with materials. (Unger, *These United States*)

    a. What is Unger's main idea?
    b. What signal word does Unger use to alert you to the second part of the main idea?

2. [1]Today about 10 percent of the Earth's land surface, amounting to some 6 million square miles (15 million km) is covered with ice. [2]More than 96 percent of that area comprises the Antarctic and Greenland ice caps. [3]In addition, many of the high mountains of the world contain glaciers, which are large natural accumulations of land ice that flow downslope or outward from their centers of accumulation. (Bergman, *Human Geography*)

    a. Besides the Antarctic and Greenland ice caps, what other areas are covered with ice?
    b. What signal phrase does Bergman use as a clue?

3. [1]The 1990s have been designated the "decade of the brain," so it is not surprising that one of the emerging specialties in psychology is concerned with brain functioning. [2]Neuropsychologists are trained to diagnose disorders of the brain. [3]Using various tests, they try to identify specific brain areas that may be malfunctioning. [4]They also conduct research to identify early symptoms that predict the development of disorders such as Huntington's disease (Diamond, White, Myers, and Mastromauro, 1992). (Davis & Palladino, *Psychology*)

    a. What do neuropsychologists do in addition to diagnosing disorders of the brain?
    b. What signal word does the author use as a clue?

4. [1]Researchers often discover that search engines are frustrating to use. [2]In addition, finding useful information with them is not easy. [3]For example, using a search engine for a search with the keywords *business management* returned 500,000 occurrences (hits) of the words *business* and *management*. [4]Many of the occurrences of these words were in job listings of companies that were advertising their services. [5]This is why

search directories are frequently an excellent resource to begin with when starting your research. [6]The search directory may lead you to the goldmine collection of electronic resources you are searching for. (Adapted from Leshin, *Student Resource Guide to the Internet*)

a. What is the relationship of sentence 2 to sentence 1? What signal phrase does Leshin use as a clue?

b. What is the relationship of sentence 3 to sentences 1 and 2? What signal phrase does Leshin use as a clue?

5. [1]Donald Cressey's book *Other People's Money* (1953) is a classic study of embezzlers. [2]On the basis of interviews with convicted embezzlers, Cressey concluded that three basic conditions are necessary before people will turn to embezzlement. [3]First, they must have a financial problem that they do not want other people to know about. [4]Second, they must have an opportunity to steal. [5]Third, they must be able to find a formula to rationalize the fact that they are committing a criminal act—such as "I'm just borrowing it to tide me over." (Kornblum & Julian, *Social Problems*)

a. What is Kornblum and Julian's main idea?

b. Do sentences 3, 4, and 5 contain major details, minor details, or irrelevant information? What signal words were helpful?

6. [1]In films, the pitch, volume, and tempo of sound effects can strongly affect our responses to any given noise. [2]High-pitched sounds are generally strident and produce a sense of tension in the listener. [3]Especially if these types of noises are prolonged, the shrillness can be totally unnerving. [4]For this reason, high-pitched sounds (including music) are often used in suspense sequences, particularly just before and during the climax. [5]Low-frequency sounds, on the other hand, are heavy, full, and less tense. [6]Often they are used to emphasize the dignity or solemnity of a scene, like the male humming chorus in *The Seven Samurai*. (Adapted from Giannetti, *Understanding Movies*)

a. What is Giannetti's main idea?

b. How do low-pitched sounds differ from high-pitched sounds? What signal phrase does Giannetti use in sentence 5 to help identify the differences?

c. Explain the purpose of the phrase "for this reason" in sentence 4.

7. [1]Understanding your audience is critical to the success of any presentation. [2]If you're communicating with someone you know well, perhaps your boss or coworkers, your audience analysis is relatively easy. [3]You can predict their reactions pretty well, without a lot of research. [4]On the other hand, your audience could be made up of strangers—customers or suppliers you've never met, a new boss, or new employees. [5]When that happens you'll have to learn all you can about them so you can adjust your message to serve them. (Adapted from Bovée, Thill, & Schatzman, *Business Communication Today*)

a. What is Bovée, Thill, and Schatzman's main idea?

b. What is the relationship of sentences 4 and 5 to sentences 2 and 3? What signal phrase is the clue?

8. [1]The age of the average worker has gradually increased over the past few decades affecting businesses in two ways. [2]First, older workers tend to put greater demand on a company's health insurance, life insurance, and retirement benefit programs. [3]And second, younger workers taking the places of retirees tend to want different things from employers—things like more opportunities for self-expression or more leisure time. (Adapted from Griffin & Ebert, *Business*)

   a. What is Griffin and Ebert's main idea?

   b. What is the relationship of sentences 2 and 3 to sentence 1? What signal words were helpful?

9. [1]The crucial importance of access to education is underscored by the difference in women's contributions to the field of photography as compared with architecture. [2]Only a few women were able to acquire the training necessary to become practicing architects in the last hundred years. [3]On the other hand, no formal training was required to become a photographer. [4]And, because photography was not originally considered an art form, its technology was equally available to men and women. [5]Thus in this chapter we will meet a group of women who are among the most innovative and important photographers since the invention of the medium. (Adapted from Slatkin, *Women Artists in History*)

   a. What is Slatkin's main idea?

   b. What is the relationship of sentences 3 and 4 to sentence 2? What signal phrase and word were helpful?

10. [1]The English made no significant contribution to Baroque painting and sculpture. [2]They were content with feeble offshoots of Van Dyck's portraiture by imported artists such as the Dutch-born Peter Lely (1618–1680) and his German successor, Godfrey Kneller (1646–1723). [3]The English achievement in architecture, however, was of genuine importance. [4]This accomplishment is all the more surprising in light of the fact that the Late Gothic Perpendicular style proved extraordinarily durable in England, which did not produce any buildings of note until Elizabethan times. (Janson & Janson, *A Basic History of Art*)

   a. What is Janson and Janson's main idea?

   b. What is the relationship of sentence 3 to sentence 1? What signal word was helpful?

Exercise 3   Determining Relationships Among Ideas

Read each paragraph and answer the questions.

1. [1]The origin of the term "Baroque" is uncertain. [2]Possibly it derives from the Portuguese word barroco, an irregularly shaped pearl. [3]Or it may have come from the Italian word baroco, a far-fetched syllogistic argument. [4]Or perhaps it came from the name of a sixteenth-century Italian painter, Frederigo Barocci. (Politoske, *Music*)

   a. What is the main idea?

   b. What is the relationship of sentences 2, 3, and 4 to sentence 1?

   c. What structure does Politoske use to develop his main idea?

2. [1]The end of World War II brought rapid international change. [2]In 1945 the Soviet Union exerted pressure not only to secure its western borders, but also to gain access to warm-water ports to the south. [3]In the following year Greece was torn apart by a Communist-led revolt sustained by supplies sent by Stalin and Marshal Josip Broz Tito, the leader of the Yugoslav Communists. [4]Meanwhile, in the months following German surrender, war-damaged, impoverished, and demoralized Western Europe seemed vulnerable to Soviet political inroads. (Adpted from Unger, *These United States*)

    a. What is the main idea?
    b. What is the relationship of sentences 2, 3, and 4 to sentence 1?
    c. What structure does Unger use to develop his main idea?

3. [1]Various behavioral theories about how we view ourselves have been studied as they relate to health. [2]Ideas and concepts such as self-efficacy, locus of control, and health locus of control are becoming more widely understood. [3]Self-efficacy refers to a person's appraisal of his or her own ability to change or to accomplish a particular task or behavior. [4]Locus of control refers to a person's perceptions of forces or factors that control his or her destiny. [5]Health locus of control focuses specifically on those factors that influence health. (Donatelle & Davis, *Access to Health*)

    a. What is Donatelle and Davis's main idea?
    b. What is the relationship of sentences 3, 4, and 5 to sentence 2?
    c. What structure do Donatelle and Davis use to develop their main idea?

4. [1]We all want to have positive influence with certain people in our personal and professional lives. [2]But how do we do it? [3]How do we powerfully and ethically influence the lives of other people? [4]There are three basic categories of influence: (1) model by example (others see); (2) build caring relationships (others feel); (3) mentor by instruction (others hear). (Covey, *Seven Habits of Highly Effective People*)

    a. What is Covey's main idea?
    b. What structure does Covey use to develop his main idea?
    c. What do you predict the paragraphs that follow this one contain?

5. [1]Being shy can cause many problems for adults. [2]They are often hesitant to seek out others and are excluded from social relationships. [3]Shy or withdrawn individuals are less likely to be promoted at work. [4]In addition, adults who are hesitant to talk with others are often taken advantage of by aggressive salespeople. (McGrath, *Self-Defeating Behaviors*)

    a. What is McGrath's main idea?
    b. What is the relationship of sentences 2, 3, and 4 to sentence 1?
    c. What structure does McGrath use to develop her main idea?

6. [1]Mechanical industries that processed tobacco, grain, soap, and canned foodstuffs dramatically increased their output through the use of continuous-process machinery. [2]A cigarette-making machine developed in 1881 was so productive that just fifteen of them satisfied America's entire annual demand for cigarettes. [3]Procter & Gamble developed a

new machine for mass-producing Ivory soap. [4]Diamond Match began using a machine that produced and boxed matches by the billions. [5]Industries that distilled and refined petroleum, sugar, animal or vegetable fats, alcohol, and chemicals reaped enormous savings from new heat and chemical technologies, giant furnaces, whirling centrifuges, converters, and rolling and finishing equipment. [6]Standard Oil, American Sugar Refining, and Carnegie Steel, among others, gained unprecedented efficiencies. [7]Metalworking industries benefited from larger and more efficient machine tools and a wider variety of semifinished materials. [8]International Harvester and Singer Sewing Machine expanded their production far beyond the imaginings of past generations. (Reich, *The Work of Nations*)

   a.   What is Reich's main idea?

   b.   What is the relationship of sentences 2, 3, and 4 to sentence 1?

   c.   What is the relationship of sentence 6 to sentence 5?

   d.   What is the relationship of sentence 8 to sentence 7?

7.   [1]How will we contend with all the mystifying dilemmas the Information Age brings us? [2]For example, new technology enables monitoring of doctor's prescriptions, with both good and bad consequences: Some medical overseers use it to make sure that doctors choose the medicine that best treats patients' ailments, while others use it to pressure doctors to prescribe not the most effective drug but the cheapest one. [3]Similarly, the existence of digital records tracking patients' medical histories can enhance treatment and promote epidemiological research, but it can also lead to invasion of patients' privacy. [4]Computers can bring new realms into the classroom, but they may divert precious funds from more sorely needed educational tools and deepen the divide between rich and poor classrooms. [5]The list of good news–bad news effects goes on and on. (Leslie, "Computer Visions: The Good, the Bad, and the Unknown," *Modern Maturity*)

   a.   What is Leslie's main idea?

   b.   What is the relationship between the first part of sentence 2 (before the colon) and the second part?

   c.   What two structures does Leslie use to develop and support his main idea?

8.   [1]A number of factors contribute to overweight and obesity in the United States population. Inactivity and overeating, in that order, are the two leading causes among both children and adults. [2]Early eating patterns, the number of fat cells acquired early in life, metabolism, age, and environmental and genetic factors also play a significant role. (Greenberg & Dintiman, *Exploring Health*)

   a.   What is Greenberg and Dintiman's main idea?

   b.   What structure do Greenberg and Dintiman use to develop and support their main idea?

9.   [1]Approximately three-fourths of the world's population live on only 5 percent of Earth's surface clustered in five regions: East Asia, South Asia, Southeast Asia, Western Europe, and Eastern North America.

[2]These five regions display some similarities. [3]For example, most of their people live near an ocean, or near a river with easy access to an ocean, rather than in the interior of major landmasses. [4]In fact, approximately two-thirds of the world's population live within 500 kilometers (300 miles) of an ocean, and 80 percent live within 800 kilometers (500 miles). [5]In addition, the five population clusters occupy generally low-lying areas, with fertile soil and temperate climate. [6]Also, the regions all are located in the Northern Hemisphere between 100 and 550 north latitude, with the exception of part of the Southeast Asia concentration. (Adapted from Rubenstein, *An Introduction to Human Geography*)

   a.   What is Rubenstein's main idea?

   b.   What is the relationship between sentence 4 and sentence 3?

   c.   What structure does Rubenstein use to develop and support his main idea?

10. [1]To be convincing, you must design your presentation graphics to fit the message and the audience. [2]First, identify the one primary idea with which you want to leave your audience—your thesis. [3]State it in a dozen words or less. [4]Second, clarify your time frame. [5]Third, develop a complete outline of what you want to say and assign the relative emphasis of each portion of your presentation. [6]Fourth, decide on the best way to illustrate your message for this audience. [7]Then, draw small sketches of each overhead, slide, or handout you want to use. (Adapted from Hengesbaugh, *Typography for Desktop Publishers*)

   a.   What is Hengesbaugh's main idea?

   b.   What structure does Hengesbaugh use to develop his main idea?

   c.   What four signal words does he use?

Exercise 4   **Determining Relationships Among Ideas**

Read each paragraph and answer the questions.

1. [1]When scientists need to measure the raging winds inside a hurricane or gather weather data above remote ocean regions, they often use dropwindsondes. [2]A dropwindsonde is a group of sensors and electronics packed inside a rigid cardboard tube that is dropped from an airplane. [3]As the sonde parachutes down, it radios information back to the plane about the changing temperature, pressure, and water vapor at different altitudes. [4]The sonde also receives and retransmits navigational signals. [5]A computer on the plane then uses these signals to calculate the speed and direction of the winds that push against the sonde. (National Center for Atmospheric Research, *Dropwindsondes*)

   a.   What is the main idea?

   b.   What structure does the author use to develop the main idea?

2. [1]Like marketers, fund-raisers are constantly on the hunt for new sources of income. [2]But selling a charity is unlike selling other products because donors are motivated by generosity, while consumers are moved by self-interest. [3]When they buy a product from the supermarket, consumers receive a tangible good. [4]With charity, donors receive a sense of good will. (Galper, "Generosity by the Numbers," *American Demographics*)

   a. What is Galper's main idea?

   b. What structure does Galper use to develop the main idea?

3. [1]Nonverbal communication differs from verbal communication in fundamental ways. [2]For one thing, it's less structured, so it's more difficult to study. [3]You can't pick up a book on nonverbal language and master the vocabulary of gestures, expressions, and inflections that are common in our culture. [4]For example, no one teaches a baby to cry or smile, yet these forms of self-expression are almost universal. [6]However, other types of nonverbal communication, such as the meaning of colors and certain gestures, vary from culture to culture. (Adapted from Bovée, Thill, & Schatzman, *Business Communication Today*)

   a. What is Bovée, Thill, and Schatzman's main idea?

   b. What structure do they use to develop the main idea?

4. [1]Animals and plants develop in dramatically different ways. [2]One difference is the timing and distribution of growth. [3]As you grew from a baby to an adult, all parts of your body became larger. [4]When you reached your adult height, you stopped growing (upward, at least!). [5]In contrast, flowering plants grow throughout their lives, never reaching a stable "adult" body form. [6]Moreover, most plants grow longer only at the tips of their branches and roots, and structures that developed earlier remain in exactly the same place; a swing tied to a tree branch does not move farther from the ground each year. [7]Why do plants grow this way? (Audesirk, Audesirk, & Byers, *Biology*)

   a. What is Audesirk, Audesirk, and Byers's main idea?

   b. What is the relationship of sentences 5 and 6 to sentences 3 and 4?

   c. Based on sentence 7, what do you predict the next paragraph is about?

5. [1]In most full-service restaurants food servers can, to a great degree, control the flow of service to create a balance within their sections. [2]To explain how this is done, I'll use an example of a typical section with four tables, each at a different point in the sequence of service. [3]One table is just sitting down, requiring a greeting. [4]Another table is in the middle of the salad course. [5]A third table is at the entrée course, and the fourth table is finishing dessert or getting ready to leave. [6]Under these circumstances service logjams are minimized because the section is in balance. (Adapted from Martin, *Providing Quality Service*)

   a. What is Martin's main idea?

   b. What structure does Martin use to develop his main idea?

6. [1]When transporting a patient by wheelchair, there are several steps you should follow. [2]First, you should cover the feet as well as the shoulders with a sheet or a blanket, making sure it does not get caught in the wheels. [3]You should push the wheelchair from behind, keeping your body close to the chair, except when entering or leaving elevators. [4]When you are moving a patient down a steep incline or ramp, you should take the chair down backward. [5]To do this, stand behind the chair with your back facing the direction you want to go. [6]Walk backward, holding the chair and moving it carefully down the ramp. [7]Glance back now and then to make sure of your direction and to avoid collisions, as if you were driving a car in reverse. (Adapted from Wolgin, *Being a Nursing Assistant*)

   a.   What is Wolgin's main idea?

   b.   What structure does Wolgin use to develop her main idea?

   c.   What is the relationship of sentences 5, 6, and 7 to sentence 4?

7. [1]Domestic wine production increased by 74 percent between 1965 and 1980. [2]In addition, in 1980 the United States imported more than nine times as much wine as it had in 1965. [3]Overall demand increased 86.6 percent. [4]Part of this increase was due to increased population, part was probably due to a change in the age distribution of the population, and part was due to a simple change in preferences. (Adapted from Case & Fair, *Economics*)

   a.   What is Case and Fair's main idea?

   b.   What is the relationship between sentence 4 and sentences 1, 2, and 3?

8. [1]Cultural changes are set in motion in three ways. [2]The first is invention, the process of creating new cultural elements. [3]Invention has given us the telephone (1876), the airplane (1903), and the computer (the late 1940s), each of which has had a tremendous impact on our way of life. [4]The process of invention goes on constantly, as indicated by the thousands of applications submitted annually to the U.S. Patent Office. (Macionis, *Sociology*)

   a.   What is Macionis's main idea?

   b.   What is the relationship of sentence 3 to sentence 2?

   c.   What do you predict the next two paragraphs discuss?

9. [1]Work and personal life can influence each other in both positive and negative ways. [2]A high level of job satisfaction tends to spill over into your personal life in many positive ways. [3]Conversely, an unsatisfactory personal life could lead to negative job attitudes. [4]Another close tie between work and personal life is that your job can affect physical and mental health. [5]Severely negative job conditions may lead to a serious stress disorder, such as heart disease. (Adapted from DuBrin, *Human Relations*)

   a.   What is DuBrin's main idea?

   b.   What structure does DuBrin use to develop his main idea?

10. [1]After 1763, Britain imposed a series of direct taxes on the American colonies. [2]The Sugar Act retained a tax on molasses and extended duties to other goods imported into the colonies. [3]The Stamp Act required that taxes be placed on all printed matter and legal documents. [4]The Townshend Revenue Acts imposed taxes on glass, lead, tea, and paper imported into the colonies. [5]The tax on tea especially irritated the colonists. [6]The most famous protest against this tax was the Boston Tea Party of December 16, 1773, in which colonists dumped chests of tea into Boston Harbor. (Adapted from Berman & Murphy, *Approaching Democracy*)

a. What is Berman and Murphy's main idea?

b. What structure do Berman and Murphy use to develop the main idea?

c. What is the relationship between sentence 6 and sentence 5?

CHAPTER 4 REVIEW QUESTIONS

1. Explain the differences among a main idea, a major detail, and a minor detail.

2. What is the purpose of signal words? Give two examples of signal words and describe how they can be used.

3. List and explain six common structures authors use to develop and support their main ideas.

4. Discuss why it is important to understand the relationships among the ideas and sentences in a paragraph.

Use Your Strategies 1

Read each paragraph and answer the questions.

1. [1]Exercise has several beneficial effects. [2]It burns calories, enhances weight loss, and increases the likelihood that weight loss will be maintained. [3]It also increases metabolism, which counteracts the opposing effects of dieting, suppresses appetite, and minimizes the loss of lean tissue. [4]Aerobic exercise in particular strengthens the heart; enhances general muscle tone, strength, and elasticity; and has a positive effect on serum lipids, coronary efficiency, and blood pressure (Brownell, 1980). [5]At the same time, aerobic exercise decreases the risk of coronary artery disease, diabetes, and high blood pressure. [6]It is also associated with decreased anxiety and depression and an enhanced sense of well-being. [7]However, exercise also carries some risks. [8]If initiated by someone who is unfit or if carried to extremes, it may result in orthopedic discomfort and injury and, more rarely, may precipitate a heart attack (Haskell, 1984). (Snyder, *Health Psychology and Behavioral Medicine*)

a. What is Snyder's main idea?

b. What structure does Snyder use to develop and support the main idea?

c. What is the relationship of sentence 7 to sentence 1?

2. [1]Computers are designed to be either special-purpose or general-purpose computing devices. [2]Special-purpose computers, also known as dedicated computers, are designed around a specific application or type of application. [3]For example, the Lunar Excursion Module (LEM), which landed the first man on the moon, had a special-purpose computer on board intended to do only one thing: control the altitude or relative position of the vehicle during descent and ascent to and from the moon. [4]On the other hand, general-purpose computers are designed

to handle a variety of tasks. [5]Thus the same combination of hardware can be used to execute many different programs. [6]General purpose computers have the advantage of versatility over special-purpose computers but typically are less efficient and slower than special-purpose computers when applied to the same task. (Adapted from Fuori & Gioia, *Computers and Information Processing*)

    a. Label the function that each sentence, 1 through 6, has in the paragraph: main idea, major detail, minor detail, combination major and minor detail, transition, irrelevant.

3. [1]In the early years of the new nation, two types of newspapers were developing. [2]One was the mercantile paper, published in the seaboard towns primarily for the trading and shipping classes interested in commercial and political news. [3]Its well-filled advertising columns reflected the essentially business interest of its limited clientele of subscribers—2000 was a good number. [4]The other type was the political paper, partisan in its appeal and relying for reader support on acceptance of its views, rather than upon the quality and completeness of its news. [5]Most editors of the period put views first and news second; the political paper deliberately shaped the news to fit its views. (Agee, Ault, & Emery, *Introduction to Mass Communications*)

    a. What is Agee, Ault, and Emery's main idea?

    b. What structure do Agee, Ault, and Emery use to develop and support their main idea?

4. [1]Earth's surface is never perfectly flat but instead consists of slopes. [2]Some are steep and precipitous; others are moderate or gentle. [3]Some are long and gradual; others are short and abrupt. [4]Some slopes are mantled with soil and covered by vegetation; others consist of barren rock and rubble. [5]Their form and variety are great. (Lutgens & Tarbuck, *Foundations of Earth Science*)

    a. Label the function that each sentence, 1 through 5, has in the paragraph: main idea, major detail, minor detail, combination major and minor detail, transition, irrelevant.

5. [1]The sociological perspective was sparked by three basic and interrelated changes. [2]First, rapid technological innovation in eighteenth-century Europe soon led to the spread of factories and an industrial economy. [3]Second, these factories drew millions of people from the countryside, causing an explosive growth of cities. [4]Third, people in these expanding industrial cities soon began to entertain new ideas about the world, leading to important political developments. (Macionis, *Sociology*)

    a. What is Macionis's main idea?

    b. What structure does Macionis use to develop and support his main idea?

    c. What signal words does Macionis use?

6. [1]About 300 million years ago the conditions for the subsequent formation of petroleum (mineral oil) were established in shallow coastal waters by the teeming tiny creatures and plants that lived and died in vast numbers. [2]The ooze formed on the bottom by the remains of these organisms was unable to decompose because of a lack of oxygen. [3]As a result of climatic changes, these coastal areas became buried under layers of earth, and the organic remains were subjected to high pressures and temperatures over periods of millions of years. [4]The fats, carbohydrates and proteins were thereby subjected to conditions in which they were decomposed and underwent extensive chemical changes. [5]As a result of these changes, a large number of compounds were formed which all enter into the composition of petroleum. (*The Way Things Work*)

a. What structure does the author use to develop and support the main idea?

b. What signal phrase does the author use in sentences 3 and 5?

7. [1]Bob Vila, host of the TV show *Bob Vila's Home Again,* says that with the right technique you can keep the wood from splitting when you're driving nails in close to the end of a board. [2]First, lay the nail flat on a scrap of wood and give the pointed end a good firm tap with your hammer to flatten the point. [3]Start hammering your nail with the flat edge aligned with the grain of the wood. [4]The flattening should allow the nail to whisk right through the wood without creating the stress that so often makes the board crack. (Adapted from Vila, "Hammer a Nail")

a. What is Vila's main idea?

b. What structure does Vila use to develop and support his main idea?

8. [1]A margin account sounds mysterious to the uninformed. [2]Actually, it is nothing more than a loan the stockbroker makes to you using your securities as collateral to support the loan. [3]Here's how it works: [4]Say you open a margin account by depositing $3,000. ([5]All brokers require a minimum deposit for a margin account, and the Board of Governors of the Federal Reserve System requires an initial margin requirement of 50 percent of the value of securities purchased.) [6]Then, you buy 100 shares of ABC stock at $50 a share. [7]Thus, you bought $5,000 worth of stock, ignoring commissions, with only a $3,000 deposit; obviously the other $2,000 came from your broker. [8]Now, what happens if the stock goes up or down in value? [9]No problem, if it goes up. [10]You can sell whenever you like and repay the $2,000 loan plus interest and pocket the difference. [11]If it goes down, keep one simple fact in mind—the loss is all yours. [12]You don't share it with the broker. So if ABC goes down to $30 a share and you then sell, the broker still gets $2,000, plus interest, and you still pocket the difference—$1,000 in this case. [13]You lose $2,000, which is $20 ($50–$30) a share times the 100 shares. (Winger & Frasca, *Personal Finance*)

a. How do Winger and Frasca define margin account?

b. What structure do Winger and Frasca use to develop and support the main idea?

9. [1]One analogy for describing the difference between a listserv mailing list and a Usenet newsgroup is to compare the difference between having a few intimate friends over for dinner and conversation (a listserv) vs. going to a Super Bowl party to which the entire world has been invited (newsgroups). [2]A listserv is a smaller, more intimate place to discuss issues of interest. [3]A Usenet newsgroup is much larger and much

more open to "everything and anything goes." (Leshin, *Student Resource Guide to the Internet*)

   a. What is the primary difference between a listserv and a newsgroup?

   b. What structure does Leshin use to explain the difference?

10. [1]Areas around the home can be classified into three categories: (1) full shade, (2) partial shade/partial sun, and (3) full sun. [2]Full shade areas are those in which the sun rarely shines directly, perhaps for only an hour per day at early morning or late afternoon when the sun's rays are the weakest. [3]These areas would include the northern sides of houses, narrow areas between houses, under large trees, and any other areas that are shaded for almost all of the day by trees, buildings, or other structures. [4]Partial shade (also known as partial sun) areas receive direct sunlight for about a third to half of the day. [5]Such areas include the east- and west-facing walls of houses (provided that the eaves are not so wide that they cast shade all day) and sites under small or finely foliaged trees that admit a dappled "filtered sun." [6]Full sun would be found on the south sides of houses or wherever there are no trees, shrubs, or structures that block the light. [7]Full sun can also be on the west side of houses in the western United States, because the afternoon sun in these areas can be very strong even though it is only shining on the area for a few hours. (Adapted from *Rice & Rice, Practical Horticulture*)

   a. What is Rice and Rice's main idea?

   b. What primary structure do Rice and Rice use to develop and support their main idea?

Use Your Strategies 2

Preview the selection, read the selection, and then answer the questions.

RICKY W. GRIFFIN AND RONALD J. EBERT

Well-known in the fields of business and education, Dr. Griffin teaches business at Texas A&M University and Dr. Ebert teaches business at the University of Missouri-Columbia. This excerpt is from their introductory text Business.

RUNNING THE SMALL BUSINESS: REASONS FOR SUCCESSES AND FAILURES

Ricky W. Griffin and Ronald J. Ebert

[1a]Why do many small businesses succeed and others fail? [1b]While there is no set pattern, there are some common causes of both success and failure.

REASONS FOR FAILURE

[2a]Four common factors contribute to small business failure. [2b]One major problem is managerial incompetence or inexperience. [2c]If managers do not know how to make basic decisions, they are unlikely to make them effectively. [2d]A second contributor to failure is neglect. [2e]That is, after the glamour and excitement of the big grand opening, some entrepreneurs get discouraged and don't concentrate as much on their business as they should. . . . [2f]Third, weak control systems can also be a cause of failure. [2g]If control systems fail to alert managers to impending problems, they are likely to be caught unprepared to deal with them. [2h]Finally, many small businesses fail because the owner does not have enough capital to keep it going. [2i]New business owners are almost certain to fail if they expect to pay the second month's rent from the first month's profits.

REASONS FOR SUCCESS

[3a]Likewise, four basic factors contribute to small business success. [3b]One factor is hard work, drive, and dedication. [3c]Owners must be committed to succeeding and willing to put in the time and effort necessary to make it happen. [3d]Another factor is market demand for the products or services being provided. [3e]If a large college town has only a single pizza parlor, a new one is more likely to succeed than if there are already thirty in operation. [3f]Managerial competence is also important. [3g]Successful small business-people have at least a modicum of ability and understanding of what they should do. [3h]And finally, luck is often a key variable in determining whether the business succeeds or fails. [3i]For example, when Debbi Fields first opened Mrs. Fields' Cookies, she literally had to give cookies away in order to tempt people to buy them. [3j]Had she not found eager customers that first day she might well have given up and quit.

Use Your Strategies 2 Questions

1. Define these words and phrases:
   A. entrepreneurs (¶ 2)
   B. impending problems (¶ 2)
   C. market demand (¶ 3)

2. What type of context clue do Griffin and Ebert use to help define market demand?

3. For each sentence in paragraphs 2 and 3, identify whether the sentence is the main idea, a major detail, or a minor detail.

4. In paragraph 2, what is the relationship of sentence 2b to sentence 2a?

5. In paragraph 2, what is the relationship of sentence 2c to sentence 2b?

6. What are four common causes of failure for small businesses?

7. What four phrases do Griffin and Ebert use in paragraph 2 to signal the four causes of failure?

8. What are four common causes of success for small businesses?

Use Your Strategies 3

Preview the selection, read the selection, and then answer the questions.

DONALD C. MEYER

Dr. Meyer, associate professor of music at Lake Forest College in Illinois, is a musicologist, an electronic music composer, and an award-winning teacher. This excerpt is from his introductory text Perspectives on Music.

THE EARLY ROMANTICS

Donald C. Meyer

[1a]Between the years 1803 and 1813 a number of significant composers were born. [1b]All of them worked in the enormous shadow of Beethoven, who pointed the way forward for both musical expression and for how a composer should live and think of himself. [1c]This generation also moved away from Beethoven's legacy in several respects, however. [1d]One of the changes in this next generation was an increasing inclination to specialize in genres. [1e]While Beethoven had composed in virtually every genre enjoyed in the classical era, the early romantics often focused their energy on two or three genres, sometimes even just one, such as opera. [1f]Another change came with their conception of musical structure. [1g]While Beethoven pioneered the breaking of rules for the sake of expression, there is usually an underlying order to his works. [1h]Some members of the next generation, however, abandoned traditional form altogether. [1i]The early romantic era was also a time of great interaction between the arts, and so, more than Beethoven, these early romantic composers took a great interest in writing, painting, and other art forms, sometimes even practicing these themselves. [1j]Another difference between Beethoven and the early romantics has to do with geography. [1k]In Beethoven's time, Vienna was the musical capital of the world, but the early romantics were a more cosmopolitan set, working and touring in Paris, London, Italy, Switzerland, the various courts of Germany, even Russia.

[2a]In general it was a good time to be a composer. [2b]Now totally free from dependency on aristocrats, composers enjoyed more freedom and independence. [2c]This also meant they were less isolated, and several of the early romantic composers were close friends and helped each other out in their careers (and some, of course, were bitter enemies, too). [2d]The slow breakdown of social classes meant a composer could be born at any level and move up to socialize with princes and princesses, all based on the composer's talent. [2e]We even begin to see the crusty old doors of sexism open—just a crack—to let the first significant women composers in several generations begin to be heard. [2f]Yes, it was a good time to be a composer. [2g]But almost without exception, the lives of the early romantic composers were marked by tragedy.

Use Your Strategies 3 Questions

1. What is the main idea of paragraph 1?

2. What structure does Meyer primarily use to develop and support his main idea in paragraph 1? Please explain.

3. What is the main idea of paragraph 2?

4. What structure does Meyer primarily use to develop and support his main idea in paragraph 2? Please explain.

5. Is sentence 2g a major detail, a minor detail, or a transition sentence?

6. What do you predict paragraph 3 (not reprinted here) will be about?

Use Your Strategies 4

Preview the selection, read the selection, and then answer the questions.

SHERRON BIENVENU AND PAUL R. TIMM

Dr. Bienvenu is associate professor in the Practice of Management Communication at the Goizueta Business School of Emory University. She also teaches in the International MBA Program at the Helsinki School of Economics and Business Administration in Finland. Dr. Timm is a professor in the Marriott School of Management at Brigham Young University. An active author, he has written more than 30 books dealing with various management and business communication topics. This selection is adapted from their introductory text Business Communication: Discovering Strategies, Developing Skills.

COMMON TYPES OF INTERVIEW QUESTIONS

Sherron Bienvenu and Paul R. Timm

[1a]The quality of an interview is largely determined by the kinds of questions asked. [1b]As interviewers, you have several types of questions to choose from, each useful under certain conditions. ([1c]The term *question* refers to any comments made to elicit responses from the other party. [1d]Sometimes these take the form of statements or commands.) [1e]Let's look at the six common types of questions.

- [2]Closed-ended questions. This type of question allows the respondent little freedom in choosing a response; typically, only one or two possible answers exist. Examples: "Did your study group meet last Tuesday?" "Have you completed the Tompkins report yet?" "How long have you been on your present job assignment?"

- [3]Open-ended questions. Unlike closed-ended questions, open-ended questions allow the respondent maximum freedom in answering because they impose no limitations on how the question may be answered. Examples: "How do you feel about working with your study group?" "What would be a better way to handle that job?" Often open-ended questions take the form of statements such as, "Tell me about your experiences with the new study group," or "Explain that procedure to me."

- [4]Probing questions. Probing questions ask the interviewee to clarify a response for better understanding. Examples: "Could you give me an example of something that happened in the study group that upset you?" "Can you clarify what you mean when you say she's ruthless?" "Can you give me more details about the problem from your perspective?"

- [5]Leading questions. While probing questions lead respondents to elaborate on their own feelings, the leading question typically suggests the response desired. Occasionally this is helpful, but more often it is a block to the emergence of authentic information. Examples: "I'm interested in how well your study group is doing. Did you learn a lot while working with this group?" (Obviously, the interviewer wants the respondent to say yes.) "Don't you think it's important for our students to learn to work in teams as they will in business?" (Of course. What else could you say?) When the question is prefaced by a remark that suggests the kind of answer the interviewer would like to hear, the range of responses is reduced. The interviewee may feel too intimidated to offer useful and honest but conflicting information.

- [6]Loaded questions. So-called loaded questions also suggest the desired response to the interviewee primarily through the use of highly emotional terms. Sometimes they are used to determine a respondent's reactions under stress and when a questioner seeks to "crack" a reluctant respondent. Interviewees who are wearing a mask or acting a role may become angry enough to let their true feelings or honest answers emerge. Examples: "How can you stand working in such a mess?" or "Everybody I've talked to says you are a pain to work with. How do you respond to that?" "I've heard reports that you are satisfied with slipshod quality. How would you respond to that?" The person hit with a loaded question may respond by attacking. The loaded question, like a loaded gun, occasionally goes off in the wrong direction. Avoid them under all but the most desperate circumstances.

- [7]Hypothetical questions. Hypothetical questions can be used to learn how a respondent might handle a particular situation. They are helpful in identifying creativity, prejudices, the ability to conceptualize the big picture, and other respondent characteristics. Examples: "If you were asked to lead the study group, what would you do differently?" "Put yourself in the shoes of the sales manager and suggest some approaches she might take to make your internship more valuable." "Let's assume that you discovered one of your co-workers was intoxicated on the job. What would you do?"

Use Your Strategies 4 Questions

1. What is the main idea of paragraph 1?
2. What are the six common types of interview questions?
3. To develop the ideas within and among paragraphs 2 through 7, do Bienvenu and Timm use (a) explanation and examples, (b) comparison and contrast, (c) cause and effect, or (d) a combination of explanation and examples, comparison and contrast, and cause and effect?
4. What is the major difference between probing questions and leading questions?
5. What is a possible result of asking loaded questions?

REFLECT AND CONNECT

A. Review the topic sentences about health care costs you wrote for the Chapter 3 "Reflect and Connect" exercise on page 86. Select one of your topic sentences. Decide on an organizational structure you think would help you develop and support that idea, such as examples, comparison/contrast, or cause and effect. Use that structure to organize one paragraph. The paragraph should include at least two major details and one minor detail that support and develop your topic sentence.

B. Using your texts or other expository material, identify one paragraph in which the author develops the main idea using primarily examples, one paragraph in which the author uses comparison and/or contrast, and one paragraph in which the author uses process, division or classification, or cause and effect.

LOG ON TO THE WEB

These Web sites contain movie reviews or links to movie reviews. Log on to one of these sites or use your favorite search engine to locate movie reviews.

http://www.mrqe.com/
http://www.moviemom.com/
http://www.suntimes.com/ebert/ebert.html

1. Find one review in which the author primarily uses examples to develop and support one of his or her main ideas.
2. Find one review in which the author uses a structure other than examples, such as comparison/contrast or cause and effect, to develop and support one of his or her main ideas.
3. Print out the two reviews. Identify the paragraph, the main idea and the structure, and turn it in to your professor.

REFERENCES

Bakken, J. P., M. A., Mastropieri, & T. E. Scruggs. (1997). "Reading Comprehension of Expository Science Material and Children with Learning Disabilities: A Comparison of Strategies." *The Journal of Special Education, 31*(3).

Conlin, M. L. (1992). *Patterns.* Boston: Houghton Mifflin.

Cook, L. K. (1983). "Instructional Effects of Text Structure-Based Reading Strategies on the Comprehension of Scientific prose." Unpublished doctoral dissertation, University of California, Santa Barbara.

Downing, J. A., J. P., Bakken, & C. K. Whedon. (2002). "Teaching Text Structure To Improve Reading Comprehension." *Intervention in School & Clinic, 37*(4).

Parker, R., J. E., Hasbrouck, & C. Denton. (2002). "How to Tutor Students With Reading Comprehension Problems." *Preventing School Failure, 47*(1).

Veit, R., C., Gould, & J. Clifford. (1990). *Writing, Reading, and Research,* 2nd ed. New York: MacMillan.

read-ing (red´in) *adj.* 1 inclined ... ad or study 2 ...
reading n. 1 the act or practic ... person who re ...
of books 2 a public entertainm ... which literar ...
aloud 3 the extent to which a ... has read 4 ...
meant to be read 5 the amoun ... asured as by a ...
thermometer 6 the form of a specified word, sente ...

CHAPTER 5

Reading Multiparagraph Selections

I cannot say whether things will get better if we change; what I can say is that we must change if they are to get better.

—G. C. Lichtenberg

AN IDEA TO THINK ABOUT

Although it seems that we are looking at comprehension as proceeding incrementally from a word to a sentence, to a paragraph, to multiparagraphs, please do not be misled. Reading is *not* just a simple combination of isolated skills or predictable procedural steps. Reading truly is a holistic process of constructing meaning (Casteel, Isom, & Jordan, 2000).

For this reason, reading and learning strategies do not exist in neat, numbered boxes that require strategy one to always be used before strategy two, strategy two before strategy three, and so on. In fact, skillful readers only choose to activate a strategy or set of strategies because of the specific needs of the task (Villaume & Brabham, 2002). The combination of strategies must vary from assignment to assignment because of elements such as

1. Your purpose for reading
2. Your knowledge of the subject
3. The author's writing style
4. The length of the reading
5. The medium (the type and form of the publication)

How large is your repertoire, or toolbox, of strategies? Which strategies do you think have helped you the most this term? How effectively have you transferred the reading and learning strategies you practice in this text to your own tasks in your content area courses?

CHAPTER FOCUS

By now you realize that comprehension doesn't just "magically" happen—for any reader. Only a very few people can read about everything from the effects of ozone depletion to the characteristics of Dixieland jazz with equal ease and success.

However, proficient readers understand the "work" required for comprehension and take responsibility for their reading (Martens, 1995). In other words, successful students select, modify, and use the strategies most appropriate to each reading task in each class. The result is that students who use comprehension strategies flexibly have higher levels of academic performance (Taraban, Rynearson, & Kerr, 2000).

Because most of your reading involves more than single paragraphs, this chapter has two major sections with strategies for reading multiparagraph selections like a text chapter or a journal article.

First, we consider four primary reasons writers write—exposition, narration, description, and persuasion/argumentation—and strategies for identifying them. The second part of the chapter provides strategies for identifying the **thesis**— the overall main idea—of a multiparagraph selection.

PRIMARY REASONS WRITERS WRITE

Most of the reading passages in the examples and exercises in the first four chapters are expository—written to report or explain facts, events, or ideas without personal interpretation. However, writers often have additional and/or different reasons for writing. Four primary purposes for writing prose (writing other than poetry) are

Exposition: The author wants to report or explain facts, events, or ideas without personal interpretation.

Description: The author wants to paint a picture in words.

Narration: The author wants to tell a story.

Persuasion/Argumentation: The author wants to influence you—by engaging your emotions or by presenting logical arguments—to believe or feel a certain way or to take a particular action.

But, just as in your own writing, authors often combine two or more purposes so they can clearly communicate their message. For example, an author can use vivid descriptions to tell a story's sequence of events or can give you facts about the consequences of inaction to persuade you to take some action.

Knowing an author's purpose helps you understand what the author writes. However, because an author doesn't often state his or her reason for writing, you must consider the information from all the sentences and infer, or put together, the reason for writing. Inferring a writer's purpose involves more than just forming an opinion or making a wild guess. Valid inferences follow logically from the information and clues the author provides.

Exposition

Many beginning undergraduate students have difficulty reading and studying college textbooks (Applebee, Langer, & Mullis, 1985). This is because **expository** text can be complex and demanding (Hiebert, Englert, & Brennan, 1983). Examples of exposition include an explanation of how gravity works in a physics book and a listing of the major paintings by Rembrandt in an art humanities book.

To establish writing as expository, look for definitions, facts, and explanations that can be verified rather than emotions, personal opinions, and reasoned judgments. For example, consider this excerpt from the chapter on Greek art from an art history textbook:

> The formative phase of Greek civilization covers about 400 years, from about 1100 to 700 B.C. We know very little about the first three centuries of this period, but after about 800 B.C. the Greeks rapidly emerge into the full light of history. The earliest specific dates that have come down to us are from that time. The main ones are the founding of the Olympian Games in 776 B.C., the starting point of Greek chronology, as well as slightly later dates for the founding of various cities. Also during that time the oldest Greek style in the fine arts, the so-called Geometric, developed. . . . (Janson & Janson, "Greek Art," *A Basic History of Art*)

When reading exposition, have a clear purpose and concentrate on identifying main ideas first and then selecting the details that meet your purpose.

EXAMPLE John Macionis is a professor of sociology and author of numerous texts in the field. This excerpt comes from his text *Sociology*.

SURVEY RESEARCH

A survey is a research method in which subjects respond to a series of items or questions in a questionnaire or an interview. Perhaps the most widely used of all research methods, surveys are particularly suited to studying what cannot be observed directly, such as political attitudes, religious beliefs, or the private lives of couples. Like experiments, surveys can be used to investigate the relationship among variables. They are also

<u>useful for</u> descriptive research, in which subject responses help a sociologist to describe a social setting, such as an urban neighborhood or gambling casino.

Explanation The underlined phrases highlight how Macioni defines his topic and give examples of its use. Taken together, you can infer his purpose is to give information about survey research.

Description

When authors want you to visualize people, places, and things, they use sight, hearing, smell, taste, and touch words to create a picture that you can see in your mind. In your reading, **description** is often combined with exposition. Examples of description in textbooks include political science—the detailed recounting of the sights and sounds of the exuberant celebration when the Berlin Wall came down, and American literature—Steinbeck allowing us to smell and feel the red dirt of the Oklahoma dust bowl in *Grapes of Wrath*.

To identify descriptive writing, look for details about the characteristics of people, places, and things that engage your senses. When reading description, use the author's words to build pictures in your mind.

For example, consider this excerpt from an article on Brienz, Switzerland, in a travel magazine:

> A woman opens a chalet window and leans out over a narrow cobblestone lane in the small Swiss town of Brienz, tipping a shiny aluminum watering can over boxes filled with flowers. Behind her the ribs of the chalet—the heavy cross beams, the wood paneling—glow in the morning sun. A black cat jumps up and settles on the sill. Smoke fragrant with pine drifts up from squat chimneys on chalets dotting the high green hills behind the town. (Masello, "Switzerland: Halfway to Heaven," *Travel Holiday*)

EXAMPLE From the title and the words that writer-naturalist Joseph Wood Krutch uses in *Desert Year*, we learn more than just that the desert is dry.

WHAT IT LOOKS LIKE

> What one finds, after one has come to take for granted the grand general simplicity, will be what one takes the trouble to <u>look for</u>—the <u>brilliant little flower springing</u> improbably out of the <u>bare, packed sand,</u> the <u>lizard scuttling with incredible speed</u> from cactus clump to spiny bush, the sudden <u>flash of a bright-colored bird.</u> This dry world, all of which seems so strange to you, is normal to them.

Explanation Notice how, with phrases like those underlined, Krutch paints us a picture of the flower, sand, bird, and lizard. We can infer that his purpose is to sketch a picture of his beloved New Mexico desert.

Narration

In the **narrative**, the author tells a story. In academic reading, you will most likely read **narration** used with exposition; the author tells the story for a purpose or to make a point. Good expository narratives use many specific details. Narration in textbooks include, for example, an excerpt from a John Kennedy biography in an American government text and an explanation of what happens during combustion in a chemistry book.

To identify narrative writing, watch for a retelling of events, situations, and experiences told in the order in which they happen.

For example, consider this excerpt from a personal remembrance story:

> On Saturday night, December 6, 1941, we dined and danced until the small hours of the morning at the Officers' Club, Pearl Harbor. The officers were resplendent in white uniforms, the ladies colorful in formal dresses with gardenia, orchid, or pikaki corsages. We dressed formally every evening in those days. We made calls on each other and left our cards. That Somerset Maugham world ended a few hours later. It felt like dawn when the distant explosions wakened us. . . ." (Marilyn Riddell, "As the Bombs Began Falling on Pearl Harbor," *MM*)

When reading narration, determine if the author is telling the story just to entertain or if he or she is making a point, explaining a process, developing an idea, or providing information.

EXAMPLE   Professor, scholar, and Pulitzer Prize–winning author N. Scott Momaday tells of his life and the traditions of his Native American ancestors in his autobiography, *The Names*.

THE END OF MY CHILDHOOD

> The day before I was to leave I went walking across the river to the red mesa, where many times before I had gone to be alone with my thoughts. And I had climbed several times to the top of the mesa and looked among the old ruins there for pottery. This time I chose to climb the north end, perhaps because I had not gone that way before and wanted to see what it was. It was a difficult climb, and when I got to the top I was spent. I lingered among the ruins for more than an hour, I judge, waiting for my strength to return. From there I could see the whole valley below—the fields, the river, and the village. It was all very beautiful, and the sight of it filled me with longing.

Explanation   An autobiography is the story of a person's life—a narrative. The underlined phrases point out how he uses the sequence of events to pull us along. We can infer his purpose is to tell a story.

Persuasion/Argumentation

In **persuasive** writing, authors present information, ideas, emotions, and opinions they hope will influence you to adopt a particular **point of view**, spend your money in a specific way, believe a concept, or do something. Authors can try to influence you by engaging your emotions or by presenting logical **arguments** to support their belief.

For our purpose, whether an author wants to convince you through an appeal to emotions or an appeal to reason, we'll call their purpose **persuasion**. (As you continue with more advanced work, you will differentiate between an appeal to emotions—persuasion—and an appeal to reason—**argumentation**.)

Examples of persuasion in textbooks include details on disk failure rates that convince you to keep back-up disks and data from the American Cancer Society on cure rates and research costs that persuade you to donate money.

To identify persuasive writing, look for information and opinions that support only one side of an issue or idea. Although skilled persuasive authors indicate they understand the other side of the issue by saying something about it, they spend their time discrediting ideas that go against their own. When reading persuasion, keep track of information without taking sides.

For example, consider this letter the American Heart Association posted on its Web site to send to members of the legislature:

> Dear [Lawmaker]:
>
> As your constituent, I am writing to you because I am deeply concerned that funding for the National Institutes of Health could slow significantly next year. I am particularly troubled about lost opportunities in the areas of heart and stroke research.
>
> Despite the fact that heart disease is our nation's No. 1 killer and stroke is the third leading cause of death, the National Institutes of Health still invests only a small portion of its budget to study these diseases, even in the wake of historic funding increases. Currently only 8 percent is spent on heart research and a mere 1 percent on stroke research.
>
> Please do your part to keep our families, friends, and neighbors healthy. Make NIH research a top priority as you make critical funding choices. The millions of Americans who are affected by heart disease and stroke will be thankful for your support.

As you see, persuasive material is not necessarily bad and should not be discredited. However, you do need to recognize the author's attempt to influence you so you can decide whether to accept the information, reject the information, or suspend judgment until you can find more information on the subject.

EXAMPLE   In this preface to his book *Quality in America: How to Implement a Competitive Quality Program*, president of Technology Research Corporation V. Daniel Hunt discusses the importance of producing quality goods.

PREFACE

Producing quality goods and services is crucial not only to the continued economic growth of the United States, but also to our national security and the well-being and standard of living of each American family. America has been recognized for its leadership in producing quality products. However, in recent years, the position of America as quality leader has been challenged by foreign competition in domestic and overseas markets. Reasserting our leadership position will require a firm commitment to quality and the Quality First™ principle of continuous quality improvement. America can, and must, excel in this area, setting new standards for world-class quality and competing vigorously in international markets. (™ held by Technology Research Corporation)

Explanation   Notice in the underlined phrases the words Hunt uses to appeal to patriotism and the desire for security to encourage readers to implement the Quality First program. We can infer his purpose is to persuade the reader to take action.

Multiple Reasons for Writing

As mentioned earlier, an author often combines two or more purposes to communicate a message more clearly. For example, consider this excerpt from an article in the National Wildlife Federation's magazine. The author describes the scene to give readers information about the conservation program:

> The vast field is littered with splintered branches, crushed red berries and dead leaves, and tire tracks indent the mud where a thicket used to stand. Sawdust fills the warm, blue sky as a trailer-sized wood chipper noisily consumes a tree trunk. . . . Despite appearances, this is part of an ambitious and nearly unprecedented conservation program: an effort to rid an entire community of weedy nonnative plants by 2010. (Cheater, "A Florida Island Battles Green Invaders," *National Wildlife*)

EXAMPLE Harvard historian and Kennedy adviser Arthur M. Schlesinger, Jr. uses a combination of narration and exposition—using story form to tell what happened—in this excerpt from his book about Kennedy, *A Thousand Days*. What clues does Schlesinger give you?

A THOUSAND DAYS

> When they arrived at Love Field, Congressman Henry Gonzalez said jokingly, "Well, I'm taking my risks. I haven't got my steel vest yet." The President, disembarking, walked immediately across the sunlit field to the crowd and shook hands. Then they entered the cars to drive from the airport to the center of the city. The people in the outskirts, Kenneth O'Donnell later said, were "not unfriendly nor terribly enthusiastic. They waved. But they were reserved, I thought." The crowds increased as they entered the city—"still very orderly, but cheerful." In downtown Dallas enthusiasm grew. Soon even O'Donnell was satisfied. The car turned off Main Street, the President was happy and waving, Jacqueline erect and proud by his side, and Mrs. Connally saying, "You certainly can't say that the people of Dallas haven't given you a nice welcome," and the automobile turning on to Elm Street and down the slope past the Texas School Book Depository, and the shots, faint and frightening, suddenly distinct over the roar of the motorcade, and the quizzical look on the President's face before he pitched over, and Jacqueline crying, "Oh, no, no . . . Oh, my God, they have shot my husband," and the horror, the vacancy.

Explanation The first narrative clues include *When they arrived,* and *The President, disembarking, walked immediately across the sunlit field to the crowd and shook hands.* What other narrative clues do you find?

EXAMPLE Malcolm Rohrbough, a history professor and historian of the American West, tells the story of *Aspen: The History of A Silver Mining Town* using description and exposition—word pictures and facts. What descriptive clues does Rohrbough use?

A THRIFTY MINING CAMP

The mining camp of Aspen lay at the end of a horseshoe, with the open end facing west down the valley of the Roaring Fork. Contact with the world of capital, supplies, technology, and people (in the form of immigrants) lay toward the east, however, across the axis of the horseshoe, by way of mountain ranges more than fourteen thousand feet high. The camp could be approached from only two directions: west from Leadville by way of Independence Pass; north from Buena Vista via the Taylor or Cottonwood Pass.

Explanation   Rather than just tell where Aspen was located on a map, Rohrbough begins drawing a word picture of the location of Aspen in the first sentence: . . . *Aspen lay at the end of a horseshoe, with the open end facing west down the valley of the Roaring Fork.*

Exercise 1   Identifying the Author's Purpose

Identify the author's primary purpose(s) for writing in each paragraph.

1. Like traditional library research, there are a number of things you should do before you go online to do research. First, decide exactly what you want to know. Next, determine which search engines you will be using and how those search engines operate. Finally, write out your search strategy so that once you are online you can proceed efficiently. (McGrath, *Magazine Article Writing Basics*)

2. Across the Great Plains, they erupt from the earth, tall and spindly with great round heads that spin and shine like galvanized bugs, twisting and clanking and spitting water. (Carrier, "Windmill Creaks Echo in West's History," *The Denver Post*)

3. Most adults in the United States get less sleep than they need. On average, adults sleep six hours and 58 minutes per night during the workweek, or about an hour less than the eight hours recommended by sleep experts. Most adults compensate for their sleep loss during the workweek by sleeping longer on weekends, with sleep time increasing by an average of about 40 minutes. (National Sleep Foundation's 1999 Sleep in America survey)

4. The primary distinction between a bill, note and bond is the length of time, or term, the security will be outstanding from the date of issue. Treasury bills are short-term obligations issued for one year or less. Treasury notes are medium-term obligations issued with a term of at least one year, but not more than ten years. Treasury bonds are long-term obligations issued with a term greater than ten years. (Department of the Treasury)

5. The National Cancer Institute recommends that you increase the amount of fiber in your diet to 20–30 grams of fiber per day. Fiber is found in fruits, vegetables, whole grains, cereals, dried beans, and peas. When shopping, read the food label. Foods that are high in fiber contain 5 or more grams of fiber in a serving. Foods that are good sources of fiber contain 2.5 to 5 grams of fiber in a serving. (National Cancer Institute, *Action Guide for Healthy Eating*)

6. By the early 1600s several religious minorities had abandoned hope of change in England and had begun to consider emigration. The first to depart was a small body of radical Puritan Separatists, the Pilgrims. In 1608 this group moved to Leiden in the Netherlands, then a refuge for religious minorities from all over Europe. For a while they prospered, but as time passed the little congregation began to fear for its survival and its orthodoxy in the face of the easygoing religious ways of the Dutch. In 1617 the Pilgrim leaders decided to move the congregation to "Virginia," where they could maintain their preferred mode of life and form of worship without distraction. (Unger, *These United States*)

7. We shy persons need to write a letter now and then, or else we'll dry up and blow away. It's true. And I speak as one who loves to reach for the phone, dial the number, and talk. I say, "Big Bopper here—what's shakin', babes?" The telephone is to shyness what Hawaii is to February, it's a way out of the woods, and yet: a letter is better. (Keillor, *How to Write a Personal Letter*)

8. First and foremost, parents must set a good example by using alcohol only in moderation, preferably with meals, and never suggesting it as a solution for stress or other emotional problems. Although parents tend to think that peer pressure is the primary influence on drinking by teenagers, youngsters say otherwise.

   According to a survey released in 1998 by the National Institute on Drug Abuse, the leading reasons given by high school seniors for drinking are to have a good time with friends, to see what it's like, to feel good, to relax or relieve tension, to relieve boredom, to get away from problems, and to cope with anger or frustration. Only 8 percent gave "to fit in with a group I like" as their reason for drinking.

   "Parents should emphasize that getting drunk is always to be avoided," said Dr. Henry Wechsler, director of College Alcohol Studies at the Harvard School of Public Health. (Brody, "Sobering Facts on Teen Drinking Reveal Disturbing Trends")

9. One of the strongest barriers to good thinking, then, is fear. Fear may show itself as anger, envy, selfishness, or hatred, but these are just expressions of our fear. And don't underrate the power of such emotions. History has shown what devastation fear and hatred among nations can wreak. Our personal fears can be just as damaging to our inner world, blinding our critical faculties with their dark energies. When we argue, then, we must be aware of what we feel as well as what we think. A good critical thinker may have to scrutinize not only the intellectual character of an argument, but its emotional temperature as well. (White, *Discovering Philosophy*)

10. I'm nearly halfway across [Kenai Fjords' North Arm] when I first notice the deep, throbbing song of the waterfall. It reminds me of the rhythmic rumblings of a distant freight train or a faraway thunderstorm. Looking through binoculars I see its white sheets cascading through a narrow slot in the bedrock. They tumble and break along canyon walls before dropping hundreds of feet in a freefall. Elegantly powerful, the waterfall is a dazzling, musical pendant strung across the mountainside. (Sherwonit, "Paddling Kenai Fjords' North Arm," *Alaska*)

Exercise 2 **Identifying the Author's Purpose**

Read the article and answer the two questions that follow.

JANA LYNN

Jana Lynn is an educational consultant in Boulder, Colorado, guiding students and parents in the college selection process.

MAKING THE GRADE IN COLLEGE

Jana Lynn

Some colleges send incoming freshmen information during the summer to get them thinking about how to be successful in their college experience.

Southern Methodist University in Texas and Old Dominion University in Virginia are two that have recently compiled informative lists describing how college is different from high school. One list begins with an obvious but thought-provoking point: High school is mandatory and free. College is voluntary and expensive.

Here are some important but perhaps subtle differences that can be helpful to prepare students to consider what habits from high school they may or may not want to take to college.

The average high school student spends six hours a day in class and a few hours a week studying. The average college course load is 15 hours a week in class. But before students get too excited about all that time sleeping late and playing ultimate Frisbee, the 15 hours comes with the expectation of studying an additional 30 or more hours per week. A rule of thumb is to study two to three hours outside of class for every hour in class.

High school teachers approach students if they think they need help or to remind them of incomplete work. College professors are usually open and helpful, but most expect the student to initiate contact if help is needed, to make use of their office hours, and to take full responsibility for assigned papers and tests.

Teachers present material to help students understand the textbook and what may be covered on the exam. Professors hold students responsible for reading and understanding the assigned material; lectures and assignments proceed from the assumption that students have done so. Lectures may be used to amplify other research about the subject.

In high school, students are expected to read short assignments that are then discussed and often re-taught in class. In college, students are assigned substantial amounts of reading and writing that may not be directly addressed in class but may be on the test. Strong comprehension skills will help immensely.

High school teachers often write key information on the board to be copied in student notes. However, professors may lecture nonstop, expecting students to identify the important points. Effective note-taking skills are critical.

In high school, testing is frequent and covers small amounts of material. In college, tests are usually infrequent and may be cumulative, covering large amounts of material. A course may have only two or three tests in a semester, and this may account for the entire grade.

Guiding principle: In high school "effort counts." Courses are usually structured to reward a "good-faith effort." In college "results count." "Good-faith effort" is necessary for the professor to be willing to help the student, but it will not substitute for results in the grading process.

Exercise 2 Questions

1. Explain Lynn's purpose(s).

2. Explain the primary structure Lynn uses to develop and support the idea that college is different from high school. Use at least two examples to support your answer.

IDENTIFY THE THESIS OF A MULTIPARAGRAPH SELECTION

Reading isolated paragraphs has been useful for practice. However, most of the reading you do in college involves multiple paragraphs like an essay or text chapter.

A multiparagraph selection is a group of related paragraphs—each with a main idea—that support and explain one overall main idea. This overall idea is called the thesis.

Just as a main idea is the unifying idea that holds a paragraph together, the thesis is the unifying idea that holds the many paragraphs of the essay or chapter together. When you know the thesis of a selection, you have the idea that helps you connect, understand, and remember all the other ideas. If you don't identify the **thesis**, you have a series of ideas with nothing to connect them. This means that when you are reading for learning, you always need to understand the thesis.

The thesis sentence is often stated in the first paragraph of a selection to prepare the reader for the rest of the paragraphs. However, the thesis can appear anywhere in the selection or, like the main idea of a paragraph, it may not be directly stated at all. This means that in many selections you must put all of the author's ideas together and infer the thesis. Like other inferences, inferring the thesis requires your best reasoned conclusion based on the information you are given.

No matter where the thesis is located, your strategy for identifying and understanding the thesis is the same:

1. Identify the topic by answering the question, Who or what is the entire selection about? (You should have identified the topic during your preview.)

2. Clarify the controlling thought by answering, What does the author want me to know or understand about the topic? (Think how each

main idea helps to develop and explain the whole multiparagraph selection.)

3. Combine the topic and controlling thought to form the thesis.
4. State the thesis in your own words.

In the same way it is important to understand how the details and sentences of a paragraph relate to the main idea and the other sentences in the paragraph, it is important to understand how a paragraph relates to the thesis and to the other paragraphs.

EXAMPLE   Your purposes for reading this selection include identifying the authors' purpose and thesis.

JERROLD S. GREENBERG AND GEORGE B. DINTIMAN

Dr. Greenberg teaches at the University of Maryland. Dr. Dintiman teaches at Virginia Commonwealth University. This selection is excerpted from their introductory text Exploring Health: Expanding the Boundaries of Wellness.

SPECIAL NUTRITIONAL NEEDS OF ATHLETES AND ACTIVE INDIVIDUALS

Jerrold S. Greenberg and George B. Dintiman

[1]Athletes and active individuals have a few special nutritional needs to meet the demands of vigorous activity, to prevent heat exhaustion and heat stroke, and to maximize and store energy from food.

MORE CALORIES

[2]If you are neither losing nor gaining weight and have sufficient energy, you are probably taking in the correct number of calories daily. Weigh yourself at the same time and under the same conditions daily, preferably upon rising. If no weight gain or loss is occurring, there is no need to keep complicated records in caloric intake and expenditure. In general, very active male college-age athletes need approximately 25 to 27 calories per pound compared to 20 to 21 per pound for female athletes. Moderately active individuals need approximately 20 to 23 (males) and 16 to 18 (females) calories per pound. Sedentary individuals, on the other hand, need approximately 15 to 18 (males) and 11 to 12 (females) calories per pound.

MORE WATER

[3]To avoid dehydration, electrolyte imbalance, and heat-related disorders, as well as early fatigue, it is necessary to hydrate approximately fifteen minutes before exercising by drinking 12–48 ounces of cold water (one to four glasses), then drinking water freely during and after exercise. Since

thirst will underestimate your needs, you must form the habit of drinking when no thirst sensations exist.

PROPER NUTRITION

[4]Electrolytes—water, sodium, potassium, and chloride—lost through sweat and water vapor from the lungs should be replaced as rapidly as possible. It is the proper balance of each electrolyte that prevents dehydration, cramping, heat exhaustion, and heat stroke. Too much salt without adequate water, for example, actually draws fluid from the cells, precipitates nausea, and increases potassium loss. Although water alone will not restore electrolyte balance, it is the single most important element in preventing heat-related disorders. Eating extra portions of potassium-rich foods several days before a contest and using extra table salt is all most individuals need. If commercial electrolyte drinks are used, they should be diluted with twice the normal amount of water to reduce the sugar content. Lower sugar content will speed absorption time and prevent the body's release of insulin and possible reduction of quick energy.

IRON SUPPLEMENTS

[5]Iron deficiency can lead to a loss of strength and endurance, early fatigue during exercise, loss of visual perception, and impaired learning. Needs vary according to age, activity level, and sex. Iron is the only nutrient that adolescent female and male athletes need in greater quantity.

Explanation   Greenberg and Dintiman's purpose is exposition—to explain facts about the special nutritional needs of athletes and active individuals. The thesis of the selection is stated in the first paragraph: "Athletes and active individuals have a few special nutritional needs to meet the demands of vigorous activity, to prevent heat exhaustion and heat stroke, and to maximize and store energy from food." Paragraphs 2 through 5 develop and support that thesis by giving examples of the special nutritional needs.

Exercise 3   **Identifying the Author's Purpose and Thesis**

Read the selection and answer the questions that follow it. Your purposes for reading include identifying the author's purpose and thesis.

LINDA WELTNER

Linda Weltner is a columnist for The Boston Globe. *Her work appears in newspapers across the country.*

AN IDEA TO THINK ABOUT

Do you always have time to do everything you want to do? How do you decide what activities to do in a day or a week and what to put off until later? *As you read,* look for Weltner's advice on how to put "first things first."

HAPPINESS IS FIRST THINGS FIRST

Linda Weltner

Resting in a hammock last week, I had time to think about the hectic pattern of my life, how I ricochet from over-busy to fairly relaxed to far too busy again. It's as if I'm asleep as this process unfolds again and again. Then, every time I wake up and look around, my calendar is somehow full to the brim.

"How did this happen?" I ask myself, bewildered for the hundredth time. Faced with too much on my plate, I can't remember the preliminary thoughts or acts that led me here, can't identify any warning signals that might have alerted me in time to make a correction. I know I've been in this mess before because I recognize the stifling feeling of being trapped, but without any idea of how I keep re-creating this situation, I lack the tools to keep history from repeating itself.

Two of my readers, Pat Steuert and Susan Porter, sent me a monthly planner they created called "A Balancing Act." It's a small spiral calendar book with unusual directions. At the beginning of each month you're instructed to take 30 minutes to make sure you schedule time for yourself.

At the back of the book, there are places to jot down those stray longings that hit you at your busiest moments: the books you'd like to read, the friends you'd like to visit, the classes you'd like to take, the movies you'd like to see, places you'd like to go, all your neglected wishes, hopes, and dreams. With these at your fingertips, every month you get a chance to make sure you make space for the things that matter.

This looking ahead and planning for the future, it seems to me, has the potential to repair anyone's badly skewed long-range perspective about time. It's a chance to see the future coming instead of having it take you by surprise. You get to anticipate everything that is sure to happen instead of having predictable events suddenly show up to haunt you. You get to decide in advance how many projects you can comfortably take on rather than discovering too late that you're swamped.

Without this corrective, many of us fill our regular calendars with so many obligations, meetings, work dates, and special events that we're left frantically trying to squeeze in what remains of our life. Our days often seem as stuffed to the gills as the Mason jar in this Norris Lee story sent to me by one of my readers, Jeanne Rudnick.

A lecturer stands in front of a class of high-powered overachievers, holding a 1-gallon wide-mouth mason jar. He fills it with good-size rocks, then asks the group, "Is this jar full?" The audience agrees that it is.

"Oh, really?" he asks. He pours in several handfuls of gravel. "Is the jar full now?" The audience is doubtful. Probably not. He pours a handful of sand into the jar, filling it to the brim. "How about now?" he asks. Not yet. He pours in a pitcher of water.

"OK," he asks. "What's the lesson to be learned here?"

"Well," says a man sitting near the front, "you've just demonstrated that no matter how full your schedule is, you can always fit more in."

"You're absolutely wrong," says the teacher. "The point I'm making is that if you don't put the rocks in first, you'll never get them in at all."

This is where you get to make your true values visible. What's your definition of a rock? A business meeting or a child's basketball game? Organizing your files or reading a book? Staying home or attending a meeting? If you don't make such choices consciously and well in advance, all the forces demanding your attention in this fast-paced world will make them for you.

Of course, if you really reflect upon it, you might not want to stuff your jar of days full of every rock, bit of gravel, grain of sand, and drop of water it will hold. There's almost no room for movement in that crowded a space, no room to breathe. Ignore this fact until after the water's in and the cover's been tightened, as I do with distressing regularity, and you will discover to your sorrow that the compacted life feels a lot like drowning.

Exercise 3 Questions

1. What is Weltner's purpose?
2. What is Weltner's thesis?
3. Why does Weltner use the Norris Lee story sent in by one of her readers? Does it fulfill its purpose? Please explain.
4. What does Weltner mean when she says that "your definition of a rock" is your true values? Please explain.

Exercise 4

Read the selection and answer the questions that follow it. Your purposes for reading include identifying the author's purpose and thesis.

RUSSELL BAKER

International Paper asked Russell Baker, winner of the Pulitzer Prize for his book Growing Up *and for his essays in* The New York Times, *to help student writers make better use of punctuation.*

AN IDEA TO THINK ABOUT

Do you ever wonder if you're using a semicolon correctly? Do you ever put a comma in a sentence and then take it out and wonder if you are correct? *As you read*, find out which of the 30 main punctuation marks Baker says are most important.

HOW TO PUNCTUATE

Russell Baker

[1]When you write, you make a sound in the reader's head. It can be a dull mumble—that's why so much government prose makes you sleepy—or it can be a joyful noise, a sly whisper, a throb of passion.

[2]Listen to a voice trembling in a haunted room:

[3]"And the silken, sad, uncertain rustling of each purple curtain thrilled me—filled me with fantastic terrors never felt before. . . ."

[4]That's Edgar Allan Poe, a master. Few of us can make paper speak as vividly as Poe could, but even beginners will write better once they start listening to the sound their writing makes.

[5]One of the most important tools for making paper speak in your own voice is punctuation.

[6]When speaking aloud, you punctuate constantly—with body language. Your listener hears commas, dashes, question marks, exclamation points, quotation marks as you shout, whisper, pause, wave your arms, wrinkle your brow.

[7]In writing, punctuation plays the role of body language. It helps readers hear you the way you want to be heard.

"GEE, DAD, HAVE I GOT TO LEARN ALL THEM RULES?"

[8]Don't let the rules scare you. For they aren't hard and fast. Think of them as guidelines.

[9]Am I saying, "Go ahead and punctuate as you please"? Absolutely not. Use your own common sense, remembering that you can't expect readers to work to decipher what you're trying to say.

[10]There are two basic systems of punctuation:

1. [11]The loose or open system, which tries to capture the way body language punctuates talk.

2. [12]The tight, closed structural system, which hews closely to the sentence's grammatical structure.

[13]Most writers use a little of both. In any case, we use much less punctuation than they used 200 or even 50 years ago. (Glance into Edward Gibbon's *Decline and Fall of the Roman Empire,* first published in 1776, for an example of the tight structural system at its most elegant.)

[14]No matter which system you prefer, be warned: punctuation marks cannot save a sentence that is badly put together. If you have to struggle over commas, semicolons and dashes, you've probably built a sentence that's never going to fly, no matter how you tinker with it. Throw it away and build a new one to a simpler design. The better your sentence, the easier it is to punctuate it.

CHOOSING THE RIGHT TOOL

[15]There are 30 main punctuation marks, but you'll need fewer than a dozen for most writing.

[16]I can't show you in this small space how they all work, so I'll stick to the ten most important—and even then can only hit highlights. For more details, check your dictionary or a good grammar book.

COMMA [,]

[17]This is the most widely used mark of all. It's also the toughest and most controversial. I've seen aging editors almost come to blows over the comma. If you can handle it without sweating, the others will be easy. Here's my policy:

1. [18]Use a comma after a long introductory phrase or clause *: After stealing the crown jewels from the Tower of London, I went home for tea.*

2. [19]If the introductory material is short, forget the comma: *After the theft I went home for tea.*

3. [20]But use it if the sentence would be confusing without it, like this: *The day before I'd robbed the Bank of England.*

4. [21]Use a comma to separate elements in a series: *I robbed the Denver Mint, the Bank of England, the Tower of London and my piggy bank.*
   [22]Notice there is no comma before *and* in the series. This is the common style nowadays, but some publishers use a comma there too.

5. [23]Use a comma to separate independent clauses that are joined by a conjunction like *and, but, for, or, nor, because,* or *so: I shall return the crown jewels, for they are too heavy to wear.*

6. [24]Use a comma to set off a mildly parenthetical word grouping that isn't essential to the sentence: *Girls, who have always interested me, usually differ from boys.*
   [25]Do not use commas if the word grouping is essential to the sentence's meaning: *Girls who interest me know how to tango.*

7. [26]Use a comma in direct address: *Your majesty, please hand over the crown.*

8. [27]And between proper names and titles: *Montague Sneed, Director of Scotland Yard, was assigned to the case.*

9. [28]And to separate elements of geographical address *: Director Sneed comes from Chicago, Illinois, and now lives in London, England.*

[29]Generally speaking, use a comma where you'd pause briefly in speech. For a long pause or completion of thought, use a period.

[30]If you confuse the comma with the period, you'll get a run-on sentence: *The Bank of England is located in London, I rushed right over to rob it.*

SEMICOLON [;]

[31]A more sophisticated mark than the comma, the semicolon separates two main clauses, but it keeps those thoughts more tightly linked than a period can: *I steal crown jewels; she steals hearts.*

DASH [—] AND PARENTHESES [( )]

³²Warning! Use sparingly. The dash SHOUTS. Parentheses whisper. Shout too often, people stop listening; whisper too much, people become suspicious of you. The dash creates a dramatic pause to prepare for an expression needing strong emphasis: *I'll marry you—if you'll rob Topkapi with me.*

³³Parentheses help you pause quietly to drop in some chatty information not vital to your story: *Despite Betty's daring spirit ("I love robbing your piggy bank," she often said), she was a terrible dancer.*

QUOTATION MARKS [" "]

³⁴These tell the reader you're reciting the exact words someone said or wrote: *Betty said, "I can't tango."* Or: *"I can't tango," Betty said.*

³⁵Notice the comma comes before the quote marks in the first example, but comes inside them in the second. Not logical? Never mind. Do it that way anyhow.

COLON [:]

³⁶A colon is a tip-off to get ready for what's next: a list, a long quotation or an explanation. This article is riddled with colons. Too many, maybe, but the message is: "Stay on your toes, it's coming at you."

APOSTROPHE [']

³⁷The big headache is with possessive nouns. If the noun is singular, add *'s: I hated Betty's tango.*

³⁸If the noun is plural, simply add an apostrophe after the *s: Those are the girls' coats.*

³⁹The same applies for singular nouns ending in *s*, like *Dickens: This is Dickens's best book.*

⁴⁰And in plural: *This is the Dickenses' cottage.*

⁴¹The possessive pronouns *hers* and *its* have no apostrophe.

⁴²If you write *it's,* you are saying *it is.*

KEEP COOL

⁴³You know about ending a sentence with a period (.) or a question mark (?). Do it. Sure, you can also end with an exclamation point (!), but must you? Usually it just makes you sound breathless and silly. Make your writing generate its own excitement. Filling the paper with !!!! won't make up for what your writing has failed to do.

⁴⁴Too many exclamation points make me think the writer is talking about the panic in his own head.

⁴⁵Don't sound panicky. End with a period. I am serious. A period. Understand?

⁴⁶Well . . . sometimes a question mark is okay.

Exercise 4 Questions

1. What is Baker's purpose?
2. Write the main idea of paragraphs 8, 9, 15, and 17.
3. What is the thesis of the selection?

Exercise 5

Read the selection and answer the questions that follow it. Your purposes for reading include identifying the author's purpose and thesis.

TERESA AUDESIRK, GERALD AUDESIRK, AND BRUCE E. BYERS

Doctors Terry and Gerry Audesirk are professors of biology at the University of Colorado at Denver, where they have taught introductory biology and neurobiology. Dr. Byers is a professor in the biology department at the University of Massachusetts, Amherst. This selection is one of a series of essays from their text Biology: Life on Earth.

AN IDEA TO THINK ABOUT

Do you know how many different kinds of living things there are on the planet? Do you think it matters—to Earth or to you—if a few become extinct each year? *As you read*, find out what biodiversity is and why the authors think we should be concerned about it.

WHY PRESERVE BIODIVERSITY?

Teresa Audesirk, Gerald Audesirk, and Bruce E. Byers

"The loss of species is the folly our descendants are least likely to forgive us."
E. O. Wilson, Professor, Harvard University

Ever since the United Nations' 1992 "Earth Summit" in Rio de Janeiro, Brazil, the word *biodiversity* has jumped out at us from magazines and news articles. What is biodiversity, and why should we be concerned with preserving it? *Biodiversity* refers to the total number of species within an ecosystem and to the resulting complexity of interactions among them; in short, it defines the "richness" of an ecological community.

Over the 3.5-billion-year history of life on Earth, evolution has produced an estimated 8 million to 10 million unique and irreplaceable species. Of these, scientists have named only about 1.4 million, and only a tiny fraction of this number has been studied. Evolution has not, how ever, merely been churning out millions of independent species. Over thousands of years, organisms in a given area have been molded by forces of natural selection exerted by other living species as well as by the nonliving environment in which they live. The outcome is the community, a highly complex web of interdependent life-forms whose interactions sustain one another. By participating in the natural cycling of water, oxygen, and other nutrients, and by producing rich soil and purifying wastes, these communities contribute to the sustenance of human life as well. The concept of biodiversity has emerged as a result of our increasing concern over the loss of countless forms of life and the habitat that sustains them.

The Tropics are home to the vast majority of all the species on Earth, perhaps 7 million to 8 million of them, living in complex communities. The rapid destruction of habitats in the Tropics, from rain forests to coral reefs, as a result of human activities is producing high rates of extinction of many species. Most of these species have never been named, and others never even discovered. Aside from ethical concerns over eradicating irreplaceable forms of life, as we drive unknown organisms to extinction, we lose potential sources of medicine, food, and raw materials for industry.

For example, a wild relative of corn that is not only very disease-resistant but also *perennial* (that is, lasts more than one growing season) was found growing only on a 25-acre plot of land in Mexico that was scheduled to be cut and burned within a week of the discovery. The genes of this plant might one day enhance the disease-resistance of corn or create a perennial corn plant. The rosy periwinkle, a flowering plant found in the tropical forest of the island of Madagascar (off the eastern coast of Africa) produces two substances that are now widely marketed for the treatment of leukemia and Hodgkin's disease, a cancer of the lymphatic organs. Only about 3% of the world's flowering plants have been examined for substances that might fight cancer or other diseases. Closer to home, loggers of the Pacific Northwest frequently cut and burned the Pacific yew tree as a "nuisance species" until the active ingredient that has since gone into making the anticancer drug Taxol® was discovered in its bark. Animals too have proven useful in fighting cancer: In 1997 researchers isolated a potent anti-cancer compound from a species of coral that dwells in the Indian Ocean.

Many conservationists are also concerned that as species are eliminated, either locally or through total extinction, the communities of which they were a part might change and become less stable and more vulnerable to damage by diseases or adverse environmental conditions. Some experimental evidence supports this viewpoint, but the interactions within communities are so complex that these hypotheses are difficult to test. Clearly, some species have a much larger role than do others in preserving the stability of a given ecosystem. Which species are most crucial in each ecosystem? No one knows. Human activities have increased the natural rate of extinction by a factor of at least 100 and possibly by as much as 1000 times the pre-human rate. By reducing biodiversity to support increasing numbers of humans and wasteful standards of living, we have ignorantly embarked on an uncontrolled global experiment, using planet Earth as our laboratory. In their book *Extinction* (1981), Stanford ecologists Paul and Anne Ehrlich compare the loss of biodiversity to the removal of rivets from the wing of an airplane. The rivet-removers continue to assume that there are far more rivets than needed, until one day, upon takeoff, they are proven tragically wrong. As human activities drive species to extinction while we have little knowledge of the role each plays in the complex web of life, we run the risk of removing "one rivet too many"

Exercise 5 Questions

1. Describe the authors' purpose(s) for writing.
2. Explain why you think this article is listed in the book as an essay.
3. What is the thesis of the selection?
4. Does the title, "Why Preserve Biodiversity?" help you to understand the purpose and/or the thesis? Please explain.

CHAPTER 5 REVIEW QUESTIONS

1. Why is it important to use your reading and study strategies flexibly?
2. List and explain four primary purposes for writing.
3. List one strategy to use for identifying each of the purposes for writing.
4. What is a thesis?
5. What is your strategy for identifying the thesis of a multiparagraph selection?

Use Your Strategies 1

Read the selection and answer the questions that follow it. Your purposes for reading include identifying the author's purpose and thesis.

JIMMY TOMLIN

Jimmy Tomlin writes columns and features for the High Point North Carolina Enterprise *and numerous national magazines. "Prest-o! Change-o!" is from Delta Airlines'* Sky *magazine.*

AN IDEA TO THINK ABOUT

Do you use a remote control to change the channel and adjust the volume on your television set? How do you react when you can't find the remote and you have to get up and walk over to the TV to make an adjustment? *As you read,* find out how the remote has changed over the years and what may be next.

PREST-O! CHANGE-O!
A short and very stationary history of the remote control

Jimmy Tomlin

[1]Oh sure, it's easy being a couch potato now. Wondrous advances in boob-tube technology, particularly during the gadget-conscious 1990s, have made the waves for channel-surfing terribly inviting.

[2]What with remote controls offering everything from picture-in-a-picture technology—which allows you to monitor one channel while merrily breezing through all the others—to on-screen programming that doesn't even require you to *look* at the remote, there's never been a more perfect climate for visual vegetation. Just add beer and pretzels, and watch yourself grow into a sofa spud.

[3]But even as we hurtle at breakneck speed toward ever-greater technological advances, let us not forget the trials and tribulations of the millions who have gone before us. For years they struggled with remote controls that sometimes changed channels or muted the volume unpredictably—almost as if possessed by some sort of prime-time demon. Though heralded as technological marvels in their heyday, today those devices look downright comical.

[4]So come along as we flash back to the 1950s. The decade may have been the Golden Age of television, but in the evolution of the remote control, it was the Stone Age.

[5]The most primitive of the remotes was developed in 1950 by Zenith Electronics (then Zenith Radio Corporation), which decades later would win an Emmy for its pioneering work in remote-control technology. Zenith's first brainchild was the aptly named "Lazy Bones," a control with a cable that connected the television to the device. Just by pushing buttons on the remote, viewers could turn the television on and off and change channels.

[6]"Prest-o! Change-o!" cried a magazine ad introducing the product. "Just press a button . . . to change a station!"

[7]The problem? "Trip-o! Fall-o!" Customers complained that the cable, besides being unsightly as it snaked across the living room floor, tripped many an unsuspecting passerby.

[8](Incidentally, in the ad's accompanying illustration of a family gathered 'round the television, it's the ostensible *man* of the house who holds the Lazy Bones control. Not that we're necessarily suggesting that's where the well-worn man-and-his-remote stereotype got its start. We're just making the observation.)

[9]It wasn't until 1955 that Zenith came out with a wireless remote. At the urging of company founder Eugene F. McDonald Jr.—who, like many Americans, *hated* commercials—Zenith engineers invented the Flash-matic, which looked like some sort of ray-gun from a cheesy science-fiction flick. The gizmo worked by firing a beam of light, which the viewer aimed at one of four photoelectric cells located in each corner of the TV cabinet around the screen. Each cell controlled a different function: on/off, channel up, channel down and mute.

¹⁰First-generation couch potatoes embraced the new technology, but there was a glaring problem—literally. Sets reacted to any kind of light—not just beams fired by the Flashmatic—so channels changed unpredictably and the sound mysteriously came and went. "So if the sun set glaringly and came through the living room window, it would hit the set and all hell would break loose," says Zenith engineer Robert Adler.

¹¹In addition, viewers—who weren't quite as technology-savvy as they are today—had trouble remembering which photo cell controlled which function.

¹²Meanwhile, other companies were experimenting with remote control by transmission of radio waves—another dud idea. Radio waves can travel right through walls, so when a viewer changed channels on his television, he might very well have been changing channels on his next-door neighbor's set as well.

¹³It was Adler, an Austrian-born immigrant with a doctorate in physics, who fathered the remote control that would dominate the industry for the next quarter-century. Pretty ironic when you consider that Adler, by his own admission, to this day watches no more than an hour of television a week.

¹⁴In 1955, when it became apparent that Zenith's latest remote was just another Flashmatic in the pan, engineers set about pursuing other ideas. Adler came up with the concept of ultrasonics—that is, high-frequency sound beyond the range of human hearing.

¹⁵Now 84 and living in Northfield, Illinois, Adler recalls that his co-workers were initially skeptical.

¹⁶"Our audio expert, who certainly knew about the subject, ventured the opinion, for some very logical reasons, that this probably would not work reliably," Adler says. "But when somebody says your idea won't work, that's a great stimulant to *make* it work. So we made some experiments and proved to ourselves and others that, oh yes, you could make it work."

¹⁷Adler and a team of engineers designed a transmitter that contained four lightweight aluminum rods, each designed to emit a distinctive, high-frequency sound. The 2 1/2-inch-long rods were carefully cut to lengths that would generate four slightly different frequencies when struck by a tiny hammer—one frequency for channel up, one for channel down, one for muting and one for power.

¹⁸Ingenious? Absolutely.

¹⁹Revolutionary? No doubt.

²⁰Foolproof? Not quite.

²¹It turned out that Adler's invention, which Zenith introduced in mid-1956 and dubbed the Space Commander 400, could be triggered by any number of metallic noises similar to those produced by the transmitter. For example, the family dog could change channels just by furiously scratching its hindquarters, thereby causing its dog tags to jingle, which would cause the television to change from Uncle Miltie to, say, a dog food commercial. A ringing telephone or jangling keys could have the same effect.

²²But the Space Commander 400, one of which is on permanent display at the Smithsonian Institution's National Museum of American History in Washington, D.C., played a major role in the evolution of the modern couch potato.

²³For one thing, the transmitter made a distinctive clicking sound when any of its buttons was pushed. That's how the remote control got its nickname—"the clicker."

[24]More significantly, though, remote control by ultrasonics remained the industry standard for nearly 25 years, quite a feat in the ever-progressive electronics industry. Adler's creation solidified its hold on the market in the early 1960s, when TV sets' bulky, expensive vacuum tubes—which were needed to pick up and process the signals from the remote, but which made the sets far more expensive—were replaced by smaller, cheaper transistors.

[25]The ultrasonic remote's decline began in 1977, when General Electric introduced a remote based on infrared technology—that is, using low-frequency light beams invisible to the human eye but detectable by a receiver in the television. *Popular Science* magazine hailed the new remote as "immune to outside interference," and by the early 1980s, infrared remotes had made the ultrasonic ones practically obsolete. Even now, the infrared type continues to be the preferred technology for the industry.

[26]Today, in the Golden Age of the remote control, some 99 percent of TV sets and all videocassette recorders sold in the United States come with remote controls, according to industry figures. So do many other electronic components, such as compact disc players, audio cassette decks and satellite dishes. "Universal" remotes, which have been around since the mid-'80s, allow you to operate several products—say, for example, the TV, the VCR and the CD player—with just one transmitter rather than three separate units. Even common household functions—switching on a light, preheating the oven, turning off a ceiling fan—can be performed today by remote control if you're willing to pay the price for such high-tech innovation and convenience.

[27]And who knows where couch-potato technology is headed from here? After all, during the 1950s, when remotes were frequently overridden by car keys, dog tags and sunsets, who would've thought there would ever be a remote that could operate all of a television's functions (volume, channel, contrast, color, etc.) without any of the snafus that characterized those primitive devices? Given that sort of progress in an industry that's continuously introducing amazing new gadgetry, can voice-activated remote control—that is, changing channels with a simple word command, like, say, "couch potato"—be very far behind? Probably not.

Use Your Strategies 1 Questions

1. Define these words and phrases:
    a. visual vegetation (¶2)
    b. heralded (¶3)
    c. ostensible (¶8)
    d. ironic (¶13)
    e. initially skeptical (¶15)
    f. emit (¶17)
    g. feat (¶24)

2. What is Tomlin's purpose?
3. Write a sentence that expresses Tomlin's thesis.

4. How does Tomlin develop and support his thesis?
5. What is the purpose of paragraph 4?
6. Why do you think paragraph 8 is in parentheses?
7. What was a major problem with the first Lazy Bones remote?
8. What was one of the problems with the Flashmatic?
9. When the Space Commander 400 was introduced in 1956, what new technology did it use? What was the problem with it?
10. What is the "preferred" technology for the industry today?

Use Your Strategies 2

RICHARD COHEN

Richard Cohen is a writer on national affairs for The Washington Post.

AN IDEA TO THINK ABOUT

Think about the various words you use to describe people. For example, do you often use physical descriptors such as attractive, plain, or sexy? Do your descriptions ever limit or exaggerate how you value the person? *As you read,* look for the many ways physical descriptors affected these two famous ladies.

[Note: Eleanor Roosevelt was the wife of President Franklin D. Roosevelt. She was an active and effective First Lady during his 13 years as President. Even after his death she continued her work as a distinguished diplomat, writer, and speaker. Alice Roosevelt Longworth was the oldest daughter of President Theodore Roosevelt. She was married in the White House to Speaker of the House Nicholas Longworth and enjoyed a long and glamorous social life.]

GLITTERING ALICE; SAD ELEANOR

Richard Cohen

[1]It is one of those coincidences of history that Alice Roosevelt Longworth, daughter of the grand and unforgettable Teddy and wife of the totally forgettable Nicholas, died the very same week two more books were published about her cousin, Eleanor. The two hated each other—at least Alice hated Eleanor—thinking probably that they had little in common but a family name. They had something else: They were prisoners of their looks.

[2]Alice, of course, was radiant and pretty—daughter of a president, a Washington debutante, a standard of style and grace, the one who gave the color Alice Blue to the nation as surely as her father gave his name to a certain kind of stuffed toy bear.

[3]She married in the White House, took the speaker of the House of Representatives for her husband, and stayed pretty much at the center of

things Washingtonian for something like 70 years. She was, as they say, formidable.

⁴Eleanor, on the other hand, was homely. She had a voice pitched at the level of chalk on a blackboard, and the teeth of a beaver. She was awkward in both speech and manner, and when she talked—when she rose to speak—the experience was painful to both her and her audience. She had a husband, but there is reason to believe that she was unloved by him. There is about Eleanor Roosevelt an aura of aching sadness, yet in her own way she, too, was formidable. She certainly endures.

⁵It is interesting to consider how their looks—the way they looked to the world—shaped these two women. It is interesting because in some ways they were so similar. They were both Roosevelts—one of the Oyster Bay branch, the other of the Hyde Park—both well-off, both of the aristocracy, and both manifestly bright.

⁶Eleanor's intelligence proclaimed itself. She threw herself into causes. She spoke for people who had no spokesperson and she spoke well. She championed the poor, the black, women and other minorities. She campaigned and lectured and gave speeches, and she did this with such intensity and such effect that it is not too much to say that before her death she was either a goddess or a witch to most Americans.

⁷I am partial to the goddess side, thinking that the worst you can call a person is not "do-gooder" but rather "do-nothinger." That is something you could never call Eleanor Roosevelt.

⁸As for Alice, she showed her intelligence in her wit. It was she who said, "The secret of eternal youth is arrested development," and who commented on Wendell Willkie after he received the presidential nomination: "He sprang from the grass roots of the country clubs of America."

⁹Her most admired remark, the one about Thomas Dewey looking like the "bridegroom on a wedding cake," was not hers at all. The reason we know is that she admitted it. She borrowed it, popularized it, but did not invent it.

¹⁰No matter. She invented enough so that Washington adored her and presidents more or less routinely elbowed themselves to her side so that they could hear what she had to say.

¹¹Yet with Alice, there it stopped. She was what she was, and what she was was beautiful. She did more or less what was expected of pretty girls. She was perfect just being—just being Alice and being pretty—and in the America of both her youth and her maturity there was nothing better than to be rich and pretty and well-married.

¹²That she was also intelligent was almost beside the point, like the gilding on a lily. And while she later became cherished for her wit, it was not because she could use it for any purpose, but because it was like her beauty itself: something of a jewel. She was the perfect appurtenance, the one men wanted seated next to them.

¹³With Eleanor, the story is different. Her looks were not her strong suit and so she had to declare herself in another way—by intellect, character, indomitability. She did this well, found causes, gave purpose to her life and left this earth with the certainty that she had mattered.

¹⁴The conventional view is to see Eleanor as sad and Alice as glittering. To an extent, I'm sure, that's true. But in reading the obituaries, in reading how Alice cruelly imitated Eleanor and mocked her good causes, you get the sense that Alice herself realized that something ironic had happened, that she had somehow become trapped by her own good looks,

by her perfection, by her wit—that she had become the eternal debutante, frozen in time. Eleanor was actually doing something.

¹⁵So now Eleanor and Alice are dead. One led a sad life, the other a glittering one. But one suspects that as the books came out on Eleanor, Alice realized the tables had turned. There is something sad about being an ugly duckling, but there is something sadder yet about being the belle of the ball after the music has stopped, the guests have gone home and the rest of the world has gone to work.

Use Your Strategies 2 Questions

1. Define these words and phrases:
    a. formidable (¶3)
    b. manifestly bright (¶5)
    c. gilding on a lily (¶12)
    d. appurtenance (¶12)
    e. indomitability (¶13)
    f. mocked (¶14)
    g. something ironic had happened (¶14)

2. Have you ever heard of Alice Roosevelt or Eleanor Roosevelt? What did you already know about either of them?

3. What is Cohen's purpose?

4. Write a sentence that expresses Cohen's thesis.

5. How does Cohen develop and support his thesis?

6. What is the relationship of paragraph 4 to paragraphs 2 and 3?

7. List three descriptors of each woman's physical appearance.

8. List three descriptors of each woman's intelligence and life's work.

9. In paragraph 15, Cohen says, "But one suspects that as the books came out on Eleanor, Alice realized the tables had turned." What do you think he means?

10. Based on Cohen's article and your previous knowledge, do you agree with his statement in paragraph 1, "They were prisoners of their looks"? Why or why not?

Use Your Strategies 3

Read the selection and answer the questions that follow it.

JOHN MACIONIS

Dr. John Macionis is professor of sociology at Kenyon College, Gambier, Ohio. In addition to his teaching, he is known for his twenty years of work as a popular textbook author. This excerpt is from Chapter 9, "Alcohol and Other Drugs" in his introductory Social Problems *text.*

AN IDEA TO THINK ABOUT:

How do you define a "drug"? How do you think your definition would compare to the definition your great-grandparents used? How about the definition today's ten-year-old might use? *As you read,* find out what makes the difference between a "useful medicine" and a "dangerous drug" and how the differences change over time.

ALCOHOL AND OTHER DRUGS

John Macionis

Like tens of thousands of other people in the United States, Jennifer Smith is a drug addict. To help understand stories like Jennifer's, this chapter explains what drugs are, what they do to the people who abuse them, and how society defines and responds to the drug problem. We begin with a basic definition.

WHAT IS A DRUG?

Broadly defined, a **drug** is *any chemical substance—other than food or water—that affects the mind or body* (Goldstein, 1994). For thousands of years, people have known that various substances cause changes in the human body. In fact, most people give little thought to the drugs they take, from the aspirin that eases a headache to a morning cup of coffee to help wake up.

But most people in the United States also think that certain drugs—like crank, described in the opening to this chapter—are a serious social problem (NORC, 1999:97). This fact raises the question of when and why people come to define particular drugs as good or as harmful.

Drugs and Culture

How people view a particular drug varies from society to society. Europeans, for example, have enjoyed drinking alcohol for thousands of years. But when Native Americans were introduced to wine and liquor by European colonists five centuries ago, they had no customs to guide its use. As a result, many native peoples fell into drunken stupors, causing tribal leaders to declare alcohol a serious problem (Mancall, 1995; Unrau, 1996).

For centuries, however, many Native American peoples had been using peyote—which alters human consciousness—as part of their religious rituals. They then shared this drug with the Europeans, many of whom became terrified by the hallucinations it produces. Europeans soon pronounced peyote a dangerous drug.

Such diverse definitions of drugs continue today. Coca—the plant used to make cocaine—is grown legally in the South American nations of Bolivia, Peru, and Colombia, as it has been for thousands of years.

Indeed, many local farmers chew the plant as they work, to give them a "lift." But officials in the United States have passed laws banning the growing of coca as well as the sale or possession of cocaine. Indeed, in the United States, most people view this drug as a dangerous cause of violence and crime (Léons & Sanabria, 1997).

Drugs and Social Diversity

We find the same varied definitions of drugs if we look back at U.S. history: A century ago, almost no one in the United States or Europe was aware of a "cocaine problem." On the contrary, famous people like Sigmund Freud used cocaine openly, and anyone could enjoy a popular new "brain tonic" called Coca-Cola, which included cocaine as one of its ingredients (Inciardi, 1996; Léons & Sanabria, 1997).

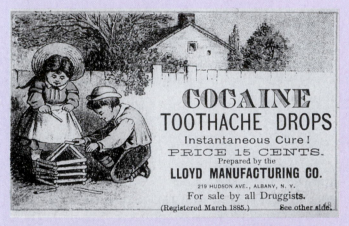

Whether a society defines a substance as a "useful medication" or a "dangerous drug" varies over time. It would suprise many poeple to learn that, a century ago, cocaine was an ingredient in a number of readily available products, such as this remedy for toothaches.

When and why did public opinion about cocaine change? Some scholars suggest that attitudes about drugs have much to do with attitudes about racial and ethnic minorities. Especially across the South a century ago, many white people feared that cocaine would encourage African Americans to break strict racial codes of conduct and perhaps even become violent toward whites. Such concerns helped push the Coca-Cola company to remove cocaine from its formula in 1903. Soon after, states began to pass laws banning this drug (Goode, 1993; Bertram et al., 1996).

Immigration, too, figured into changing views of drugs. As immigrants came to the United States in ever-increasing numbers during the nineteenth century, they brought not only their dreams but their favored drugs. In the 1850s, for example, many Chinese immigrants in California smoked opium (a practice they had picked up from the British). Anti-Chinese feelings prompted eleven Western states to ban opium, although, elsewhere, opiates were readily available, even through the Sears Roebuck mail-order catalogue.

As immigration increased, the U.S. Congress passed the 1914 Harrison Act, which restricted the sale of many drugs, including heroin and cocaine. Then, in 1919, the law stated that even doctors could no longer write prescriptions for these drugs. But, by 1920, the nation's attention had turned to a new controversy over a much more widely used drug—alcohol.

Alcohol an Important (and Controversial) Drug

Alcohol is one of the most widely used drugs in the United States, with more than 55 percent of the adult population reporting regular drinking of some alcoholic beverage (U.S. Department of Health and Human Services, 2000). This popularity is nothing new: From the time of the first European colonies in the Americas, people enjoyed alcoholic drinks, and few thought of alcohol as a problem. But, as the tide of immigration rose during the nineteenth century, public opinion began to turn against alcohol. Why? Many people held stereotypes that linked the Germans with beer, the Irish with whiskey, and the Italians with wine. In short, they concluded, a million immigrants entering the country each year was bad enough, but immigrants drinking alcohol added up to a serious social problem (Pleck, 1987; Unrau, 1996).

As opposition to immigration increased . . . , so did the strength of the Temperance Movement, a national organization seeking to ban alcohol. In 1920, the movement succeeded in pushing Congress to pass the Eighteenth Amendment to the Constitution, which outlawed the manufacture and sale of alcohol across the country.

Given people's desire to drink, no one was surprised that Prohibition did not get rid of alcohol. But it did drive up prices. With so much money to be made in illegal sales, many people began smuggling liquor from Canada or distilling it themselves. In the rural South, for example, poor mountain people made "moonshine" in local stills. In the urban North, notorious gangsters like Al Capone made fortunes smuggling and distributing liquor to "speakeasy" nightclubs.

Prohibition gave organized crime more power and money than ever before. Many people, therefore, came to see Prohibition not as a solution but as a problem itself. In 1933, Congress repealed the Eighteenth Amendment, bringing the "Great Experiment" to an end.

THE EXTENT OF DRUG USE

What about today? What is the extent of drug use? The answer, of course, depends on which drugs one is talking about. If we define drugs in a broad way—to include substances like aspirin and caffeine—almost everyone is a "user." Moreover, parents give antibiotics to infants and many also give Ritalin to overactive school children; college students take appetite suppressants to control their weight; and adults reach for antidepressants, tranquilizers, and even pills to restore sexual functioning. In short, most people in the United States look to drugs to go to sleep, to wake up, to relax, or to ease pain.

With such a widespread reliance on chemicals, we might well describe our way of life as a "drug culture." Even so, most people do not define this kind of drug use as a problem, simply because it is so routine. On the contrary, most people define the drug problem as the use of *illegal* drugs.

Use Your Strategies 3 Questions

1. What is Macionis's purpose?
2. Write the main idea of these two sections: "Drugs and Culture" and "The Extent of Drug Use Today."
3. Write a sentence that expresses Macionis's thesis.

Use Your Strategies 4

Read the selection and answer the questions that follow it.

KARL E. CASE AND RAY C. FAIR

Dr. Case is the Katherine Coman and A. Barton Hepburn professor of economics at Wellesley College and is a visiting scholar at the Federal Reserve Bank of Boston. Dr. Fair is professor of economics at Yale University. This excerpt is from their text Principles of Economics, *sixth edition.*

IDEAS TO THINK ABOUT

Have you ever bought anything on sale? Do you know if the product was on sale because the store had too many similar items in stock? Have you ever "bargained" with a salesperson to get a lower price on an item? What made you think the person would be tempted to accept your offer? *As you read,* find out what causes an excess supply or surplus and what typically happens when there is a surplus.

EXCESS SUPPLY

Karl E. Case and Ray C. Fair

EXCESS SUPPLY

[1]**Excess supply,** or a **surplus,** exists when the quantity supplied exceeds the quantity demanded at the current price. As with a shortage, the mechanics of price adjustment in the face of a surplus can differ from market to market. For example, if automobile dealers find themselves with unsold cars in the fall when the new models are coming in, you can expect to see price cuts. Sometimes dealers offer discounts to encourage buyers; sometimes buyers themselves simply offer less than the price initially asked. In any event, products do no one any good sitting in dealers' lots or on warehouse shelves. The auction metaphor introduced earlier can also be applied here: If the initial asking price is

too high, no one bids, and the auctioneer tries a lower price. It is almost always true, and 2000 was no exception, that certain items do not sell as well as anticipated during the Christmas holidays. After Christmas, most stores have big sales during which they lower the prices of over-stocked items. Quantities supplied exceeded quantities demanded at the current prices, so stores cut prices.

[2]Across the state from Boomville is Bustville, where last year a drug manufacturer shut down its operations and 1,500 people found themselves out of work. With no other prospects for work, many residents decided to pack up and move. They put their houses up for sale, but there were few buyers. The result was an excess supply, or surplus, of houses: The quantity of houses supplied exceeded the quantity demanded at the current prices.

[3]As houses sit unsold on the market for months, sellers start to cut their asking prices. Potential buyers begin offering considerably less than sellers are asking. As prices fall, two things are likely to happen. First, the low housing prices may attract new buyers. People who might have bought in a neighboring town see that there are housing bargains to be had in Bustville, and quantity demanded rises in response to price decline. Second, some of those who put their houses on the market may be discouraged by the lower prices and decide to stay in Bustville. Developers are certainly not likely to be building new housing in town. Lower prices thus lead to a decline in quantity supplied as potential sellers pull their houses from the market. This was exactly the situation in New England and California in the early 1990s.

[4]Figure 3.10 illustrates another excess supply/surplus situation. At a price of $3 per bushel, farmers are supplying soybeans at a rate of 40,000 bushels per year, but buyers demand only 20,000. With 20,000

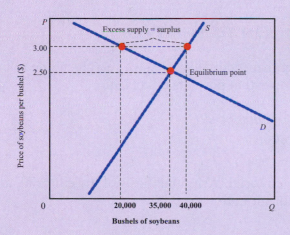

FIGURE 3.10
Excess Supply, or Surplus

At a price of $3, quantity supplied exceeds quantity demanded by 20,000 bushels. This excess supply will cause price to fall.

(40,000 minus 20,000) bushels of soybeans going unsold, the market price falls. As price falls from $3 to $2.50, quantity supplied decreases from 40,000 bushels per year to 35,000. The lower price causes quantity demanded to rise from 20,000 to 35,000. At $2.50, quantity demanded and quantity supplied are equal. For the data shown here, $2.50 and 35,000 bushels are the equilibrium price and quantity.

> [5]Early in 1999, crude oil production worldwide exceeded the quantity demanded, and prices fell significantly as competing producer countries tried to maintain their share of world markets. Although the mechanism by which price is adjusted is different for automobiles, housing, soybeans, and crude oil, the outcome is the same.

Use Your Strategies 4 Questions

1. What is Case and Fair's purpose?
2. Write a sentence that expresses the thesis.
3. How do Case and Fair develop and support their thesis?

REFLECT AND CONNECT

A. At the end of Chapter 1, reread Use Your Strategies 1, "How to Read Faster," by Bill Cosby. Identify Cosby's purpose(s) and his thesis.
B. Using the topic "cheating on a college exam," write a thesis statement for an expository essay and a thesis statement for a persuasive essay.
C. Identify three articles from recent newspapers and magazines, one in which the author's purpose is exposition, one in which it is persuasion, and one in which it is description and/or narration. Write the thesis of each article you select.

LOG ON TO THE WEB

Log on to one of these newspaper index sites or use a search engine to locate a current edition of a newspaper that posts its editorials.

http://headlinespot.com/opinion/oped/

http://www.newspaperlinks.com

http://www.ipl.org/reading/news/

Read and print out one editorial. Write the thesis of the editorial, attach it to the printout, and turn it in to your professor.

REFERENCES

Applebee, A., J. Langer, & I. Mullis. (1985). The Reading Report Card (NAEP Report No. 15-R-01). Princeton, NJ: Educational Testing Service.

Casteel, P., B. A. Isom, & K. F. Jordan. (2000). "Creating Confident and Competent Readers." *Intervention in School & Clinic,* 36(2).

Hiebert, E. H., C. S. Englert, & S. Brennan. (1983). "Awareness of Text Structure in Recognition and Production of Expository Discourse." *Journal of Reading Behavior,* 15(4), 63–79.

Martens, P. (1995). "Empowering Teachers and Empowering Students." *Primary Voices,* 3(4), 39–44.

Pressley, M., & P. Afflerbach. (1995). *Verbal Protocols of Reading: The Nature of Constructively Responsive Reading.* Hillsdale, NJ: Erlbaum.

Taraban, R., K. Rynearson, & M. S. Kerr. (2000). "Metacognition and Freshman Academic Performance." *Journal of Developmental Education,* 24(1).

Villaume, S. K., & E. G. Brabham. (2002). "Comprehension Instruction: Beyond Strategies." *The Reading Teacher,* 55(7), 672.

CHAPTER

6 Reading Graphics

One picture is worth a thousand words.

—Frederick R. Barnard

AN IDEA TO THINK ABOUT

Publicist Frederick Barnard first used this popular phrase, "A picture is worth a thousand words," in 1927 in the advertising trade journal *Printer's Ink*. He wanted to convince his advertising colleagues that supplementing the words with an attractive photograph of the product being used would communicate the message more quickly and effectively than just using the words.

Today, thanks to modern computer technology, authors can create an ever-increasing array of "pictures" to give us information. But their reasons for using the graphs, tables, diagrams, and illustrations are the same as Barnard's: to communicate information quickly and effectively.

For example, are you more likely to understand an author's main idea if you read an illustration or read a few paragraphs of detailed information? How about if you read the illustration in combination with reading the text?

As you preview this chapter, think about the **graphics** you have seen recently in text assignments, newspapers, magazines, and on television. Did you read the graphic? If so, did you understand the main idea? If you read the graphic, did you skip over the words? Did you read both the words and the graphic? Did you compare the information between the words and the graphic?

CHAPTER 6 AT A GLANCE

CHAPTER FOCUS

Graphics such as **graphs**, **tables**, and **diagrams** are a unique fusion of images and words. I say they are a fusion because the images and words work together to communicate the information. They are used to complement and supplement text. Graphics are powerful learning devices (DuPlass, 1996).

However, the ability of the American public to understand graphics is suspect (Kamm, Askov, & Klumb, 1977; Kirsch & Jungeblut, 1986; Piston, 1992). This is unfortunate because studies comparing the performance of students who were presented material with and without graphic displays provide convincing evidence that comprehension improves for those who are taught with graphics (Arnold & Dwyer, 1975; Booher, 1975; Decker & Wheatly, 1982; Holiday, Brunner, & Donais, 1977; Rigney & Lutz, 1976).

Therefore, this chapter suggests a general strategy for reading graphics and provides practice reading several common types of graphics.

A general strategy for reading graphics is as follows:

1. Determine the topic and main idea. Do not assume the graphic is merely repeating the nearby text. Read the title or caption. Determine what information the author wants you to gain from the graphic.

2. Determine how the graphic is organized. Understand the symbols, abbreviations, and units of scale or measurement used in the **key** or **legend**.

3. Identify what trends, patterns, or relationships the graphic is intended to show. As you do when reading text, identify the relationships among the details.

4. Confirm the source of the data. Just as you do with text, consider the source or quality of the graphic's data. Information about who collected and prepared the data should be included in the graphic's caption or footnote.

5. Compare the information in the graphic with the information in the text. Is the information the same, or are there differences? Does the graphic clarify or simplify the text, emphasize a concept, illustrate or give an example of the text, summarize, or add details to the written material?

6. Based on your overall purpose for reading, decide how much of the graphic's information you need to remember. As you do when reading text, determine what data and concepts you need to remember and develop a plan to accomplish your goal.

READING GRAPHICS

Reading graphics is often challenging because graphics lack the familiar structures and clues we use to understand written text. In addition, graphics do not supply the verbs to connect the nouns that are the substance of most graphics (DuPlass, 1996). Therefore, to understand a graphic, you must intuitively supply the verbs that will help you to decipher the information (Boardman, 1976; Monk, 1988).

The type and form of graphic selected by an author to convey information is sometimes an artistic or aesthetic consideration. However, certain graphic forms do convey some information better than others, and authors typically select the graphic that will best achieve their purpose. Among the reasons authors use graphics are to

1. clarify
2. simplify
3. emphasize
4. summarize
5. illustrate
6. add details to their written material

Building on the work of Gillespie (1993), I divide graphics into four major categories:

1. Graphs: bar graphs, line graphs, pictographs, and pie charts/circle graphs
2. Tables: multirow and column matrices
3. Diagrams: Venn diagrams, flowcharts, timelines, maps, and process charts
4. Illustrations: photos, drawings, and art work

GRAPHS

Graphs use bars, lines, or objects to show patterns, distributions, or trends in quantitative information. Graphs can be used in almost every subject. For example, a graph can be used in a mass communications text to show the change in the number of newspapers published in the United States over the last fifty years, in a psychology text to show the divorce rates by sex and age, or in your reading class to show the distribution of grades on the last exam.

When reading a graph, you are concerned with at least two variables—one indicated, or labeled, on the vertical axis (up and down the side), and the other labeled on the horizontal axis (across the bottom). A graph's scales usually start at zero, and the axis interval increments should be constant.

The main idea of the graph is often summarized in its title or in the written discussion of the graph. Source lines or captions under the graph typically give the source of the information. A key, or reference center, defines any other codes being used. Common types of graphs are bar graphs, pictographs, stacked bar graphs, line graphs, and pie charts/circle graphs.

Bar Graphs

An author typically uses a bar graph to compare one item with another or to show the comparison of quantities within a category. Example 1.1 uses a bar graph to show a comparison of the number of gallons (vertical axis) of three kinds of milk (key) consumed in the United States during five consecutive years (horizontal axis) according to data from the U.S. Census Bureau (source note).

EXAMPLE 1.1 BAR GRAPH

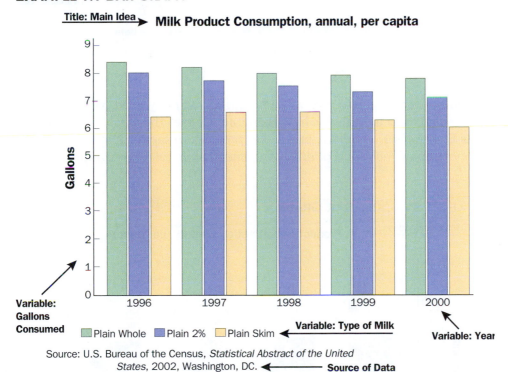

Source: U.S. Bureau of the Census, *Statistical Abstract of the United States*, 2002, Washington, DC. ← **Source of Data**

Pictographs

A graph that uses symbols or graphics of the data items instead of plain bars is known as a pictograph. Authors use a pictograph because it can convey more of the message visually. See how the pictograph in Example 1.2 presents the same data as Example 1.1 with graphics rather than plain bars representing the different types of milk.

EXAMPLE 1.2 PICTOGRAPH

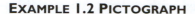

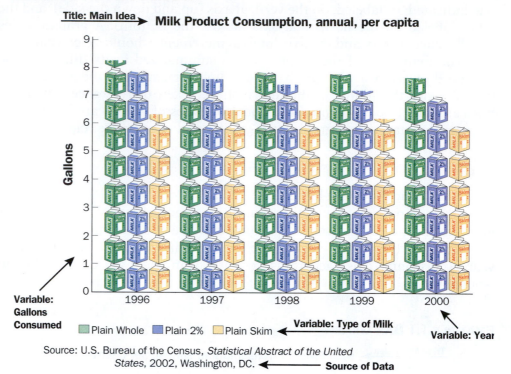

Stacked Bar Graphs

A stacked bar graph is effective when an author wants you to concentrate on component parts of a total. See how Example 1.3 uses the same data and variables as Examples 1.1 and 1.2, but makes it easier to see the slight changes in the proportion of each kind of milk consumed to the total consumption.

EXAMPLE 1.3 STACKED BAR GRAPH

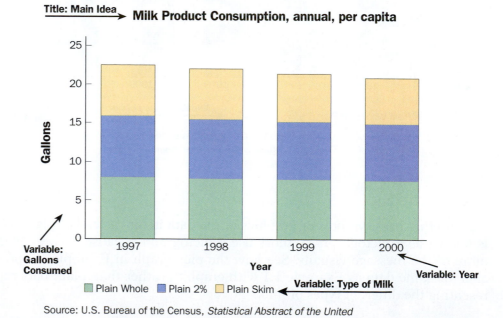

Reading and Integrating a Graph and Text

Read the paragraph, read Figure 6.5, integrate the information, and answer the questions.

Financing the Small Business. Although determining whether to start from scratch or buy an existing firm is an important decision, it is meaningless unless a small businessperson can obtain the money to set up shop or purchase a business. As Figure 6.5 shows, a bewildering variety of monetary resources—ranging from private to governmental—await the small businessperson. (Griffin and Ebert, *Business*)

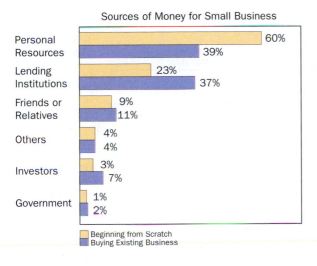

Sources of Money for Small Business

Personal Resources: 60% Beginning from Scratch, 39% Buying Existing Business
Lending Institutions: 23% Beginning from Scratch, 37% Buying Existing Business
Friends or Relatives: 9% Beginning from Scratch, 11% Buying Existing Business
Others: 4% Beginning from Scratch, 4% Buying Existing Business
Investors: 3% Beginning from Scratch, 7% Buying Existing Business
Government: 1% Beginning from Scratch, 2% Buying Existing Business

Beginning from Scratch
Buying Existing Business

Figure 6.5

1. What is the topic of Figure 6.5?
2. The paragraph refers to "a bewildering variety of monetary resources." How is the graph more specific?
3. What is the largest source of money for a small businessperson starting a new business from scratch?
4. What is the second largest source of money for a small businessperson buying an existing business?

Line Graphs

A line graph illustrates trends over time or plots the relationship of two variables. An author uses a line graph to focus your attention on the pattern or an upward or downward trend. Typically, the vertical axis shows the amount, and the horizontal axis shows the time or quantity being measured. Although both scales ordinarily begin at zero and proceed in equal increments, you should always check what values are being used.

See how the line graph in Example 1.4, using the same U.S. Census Bureau data as before, directs your attention to the downward trend in milk consumption, especially in whole milk consumption.

EXAMPLE 1.4 LINE GRAPH

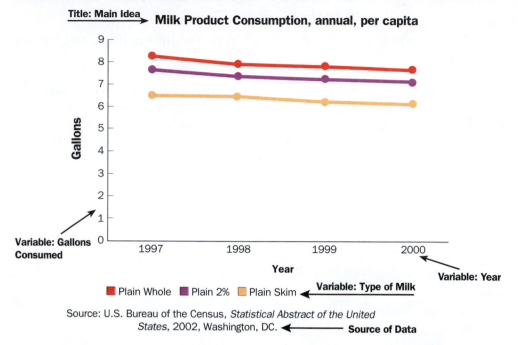

Title: Main Idea → **Milk Product Consumption, annual, per capita**

Variable: Gallons Consumed

Gallons

Year

Variable: Year

■ Plain Whole   ■ Plain 2%   ■ Plain Skim ← Variable: Type of Milk

Source: U.S. Bureau of the Census, *Statistical Abstract of the United States*, 2002, Washington, DC. ← Source of Data

Exercise 2   Reading and Integrating a Graph and Text

Read the paragraph, read Figure 2.1, integrate the information, and answer the questions.

Oceans respond very differently than do continents to the arrival of solar radiation. In general, land heats and cools faster and to a greater degree than does water. Therefore, both the hottest and coldest areas of the Earth are found in the interiors of continents, distant from the moderating influence of oceans. In the study of the atmosphere, probably no single geographical relationship is more important than the distinction between continental and maritime climates. A continental climate experiences greater seasonal extremes of temperature—hotter in summer, colder in winter—than does a maritime climate (see Figure 2.1). (Bergman & McKnight, *Introduction to Geography*)

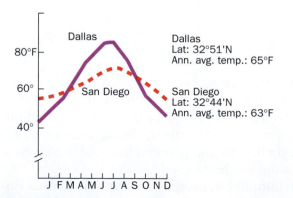

Dallas

San Diego

Dallas
Lat: 32°51'N
Ann. avg. temp.: 65°F

San Diego
Lat: 32°44'N
Ann. avg. temp.: 63°F

J F M A M J J A S O N D

FIGURE 2.1 Temperature Curves for San Diego and Dallas: San Diego, situated on the coast, experiences milder temperature in both summer and winter than inland Dallas.

1. What is the topic of Figure 2.1?
2. What is the purpose of the line graph—does it clarify, emphasize, or illustrate?
3. If your purpose for reading this selection is to understand why there is a difference between continental and maritime climates, would you need to memorize the details from the graph? Please explain.

Pie Charts/Circle Graphs

Authors use pie charts (also called circle graphs) to illustrate the ratio of the values of a category to the total. The whole pie, or circle, represents 100 percent when percentages are used or the total number of "units" when another measurement is used.

Each segment, or piece of the pie, is labeled to show its relative value; the larger the pie wedge, the larger fraction of the total it represents. The segments should total 100 percent or units. Typically, the largest or most important slice of the pie is placed at the twelve o'clock position and the rest are arranged clockwise in a logical order such as size.

As with other graphics, use the title, labels, and key to identify the topic and main idea—what 100 percent of the pie represents. Next, check the key to see how many segments are included and what they represent. Check the caption or footnote for the source of the information.

Pie charts can be used to illustrate a variety of data. For example, a study skills author might use one to illustrate the percentage of time a student spends in various activities—for example, studying, working, sleeping; or an accounting text author could use a pie chart to show the relative amounts to budget for household expenses—for example, rent, food, clothing.

Look at the pie chart in Example 1.5 that displays Social Security benefits data from the U.S. Census Bureau. The whole pie represents all people (100 percent) who received monthly Social Security benefits in 2002. The pieces of the pie represent the proportion of the total received by each eligible category.

EXAMPLE 1.5 PIE CHART/CIRCLE GRAPH

Types of Persons Receiving Monthly Social Security Benefits in 2002

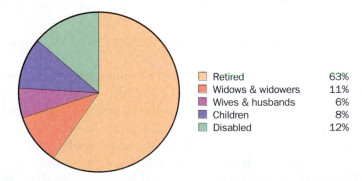

Retired	63%
Widows & widowers	11%
Wives & husbands	6%
Children	8%
Disabled	12%

Source: U.S. Bureau of the Census, *Statistical Abstract of the United States*, 2002, Washington, DC.

Reading and Integrating a Pie Chart and Text

Read the paragraph, read Figure 19.2, integrate the information, and answer the questions.

> Nondirect distribution channels do mean higher prices to the ultimate consumer. The more members involved in the channel, the higher the final price to the purchaser. After all, each link in the distribution chain must charge a markup or commission in order to make a profit. Figure 19.2 shows typical markup growth through the distribution channel. (Griffin and Ebert, *Business*)

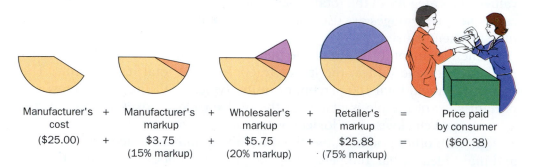

Manufacturer's cost	+	Manufacturer's markup	+	Wholesaler's markup	+	Retailer's markup	=	Price paid by consumer
($25.00)	+	$3.75 (15% markup)	+	$5.75 (20% markup)	+	$25.88 (75% markup)	=	($60.38)

FIGURE 19.2 Typical Price Markup: Manufacturer to Consumer

1. What is the topic of Figure 19.2?

2. What is the purpose of Figure 19.2—to emphasize one portion of the paragraph, illustrate with a specific example of the concept, or summarize the paragraph?

3. What is the manufacturer's cost for the item? What does the consumer pay for the item?

4. Why does each member of the distribution chain mark up the item? Where did you find that information?

TABLES

Authors use a table when they want to present several pieces of detailed, specific information that would be difficult or tedious to put in the text. Most tables contain standard parts: the data arranged systematically in **rows** (horizontal) and **columns** (vertical), with useful headings along the top and side.

Although the data is usually numbers or percentages—comparing qualities or quantities or showing how things change over time (the trend)—a table can contain words to compare various items against a standard.

When reading a table, use the title or text reference to the table to predict the topic and main idea. Next, identify the variables by reading the column labels (across the top of the table) and the row labels (down the left side of the table). Clarify the type of data presented for each variable—for example, raw numbers, percentages. And, as always, check the source line and/or caption for source information and clarification.

Tables can be used to display data in almost any subject. For example, a table might display the growth of government spending, the number of calories found in alcoholic beverages, or a summary of survey findings.

See how the table in Example 1.6 displays the complete data from the U.S. Census Bureau on dairy product consumption.

EXAMPLE 1.6 TABLE   Column Labels: Variables

Title: Main Idea → **Per Capita Consumption of Diary Products: 1995 to 2000**

COMMODITY	UNIT	1995	1996	1997	1998	1999	2000
Beverage milks	Gallons	24.2	24.3	24.0	23.4	23.2	22.7
Plain whole milk	Gallons	8.4	8.4	8.2	8	7.9	7.8
Plain reduced-fat milk (2%)	Gallons	8.2	8	7.7	7.5	7.3	7.1
Plain light and skim milks	Gallons	6.2	6.4	6.6	6.6	6.3	6.1
Flavored whole milk	Gallons	0.3	0.3	0.3	0.3	0.4	0.4
Flavored milks other than whole	Gallons	0.8	0.9	0.9	1	1	1
Buttermilk	Gallons	0.3	0.3	0.3	0.3	0.3	0.3
Yogurt (excl. frozen)	1/2 pints	9.4	8.9	9.5	9.3	9	9.9
Fluid cream products[1]	1/2 pints	15.9	16.4	17	17.3	17.9	18.6
Cream[2]	1/2 pints	9.5	10.2	10.7	10.9	11.4	11.8
Sour cream and dips	1/2 pints	5.5	5.4	5.6	5.7	5.7	6.2
Condensed and evaporated milks	Pounds	6.9	6.4	6.6	6.4	6.5	5.8
Whole milk	Pounds	2.3	2.3	2.6	2.2	2.1	1.8
Skim milk	Pounds	4.5	4.1	4 4.	1	4.4	3.8
Cheese[3]	Pounds	27.3	27.7	28	28.4	29	29.8
American	Pounds	11.8	12	12	12.2	12.6	12.7
Cheddar	Pounds	9.1	9.2	9.6	9.6	10.1	(NA)
Italian	Pounds	10.4	10.8	11	11.3	11.8	(NA)
Mozzarella	Pounds	8.1	8.5	8.4	8.7	9.2	(NA)
Other[4]	Pounds	5	5	5	4.8	5	(NA)
Swiss	Pounds	1.1	1.1	1	1	1.1	(NA)
Cream and Neufchatel	Pounds	2.1	2.2	2.3	2.3	2.4	(NA)
Cottage cheese, total	Pounds	2.7	2.6	2.7	2.7	2.6	2.6
Lowfat	Pounds	1.2	1.2	1.3	1.3	1.3	1.3
Frozen dairy products[5]	Pounds	29.4	28.6	28.8	29.6	28.6	27.8
Ice cream	Pounds	15.7	15.9	16.4	16.6	16.7	16.5
Lowfat ice cream	Pounds	7.5	7.6	7.9	8.3	7.5	7.3
Sherbet	Pounds	1.3	1.3	1.3	1.4	1.3	1.2
Frozen yogurt	Pounds	3.5	2.6	2.1	1.9	1.9	1.8

NA Not available. 1 Includes eggnog, not shown separately. 2 Heavy cream, light cream, and half and half. 3 Excludes full-skim American, cottage, pot and baker's cheese. 4 Includes other cheeses not shown separately. 5 Includes other frozen dairy products not shown separately.

Footnote

Source: U.S. Bureau of the Census, *Statistical Abstract of the United States*, 2002, Washington, D.C., 2002 Source of Data

Row Labels: Variables

Exercise 4   **Reading and Integrating a Table and Text**

Read the paragraph, read Table 19.1, integrate the information, and answer the questions.

The United States was among the first countries to set a goal of mass education. By 1850, about half the young people between the ages of five and nineteen were enrolled in school. In 1918, the last of the states passed a mandatory education law requiring children to attend school until the age of sixteen or completion of the eighth grade. Table 19.1 shows that a milestone was reached in the mid-1960s when, for the first time, a majority of U.S. adults had high school diplomas. Today, more than four out of five have a high school education, and almost one in four a four-year college degree. (Macionis, *Sociology*)

TABLE 19.1 **Educational Achievement in the United States, 1910–1996***

Year	High School Graduates	College Graduates	Median Years of Schooling
1910	13.5%	2.7%	8.1
1920	16.4	3.3	8.2
1930	19.1	3.9	8.4
1940	24.1	4.6	8.6
1950	33.4	6.0	9.3
1960	41.1	7.7	10.5
1970	55.2	11.0	12.2
1980	68.7	17.0	12.5
1990	77.6	21.3	12.4
1996	81.7	23.6	12.7

*For persons twenty-five years of age and over. Percentage for high school graduates includes those who go on to college. Percentage of high school dropouts can be calculated by subtracting percentage of high school graduates from 100 percent.

Source: U.S. Bureau of the Census (1997)

1. What is the topic of Table 19.1?

2. Is the purpose of Table 19.1 to emphasize one portion of the paragraph, summarize the paragraph, or add details to the paragraph?

3. The paragraph says "a milestone was reached in the mid-1960s when, for the first time, a majority of U.S. adults had high school diplomas." What specific data from the table supports this statement?

4. What was the percentage of high school dropouts in 1996? How did you arrive at your answer?

DIAGRAMS

A **diagram** is any of an assortment of graphics authors use to help you understand ideas, objects, plans, processes, or sequences. Diagrams include everything from a timeline in a history text, to an organizational chart in a management text, to a complex correlation-and-cause diagram in a sociology text.

When reading a diagram, begin by identifying the topic and main idea. Next, try to establish the purpose of the diagram—what it shows and why the author is using it. In addition, clarify what each portion of the diagram represents.

Venn Diagrams

Using circles, Venn diagrams help readers view interrelated and independent aspects of concepts. In a Venn diagram, similar points appear in the areas where the circles overlap, and dissimilar points appear in the areas of the circles outside the overlap.

For example, look at the diagram in Example 1.7 that I developed for the chapter on "researching information" in my *Magazine Article Writing Basics* text. It shows (with the filled circles) and tells (in words) the differences in the information you will find when you use the three key terms of Boolean Logic.

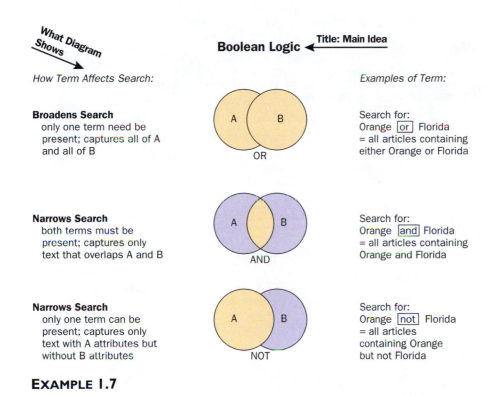

EXAMPLE 1.7

Flowcharts

A flowchart is a type of diagram that illustrates a step-by-step sequence of events from start to finish. The various elements in the sequential process are listed in boxes, rectangles, diamonds, or circles, with connecting lines and arrows. They should be read in the direction the arrows point, such as top to bottom or left to right.

Flowcharts can be constructed to show many different kinds of processes, such as how a computer program operates, the procedure for analyzing the elements in a laboratory sample, or how to write an essay, as shown in Example 1.8 that I developed for students in my writing classes.

**EXAMPLE 1.8
Flowchart**

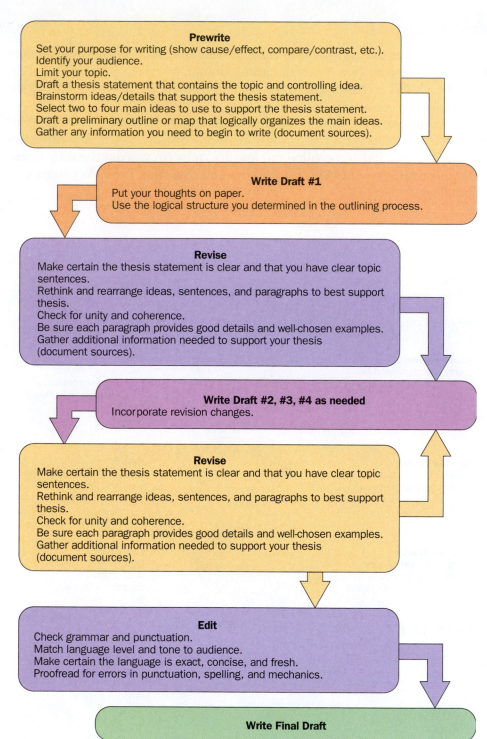

Prewrite
Set your purpose for writing (show cause/effect, compare/contrast, etc.).
Identify your audience.
Limit your topic.
Draft a thesis statement that contains the topic and controlling idea.
Brainstorm ideas/details that support the thesis statement.
Select two to four main ideas to use to support the thesis statement.
Draft a preliminary outline or map that logically organizes the main ideas.
Gather any information you need to begin to write (document sources).

Write Draft #1
Put your thoughts on paper.
Use the logical structure you determined in the outlining process.

Revise
Make certain the thesis statement is clear and that you have clear topic sentences.
Rethink and rearrange ideas, sentences, and paragraphs to best support thesis.
Check for unity and coherence.
Be sure each paragraph provides good details and well-chosen examples.
Gather additional information needed to support your thesis (document sources).

Write Draft #2, #3, #4 as needed
Incorporate revision changes.

Revise
Make certain the thesis statement is clear and that you have clear topic sentences.
Rethink and rearrange ideas, sentences, and paragraphs to best support thesis.
Check for unity and coherence.
Be sure each paragraph provides good details and well-chosen examples.
Gather additional information needed to support your thesis (document sources).

Edit
Check grammar and punctuation.
Match language level and tone to audience.
Make certain the language is exact, concise, and fresh.
Proofread for errors in punctuation, spelling, and mechanics.

Write Final Draft

Maps

A map is a diagram that depicts all or part of the earth's three-dimensional surface on a two-dimensional flat surface. Maps translate data into spatial patterns by using distance, direction, size, and shape. Maps are based on real images—a map of Africa is based on the form of the African continent—whereas many other graphics are abstract images—bars, circles, lines.

Maps are used in geography and history to show the locations of places and events, but they can also be used to show everything from distributions

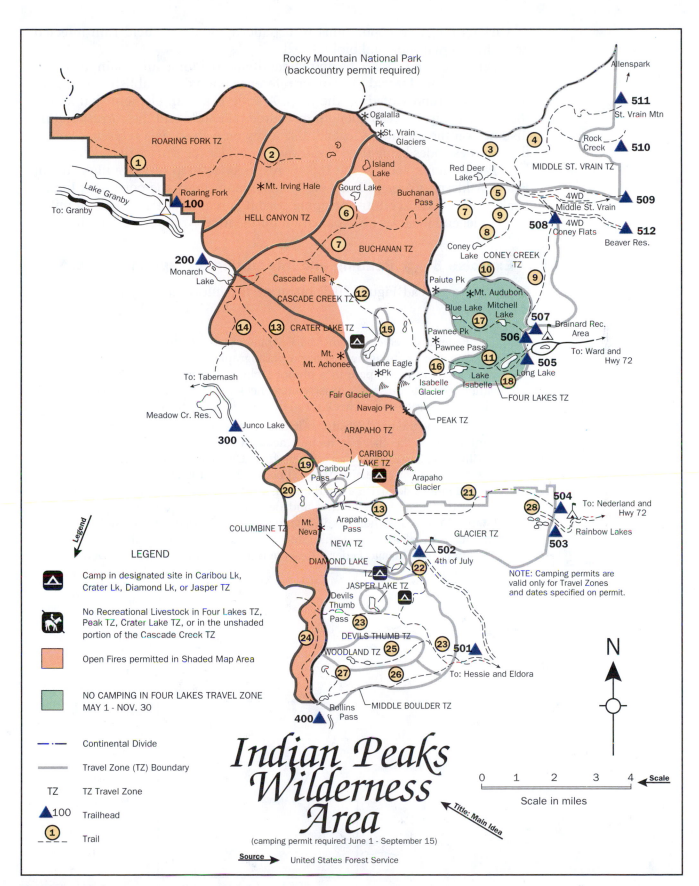

Rocky Mountain National Park
(backcountry permit required)

LEGEND

Camp in designated site in Caribou Lk, Crater Lk, Diamond Lk, or Jasper TZ

No Recreational Livestock in Four Lakes TZ, Peak TZ, Crater Lake TZ, or in the unshaded portion of the Cascade Creek TZ

Open Fires permitted in Shaded Map Area

NO CAMPING IN FOUR LAKES TRAVEL ZONE MAY 1 - NOV. 30

— ∙ — Continental Divide

—— Travel Zone (TZ) Boundary

TZ TZ Travel Zone

▲100 Trailhead

① Trail

*Indian Peaks
Wilderness
Area*

(camping permit required June 1 - September 15)

Source ➤ United States Forest Service

NOTE: Camping permits are valid only for Travel Zones and dates specified on permit.

Scale
0 1 2 3 4
Scale in miles

EXAMPLE 1.9

of various religious populations in a philosophy text to acid rain affected areas in an environmental biology text.

When reading a map, begin by identifying the topic and main idea. Use the words, **scale**, **legend**, and other reference points to establish how the information is represented on the map. A scale is a map element that shows the relationship between a length measured on a map and the corresponding distance on the ground. A legend, like a key on a chart, is a reference center that defines codes being used. As always, consider the source of the data.

For example, look at the U.S. Forest Service map of Colorado's Indian Peaks Wilderness Area in Example 1.9. The map shows the portion of Indian Peaks where a backcountry camping permit is required. Its scale is in miles, and the legend includes an explanation for the nine symbols used on the map.

Exercise 5 **Reading and Integrating a Diagram and Text**

Read the text, read Figure 20.3, integrate the information, and answer the questions.

The Federal Reserve System (the Fed) also serves commercial banks by clearing checks. Imagine you are a photographer living in New Orleans, who wants to participate in a photography workshop in Detroit, Michigan. In order to do so you must send a check for $50 to the Detroit studio. Figure 20.3 traces your check through the clearing process.

After the studio deposits your check in a Detroit bank (step 1), the bank deposits the check in its own account at the Federal Reserve Bank of Chicago (step 2). The check is sent from Chicago to the Atlanta Federal Reserve bank for collection (step 3) because you, the check writer, are in the Atlanta Federal Reserve Bank district. Your New Orleans bank receives the check from Atlanta and deducts the $50 from your account (step 4). Your bank then has $50 deducted from its deposit account at the Atlanta Federal Reserve Bank (step 5). Finally, the $50 is shifted from Atlanta to the Chicago Federal Reserve Bank (step 6). The studio's Detroit

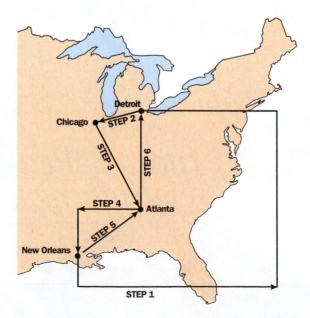

Figure 20.3

bank gets credited, and the studio's account then gets credited $50, normally within two weeks. Your bank then returns the canceled check to you by mail. (Griffin and Ebert, *Business*)

1. What is the purpose of Figure 20.3—to emphasize one portion of the text, illustrate the text, summarize the text, or add details to the paragraph?

2. Do you think Griffin and Ebert want you to concentrate on remembering the names of the cities? Why or why not?

3. What main idea do the authors want you to remember from the paragraph and graphic?

ILLUSTRATIONS

Illustrations are graphics such as photographs and drawings that provide realistic representations of the information in the text. Illustrations are used for everything from a simple labeled line drawing of the parts of a flower in a biology text, to photographs of examples of facial expressions in a speech communications text, to caste marks of Indian society in a sociology text.

Photographs

Photographs generally lack a title or labels common to other graphics, but usually include a caption—a brief description of the contents of the illustration. Use the caption to direct your attention to specific elements.

Example 1.10 Photograph

(Photo by Lary McGrath)

Photo A

Photo B

Example 1.10. In many cases, selecting a slightly different vantage point and/or using a different lens permits the photographer to exclude distracting elements in a picture. Notice how the distracting wires and lightpost in Photo A have been eliminated in Photo B by moving closer to the chapel and changing from a normal to a wide-angle lens.

Look at the two photographs in Example 1.10 from Larry McGrath's *Travel Photography Handbook*. Note how the caption points out the main idea of Photo A and Photo B.

Drawings

Drawings, especially line drawings in science texts, contain extensive labeling to clarify and direct your attention to critical aspects and/or information. Example 1.11 from Rice and Rice's *Practical Horticulture* text is typical of labeled line drawings.

EXAMPLE 1.11 LINE DRAWING

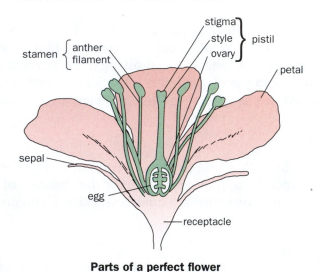

Parts of a perfect flower

Exercise 6 ▶ **Reading and Integrating an Illustration and Text**

Read the text and the illustration, integrate the information, and answer the questions.

To see how the mind can shape what we perceive, look at these two pictures:

What do you see? Each would present you with two distinctly different images. When you look at the first one in one way, you see a vase. Look at it differently and you see two faces. The second picture presents either a beautiful young woman facing away from you or an ugly old crone in profile. How is this possible? The sense data that your eyes take in—the arrangement of lines and shading—remain the same. But you can "shift" the pictures you see. What you "see," then, is the meaning your mind imposes on the data, and your mind can reprocess that data so that they represent something different. (White, *Discovering Philosophy*)

1. What is the purpose of the illustration in this example?
2. What do you think White wants you to remember from the illustration?

Exercise 7

Read the selection and answer the questions that follow it.

PAULA KURTZWEIL

Paula Kurtzweil is a member of the Food and Drug Administration's (FDA) public affairs staff. This selection is adapted from an FDA Consumer article that originally appeared in June 1996 and was revised after the Sunscreen Regulations were finalized in May 1999.

AN IDEA TO THINK ABOUT

Sunburn can be painful and dangerous. What steps do you take to make sure you don't get sunburned? *As you read,* find out what UV radiation has to do with sunburn, what the UV Index (UVI) is, and what steps you can take to prevent sunburn.

SEVEN STEPS TO SAFER SUNNING

Paula Kurtzweil

[1]Put away the baby oil. Toss out that old metal sun reflector. Cancel your next appointment to the local tanning salon.

[2]These are new days with new ways of sunning, and the practices that traditionally have gone into obtaining the so-called healthy tanned look are on the verge of fading into history.

[3]In their place: safer sun practices that preserve people's natural skin color and condition.

[4]That's what health experts are hoping for as the evidence against exposure to the sun and sunlamps continues to mount. Both emit harmful ultraviolet (UV) radiation that in the short term can cause painful sunburn and in the long term may lead to unsightly skin blemishes, premature aging of the skin, cataracts and other eye problems, skin cancer, and a weakened immune system.

[5a]The problems may become more prevalent, too, if, as some scientists predict, the Earth's ozone layer continues to be depleted. [b]According to the Environmental Protection Agency, scientists began accumulating evidence in the 1980s that the ozone layer—a thin shield in the stratosphere that protects life from UV radiation—is being depleted by certain chemicals used on Earth. [c]According to the most recent estimates from the National Aeronautics and Space Administration, the ozone layer is being depleted at a rate of 4 to 6 percent each decade. [d]This means additional UV radiation reaching Earth's surface—and our bodies.

[6]Although people with light skin are more susceptible to sun damage, darker skinned people, including African Americans and Hispanic Americans, also can be affected.

[7]You may have already started to take precautions. But are you doing all you can?

[8]The following recommendations come from various expert organizations, including the American Academy of Dermatology, American Cancer Society, American Academy of Ophthalmology, Skin Cancer Foundation, American Academy of Pediatrics, National Cancer Institute, National Weather Service, and Food and Drug Administration. FDA regulates many items related to sun safety, including sunscreens and sunblocks, sunglasses, and sun-protective clothing that makes medical claims. The agency also sets performance standards for sunlamps.

[9]Here are seven steps to safer sunning:

1. AVOID THE SUN.

[10]This is especially important between 10 a.m. and 3 p.m., when the sun's rays are strongest. Also avoid the sun when the UV Index is high in your area.

[11]The UV Index is a number from 0 to 10+ that indicates the amount of UV radiation reaching the Earth's surface during the hour around noon. The higher the number, the greater your exposure to UV radiation if you go outdoors. The National Weather Service forecasts the UV Index daily in 58 U.S. cities, based on local predicted conditions (See Table 1). The index covers about a 30-mile radius from each city. Check the local newspaper or TV and radio news broadcasts to learn the UV Index in your area. It also may be available through your local phone company and is available on the Internet at the National Weather Service Climate Prediction Center's home page.

[12]Don't be fooled by cloudy skies. Clouds block only as much as 20 percent of UV radiation. UV radiation also can pass through water, so don't assume you're safe from UV radiation if you're in the water and feeling cool. Also, be especially careful on the beach and in the snow because sand and snow reflect sunlight and increase the amount of UV radiation you receive.

[13]People with darker skin will resist the sun's rays by tanning, which is actually an indication that the skin has been injured. Tanning occurs when ultraviolet radiation is absorbed by the skin, causing an increase in the activity and number of melanocytes, the cells that produce the pigment melanin. Melanin helps to block out damaging rays up to a point.

[14]Those with lighter skin are more likely to burn. Too much sun exposure in a short period results in sunburn. A sunburn causes skin redness, tenderness, pain, swelling, and blistering. Although there is no quick cure,

Table 1   NOAA/EPA Ultraviolet Index (UVI) Forecast*

City	State	UVI	City	State	UVI
Albuquerque	NM	9	Little Rock	AR	6
Anchorage	AK	2	Los Angeles	CA	8
Atlantic City	NJ	6	Louisville	KY	4
Atlanta	GA	5	Memphis	TN	6
Baltimore	MD	6	Miami	FL	9
Billings	MT	6	Milwaukee	WI	5
Bismarck	ND	5	Minneapolis	MN	3
Boise	ID	6	Mobile	AL	8
Boston	MA	3	New Orleans	LA	9
Buffalo	NY	4	New York	NY	5
Burlington	VT	3	Norfolk	VA	7
Charleston	WV	5	Oklahoma City	OK	6
Charleston	SC	6	Omaha	NE	6
Cheyenne	WY	8	Philadelphia	PA	6
Chicago	IL	4	Phoenix	AZ	9
Cleveland	OH	6	Pittsburgh	PA	6
Concord	NH	3	Portland	ME	3
Dallas	TX	7	Portland	OR	5
Denver	CO	7	Providence	RI	4
Des Moines	IA	5	Raleigh	NC	6
Detroit	MI	6	Salt Lake City	UT	7
Dover	DE	6	San Francisco	CA	8
Hartford	CT	3	San Juan	PU	11
Honolulu	HI	10	Seattle	WA	4
Houston	TX	11	Sioux Falls	SD	3
Indianapolis	IN	4	St. Louis	MO	5
Jackson	MS	7	Tampa	FL	9
Jacksonville	FL	7	Washington	DC	7
Las Vegas	NV	7	Wichita	KS	8

The UV Index is categorized by EPA as follows

UVI	Exposure Level
0 1 2	Minimal
3 4	Low
5 6	Moderate
7 8 9	High
10 And Greater	Very High

*Valid May, 2003, Approximately Noon Local Standard Time

Source: Climate Prediction Center, National Weather Service, Washington DC

the American Academy of Dermatology recommends using wet compresses, cool baths, bland moisturizers, and over-the-counter hydrocortisone creams.

[15]Sunburn becomes a more serious problem with fever, chills, upset stomach, and confusion. If these symptoms develop, see a doctor.

2. USE SUNSCREEN.

[16]With labels stating "sunscreen" or "sunblock," these lotions, creams, ointments, gels, or wax sticks, when applied to the skin, absorb, reflect or scatter some or all of the sun's rays.

[17]Some sunscreen products, labeled "broad-spectrum," protect against two types of radiation: UVA and UVB. Scientists now believe that both UVA and UVB can damage the skin and lead to skin cancer.

[18]Other products protect only against UVB, previously thought to be the only damaging type.

[19]Some cosmetics, such as some lipsticks, also are considered sunscreen products if they contain sunscreen and their labels state they do.

[20]Sunblock products block a large percentage of UV radiation.

[21]FDA requires the labels of all sunscreen and sunblock products to state the product's sun protection factor, or "SPF," from 2 on up. The higher the number, the longer a person can stay in the sun before burning. Beginning in 1993, FDA suggested 30 as the upper SPF limit because it was felt that anything above this offers little additional benefit and might expose people to dangerous levels of chemicals.

[22]FDA also advised manufacturers that "water-resistant" or "sweat-resistant" products must list an SPF for both before and after being exposed to water or sweat. FDA also proposed that products claiming to be sunblocks have an SPF of at least 12 and contain titanium dioxide, the only opaque agent that blocks light. Also, any tanning product that doesn't contain a sunscreen would have to state on the label that the product does not contain a sunscreen.

[23]Experts recommend broad-spectrum products with SPFs of at least 15. They also suggest applying the product liberally—about 30 milliliters (1 ounce) per application for the average-size person, according to the Skin Cancer Foundation—15 to 30 minutes every time before going outdoors. It should be applied evenly on all exposed skin, including lips, nose, ears, neck, scalp (if hair is thinning), hands, feet, and eyelids, although care should be taken not to get it in the eyes because it can irritate them. If contact occurs, rinse eyes thoroughly with water.

[24]Sunscreens should not be used on babies younger than 6 months because their bodies may not be developed enough to handle sunscreen chemicals. Instead, use hats, clothing, and shading to protect small babies from the sun. If you think your baby may need a sunscreen, check with your pediatrician.

[25]For children 6 months to 2 years, use a sunscreen with at least an SPF of 4, although 15 or higher is best.

3. WEAR A HAT.

[26]A hat with at least a 3-inch brim all around is ideal because it can protect areas often exposed to the sun, such as the neck, ears, eyes, and scalp. A shade cap (which looks like a baseball cap with about 7 inches of material draping down the sides and back) also is good. These are often sold in sports and outdoor clothing and supply stores.

[27]A baseball cap or visor provides only limited protection but is better than nothing.

4. WEAR SUNGLASSES.

[28]Sunglasses can help protect your eyes from sun damage.

[29a]The ideal sunglasses don't have to be expensive, but they should block 99 to 100 percent of UVA and UVB radiation. [b]Check the label to see that they do. [c]If there's no label, don't buy the glasses.

[30]And, don't go by how dark the glasses are because UV protection comes from an invisible chemical applied to the lenses, not from the color or darkness of the lenses.

[31]Large-framed wraparound sunglasses are best because they can protect your eyes from all angles.

[32]Children should wear sunglasses, too, starting as young as 1, advises Gerhard Cibis, a pediatric ophthalmologist in Kansas City, Mo. They need smaller versions of real, protective adult sunglasses—not toy sunglasses. Kids' sunglasses are available at many optical stores, Cibis says.

[33]Ideally, says the American Academy of Ophthalmology, all types of eyewear, including prescription glasses, contact lenses, and intraocular lens implants used in cataract surgery, should absorb the entire UV spectrum.

5. COVER UP.

[34]Wear lightweight, loose-fitting, long-sleeved shirts, pants or long skirts as much as possible when in the sun. Most materials and colors absorb or reflect UV rays. Tightly weaved cloth is best.

[35]Avoid wearing wet clothes, such as a wet T-shirt, because when clothes get wet, the sun's rays can more easily pass through. If you see light through a fabric, UV rays can get through, too.

6. AVOID ARTIFICIAL TANNING.

[36]Many people believe that the UV rays of tanning beds are harmless because sunlamps in tanning beds emit primarily UVA and little, if any, UVB, the rays once thought to be the most hazardous. However, UVA can cause serious skin damage, too. According to some scientists, UVA may be linked to the most serious form of skin cancer, melanoma. A 1996 unpublished risk analysis by FDA scientists Sharon Miller, Scott Hamilton and Howard Cyr, Ph.D., concluded that people who use sunlamps about 100 times a year may be increasing their exposure to "melanoma-inducing" radiation by up to 24 times compared with the amount they would receive from the sun.

[37]Because of sunlamps' dangers, health experts advise people to avoid them for tanning.

[38]Several products that claim to give a tan without UV radiation carry safety risks, too. These include so-called "tanning pills" containing carotenoid color additives derived from substances similar to beta-carotene, which gives carrots their orange color. The additives are distributed throughout the body, especially in skin, making it orange. Although FDA has approved some of these additives for coloring food, it has not approved them for use in tanning agents. And, at the high levels that are consumed in tanning pills, they may be harmful. According to John Bailey, Ph.D., acting director of FDA's Office of Cosmetics and Colors, the main ingredient in tanning pills, canthaxanthin, can deposit in the eyes as crystals, which may cause injury and impaired vision.

[39]Tanning accelerators, such as those formulated with the amino acid tyrosine or tyrosine derivatives, are ineffective and also may be dangerous. Marketers promote these products as substances that stimulate the body's own tanning process, although the evidence suggests they don't work, Bailey says. FDA considers them unapproved new drugs that have not been proved safe and effective.

[40]Two other tanning products, bronzers and extenders, are considered cosmetics for external use. Bronzers, made from color additives approved by FDA for cosmetic use, stain the skin when applied and can be washed off with soap and water. Extenders, when applied to the skin, interact with protein on the surface of the skin to produce color. The color tends to wear off after a few days. The only color additive approved for extenders is dihydroxyacetone.

[41]Although they give skin a golden color, these products do not offer sunscreen protection. Also, the chemicals in bronzers may react differently on various areas of your body, producing a tan of many shades.

7. CHECK SKIN REGULARLY.

[42]You can improve your chances of finding precancerous skin conditions, such as actinic keratosis—a dry, scaly, reddish, and slightly raised lesion—and skin cancer by performing simple skin self-exams regularly. The earlier you identify signs and see a doctor, the greater the chances for successful treatment.

[43]The best time to do skin exams is after a shower or bath. Get used to your birthmarks, moles, and blemishes so that you know what they usually look like and then can easily identify any changes they undergo. Signs to look for are changes in size, texture, shape, and color of blemishes or a sore that does not heal.

[44]If you find any changes, see your doctor. Also, during regular checkups, ask your doctor to check your skin.

[45]The more of these practices you can incorporate into your life, the greater your chances of reducing the damage sun can cause. And by teaching these same practices to children, you can help them get off to a lifetime of safer sun practices.

Exercise 7 Questions

In questions 1 and 2, define the underlined words.

1. "...practices that traditionally have gone into obtaining the so-called 'healthy tanned' look are on the <u>verge</u> of fading into history." (¶2)

2. "Although people with light skin are more <u>susceptible</u> to sun damage...." (¶6)

In questions 3 and 4, if the statement is false, rewrite it to make it true.

T F **3.** Both UVA and UVB can damage the skin and lead to skin cancer.

T F **4.** The lower the SPF number on a sunscreen or sunblock product, the longer a person can stay in the sun before burning.

5. Write a sentence that expresses Kurtzweil's thesis.

6. In paragraph 5, what is the relationship of sentence d to sentence c?

7. List Kurtzweil's seven steps to safer sunning.

8. **a.** List three of the organizations that contributed to Kurtzweil's recommendations for safer sunning.

    b. List the source of the Ultraviolet Index (UVI) Forecast in Table 1.

9. What is the purpose of Table 1?

10. List the city or cities predicted to have the highest UVI exposure level. What UVI exposure level was predicted for the city closest to your home?

CHAPTER 6 REVIEW QUESTIONS

1. List six common reasons authors use graphics.
2. List and describe four common categories of graphics.
3. How can you identify the source and reliability of the information?
4. Why is it important to integrate text and graphics?
5. Describe your general strategy for reading graphics.

Use Your Strategies 1

Read the text and the graphic, integrate the information, and answer the questions.

1. Several programs have been proposed to provide job opportunities for America's inner-city unskilled. One is to rebuild the blue-collar economies of the central cities by encouraging industry to locate there in urban enterprise zones, where manufacturers receive government subsidies. The federal government has been slow to act, but several states and cities have designated such zones in their poorest communities (see Figure 9.27). (Bergman & McKnight, *Introduction to Geography*)

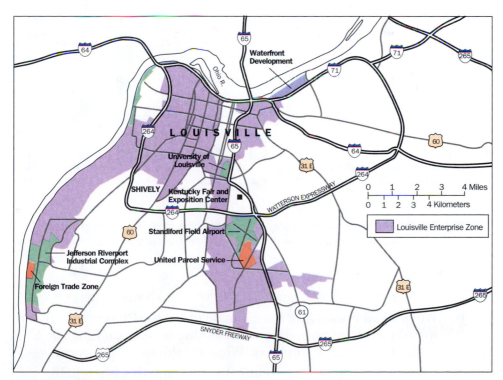

FIGURE 9.27

    a. Is the purpose of Figure 9.27 to emphasize one portion of the text, illustrate with an example of the concept, or summarize the text?

    b. Which portion of which city is represented on this map?

    c. What type of businessperson might be interested in looking at this map? Why?

2. Only those workers with dependents need life insurance, but every worker needs disability income protection. Young workers often purchase life insurance while ignoring the much greater risk of disability. This is especially unfortunate because your chances of suffering a serious disability are surprisingly high. The Social Security Administration estimates that a 20-year-old has over a 20 percent probability of experiencing an insured disability before reaching age 65 (see Figure 7.7). Since the requirements for an insured disability are rather strict, it is likely that many more individuals will experience a significant earnings loss at some point in their work life. In fact, over one-fifth of 55- to 64-year-olds state that they have a work disability that limits the kind or amount of work they do. (Winger & Frasca, *Personal Finance*)

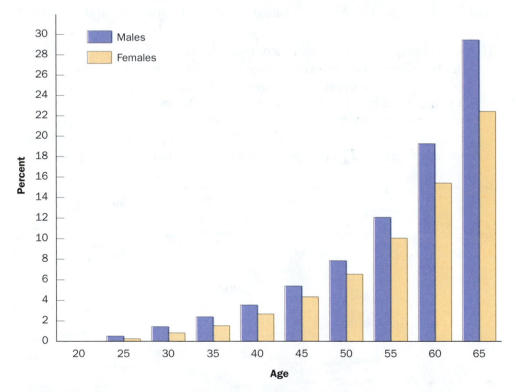

FIGURE 7.7 Probability of Social Security insured disability from age 20 to given age. *Source:* U.S. Department of Health and Human Services, A death and disability life table for the 1996 birth cohort.

    a. Explain the topic of Figure 7.7 and what it shows.

    b. Winger and Frasca give the estimate of "over a 20 percent probability" of experiencing an insured disability before reaching age 65, rather than specific numbers. What are the specific percentages?

    c. What is the source of the data? Do you think this is a reliable source? Why or why not?

3. Management is the process of planning, organizing, leading, and controlling an enterprise's financial, physical, human, and information resources in order to achieve the organization's goals of supplying various products and services. . . . The planning, organizing, leading, and controlling aspects of a manager's job are interrelated, as shown in Figure 5.1. But note that while these activities generally follow one another in a logical sequence, sometimes they are performed simultaneously or in a different sequence altogether. In fact, any given manager is likely to be engaged in all these activities during the course of any given business day. (Griffin & Ebert, *Business*)

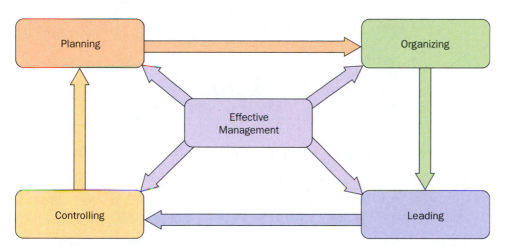

FIGURE 5.1 The Management Process

    a. What is the purpose of Figure 5.1?

    b. Why do you think Griffin and Ebert chose a flowchart to illustrate the management process?

    c. Assume you are preparing for a test on the management process. List the information you would need to remember.

4. Fruit thinning is the removal of a portion of the fruits on a tree while they are still small. Many deciduous fruit trees (nut trees are excluded) produce more fruit than can fully mature. If unthinned, the fruit will be undersized and frequently poorly colored. In addition, the excessive fruit load may weaken the tree. Bearing in alternate years may result, with the fruitless year devoted to regaining the vigor of the tree. Because most gardeners want fruit every year, the advantages of thinning are obvious.

    Fruits should be thinned when they are 1/2 to 3/4 inch (13–20 millimeters) in diameter, and after the natural drop of young fruit has occurred. Twisting fruits will remove them quickly and easily.

    The number of fruits that should be left on a tree depends on the species. Table 7.1 lists approximate distances that should be left between fruits along a branch for moderate fruit load. In practice, fruits are not spaced evenly but are close together on strong branches and far apart on weak ones. The spacing guidelines should be taken only as a guide and not an absolute. The largest, healthiest fruits should always be left on the tree, regardless of their relative spacing on a branch. (Rice & Rice, *Practical Horticulture*)

Table 7-1 Suggested Fruit Load after Thinning for Common Fruit Species

Species	Distance between fruits
apples	6–8 in. (15–20 cm)
apricots	1½–2 in. (4–5 cm)
avocados	Thinning not necessary
cherries	Thinning not necessary
citrus, figs, mulberries	Thinning not necessary
nectarines, olives	4–5 in. (10–13 cm)
peaches	6–8 in. (15–20 cm) for early varieties, 4–5 in. (10–13 cm) for later ones
pears	Thinning not necessary but can be thinned lightly to increase size
persimmons	Thinning not necessary
plums, European	Thinning not necessary
plums, Japanese	2–4 in. (5–10 cm)
quinces	Thinning not necessary

a. What information does Table 7.1 provide?

b. Who is the source of the information in Table 7.1?

c. Is the information in Table 7.1 true for every tree in every climate every year? Please explain.

5. All insects undergo metamorphosis. (Species from many other animal groups do as well.) This transformation can be subtle or it can be spectacular. For example, a series of molts gradually changes the grasshopper from a wingless, sexually immature juvenile form to a sexually mature adult that is capable of flight (Figure 30.14a). Throughout this process, grasshoppers feed on the same food source in the same way—they chew leaves. This type of metamorphosis is called hemimetabolos. Literally translated, the name means half-change; it refers to the limited morphological differences between juveniles and adults. Hemimetabolous development is a one-step process of sexual maturation—from juvenile to adult.

A fruit fly, in contrast, changes from a worm-like larva that burrows through rotting fruit to a flying adult that feeds by lapping up yeast from the surface of fruit (Figure 30.14b). This more drastic type of metamorphosis is referred to as holometabolous (holo means "whole"). Holometabolous development is a two-step maturation process, from larva to pupa to adult, involving dramatic changes in morphology and habitat use. (Freeman, *Biological Science*)

a. What is the purpose of Figure 30.14?

b. In Figure 30.14, what is the relationship of (a) to (b)? Is it illustrating similarities, differences, or cause and effect?

c. Could Freeman have selected insects other than the grasshopper and fruit fly to illustrate his concepts? Please explain.

6. As the number of elderly people in Western societies increases, mandatory retirement is an issue of considerable concern in many countries. Government policies and attitudes on compulsory retirement vary widely. Representative samples in four countries were asked the same

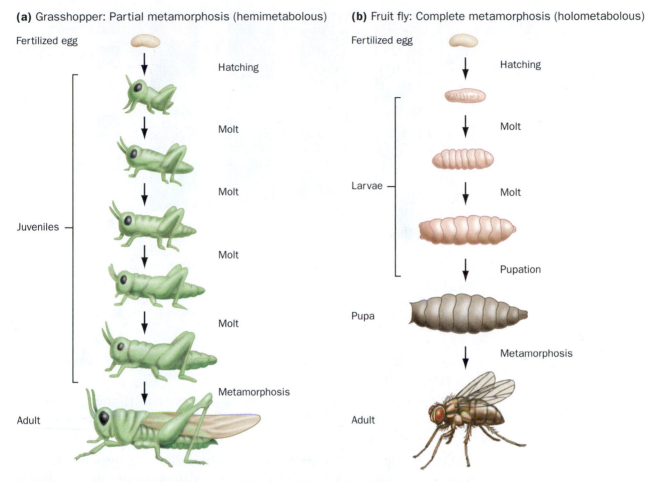

(a) Grasshopper: Partial metamorphosis (hemimetabolous)

Fertilized egg

Hatching

Molt

Molt

Juveniles

Molt

Molt

Metamorphosis

Adult

(b) Fruit fly: Complete metamorphosis (holometabolous)

Fertilized egg

Hatching

Molt

Larvae

Molt

Pupation

Pupa

Metamorphosis

Adult

FIGURE 30.14 Insect Metamorphosis Occurs in One of Two Ways
(a) Hemimetabolous development is a one-step process—from juvenile to adult. **(b)** Holometabolous development is a two-step process—from larva to pupa to adult.

question: "Do you think that all employees should be required to retire at any age set by law?" As shown in Figure 8.3, attitudes in the two European countries were in favor of mandatory retirement, while attitudes in the U.S. were opposed (Hayes and VandenHeuvel, 1994).

A number of factors, psychological, social, economic, and political, contribute to these differences in attitudes. Several factors are of interest from the perspective of the psychology of aging. Those in support of mandatory retirement view it as a mechanism for providing employment and promotion opportunities for younger workers, women, and minorities. The elderly are viewed as a reserve labor force that can and should be displaced when necessary. Other arguments suggest that it is a humane way to retire older workers who might otherwise be forced to retire on the basis of inadequate job performance; mandatory retirement is said to provide employers with a means to avoid both the difficult and controversial task of making case-by-case decisions. (Schaie and Willis, *Adult Development and Aging*)

a. What information is presented in Figure 8.3?

b. The text presents summary information about the attitudes of people in three of the countries. Which country did the authors leave

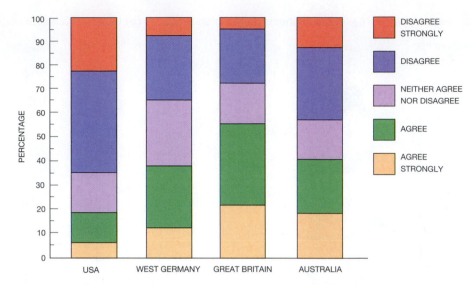

Figure 8.3 Attitudes toward Mandatory Retirement: U. S. A., West Germany, Great Britain, and Australia. Source: Hayes, B.C., and VandenHeuvel, A. (1994). Attitudes toward mandatory retirement: An international comparsion. *Aging and Human Development*, 39, 209-231.

out of the text, and how would you characterize the views of the people in that country?

c. What kinds of factors do the authors believe contribute to these differences in attitudes? Did you find that information in the text or the graphic?

7. Americans are living longer, a phenomenon called the "graying of America" (Figure 5.8). Moreover, given the size of the population, fewer babies are being born. This demographic change is having important consequences; it has increased the demand for medical care, retirement benefits, and a host of other age-related services. Persons over the age of 65 constitute less than 13 percent of the population yet account for 31 percent of the total medical expenditures.

Older Americans have political concerns, and they vote. Past legislative victories have changed the lives of older citizens. For instance, the poverty rate among this group dropped from 35 percent in 1959 to 10 percent in 1997, a change partly due to improved medical benefits passed during the 1960s. As a group, older Americans fight to ensure

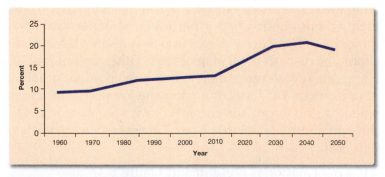

FIGURE 5.8   Percent of Population over Age 65, 1960–2050

Source: U.S. Bureau of the Census, "Aging in the United States, Past Present and Future," at www. census. gov/ipc/prod/97agewc.pdf.

that Social Security is protected; they value Medicare and favor prescription drug coverage.

a. What does Figure 5.8 show?

b. What is this trend called?

c. What are three consequences of this demographic change?

Use Your Strategies 2

Read the text and the graphics, integrate the information, and answer the questions.

JERROLD S. GREENBERG AND GEORGE B. DINTIMAN

Dr. Greenberg teaches at the University of Maryland. Dr. Dintiman teaches at Virginia Commonwealth University. This selection is from their introductory text Exploring Health.

AN IDEA TO THINK ABOUT

Can you be "well" regardless of whether you are ill or healthy? *As you read,* find out how Greenberg and Dintiman answer this question.

THE HEALTH-ILLNESS CONTINUUM

Jerrold S. Greenberg and George B. Dintiman

[1]It is important to consider health as being separate from illness. You may wonder why, for many people define illness as lack of health, and health as lack of illness. These people might depict health and illness as a straight line and call that line a "health continuum," with ill health at one end and perfect health at the other (see Figure 1.1).

FIGURE 1.1 The Health Continuum

[2]However, when we consider illness and health as separate entities, the continuum will not show them overlapping. That is, at some point one must stop and the other must begin. Figure 1.2 shows the model for this conceptualization. Illness occupies the right half of the continuum and ends at the midpoint; health begins there and occupies the left half of the continuum.

FIGURE 1.2 The Health-Illness Continuum

[3]Of course, one may argue that even if someone is ill, that person may have some degree of health. For example, a physically handicapped person who exercises regularly and participates in the Wheelchair Olympics may be healthier than a person who is not ill, but who is not physically fit. For now, though, let's withhold objection until we can explain how we intend to use the health-illness continuum.

WELLNESS

[4]We'd now like you to look at the health-illness continuum under a microscope. Notice that the line isn't a line at all, but a series of dots. The continuum would then look like Figure 1.3.

```
Perfect
health        Health          Illness          Death
|················|················|················|
```

FIGURE 1.3 The Magnified Health-Illness Continuum

[5]If we could get an even more powerful microscope and focus it on just one of the dots on the continuum, you might see something like Figure 1.4. Each dot on the continuum, then, is composed of the five components of health. When we integrate social, mental, emotional, spiritual, and physical health at any level of health or illness, we achieve what we will call wellness. Put another way, you can be well regardless of whether you are ill or healthy. Paraplegics, for example, may not be defined as healthy; but they could have achieved high-level wellness by maximizing and integrating the five components of health so that, within their physical limitations, they are living a quality life. They may interact well with family and friends (social health); they may succeed at school, on the job, or with a hobby (mental health); they may be able to express their feelings when appropriate (emotional health); they may have a sense of how they fit into the "grand scheme of things" through a set of beliefs (spiritual health); and they may exercise within the boundaries of their capabilities, for example, by finishing a marathon on crutches or in a wheelchair (physical health).

FIGURE 1.4 The Single Health-Illness Continuum Dot

1. Define continuum. How do Greenberg and Dintiman use a graphic to represent a continuum?

2. What is the difference between the health continuum (Figure 1.1) and the health-illness continuum (Figure 1.2)? Did you find the written or the graphic explanation easier to understand? Why?

3. How is the continuum graphic in Figure 1.3 different than the one in Figure 1.2?

4. What is the relationship of Figure 1.4 to the health-illness continuum in Figure 1.3?

5. What are the five components of health? Where is this information stated?

6. How do Greenberg and Dintiman define wellness? What example do they use to support and develop their definition of wellness?

Use Your Strategies 3

Read the text and the graphics, integrate the information, and answer the questions.

FRANK SCHMALLEGER

Dr. Schmalleger is director of the Justice Research Association, a private consulting firm and think tank focusing on issues of crime and justice. This one-page excerpt is from Chapter 2, "The Crime Picture," in his text Criminal Justice Today: An Introductory Text for the 21st Century.

AN IDEA TO THINK ABOUT

Have you been the victim of a violent street crime? Has someone you know been a victim? *As you read*, find out some of the reasons why our fear of being a victim of crime may be out of out of proportion with reality.

THE FEAR OF CRIME

Frank Schmalleger

[1]Although we may read in newspapers or in books that violent street crime is decreasing, we may not fully believe it. In fact we may be just as afraid as ever. As some authors point out, the fear of crime is often out of proportion to the likelihood of criminal victimization. Table 2.5 compares the chance of death from homicide with other causes of death for persons in this country aged 15 to 25. For most people, regardless of age, the chance of accidental death is far greater than the chance of being murdered.

Table 2.5	Deaths and Death Rates for the Ten Leading Causes of Death for Americans Aged 15-24	
CAUSE OF DEATH	NUMBER OF DEATHS	RATES PER 100,00
Accident (except motor vehicle)	17,120	47.3
Motor vehicle accident	10,624	29.3
Homicide	6,548	18.1
Suicide	4,369	12.1
Cancer	1,642	4.5
Heart disease	920	2.5
HIV/AIDS	420	1.2
Congenital anomaly	387	1.1
Lung disease/asthma	230	0.6
Pneumonia and influenza	174	0.5
Stroke/brain hemorrhage	174	0.5
All other causes	3,940	10.9
Total	32,699	90.3

Source: National Center for Health Statistics, *Annual Report* (Washington, D.C.: U.S. Government Printing Office, 2000)

[2]The Bureau of Justice Statistics says that "fear of crime affects many people, including some who have never been victims of crime." Sources of fear are diverse. Some flow from personal experience with victimization, but most people fear crime because of dramatizations of criminal activity on television and in movies and because of frequent newspaper and media reports of crime. Feelings of vulnerability may result from learning that a friend has been victimized or from hearing that a neighbor's home has been burglarized.

[3]Speaking to a session of the American Psychiatric Association in 1999, following the Columbine High School Shootings, Kathleen M. Fisher of Pennsylvania State University said that schools are much safer today than they were ten years ago. "Schools are safe, that is the reality," said Fisher. Still, she noted, the fear generated by high school shootings makes parents everywhere afraid for the safety of their children and contributes to the general perception in American society that violent crime is out of control.

[4]At least one social commentator suggests that fear of crime is directly related to the amount and type of crime presented by the news media: Indira Lakshmanan, a columnist for the *Boston Globe*, says, "How about this for a theory: crime news is a product. Like all manufacturers, the makers of crime news strive to constantly broaden their market. They try to diversify their product line, increase public awareness of its existence, raise its quality, and increase its quantity." It may be that what people fear the most is the chance of becoming the victim of a random act of violence. As a consequence, even in an environment where crime rates are falling, the fear of crime remains high—and may be increasing.

[5]Interestingly, the groups at highest risk of becoming crime victims are not the ones who experience the greatest fear. The elderly and women report the greatest fear of victimization, even though they are among the lowest-risk groups for violent crimes. Young males, on the other hand, who stand the greatest statistical risk of victimization, often report feeling the least fear.

Use Your Strategies 3 Questions

1. State Schmalleger's thesis.
2. How does the information in Table 2.5 help to support and develop Schmalleger's thesis?
3. For Americans between the ages of 15 and 24, what is the most likely cause of death?
4. Although there are many reasons for our fear of being a victim of crime, why does Schmalleger believe most people fear crime?
5. Explain what Schmalleger means when he says, "Interestingly, the groups at highest risk of becoming crime victims are not the ones who experience the greatest fear."

Use Your Strategies 4

Read the text and the graphics, integrate the information, and answer the questions.

B. E. (BUZZ) PRUITT, KATHY TEER CRUMPLER, AND DEBORAH PROTHROW-STITH

Dr. Pruitt is professor of health education at Texas A&M University. Dr. Crumpler is health and safety supervisor for the Onslow County School in Jacksonville, North Carolina. Dr. Prothrow-Stith is associate dean for faculty development at the Harvard School of Public Health. This excerpt is from Chapter 2, "Theories of Personality," in their introductory text Health Skills *for* Wellness.

AN IDEA TO THINK ABOUT

Can you concentrate and study when you are hungry or thirsty? *As you read*, find out how Maslow's hierarchy of needs may explain some of our behaviors.

MASLOW

B. E. (Buzz) Pruitt, Kathy Teer Crumpler, and Deborah Prothrow-Stith

MASLOW

[1]An American psychologist named Abraham Maslow theorized that everyone has a basic drive to achieve his or her fullest potential. Maslow used the term **self-actualization** to describe the process by which each person strives to be all that he or she can be. To define the characteristics of a self-actualized person, Maslow studied people who, in his view, had attained self-actualization. These people included Abraham Lincoln, Albert

Einstein, Eleanor Roosevelt, and many others. Based on these studies, Maslow arrived at the list of ideal personality traits shown in Figure 2.7.

Personality Traits of Self-Actualized People

- Realistic
- Accepting
- Independent, self-sufficient
- Appreciative of life
- Concerned about humankind
- Capable of loving others
- Fair, unprejudiced
- Creative
- Hardworking
- Not afraid to be different

Figure 2.7 *According to Maslow, self-actualized people show many of these personality traits. What other traits would you add to the list?*

[2]Maslow found that few people ever reach their full potential. He developed a theory to explain why. Maslow suggested that before people could achieve self-actualization, their basic needs had to be met. Maslow put these needs in an ascending order, called the **hierarchy of needs**. Notice that the hierarchy, shown in Figure 2.8, is a pyramid, with self-actualization at the top. At the base is what Maslow considered to be a person's most urgent needs: physical needs of the body. These include getting enough sleep, exercising, and satisfying hunger and thirst. If these basic needs are not met, a person has little or no energy to pursue higher needs.

[3]Look again at Figure 2.8. The next need is safety. This includes the needs for adequate shelter, adequate income, and protection from danger. Once the need for safety is met, a person has the energy to pursue the next level of Maslow's hierarchy: social needs. Social needs include the need for friends, love, and acceptance.

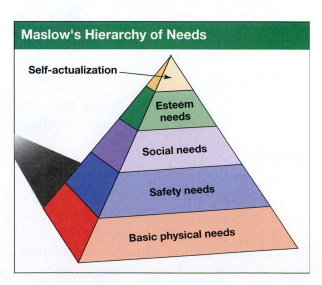

Maslow's Hierarchy of Needs

Self-actualization
Esteem needs
Social needs
Safety needs
Basic physical needs

Figure 2.8 *Which needs did Maslow feel must be satisfied before social needs can be met?*

Use Your Strategies 4 Questions

1. Define the term *self-actualization* as used by Maslow.
2. How did Maslow develop the list of traits in Figure 2.7?
3. Explain the term *hierarchy* in the phrase *hierarchy of needs*.
4. Why are "Basic physical needs" at the base of the pyramid in Figure 2.8?
5. Once safety needs are met, what needs can people can direct their energies toward meeting? Give an example of those needs.

REFLECT AND CONNECT

A. Reread the first portion of Chapter 1. What does the Plan»Do»Review flowchart on page 4 show? Why do you think I selected a flowchart? Does it fulfill its purpose? Why or why not?

B. Select a text assignment from another class that includes at least one graphic. What is the purpose of the graphic? How do the words help you understand the graphic? How does the graphic help you understand the words?

LOG ON TO THE WEB

These Web sites contain graphics or links to sites with graphics. Log on to one of these sites or use a search engine to locate two different types of informational graphics.

> www.nal.usda.gov/fnic/foodcomp
> www.druglibrary.org/schaffer/library/graphs/graphs.htm
> www.energy.ca/CG.html
> www2.nature.nps.gov/ard/parkhp.html

Print out both graphics. For each graphic write the topic of the graphic, what the data in the graphic depicts, the source of the data, and the date of the data. Attach your answers to the printouts and turn them in to your professor.

REFERENCES

Arnold, T., & F. Dwyer. (1975). "Realism in Visualized Instruction." *Perception and Motor Skills*, 40(4), 369–370.

Booher, R. (1975). "Relative Comprehensibility of Pictorial Information and Printed Words in Proceduralized Instruction." *Human Factors*, 17, 266–277.

Boardman, D. (1976). "Graphics in the Curriculum." *Educational Review*, 28(2), 118–125.

Decker, W., & P. Wheatly. (1982). "Spatial Grouping, Imagery, and Free Recall." *Perception and Motor Skills*, 55(1), 45–46.

DuPlass, James A. (1996). "Charts, Tables, Graphs, and Diagrams: An Approach for Social Studies Teachers." *Social Studies*, 87(1).

Gillespie, C. S. (1993). "Reading Graphic Displays: What Teachers Should Know." *Journal of Reading*, 36(5), 350.

Holliday, W. G. (1975). "What's in a Picture?" *The Science School Teacher*, 42(2), 21–22.

Kamm, K., E. Askov, & R. Klumb. (1977). "Study-skills Mastery among Middle and High School Students." (ERIC Document No. Ed 141 780).

Kirsch, I., & A. Jungeblut. (1986). "Literacy: Profile of America's Young Adults." (ERIC Document No. Ed 275692).

Monk, G. S. (1988). "Students' Understanding of Functions in Calculus." *Humanistic Mathematics Network Newsletter*, 2, 236–41.

Piston, C. (1992). "Supplementing the Graphing Curriculum." *Mathematics Teacher*, 84(6), 336.

Rigney, J. W., & K. Lutz. (1976). "Effect of Graphic Analogies of Concepts in Chemistry on Learning and Attitude." *Journal of Educational Psychology*, 68(4), 305–311.

read-ing (red´in) *adj.* 1 inclined ...d or study 2 ma
reading n. 1 the act or practic... ...erson who reac...
of books 2 a public entertainm... ...which literary
aloud 3 the extent to which a ... ...n has read 4 ma
meant to be read 5 the amoun... ...asured as by a ba
thermometer 6 the form of a specified word, senten...

Understanding the Author's Point of View

It is the mark of an educated mind to be able to entertain a thought without accepting it.

—Aristotle

AN IDEA TO THINK ABOUT

We all know that Cinderella was mistreated by her stepsisters. Or was she? Do we know her stepsisters' side of the story? Was the Giant at the top of Jack's beanstalk really a monster, or have we just never heard the Giant's version of the story?

I'm not saying that the common versions of these stories are wrong. However, I am suggesting that in fairy tales, as in real life, there may be more than one point of view.

As you prepare to read this chapter, think about your point of view, or position, on an issue—for example, getting older. Consider what words and actions you use when you want to let others know how you feel about your coming birthday. How do you communicate that you're delighted about finally getting older or, on the other hand, that you're feeling ancient and need some quiet understanding?

Even if you have strong feelings about the issue, could you write an essay that equally presents the positive and negative aspects of getting older? What precautions would you take if you wanted to make sure you were presenting both sides of the issue? Do you think it would be wrong if you wrote only your feelings? Do you think it would be important for someone reading your essay to know if you had personal feelings about aging that influenced what you wrote?

By the way, if you want to read classic fairy tales from another point of view, check out *That Awful Cinderella* and *Jack and the Beanstalk: Giants Have Feelings,*

Too, in the Point of View series by Alvin Granowsky or *The True Story of the 3 Little Pigs!* by Jon Scieszka.

CHAPTER FOCUS

Point of view can refer to the perspective from which an author writes: a *first-person, second-person,* or *third-person* point of view. However, as I use the term in this chapter, an author's point of view is his or her fundamental attitude, position, or opinion about the topic. Understanding the author's point of view gives you additional perspective on the author's message and is essential to comprehension (Novelli, 1999a).

Unfortunately, an author does not usually directly state his or her point of view. So, as you have done when you have made other inferences, you must carefully combine what the author says with clues the author provides and your own knowledge to infer the point of view.

As noted in previous chapters, an inference is a *reasonable* conclusion—a logical guess based on what the author says. To increase your ability to make valid, appropriate inferences,

1. Be sure you understand what is stated. It's almost impossible to make a statement about what *is not known* if you are unclear about what *is known.*

2. Make certain your inferences are based on and supported by the information the author does give.

3. Check that your inferences are not contradicted by any of the author's stated information.

To identify point of view in writing, use clues such as the author's knowledge and reliability, tone, and the type of information.

KNOWLEDGE AND RELIABILITY

Think about the last time you had to talk with someone you didn't know. Remember how difficult that first conversation was? But do you also recall that as you learned about his or her background, job, hobbies, friends, and language, the talking and understanding became easier?

This also holds true for the silent conversation that takes place between you and the author during reading. Reading without knowing the writer, like talking with someone you don't know, makes communication difficult.

There are strategies you can use to get to know an author and his or her credibility, or qualification for writing. In books, look on the title page for basic data such as where the author teaches or what he or she does. Information about an author's background and professional activities is often included in the preface or a special "About the Author" section. Journals and magazines usually run a byline and short biography. Professors and librarians can also provide background data on authors. The more comprehensive picture of the author you construct, the more insight you will have for understanding what he or she is saying.

In addition to knowing about the author's expertise, it is important to know if he or she is reliable—that is, whether you can trust the author to give you a fair analysis of the topic without undue influence from others. An expert is an authority, a specialist. Experts work to uncover the accuracy and exactness of a view or position. On the other hand, an advocate is a supporter or defender of a particular position or point of view. Advocates attempt to prove that their view or position is right.

For example, a professional athlete and a sports medicine doctor could both write knowledgeably on the topic of athletic footwear—from different perspectives, but with knowledge about the topic. In other words, they would both be experts on the topic. It would be difficult to know, however, whether they are writing as experts or whether they are advocating a point of view because of influence from a sponsor or manufacturer.

Most of what you read in print-on-paper resources such as journals, magazines, and textbooks has been reviewed by experts or editors for content and style before publication. This editorial process gives some assurance the material is valid and reliable. Or, at the very least, it provides author and source information you can review.

Unfortunately, this traditional filtering system does not exist for most of the material you read on the Internet. For this reason, one of the great strengths of the Internet—that anyone anywhere can put up any information he or she wants—becomes its biggest weakness. Although you can run a Web search and locate hundreds of sites with information related to your topic, sources are not equally knowledgeable or reliable. In cyberspace, you are not just a reader, you are also the editor reviewing the information for legitimate content and understandable style. This means that you must be extra cautious when reading information on the Internet.

Passively accepting any information as accurate and reliable makes you vulnerable to a variety of problems—from small inconveniences like seeing a highly rated movie that you hate to major disasters like submitting to your boss a report containing flawed information. To increase your chances of using knowledgeable and reliable information, use an active, strategic approach to reading.

TONE

Tone is the emotional feeling or attitude we create with our words. As illustrated in Chapter 2, words by themselves don't have much meaning. For example, the words "I don't care" can be a simple phrase meaning "I just don't have a preference" or a complex of emotions meaning "you've made me so angry it doesn't matter." The problem is, if you misunderstand the meaning, you can be in big trouble. But how do you know which meaning to select?

When you're talking with someone, you identify tone by listening to the pitch and volume of his or her voice and watching gestures and facial expressions. Using these clues, you determine if someone is being serious, humorous, straightforward, or ironic. And this knowledge helps you understand their meaning.

Like a speaker, a writer can create any emotion. In some of your reading assignments, you may need to narrowly define the author's tone—for example, decide whether the tone is funny, witty, whimsical, or comical. However, most of the time you can place the tone of the writing into one of seven general groupings.

General Types of Tone		
	General Description of Tone	**Similar Types of Tone**
straightforward	objective; without bias	honest, objective, fair
emotional	subjective; with strong feeling	passionate, sympathetic, fervent
humorous	intended to be funny and enjoyable	whimsical, witty, comical
ironic	means opposite of what it says	contradictory, paradoxical
satire/sarcastic	biting humor	mocking, acerbic
positive	confident and upbeat attitude	optimistic, enthusiastic, hopeful
negative	skeptical and gloomy attitude	cynical, angry, grim, pessimistic

Identifying Tone

Although you don't have a speaker's verbal or visual clues available when you are reading, you can understand the author's tone by watching for words and phrases that have special connotations and details the author chooses to use or to leave out. Using these clues, along with what the author says directly and your own knowledge, will help you correctly infer the author's tone.

EXAMPLE   Read to determine the author's tone in these paragraphs. How does the author want you to feel about the person being described? What elements contribute to the differences?

Description A: He had apparently not shaved for several days and his face and hands were covered with dirt. His shoes were torn and his coat, which was several sizes too small for him, was spotted with dried mud.

Description B: Although his face was bearded and neglected, his eyes were clear and he looked straight ahead as he walked rapidly down the road. He looked very tall; perhaps the fact that his coat was too small for him emphasized that impression. He was carrying two books snugly under his left arm and a small terrier puppy ran at his heels.

Explanation Both paragraphs could be describing the same man, but the words and details the author has chosen present two very different impressions of the man. Notice how the negatives in description A (unshaven, coat too small) have been reworded and turned into assets in description B. Also, leaving out details (like torn shoes) and adding details like the books and the puppy in description B contributes to the different tone.

Exercise 1

1. There are those who believe that a rapidly advancing computer technology exhibits little regard for the future of the human race. They contend that computers are overused, misused, and generally detrimental to society. This group argues that the computer is dehumanizing and is slowly forcing society into a pattern of mass conformity. To be sure, the computer revolution is presenting society with complex problems, but they can be overcome. (Long, *Introduction to Computers and Information Systems*)

   a. What is Long's point of view about computers?

   b. Would you describe Long's tone as positive or negative? Why?

2. Donald Trump had not granted an interview or smirked into a camera in nearly a month. It was his longest media dry spell since 1986—when he started taking reporters on grand tours aboard his black Puma helicopter, laying claim to the Manhattan-to-Atlantic City landscape with a lordly wave of his hand. At forty-four, despite almost daily, banner-headlined catastrophes since the beginning of 1990, he was still willing to play poster-boy, and a birthday was a great photo opportunity. So, after weeks of hiding from a suddenly carnivorous press, he decided to surface at a birthday blast organized by his casino dependents. With his golden hair backing up beneath his starched collar, a wounded half smile on his silent lips, and perfectly protected by his ever-present blue pin-striped suit, the icon of the eighties—slowed in the first six months of the new decade to an uncertain pace—worked his way out onto a Boardwalk blanketed by a mid-June haze. (Barrett, *Trump: The Deals and the Downfall*)

   a. What is Barrett's point of view about Trump?

   b. How would you describe Barrett's tone? Why?

3. One of the strongest barriers to good thinking, then, is fear. Fear may show itself as anger, envy, selfishness, or hatred, but these are just expressions of our fear. And don't underrate the power of such emotions. History has shown what devastation fear and hatred among nations can wreak. Our personal fears can be just as damaging to our inner world, blinding our critical faculties with their dark energies. When we argue, then, we must be aware of what we feel as well as what we think. A good critical thinker may have to scrutinize not only the intellectual character of an argument, but its emotional temperature as well. (White, *Discovering Philosophy*)

   a. What is White's point of view about the impact of fear?

   b. How would you describe White's tone? Why?

4. Two new books—*Built from Scratch* by founders Bernie Marcus and Arthur Blank (Times Business, 332 pages, $24.95) and *Inside Home Depot* by journalist Chris Roush (McGraw-Hill, 266 pages, $24.95)—tell the story of how Home Depot succeeded beyond anyone's dreams. . . . Alas, much of *Inside Home Depot* smacks of old interview notes, faded newspaper clippings and public-relations puff. The dust jacket for Mr. Roush's book proclaims: "Unauthorized! Not sponsored or approved by The Home Depot." If Home Depot executives were nervous about what Mr. Roush would build from scratch, they can relax. (Hagerty, "Bookshelf: Do-It-Yourself Dreams," *Wall Street Journal*)

   a. What is Hagerty's point of view about *Inside Home Depot?*
   b. How would you describe Hagerty's tone? Why?

5. Although John was most significant in the early 1970s, that is up to 1975, he has remained active and is not yet nostalgic. He is still progressing. Like all rock stars who pass the age of thirty, he has become old by commercial standards. He is no longer the new sensation, but he remains a genius in the context of his time. Although some critics have suggested that his singing is mechanical and nonexpressive, I believe this charge to be false. Elton John expresses his words in the context of the melodic and musical line, and within the appropriate context, his singing is both expressive and musical. (Brown, *The Art of Rock and Roll*)

   a. What is Brown's point of view about Elton John as a musician?
   b. How would you describe Brown's tone? Why?

Irony

Irony is a powerful rhetorical tool whose role in creating meaning should not be underestimated (Shugart, 1999). This is because an author using an ironic tone doesn't intend for the reader to take his or her words literally: If you don't realize that the author is being ironic—saying the opposite of what he or she means—you totally misinterpret the message.

Although there are many types of irony, such as literary irony and dramatic irony, which have slightly more specific definitions, I use the term to mean anytime the intended meaning of the words is the direct opposite of their usual meaning.

Sometimes funny, sometimes sad, Holman (1980) defines irony as "a figure of speech in which the actual intent is expressed in words which carry the opposite meaning. . . . Characteristically it speaks words of praise to imply blame and words of blame to imply praise" (236). However, unlike other forms of nonliteral language, such as a metaphor, an ironic statement provides a clue to the speaker's intentions and helps reveal his or her attitude toward the topic (Winner et al., 1988).

EXAMPLE   Consider this portion of a scientist's presentation to his colleagues. If they take his words literally and follow his principles of good writing, will they be good writers?

THE PRINCIPLES OF GOOD WRITING

Write hurriedly, preferably when tired. Have no plans; write down items as they occur to you. The article will thus be spontaneous and poor. Hand in your manuscript the moment it is finished. Rereading a few days later might lead to revision—which seldom, if ever, makes the writing worse. If you submit your manuscript to colleagues (a bad practice), pay no attention to their criticisms or comments. Later, resist any editorial suggestions. Be strong and infallible; don't let anyone break down your personality. The critic may be trying to help you or he may have an ulterior motive, but the chance of his causing improvement in your writing is so great that you must be on guard.

Explanation   The scientist's title tells us that his purpose is to give information on techniques for good writing. But, when his first details—writing hurriedly, when tired, and without plans—seem to contradict what you know about good writing practices, you begin to question his real meaning. Then, in his third sentence, when he actually says his advice will lead to a poor article—the opposite of his stated purpose—you know that he's being ironic. Rather than just listing the practices of good writing, he uses a bit of ironic humor to make his point.

Satire and Sarcasm

Although the terms irony, **satire**, and **sarcasm** may sound like they all describe the same kind of tone, they do not. They differ in the way they are used—what the author wants to accomplish.

Irony is simply intended to amuse or provoke thought.

Satire is intended to reform. It uses humor and ironic statements to poke fun at people and deride foolish or dishonest human behaviors or institutions. It is funny even when it is painful. For example, political satire mocks politics and politicians in an effort to bring about public awareness or change.

Sarcasm is intended to deride, embarrass, or cause injury. Sarcasm is a much more aggressive device with a bitter, caustic quality.

These types of biting humor are used by cartoonists like *Doonesbury*'s Gary Trudeau and comedians on shows like *Saturday Night Live*. When you're reading a cartoon or watching one of these comedy shows and you understand the words but don't understand that they are making fun of the subject, you miss the point and the humor. You also miss the point when you don't understand that an author is using satire or sarcasm.

Exercise 2

E. J. MONTINI

E. J. Montini writes on social and political issues and their effects on people. This selection is from the Arizona Republic, *the daily newspaper in Phoenix.*

EXECUTION HAS BENEFITS—DOESN'T IT?

E. J. Montini

[1]Now that Don Harding is dead, now that we've killed him, it's time to reap the rewards, to count up the ways we're benefiting from his death. There must be plenty.

[2]Two days ago, the convicted murderer was alive and in prison. Today, he's dead. He was killed at our expense. In our name. By us. Which means we must have thought it was important to kill him. We must have believed there were benefits in it for us.

[3]Like, for instance, safety.

[4]Maybe we're safer today than we were Sunday, when Harding was still alive.

[5]No, that's not it.

[6]Harding was in a maximum-security prison cell Sunday, as he had been every day for the past 10 years. We were as safe from him then, while he was alive, as we are from him now.

[7]It must be something else. There must be some other benefit to having strapped Harding into a chair in a tiny room and filled the space with poison gas. It took him about 10 minutes to die.

$16,000 TO KEEP HIM ALIVE

[8]How about money?

[9]Some people say that killing Harding saved us a lot of money. It was costing us $16,000 a year to keep him alive, and we no longer have to spend the cash. That's the benefit, right?

[10]Wrong.

[11]Our efforts to kill Harding (and anyone else on death row) probably cost us more than it would have cost to keep him in prison for life. In fact, several states have abolished the death penalty partly because it costs so much.

[12]It must be something else.

[13]There must be some other extremely beneficial reason for standing by calmly as the tiny capillaries in Harding's lungs were exploded by the cyanide gas, filling his chest with blood. Drowning him from the inside.

[14]Maybe we figured that, if we execute Harding, others will think twice before killing. That would be nice.

[15]Too bad it's not true. Not even those who foam at the mouth at the thought of executing people, like high-profile proponent Arizona Attorney General Grant Woods, believe the death penalty is a deterrent. Studies in states that execute people—as we now do—show that it's not, that murder rates don't go down.

[16]It must be something else.

WE DON'T KILL ALL MURDERERS

[17]I know. Everyone says there's a benefit to the families of the victims. We kill people like Harding for them. So the families can get revenge.

[18]What about other cases, though?

[19]There are hundreds of inmates in Arizona prisons who have killed people. Yet there are only 99 on death row. We don't kill all murderers, even though the families of all victims suffer the same loss.

[20]We're willing to kill 100 but not 1,000. Killing 1,000 would be considered too barbaric, wouldn't it? A little death goes a long way.

[21]Still, the fact that we don't kill all murderers proves we're really not interested in satisfying the revenge of all victims' families.

[22]If there's a benefit to having killed Harding, it must be something else.

²³Like the fact that it freed up a prison cell. That's something. We might say there's now room for one more criminal in Arizona prisons.

²⁴Except, unfortunately, there isn't. The prisons already contain about 1,000 more inmates than they're designed to handle. Killing one or two people won't help. We'd have to kill a thousand or so, and, like I said, we don't have the stomach for that.

²⁵So, it must be something else.

²⁶Maybe the benefit we got from killing Harding is less tangible. Maybe we killed him only to prove, as Attorney General Woods likes to say, that "justice is being served."

²⁷In other words, to send a message. To teach a lesson.

²⁸That must be it. The execution was a lesson. Our children, I figure, will learn something by it. They'll find out we're willing to strap a man down, poison him, then stand around and watch him slowly and painfully die.

²⁹That's the benefit.

³⁰The boys and girls we sent to bed Sunday night, before the killing, eventually will learn something very important from what we did. They'll learn what type of people their parents really are.

Exercise 2 Questions

1. What is Montini's purpose?
2. What is his thesis?
3. What is Montini's point of view on the death penalty?
4. What is his tone?
5. Do you think he has the knowledge to write this article? Why or why not?
6. Do you think he is reliable? That is, do you think anything could cause him to change his point of view? Why or why not?
7. Montini lists and discounts five "benefits" of Harding's execution. Name them.
8. What is the "benefit" that Montini decides "must be it"? Does he really think it is a benefit?
9. Montini says that children will "learn what type of people their parents really are." What does he mean?
10. If you wanted to get more information on the death penalty, list one source that would likely provide factual information and one source that would likely provide opinions.

FACTS, OPINIONS, AND REASONED JUDGMENTS

Although any author can use **facts**, **opinions**, or a combination of facts, opinions, and **reasoned judgments** to support his or her point of view, readers tend to expect expository pieces such as textbooks to contain only facts and persuasive works like editorials to include only opinions. However, no such rule exists. For this reason, learning to differentiate between facts—

statements that can be proved true—and opinions—statements that express judgments or ideas—helps boost reading comprehension (Novelli, 1999b).

Facts

A fact is an objective statement that can be proved true or false. A fact can be verified—no matter where you look or whom you ask, the information is the same. Examples of facts include the following:

- In the mid-1800s the work of Louis Pasteur and others revealed that microorganisms cause epidemic diseases.
- A lobbyist is a person hired by an individual, interest group, company, or industry to represent its interests with government officials.

Statements of facts will pass one of these three tests (Welker, 1999):

1. Can it be observed? (Example: Last Saturday, it rained all day.)
2. Has it been established by use over the years; is it supported by data? (Example: A car will stop when it runs out of gas.)
3. Can it be tested and yield results which are not open to interpretation? (Example: Water will boil at 212° Fahrenheit or 100° Celsius.)

However, as Caywood (1998) reminds us, "The rate of change in human knowledge demands thinking skills, not simply pat answers. We can no longer assume that facts we learned in school will stay the same through our lifetimes. What I learned to call blue-green algae in biology is now called cyanobacteria and isn't even considered a plant any more . . . knowledge is an ongoing process, not a frozen collection of facts."

Opinions

A statement of opinion can be very well thought out, but it cannot be verified—it is always open to debate. It is a subjective statement that cannot be proved true or false; the information can change depending on where you look or whom you ask. Examples of opinions include the following:

- Louis Pasteur made the most significant contributions to the world of medicine of any scientist in history.
- Lobbyists are the primary cause of problems in the government today.

The following tips can help you spot opinions:

1. Look for word clues that signal
   - the author is stating an opinion, such as *think, believe, assume, imagine, feel, contend, conjecture, suppose, surmise,* or *suggest;*
   - there may be room for different interpretations, such as *may, believed to have, might have, probably, perhaps,* or *usually;*
   - judgment, such as *bad, good, greatest, finest, best, worst, most, tremendous, outstanding, beautiful,* or *dangerous.*
2. Look for ideas and concepts that create passionate responses. (Example: Abortion should be illegal/legal.)
3. Look for statements that can be argued. (Example: That is the best restaurant in town.)

Reasoned Judgments

An opinion is not inherently right or wrong, or good or bad. However, depending on the amount and type of evidence the author considered before forming the opinion, it can be valid or invalid. Invalid opinions are often based on emotion, peer pressure, politics, and trends more than on evidence. You should be skeptical of these opinions.

On the other hand, valid opinions can be helpful. Reasoned judgments are thoughtful, coherent evaluations that informed individuals make from available evidence. Articles, essays, and even textbooks rarely use only verifiable facts, and most of the time we're grateful because it's the author's insight, wisdom, and conclusions—his or her reasoned judgments—that help us understand ideas, concepts, and issues.

EXAMPLE   Liz Caile was a passionate political and environmental columnist. These are the first three paragraphs from a column she wrote for *The Mountain-Ear*, a small Colorado mountain town weekly newspaper. Consider her knowledge, reliability, tone, and use of facts, opinions, and reasoned judgments to discover her point of view about computers and humans.

COMPUTERS CAN'T TEACH AWARENESS

In a recent discussion of careers, young people were told to master computer skills and math if they wanted to "work for the environment." That stuck in my mind the way the limited concept of outdoor education sometimes sticks. It's OK as far as it goes, but are we going to solve global warming or ozone holes with computers, or just diagnose them that way? Are we going to reverse population growth through mathematical models, or just extrapolate the possibilities?

The key to solutions is awareness of what constitutes a healthy environment. You can't get that awareness staring into a glass tube lit by electricity generated someplace out of sight, out of mind (in our neighborhood by burning coal). You can't feel the complex relationships of air, water, plants and animals. No matter how sophisticated our technology gets, it will never be as intricate as the real thing. Would you like to make love to your computer? They're making great strides in "virtual reality," but. . . .

Holly Near has a line in one of her songs, a song both political and environmental, "love disarms." Being disarmed is part of being aware. Disarmed, we become observers. We enlarge our receptiveness to the planet's needs to balance out our active manipulations of it. Awareness requires that we love wild ecosystems as much as ourselves—that we give them life and soul. That kind of awareness can't be taught by a computer.

Explanation   With the questions she asks and the words she uses, Caile makes it clear from the beginning that she believes it's up to people, not computers, to help the environment. Her passionate tone and primary use of opinions should not necessarily enhance or diminish her point of view.

EXAMPLE   Professors Fuori and Gioia conclude the final chapter in their text *Computers and Information Processing* with the following paragraphs. Consider their knowledge, reliability, tone, and use of facts, opinions, and reasoned judgments to discover their point of view about computers and humans.

COMPUTERS DOWN THE ROAD

Whereas some computer experts believe that computers hold the key to great progress for the human race, others feel that computers will eventually lead to depersonalization, unemployment, an invasion of our privacy, and the nuclear destruction of our planet. While some are moving with the flow and striving to acquire computer knowledge and skills, others are laying back and hoping computer technology will not disrupt their lives too much.

As with any powerful scientific advancement, the computer can be a curse or a blessing. Historically, human beings have never reached a new level of technological advancement and deemed it too dangerous to use. Despite its destructive capabilities, there is little chance that we will ever ban the use of nuclear energy; similarly, it looks as though computers are here to stay. But is it the computer we should fear? Or is it the nature of those who would harness its power for good or evil? As always, it is not the tool but the tool user that must be monitored.

One of the goals of artificial intelligence research is to help us determine how we think, why we interpret as we do, and ultimately, who we are. We humans have been perplexed by our existence since earliest history. By providing us with a clearer understanding of the human mental process, perhaps AI research may eventually lead us to a better understanding of self. As was once said many years ago, "The answer lies within."

Explanation   Fuori and Gioia do say there are two sides of the controversial technology issue. But, with the questions they ask in the second paragraph, and the words they use, they make it clear they believe computers do have a vital role. Their straightforward tone and primary use of opinions should not necessarily enhance or diminish their point of view.

Exercise 3

Indicate whether each sentence is fact, opinion, reasoned judgment, or contains a combination of types of information.

1. [a]In managing the planning process, more and more firms have adopted a management by objectives (MBO) approach. [b]MBO is a system of collaborative goal setting that extends from the top of the organization to the bottom. [c]Under this system, managers meet with each of their subordinates individually to discuss goals. [d]This meeting usually occurs annually and focuses on the coming year. [e]The manager and the subordinate agree on a set of goals for the subordinate. [f]The goals are stated in quantitative terms (for example, "I will decrease turnover in my division by 3 percent") and written down. [g]A year later, the subordinate's performance is evaluated in terms of the extent to which the goals were met. [h]MBO has been shown to be quite effective when applied at all levels of the company. [i]Tenneco, Black & Decker, General Motors, General Foods, and Alcoa have all reported success using MBO. [j]However, MBO involves quite a bit of paperwork and is sometimes used too rigidly. (Griffin & Ebert, *Business*)

2. [a]A major federal program aimed at identifying and cleaning up existing waste sites was initiated by the Comprehensive Environmental Response, Compensation, and Liability Act of 1980, popularly known as Superfund. [b]Through a tax on chemical raw materials, this legislation

provided a fund of 1.6 billion over the period 1980–1985 to identify and clean up sites that posed a threat to groundwater. [c]However, the Environmental Protection Agency's (EPA's) record in administering this program over the first five years was disgraceful. (Nebel, *Environmental Science*)

3. [a]American adults consume an average of 32.0 gallons of beer, 2.5 gallons of wine, and 1.8 gallons of distilled spirits a year (*Statistical Abstract*, 1996). [b]Despite these high rates of consumption, the problems associated with alcohol abuse—chronic inebriation, vagrancy, drunken driving—arouse less interest and concern than the abuse, or even the use, of other drugs. [c]In contrast to other drugs, alcohol is thoroughly integrated into Western culture. [d]It may also be better adapted to our complex lifestyle because, in addition to relieving tension and reducing sexual and aggressive inhibitions, alcohol seems to facilitate interpersonal relations, at least superficially, whereas other drug experiences, even in groups, are often highly private. (Kornblum & Julian, *Social Problems*)

4. [a]Inflation is a perennial problem. [b]We are not likely to repeat in the near future the double-digit inflation numbers of the 1970s and early 1980s, but more modest amounts are very possible. [c]Recent annual rates have been between 2 and 4 percent, a range that is likely to continue. [d]Although these numbers suggest a tame inflationary environment, over long periods of time they can seriously erode the value of your savings. [e]Your investments must earn more that the inflation rate if you hope to grow your wealth in real terms. [f]Unfortunately, many people have been content to leave too much of their money in low-yielding savings accounts that often only match, or fall short of, inflation rates. [g]We hope you won't make that mistake. (Winger & Frasca, *Personal Finance*)

5. [a]A generation ago, the elderly were the ones most likely to be poor. [b]Today, however, the age category at greatest risk of poverty is children, who make up 37.5 percent of the U.S. poor. [c]In 1999, 12.1 million young people (16.9 percent of people under eighteen) were living in poor households. [d]More seriously, 40 percent of these children live in families with incomes no more than half the poverty line ($8,500 or less). (Macionis, *Social Problems*)

Exercise 4

Answer the questions following each selection.

SELECTION 1

Most books about what's wrong with baseball and how to fix it make you feel as if you've been cornered by a drunk at a noisy party. Bob Costas's *Fair Ball: A Fan's Case for Baseball* puts you more in mind of a good conversation during a rainout that makes you forget the game is on hold.

Mr. Costas, who says he is "a 'Bull Durham' guy, not a 'Field of Dreams' guy," makes his points with neat, forceful prose. In arguing persuasively against the current set-up of a divisional winners race plus wild-card race, he writes that "baseball doesn't offer slam-bam moment-to-moment action. It isn't easily enhanced by hype. It draws drama from context." Which is a better way of saying that more playoffs—á la hockey and basketball—detract from the primary appeal of baseball: the long season and the pennant race. . . . (book review by Allen Barra)

1. We can infer that Barra

   a. dislikes Costas's book.

   b. likes Costas's book.

   Please explain what Barra said that leads you to infer your answer.

2. We can infer that Barra

   a. thinks Costas is a good writer.

   b. thinks Costas is a poor writer.

   Please explain what Barra said that leads you to infer your answer.

SELECTION 2

When you annotate a reading selection, you do things such as circle unfamiliar words and define them in the margin, bracket significant sentences or paragraphs and paraphrase them in the margin, and restate the thesis and main ideas in your own words. Rephrasing an idea into your own words makes you think the idea through and process its meaning. Using your own words to annotate is an active notetaking process that requires thinking.

On the other hand, using colored pens to highlight text is a passive notetaking activity. Often, students don't even understand the material they highlight. Whenever they think something may be important, they mark it and promise to go back and read it later. In essence, they just postpone the reading assignment. (adapted from McGrath, *Understanding Diverse Viewpoints*)

1. We can infer that I recommend

   a. annotating more than highlighting.

   b. highlighting more than annotating.

   Please explain what I said that leads you to infer your answer.

2. We can infer that I believe

   a. students learn the same by rephrasing ideas as by highlighting sentences.

   b. students learn more by rephrasing ideas in their own words than by highlighting a sentence.

   Please explain what I said that leads you to infer your answer.

SELECTION 3

There are three forms of communication between people. One is the written form—letters, memos, faxes, e-mails, etc. The second is the verbal form—face-to-face conversations, telephone conversations, voice mail, intercom discussions, video conferencing, etc. The third involves the transmission of attitudes.

The first two forms of communication are so important to the profitable operation of an organization that we tend to think they are the only ones. We forget that we also communicate our attitudes through facial expressions, hand gestures, and other more subtle forms of body language. Sometimes people will greet others with a positive voice, but their body language (negative facial expression) sends a contrasting signal. As the expression claims, sometimes your attitude speaks so loudly that others cannot hear what you say. (Chapman & O'Neil, *Your Attitude Is Showing*)

1. We can infer that Chapman and O'Neil think that

   a. of the three forms of communication, only written and verbal are important.

   b. all three forms of communication are very important.

   Please explain what Chapman and O'Neil said that leads you to infer your answer.

2. We can infer that Chapman and O'Neil think that

   a. educating people about how we communicate our attitudes through facial expressions, hand gestures, and other forms of body language would improve interpersonal communication.

   b. the traditional emphasis on written and verbal skills is all that's needed for good interpersonal communication.

   Please explain what Chapman and O'Neil said that leads you to infer your answer.

SELECTION 4

Spend a few minutes on the road and you'll realize that many beginning drivers lack basic knowledge of driving courtesy, safe driving practices and crash-avoidance techniques. The amount of training most teens receive before they drive is not sufficient considering the dense and intense driving environment many of them will face.

Most teens think "driver's ed" is a joke. In some respects, they're right. Teaching young drivers when to use turn signals and how to parallel park is simply not enough.

Now there is a growing clamor for graduated driver-licensing programs. The concept is to gradually phase in driving privileges for new licensees as they "demonstrate growth in driving skills and responsible operation of motor vehicles." The misguided premise for graduated licensing is that time is a substitute for training. . . . (adapted from Franklin, "Point of View," *USA Today*)

1. We can infer that Franklin believes America's driver's education system

   a. is working fine.

   b. needs changing.

   Please explain what Franklin said that leads you to infer your answer.

2. We can infer that Franklin believes a graduated driver-licensing program

   a. is not a good way to improve the skills of beginning drivers.

   b. is a good way to improve the skills of beginning drivers.

   Please explain what Franklin said that leads you to infer your answer.

Exercise 5

1. Cigarette smoking accelerates artery clogging and greatly increases the risk of death from coronary artery disease, heart attack, and stroke in the adult years. The incidence of cancer, chronic bronchitis, and emphysema also increases. (Greenberg & Dintiman, *Exploring Health*)

   a. What do Greenberg and Dintiman think about smoking?

   b. Do you think they are reliable? Why or why not?

   c. What point of view might a representative of the tobacco industry have?

   d. Assume that you have to write a research paper on the effects of smoking. Why would it be necessary to read more than one source for your research?

2. We are tempted to say that [Elvis] Presley did not evolve with the times, but a careful listening to his recordings from the end of his career would suggest the opposite. Retained in his music were country and blues roots, but the instrumental backing was constantly updated. He used contemporary music where it fit, and his performances made use of modern technology—additional musical resources and contemporary subjects. Although Presley was tied to his background, he changed as his background changed. His last performance in Las Vegas was exciting and filled with energy. (Brown, *The Art of Rock and Roll*)

   a. How does Brown feel about Elvis Presley's music in his last years?

   b. How would you describe Brown's knowledge on this topic?

   c. Who might have a different point of view about Elvis Presley's music in his last years?

3. As long as Americans spend more time watching [TV] than reading, educators must address the need for critical viewing as well as critical reading. If readers are trained to read interpretively, so too must viewers be taught to look critically at TV. And if we succeed with this teaching, we'll have changed the present pattern in which 70 percent of what Americans hear in a political campaign consists of thirty- and sixty-second commercials consisting of half-truths and innuendo. . . .
   As E. B. White noted a half century ago, television is "the test of the modern world." Used correctly, it can inform, entertain, and inspire. Used incorrectly, television will control families and communities, limiting our language, dreams, and achievements. It is our "test" to pass or fail. (Trelease, "Television")

   a. What does Trelease think about our current television viewing habits?

   b. Who might have a different point of view about the effects of television?

   c. What is your point of view about the effects of television?

4. WYSIWYG. Say it again: What you see is what you get. When we looked at Dreamweaver 1.0 (May/98), we affirmed its reputation as the first respectable WYSIWYG Web-authoring package because it got the "what you get" part—the HTML source code. Dreamweaver 2.0's HTML tools are even more powerful, offering precise control over HTML for-

matting and find-and-replace functions that make the bundled BBEdit nearly redundant. In visual mode Dreamweaver 2.0 makes it easier than ever to arrange "what you see" while building interactive Web sites with all the latest Dynamic HTML tricks, like the proverbial bells and whistles of JavaScript and Cascading Style Sheets. (Coucouvanis, "Reviews: Dreamweaver 2.0," *MAC Addict*)

    a. What does Coucouvanis think of Dreamweaver 2.0 Web-authoring software?

    b. Do you think he is reliable? Why or why not?

    c. Who might have a different point of view?

5. New scientific advances promise to multiply future food yields. Biotechnology offers genetically altered crops that can be custom designed to fit the environment, produce bountiful harvests, and resist plant diseases. One bacterial gene eliminates the need for chemicals to kill worms by producing a natural protein that disintegrates the worms' digestive system. Genetically engineered viruses can be used as pesticides. In 1988 scientists mapped the genome of rice—the set of 12 chromosomes that carries all the genetic characteristics of rice. This development could enable geneticists to produce improved strains of rice. Biotechnology can replace chemical pesticides and fertilizers, whose biological or even genetic impact on our own bodies is not fully understood. (Bergman & McKnight, *Introduction to Geography*)

    a. What do Bergman and McKnight think about the impact of biotechnology?

    b. What point of view might a person who prefers health foods or natural foods have?

    c. What point of view might a representative of a pesticide company have?

READING AN EDITORIAL CARTOON

An editorial expresses a point of view in a short, persuasive essay. An editorial cartoon expresses a point of view in using simple text and a single image. Or, as Ranan R. Lurie, former *New York Times* editorial cartoonist says, "A picture shows—A cartoon shows and thinks."

This is why editorial cartoons have been popular vehicles for public criticism and political commentary since the mid-1700s, according to Toby Graham, Special Collections Librarian at the University of Southern Mississippi. They take just seconds to read and decipher, yet they encourage the reader to develop an opinion about someone or something in the news.

Cartoons are a visual medium, but they communicate a point of view very effectively. It seems that the overall nature of sarcasm, satire, and parody inherent in cartoons makes the absurdities or truths more obvious than does written text.

In fact, Pulitzer Prize–winner Paul Conrad views the actual art of his editorial cartoons to be but the vehicle for getting across his ideas. He even goes so far as to say that an editorial cartoon is 90 percent idea, 10 percent drawing.

Strategies for Understanding an Editorial Cartoon

- Determine the topic. What issue is addressed? Did a specific event or issue inspire the cartoon? What is the history of the topic or issue?

- Identify who is portrayed in the cartoon. Are there any real people?

- Identify any symbols used. What do the symbols represent?

- Determine which of these common components is used and why: stereotype, exaggeration, caricature. (A caricature is a drawing that pokes fun at a well-known person by exaggerating his or her physical and facial characteristics.)

- Understand the information and impact of the caption or words in the cartoon. Is the caption in straightforward language, or does it contain features of satire, sarcasm, or irony?

- Identify the cartoonist's point of view. What are the opposing or varying points of view on the issue?

- Clarify the cartoonist's purpose and intended audience. What does he or she want the reader to do or think after reading this cartoon?

EXAMPLE   Pulitzer Prize–winning editorial cartoonist Clay Bennett has been with *The Christian Science Monitor* since 1998. In addition to producing five full-color cartoons each week for *The Christian Science Monitor,* he produces fully animated editorial cartoons for the Internet and draws cartoons for distribution through King Features Syndicate. Use the strategies suggested above to understand Bennett's message.

(The Christian Science Monitor/Clay Bennett)

Explanation   The topic is "endangered species." The symbols are the rhinoceros, an endangered species in Southern Africa; the panda, an endangered species in Western China; the dove of peace, an "endangered species" in the

Middle East. Bennett's point of view is that peace is "in danger" in the Middle East. He wants the reader to think about the fragile Middle East situation.

Read other cartoons in your daily newspaper or log on to these sites:

http://cagle.slate.msn.com/
http://www.claybennett.com/
http://lcweb.loc.gov/rr/print/swann/herblock/cartoon.html
http://www.unitedfeatures.com/ufs/EDITOONS.html

Exercise 6

CLAY BENNETT

This Clay Bennett cartoon first appeared in The Christian Science Monitor.

AN IDEA TO THINK ABOUT

In 1901, the last five lines of the sonnet "The New Colossus" by the U.S. poet Emma Lazarus were inscribed on a bronze plaque at the base of the Statue of Liberty:

> Give me your tired, your poor,
> Your huddled masses yearning to breathe free,
> The wretched refuse of your teeming shore.
> Send these, the homeless, tempest-tossed to me,
> I lift my lamp beside the golden door!

What do you think Lazarus and the people responsible for inscribing the sonnet wanted to communicate?

(The Christian Science Monitor/Clay Bennett)

Exercise 6 Questions

1. What is the topic or issue?
2. Who is portrayed in the cartoon?
3. Identify any symbols and what they represent.
4. How do Bennett's words change the original message?
5. What is Bennett's point of view?
6. What does Bennett want the reader to do or think after reading this cartoon?

Please Remember

Since writers are human, most writing, from classic fairy tales to magazine and newspaper articles to textbooks, to some degree reflects what the author thinks—the author's bias. That does not make the writing good or bad—as long as you identify the author's point of view and factor that into your comprehension of the information.

CHAPTER 7 REVIEW QUESTIONS

1. What is point of view?
2. Why is it important to know an author's expertise?
3. What is the difference between an expert and an advocate?
4. What is tone?
5. How does tone, especially irony, satire, and sarcasm, affect comprehension?
6. Define fact, opinion, and reasoned judgment.
7. Describe your general strategy for reading an editorial cartoon.

Use Your Strategies 1

ROGER ROSENBLATT

Mr. Rosenblatt is an essayist for Time, The New Republic, *and the* NewsHour with Jim Lehrer *on PBS. This essay is from* MM, *where he is a contributing editor.*

AN IDEA TO THINK ABOUT

Have you ever used a typewriter? Do you think there are any advantages to using a typewriter rather than a computer? *As you read,* find out why Rosenblatt "doesn't compute."

WHY I DON'T COMPUTE

Roger Rosenblatt

[1]It says something that I have been able to survive the past 15 years without using a word processor. Forbearing editors have been willing to enter my typewritten pieces into systems for me. Other than that kind accommodation, I have had no contact with that so-called invention for which people like Steve Jobs and Bill Gates have claimed evangelical powers. In my line of "work," I could not get along for a day without the telephone, TV, radio, automobile, and fax. But I shall happily live out my days computer-free.

[2]Fact is, I think that Jobs, Gates, and all the other cyberspace billionaires have bamboozled the world. Not only is a computer slower than a typewriter in the long run, its research function is also faulty; and worst of all, it encourages a society of increasing isolations (though it claims the opposite). What the computer has done is to make a few clever fellows rich.

[3]Slower than a typewriter? Yes, even slower than a Bic ballpoint pen, my principal machine, because a word processor (what a name!) facilitates bad writing by way of fast and easy corrections. When something is wrong with a piece, it is usually all wrong. A writer needs to start from scratch, not to transpose paragraph 19 for 36. Writers need writing to be difficult. An honest writer, looking at a screen full of patched copy, will begin again. He would've gone faster if he'd gone slower.

[4]The research function faulty and inadequate? Of course it is. People use NEXIS, LEXIS, and "SEXIS" to look up all sorts of things, and they think they're doing research. But real research requires happy accidents. A computer offers nowhere near the same capacity for serendipity that a stroll through the stacks of a library offers. It also suggests that we always know what we want to learn. What happens to the meandering dream state necessary for learning? Computers turn dream states into theme parks.

[5]As for encouraging increasing isolations, that's self-evident. I grew up in a world in which the declared enemy of the human mind was mechanization. Science fiction would routinely scare you silly by presenting people becoming machines. (Read *R.U.R.*) Or people would be warned of losing control to machines. (See *2001.*) Computer salesmen want us to join machines, not to beat 'em.

[6]But the deeper isolations occur within those very functions of computer life that hackers praise most lavishly. Take a trip on the Internet and link up with people exactly like yourself. The emerging technologies are simply imposing a new class system on the existing ones. Their overarching context is the ability to use computers at all; if everyone has one, everyone belongs to the same class. But within that class lie thousands of subclasses—from chess players to militia members to nuts of every stripe. What is gained if everybody still hangs out with his or her own kind?

[7]Information, the god of these gizmos, is not only a poor form of learning, it's the dumbest form of communication. Give me a good face-to-face conversation any time, or a bad one. And even good communication

should not be confused with sympathetic social existence. There's still a difference between talking and living.

[8]A magazine once gave me a PC to try to allure me into modern America. I used it as a planter. Don't compare these things with real inventions. A stick with a small ball at one end that dispenses ink from a plastic tube: That's an invention.

Use Your Strategies 1 Questions

1. What is Rosenblatt's purpose?
2. What is his thesis?
3. How does he support and develop his thesis?
4. What is Rosenblatt's point of view on computers?
5. What is his tone?
6. Do you feel Rosenblatt has the knowledge to write this article? Why or why not?
7. Do you feel he is reliable? Why or why not?
8. What are three reasons Rosenblatt won't use computers?
9. What does he believe is the "worst" thing about computers?
10. Generally the word *isolation* means to be alone. What does Rosenblatt mean by the "deeper isolations" in paragraph 6?

Use Your Strategies 2

KURT VONNEGUT

International Paper Company asked author Kurt Vonnegut to help college students understand "How to Write with Style." His critically acclaimed novels include Slaughterhouse-Five, Jailbird, *and* Cat's Cradle.

AN IDEA TO THINK ABOUT

Do you like to read some authors more than others? What makes those authors more enjoyable or easier to understand? *As you read,* find out how Vonnegut suggests you make your writing more enjoyable to read.

HOW TO WRITE WITH STYLE

Kurt Vonnegut

[1]Newspaper reporters and technical writers are trained to reveal almost nothing about themselves in their writings. This makes them freaks in the world of writers, since almost all of the other ink-stained wretches in that world reveal a lot about themselves to readers. We call these revelations, accidental and intentional, elements of style.

[2]They tell us as readers what sort of person it is with whom we are spending time. Does the writer sound ignorant or informed, crooked or honest, humorless or playful? And on and on.

[3]Why should you examine your writing style with the idea of improving it? Do so as a mark of respect for your readers, whatever you're writing. If you scribble your thoughts any which way, your readers will surely feel that you care nothing about them. They will mark you down as an egomaniac or a chowderhead, or worse, they will stop reading you.

[4]The most damning revelation you can make about yourself is that you do not know what is interesting and what is not. Don't you yourself like or dislike writers mainly for what they choose to show you or make you think about? Did you ever admire an empty-headed writer for his or her mastery of the language? No.

[5]So your own winning style must begin with ideas in your head.

FIND A SUBJECT YOU CARE ABOUT.

[6]Find a subject you care about and which you feel others should care about. It is this genuine caring, and not your games with the language, which will be the most compelling and seductive element in your style.

[7]I am not urging you to write a novel—although I would not be sorry if you wrote one, provided you genuinely cared about something. A petition to the mayor about a pothole in front of your house or a love letter to the girl next door will do.

KEEP IT SIMPLE.

[8]As for your use of language: Remember that two great masters, William Shakespeare and James Joyce, wrote sentences which seemed almost childlike when their subjects were most profound. "To be or not to be?" asks Shakespeare's Hamlet. The longest word is three letters long. Joyce, when he was frisky, could put together a sentence as intricate and as glittering as a necklace for Cleopatra, but my favorite sentence in his short story "Eveline" is this one: "She was tired." At that point in the story, no other words could break the heart of a reader as those three words do. Simplicity of language is not only reputable, but perhaps even sacred. Your rule might be this: If a sentence, no matter how excellent, does not illuminate your subject in some new and useful way, scratch it out.

SOUND LIKE YOURSELF.

[9]The writing style which is most natural for you is bound to echo the speech you heard when a child. English was the novelist Joseph Conrad's third language, and much that seems piquant in his use of English was no doubt colored by his first language, which was Polish. And lucky indeed is the writer who has grown up in Ireland, for the English spoken there is so amusing and musical. I myself grew up in Indianapolis, where common speech sounds like a band saw cutting galvanized tin, and employs a vocabulary as unornamental as a monkey wrench.

[10]In some of the more remote hollows of Appalachia, children still grow up hearing songs and locutions of Elizabethan times. Yes, and many Americans grow up hearing a language other than English, or an English dialect a majority of Americans cannot understand.

¹¹All these varieties of speech are beautiful, just as the varieties of butterflies are beautiful. No matter what your first language, you should treasure it all your life. If it happens not to be standard English, and if it shows itself when you write standard English, the result is usually delightful, like a very pretty girl with one eye that is green and one that is blue.

¹²I myself find that I trust my own writing most, and others seem to trust it most, too, when I sound most like a person from Indianapolis, which is what I am. What alternatives do I have? The one most vehemently recommended by teachers has no doubt been pressed on you as well: to write like cultivated Englishmen of a century or more ago.

SAY WHAT YOU MEAN TO SAY.

¹³I used to be exasperated by such teachers, but am no more. I understand now that all those antique essays and stories with which I was to compare my own work were not magnificent for their datedness or foreignness, but for saying precisely what their authors meant them to say. My teachers wished me to write accurately, always selecting the most effective words, and relating the words to one another unambiguously, rigidly, like parts of a machine. The teachers did not want to turn me into an Englishman after all. They hoped that I would become understandable—and therefore understood. And there went my dream of doing with words what Pablo Picasso did with paint or what any number of jazz idols did with music.

¹⁴If I broke all the rules of punctuation, had words mean whatever I wanted them to mean, and strung them together higgledy-piggledy, I would simply not be understood. So you, too, had better avoid Picasso-style or jazz-style writing if you have something worth saying and wish to be understood.

¹⁵Readers want our pages to look very much like pages they have seen before. Why? This is because they themselves have a tough job to do, and they need all the help they can get from us.

FOR REALLY DETAILED ADVICE.

¹⁶For a discussion of literary style in a narrower sense, in a more technical sense, I commend to your attention *The Elements of Style* by William Strunk, Jr., and E. B. White (Macmillan, 1979). E. B. White is, of course, one of the most admirable literary stylists this country has so far produced. ¹⁷You should realize, too, that no one would care how well or badly Mr. White expressed himself if he did not have perfectly enchanting things to say.

Use Your Strategies 2 Questions

1. What is Vonnegut's purpose?
2. What is his thesis?
3. How does he develop and support his thesis?
4. What is his point of view on writing style?
5. What is Vonnegut's tone?
6. In paragraph 11, Vonnegut uses two figurative expressions (similes) to support his main idea. What are they? How do they add to the paragraph?

7. Why does he think his teachers, and your teachers, require students to read all those "antique essays and stories"?

8. What does he believe would happen if authors had words mean whatever they wanted and broke the rules of punctuation and grammar?

9. According to Vonnegut, readers "have a tough job to do." Explain what he means.

Use Your Strategies 3

MIKE ROYKO

The funny, acerbic syndicated columnist Mike Royko took on any and all social and political issues in his column that appeared in hundreds of newspapers daily. This selection was reprinted in a collection of his columns titled Dr. Kookie, You're Right.

AN IDEA TO THINK ABOUT

If an ad agency offered you a week's pay to film a short commercial for a fruit juice you drank every day, would you do it? If that same agency offered you a week's pay to film a short commercial for a juice drink you were allergic to and never drank, would you do it? *As you read,* see how Royko feels about commercial endorsements.

ENDORSEMENTS JUST A SHELL GAME

Mike Royko

¹The man from an advertising agency had an unusual proposition.

²His agency does the TV commercials for a well-known chain of Mexican restaurants in Chicago.

³"You may have seen our commercials," he said. "They include a cameo appearance by Lee Smith and Leon Durham of the Cubs. It shows them crunching into a tortilla."

⁴No, I somehow missed seeing that.

⁵"Well, anyway, we'd like to have you in a commercial."

⁶Doing what?

⁷"Crunching into a tortilla."

⁸I thought tortillas were soft. I may be wrong, but I don't think you can crunch into a tortilla. Maybe you mean a taco.

⁹"Well, you'd be biting into some kind of Mexican food."

¹⁰What else would I have to do?

¹¹"That's it. It would be a cameo appearance. You'd be seen for about four seconds. You wouldn't have to say anything."

¹²I'd just bite into a piece of Mexican food?

[13]"Right. For a fee, of course."

[14]How big a fee?

[15]He named a figure. It was not a king's ransom, but it was more than walking-around money.

[16]"It would take about forty-five minutes to film," he said.

[17]Amazing. In my first newspaper job almost thirty years ago, I had to work twelve weeks to earn the figure he had mentioned.

[18]It was a small, twice-a-week paper, and I was the only police reporter, the only sports reporter, the only investigative reporter and the assistant political writer, and on Saturday I would edit the stories going into the entertainment page. The publisher believed in a day's work for an hour's pay.

[19]Now I could make the same amount just for spending forty-five minutes biting into a taco in front of a TV camera.

[20]And when I was in the military, it would have taken eight monthly paychecks to equal this one taco-crunching fee. Of course, I also got a bunk and meals and could attend free VD lectures.

[21]"Well, what do you think?" he asked.

[22]I told him I would think about it and get back to him.

[23]So I asked Slats Grobnik, who has sound judgment, what he thought of the deal.

[24]"That's a lot of money just to bite a taco on TV. For that kind of scratch, I'd bite a dog. Grab the deal."

[25]But there is a question of ethics.

[26]"Ethics? What's the ethics in biting a taco? Millions of people bite tacos every day. Mexicans have been biting them for hundreds of years. Are you saying that Mexicans are unethical? Careful, some of my best friends are Mexicans."

[27]No, I'm not saying that at all. I like Mexicans, though I'm opposed to bullfighting.

[28]"Then what's unethical?"

[29]The truth is, I can't stand tacos.

[30]"What has that got to do with it? I can't stand work, but I do it for the money."

[31]It has everything to do with it. If I go on TV and bite into a taco, won't I be endorsing that taco?

[32]"So what? You've endorsed politicians and I've never met a politician that I liked better than a taco."

[33]But endorsing a taco I didn't like would be dishonest.

[34]"Hey, that's the American way. Turn on your TV and look at all the people who endorse junk. Do you think they really believe what they're saying?"

[35]Then it's wrong. Nobody should endorse a taco if they don't like a taco.

[36]"Then tell them you'll bite something else. A tortilla or an enchilada."

[37]But I don't like them either. The truth is, I can't stand most Mexican food. The only thing I really like is the salt on the edge of a margarita glass. Oh, and I do like tamales.

[38]"Good, then bite a tamale."

[39]No, because the only tamales I like are the kind that used to be sold by the little Greeks who had hot dog pushcarts on the streets. They were factory-produced tamales about the size and weight of a lead pipe. But I don't think anybody would want me to do a TV commercial for hot dog stand tamales.

[40]"Can't you just bite the taco and spit it out when the camera is turned off?"

[41]That would be a sham. Besides, even if I liked tacos or tortillas, what does it matter? Why should somebody eat in a restaurant because they see me biting into that restaurant's taco? Am I a taco expert? What are my credentials to tell millions of people what taco they should eat? I'm not even Mexican.

[42]"Well, you're a sucker to turn it down. Why, it's almost un-American. Do you think that in Russia any newsman would ever have an opportunity to make that much money by biting into a pirogi?"

[43]That may be so. But maybe someday a food product will come along that I can lend my name to, something I can truly believe in.

[44]"I doubt it. Not unless they start letting taverns advertise shots and beers on TV."

Use Your Strategies 3 Questions

1. Explain these phrases or figures of speech:
   a. shell game (title)
   b. cameo appearance (¶3)
   c. king's ransom (¶15)
   d. walking-around money (¶15)
   e. that kind of scratch (¶24)
2. What is Royko's purpose?
3. What is his thesis?
4. How does Royko's thesis match or contradict your concept of reliability? Please explain.
5. What is his tone?
6. What did the advertising agency want Royko to do?
7. Do you think Royko made the commercial? Why or why not?
8. How much of a factor do you think money was in Royko's decision?
9. If you were in Royko's position, what would you have decided to do? Why?
10. This type of situation is often referred to as a moral dilemma. Have you ever had a moral dilemma? How did you resolve the dilemma?

Use Your Strategies 4

JOHN J. MACIONIS

Dr. Macionis is professor of sociology at Kenyon College, Gambier, Ohio. In addition to his teaching, he is known for his twenty years of work as a popular textbook author. This excerpt is from Chapter 22, "Population, Urbanization, and Environment" in his introductory text Sociology, *ninth edition.*

AN IDEA TO THINK ABOUT

Do you think the people in your town could eventually use up your supply of a "resource" like water or energy? Do you think we should do anything "today" to make sure it doesn't happen "tomorrow"? *As you read,* find out what Macionis thinks.

LOOKING AHEAD: TOWARD A SUSTAINABLE WORLD

John J. Macionis

[1]The demographic analysis presented in this chapter points to some disturbing trends. We see first that Earth's population has reached record levels because birth rates remain high in poor nations and death rates have fallen just about everywhere. Lowering fertility will remain a pressing problem throughout this century. Even with some recent decline in population increase, the nightmare Thomas Malthus described is still a real possibility. (More than two centuries ago Malthus predicted that population would outstrip the Earth's resources and plunge humanity into war and suffering.)

[2]Furthermore, population growth remains greatest in the poorest countries of the world, those without the means to support their present populations, much less their future ones. Supporting 77 million additional people on our planet each year—almost 74 million of whom are in low-income societies—will require a global commitment to provide not only food but housing, schools, and employment. The well being of the entire world may ultimately depend on resolving the economic and social problems of poor, overly populated countries and bridging the widening gulf between "have" and "have-not" societies.

[3]Urbanization, too, is continuing, especially in poor countries. Throughout human history, people have sought out cities with the hope of finding a better life. But the sheer numbers of people who live in the emerging global supercities—Mexico City, São Paulo (Brazil), Kinshasa (Democratic Republic of the Congo), Bombay (India), and Manila (the Philippines)—have created urban problems on a massive scale.

[4]Throughout the entire world, humanity is facing a serious environmental challenge. Part of this problem is population increase, which is greatest in poor societies. But another part of the problem is the high levels of consumption typical of rich nations such as our own. By increasing the planet's environmental deficit, our present way of life is borrowing against the well being of our children and their children. Globally, members of rich societies, who currently consume so much of the Earth's resources, are mortgaging the future security of the poor countries of the world.

[5]The answer, in principle, is to form an **ecologically sustainable culture,** *a way of life that meets the needs of the present generation without threatening the environmental legacy of future generations.* Sustainable living depends on three strategies.

[6]First, the world needs to bring population growth under control. The current population of more than 6 billion is already straining the natural environment. Clearly, the higher the world's population climbs, the more difficult environmental problems will become. Even if the recent slowing of population growth continues, the world will have 8 billion people by 2050. Few analysts think that the Earth can support this many people; most argue that we must hold the line at about 7 billion, and some argue that we must decrease population in the coming decades (Smail, 1997).

[7]A second strategy is conservation of finite resources. This means meeting our needs with a responsible eye toward the future by using resources efficiently, seeking alternative sources of energy, and, in some cases, learning to live with less.

[8]A third strategy is reducing waste. Whenever possible, simply using less is the best solution. But recycling programs also are part of the answer.

[9]In the end, making all these strategies work depends on a more basic change in the way we think about ourselves and our world. Our egocentric outlook sets our own interests as standards for how to live, but a sustainable environment demands an ecocentric outlook that helps us see how the present is tied to the future and why everyone must work together. Most nations in the southern half of the world are underdeveloped, unable to meet the basic needs of their people. At the same time, most countries in the northern half of the world are overdeveloped, using more resources than the Earth can sustain over time. Changes needed to create a sustainable ecosystem will not come easily. But the cost of not responding to the growing environmental deficit will certainly be greater (Humphrey & Buttel, 1982; Burke, 1984; Kellert & Bormann, 1991; Brown et al., 1993; Population Action International, 2000).

[10]In closing, consider that the great dinosaurs dominated this planet for some 160 million years and then perished forever. Humanity is far younger, having existed for a mere 250,000 years. Compared to the dimwitted dinosaurs, our species has the gift of great intelligence. But how will we use this ability? What are the chances that our species will continue to flourish 160 million years—or even 1,000 years—from now? The shape of tomorrow's world depends on the choices we make today.

Use Your Strategies 4 Questions

1. What is Macionis's purpose(s)?
2. What is his thesis?
3. What is his point of view toward a "sustainable world"?
4. How does his point of view relate to his thesis?
5. Macionis says, "Sustainable living depends on three strategies." List them.
6. What needs to happen to make all these strategies work?
7. Compare an egocentric outlook and an ecocentric outlook.
8. Explain what Macionis means in paragraph 9 when he says, "But the cost of not responding to the growing environmental deficit will certainly be greater."

9. Who does Macionis believe is responsible for our world?
10. Who do you think might have a different point of view? Please explain.

REFLECT AND CONNECT

A. Make a list of the following:

Things you have bought recently (like shoes, jeans, cereal, a car)

Things you have done recently (such as gone to a movie, drunk a soft drink, voted)

Views you have adopted (such as for or against abortion, nuclear energy, affirmative action)

Can you identify who or what you saw or read that influenced you to buy, do, or believe? Did you realize you were being influenced? What types of things will you watch for in the future?

B. In "Looking Ahead: Toward A Sustainable World," page 218–219 , Dr. Macionis clearly states his view on the need to form an ecologically sustainable culture. Do you think it is acceptable for textbook authors to include their point of view in a textbook? Why or why not?

LOG ON TO THE WEB

These Web sites contain book reviews or links to book reviews. Log on to one of these sites or use a search engine to locate two reviews (of the same book, if possible).

http://www.bookwire.com/bbr/bbr-home.html
http://www.suntimes.com/index/kisor.html
http://www.anatomy.usyd.edu.au/danny/book-reviews/
http://dir.yahoo.com/Arts/Humanities/Literature/Reviews/

A. Print out the two reviews.
B. For each review write
    1. the reviewer's name and whether you believe he or she is reliable, including your reasoning;
    2. the reviewer's point of view;
    3. the reviewer's tone.
C. Attach your answers to the printouts and turn them in to your professor.

REFERENCES

Booth, W. C. (1978). "The Pleasures and Pitfalls of Irony: Or, Why Don't You Say What You Mean?" In D. M. Burks (Ed.), *Rhetoric, Philosophy, and Literature: An Exploration* (pp. 1–13). West Lafayette, IN: Purdue University Press.

Caywood, Carolyn, (1998). "The Facts of the Matter." *School Library Journal,* 44(4).

Foss, K. A., & S. W. Littlejohn. (1986). "The Day After: Rhetorical Vision in an Ironic Frame." *Critical Studies in Mass Communication,* 3, 316–336.

"Humor in Literature from Swift to The Simpsons," (2003). *Literary Cavalcade,* 55(4).

Holman, C. H. (1980). *Handbook to Literature.* Indianapolis, IN: Bobbs Merrill.

Novelli, Joan. (1999a). "Focus on point of view." *Instructor,* 108(7).

Novelli, Joan, (1999b). "Fact Vs. Opinion." *Instructor-Intermediate,* 108(6).

Shugart, Helene A. (1999). "Postmodern Irony As Subversive Rhetorical Strategy." *Western Journal of Communication,* 63(4).

Welker, William A. (1999). "The Critics Procedure." *Journal of Adolescent & Adult Literacy,* 43(2).

Winner, E., J. Levy, J. Kaplan, & E. Rosenblatt. (1988). "Children's Understanding of Nonliteral Language." In H. Gardner and D. Perkins (Eds.), *Art, Mind, and Education: Research from Project Zero.* Urbana: University of Illinois Press.

read-ing (red´in) *adj.* **1** inclined to read or study **2**
reading n. **1** the act or practice person who re
of books **2** a public entertainm   which literar
aloud **3** the extent to which a   has read **4**
meant to be read **5** the amoun   asured as by a
thermometer **6** the form of a specified word, sente

CHAPTER
8

Organizing the Information You Need

*I can give you a six-word formula for success: Think things through—
then follow through.*

Edward Rickenbacker

AN IDEA TO THINK ABOUT

We often hear the phrase, "I've got to get organized!" But what exactly does "getting organized" mean, and what do people hope to accomplish? The dictionary says you organize something by "systematically arranging a collection of interdependent parts with relation to the whole." In other words, you introduce an overall order to things.

You organize, or bring order to things, because it helps your memory and allows you to complete tasks more efficiently. When you're organized, you're more likely to be successful at work and at home.

For example, you prioritize a list of tasks you have to get done, develop a system for remembering client's names, arrange a group of details in sequential order, or, like Luann's dad in this cartoon, you develop a system to organize items for storage.

LUANN

(Copyright ©2002 GEC, Inc., Distributed by United Feature Syndicate, Inc.)

However, there is no one best way to organize all objects, activities, and information for all people. And, if the method of organization is not logical and meaningful to *you,* you will wind up like Luann and her family—confused.

(Copyright ©2002 GEC, Inc., Distributed by United Feature Syndicate, Inc.)

As you develop your plan for this chapter, consider how you organize various tasks and information. Do you consciously spend part of each day "getting organized," or do you unconsciously order things? When you've gathered information from several sources, how do you put it together? Do you have different organizational strategies for different kinds of tasks and different kinds of information? Does anyone ever say they wish you were better organized? What do you think they mean?

CHAPTER 8 AT A GLANCE

CHAPTER FOCUS

In everyday life, you keep track of a variety of information—tax records, baseball cards, recipes, mailing lists, appointments. Since there isn't just one way to organize and store all information, you consider your purpose and the type of information. Then, you design an appropriate organizational strategy: a way to sort, organize, and store the information so you can easily find and use it when you want it. For example, you might organize tax receipts by deduction category, recipes by meal course, mailing lists alphabetically by last name, and appointments sequentially by date.

In academic life, you also have to keep track of a variety of information within a single text and across texts, supplemental readings, and lecture and study group notes.

And, just as you do with everyday information, you start by clarifying your purpose and the type of information you need to know—thesis, main ideas, major details, minor details. Then, you design a strategy for organizing and storing it so you can access and use it.

Common strategies include annotating, creating a **graphic organizer**, and summarizing.

In some situations with some text you may need to use multiple strategies. For example, Bean, Singer, Sorter, and Frasee (1986) reported that comprehension was enhanced when students used graphic organizers in combination with other strategies such as summarizing.

ANNOTATE

Annotate means to write brief, useful notes in your own words in the margins of your text. Annotating is an effective strategy because it requires you to be an active reader; to think about and restate the author's words and ideas. In addition, since you must fit your notes legibly into the text's margins, annotating encourages you to carefully sift and sort ideas. Therefore, when it comes time to review, you have the information you need in concise, meaningful groupings.

Annotating your text is very different than marking text with a highlighter or underlining. This is because highlighting and underlining encourage you to passively mark the author's words without regard to the type or level of information. Therefore, you often wind up with too much information marked, and review is difficult.

The more clear and appropriate your annotations—the more effectively you have identified the ideas and concepts that are important to your purpose—the more organized and useful the annotations will be when you need them for your review.

Although how you annotate a section of text varies with your purpose and the type of information, typically you follow these steps:

Step 1: Read the section of text and clarify what you need to know.

Step 2: Reread the portion you need to annotate.

Step 3: Write the thesis and/or main ideas in your own words.

Step 4: Mark the other information you need to know, such as key words, major details, and examples. In addition to restating information in the margins, common symbols you might use include **T** for *thesis*; **MI** for *main idea;* **EX** for *example;* **S** for *summary;* **DEF** for *definition;* **1, 2, 3** for *major points;* **F** for *fact;* **O** for *opinion;* **?** for *items to be clarified,* and ***** for *important concepts.* Underline judiciously.

Step 5: Note relationships and structures such as cause/effect, comparison/contrast.

Step 6: Restate information from graphics.

Step 7: Tag confusing ideas you need to clarify.

Step 8: Review your annotations. Is all the information you need noted? Is any unimportant information noted that you should erase? Is everything clear?

EXAMPLE In this paragraph from Grassian's *Moral Reasoning* text, I need to remember the main idea and the five definitions he uses to develop and support the idea. I've used notations that make sense to me; yours would be similar, but not exactly the same.

MI: term euthanasia is used to mean many things

original

today

1 easy, painless death

2 a Doc reducing pain of dying

3 mercy killing

4 causing a merciful, painless death

5 giving lethal drug to ease painful death

The concept of euthanasia is used today with varying meanings. In its original Greek meaning, "euthanasia" meant no more than an easy and painless death (eu = well; thanatos = death) and was later extended to refer to the work of a physician in alleviating as far as possible the suffering of dying. Today, however, "euthanasia" is often used synonymously with "mercy killing" and as such entails the bringing about of death. The *American Heritage Dictionary* (1975) defines "euthanasia" as "the action of inducing the painless death of a person for reasons assumed to be merciful." As this definition demonstrates, central to our current concept of euthanasia is the idea that such an action be motivated by a desire to be merciful to or to do good to the recipient. As such, when most people are asked to think of a case of euthanasia, they imagine a person who is dying of a painful terminal illness, such as cancer, and is given some lethal drug or injection that is meant to "put him out of his misery."

Explanation These annotations organize the information I need to know: the main idea (term euthanasia is used to mean many things) and five definitions of the word from the original Greek meaning to today's more common meaning.

EXAMPLE In this paragraph from Lapp, Flood, and Farnan's *Content Area Reading and Learning,* I need to remember the main idea and the three major examples they use to develop and support their idea.

MI: many kinds of life exist in glaciers

EX:
• fish
• ice worms
• flowers

Glaciers, despite their barren, stationary appearance, support many kinds of life. Fish thrive in the rivers of ice melt that flow underneath. Ice worms tunnel through the surface and eat pollen that blows in from nearby forests. Flowers sometimes bloom in the dust that collects on the edges. Some of these ice flowers grow as high as four feet.

Explanation These annotations organize the information I need to know: the main idea (many kinds of life exist in glaciers) and three examples (fish, ice worms, and flowers).

EXAMPLE In this paragraph from Macionis's *Sociology* text, I need to remember the main idea and the major details.

Surveys good for:
1: studying what can't be seen
2: studying relationships among variables (like experiments)
3: descriptive research

A survey is a widely used research method in which subjects respond to a series of items or questions in a questionnaire or an interview. Surveys are particularly suited to studying what cannot be observed directly, such as political attitudes, religious beliefs, or the private lives of couples. Like experiments, surveys can be used to investigate the relationship among variables. They are also useful for descriptive research, in which subject responses help a sociologist to describe a social setting, such as an urban neighborhood or gambling casino.

MI: a survey is a widely used research technique where people answer questions

Explanation   These annotations organize the information I need to know: the main idea (a survey is a widely used research technique where people answer questions) and the three major details used to develop and support the idea: surveys are good for studying what can't be seen; relationships among variables, like experiments; and descriptive research.

Exercise 1   Annotating Text

As you read, assume you are preparing to answer an essay question about how to read history effectively. Annotate it only after you have read and thought about the material and have a clear understanding of what you need to know.

ROBERT WEISS

This excerpt from the essay "Writing about History" by noted historian and author Dr. Robert Weiss provides fundamental principles for reading historical reports and essays. It is reprinted from Unger's These United States, *concise edition.*

READING HISTORY

Robert Weiss

An understanding of the fundamentals of historical writing will make the student of history a more discerning and selective reader. Although no two historical works are identical, most contain the same basic elements and can be approached in a similar manner by the reader. When reading a historical monograph, concentrate on . . . two basic issues: . . . facts and interpretation.

INTERPRETATION

The first question the reader should ask is: What is the author's argument? What is his theme, his interpretation, his thesis? A theme is not the same as a topic. An author may select the Civil War as a topic, but he then must propose a particular theme or argument regarding some aspect of the war. (The most common, not surprisingly, is why the war occurred.)

Discovering the author's theme is usually easy enough because most writers state their arguments clearly in the preface to their book. Students often make the crucial error of skimming over the preface—if they read it at all—and then moving on to the "meat" of the book. Since the preface indicates the manner in which the author has used his data to develop his arguments, students who ignore it often find themselves overwhelmed with details without understanding what the author is attempting to say. This error should be avoided always.

The more history you read, the more you will appreciate the diversity of opinions and approaches among historians. While each author offers a unique perspective, historical works fall into general categories, or "schools," depending on their thesis and when they were published. The study of the manner in which different historians approach their subjects is referred to as historiography. Every historical subject has a historiography, sometimes limited, sometimes extensive. As in the other sciences, new schools of thought supplant existing ones, offering new insights and challenging accepted theories. Below are excerpts from two monographs dealing with the American Revolution. As you read them, note the contrast in the underlying arguments.

1. "Despite its precedent-setting character, however, the American revolt is noteworthy because it made no serious interruption in the smooth flow of American development. Both in intention and in fact, the American Revolution conserved the past rather than repudiated it. And in preserving the colonial experience, the men of the first quarter century of the Republic's history set the scenery and wrote the script for the drama of American politics for years to come."*

2. "The stream of revolution, once started, could not be confined within narrow banks, but spread abroad upon the land. Many economic desires, many social aspirations were set free by the political struggle, many aspects of colonial society profoundly altered by the forces thus set loose. The relations of social classes to each other, the institution of slavery, the system of landholding, of business, the forms and spirit of the intellectual and religious life, all felt the transforming hand of revolution, all emerged from under it in shapes advanced many degrees nearer to those we know."†

What you have just read is nothing less than two conflicting theories of the fundamental nature of the American Revolution. Professor Jameson portrays the Revolution as a catalyst for major social, economic, and political

---

*Carl N. Degler, *Out of Our Past*, rev. ed. (New York: Harper and Row, Harper Colophon Books, 1970), p. 73.

†J. Franklin Jameson, *The American Revolution Considered as a Social Movement* (Boston: Beacon Press, 1956), p. 9.

change, while Professor Degler views it primarily as a war for independence that conserved, rather than transformed, colonial institutions. The existence of such divergent opinions makes it imperative that the reader be aware of the argument of every book and read a variety of books and articles to get different perspectives on a subject.

All historical works contain biases of some sort, but a historical bias is not in itself bad or negative. As long as history books are composed by human beings, they will reflect the perspectives of their authors. This need not diminish the quality of historical writing if historians remain faithful to the facts. Some historians, however, have such strong biases that they distort the evidence to make it fit their preconceived notions. This type of history writing (which is the exception rather than the rule) is of limited value, but when properly treated can contribute to the accumulation of knowledge by providing new insights and challenging the values—and creative abilities—of other historians.

EVIDENCE

Once you are aware of the author's central argument, you can concentrate on his use of evidence—the "facts"—that buttress that argument. There are several types of questions that you should keep in mind as you progress through a book. What types of evidence does the author use? Is his evidence convincing? Which sources does he rely on, and what additional sources might he have consulted? One strategy you might adopt is to imagine that you are writing the monograph. Where would you go for information? What would you look at? Then ask yourself: Did the author consult these sources? Obviously no writer can examine everything. A good historical work, however, offers convincing data extracted from a comprehensive collection of materials.

As you begin to ask these questions, you will develop the skill of critical reading. Used in this sense the word critical does not mean reading to discern what is wrong with the narrative. Rather, it refers to analytic reading, assessing the strengths and weaknesses of the monograph, and determining whether the argument ultimately works. All historical works should be approached with a critical—but open—mind.

One important point to remember is that you need not accept or reject every aspect of a historical monograph. In fact, you most likely will accord a "mixed review" to most of the books you read. You may accept the author's argument but find his evidence inadequate, or you may be impressed by his data but draw different conclusions from it. You may find some chapters tightly argued, but others unconvincing. Even if you like a particular book, almost inevitably you will have some comments, criticisms, or suggestions.

Exercise 2 **Annotating Text**

In Chapter 5, Use Your Strategies 3, pages 146–150you identified Macionis's purpose and thesis. Now, annotate the excerpt in preparation for a test that will have multiple-choice and short-answer questions on the content.

JOHN MACIONIS

Dr. Macionis, is professor of sociology at Kenyon College, Gambier, Ohio. This two-page excerpt is from Chapter 9, "Alcohol and Other Drugs," in his newest text, Social Problems.

ALCOHOL AND OTHER DRUGS

John Macionis

Like tens of thousands of other people in the United States, Jennifer Smith is a drug addict. To help understand stories like Jennifer's, this chapter explains what drugs are, what they do to the people who abuse them, and how society defines and responds to the drug problem. We begin with a basic definition.

WHAT IS A DRUG?

Broadly defined, a **drug** is *any chemical substance—other than food or water—that affects the mind or body* (Goldstein, 1994). For thousands of years, people have known that various substances cause changes in the human body. In fact, most people give little thought to the drugs they take, from the aspirin that cases a headache to a morning cup of coffee to help wake up.

But most people in the United States also think that certain drugs—like crank, described in the opening to this chapter—are a serious social problem (NORC, 1999:97). This fact raises the question of when and why people come to define particular drugs as good or as harmful.

Drugs and Culture

How people view a particular drug varies from society to society. Europeans, for example, have enjoyed drinking alcohol for thousands of years. But when Native Americans were introduced to wine and liquor by European colonists five centuries ago, they had no customs to guide its use. As a result, many native peoples fell into drunken stupors, causing tribal leaders to declare alcohol a serious problem (Mancall, 1995; Unrau, 1996).

For centuries, however, many Native American peoples had been using peyote—which alters human consciousness—as part of their religious rituals. They then shared this drug with the Europeans, many of whom became terrified by the hallucinations it produces. Europeans soon pronounced peyote a dangerous drug.

Such diverse definitions of drugs continue today. Coca—the plant used to make cocaine—is grown legally in the South American nations of Bolivia, Peru, and Colombia, as it has been for thousands of years. Indeed, many local farmers chew the plant as they work, to give them a "lift." But officials in the United States have passed laws banning the growing of coca as well as the sale or possession of cocaine. Indeed, in the United

States, most people view this drug as a dangerous cause of violence and crime (Léons & Sanabria, 1997).

Drugs and Social Diversity

We find the same varied definitions of drugs if we look back at U.S. history. A century ago, almost no one in the United States or Europe was aware of a "cocaine problem." On the contrary, famous people like Sigmund Freud used cocaine openly, and anyone could enjoy a popular new "brain tonic" called Coca-Cola, which included cocaine as one of its ingredients (Inciardi, 1996; Léons & Sanabria, 1997).

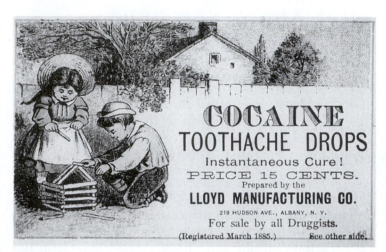

Whether a society defines a substance as a "useful medication" or a "dangerous drug" varies over time. It would surprise many people to learn that, a century ago, cocaine was an ingredient in a number of readily available products, such as this remedy for toothaches.

When and why did public opinion about cocaine change? Some scholars suggest that attitudes about drugs have much to do with attitudes about racial and ethnic minorities. Especially across the South a century ago, many white people feared that cocaine would encourage African Americans to break strict racial codes of conduct and perhaps even become violent toward whites. Such concerns helped push the Coca-Cola company to remove cocaine from its formula in 1903. Soon after, states began to pass laws banning this drug (Goode, 1993; Bertram et al., 1996).

Immigration, too, figured into changing views of drugs. As immigrants came to the United States in ever-increasing numbers during the nineteenth century, they brought not only their dreams but their favored drugs. In the 1850s, for example, many Chinese immigrants in California smoked opium (a practice they had picked up from the British). Anti-Chinese feelings prompted eleven Western states to ban opium, although, elsewhere, opiates were readily available, even through the Sears Roebuck mail-order catalogue.

As immigration increased, the U.S. Congress passed the 1914 Harrison Act, which restricted the sale of many drugs, including heroin and cocaine. Then, in 1919, the law stated that even doctors could no longer write prescriptions for these drugs. But, by 1920, the nation's attention had turned to a new controversy over a much more widely used drug—alcohol.

Alcohol An Important (and Controversial) Drug

Alcohol is one of the most widely used drugs in the United States, with more than 55 percent of the adult population reporting regular drinking of some alcoholic beverage (U.S. Department of Health and Human Services,

2000). This popularity is nothing new: From the time of the first European colonies in the Americas, people enjoyed alcoholic drinks, and few thought of alcohol as a problem. But, as the tide of immigration rose during the nineteenth century, public opinion began to turn against alcohol. Why? Many people held stereotypes that linked the Germans with beer, the Irish with whiskey, and the Italians with wine. In short, they concluded, a million immigrants entering the country each year was bad enough, but immigrants drinking alcohol added up to a serious social problem (Pleck, 1987; Unrau, 1996).

As opposition to immigration increased . . ., so did the strength of the Temperance Movement, a national organization seeking to ban alcohol. In 1920, the movement succeeded in pushing Congress to pass the Eighteenth Amendment to the Constitution, which outlawed the manufacture and sale of alcohol across the country.

Given people's desire to drink, no one was surprised that Prohibition did not get rid of alcohol. But it did drive up prices. With so much money to be made in illegal sales, many people began smuggling liquor from Canada or distilling it themselves. In the rural South, for example, poor mountain people made "moonshine" in local stills. In the urban North, notorious gangsters like Al Capone made fortunes smuggling and distributing liquor to "speakeasy" nightclubs.

Prohibition gave organized crime more power and money than ever before. Many people, therefore, came to see Prohibition not as a solution but as a problem itself. In 1933, Congress repealed the Eighteenth Amendment, bringing the "Great Experiment" to an end.

THE EXTENT OF DRUG USE

What about today? What is the extent of drug use? The answer, of course, depends on which drugs one is talking about. If we define drugs in a broad way—to include substances like aspirin and caffeine—almost everyone is a "user." Moreover, parents give antibiotics to infants and many also give Ritalin to overactive school children; college students take appetite suppressants to control their weight; and adults reach for antidepressants, tranquilizers, and even pills to restore sexual functioning. In short, most people in the United States look to drugs to go to sleep, to wake up, to relax, or to ease pain.

With such a widespread reliance on chemicals, we might well describe our way of life as a "drug culture." Even so, most people do not define this kind of drug use as a problem, simply because it is so routine. On the contrary, most people define the drug problem as the use of *illegal* drugs.

CREATE A GRAPHIC

Another way to organize the information you need is in a graphic or picture format. You can write it on paper in a way that shows the relationships between and among the various ideas and details.

Two general types of graphic organizers are **informal outlines** and **information maps**. **Graphic organizers** such as these are especially effective when you are a visual learner and you need to order several pieces of information of different levels of importance.

Constructing a graphic organizer as a post-reading activity allows you to view the ideas, words, and concepts you need in an orderly pattern. Because graphic organizers help readers make meaningful connections, they facilitate comprehension and retention of new text (Flood & Lapp, 1988; Heimlich & Pittelman, 1986; Hawk, 1986).

Although graphic organizers can also be used as prereading tools—in fact, many professors distribute or post blank organizers for you to complete as you read a chapter or listen to a lecture—research on graphic organizers by Alvermann and Boothby (1986) suggests that comprehension is increased when the graphics are at least partially constructed by students as a during-reading or post-reading activity.

To create an effective graphic organizer, follow these steps:

Step 1: Clarify what you need to know and reread the portion you need to organize.

Step 2: Write the thesis or main idea in your own words in the "prime" location in your graphic.

Step 3: Arrange the other information you need in the way that best illustrates the relationships between and among ideas.

Step 4: Review your graphic. Is any important information missing? Is any unimportant information included that you can delete? Are the relationships between and among the information correct and clear?

Informal Outline

When you create a formal **outline**, you must follow strict rules of convention such as designating various levels of information with the appropriate Roman numerals, capital letters, Arabic numbers, and lowercase letters. However, when you create an informal outline, you are not bound by those rules. In an informal outline, you simply want to create a picture of the relationships among ideas by using differing amounts of indentation, or space, at the start of each line.

To create an informal outline, identify the thesis, main idea(s), and major and minor details you need to know. Then, write each piece of information indented under the information it supports and explains.

For example, if you were creating an informal outline of a paragraph, it might look like this:

Main Idea (of whole paragraph)
    Major Detail
    Major Detail
        Minor Detail
    Major Detail

If you were creating an informal outline of a multiparagraph selection, it might look like this:

Thesis (of the whole selection)
    Main Idea (of first paragraph)
        Major Detail
           Minor Detail
    Main Idea (of second paragraph)
        Major Detail
        Major Detail
           Minor Detail
           Minor Detail
        Major Detail

EXAMPLE   If you needed to remember the main idea and the five definitions in Grassian's paragraph on euthanasia, your informal outline might look like this:

The term euthanasia is used to mean many things.
    an easy and painless death (original)
    a doctor easing the suffering of dying
    mercy killing
    causing a merciful, painless death
    giving a lethal drug to ease painful death (common today)

EXAMPLE   If you needed to remember the main idea and the three examples in Lapp, Flood, and Farnan's paragraph on glaciers, your outline might look like this:

Many kinds of life exist in glaciers.
    fish
    ice worms
    flowers

EXAMPLE   Reread Macionis's paragraph on surveys.

A survey is a widely used research method in which subjects respond to a series of items or questions in a questionnaire or an interview. Surveys are particularly suited to studying what cannot be observed directly, such as political attitudes, religious beliefs, or the private lives of couples. Like experiments, surveys can be used to investigate the relationship among variables. They are also useful for descriptive research, in which subject responses help a sociologist to describe a social setting, such as an urban neighborhood or gambling casino.

Now, assume you need to remember all the information, including the minor details, and complete this informal outline.

A survey is a widely used research technique where people answer questions.

    Good for studying what can't be seen

        Examples: political attitudes, religious beliefs, or private lives

    Good for studying relationships among variables (like experiments)

_____

_____

As you see, the information in an informal outline is the same as, or at least very similar to, the information in that paragraph's annotations—only the method of organization changes.

Information Maps

Another graphic, or visual, way you can organize information is to map it. Just like a road map that shows the relationships among small towns, cities, and metropolitan areas with different sized dots and different sizes and styles of type, an information map shows the relationships among information. You can use any type of graphic that makes sense to you—a classic Venn diagram, an information "web," a branching tree, or something unique you create using different sized boxes, circles, lines, and type.

Like the process of creating an informal outline, your first step in creating an information map is to clarify what information you need to know. Only then can you begin to construct a map that will show the relationships among the different levels of information.

Begin by writing the thesis or main idea inside a large box or circle in a prime location on your paper. Then, add the major supporting information as "branches" off the central idea. Continue adding branches for each level of detail you need to know.

As you will see, the information in a map is the same as, or at least very similar to, the information in that paragraph's annotations and informal outline—only the method of organization changes.

EXAMPLE   If you needed to remember the main idea and the five definitions in Grassian's paragraph on euthanasia, your map might look like this:

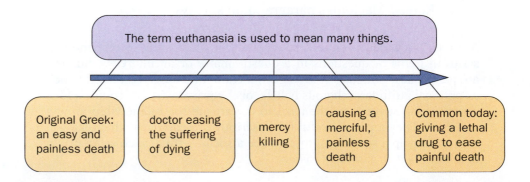

EXAMPLE   If you needed to remember the main idea and the three examples in Lapp, Flood, and Farnan's paragraph on glaciers, your map might look like this:

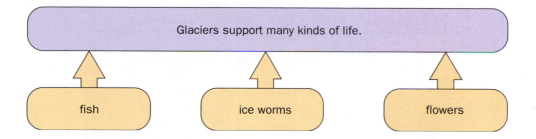

EXAMPLE If you needed to remember all the information from Macionis's paragraph on surveys, your map might look like this:

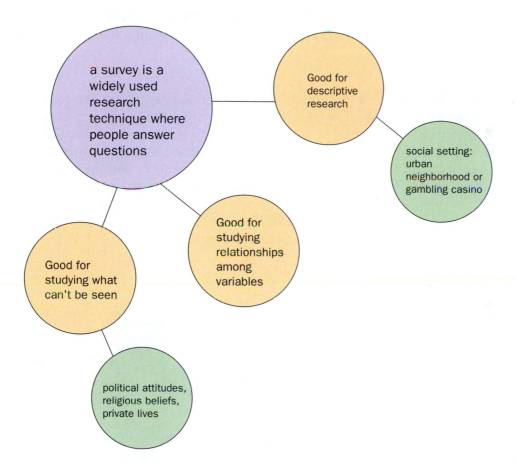

You can also create your map to reinforce the author's structure.

EXAMPLE A map of Long's comparison paragraph from his *Introduction to Computers and Information Processing* text might look like the one that follows the paragraph.

A computer system can also be likened to the biological system of the human body. Your brain is the processing component. Your eyes and ears are input components that send signals to the brain. If you see someone approaching, your brain matches the visual image of this person with others in your memory (storage component). If the visual image matches that of a friend, your brain sends signals to your vocal cords and right arm (output components) to greet your friend with a hello and a handshake. Computer system components interact in a similar way.

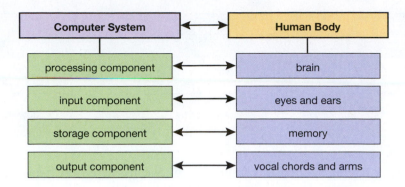

EXAMPLE   If an author wanted you to understand the steps of a process, like Tocquet does in this paragraph, your map might look like the one that follows the paragraph.

> For the extraction of a square root, the mental calculation broadly follows the normal method: first, you divide the number into groups of two figures, you look for the largest square contained in the first group, you carry the root as the first result and subtract this square from the first group. Next, you mentally add on to the remainder the first figure of the second group and divide the number thus obtained by twice the first figure carried; you retain this quotient as the second figure of the root required. As can be seen, the process is rather complicated and lengthy. (Tocquet, *The Magic of Numbers*)

To calculate square root mentally:

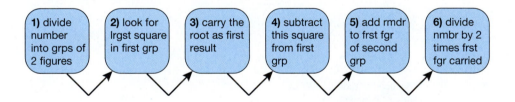

EXAMPLE   Look again at this one-page excerpt from Wade and Tavris's *Invitation to Psychology,* second edition, that begins the discussion of "The Three-Box Model of Memory." If you needed to organize the details of and about the three separate memory systems (boxes), you could create an information map such as the one that follows the excerpt.

THE THREE-BOX MODEL OF MEMORY

Wade and Tavris

THE THREE-BOX MODEL OF MEMORY

The information-processing model of three separate memory systems—sensory, short-term, and long-term—remains a leading approach because it offers a convenient way to organize the major findings on memory, does a good job of accounting for these findings, and is consistent with the biological facts about memory. . . . Let us now peer into each of the "boxes."

Sensory Memory: Fleeting Impressions

In the three-box model, all incoming sensory information must make a brief stop in **sensory memory,** the entryway of memory. Sensory memory includes a number of separate memory subsystems, as many as there are senses. Visual images remain in a visual subsystem for a maximum of half a second. Auditory images remain in an auditory subsystem for a slightly longer time, by most estimates up to two seconds or so.

Sensory memory acts as a holding bin, retaining information in a highly accurate form until we can select items for attention from the stream of stimuli bombarding our senses. It gives us a brief time to decide whether information is extraneous or important; not everything detected by our senses warrants our attention. **Pattern recognition,** the identification of a stimulus on the basis of information already contained in long-term memory, occurs during the transfer of information from sensory memory to short-term memory.

Information that does not quickly go on to short-term memory vanishes forever, like a message written in disappearing ink. That is why people who see an array of 12 letters for just a fraction of a second can report only 4 or 5 of them; by the time they answer, their sensory memories are already fading (Sperling, 1960). The fleeting nature of sensory memory is actually beneficial; it prevents multiple sensory images—"double exposures"—that might interfere with the accurate perception and encoding of information.

Short-term Memory: Memory's Scratch Pad

Like sensory memory, **short-term memory (STM)** retains information only temporarily—for up to about 30 seconds by most estimates, although some researchers think that the maximum interval may extend to a few minutes. In short-term memory, the material is no longer an exact sensory image but is an encoding of one, such as a word or a phrase. This material either transfers into long-term memory or decays and is lost forever.

Individuals with brain injury, such as H. M., demonstrate the importance of transferring new information from short-term memory into longterm memory. H. M., you will recall, can store information on a short-term basis; he can hold a conversation and he appears to be fine when you first meet him. He also retains implicit memories. However, for the most part, H. M. cannot retain explicit information about new facts and events for longer than a few minutes. His terrible memory deficits involve a problem in transferring explicit memories from short-term storage into long-term storage. With a great deal of repetition and drill, H. M. can learn some new visual information, retain it in long-term memory, and recall it normally (McKee & Squire, 1992). But usually information does not get into long-term memory in the first place.

Besides retaining new information for brief periods while we are learning it, short-term memory holds information that has been retrieved from long-term memory for temporary use, providing the mental equivalent of a scratch pad. Thus short-term memory functions in part as a *working memory*. When you do an arithmetic problem, your working memory contains the numbers and the instructions for doing the necessary operations, plus the intermediate results from each step. The ability to bring information from long-term memory into working memory is not disrupted in patients like H. M. They can do arithmetic, converse, relate events that predate their injury, and do anything else that requires retrieval of information from long-term into short-term memory. . . .

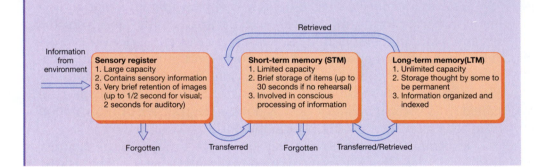

Exercise 3   Creating a Graphic Organizer

Assume you are instructed to read "Reading History" by Dr. Robert Weiss (pages 226–228) as preparation for answering an essay question about how to read history effectively. After you have read and thought about the material and have a clear understanding of what you need to know, create a graphic organizer to help you prepare.

Exercise 4   Creating a Graphic Organizer

Part A: Assume you are instructed to read this article as preparation for writing a brief comparison/contrast essay on nurse practitioners and physician's assistants covering how they are supervised, their clinical roles, and their approach to patient care. Identify the information you need and then create a graphic organizer to help you prepare.

MARCIE BAKER

Marcie Baker is a physician's assistant at the Carl T. Hayden Veterans Affairs Medical Center in Phoenix, Arizona. This selection is adapted from an article she wrote for The Arizona Republic's *"To Your Health" column.*

A NURSE PRACTITIONER IS SIMILAR TO A PHYSICIAN'S ASSISTANT

Marcie Baker

There are many similarities in the clinical roles of the physician's assistant (PA) and nurse practitioner (NP). Both perform such services as recording medical histories; performing physical examinations; ordering and interpreting laboratory and X-ray studies; diagnosing and treating illness; prescribing and dispensing medications; and counseling patients and their families.

The major difference stems from the oversight of these two positions. NPs are autonomous. PAs work with a supervising physician and cannot practice independently. The supervising physician is available to the PA either in person or by electronic means. Both consult with a physician or specialist on complicated, unusual or hard-to-manage cases.

Both NPs and PAs enhance their learning and skills through continuing medical education and interaction with other health-care professionals. NPs must have periodic peer reviews and evidence of continuing professional development and maintenance of clinical skills. PAs are required to log 100 hours of continuing medical education units every two years and take a national recertifying exam every six years if they wish to maintain their national certification.

However, their training and approach to patient care differs. NPs are registered nurses who have attained advanced expertise in the clinical management of health problems. NPs assess and manage from a medical and nursing perspective, which emphasizes health promotion and disease prevention as well as treatment of acute and chronic disease. Typically, the education of the NP is at a master's level. NPs are certified nationally in their areas of expertise, which can be nurse midwife, pediatric, family, adult, geriatric, psychiatric, school nurse and neonatal nurse practitioner.

PAs also emphasize patient education and preventive medicine. However, PAs are educated in the medical model, sometimes along with medical students, designed to complement physician training. PAs come from various medical backgrounds, such as physical therapists, radiologic technologists, nurses, and emergency medical technologists.

Each candidate has at least four years' experience in the medical profession and at least a two-year college degree; most have a four-year degree on entry or will earn it in the course of their training. There are also some master's level programs available.

PAs are graduates of a nationally accredited PA program and must pass a national certifying exam upon graduation. State licensure requires graduation from an accredited program, passage of the national certifying exam, and continuing medical education. A recertifying exam every six years is required to maintain national certification and the title "physician's assistant."

The PA profession was founded in the mid-1960s, when it was recognized that there was a shortage and uneven distribution of primary-care physicians. Dr. Eugene Stead of Duke University Medical Center in Durham, N.C., put the first class of PAs together in 1965. He selected Navy corpsmen who received considerable medical training during their military service and the Vietnam War but had no comparable civilian employment.

"Midlevel" practitioners such as PAs and NPs may have different educational backgrounds and licensure, but they deliver high-quality patient care, compassion, and a desire to educate the patients and their families regarding prevention and treatment of medical conditions.

Part B: Assume that instead of preparing to write a comparison/contrast essay, you are preparing to write a short essay on the history and role of physician's assistants. What, if anything, would you do differently? Explain.

SUMMARIZE

A **summary** is a condensed version of the original text in your own words. A summary is useful when you need to concentrate on just the thesis and main ideas or on the main ideas and major details. A summary does not usually include examples and minor details that may be included in other organizational strategies.

A summary must be

In your own words: **Paraphrase**—put the information in your own words—to be sure you understand the author's ideas. Do not copy from the original.

In standard paragraph form: Use good writing techniques, that is, complete sentences with capital letters, transitions, and punctuation.

Brief: Include only the thesis and main ideas from a multiparagraph selection or main idea and major details from a paragraph.

Complete: Do not leave out any main ideas from a multiparagraph selection or major details from a paragraph.

Objective: Include only the author's information; do not include your opinion of the information.

To write an effective summary, follow these steps:

Step 1: Clarify what you need to know and reread the portion you need to summarize.

Step 2: Write the thesis or main idea in your own words. As with all thesis or main idea statements, do not include your opinion.

Step 3: Paraphrase each main idea or major detail into a sentence. Include the ideas or details in the same order and with the same emphasis as the original.

Step 4: Revise your summary. Is your summary an accurate capsule version of the original? Is any important information missing? Is there any unimportant information included that should be deleted? Is anything unclear?

Step 5: Edit your summary.

EXAMPLE Because you must use your own words in a summary, the one you write for Grassian's paragraph would not be exactly like this one. However, the basic content would be the same.

Over the years, the term euthanasia has been used to mean many things. In the original Greek, it meant an easy and painless death. Next, it referred to a doctor easing the suffering of dying. More recently it has come to be synonymous with "mercy killing" or causing a merciful, painless death. Today it is thought of as giving a lethal drug to ease painful death.

EXAMPLE A summary of Lapp, Flood, and Farnan's paragraph could say

Among the many kinds of life that can exist in glaciers are fish, ice worms, and flowers.

EXAMPLE A summary of Macionis's paragraph could say

A survey is a common research technique asking people to answer written or oral questions. Surveys are very useful for studying things that can't be seen, examining the connections among variables, and for descriptive research.

As you have seen, the information in a summary is very similar to the information in that paragraph's annotations and graphic organizer—only the method of organization changes.

Exercise 5 ▶ Writing a Summary

Assume you are instructed to read "Reading History" by Dr. Robert Weiss (pages 226–228) as preparation for answering an essay question about how to read history effectively. After you have read and thought about the material, write a summary of the excerpt.

Exercise 6 ▶ Writing a Summary

Assume you are instructed to read this selection as preparation for answering two essay questions: (1) the severity and dangers of overweight and obesity in America, and (2) keys to losing weight. After you have read and thought about the material, write a summary of the selection.

LINDA BREN

Ms. Bren is a staff writer for the FDA Consumer. *This selection is based on her article in the January-February 2002* FDA Consumer *and contains revisions made in April 2002. For the complete article, see Publication No. (FDA) 02–1231.*

LOSING WEIGHT: MORE THAN COUNTING CALORIES

Linda Bren

[1]Americans are getting fatter. We're putting on the pounds at an alarmingly rapid rate. And we're sacrificing our health for the sake of supersize portions, biggie drinks, and two-for-one value meals, obesity researchers say.

[2]More than 60 percent of U.S. adults are either overweight or obese, according to the Centers for Disease Control and Prevention (CDC). While the number of overweight people has been slowly climbing since the 1980s, the number of obese adults has nearly doubled since then.

OVERWEIGHT AND OBESITY

[3]Overweight refers to an excess of body weight, but not necessarily body fat. Obesity means an excessively high proportion of body fat. Health professionals use a measurement called body mass index (BMI) to classify an adult's weight as healthy, overweight, or obese. BMI describes body weight relative to height and is correlated with total body fat content in most adults.

[4]To get your approximate BMI, multiply your weight in pounds by 703, then divide the result by your height in inches, and divide that result by your height in inches a second time. (Or you can use the interactive BMI calculator at *www.nhlbisupport.com/bmi/bmicalc.htm.*)

[5]A BMI from 18.5 up to 25 is considered in the healthy range, from 25 up to 30 is overweight, and 30 or higher is obese. Generally, the higher a person's BMI, the greater the risk for health problems, according to the National Heart, Lung and Blood Institute (NHLBI). However, there are some exceptions. For example, very muscular people, like body builders, may have a BMI greater than 25 or even 30, but this reflects increased muscle rather than fat. "It is excess body fat that leads to the health problems such as type 2 diabetes, high blood pressure, and high cholesterol," says Eric Colman, M.D., of the Food and Drug Administration's Division of Metabolic and Endocrine Drug Products.

[6]In addition to a high BMI, having excess abdominal body fat is a health risk. Men with a waist of more than 40 inches around and women with a waist of 35 inches or more are at risk for health problems.

NO LAUGHING MATTER

[7]Excess weight and physical inactivity account for more than 300,000 premature deaths each year in the United States, second only to deaths related to smoking, says the CDC. People who are overweight or obese are more likely to develop heart disease, stroke, high blood pressure, diabetes, gallbladder disease, and joint pain caused by excess uric acid (gout). Excess weight can also cause interrupted breathing during sleep (sleep apnea) and wearing away of the joints (osteoarthritis).

[8]Carrying extra weight also means carrying an extra risk for certain types of cancer. "[Our] researchers have concluded that obesity increases the risk for many of the most common cancers worldwide, and perhaps cancer in general," says Melanie Polk, R.D., director of nutrition education at the American Institute for Cancer Research (AICR), a nonprofit research and education organization in Washington, D.C.

[9]In their review of more than 100 studies and international reports on obesity and cancer risk, completed in October 2001, researchers at the AICR concluded that obesity is consistently linked to post-menopausal breast cancer, colon cancer, endometrial cancer, prostate cancer, and kidney cancer.

[10]Obesity, once thought by many to be a moral failing, is now often classified as a disease. The NHLBI calls it a complex chronic disease involving social, behavioral, cultural, physiological, metabolic, and genetic factors. Although experts may have different theories on how and why people become overweight, they generally agree that the key to losing weight is a simple message: Eat less and move more. Your body needs to burn more calories than you take in.

SETTING A GOAL

[11]The first step to weight loss is setting a realistic goal. By using a BMI chart and consulting with your health-care provider, you can determine what is a healthy weight for you.

[12]Studies show that you can improve your health with just a small amount of weight loss. "We know that physical activity in combination with reduced calorie consumption can lead to the 5 to 10 percent weight loss necessary to achieve remission of the obesity-associated complications," says William Dietz, M.D., Ph.D., director of the Division of Nutrition and Physical Activity at the CDC. "Even these moderate weight losses can improve blood pressure and help control diabetes and high cholesterol in obese or overweight adults."

[13]To reach your goal safely, plan to lose weight gradually. A weight loss of one-half to 2 pounds a week is usually safe, according to the Dietary Guidelines for Americans. This can be achieved by decreasing the calories eaten or increasing the calories used by 250 to 1,000 calories per day, depending on current calorie intake. (Some people with serious health problems due to obesity may lose weight more rapidly under a doctor's supervision.) If you plan to lose more than 15 to 20 pounds, have any health problems, or take medication on a regular basis, a doctor should evaluate you before you begin a weight-loss program.

CHANGING EATING HABITS

[14]Dieting may conjure up visions of eating little but lettuce and sprouts—but you can enjoy all foods as part of a healthy diet as long as you don't overdo it on fat (especially saturated fat), protein, sugars, and alcohol. To be successful at losing weight, you need to change your lifestyle—not just go on a diet, experts say.

[15]Limit portion sizes, especially of foods high in calories, such as cookies, cakes and other sweets; french fries; and fats, oils and spreads.

Reducing dietary fat alone—without reducing calories—will not produce weight loss, according to the NHLBI's guidelines on treating overweight and obesity in adults.

[16]Use the Food Guide Pyramid, developed by the U.S. Department of Agriculture (USDA) and the Department of Health and Human Services, to help you choose a healthful assortment of foods that includes vegetables, fruits, grains (especially whole grains), fat-free milk, and fish, lean meat, poultry, or beans. Choose foods naturally high in fiber, such as fruits, vegetables, legumes (such as beans and lentils), and whole grains. The high fiber content of many of these foods may help you to feel full with fewer calories.

[17]All calorie sources are not created equal. Carbohydrate and protein have about 4 calories per gram, but fat has more than twice that amount (9 calories per gram). Just as for the general population, weight-conscious consumers should aim for a daily fat intake of no more than 30 percent of total calories.

[18]Keep your intake of saturated fat at less than 10 percent of calories. Saturated fats increase the risk for heart disease by raising blood cholesterol. Foods high in saturated fats include high-fat dairy products (like cheese, whole milk, cream, butter, and regular ice cream), fatty fresh and processed meats, the skin and fat of poultry, lard, palm oil, and coconut oil.

[19]If you drink alcoholic beverages, do so in moderation. Alcoholic beverages supply calories but few nutrients. A 12-ounce regular beer contains about 150 calories, a 5-ounce glass of wine about 100 calories, and 1.5 ounces of 80-proof distilled spirits about 100 calories.

[20]Limit your use of beverages and foods that are high in added sugars—those added to foods in processing or preparation, not the naturally occurring sugars in foods such as fruit or milk. Foods containing added sugars provide calories, but may have few vitamins and minerals. In the United States, the major sources of added sugars include non-diet soft drinks, sweets and candies, cakes and cookies, and fruit drinks and fruitades.

INCREASING PHYSICAL ACTIVITY

[21]Most health experts recommend a combination of a reduced-calorie diet and increased physical activity for weight loss. Most adults should get at least 30 minutes and children should get 60 minutes of moderate physical activity on most, and preferably all, days of the week. But fewer than 1 in 3 U.S. adults gets the recommended amount of physical activity, according to *The Surgeon General's Call to Action to Prevent and Decrease Overweight and Obesity.*

[22]In addition to helping to control weight, physical activity decreases the risk of dying from coronary heart disease and reduces the risk of developing diabetes, hypertension, and colon cancer. Researchers also have found that daily physical activity may help a person lose weight by partially lessening the slow-down in metabolism that occurs during weight loss.

[23]Exercise does not have to be strenuous to be beneficial. And some studies show that short sessions of exercise several times a day are just as effective at burning calories and improving health as one long session.

[24]To lose weight and to maintain a healthy weight after weight loss, many adults will likely need to do more than 30 minutes of moderate physical activity daily.

WORTH THE EFFORT

[25]"Losing weight requires major lifestyle changes, including diet and nutrition, exercise, behavior modification, and—when appropriate—intervention with drug therapy," says Judith S. Stern, Sc.D., professor of nutrition and internal medicine at the University of California, Davis, and vice president of the American Obesity Association. "But it is always worth making the effort to improve your health."

CHAPTER 8 REVIEW QUESTIONS

1. What is annotating? Describe your basic strategy for annotating a selection.
2. What are two reasons it is better to annotate than to use a highlighter or underline?
3. What are graphic organizers? When would you use a graphic organizer as a strategy for organizing information?
4. What does paraphrase mean?
5. What is a summary? When would you use summarizing as a strategy for organizing information?

Use Your Strategies 1

Assume your instructor has instructed you to read this excerpt to prepare for a quiz. You will need to explain (1) what feedback is, (2) the two types of feedback, and (3) three functions of feedback.

KITTIE W. WATSON

Kittie Watson is an associate professor at Tulane University and an authority on listening and feedback. This selection is excerpted from her chapter on listening in Barker and Barker's text Communication.

AN IDEA TO THINK ABOUT

If you were talking with two friends and one smiled and nodded enthusiastically while the other one just stared at you with a blank expression, what would you think? *As you read,* find out why those smiles, nods, blank stares, and other forms of feedback are useful.

FEEDBACK

Kittie W. Watson

[1]Communication is a circular process. As a message is transmitted from sender to receiver, a return message, known as feedback, is transmitted in the opposite direction. Feedback is a message that indicates the level of understanding or agreement between two or more people in communication in response to an original message. Feedback represents a listener's verbal or nonverbal commentary on the message being communicated.

[2]Feedback is an ongoing process that usually begins as a reaction to various aspects of the initial message. For example, a definite response is being fed back to the speaker when we shake our heads affirmatively or look quizzically at the speaker. Feedback plays an essential role in helping us to determine whether or not our message has been understood; whether it is being received positively or negatively; and whether our audience is open or defensive, self-controlled or bored. Feedback can warn us that we must alter our communication to achieve the desired effect. If we are not aware of feedback or don't pay any attention to it, there is a strong possibility that our efforts at communicating will be completely ineffective.

[3]To emphasize the importance of the feedback mechanism in communication, you need only imagine yourself growing up for the last 18 years or so, never having received any feedback. No one has praised you as you learned to walk or ride a bike. No one has warned you not to chase a ball into the street or to put your hand on a hot stove. No one has shared your tears or laughter. You probably would not function well at all. How would you appraise your self-concept? What values or morals would you possess? While such an existence is impossible, since a certain amount of feedback comes from you yourself as well as from others in the environment, this example does suggest the various functions and effects of feedback in the communication process.

TYPES OF FEEDBACK

[4]There are two types of feedback: self-feedback and listener feedback. See Figure 3.5.

[5]Self-feedback applies to the words and actions that are fed back into your central nervous system as you perceive your own muscular movements and hear yourself speak. Feeling your tongue twist as you mispronounce a word or, in a library, suddenly realizing that you are speaking too loudly are examples of self-feedback. Another example would be hearing yourself use a word incorrectly, or reversing sounds—for example, asking, "Were you sappy or had?" instead of "happy or sad."

[6]Research indicates that self-feedback plays an important role in the nature and form of our judgmental processes, especially when listener feedback is absent. For example, Hagafors and Brehmer have

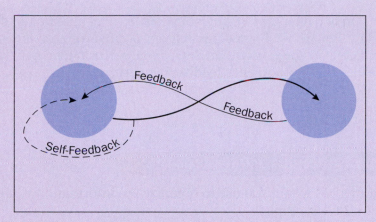

FIGURE 3.5 Self-Feedback and Listener Feedback

found that our judgments become more consistent when we are required to justify them to others and when no other form of listener feedback is present. In addition, under these conditions our judgments seem to become more analytical and less intuitive. It seems that self-feedback in the form of justification alters the nature and form of our overall judgmental process.

[7]The other major type of feedback, listener feedback, involves verbal and nonverbal responses. Verbal feedback may take the form of questions or comments. A listener may, for instance, ask a speaker to explain the last point or give praise for making the story so interesting. Nonverbal feedback may be transmitted by applause or laughter, to indicate approval, or by a blank stare, which might indicate disinterest or confusion. Even silence can act as feedback. If a teacher asks a question and no one answers, the silence may indicate understanding, or perhaps dislike of the teacher. If a father asks his son if he has finished his homework and the son doesn't reply, that silence is meaningful.

FUNCTIONS OF FEEDBACK

[8]Feedback serves various functions in the communication process. The first of these functions is to evaluate what is right or wrong about a particular communication. If you give a speech to the class, your teacher will offer criticism and suggestions for improving your delivery. If someone is watching you hang a painting, he or she will give you feedback as you try various positions, to help you find the right place for it. . . . [N]onverbal feedback, in the form of nods and hand movements, helps to regulate turn taking in conversation.

[9]Secondly, feedback can serve to stimulate change. For example, a popular soft-drink company, after changing its century-old formula, received so much mixed feedback in the form of letters and phone calls that the company not only retained the new formula but brought back the original formula and placed both on grocery-store shelves.

[10]A third function of feedback is to reinforce, to give reward or punishment. A father says, "I'm proud of you, son," or "Jim, can't you ever keep quiet!" When used in this way, rewarding feedback encour-

ages certain behaviors, while punishing feedback is intended to discourage certain behaviors. Comedians rely on positive reinforcement from their audience in the form of laughter; their performance may improve if they sense that the audience feedback is positive.

Use Your Strategies 1 Questions

1. What method would you use to organize the information you need for the quiz? Please explain.
2. Write a sentence that expresses Watson's thesis.
3. What is feedback?
4. List the two types of feedback.
5. List three major functions of feedback.
6. What is the purpose of Figure 3.5?
7. How would your organization strategy change if you were preparing to write a paragraph on the importance of feedback in the communication process?

Use Your Strategies 2

Assume you are reading this selection to prepare to write a short essay on the importance of toys and play.

THE TOY MANUFACTURERS OF AMERICA AND THE AMERICAN TOY INSTITUTE

This article is excerpted from Guide to Toys and Play *by the Toy Manufacturers of America and the American Toy Institute.*

AN IDEA TO THINK ABOUT

What are some of the things a child might learn from playing with toys such as balls, puzzles, teddy bears, and craft kits? *As you read,* find out why many people think "playing" is essential to a child's development.

LEARNING THROUGH TOYS AND PLAY

*The Toy Manufacturers of America
and the American Toy Institute*

INTRODUCTION

[1]One of the most important things a child can do is play. Play is the essential joy of childhood and is also the way children learn about themselves, their environment and the people around them. As they play, children learn to solve problems, get along with other people and control their bodies as they enrich their creativity and develop leadership skills. When children play with a broad variety of toys, the experiences help them to develop to their fullest potential.

[2]Children bring boundless energy and imagination to their play with toys and are constantly developing new and creative ways to play. Because there are so many different kinds of toys and novel ways to play with them, children learn that the world is a diverse place with unlimited possibilities. Toys thus have an exciting role in helping children to become mature, confident and imaginative adults.

LEARNING THROUGH PLAY

[3]Play is essential to a child's development and is the way that youngsters learn the skills they will need for a happy and capable adulthood. According to child development specialist Mary Sinker, these are just some of the ways a child learns while playing:

[4]Physical skills are developed through movement as a child learns to reach, grasp, crawl, run, climb and balance. Dexterity develops as he or she handles objects in play.

[5]Language develops as a child plays and interacts with others. Beginning with cooing games with a parent and evolving to sophisticated levels such as telling stories and jokes, the ability to use language increases as the child plays.

[6]Social skills grow as the child plays. Learning to cooperate, negotiate, take turns and play by the rules are all important skills learned in early games. It is through imaginative play that the child begins to learn some of the roles and rules of society.

[7]Understanding how the world works develops as result of problem solving with toys. What fits here? How big is that? Is this color the same as that color? How can I balance these? A child moves on to higher levels of thought as he or she plays in a stimulating environment.

[8]Emotional well being develops through positive play experiences. When children feel successful and capable as they play, they acquire important ingredients for emotional health. Sharing play experiences also forges strong bonds between parent and child throughout childhood.

WHY TOYS ARE LABELED

[9]Labels on toy packages make choosing safe, appropriate toys much easier. However, no package label can tell you exactly which toys are right for your child, and not all toys are appropriate for every youngster. On the other hand, child development experts agree that children develop in a sequence of stages, and toymakers use this information to indicate which types of toys are safe and appropriate for children of various ages. Product labels help consumers distinguish among the vast number of toys on the market to make the most appropriate purchases.

[10]Remember, each child is unique and develops at his or her own pace. The best thing adults can do when purchasing toys is to know the maturity, skill level and interests of the child, read the age labels carefully and use them as guides and, above all, use common sense. Nobody knows your child better than you do.

HOW TOYS ARE AGE LABELED

[11]Toymakers follow the age grading guidelines of the Consumer Product Safety Commission, which consist of four main criteria:

- the ability of a child to physically manipulate and play with features of a toy
- the ability of a child to understand how to use a toy
- the child's play needs and interests at different developmental levels
- the safety aspects of the toy itself

A child's abilities, interests and play needs will, of course, vary at each level of development.

[12]New toys are frequently tested by children in play settings to determine durability, age-appropriateness and play patterns. At least one large toy manufacturer maintains an in-house, year-round nursery school for this purpose, while others establish relationships with universities and other educational facilities. Manufacturers also may involve parents, teachers and others who care for children for their first-hand knowledge and valuable insights. In addition, a toymaker may have a child development specialist, psychologist or physician on staff or working as a consultant.

TOY SELECTION

[13]The following are some suggestions for suitable toys for children of various ages. They are offered as a guide to help in your selection, but remember that all children are different. Study your child and get to know his or her interests, abilities and limitations. Not all children enjoy the same kinds of play: one child will be interested in building with blocks or doing puzzles; another may prefer riding bikes or playing ball; your child may enjoy pretending with a dollhouse or playing board games. Try to match the toy to your child and keep in mind that his or her interest in a toy will often carry through more than one age group.

Babies: Birth to One Year

[14]Experts agree that even babies need an assortment of toys. Since infants respond to smell, taste, sound, touch and sight, properly selected toys

provide a small baby with opportunities to learn about size, shape, sound, texture and how things work.

[15]Choose toys that:

- have pieces that are too large to swallow
- are lightweight for handling and grasping
- have no sharp edges or points
- are brightly colored
- are non-toxic

[16]Brightly colored, lightweight toys of various textures stimulate a baby's senses. For young infants, toys to look at and listen to are best. Rattles, squeaky toys and crib gyms are ideal for grasping when the baby is ready to hold objects.

[17]Soft dolls or stuffed animals made of non-toxic materials are fun to touch and hug but are not designed for sucking or chewing. Make sure the seams cannot be easily torn or bitten open and that eyes and noses are securely fastened.

[18]A baby who is sitting up is ready for blocks with pictures or bright colors. Nesting cups or boxes and stacking rings are also favorites. Babies at this age enjoy their first sturdy picture books showing familiar objects. Balls and push-pull toys are good choices when a baby can crawl and walk.

Toddlers: One to Three Years

[19]A busy toddler needs toys for active physical play—especially things to ride and climb on, such as a low tricycle or a wagon to ride in and pull. Outdoor toys such as large balls, inflatable toys, a wading pool and a sandbox with digging tools are all good choices.

[20]Toddlers begin to enjoy make-believe play just before their second birthdays. To imitate the adult world around them, they use play food, appliances and utensils, child-sized play furniture, simple dress-up clothes and dolls. Children in this age group are particularly interested in sorting and fitting toys, all kinds of blocks and simple puzzles. Toddlers also enjoy musical instruments such as tambourines, toy pianos, horns and drums, as well as listening to tapes.

Pre-Schoolers: Three to Five Years

[21]Pre-schoolers are masters of make-believe. They like to act out grown-up roles and create imaginary situations. Costumes and equipment that help them in their pretend worlds are important at this stage. Some of the many possibilities include pretend money, play food, a toy cash register or telephone, a make-believe village, fort, circus, farm, gas station or restaurant, a puppet theater and play with dolls and doll furniture.

[22]In a child's private world, a favorite toy is both a companion and protector. Dolls and teddy bears, for example, have helped countless children to cope with difficult moments. Children will sometimes express their feelings to toy "confidants" and share emotions with them that they might otherwise keep to themselves.

[23]Transportation is fascinating to young children. Trucks, cars, planes, trains, boats and tractors are all fun at this age and beyond. Larger outdoor toys, including gym equipment, wheeled vehicles and a first two-wheeled bicycle with helmet and training wheels, are appropriate now.

[24]Visualization and memory skills can be sharpened by play that requires use of imagination or mental computation, with the introduction of board games, electronic toys and word and matching games geared specifically for this group. Construction sets, books and tapes, coloring sets, paints, crayons, puzzles, stuffed toys and dolls continue to be favorites.

School Age: Six to Nine Years

[25]Board games, tabletop sports games and classics like marbles and model or craft kits help develop skills for social and solitary play. In experimenting with different kinds of grownup worlds, fashion and career dolls and all kinds of action figures appeal to girls and boys. Printing sets, science and craft kits, electric trains, racing cars, construction sets and hobby equipment are important to children for examining and experimenting with the world around them.

[26]For active physical play, a larger bicycle, ice or roller skates, a pogo stick, scooter, sled and other sports equipment, along with protective gear, are appropriate. Even though group play is enjoyed, children at this stage also play well by themselves. Paints, crayons and clay are still good selections, as are costumes, doll houses, play villages, miniature figures and vehicles, all of which help children to develop their imaginations and creativity.

[27]Many games and electronic toys geared to children in this age group are labeled "educational" because they have been designed to help children learn specific skills and concepts, such as games which require forming words, matching letters of the alphabet with various objects or learning about money through handling play coins and currency.

[28]Video games appeal to children, teenagers and adults. Many games offer increasingly challenging levels of play, as well as opportunities to develop coordination skills and a sense of the meaning of strategies in relationships, usually through competition against an opponent.

Nine to Twelve Years

[29]Children begin to develop specific skills and life-long interests at this age. Give considerable attention to hobbies and crafts, model kits, magic sets, advanced construction sets, chemistry and science kits and puzzles. Peer acceptance is very important at this age. Active physical play now finds its expression with team play in a variety of sports. Social and intellectual skills are refined through board, card and electronic games, particularly those requiring strategy decisions.

[30]Video and electronic games, table tennis and billiards (pool) are very popular at this stage. Dramatic play holds great appeal. Youngsters in this age group like to plan complete productions including props, costumes, printed programs, puppets and marionettes. Painting, sculpting, ceramics and other forms of artistic expression continue to be of interest, as do books, tapes and musical instruments.

Teenagers

[31]After age twelve, children's interests in toys begin to merge with those of adults. This is apparent in the growing market for sophisticated electronic games and computer-based systems, which are often considered "family entertainment" rather than toys. They also will be interested in board and adventure games. Collectors of dolls, model cars, trains, miniatures and stuffed animals often begin their hobbies in the teenage years.

CONCLUSION

[32]Choose toys with care. Get involved and encourage your youngster to be creative through play. Children tend to remember lessons they learn while having fun, so set good examples for proper use and maintenance of toys. Remember, youngsters who are creative at play tend to be more creative, well adjusted and secure as adults.

Use Your Strategies 2 Questions

1. Based on your need to prepare to write a short essay on the importance of toys and play, what method would you use to organize the information? Explain your selection.
2. Write a sentence that expresses the thesis.
3. What are three positive things children learn through play?
4. How do toys help children play?
5. Why are toys labeled for age ranges?
6. What impact, if any, does play have on children as they become adults?
7. Assume you are preparing to take a true/false and multiple-choice test on what toys are suitable for children of various ages. Would the information you need and/or the method you use to organize the information be different than when you were preparing to write an essay on the importance of toys and play? Please explain.
8. Use the organization strategy of your choice on this selection.

Use Your Strategies 3

Assume you are reading this selection to prepare to discuss the importance of drive and determination to success.

CAROLE WADE AND CAROL TAVRIS

Dr. Wade developed the first course on the psychology of gender at the University of New Mexico. She has taught at San Diego Mesa College, College of Marin, and is now affiliated with Dominican University of California. Dr. Tavris is a writer and lecturer on the importance of critical and scientific thinking in psychology. She has taught at UCLA and the Human Relations Center for the New School for Social Research in New York. This selection is from Chapter 6, "Thinking and Intelligence," in their text Invitation to Psychology, *second edition.*

AN IDEA TO THINK ABOUT

Are the smartest people—the ones with the highest IQ—always rich and successful? Can someone with average intelligence become rich and successful? *As you read,* find out what factors other than intelligence play a role in our success.

ATTITUDES, MOTIVATION, AND INTELLECTUAL SUCCESS

Carole Wade and Carol Tavris

[1]Even with a high IQ, emotional intelligence, genetic advantages, talent, and practical know-how, you still might get nowhere at all. Talent, unlike cream, does not inevitably rise to the top; success also depends on drive and determination.

[2]Consider a finding from one of the longest-running psychological studies ever conducted. Since 1921, researchers at Stanford University have been following more than 1,500 people with childhood IQ scores in the top 1 percent of the distribution. As boys and girls, these subjects were nicknamed "Termites," after Lewis Terman, who originally directed the research. The Termites started out bright, physically healthy, sociable, and well adjusted. As they entered adulthood, most became successful in the traditional ways of the times: men in careers and women as homemakers (Sears & Barbee, 1977; Terman & Oden, 1959). However, some gifted men failed to live up to their early promise, dropping out of school or drifting into low-level work. When the researchers compared the 100 most successful men with the 100 least successful, they found that motivation made the difference. The successful men were ambitious, were socially active, had many interests, and were encouraged by their parents. The least successful men drifted casually through life. There was *no* average difference in IQ between the two groups.

[3]Motivation to work hard at intellectual tasks depends in turn on your attitudes about intelligence and achievement. For many years, Harold Stevenson and his colleagues have been studying such attitudes in Asia and the United States. Since 1980 they have been comparing large samples of grade-school children, parents, and teachers in Minneapolis, Chicago, Sendai (Japan). Taipei (Taiwan), and Beijing (Stevenson & Stigler, 1992). In 1990, Stevenson, along with Chuansheng Chen and Shin-ying Lee (1993), revisited the original schools to collect new data on fifth-graders, and they also retested many of the children who had been in the 1980 study and who were now in the eleventh grade. Their results have much to teach us about the cultivation of intellect.

[4]In 1980, the Asian children far outperformed the American children on a broad battery of mathematical tests. (A similar gap existed between the Chinese and American children on reading tests.) On computations and word problems, there was virtually no overlap between schools, with the lowest-scoring Beijing schools doing better than the highest-scoring Chicago schools. By 1990, the gap between the Asian and American children had grown even greater. Only 4 percent of the Chinese children and 10 percent of the Japanese children had scores as low as those of the *average* American child. These differences could not be accounted for by educational resources: The Chinese schools had worse facilities and larger classes than the American ones, and on aver-

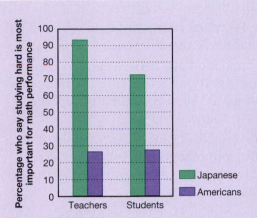

Figure 6.7
What's the Secret of Math Success?
Japanese school teachers and students are much more likely than their American counterparts to believe that the secret to doing well in math is working hard. Americans tend to think that you either have mathematical intelligence or you don't.

age, the Chinese parents were poorer and less educated than the American parents. Nor did it have anything to do with intellectual ability in general; the American children were just as knowledgeable and capable as the Asian children on tests of general information.

[5]But this research found that Asians and Americans are worlds apart in their attitudes, expectations, and efforts:

- *Beliefs about intelligence.* American parents, teachers, and children are far more likely than Asians to believe that mathematical ability is innate (see Figure 6.7). They think that if you "have it," you don't have to work hard, and if you don't have it, there's no point in trying.

- *Standards.* American parents have far lower standards for their children's performance; they are satisfied with scores barely above average on a 100-point test. In contrast, Chinese and Japanese parents are happy only with very high scores.

- *Values.* American students do not value education as much as Asian students do, and they are more complacent about mediocre work. When asked what they would wish for if a wizard could give them anything they wanted, more than 60 percent of the Chinese fifth-graders named something related to their education. Can you guess what the American children wanted? A majority said money or possessions.

[6]When it comes to intellect, then, it's not just what you've got that counts but what you do with it. Complacency, fatalism, or low standards can prevent people from recognizing what they don't know and reduce their efforts to learn.

Use Your Strategies 3 Questions

1. Based on your need to prepare to discuss the importance of drive and determination to success, what method would you use to organize the information? Please explain.

2. Write a sentence that expresses the thesis.

3. When researchers compared the 100 most successful men with the 100 least successful, what did they find made the difference?

4. What do most Japanese teachers and students believe is the secret to doing well in math? What do most American teachers and students believe is the secret to doing well in math? How does their difference in views seem to impact student performance?

5. In the last sentence, Wade and Tavris say, "Complacency, fatalism, or low standards can prevent people from recognizing what they don't know and reduce their efforts to learn." Give an example from the text or your own experience that shows what they mean.

6. Use the organization strategy of your choice on this selection.

Use Your Strategies 4

Assume you are preparing to take a test on how the materials used in architecture have changed through the years.

H. W. JANSON AND ANTHONY F. JANSON

Dr. H. W. Janson is a legendary name in art history. He was Professor of Fine Arts at New York University for more than twenty-five years, and his world-famous History of Art *has been translated into more than a dozen languages. Dr. Anthony F. Janson has forged a distinguished career as an author, museum professional, and teacher, and is currently on the faculty at the University of North Carolina, Wilmington. This selection is from Chapter 23, "Realism and Impressionism," in* A Basic History of Art, *the sixth edition of their beginning art history text.*

AN IDEA TO THINK ABOUT

Suppose you needed to build a bridge over a small stream. What materials would you want to use—wood, iron, steel, concrete, a combination of materials? What factors do you think you would need to consider? *As you read,* look for information about materials and factors architects consider when they build bridges, railway stations, decorative structures, and buildings.

THE MATERIALS OF MODERN ARCHITECTURE

H. W. Janson and Anthony F. Janson

[1]After about 1780, in the world of commercial architecture we find the gradual introduction of new materials and techniques that were to have a profound effect on architectural style by 1900. Of these by far the most

important was iron, which was used as early as the fourth millennium B.C. and began to be made on a large scale beginning in the fourteenth century Pig iron, smelted in blast furnaces, can be poured into molds to make cast iron, which has relatively high amounts of carbon and impurities (slag), so that it is brittle. Wrought iron, introduced around 1820, is soft and malleable hence its name but, having less carbon and slag, possesses greater tensile strength, making it ideal for bolts, ties and trusses. Steel is an even stronger alloy of iron and small amounts of carbon that is also ductile and corrosion-resistant. (Technically, most nineteenth-century steel was really a form of wrought iron, since it lacked other elements, such as nickel, chromium, and aluminum, which were added after 1900 for greater hardness.) It was handmade until the 1850s, when the Englishman Henry Bessemer and the American William Kelly independently invented a commercial process to remove the impurities by introducing oxygen, which also heated the iron in a converter of steel lined with silica. The open-hearth furnace, devised in 1864 by William and Frederick Stemens, used regenerative preheating of air to smelt a combination of iron ore and pig iron at extremely high temperatures. The only major advances since then have been the basic-oxygen process and the electric furnace.

[2]CAST IRON was first mass-produced for rails by Abraham Darby in 1767. Fires at textile mills led to the use of cast-iron pillars in the 1780s, then beams during the following decade. Cast-iron columns were also introduced in churches as early as the 1780s; soon the structural elements of churches were being built almost entirely of iron—for example, St. George at Merseyside, erected in 1812–13 by the architect Thomas Rickman and iron founder John Cragg, which uses an extremely sophisticated structural system, including tension rods to tie it together. Cast iron has the advantage of being stronger and more fire-resistant than wood, but it is subject to corrosion and being an excellent heat conductor, expands and contracts, thereby causing condensation that further contributes to the problem of rust. Iron and steel proved especially useful for bridge spans. The first iron bridge was built in 1777–79 at Coalbrookdale by Abraham Darby III from a design by the architect Thomas Pritchard. Construction was greatly improved during the first half of the nineteenth century by the introduction of new truss systems and the riveted I beam. Within a few decades of their first appearance, iron columns and arches became the standard means of supporting roofs over the large spaces required by railroad stations. The first railway shed, built in 1830, was a modest structure using straight beams; the arch became an important form only in the 1840s, as rail lines became increasingly common, first throughout Europe, then in America, and large terminals began to be erected.

[3]Because it can be manufactured with great consistency, iron can be used in predictable ways that can be calculated by using standard mathematical formulas. This property gave rise to new structural systems (notably those by James Bogardus in the 1840s and '50s) that are extremely stable yet lightweight, though they almost always remained completely hidden from view. Technology produced a fundamental

change in the practice of architecture, which became increasingly dependent on engineering. As a consequence, the tradition of artists and gifted amateurs practicing as architects was over by 1880. The triumph of the iron age was announced at the world's fair held in Paris in 1889 by the Hall of Machines, designed by Charles Dutert with the engineering team of Contamin, Pierron, and Charton. . . . The Eiffel tower itself was a miracle of engineering, manufacturing, and construction. In addition to being extremely lightweight, it was precast so precisely that no fabrication or cutting was done on the site, only riveting, and planned so carefully that not a single worker was killed. (Interestingly enough, Eiffel added the arches at the base, similar to those on his bridges, to assure the viewer that the tower would stand, though they were not structurally necessary.) By this time, iron was already being rapidly supplanted by STEEL. Steel mills sprang up everywhere after 1865 to serve the rail industry, but it was not until the 1880s that long rolled-steel beams began to be produced in large quantities, thanks to the widespread use of the open-hearth furnace. This innovation in turn made possible steel-frame construction, essential to skyscrapers, whose potential was first explored during the same decade in New York and Paris, and then in Chicago.

[4]The difficulty with iron and steel is that they rust and can be damaged by fire. To overcome these limitations, they were embedded in concrete, to make FERROCONCRETE, which is fire- and water-resistant, but has low tensile strength and is subject to erosion. Ferroconcrete thus unites the best of both materials. CONCRETE is made by heating limestone and clay until they almost fuse, then grinding and mixing them with water and stone, sand, or gravel. Used widely by the Romans, it was rediscovered in 1774 by John Smeaton of England. PORTLAND CEMENT, which is stronger and more durable, was invented in 1824 by another Englishman, Joseph Aspdin. The process of making it is similar to that of concrete but uses different materials. Lime, silica, alumina, sulfates, and iron oxide are heated until they nearly coalesce before being ground up and mixed with gypsum. Though a concrete house was built as early as 1837 by J. B. White of England, cement did not become widely adopted until the 1850s and '60s, when it was employed for sewer systems. It nevertheless remained too expensive for large-scale use before the early 1900s.

[5]Ferroconcrete incorporating tension rods was first patented in 1856 by François Coignet. Iron beams were substituted in patents issued in 1867 and 1878 to Joseph Monier, whose system was improved further by Gustav Adolf Wayss in his important publication of 1887. In 1892 the Belgian François Hennebique replaced iron with steel and enclosed girders in cement for the first time to protect them from fire and corrosion, as well as from the chemical fumes found in factories. Equally important, he combined all supports, walls, and ceilings into a single unit using hooked connections that was far more stable. The final step was taken in the early 1900s by Eugène Freyssinet, who recalculated all the formulas for reinforced concrete and in the process invented PRESTRESSED CONCRETE, which enables curved supports to carry much greater loads and counteracts deterioration of the concrete itself under pressure.

⁶As important as these developments were, modern architecture would not have been possible without others that we now take for granted. PLATE GLASS was introduced in the 1820s, followed by the cheaper SHEET GLASS around 1835. The repeal of the excise tax on glass in 1845 in England finally made sheet glass an affordable material on a large scale. Used in conjunction with cast iron, ever-larger panes of glass gave rise to the modern storefront, which became ubiquitous after midcentury. Massive windows, used serially, were also incorporated first into department stores and eventually skyscrapers from the late 1870s onward. Equally essential to the skyscraper was the invention of the PASSENGER ELEVATOR by Elisha Otis in 1857. The humble BRICK became an important building material in the 1850s with the advent of the modern kiln, which produced it cheaply in vast quantities. Other amenities included gas lighting (1840s), toilets (c. 1870), electricity (1880s), telephones (1880s), and central heat (1890s).

⁷Finally, we should mention RUBBER. It was at first limited chiefly to waterproofing as the result of a process for applying it to fabrics devised by Samuel Peale in 1791, though it was the chemist Charles Mackintosh who opened the first factory in Glasgow in 1823. Its widespread use as insulation and for other applications was made possible only in 1839, when Charles Goodyear, relying on the work of the German chemist Friedrich Ludersdorf and the American chemist Nathaniel Hayward, discovered VULCANIZATION, which involved cooking the rubber with sulfur to prevent it from melting in hot weather and becoming brittle in cold. Synthetic rubber was initially developed in Germany during World War I because natural rubber was hard to come by, but it was not commercially viable until after 1930, when the chemistry of polymers was finally understood through the efforts of Wallace Hume Carothers of the United States and Hermann Staudinger of Germany. The result was the production of neoprene (1931), Buna (1935), butyl rubber (1940), and GR-5 (Government Rubber-Styrene, used in World War II).

Use Your Strategies 4 Questions

1. Based on your need to take a test on how the materials used in architecture have changed through the years, what method would you use to organize the information? Please explain.
2. What material do Janson and Janson say had "by far the most important" effect on architectural style?
3. What are the advantages using cast iron rather than wood? What are the disadvantages?
4. What innovation made steel-frame construction possible?
5. What advantage does ferroconcrete have over iron and steel?
6. What is the advantage of prestressed concrete?
7. List five additional developments Janson and Janson cite as important to modern architecture.
8. Use the organization strategy of your choice on this selection.

REFLECT AND CONNECT

A. Select a five-paragraph reading assignment from another class. Based on your purpose and the content, use one of these strategies: annotate it, create an informal outline or map, or write a summary of the selection.

B. Does anyone ever tell you that he or she wishes you were better organized? What changes do you think he or she wants you to make? Do you ever wish other people were more organized? What advice would you give them?

LOG ON TO THE WEB

These Web sites contain information on people or events in history or links to sites with such information. Log on to one of these sites or use a search engine to locate a multiparagraph narrative or expository article on a person or event in history.

http://www.thehistorynet.com/THNarchives/AmericanHistory/

http://www.americaslibrary.gov/

http://www.pbs.org/lewisandclark/

A. Print out the article.

B. Assume you are going to answer an essay question about the importance of the person or event or a sequence of events in history.

C. Annotate the article, create an informal outline or information map of it, or write a summary of it.

D. Turn in your annotated printout or the printout along with your outline, map, or summary.

REFERENCES

Alvermann, D. E., & P. R. Boothby. (1986). "Children's Transfer of Graphic Organizer Instruction. *Reading Psychology: An International Quarterly,* 7, 87–100.

Merkley, Donna M., & Debra Jefferies. (2000). "Guidelines for Implementing a Graphic Organizer." *Reading Teacher,* 54(4).

Bean, T. W., H. Singer, J. Sorter, & C. Frasee. (1986). "The Effect of Metacognitive Instruction in Outlining and Graphic Organizer Construction on Students' Comprehension in a Tenth-Grade World History Class." *Journal of Reading Behavior,* 18, 153–169.

Flood, J., & D. Lapp. (1988). "Conceptual Mapping Strategies for Understanding Information Texts." *Reading Teacher,* 41(8), 780–783.

Griffin, C. C., & B. L. Tulbert. (1995). "The Effect of Graphic Organizers on Students' Comprehension and Recall of Expository Text: A Review of the Research and Implications for Practice." *Reading and Writing Quarterly,* 11, 73–89.

Hawk, P. P. (1986). "Using Graphic Organizers to Increase Achievement in Middle School Life Science." *Science Education,* 70, 81–87.

Heimlich, J. E., & S. D. Pittelman. (1986). *Semantic Mapping: Classroom Applications.* Newark, DE: International Reading Association.

Nelson, J. R., & D. J. Smith. (1992). "The Effects of Teaching a Summary Skills Strategy to Students Identified as Learning Disabled on Their Comprehension of Science Text." *Education and Treatment of Children,* 15, 228–243.

read-ing (red´in) *adj.* **1** inclined to read or study **2** reading n. **1** the act or practice of a person who reads of books **2** a public entertainment in which literary aloud **3** the extent to which a person has read **4** meant to be read **5** the amount measured as by a thermometer **6** the form of a specified word, sentence

CHAPTER 9

Becoming a More Critical Reader

Readers may be divided into four classes:

1. *Sponges, who absorb all that they read and return it in nearly the same state, only a little dirtied.*
2. *Sand-glasses, who retain nothing and are content to get through a book for the sake of getting through the time.*
3. *Strain-bags, who retain merely the dregs of what they read.*
4. *Mogul diamonds, equally rare and valuable, who profit by what they read and enable others to profit by it also.*

—Samuel Taylor Coleridge

AN IDEA TO THINK ABOUT

How will you decide whom to vote for during the next election? If you want to buy a new car or truck, where will you look for information on the most reliable models and best buys? Among all the organizations that ask for contributions, how will you decide which one(s) get your time and money?

If you're like most people, you'll gather information in two ways: you'll listen to friends, experts, and analysts, and you'll read an assortment of print materials—everything from advertisements to newspapers to Web pages.

The problem is, sometimes you're investigating a topic you don't know much about. In addition, you often find conflicting viewpoints. For example, suppose you are reading information on genetically altered food. The first journal article is by a scientist who concludes that "genetically altered food is hazardous to our health and should be banned." The next article is by a scientist who suggests that "genetically altered food poses no threat to human health." Your Web search locates more than 800 pages with information about genetically altered food—from those with predictions that genetically altered food will lead to global catastrophe to those declaring it will save the people of many nations from starvation.

As you read each article, book, and Web page, most of the information seems reasonable and the examples appear plausible. Yet the selections contain different and sometimes contradictory information.

What do you do? Do you just keep searching until you find *the* journal or book or Web site that contains the "right" information? If you tried this approach on genetically altered food, or almost any other topic, your search would never end. This is because most fields of study require humans to interpret information, make inferences, and reach reasoned conclusions. Therefore, it is quite common for even rational professionals to have different points of view.

This means you must become an effective **critical reader**. As Mursell (1951) says in *Using Your Mind Effectively,*

> There is one key idea which contains, in itself, the very essence of effective reading, and on which the improvement of reading depends: *Reading is reasoning.* When you read properly, you are not merely assimilating. You are not automatically transferring into your head what your eyes pick up on the page. What you see on the page sets your mind at work, collating, criticizing, interpreting, questioning, comprehending, comparing. When this process goes on well, you read well. When it goes on ill, you read badly.

What are some of the steps you take to make sure you are collating, criticizing, interpreting, questioning, comprehending, and comparing rather than merely assimilating?

CHAPTER 9 AT A GLANCE

CHAPTER FOCUS

Many research studies have investigated what expert readers do and think while reading text. In reviewing the research, Asselin (2002) found that proficient readers most commonly use these Plan→Do→Review cycle kinds of strategies:

- Set a purpose for reading, such as for pleasure, to find information;

- Preview text for relevancy to reading purpose and identify key parts;

- Make and revise predictions about the text;

- Read selectively;
- Figure out meanings of new words in context;
- Note important points;
- Associate ideas in text with prior knowledge;
- Evaluate text quality; and
- Review the text.

In addition, once readers understood the author's information and had accomplished their primary purpose, they critically examined the information and

- Revised prior knowledge based on reading, and
- Thought about how to apply new information from the text.

Therefore, we can extend the basic Plan→Do→Review cycle:

Extended Plan→Do→Review Cycle

Plan to read

Do the reading

Review what you read

Revise prior knowledge based on reading
Think about how to apply new information from the reading

This chapter introduces reading strategies that provide a base for the more sophisticated critical analysis techniques you will encounter in advanced course work.

BECOMING A CRITICAL READER

Critical readers are not negative people who enjoy finding fault with or being critical of what they read. Critical readers are open-minded individuals who appreciate the rich diversity of values, contexts, and ideas in our world. They ask questions so they can find inconsistencies in their own thinking as well as the thinking of others. They seek to understand different points of view so they can better understand their own views. They take time to objectively evaluate information rather than immediately accept or reject it.

They learn to compare sources, look for **biases**, demand clear citations for facts, and critically assess information, whether it comes from a Web site, a magazine, a broadcast documentary, or a respected reference book (Caywood, 1998).

KEEP AN OPEN MIND

Although we don't like to admit it, the old saying "Don't confuse me with the facts; my mind's already made up" often describes our behavior. Because we're human, our first inclination is to agree with authors who provide information that supports our views and to discount authors who give information that contradicts our views.

However, you want to behave exactly the opposite of that old saying. You want to examine what the author says and then make up your mind.

Monitor Assumptions and Biases

One of the best defenses against opinionated or impulsive reactions to an author's ideas and information is to maintain an honest awareness of your own **assumptions** and **biases**.

Assumptions are personal beliefs we take for granted; *biases* are assumptions that keep us from considering the **evidence** fairly. Statements such as "I don't care what anybody says, I know it's not true" or "That's my opinion and nothing is going to change it" are prime examples of accepting or rejecting a conclusion based on our biases rather than evidence. A critical reader asks questions such as, "What are the author's assumptions? What are my assumptions? What evidence supports or refutes this argument? Is the evidence reliable?"

This does not mean, however, that asking questions—being open-minded—means never accepting information, forming opinions, or taking a position. "It's good to be open-minded," philosopher Jacob Needlerman once said, "but not so open that your brains fall out."

EXAMINE THE INFORMATION AND EVIDENCE

When you have an accurate understanding of what the author says and means, you can thoughtfully and impartially examine the information and evidence the author uses to develop and support the thesis. In other words, you set aside your biases and examine it objectively.

First, differentiate among the facts, opinions, and reasoned judgments—the information and evidence—the author uses to develop and support the thesis. Then, weigh the merits of each. You can have confidence in facts, valid opinions, and reasoned judgments, but you should be skeptical of unsubstantiated opinions.

Next, determine if each piece of information and evidence is

1. **Relevant**: Does it have a clear, supportive connection to the thesis? Relevant evidence includes pertinent and specific details that advance the author's position. Do not be misled by interesting but irrelevant information.

2. **Consistent**: Does each piece of information work together to develop and support the thesis? Together, the information should clarify the author's thesis.
3. **Reliable**: Does the information appear to be trustworthy and accurate? Also review the sources the author used. Are they sufficient and reputable?

The more relevant, consistent, and reliable information the author provides, the stronger the thesis.

In addition, determine if the author presents, but then discounts either directly or with subtle language, all the information except that which supports his or her view.

EXAMINE THE REASONING

When we ask someone to "be logical—don't jump to conclusions," we are asking them to use a process of reasoning from evidence rather than making snap judgments or responding from emotion. Common labels for this process include terms such as *infer, deduce, conclude,* and *generalize.* All these words imply arriving at a sensible, rational, reliable inference at the end of a chain of reasoning; reaching a statement about what isn't known or hasn't happened on the basis of what is known or has happened. In formal logic, each term has a distinct meaning, but in everyday language, we often use these terms interchangeably.

When you examine the author's reasoning, you look at the thesis and information/evidence as a whole to determine if it is logical, complete, and fair. You want to make sure the author's ideas have evolved from a process of reasoning from evidence rather than from emotion. You're looking for any **fallacies**. Fallacies are errors in reasoning due to faulty evidence or incorrect inferences.

It is crucial that both you and the author use sound reasoning.

REACH A REASONED JUDGMENT

> There are two ways to slice easily through life: to believe everything or to doubt everything. Both ways save us from thinking.
>
> —Alfred Korzybski, Polish-American linguist

You want authors to provide relevant information, evidence, and reasoned judgments to support their thesis. In the same way, you want to be certain the inferences you draw from the author's work are accurate and reasonable. This is because your reasoned judgments form the basis for accepting, rejecting, or suspending judgment on what the author says.

You do not, of course, have to accept or reject every aspect of what an author says. You may give a "mixed review" to what you read. For example, you might accept an author's thesis, but think some of the data is too old. You may think the author has used good sources, but feel there isn't enough information and that you need to suspend judgment to seek additional information.

Also remember that you can always change your decision to accept, reject, or suspend judgment. As a critical reader, you are open-minded: new information, changing facts, a fresh perspective always give you the opportunity to review and rethink.

APPLY NEW INFORMATION

The worth of any reading, whether you accept what the writer said, reject it, or seek additional information, is the way it increases your knowledge and experience. The ideas, information, and points of view should come together to inform and enlighten.

Think about each new idea. Consider how it reinforces existing knowledge and/or what new perspective it adds. Connect the idea to issues and events in your life. And, when you gather new evidence and updated information, review, rethink, and grow.

Exercise 1

LINDA BREN

Ms. Bren is a staff writer for the FDA Consumer *magazine, a publication of the U.S. Food and Drug Administration. This article appeared in the November–December 2002 issue.*

AN IDEA TO THINK ABOUT

If you have healthy lungs, can more oxygen help you perform better? Can you ever have too much oxygen? *As you read,* find out what the FDA thinks of the oxygen bar trend.

OXYGEN BARS: IS A BREATH OF FRESH AIR WORTH IT?

Linda Bren

[1]Peppermint, bayberry, cranberry, wintergreen. Breath mints? Scented candles? No—they're "flavors" of oxygen offered at your local oxygen bar. Since oxygen bars were introduced in the United States in the late 1990s, the trend has caught on, and customers are bellying up to bars around the country to sniff oxygen through a plastic hose (cannula) inserted into their nostrils. And many patrons opt for the "flavored" oxygen produced by pumping oxygen through an aroma en route to the nose.

[2]The oxygen experience in a bar can last from a few minutes to about 20 minutes, depending on customers' preferences and the size of their wallets. The price of about a dollar a minute could leave you gasping for air, but frequent inhalers may get a discount.

[3]Most oxygen bar proprietors are careful not to make medical claims for their product, and state that their oxygen is not a medical gas—it's made and offered strictly for recreational use. But under the Federal Food, Drug, and Cosmetic Act, any type of oxygen used by people for breathing and administered by another person is a prescription drug. "It doesn't matter what they label it," says Melvin Szymanski, a consumer safety officer in the Food and Drug Administration's Center for Drug Evaluation and Research (CDER). "At the other end of the hose is oxygen, and the individual that provides you with the nasal cannula and turns on the canister for your 20-minute supply is actually dispensing the prescription drug oxygen to you."

[4]Although oxygen bars that dispense oxygen without a prescription violate FDA regulations, the agency applies regulatory discretion to permit the individual state boards of licensing to enforce the requirements pertaining to the dispensing of oxygen, says Szymanski. Many states choose to allow oxygen bars; others discourage the businesses by requiring strict compliance with the law. However, serious health claims made for oxygen, such as curing cancer or AIDS, or helping ease arthritis pain, would be investigated by the FDA, adds Szymanski.

HEALTHY OR JUST HYPE?

[5]Oxygen fans tout the benefits of oxygen as reducing stress, increasing energy and alertness, lessening the effects of hangovers, headaches, and sinus problems, and generally relaxing the body. But there are no long-term, well-controlled scientific studies that support these claims for oxygen in healthy people. And people with healthy lungs don't need additional oxygen, says Mary Purucker, M.D., Ph.D., a pulmonary specialist in CDER. "We've evolved for millions of years in an atmosphere of about 21 percent oxygen."

[6]The American Lung Association says that inhaling oxygen at oxygen bars is unlikely to have a beneficial physiological effect, but adds "there is no evidence that oxygen at the low flow levels used in bars can be dangerous to a normal person's health."

[7]People with certain medical conditions are another matter. Some need supplemental oxygen, but should not go to oxygen bars, says Purucker. People with some types of heart disease, asthma, congestive heart failure, pulmonary hypertension, and chronic obstructive pulmonary diseases, such as emphysema, need to have their medical oxygen regulated carefully to oxygenate their blood properly, says Purucker. "If they inhale too much oxygen, they can stop breathing."

[8]People who have received bleomycin, a chemotherapy used to treat some types of cancer, are in danger if they are exposed to high levels of oxygen for too long, adds Purucker. "People think oxygen is good, but more is not necessarily better."

[9]One of the FDA's biggest concerns about oxygen bars is the use of "flavored" oxygen, says Purucker. The flavor is produced by bubbling oxygen through bottles containing aromatic solutions and then pumping the vaporized scent through the hose and into the nostrils. Some bars use oil-free, food-grade particles to produce the aroma, but others may use aroma oils. Inhaling oily substances can lead to a serious inflammation of the lungs, known as lipoid pneumonia. Even if an oil-free medium is used, the

purity or sterility of the aerosol that is generated cannot be guaranteed. Susceptible customers run the risk of inhaling allergens or irritants that may cause them to wheeze. Inhalation of live contaminants such as bacteria or other pathogens may lead to infection.

OTHER OXYGEN HAZARDS

[10]Although oxygen doesn't burn, it does fuel the combustion process. "Smoking anywhere near oxygen, even in the same room, can be extremely dangerous," says Duane Sylvia, a consumer safety officer in CDER. While some oxygen bars are located in health spas or other facilities that don't allow smoking, others are found in nightclubs or casinos where smoking is common. Another fire hazard is the addition of substances, such as oils, in an oxygen-enriched environment.

[11]Improper maintenance of oxygen equipment presents a potential danger. Some oxygen concentrators use clay filters, which can start growing pathogenic microorganisms that can cause infection if they are not changed regularly.

[12]And oxygen cylinders can be very hazardous if they are stored on their sides or not kept in a well-ventilated area, says Sylvia.

PUMPING OXYGEN

[13]Most oxygen bars use either "aviators breathing oxygen" or oxygen extracted out of the air in the bar. Aviators breathing oxygen (ABO) is a medical-grade oxygen, not less than 99.0 percent pure, intended for commercial or private aircraft use. ABO should not be used for recreational inhalation or medical therapeutic treatment of humans or animals.

[14]Many oxygen bars use a concentrator, which filters out the nitrogen and other gases in the air circulating in the room, and then delivers the concentrated oxygen, about 95 percent pure, through a hose at a continuous flow rate. But oxygen users inhale the surrounding air along with the oxygen pumped through the nose hose, which decreases the concentration. The concentration is further decreased when oxygen is pumped through an aroma. According to one oxygen bar supplier, the customer gets less than 50 percent pure oxygen.

[15]Although breathing these low levels of oxygen may not hurt a healthy person, "people have nothing to gain by frequenting oxygen bars, and subject themselves to unnecessary risk," says Purucker.

Exercise 1 Questions

1. What is Bren's thesis?
2. Describe the information and evidence Bren provides to develop and support the thesis.
3. Who would likely present information and evidence to contradict Bren's thesis?
4. At this time, what is your reasoned judgment about the positives and negatives of frequenting an oxygen bar? If you feel you need more information before you make a judgment, where would you research the topic? Please explain.
5. How could you use this information?

Exercise 2

ELLIOT ARONSON, TIMOTHY D. WILSON, AND ROBIN M. AKERT

Dr. Aronson has done pioneering work in the areas of social influence and persuasion. He is professor emeritus at the University of California Santa Cruz and a visiting professor at Stanford University. Dr. Wilson is a professor of psychology at the University of Virginia and has written extensively in the areas of introspection, attitude change, self-knowledge, and affective forecasting. Dr. Akert is a professor of psychology at Wellesley College, where she was awarded the Pinanski Prize for Excellence in Teaching. She publishes primarily in the area of nonverbal communication. This excerpt is from Chapter 7, "Attitudes and Attitude Change," in their text Social Psychology, *fourth edition.*

AN IDEA TO THINK ABOUT

Does advertising ever influence you to take a particular action or buy a specific product? Does advertising ever influence anyone you know? *As you read,* find out what the research tells us about the power of advertising.

THE POWER OF ADVERTISING

Elliot Aronson, Timothy D. Wilson, and Robin M. Akert

[1]We began this chapter with a discussion of daily assaults on our attitudes by advertisers. The world of advertising is rich with examples of the principles of attitude and behavior change we have been discussing. But is there evidence that advertising really works? Most of the research we have discussed was conducted in the laboratory with college students. What about changes in attitudes and behavior out there in the real world? If we see an ad campaign for ScrubaDub detergent, are we really more likely to buy ScrubaDub when we go to the store? Or are companies wasting the billions of dollars a year they are spending on advertising?

[2]A curious thing about advertising is that most people think it works on everyone but themselves (Wilson & Brekke, 1994). A typical comment is, "There is no harm in watching commercials. Some of them are fun, and they don't have much influence on me." People can be influenced, however, more than they think (Wilson, Houston, & Meyers, 1998). In fact, substantial evidence indicates that advertising can have powerful effects (Abraham & Lodish, 1990; Liebert & Sprafkin, 1988; Ryan, 1991; Wells, 1997). The best evidence that advertising works comes from studies using what are called *split cable market tests*. Here advertisers work in conjunction with cable television companies and grocery stores, showing a target commercial to a randomly selected group of people. They keep track of

what people buy by giving potential consumers special ID cards that are scanned at checkout counters; thus they can tell whether people who saw the commercial for ScrubaDub actually buy more ScrubaDub—the best measure of advertising effectiveness.

[3]Magid Abraham and Lennard Lodish (1990) have conducted more than three hundred split cable market tests. Their findings indicate that advertising does work, particularly for new products (Lodish et al., 1995). About 60 percent of the advertisements for new products led to an increase in sales, compared to 46 percent of the advertisements for established brands. When an ad was effective, how much did it increase sales? The difference in sales between people who saw an effective ad for a new product and those who did not averaged 21 percent. Although this figure might seem modest, it translates into millions of dollars when applied to a national advertising campaign. Further, these effective ads worked quickly, increasing sales substantially within the first six months they were shown.

HOW ADVERTISING WORKS

[4]How does advertising work, and which types of ads work best? The answers follow from our earlier discussion of attitude change. By way of review, advertisers should consider the kind of attitude they are trying to change. If they are trying to change an affectively based attitude, then, as we have seen, it is best to fight emotions with emotions. Many advertisements take the emotional approach—for example, ads for different brands of soft drinks. Given that different brands of colas are not all that different, many people do not base their purchasing decisions on the objective qualities of the different brands. Consequently, soda advertisements do not stress facts and figures. As noted by one advertising executive, "The thing about soda commercials is that they actually have nothing to say" ("Battle for Your Brain," 1991). Instead of presenting facts, soda ads play to people's emotions, trying to associate feelings of excitement, youth, energy, and sexual attractiveness with the brand.

[5]If people's attitudes are more cognitively based, then we need to ask an additional question: How personally relevant is the issue? Does it have important consequences for people's everyday lives, or is it a remote issue that does not directly affect them? Consider, for example, the problem of heartburn. This is not a topic that evokes strong emotions and values in most people. Thus it is more cognitively based. To people who suffer from frequent heartburn, however, it is clearly of direct personal relevance. In this case, the best way to change people's attitudes is to use logical, fact-based arguments—convince people that your product will reduce heartburn the best or the fastest, and people will buy it (Chaiken, 1987; Petty & Cacioppo, 1986).

[6]What if you are dealing with a cognitively based attitude that is not of direct personal relevance to people? For example, what if you are trying to sell a heartburn medicine to people who experience heartburn only every now and then and do not consider it that big a deal? Here you have a problem, because people are unlikely to pay close attention to your advertisement. You might succeed in changing their attitudes via the peripheral route, such as having attractive movie stars endorse your product. The problem here, as we have seen, is that attitude change triggered by simple peripheral cues is not long-lasting (Chaiken, 1987; Petty & Cacioppo,

1986). Thus if you have a product that does not engage people's emotions and is not of direct relevance to people's everyday lives, you are in trouble.

[7]But don't despair. The trick is to *make* your product personally relevant. Let's take a look at some actual ad campaigns to see how this is done. Consider the case of Gerald Lambert, who early in the twentieth century inherited a company that made a surgical antiseptic used to treat throat infections—Listerine. Seeking a wider market for his product, Lambert decided to promote it as a mouthwash. The only problem was that no one at the time used a mouthwash or even knew what one was. So, having invented the cure, Lambert invented the disease. Look at the ad at the bottom of this page, which appeared in countless magazines over the years.

[8]Even though today we would find this ad incredibly sexist, at the time most Americans did not find it offensive. Instead, the ad successfully played on people's fears about social rejection and failure. The phrase "She was often a bridesmaid but never a bride" became one of the most famous in the history of advertising. In a few cleverly chosen, manipulative words, it succeeded in making a problem—*halitosis*—personally relevant to millions of people. Listerine became a best-selling product that has since earned a fortune. Incidentally, you might think *halitosis* is the official term of the American Medical Association for bad breath. In fact, it was a quite obscure term until Gerald Lambert and his advertising team made it a household word,

This ad is one of the most famous in the history of advertising. Although today it is easy to see how sexist and offensive it is, when it appeared in 1936 it succeeded in making a problem (bad breath) personally relevant by playing on people's fears and insecurities about personal relationships. Can you think of any contemporary ads that try to raise similar fears?

making it sound like a dreadful disease that we must avoid at all costs—by going to the nearest drugstore and stocking up on mouthwash.

[9]Lambert's success at playing to people's fears and sense of shame was not lost on other advertisers. Similar ads have been designed to create new markets for many new products, most having to do with personal hygiene or health: underarm deodorants, deodorant soaps, vitamin supplements, oat bran, fish oil, and more. These campaigns work by convincing people that they have problems of great personal relevance and that the advertised product can solve these problems.

[10]Many advertisements also try to make people's attitudes more affectively based by associating the product with important emotions and values (recall our earlier discussion of classical conditioning). Consider, for example, advertisements for long-distance telephone service. This topic does not, for most of us, evoke deep-rooted emotional feelings—until, that is, we see an ad in which a man calls his long-lost brother to tell him he loves and misses him or a man calls his mother to tell her he has just bought her a plane ticket so that she can come visit him. There is nothing logically compelling about these ads. After all, there is no reason to believe that using AT&T will magically make you closer to your family than using MCI or Sprint. However, by associating positive emotions with a product, an advertiser can turn a bland product into one that evokes feelings of nostalgia, love, warmth, and general goodwill.

SUBLIMINAL ADVERTISING: A NEW FORM OF MIND CONTROL?

[11]We cannot leave the topic of advertising without returning to one of its most controversial aspects—the use of **subliminal messages,** defined as words or pictures that are not consciously perceived but nevertheless supposedly influence people's judgments, attitudes, and behaviors. Did the word RATS embedded in the Bush campaign ad really have any effect on people's attitudes? Most members of the public believe that subliminal messages can shape their attitudes and behaviors, even though they do not know the messages have entered their minds (Zanot, Pincus, & Lamp, 1983). Given the near-hysterical claims that have been made about subliminal advertising, it is important to discuss whether it really works.

[12]In the late 1950s, James Vicary convinced a movie theater in New Jersey to try a novel approach to selling drinks and popcorn. Imagine that you happened to go to the theater that day to see *Picnic,* a popular movie at the time. Unbeknown to you or the other patrons, you see more than the movie. Messages are flashed on the screen at speeds so quick that they are not consciously perceived, messages that urge you to "drink Coca-Cola" and "eat popcorn." Vicary claimed that these messages registered in the audience members' unconscious minds and caused them to develop a sudden hankering for soda and popcorn. Coca-Cola sales at the concession counter increased by 18 percent, he said, and popcorn sales increased by 58 percent.

[13]When Vicary revealed what he had done, the public reaction was swift. Journalists blasted Vicary's sneaky attempt to boost sales. Minds have been "broken and entered," decried the *New Yorker* (September 21, 1957, p. 33), and the *Nation* called it "the most alarming and outrageous discovery since Mr. Gatling invented his [machine] gun" (October 5, 1957, p. 206). . . .

Exercise 2 Questions

1. What is the authors' thesis?
2. Describe the information and evidence the authors provide to develop and support the thesis.
3. At this time, what is your reasoned judgment about the effects of advertising? If you feel you need more information before you make a judgment, where would you research the topic? Please explain.
4. How could you use this information?

CHAPTER 9 REVIEW QUESTIONS

1. Describe what it means to be a critical reader.
2. Why is it important to keep and open mind?
3. Describe some of the elements you look for when you examine the author's information and evidence.
4. Describe some of the elements you look for when you examine the author's reasoning.
5. I've said that in my opinion the "worth of any reading is the way it increases your knowledge and experience." In what ways do you agree and/or disagree?

Use Your Strategies 1: Two Articles on Irradiated Food

Read both articles and then complete the questions at the end of article B.

JOHN HENKEL

John Henkel is a staff writer for the FDA Consumer *magazine, a publication of the U.S. Food and Drug Administration. This article first appeared in the May–June 1998 issue and was updated in January 2000.*

IDEAS TO THINK ABOUT

Do you know how and why foods are irradiated? When you're grocery shopping, do you look at labels to see if food has been irradiated? *As you read,* find out why some people favor irradiating foods and others dislike the process.

A. FOOD IRRADIATION: A SAFE MEASURE

John Henkel

[1]Food safety is a subject of growing importance to consumers. One reason is the emergence of new types of harmful bacteria or evolving forms of older ones that can cause serious illness. A relatively new strain of *E. coli,*

for example, has caused severe, and in some cases life-threatening, outbreaks of food-borne illness through contaminated products such as ground beef and unpasteurized fruit juices.

[2]Scientists, regulators and lawmakers, working to determine how best to combat food-borne illness, are encouraging the use of technologies that can enhance the safety of the nation's food supply.

[3]Many health experts agree that using a process called irradiation can be an effective way to help reduce food-borne hazards and ensure that harmful organisms are not in the foods we buy. During irradiation, foods are exposed briefly to a radiant energy source such as gamma rays or electron beams within a shielded facility. Irradiation is not a substitute for proper food manufacturing and handling procedures. But the process, especially when used to treat meat and poultry products, can kill harmful bacteria, greatly reducing potential hazards.

[4]The Food and Drug Administration has approved irradiation of meat and poultry and allows its use for a variety of other foods, including fresh fruits and vegetables, and spices. The agency determined that the process is safe and effective in decreasing or eliminating harmful bacteria. Irradiation also reduces spoilage bacteria, insects and parasites, and in certain fruits and vegetables it inhibits sprouting and delays ripening. For example, irradiated strawberries stay unspoiled up to three weeks, versus three to five days for untreated berries.

[5]Food irradiation is allowed in nearly 40 countries and is endorsed by the World Health Organization, the American Medical Association and many other organizations.

[6]Irradiation does not make foods radioactive, just as an airport luggage scanner does not make luggage radioactive. Nor does it cause harmful chemical changes. The process may cause a small loss of nutrients but no more so than with other processing methods such as cooking, canning, or heat pasteurization. Federal rules require irradiated foods to be labeled as such to distinguish them from non-irradiated foods.

[7]Studies show that consumers are becoming more interested in irradiated foods. For example, the University of Georgia created a mock supermarket setting that explained irradiation and found that 84 percent of participating consumers said irradiation is "somewhat necessary" or "very necessary." And consumer research conducted by a variety of groups, including the American Meat Institute, the International Food Information Council, the Food Marketing Institute, the Grocery Manufacturers of America, and the National Food Processors Association, has found that a large majority of consumers polled would buy irradiated foods.

[8]Some special interest groups oppose irradiation or say that more attention should be placed on food safety in the early stages of food processing such as in meat plants. Many food processors and retailers reply that irradiation can be an important tool for curbing illness and death from food-borne illness. But it is *not* a substitute for comprehensive food safety programs throughout the food distribution system. Nor is irradiation a substitute for good food-handling practices in the home.

LINDA GREENE

Linda Greene is a feature writer for Vitality, *a magazine devoted to health and fitness.*

B. IRRADIATED FOOD: SOME FACTS TO CONSIDER

Linda Greene

[1]The idea of irradiated food may conjure up images of glowing vegetables that would send a Geiger counter reading through the ceiling. But does irradiation make food radioactive?

[2]When food is irradiated, it is sent on a conveyor belt into a room containing cobalt 60 rods (a radioactive isotope). The room is then flooded with gamma rays. After treatment, the food looks and tastes the same as before.

[3]According to Edward Josephson, professor of food science and nutrition at the University of Rhode Island in West Kingston, irradiated food is no more radioactive than luggage is after it passes through an airport X-ray machine. The gamma rays used to irradiate food pass right through without leaving waste products behind.

[4]However, Michael F. Jacobson, Ph.D., executive director of the Center for Science in the Public Interest in Washington, D.C., explains that just because the food isn't radioactive doesn't mean it is safe to eat. Research indicates that irradiated food contains tiny amounts of a few unsavory chemicals. And the amount of nutrients in the food are reduced by the process.

IRRADIATED FOOD—THE PROS

[5]The reasons to treat foods with radiation sound reasonable in theory. Radiation can kill bacteria (such as salmonella) that cause food poisoning and parasites that cause disease. It can destroy insects in produce, lengthen the shelf life of fruits and vegetables and offer an alternative to the use of certain fumigants and chemicals that have been linked to cancer. Irradiation holds the promise of dramatically reducing food-related disease and expanding the world food supply.

[6]Currently, the FDA has approved the use of radiation to treat fruit, vegetables, grains, pork, poultry, wheat and wheat flour, white potatoes, spices and dry or dehydrated enzyme preparations used in many processed foods.

IRRADIATED FOOD—THE CONS

[7]Irradiation eliminates some problems with food but has the potential to create others. The process causes molecules to break down, and a few stray parts called free radicals may recombine into new derivatives called

radiolytic products (such as benzene and formaldehyde), some of which have been linked to cancer.

[8]With low doses of radiation, the number of radiolytic products produced is minimal. Moreover, some radiolytic products also occur naturally in foods and are sometimes created during cooking or processing. But no tests exist that can detect food that has received abnormally high doses of radiation and that could contain many radiolytic products. Also, some scientific research indicates irradiated foods have a degree of toxicity.

[9]An additional concern is irradiation's effect on food nutrients. Studies have shown that irradiation reduces levels of vitamin C, thiamin, vitamin E and polyunsaturated fats. This may prove to be a critical problem because the FDA estimates that, eventually, as much as 40 percent of the food we eat could be irradiated.

THE BOTTOM LINE

[10]Much of the food we eat will never undergo irradiation. Some foods, such as dairy products and water-based vegetables, aren't suitable for the process. And because U.S. food distribution and hygiene systems are good, irradiation is not cost-effective for most products. If you don't want to eat irradiated food until more research has been completed, pay attention to packaging in the grocery store: All radiation-treated foods must bear a special green symbol. Avoiding them when eating out is more of a challenge because restaurants aren't required to identify dishes made with irradiated ingredients. Each of us, weighing the pros and cons, will have to make our own decision about eating irradiated food. Irradiated food can lower our risk of food poisoning, but its long-range cancer-causing potential is still largely unknown.

Use Your Strategies 1 Questions

1. What is Henkel's thesis in Article A?
2. Describe the information and evidence Henkel provides to develop and support the thesis.
3. What is Greene's thesis in Article B?
4. Describe the information and evidence Greene provides to develop and support the thesis.
5. At this time, what is your reasoned judgment about irradiated foods? If you feel you need more information before you make a judgment, where would you research the topic? Please explain.
6. How could you use this information?

Use Your Strategies 2

BERNARD J. NEBEL AND RICHARD T. WRIGHT

Dr. Nebel is professor emeritus of biology at Catonsville Community College in Maryland. Dr. Wright is chairman of the Division of Natural Sciences, Mathematics, and Computer Science at Gordon College in Massachusetts. Both are known for their many professional and environmental endeavors. This selection is from their text Environmental Science.

AN IDEA TO THINK ABOUT

Should some jobs be protected from layoffs more than others? Should some companies and sectors of the economy be protected more than others? *As you read,* decide if you agree with Nebel and Wright that our planet's ecosystems are much like private sector corporations.

IN PERSPECTIVE: NATURE'S CORPORATIONS

Bernard J. Nebel and Richard T. Wright

[1]The Spotted Owl controversy pits jobs against the preservation of the old-growth forests of the West. Timber interests maintain that preservation will result in 20,000 lost jobs. In their view, the controversy comes down to this: We should continue to cut the old-growth forests for the sake of keeping loggers employed.

[2]General Motors and other major businesses facing hard times lay off thousands of workers, and no one questions their need or right to do so. Clearly, the survival of General Motors is more important than keeping all their workers employed. It is assumed that those laid off will find other employment. According to conventional wisdom, corporate America must survive if the economy is to have a chance of recovering from economic bad times.

[3]In a real sense, ecosystems are the corporations that sustain the economy of the biosphere. If we want those ecosystems to survive and recover, we may have to tighten our belt and withdraw some of the work force engaged in exploiting them. The maintenance of these systems is obviously more important than some jobs. Why can't laid-off loggers seek other employment the way laid-off autoworkers, steelworkers, or computer engineers do? Why should a natural ecosystem be "bankrupted" just to maintain the temporary employment of a few (temporary because the loggers will be out of a job in a few years when the old-growth forests are finally all cut)?

[4]Clearly, it is short-sighted to assume that ecosystems are there just to provide jobs and that the jobs are more important than the ecosystems. When the old-growth forests are gone, we shall have lost more than just loggers' jobs—we shall have lost a priceless heritage and a major part of the natural world that provides us with vital services.

Use Your Strategies 2 Questions

1. What is Nebel and Wright's purpose?
2. What is Nebel and Wright's thesis?
3. To what do Nebel and Wright compare ecosystems? Do you think this is a valid comparison? Why or why not?

4. Describe the information and evidence Nebel and Wright provide to develop and support the thesis.

5. At this time, do you accept, reject, or suspend judgment on their thesis? Please explain.

6. How could you use this information?

Use Your Strategies 3

JOHN J. MACIONIS

Dr. Macionis is professor of sociology at Kenyon College in Gambier, Ohio. He is the author of numerous articles and papers on topics such as community life in the United States, interpersonal relationships in families, effective teaching, and humor. This selection is from Chapter 20, "Education," in Sociology, *Ninth edition.*

AN IDEA TO THINK ABOUT

What do you think is the most serious educational issue facing Americans today? *As you read,* find out what Macionis thinks the most serious problem is and why.

ACADEMIC STANDARDS

John J. Macionis

¹Perhaps the most serious educational issue confronting our society is the quality of schooling. *A Nation at Risk,* a comprehensive report on the quality of U.S. schools published in 1983 by the National Commission on Excellence in Education, begins with this alarming statement:

²If an unfriendly foreign power had attempted to impose on America the mediocre educational performance that exists today, we might well have viewed it as an act of war. As it stands, we have allowed this to happen to ourselves. (1983:5)

³Supporting this conclusion, the report notes that "nearly 40 percent of seventeen-year-olds cannot draw inferences from written material; only one-fifth can write a persuasive essay; and only one-third can solve mathematical problems requiring several steps" (1983:9). Furthermore, scores on the Scholastic Aptitude Test (SAT) have declined in recent decades. In 1967, median scores for students were 516 on the mathematical test and 543 on the verbal test; by 2000, despite a recovery during the last few years, the averages were 514 and 505, respectively. Nationwide, about one-third of high school students—and more than half in urban schools—fail to master even the basics in reading, math, and science on the National Assessment of Education Progress examination (Sanchez, 1998; Marklein, 2000).

⁴For many, even basic literacy is at issue. Functional illiteracy, a lack of reading and writing skills needed for everyday living, is a problem for one in eight children who leave U.S. secondary schools. For older people, the problem is even worse, so that, overall, some 40 million U.S. adults (roughly 20 percent of the total) read and write at an eighth-grade level or below. As Figure 20-4 shows, the extent of functional illiteracy in the United States is below that of middle-income nations (such as Poland) but higher than in other high income countries (such as Canada and Sweden).

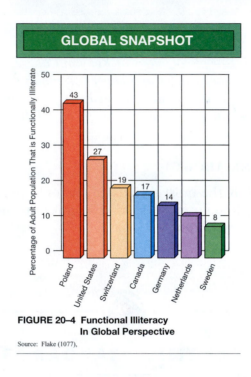

GLOBAL SNAPSHOT

**FIGURE 20–4 Functional Illiteracy
In Global Perspective**

Source: Flake (1077),

⁵To improve our educational system, *A Nation at Risk* called for drastic measures. First, all schools should require students to complete several years of English, mathematics, social studies, general science, and computer science courses. Second, schools should not promote failing students from grade to grade; instead, students should remain in the classroom as long as necessary to learn basic skills. Third, teacher training must improve, and teachers' salaries should rise to attract talent into the profession. *A Nation at Risk* concluded that educators must ensure that schools meet public expectations and that citizens must be prepared to bear the costs of good schools.

⁶What has happened in the years since this report was issued? In some respects, schools have improved. A report by the Center on Education Policy (2000) noted a decline in the dropout rate, a trend toward schools offering more challenging courses, and a larger share of high school graduates going on to college. Despite several tragic cases of shootings, overall school violence was down during the 1990s. At the same time, the evidence suggests that a majority of elementary school students are falling below standards in reading; in many cases, they can't read at all. In short, although some improvement is evident, there remains much to be done.

⁷A final concern is the low performance of U.S. students in a global context. Although per-student spending is greater in this country than almost anywhere else, U.S. eighth graders still place seventeenth in the

world in science achievement and twenty-eighth in mathematics (Bennett, 1997; Finn & Walberg, 1998). Cultural values play a big part in international comparisons. For example, U.S. students generally are less motivated than their counterparts in Japan and also do less homework. Moreover, Japanese young people spend sixty more days in school each year than U.S. students. Perhaps one approach to improving schools is simply to have students spend more time there.

Use Your Strategies 3 Questions

1. What is Macionis's thesis?
2. Describe the information and evidence Macionis provides to develop and support the thesis.
3. At this time, do you accept, reject, or suspend judgment on his thesis? Please explain.
4. How could you use this information?

Use Your Strategies 4

HARVEY MACKAY

Mackay is the author of several New York Times *bestsellers, including* Swim with the Sharks Without Being Eaten Alive, Beware the Naked Man Who Offers You His Shirt, *and* Pushing the Envelope: All the Way to the Top. *His nationally syndicated column appears in 52 newspapers around the country. He is also one of America's most popular and entertaining business speakers, chairman and CEO of Mackay Envelope Corporation, an $85 million company he founded at age 26, and an avid runner and marathoner.*

IDEAS TO THINK ABOUT

How would you characterize your chances of success in life? What are some of the things you think will help you achieve success? What are some of the things you think will keep you from achieving success? *As you read,* find out how Mackay answers those questions.

THE ROAD TO SUCCESS IS PAVED WITH DETERMINATION, FOCUS

Harvey Mackay

[1]There were only two times in my life when I wanted to be older. When I was 15 and the minimum age for a driver's license was 16. And when I was 59, and a marathoner, I knew the next year I'd be ranked against 60- to 64-year-olds instead of 55- to 59-year-olds.

[2]I ran in the Boston Marathon this year. By Mile 10, I didn't think I was going to get even a minute older. It was my 10th marathon and the toughest. With one mile to go, I hooked up with an old friend, Hal Higdon, editor of the fabulous magazine *Runners' World*. He was just about to complete his 100th (and this is not a typo, folks) marathon—100th Boston and his own 100th. He was grimacing and not looking too good, so I hollered out, "What's wrong?. . . You should be on Cloud 9 . . . They can't take this away from us!"

[3]He said he had fallen apart at Mile 10, a point at which, for the running elite, the real race hasn't even started. For the past 15 miles, he was just gutting it out.

[4]Twenty-five yards from the finish line, I had to slow down and take in the whole scene. My running partner, Bill Wenmark, had taken out his camera so he could take a picture as I crossed the finish line.

[5]At that moment, Higdon, who by now was five to 10 runners ahead of me, turned back, cupped his hands and said, "Harvey, that will teach you to stop for a picture."

[6]Hal Higdon, my hero, a gutsy performer, his competitive juices still flowing down to the last nanosecond. The truth is, except for the elite, marathoners do not compete against each other.

[7]When you are running with 38,000 other people, how can it really matter whether you finish 8,651st, 18,651st or 28,651st?

[8]What matters is, you finish . . . period.

[9]There is only one thing runners really compete against: It is the little voice that grows louder at every split that says: "Stop."

[10]It is, unfortunately, a familiar sound. We hear it all our lives, at work, at school, in our personal relations.

[11]It tells us we cannot succeed.

[12]We cannot finish.

[13]The boss expects too much.

[14]The company is too demanding.

[15]The homework assignment takes too long.

[16]Our family is too unappreciative.

[17]The truth is that many successful people are no more talented than unsuccessful people.

[18]The difference between them lies in the old axiom that successful people do those things that unsuccessful people don't like to do.

[19]Successful people have the determination, the will, the focus, the drive to complete the tough jobs.

[20]Why run 26 miles, 385 yards?

[21]Why torture yourself to achieve a goal with no tangible reward or significance other than what you yourself assign to it?

[22]The answer lies in the question.

[23]Because only you can know what it means, only you are able to make yourself do it.

[24]When you do, then you know there isn't anything you can't do.

[25]No amount of hype, no cheering section, no personal glory, no place in the annals of history can carry you all those miles.

[26]You have to do it yourself.

[27]Your chances of success in life are probably just as good as anyone else's.

²⁸Don't shortchange yourself through fear or a preconceived notion that the cards are stacked against you.

²⁹At the Boston Marathon, Heartbreak Hill is at Mile 18. There are Mile 18s in everyone's life.

³⁰Some come earlier in the race. Some later.

³¹But wherever you find them, you can overcome them.

³²Running a marathon is not about winning the race against 38,000 other runners. It's about winning the race against yourself.

MACKAY'S MORAL:

Nothing in the world can take the place of persistence. Talent will not. . . . Genius will not. . . . Education will not. . . . Persistence and determination alone are omnipotent. Press on.

—Ray Kroc, McDonald's founder

Use Your Strategies 4 Questions

1. What is Mackay's thesis? What does he want you to do?
2. What analogy does Mackay use to develop and support his thesis?
3. What does Mackay say are the main differences between successful people and unsuccessful people? Do you agree or disagree? Why?
4. At this time, do you accept, reject, or suspend judgment on his thesis? Please explain.
5. How could you use this information?

REFLECT AND CONNECT

A. In the Introduction to Chapter 7, I asked a series of questions: "Even if you have strong feelings about the issue, could you write an essay that equally presents the positive and negative aspects of getting older? What precautions would you take if you wanted to make sure you were presenting both sides of the issue? Do you think it would be wrong if you wrote only your feelings? Do you think it would be important for someone reading your essay to know if you had personal feelings about aging that influenced what you wrote?" Please discuss your answers to those questions.

B. During most of your prior school experience, you probably were taught to accept the information in textbooks without question. What changes in this approach, if any, would you suggest to elementary and high school teachers? What is an advantage of accepting text information without question? What is a disadvantage?

LOG ON TO THE WEB

Log on and locate two articles on a topic that interests you.

A. Print out both articles, making sure to include the URLs.

B. For each article,

1. State the author's thesis.

2. Describe the information and evidence the authors provide to develop and support the thesis.

3. Explain what you see as the primary similarity and/or difference between the two articles.

4. Explain your judgment about each author's information.

5. Describe how you could use this information.

C. Attach your answers to the print outs and turn them in to your professor.

REFERENCES

Asselin, Marlene. (2002). "Comprehension Instruction: Directions from Research." *Teacher Librarian,* 29(4), 55.

Caywood, Carolyn. (1998). "The Facts of the Matter." *School Library Journal,* 44(4).

Mursell, James. (1951). *Using Your Mind Effectively.* New York: McGraw-Hill, pp. vi–vii.

First Amendment Freedoms

Congress shall make no law respecting an establishment of religion, or prohibiting the free exercise thereof; or abridging the freedom of speech, or of the press, or the right of the people peaceably to assemble, and to petition the Government for a redress of grievances. *[First Amendment of the Constitution proposed by Congress on September 25, 1789, and ratified by the necessary three-fourths of the States on December 15, 1791.]*

The 45 words of the First Amendment have gone unchanged since they were adopted as one of the ten amendments to the Constitution known as the Bill of Rights. However, unchanged does not mean unchallenged.

While most Americans celebrate the freedoms guaranteed by the First Amendment, many also feel that those freedoms are sometimes dangerous. For example: Can teachers and students say anything they want to in a classroom? Can newspapers print anything they want about anyone? Can librarians have any books they want in a school or other public library? Can employees email any type of jokes and pictures?

If they cannot do these things, who decides what can be said or printed or shelved or emailed?

Perhaps, as Oliver Wendell Holmes said, "The only useful test of whether someone believes in the First Amendment is whether he or she would vigorously protect the views of the people they hate."

Many Americans believe that people in the public eye, such as professional athletes, movie stars, rap musicians, and politicians, should be free to express personal opinions without the threat of punishment. Others believe that people in positions of influence should be held to a higher standard, although it is unclear who defines and sets the "higher standard."

Some Americans combine "freedom of speech, or of the press" into "freedom of expression." They then call anything that is said, printed, projected, or performed "expression" and therefore feel it is covered under the First Amendment. Others, however, feel that when freedom of expression is stretched to protect things such as gossip, racial slurs, obscenity, and pornography, the concept is questionable.

"The First Amendment generally, and freedom of expression in particular, are not absolute concepts, and that is why they are at once so difficult to administer and so essential to a free society and an educated citizenry," says Kermit L. Hall, president and professor of history at Utah State University.

How we react to the situations and controversies created by our "freedoms" helps define who we are and how we want our society to behave. Paul McMasters, ombudsman with the First Amendment Center, says it is possible that "without the First Amendment, our society—and our lives—might be calmer, safer, even more civil." However, he quickly adds that there is also "little doubt that we would be considerably less free."

Authors in this theme provide historical perspectives, current information, and personal insights about the freedoms guaranteed by the First Amendment.

"First Amendment Freedoms," Chapter 16 in *Government by the People* by Burns, Peltason, Cronin, Magleby, O'Brien, and Light, opens the theme and provides an overview and historical perspective of the freedoms.

To see how much you know about our First Amendment rights in everyday life, take *USA Weekend*'s "Five Tests of Your Freedoms." Next, Ken Paulson's foreword to the *State of the First Amendment 2003*, a report from the First Amendment Center, provides a snapshot of Americans' views about our First Amendment freedoms.

Charles Haynes asks us, "How Much Religious Freedom Is Too Much?" Ken Paulson encourages us to consider the implications of "'Free' and Other 4-Letter Words," and then Dilbert creator Scott Adams illustrates the slippery slope of censoring speech.

Newspaper columnist Bill Thompson asks, "Well, Would You Rather Have an Unfree Press?" and then Adam Newton closes the theme with a concise history of "Our Right to Petition" and what it means to us today.

First Amendment Freedoms

JAMES MACGREGOR BURNS, J. W. PELTASON, THOMAS E. CRONIN, DAVID B. MAGLEBY, DAVID M. O'BRIEN, AND PAUL C. LIGHT

Dr. Burns is a senior scholar at the Academy of Leadership, University of Maryland, College Park, and Woodrow Wilson professor emeritus of government at Williams College. Burns has written numerous books and been awarded numerous prizes, including a Pulitzer Prize in history. Dr. Peltason is a leading scholar on the judicial process and public law, and is professor emeritus of political science at the University of California, Irvine. Peltason is past president of the American Council on Education. Dr. Cronin teaches at and serves as president of Whitman College and is a leading scholar of the American presidency and leadership. Cronin was a White House Fellow, a White House aide, and president of the Western Political Science Association. Dr. Magleby is professor of political science at Brigham Young University and nationally recognized for his expertise on direct democracy, voting behavior, and campaign finance. Magleby has received numerous teaching awards and was a Fulbright scholar at Oxford University. Dr. O'Brien is the Leone Reaves and George W.

Spicer professor at the University of Virginia. O'Brien was a judicial fellow and research associate at the Supreme Court of the United States, a Fulbright lecturer at Oxford University, a Fulbright researcher in Japan, and held the Fulbright chair for Senior Scholars at the University of Bologna. Dr. Light is the Paulette Goddard professor of public service at New York University's Wagner School of Public Service and Douglas Dillon senior fellow at the Brookings Institution. This is Chapter 16 from their twentieth edition of Government by the People.

VOCABULARY

Key vocabulary words and phrases are in boldface type and are defined in the chapter and in marginal annotations.

AN IDEA TO THINK ABOUT

The Constitution guaranteed only a few basic rights to citizens, and many of the states would not ratify it until the more specific Bill of Rights was added. If we did not have the Bill of Rights—specifically the First Amendment— how do you think our lives would be different? *As you read,* look for specific ways our freedom of religion, speech, press, assembly, and petition impact our daily lives.

CHAPTER 16

FIRST AMENDMENT FREEDOMS

CONGRESS SHALL MAKE NO LAW," DECLARES THE FIRST AMENDMENT, "RESPECTING AN ESTABLISHMENT OF RELIGION, OR PROHIBITING the free exercise thereof, or abridging the freedom of speech, or of the press, or the right of the people peaceably to assemble, and to petition the Government for a redress of grievances." In this one sentence, our Constitution lays down the fundamental principles of a free society: freedom of conscience and freedom of expression. These freedoms are essential to our individual self-determination and to our collective self-governance—to government by the people. Yet they are also vulnerable during times of war and now with recent security measures put into place to combat international terrorism.[1]

These freedoms were not constitutionally guaranteed, though, until the addition in 1791 of the first ten amendments, the Bill of Rights. For that reason, we begin this chapter by discussing the rights in the original Constitution and in the Bill of Rights as applied to both the national and state governments before turning to the "first freedoms" of religion, speech, press, and assembly.

Rights in the Original Constitution

Even though most of the framers did not think a bill of rights was necessary, they considered certain rights important enough to be spelled out in the Constitution. These rights included the writ of habeas corpus and protection against *ex post facto* laws and bills of attainder.

Foremost among constitutional rights is the **writ of habeas corpus**. Literally meaning "produce the body," this writ is a court order directing any official having a person in custody to produce the prisoner in court and explain why the prisoner is being held. As originally used, the writ was merely a judicial inquiry to determine whether a person in custody was being held as the result of the action of a court with proper jurisdiction. But over the years, it developed into a remedy for any illegal confinement. People being held

Rights in the Original Constitution

1. Habeas corpus
2. No bills of attainder
3. No *ex post facto* laws
4. No titles of nobility
5. Trial by jury in national courts
6. Protection for citizens as they move from one state to another, including the right to travel
7. Protection against using crime of treason to restrict other activities; limitation on punishment for treason
8. Guarantee that each state has a republican form of government
9. No religious test oaths as a condition for holding a federal office

writ of habeas corpus
Court order requiring explanation to a judge why a prisoner is being held in custody.

ex post facto law
Retroactive criminal law that works to the disadvantage of an individual; forbidden in the Constitution.

bill of attainder
Legislative act inflicting punishment, including deprivation of property, without a trial, on named individuals or members of a specific group.

due process clause
Clause in the Fifth Amendment limiting the power of the national government; similar clause in the Fourteenth Amendment prohibiting state governments from depriving any person of life, liberty, or property without due process of law.

can appeal to a judge, usually through an attorney, stating why they believe they are held unlawfully and should be released. The judge then orders the jailer or a lower court to show cause why the writ should not be issued. If a judge finds a petitioner is detained unlawfully, the judge may order the prisoner's immediate release. Although state judges lack jurisdiction to issue writs of habeas corpus to find out why federal authorities are holding persons, federal district judges may do so to find out if state and local officials are holding people in violation of the Constitution or national laws.

In recent years, the use of the writ of habeas corpus by federal courts to review convictions by state courts has been widely criticized. Some people believe the writ has been abused by state prisoners to get an endless and expensive round of reviews, which sometimes lead to convictions' being set aside by a federal judge after the matter has been reviewed by two or more state courts. Partly because of concerns about maintaining the principles of federalism and partly because of the growing caseloads of federal courts, the Supreme Court and Congress have severely restricted the habeas corpus jurisdiction of federal judges. The Antiterrorism and Effective Death Penalty Act of 1996, for example, restricts the number of times a person may be granted a habeas corpus review, stops appeals for most habeas petitions at the level of the U.S. Court of Appeals, and calls for deference by federal judges to the decisions of state judges unless they are clearly "unreasonable."[2]

An ***ex post facto* law** is a retroactive criminal law making a particular act a crime that was not a crime when an individual committed it, increasing punishment for a crime after the crime was committed, or lessening the proof necessary to convict for a crime after it was committed. This constitutional prohibition does not prevent the retroactive application of laws that work to the benefit of an accused person—a law decreasing punishment, for example—or prevent the retroactive application of civil law, such as an increase in income tax rates applied to income already earned.

Bills of attainder are legislative acts inflicting punishment, including deprivation of property, on named individuals or members of a specified group without a trial. For example, when Congress adopted a rider to an appropriations bill denying payment of the salaries of three federal employees for "disloyalty," the Supreme Court struck down the rider for being a bill of attainder.[3]

The Bill of Rights and the States

Although it was the framers who wrote the Constitution, in a sense it was the American people who drafted our basic charter of rights. The Constitution drawn up in Philadelphia included guarantees of a few basic rights but lacked a specific bill of rights similar to those in most state constitutions. The Federalists argued that the Constitution established a limited government that would not threaten individual freedoms, and therefore a bill of rights was unnecessary. The Antifederalists were not persuaded, and the omission aroused widespread suspicion. As a result, to persuade delegates to the state ratification conventions to vote for the Constitution, the Federalists promised to correct this deficiency. In its first session, the new Congress made good on that promise by proposing 12 amendments, ten of which were promptly ratified and became part of the Constitution.[4]

Note that the Bill of Rights applies *only to the national government*, not state governments.[5] Why not the states? The framers were confident that citizens could control their own state officials, and most state constitutions already had bills of rights. It was the new and distant central government the people feared. As it turned out, those fears were largely misdirected. The national government has generally shown less tendency to curtail civil liberties than state and local governments have.

When the Fourteenth Amendment, which applies to the states, was adopted in 1868, supporters contended that its **due process clause**—which states that no person shall be deprived by a state of life, liberty, or property without due process of law—limits states in precisely the same way the Bill of Rights limits the national government. At least, they argued, freedom of speech is protected by the Fourteenth

Key Concepts

At the outset, it is helpful to clarify certain terms—*liberties, rights, freedoms,* and *privileges*—that are often used interchangeably in discussions of rights and freedoms. We offer the following definitions.

Civil liberties The freedoms of all persons that are constitutionally protected against governmental restraint; the freedoms of conscience, religion, and expression, for example, which are secured by the First Amendment. These civil liberties are also protected by the due process and equal protection clauses of the Fifth and Fourteenth Amendments.

Civil rights The constitutional rights of all persons, not just citizens, to due process and the equal protection of the laws; the constitutional right not to be discriminated against by governments because of race, ethnic background, religion, or gender. These civil rights are protected by the due process and equal protection clauses of the Fifth and Fourteenth Amendments and by the civil rights laws of national and state governments.

Rights of persons accused of crimes The rights of all persons, guilty as well as innocent, to protection from abusive use by the government of the power to prosecute and punish persons accused of vio-

lating criminal laws. These rights are secured by the Fourth, Fifth, Sixth, Eighth, and Fourteenth Amendments.

Political rights The rights of citizens to participate in the process of governance flowing from the right to vote. These rights are secured by the Fourteenth, Fifteenth, Nineteenth, and Twenty-Third Amendments.

Legal privileges Privileges granted by governments to which we have no constitutional right and which may be subject to conditions or restrictions; for example, the right to welfare benefits or to a driver's license. But once such privileges are granted, we may have a legal right to them, and they cannot be denied except for "reasonable reasons" and by appropriate procedures.

Common law Judge-made law based on the interpretation and application of legal principles—the principle of freedom of speech, for example. Australia, England, and the United States are *common law* countries, in contrast with *civil law* countries on the European Continent.

Civil law Law evolved from Roman law and based on codes that are strictly applied by judges. *Civil law* also applies to disputes between individuals and the government that carry no criminal penalties.

Amendment. But for decades, the Supreme Court refused to interpret the Fourteenth Amendment in this way. Then in *Gitlow* v. *New York* (1925), the Court announced that it assumed "that freedom of speech and of the press—which are protected by the First Amendment from abridgment by Congress—are among the fundamental personal rights and 'liberties' protected by the due process clause of the Fourteenth Amendment from impairment by the States."[6]

Gitlow v. *New York* was a revolutionary decision. For the first time, the U.S. Constitution protected freedom of speech from abridgment by state and local governments. In the 1930s and continuing at an accelerated pace during the 1960s, through the **selective incorporation** of provision after provision of the Bill of Rights into the due process clause, the Supreme Court applied the most important of these rights to the states.[7] Today the Fourteenth Amendment imposes on the states all the provisions of the Bill of Rights except those of the Second and Third Amendments, the Fifth Amendment provision for indictment by a grand jury, the Seventh Amendment right to a jury trial in civil cases, and the Ninth and Tenth Amendments (see Table 16-1).

Selective incorporation of most provisions of the Bill of Rights into the Fourteenth Amendment is probably the most significant constitutional development since the writing of the Constitution. It has profoundly altered the relationship between the national government and the states. It made the federal courts, under the guidance of the Supreme Court of the United States, the most important protectors of our liberties.

Recently, however, there has been a renewal of interest in state constitutions as independent sources of additional protections for civil liberties and civil rights.[8] Advocates of what has come to be called the *new judicial federalism* contend that the U.S. Constitution should set minimum but not maximum standards to protect our rights. State bills of rights sometimes provide more protection of rights—the rights to equal education and personal privacy, for instance—than the national Bill of Rights or the Supreme Court's rulings on its guarantees. Despite the revival of interest in state bills of rights, the U.S. Supreme Court and the national Bill of Rights remain the dominant protectors of civil liberties and civil rights.

selective incorporation
The process by which provisions of the Bill of Rights are brought within the scope of the Fourteenth Amendment and so applied to state and local governments.

"In God We Trust" Mottos in Public Schools

The patriotic fervor ignited in the aftermath of the terrorist attacks of September 11, 2001, fueled a movement to post the motto "In God We Trust" in public school classrooms across the country. Before the attacks, only Mississippi had enacted a law requiring the posting. But three months afterward, Michigan adopted the requirement as part of its homeland security legislation. South Carolina, Utah, and Virginia, among other states, are considering similar legislation.

The American Family Association, a fundamentalist Christian organization, began a campaign in 1999 to get states to require the display of the national motto in public schools. The American Civil Liberties Union has fought the effort, claiming that it is simply a way to promote religion in schools and that it violates the First Amendment. The motto "In God We Trust" was adopted in 1956, during the cold war, and replaced *E Pluribus Unum* ("From Many, One").

SOURCE: Debbie Howlett, "'In God We Trust' Pressed for Schools," *USA Today,* February 20, 2002, A3.

TABLE 16–1   Selective Incorporation and the Application of the Bill of Rights to the States

Right	Amendment	Year
Public use and just compensation for the taking of private property by the government	5	1897
Freedom of speech	1	1925
Freedom of the press	1	1931
Fair trial	6	1932
Freedom of religion	1	1934
Freedom of assembly	1	1937
Free exercise of religion	1	1940
Separation of religion and government	1	1947
Right to a public trial	6	1948
Right against unreasonable searches and seizures	4	1949
Freedom of association	1	1958
Exclusionary rule	4	1961
Ban against cruel and unusual punishment	8	1962
Right to counsel in felony cases	6	1963
Right against self-incrimination	5	1964
Right to confront witness	6	1965
Right of privacy	1,3,4,5,9	1965
Right to an impartial jury	6	1966
Right to a speedy trial and compulsory process for obtaining witnesses	6	1967
Right to a jury trial in nonpetty cases	6	1968
Protection against double jeopardy	5	1969

Freedom of Religion

The first words of the First Amendment are emphatic and brief: "Congress shall make no law respecting an establishment of religion, or prohibiting the free exercise thereof." Note that there are *two* religion clauses: the *establishment* clause and the *exercise* clause. The Supreme Court has struggled to reconcile these two clauses, both of which are cast in absolute terms, and either of which, if expanded to a logical extreme, would clash with the other. Does a state scholarship for blind students given to a college student who decides to attend a college to become a minister violate the establishment clause by indirectly aiding religion? Or would denying the scholarship violate the student's free exercise of religion? The Supreme Court has held that giving such benefits does not violate the establishment clause.[9]

The Establishment Clause

In writing what has come to be called the **establishment clause**, the framers were reacting to the English system, wherein the crown was the head not only of the government but also of the established church—the Church of England—and public officials were required to take an oath to support the established church as a condition of holding office. The establishment clause goes beyond merely separating government from religion by forbidding the establishment of a state religion. It is designed to prevent three evils: government sponsorship of religion, government financial support of religion, and government involvement in religious matters. However, the clause does not prevent governments from "accommodating" religious needs. To what extent and under which conditions governments may accommodate these needs are at the heart of much of the debate in the Supreme Court and the country over interpreting the clause.

establishment clause
Clause in the First Amendment that states that Congress shall make no law respecting an establishment of religion. It has been interpreted by the Supreme Court as forbidding governmental support to any or all religions.

Controversies over the establishment clause are not easy to resolve. They stir deep feelings and frequently divide the justices among themselves. The prevailing interpretation stems from the decision in *Everson* v. *Board of Education of Ewing Township* (1947) that the establishment clause creates a "wall of separation" between church and state and prohibits any law or governmental action designed to specifically benefit any religion, even if all religions are treated the same.[10] That decision, though, was decided by a bare majority and upheld state support for transportation of children to private religious schools as a "child benefit."

The separation of church and state was further elaborated in *Lemon* v. *Kurtzman* (1971), which laid down a three-part test: (1) A law must have a secular legislative purpose, (2) it must neither advance nor inhibit religion, and (3) it must avoid "excessive government entanglement with religion."[11] This so-called *Lemon test* is often, but not always, used because the justices remain divided over how much separation between government and religion is required by the First Amendment.

Another test, championed by Justice Sandra Day O'Connor, is the *endorsement test*. Justice O'Connor believes that the establishment clause forbids governmental practices that a reasonable observer would view as endorsing religion, even if there is no coercion.[12] The endorsement test has been honed in a series of decisions as the Court struggled with the question of whether governments may allow religious symbols to be displayed on, in, or near public properties and in public places. For example, the Court concluded that when a nativity scene was displayed in a shopping district together with Santa's house and other secular and religious symbols of the Christmas season, there was little danger that a reasonable person would conclude that the city was endorsing religion.[13] But the Constitution does not permit a city government to display the nativity scene on the steps of the city hall, because in this context, the city gives the impression that it is endorsing the display's religious message.[14]

In this classroom at Pearl Upper Elementary School in Pearl, Mississippi, the controversial "In God We Trust" motto is on display. Before September 11, 2001, Mississippi was the only state to require the display of this motto; however, since this time, Michigan adopted the requirement as well and several other states are considering similar legislation.

The Court's three most conservative justices—Chief Justice William Rehnquist and Justices Antonin Scalia and Clarence Thomas—support a *nonpreferentialist test*.[15] They believe the Constitution prohibits favoritism toward any particular religion but does not prohibit government aid to *all* religions. In their view, government may accommodate religious activities and even give nonpreferential support to religious organizations so long as individuals are not legally coerced into participating in religious activities and religious activities are not singled out for favorable treatment.[16]

By contrast, the more liberal justices—Justices David H. Souter, John Paul Stevens, Ruth Bader Ginsburg, and Stephen Breyer—usually maintain that there should be *strict separation* between religion and the state.[17] They generally hold that even indirect aid for religion, such as scholarships or teaching materials and aids for students attending private religious schools, crosses the line separating the government from religion.

Applying these generalizations, we find that the establishment clause forbids states—including state universities, colleges, and school districts—from introducing devotional exercises into the public school curriculum, including school graduations and events before football games.[18] However, the Supreme Court has not, as some people assume, entirely prohibited prayer in public schools. It is not unconstitutional for students to pray in a school building. What is unconstitutional is sponsorship or encouragement of prayer *by public school authorities*.[19] Devotional reading of the Bible, recitation of the Lord's Prayer, and posting of the Ten Commandments on the walls of classrooms in public schools have also been ruled to be unconstitutional. A state may not forbid the teaching of evolution or require the teaching of "creation science"—the belief that human life did not evolve but rather was created by a single act of God.[20]

Tax exemptions for church properties, similar to those granted to other nonprofit institutions, are constitutional. State legislatures and Congress may also hire chaplains to open each day's legislative session—a practice that has continued without interruption since the first session of Congress. But if done in a public school, this practice would be unconstitutional. Apparently, the difference is that legislators, as adults, are not "susceptible to religious indoctrination or peer pressure."[21] Also, as the joke goes, legislators need the prayer more.

Vouchers and State Aid for Religious Schools

A troublesome area involving the separation of religion and government has revolved around states' providing financial assistance to parochial and other religious schools. The Supreme Court has tried to draw a line between permissible tax-provided aid to schoolchildren and impermissible aid to religion.

At the college level, the problems are relatively simple. Tax funds may be used to construct buildings and operate educational programs at church-related schools as long as the money is not spent directly on buildings used for religious purposes or on teaching religious subjects. Even if students choose to attend religious schools and become ministers, government aid to these students is permissible, because such aid has a secular purpose. Its effect on religion is the result of individual choice "and it does not confer any message of state endorsement of religion."[22]

At the level of elementary and secondary schools, however, the constitutional problems are more complicated. Here the secular and religious parts of institutions and instruction are much more closely interwoven. Also, students are younger and more susceptible to indoctrination, so the chances are greater that aid to church-operated schools aids religion in violation of the establishment clause.

Despite the constitutional obstacles, some states have provided tax credits or deductions for parents who send their children to private, largely religious-run schools. Such deductions or credits available *only* to parents of children attending nonpublic schools are unconstitutional, but allowing taxpaying parents to deduct or take a credit from their state income taxes for what they paid for tuition and other costs to send their children to school—public or private—is constitutional, even if most of the benefit goes to those sending their children to private religious schools.[23]

The Supreme Court has also approved using tax funds to provide students who attend primary and secondary church-operated schools (except those that deny admission because of race or religion) with textbooks, standardized tests, lunches, transportation to and from school, diagnostic services, sign language interpreters, and teachers for remedial and enrichment classes, as well as computers and software for both public and parochial schools.[24]

One hot controversy that the Supreme Court avoided for years involved whether states may also use tax money to give parents **vouchers** for the tuition of children to attend schools of their choice, including religious schools. Maine and Vermont have long had voucher programs for students living in rural areas. But Cleveland, Milwaukee, and the state of Florida experimented with voucher programs, permitting the payment of tuition at religious schools, that faced challenges in the courts.[25] Opponents argue that such programs violate the establishment clause, while supporters counter that they do not and argue that the denial of vouchers for attending religious schools violates the free exercise clause and denies parents the freedom of school choice in opting out of dysfunctional public schools.

The Supreme Court finally addressed the constitutionality of voucher programs in *Zelman* v. *Simmons-Harris* (2002),[26] and by a 5-to-4 vote found Ohio's program to be neutral and permissible. Ohio's law provides low-income families in Cleveland with vouchers of up to $2,250 per child to put toward the cost of their children's attending public or private schools outside of the failing inner-city school district, and 96 percent of the vouchers went to religious schools. As a result of this ruling, there may be increased pressure on state legislatures and school boards to adopt voucher programs.

The Free Exercise Clause

The right to hold any or no religious belief is one of our few absolute rights. The **free exercise clause** affirms that no government has authority to compel us to accept any creed or to deny us any right because of our beliefs or lack of them. Requiring religious oaths as a condition of public employment or as a prerequisite to running for public office is unconstitutional. In fact, the original Constitution states, "No religious Test shall ever be required as a Qualification to any Office or public Trust under the United States" (Article VI).

vouchers
Money provided by the government to parents for payment of their children's tuition in a public or private school of their choice.

free exercise clause
Clause in the First Amendment that states that Congress shall make no law prohibiting the free exercise of religion.

CHAPTER 16 *First Amendment Freedoms* 411

Although carefully protected, the right to practice a religion has had less protection than the right to hold particular beliefs. Prior to 1990, the Supreme Court carefully scrutinized laws allegedly infringing on religious practices and insisted that the government provide some compelling interest to justify actions that might infringe on somebody's religion. In other words, the First Amendment was thought to throw a "mantle of protection" around religious practices, and the burden was on the government to justify interfering with them in the least restrictive way.

Then, in *Employment Division* v. *Smith* (1990), the Rehnquist Court significantly altered the interpretation of the free exercise clause by discarding the compelling governmental interest test for overriding the interests of religious minorities.[27] As long as a law is generally applicable and does not single out and ban religious practices, the law may be applied to conduct even if it burdens a particular religious practice.

The ruling in *Employment Division* v. *Smith* was controversial and led Congress to enact the Religious Freedom Restoration Act of 1993 (RFRA), which aimed to override the *Smith* decision and to restore the earlier test prohibiting the government—federal, state, or local—from limiting a person's exercise of religion unless the government demonstrates a compelling interest that is advanced by the least restrictive means. Congress asserted its power to pass the RFRA because the Fourteenth Amendment gives it the authority to enforce rights secured by that amendment, including the right to free exercise of religion.

However, when the Catholic archbishop of San Antonio was denied a building permit in 1997 to enlarge a church in Boerne, Texas, because the remodeling did not comply with the city's historical preservation plan, he claimed that the city's denial of a building permit interfered with religious freedom as protected by the Religious Freedom Restoration Act. The Supreme Court then ruled the RFRA to be unconstitutional because Congress was attempting to define, rather than enforce or remedy, constitutional rights and was thereby assuming the role of the courts, which contradicted "vital principles necessary to maintain separation of powers and the federal balance."[28]

Tensions between the establishment and free exercise clauses have recently become more prominent. On the one hand, the University of Virginia denied a Christian student group funds to pay for the printing of its newspaper, *Wide Awake*, because it interpreted the establishment clause to forbid allocating student fee money to a newspaper that "primarily promotes a belief in or about a deity." The students argued that the university deprived them of their freedom of speech, including religious speech, and the Supreme Court agreed with the students.[29] On the other hand, some Christian students at the University of Wisconsin objected to the use of mandatory student activity fees for funding groups they deemed offensive and contrary to their religious beliefs. They argued that they should be exempt from paying that portion of their fees, but the Supreme Court rejected their claim.[30]

Reverend Anthony Cummins, pastor of St. Peter the Apostle Church, in front of his church in Boerne, Texas, after a battle with city officials who denied the church permission to build an addition to the historic structure.

Free Speech and Free People

Government by the people is based on every person's right to speak freely, to organize in groups, to question the decisions of the government, and to campaign openly against them. Only through free and uncensored expression of opinion can government be kept responsive to the electorate and political power transferred peacefully. Elections, separation of powers, and constitutional guarantees are meaningless unless all persons have the right to speak frankly and to hear and judge for themselves the worth of what others have to say. As Justice Oliver Wendell Holmes observed, "The best test of truth is the power of the thought to get itself accepted in the competition of the market. . . . That at any rate is the theory of our Constitution. It is an experiment, as all life is an experiment."[31]

Free speech is not simply the personal right of individuals to have their say; it is also the right of the rest of us to hear them. John Stuart Mill, whose *Essay on Liberty* (1859) is the classic defense of free speech, put it this way: "The peculiar evil of silencing the expression of opinion, is that it is robbing the human race. . . . If the opinion is right, they are deprived of the

Police arrest Scott Tyler of Chicago after he set fire to an American flag on the steps of the Capitol building in Washington. The Supreme Court ruled that freedom of speech even covers "symbolic speech" like burning the U.S. flag.

opportunity of exchanging error for truth; if wrong, they lose what is almost as great a benefit, the clearer perception and livelier impression of truth, produced by its collision with error."[32]

Americans overwhelmingly support the principle of freedom of expression in general. Yet some who say they believe in free speech draw the line at ideas they consider dangerous or when speech attacks them or is critical of their race, religion, or ethnic origin. But what is a dangerous idea? Who decides? In the realm of political ideas, who can find an objective, eternally valid standard of right? The search for truth involves the possibility—even the inevitability—of error. The search cannot go on unless it proceeds freely in the minds and speech of all. This means, in the words of Justice Robert Jackson, that "freedom to differ is not limited to things that do not matter much. That would be a mere shadow of freedom. The test of its substance is the right to differ as to things that touch the heart of the existing order."[33]

Even though the First Amendment explicitly denies Congress the power to pass any law abridging freedom of speech, the amendment has never been interpreted in absolute terms. Like almost all rights, the freedoms of speech and of the press are limited. In discussing the constitutional power of government to regulate speech, it is useful to distinguish among *belief, speech,* and *action.*

At one extreme is the right to *believe* as we wish. Despite occasional deviations in practice, the traditional American view is that government should not punish a person for beliefs or interfere in any way with freedom of conscience. At the other extreme is *action,* which is usually subject to governmental restraint. As has been said, "The right to swing your fist ends where my nose begins."

Speech stands somewhere between belief and action. It is not an absolute right, like belief, but neither is it as exposed to governmental restraint, like action. Some kinds of speech—libel, obscenity, fighting words, and commercial speech—are not entitled to constitutional protection in all circumstances. Many problems arise in distinguishing between what does and does not fit into the categories of nonprotected speech. People disagree, and it usually falls to the courts to decide and to defend the free speech of individual and minority dissenters.

Judging: Drawing the Line

Plainly, questions of free speech require that judges weigh a variety of factors: What was said? In what context? How was it said? Which level of government is attempting to regulate the speech—a city council speaking for a few people, or Congress, speaking for many? (The Supreme Court is much more deferential to acts of Congress than to those of a city council or state legislature.) How is the government attempting to regulate the speech—by prior restraint (censorship) or by punishment after the speech? Why is the government doing so—to preserve the public peace or to prevent criticism of the people in power? These and scores of other considerations are involved in the never-ending process of determining what the First Amendment permits and what it forbids.

Historical Constitutional Tests

It is useful to start with the three constitutional tests developed in the first part of the twentieth century: the bad tendency test, the clear and present danger test, and the preferred position doctrine. Although they are no longer applied, they provide a background for the current judicial approach to governmental regulation of speech and to the courts' expanding protection for free speech.

THE BAD TENDENCY TEST   This test was rooted in English common law. According to the **bad tendency test,** judges presumed it was reasonable to forbid speech that has a tendency to corrupt society or cause people to engage in illegal acts. The test was abandoned because it swept too broadly and ran "contrary to the fundamental premises underlying the First Amendment as the guardian of our democracy."[34] Some legislators still appear to hold this position today, and it also seems to be the view of some college students, who want to see their institution punish student colleagues or faculty who express "hateful" or "offensive" ideas.

bad tendency test
Interpretation of the First Amendment that would permit legislatures to forbid speech encouraging people to engage in illegal action.

SHOULD THE BILL OF RIGHTS BE AMENDED TO PROHIBIT FLAG BURNING?

You Decide... The American flag arouses patriotic emotions in Americans, many of whom fought and saw friends die under that banner. It is understandable that they would be angry to see that flag burned by protesters. Do you think the Constitution should be amended to give Congress the right to prohibit desecration of the American flag? Or would a constitutional amendment to prohibit flag burning be an unconstitutional violation of free speech?

Thinking It Through... On June 21, 1989, the Supreme Court, in *Texas* v. *Johnson,* decided by a 5-to-4 vote that the First Amendment protects the act of burning the flag as freedom of expression. President George H. W. Bush denounced the decision and called for a constitutional amendment that would nullify it. Congress responded by passing a federal law that would make it a crime to burn or deface the flag, whatever one's purposes or intent. In June 1990, the Supreme Court declared that law unconstitutional in *United States* v. *Eichman.*

An amendment to the Constitution would give Congress the power to prohibit flag desecration. Public opinion polls show strong support for it. Forty-nine state legislatures have already indicated they would ratify such an amendment, far more than the 36 needed. A Senate majority has several times voted in favor of such an amendment but has fallen short of the two-thirds majority needed to pass a constitutional amendment.

Before you decide, you might want to read the opinions of the Supreme Court justices in *Texas* v. *Johnson,* 491 U.S. 397 (1989), and *United States* v. *Eichman,* 496 U.S. 310 (1990). You may listen to the oral arguments in these cases by going to the Oyez Web site at www.oyeznwu.edu.

THE CLEAR AND PRESENT DANGER TEST   This is perhaps the most famous test. The **clear and present danger test** was formulated by Justice Oliver Wendell Holmes Jr. in *Schenck* v. *United States* (1919) as an alternative to the bad tendency test. In the words of Justice Holmes, "The question in every case is whether the words are used in circumstances and are of such a nature as to create a clear and present danger that they will bring about substantive evils that Congress has a right to prevent."[35] A government should not be allowed to interfere with speech unless it can prove, ultimately to a skeptical judiciary, that the particular speech in question presents an immediate danger—for example, speech leading to a riot, the destruction of property, or the corruption of an election.

Supporters of the clear and present danger test concede that speech is not an absolute right. Yet they believe free speech to be so fundamental to the operations of a constitutional democracy that no government should be allowed to restrict speech unless it can demonstrate a close connection between the speech and an imminent lawless action. To shout "Fire!" falsely in a crowded theater is the most famous example of unprotected speech.

THE PREFERRED POSITION DOCTRINE   This was advanced in the 1940s when the Court applied all of the guarantees of the First Amendment to the states. The **preferred position doctrine** came close to the position that freedom of expression—the use of words and pictures—should rarely, if ever, be curtailed. This interpretation of the First Amendment gives these freedoms, especially freedom of speech and of conscience, a preferred position in our constitutional hierarchy. Judges have a special duty to protect these freedoms and should be most skeptical about laws trespassing on them. Once that judicial responsibility was established, judges had to draw lines between nonprotected and protected speech, as well as between speech and nonspeech.

clear and present danger test
Interpretation of the First Amendment that holds that the government cannot interfere with speech unless the speech presents a clear and present danger that it will lead to evil or illegal acts. To shout "Fire!" falsely in a crowded theater is Justice Oliver Wendell Holmes's famous example.

preferred position doctrine
Interpretation of the First Amendment that holds that freedom of expression is so essential to democracy that governments should not punish persons for what they say, only for what they do.

Nonprotected and Protected Speech

Today the Supreme Court holds that only four narrow categories of speech—*libel, obscenity, fighting words,* and *commercial speech*—are **nonprotected speech** because they lack social redeeming value and are not essential to democratic deliberations and self-governance.

The fact that nonprotected speech does not receive First Amendment protection does not mean that the constitutional issues relating to these kinds of speech are simple. How we prove libel, how we define obscenity, how we determine which words are fighting words, and how much commercial speech may be regulated remain hotly contested issues.

Libel

At one time, newspaper publishers and editors had to take considerable care about what they wrote for fear they might be prosecuted for **libel**—published defamation or false statements—by the government or sued by individuals. Today, through a progressive elevation of constitutional standards, it has become more difficult to win a libel suit against a newspaper or magazine.

Seditious libel—defaming, criticizing, and advocating the overthrow of government—was once subject to criminal penalties but no longer is. Seditious libel was rooted in the common law of England, which has no First Amendment protections. In 1798, only seven years after the First Amendment had been ratified, Congress enacted the first national law against **sedition**, the Sedition Act of 1798. Those were perilous times for the young Republic, for war with France seemed imminent. The Federalists, in control of both Congress and the presidency, persuaded themselves that national safety required some suppression of speech. But popular reaction to the Sedition Act helped defeat the Federalists in the elections of 1800, and the Sedition Act expired in 1801. The Federalists had failed to grasp the democratic idea that a person may criticize the government, oppose its policies, and work for the removal of the individuals in power yet still be loyal to the nation. They also failed to grasp the distinction between *seditious speech* and *seditious action*—conspiring to commit and engaging in violence against the government, which can be prosecuted and punished.

Another attempt to limit political criticism of the government was the Smith Act of 1940. That law forbade advocating the overthrow of the government, distributing material advocating the overthrow of government by violence, and organizing any group having such purposes. In 1951, during the cold war, the Supreme Court agreed that the Smith Act could be applied to the leaders of the Communist party who had been charged with conspiring to advocate the violent overthrow of the government.[36]

Since then, however, the Court has substantially modified constitutional doctrine, giving all political speech First Amendment protection. In *New York Times* v. *Sullivan* (1964), seditious libel was declared unconstitutional.[37] Now neither Congress nor any government may outlaw mere advocacy of the abstract doctrine of violent overthrow of government: "The essential distinction is that those to whom the advocacy is addressed must be urged to do something now or in the future, rather than merely to believe in something."[38] Moreover, advocacy of the use of force may not be forbidden "except where such advocacy is directed to inciting or producing imminent lawless action and is likely to incite or produce such action."[39]

In the landmark ruling in *New York Times* v. *Sullivan* and subsequent cases, the Supreme Court established guidelines for libel cases and severely limited state power to award monetary damages in libel suits brought by public officials against critics of official conduct. Neither public officials nor public figures can collect damages for comments made about them unless they can prove with "convincing clarity" that the comments were made with "actual malice." *Actual malice* means not merely that the defendant made false statements but that the "statements were made with a knowing or reckless disregard for the truth."[40]

Public figures cannot collect damages even when subject to outrageous, clearly inaccurate parodies and cartoons. Such was the case when *Hustler* magazine printed a

---

nonprotected speech
Libel, obscenity, fighting words, and commercial speech, which are not entitled to constitutional protection in all circumstances.

libel
Written defamation of another person. Especially in the case of public officials and public figures, the constitutional tests designed to restrict libel actions are very rigid.

sedition
Attempting to overthrow the government by force or to interrupt its activities by violence.

parody of the Reverend Jerry Falwell; the Court held that parodies and cartoons cannot reasonably be understood as describing actual facts or actual events.[41] Nor does the mere fact that a public figure is quoted as saying something that he or she did not say amount to a libel unless the alteration in what the person said was made deliberately, with knowledge of its falsity, and "results in material change."[42]

Constitutional standards for libel charges brought by private persons are not as rigid as those for public officials and figures. State laws may permit private persons to collect damages without having to prove actual malice if they can prove the statements made about them are false and were negligently published.[43]

Obscenity and Pornography

Obscene publications are not entitled to constitutional protection, but members of the Supreme Court, like everybody else, have great difficulty in defining obscenity. As Justice Potter Stewart put it, "I know it when I see it."[44] Or, as the second Justice John Marshall Harlan explained, "One man's vulgarity is another man's lyric."[45]

In *Miller* v. *California* (1973), the Court finally agreed on a constitutional definition of **obscenity**. A work may be considered legally obscene if (1) the average person, applying contemporary standards of the particular community, would find that the work, taken as a whole, appeals to a prurient interest in sex; (2) the work depicts or describes in a patently offensive way sexual conduct specifically defined by the applicable law or authoritatively construed; and (3) the work, taken as a whole, lacks serious literary, artistic, political, or scientific value.[46]

Before *Miller,* the distinction between *pornography* and *obscenity* was not clear. The *Miller* standard clarified that only hard-core pornography is constitutionally unprotected. X-rated movies and adult theaters that fall short of the constitutional definition of obscenity are entitled to some constitutional protection, but less protection than political speech, and they are subject to greater government regulation. Cities may, as New York City has done, also regulate where adult theaters may be located by zoning laws,[47] and they may ban totally nude dancing in adult nightclubs.[48] Under narrowly drawn statutes, state and local governments can also ban the sale of "adult" magazines to minors, even if such materials would not be considered legally obscene if sold to adults.

The Court has also held that *child pornography*—sexually explicit materials either featuring minors or aimed at them—is not protected by the First Amendment.[49] Just as the government may protect minors, so apparently may it protect members of the armed forces. The Supreme Court left standing a ruling of a lower court upholding an act of Congress forbidding the sale or rental on military property of magazines or videos whose "dominant theme" is to portray nudity "in a lascivious way."[50]

Pressure for regulating pornography came primarily from political conservatives and religious fundamentalists concerned that it undermines moral standards. More recently, some feminists have joined them, arguing that pornography is degrading and perpetuates sexual discrimination and violence. They argue that just as sexually explicit materials featuring minors are not entitled to First Amendment protection, so should there be no protection for pornographic materials. They contend that pornography promotes the sexual abuse of women and maintains the social subordination of women as a class. Some feminists define pornographic materials more broadly than the Court has and would include sexually explicit pictures or words that depict women as sexual objects enjoying pain and humiliation or that present abuse of women as a sexual stimulus for men.[51]

Not all feminists favor antipornography ordinances, yet those who do have been joined by social conservatives, and thus a new battle over pornography continues to be fought. For this new antipornography coalition to be successful, a substantial alteration in constitutional doctrine will be required. Unlike the Canadian Supreme Court, which redefined obscenity to include materials that degrade women,[52] the U.S. Supreme Court does not appear willing to substantially change current doctrine.

Hustler *publisher Larry Flynt agrees to a plea bargain in which obscenity charges were dropped and a fine imposed if Flynt removed X-rated videos from a downtown store.*

obscenity
Quality or state of a work that taken as a whole appeals to a prurient interest in sex by depicting sexual conduct in a patently offensive way and that lacks serious literary, artistic, political, or scientific value.

IN COMPARATIVE PERSPECTIVE

Hate Speech in Canada

Although the Supreme Court of Canada, in interpreting the nation's Charter of Rights, generally follows the rulings on freedom of speech of the Supreme Court of the United States, it refused to do so with respect to hate speech. Whereas the U.S. Supreme Court held that the First Amendment bars making hate speech a crime,* the Canadian Supreme Court upheld a law making it a crime to express "hatred against any indentifiable group . . . distinguished by colour, race, religion, or ethnic origin."

James Keegstra.

James Keegstra, a high school teacher, was convicted of communicating anti-Semitic teachings to his students. His conviction, however, was overturned by an appeals court on the ground that the law punishing hate speech violated the Charter's guarantee of freedom of expression. In reversing the lower court and upholding Keegstra's conviction and Canada's hate speech law, the Supreme Court observed:

The international commitment to eradicate hate propaganda and, most importantly, the special role given equality and multiculturalism in the Canadian Constitution necessitate a departure from the view, reasonably prevalent in America at present, that the suppression of hate propaganda is incompatible with the guarantee of free expression. . . .

At the core of freedom of expression lies the need to ensure that truth and the common good are attained, whether in scientific and artistic endeavors or in the process of determining the best course to take in our political affairs. . . . Nevertheless, the argument from truth does not provide convincing support for the protection of hate propaganda. Taken to its extreme, this argument would require us to permit the communication of all expression, it being impossible to know with *absolute* certainty which factual statements are true, or which ideas obtain the greatest good. . . . There is very little chance that statements intended to promote hatred against an identifiable group are true, or that their vision of society will lead to a better world. To portray such statements as crucial to truth and the betterment of the political and social milieu is therefore misguided.†

*R.A.V. v. St. Paul, 505 U.S. 377 (1992).
†Regina v. Keegstra, 3 S.C.R. 697 (1990).

Fighting Words

Fighting words were held to be constitutionally unprotected because "their very utterance may inflict injury or tend to incite an immediate breach of peace."[53] That the words are abusive, offensive, and insulting or that they create anger, alarm, or resentment is not sufficient. Thus a four-letter word worn on a sweatshirt was not judged to be a fighting word in the constitutional sense, even though it was offensive and angered some people.[54] In recent years, the Court has overturned convictions for uttering fighting words and struck down laws that criminalized "hate speech"—insulting racial, ethnic, and gender slurs.[55]

Commercial Speech

Commercial speech—such as advertisements and commercials—used to be unprotected because it was deemed to have lesser value than political speech. But in recent years, the Court has reconsidered and extended more protection to commercial speech, as it has to fighting words. In *44 Liquormart, Inc.,* v. *Rhode Island* (1996), for instance, the Court struck down a law forbidding the advertising of the price of alcoholic drinks.[56] It now appears that states may forbid and punish only false and misleading advertising, along with advertising the sale of anything illegal—for example, narcotics. Although the Supreme Court has not specifically removed it from the nonprotected category, the Court has interpreted the First, Fifth, and Fourteenth Amendments so as to provide considerable constitutional protection for commercial speech.

fighting words
Words that by their very nature inflict injury on those to whom they are addressed or incite them to acts of violence.

commercial speech
Advertisements and commercials for products and services; they receive less First Amendment protection, primarily to discourage false and misleading ads.

Protected Speech

Apart from these four categories of nonprotected speech, all other expression is constitutionally protected, and courts strictly scrutinize government regulation of such speech. The Supreme Court uses the following doctrines to measure the limits of governmental power to regulate speech.

PRIOR RESTRAINT   Of all the forms of governmental interference with expression, judges are most suspicious of those that impose **prior restraint**—censorship before publication. Prior restraints include governmental review and approval before a speech can be made, before a motion picture can be shown, or before a newspaper can be published. Most prior restraints are unconstitutional, as the Court has said: "Any system of prior restraints of expression comes to this Court bearing a heavy presumption against its constitutional validity."[57] About the only prior restraints approved by the Court relate to military and national security matters—such as the disclosure of troop movements[58]—and to high school authorities' control over student newspapers.[59] Student newspapers at colleges and universities receive the same protections as other newspapers because they are independent and financially separate from the college or university.

VOID FOR VAGUENESS   Laws must not be so vague that people do not know whether their speech would violate the law and hence are afraid to exercise protected freedoms. Laws must not allow the authorities who administer them so much discretion that they may discriminate against people whose views they dislike. For these reasons, the Court strikes down laws under the void for vagueness doctrine.

LEAST DRASTIC MEANS   Even for an important purpose, a legislature may not pass a law that impinges on First Amendment freedoms if other, less drastic means are available. To illustrate, a state may protect the public from unscrupulous lawyers, but it may not do so by forbidding attorneys from advertising their fees for simple services. The state could adopt other ways to protect the public from such lawyers that do not impinge on their freedom of speech; it could, for example, provide for the disbarment of lawyers who mislead their clients.

CONTENT AND VIEWPOINT NEUTRALITY   Laws concerning the time, place, or manner of speech that regulate some kinds of speech but not others or that regulate speech expressing some views but not others are much more likely to be struck down than those that are content-neutral or viewpoint-neutral, that is, laws that apply to *all* kinds of speech and to *all* views. For example, the Constitution does not prohibit laws forbidding the posting of handbills on telephone poles. Yet laws prohibiting only religious handbills or only handbills advocating racism or sexism would in all probability be declared unconstitutional because they would relate to the kinds of handbills or what is being said rather than to all handbills regardless of what they say.

The lack of viewpoint neutrality was the grounds for the Court's striking down a St. Paul, Minnesota, ordinance that prohibited the display of a symbol that would arouse anger on the basis of race, color, creed, religion, or gender. The ordinance was not considered viewpoint-neutral because it did not forbid displays that might arouse anger for other reasons, for example, because of political affiliation.[60]

Freedom of the Press

Courts have carefully protected the right to publish information, no matter how journalists get it. But some reporters, editors, and others argue that this is not enough. They insist that the First Amendment gives them the right to ignore legal requests and to withhold information. They also contend that the First Amendment gives them a *right of access*, a right to go wherever they need to go to get information.

prior restraint
Censorship imposed before a speech is made or a newspaper is published; usually presumed to be unconstitutional.

Does the Press Have the Right to Withhold Information?

Although most reporters have challenged the right of public officials to withhold information, they claim the right to do so themselves, including the right to keep information from grand juries and legislative investigating committees. Without this right to withhold information, reporters insist, they cannot assure their sources of confidentiality, and they will not be able to get the information they need to keep the public informed.

The Supreme Court, however, has refused to acknowledge that reporters, and presumably scholars, have a constitutional right to ignore legal requests such as subpoenas and to withhold information from governmental bodies.[61] It is up to Congress and the states to provide such privileges for news reporters, and many states have passed *press shield laws* providing some protection for reporters from state court subpoenas.

Does the Press Have the Right to Know?

The press has argued that if reporters are excluded from places where public business is conducted or are denied access to information in government files, they are not able to perform their traditional function of keeping the public informed. In similar fashion, some reporters argue that they may enter facilities such as food markets, child care centers, and homes for the mentally ill, even using false identities, to expose racial discrimination, employment discrimination, and financial fraud. The Supreme Court, however, has refused to acknowledge a constitutional right of the press to know, although it did concede that there is a First Amendment right for the press, along with the public, to be present at criminal trials.[62]

Although they have no constitutional obligation to do so, many states have adopted *sunshine laws* requiring government agencies to open their meetings to the public and the press. Congress requires most federal executive agencies to open hearings and meetings of advisory groups to the public, and most congressional committee meetings are open to the public. Federal and state courtroom trials are also open, but judicial conferences, in which the judges discuss how to decide the cases, are not.

Congress has authorized the president to establish a classification system to keep some public documents and governmental files secret, and it is a crime for any person to divulge such classified information. So far, however, although they have been threatened, no newspapers have been prosecuted for doing so.

The Freedom of Information Act (FOIA) of 1966, since amended, liberalized access to nonclassified federal government records. This law makes the records of federal executive agencies available to the public, with certain exceptions, such as private financial transactions, personnel records, criminal investigation files, interoffice memorandums, and letters used in internal decision making. If federal agencies fail to act promptly on requests for information, applicants are entitled to speedy judicial hearings. The burden is on an agency to explain its refusal to supply material, and if the judge decides the government has improperly withheld information, the government has to pay the legal fees. Since the inception of FOIA, more than 250,000 people have requested information, and more than 90 percent of these requests have been granted.

President Bill Clinton issued an executive order calling for automatic declassification of almost all government documents after 25 years. Any person who wants access to documents that are not declassified can appeal to an Interagency Security Classification Appeals panel, which has a record of ruling in favor of releasing documents. The Electronic Freedom of Information Act of 1996 requires most federal agencies to put their files online and to establish an index of all their records. The National Aeronautics and Space Administration (NASA) has done the most of the federal agencies (see www.nasa.gov). One of the most frequent requests to NASA's Electronic Reading Room is for documents relating to unidentified flying objects (UFOs).

Free Press Versus Fair Trials

When newspapers and television report in vivid detail the facts of a crime, interview prosecutors and police, question witnesses, and hold press conferences for defendants and their attorneys—as in the O. J. Simpson murder and Oklahoma City bombing cases—they may so inflame the public that finding a panel of impartial jurors and conducting a fair trial is difficult. In England, strict rules determine what the media may report, and judges do not hesitate to punish newspapers that comment on pending criminal proceedings. In the United States, in contrast, free comment is protected. Yet the Supreme Court has not been indifferent to protecting persons on trial from inflammatory publicity. Judges may impose "gag orders" on lawyers and jurors, but not reporters, restraining them from talking about an ongoing trial, and new trials may be ordered as a remedy for prejudicial publicity. Trials may, on rare occasions, be closed to the press and the public. Although federal rules of criminal procedure forbid radio or photographic coverage on criminal cases in federal courts, most states permit televising courtroom proceedings, and court TV programs have become very popular.

Other Media and Communications

When the First Amendment was written, freedom of "the press" referred to leaflets, newspapers, and books. Today the amendment protects other media as well—the mails, motion pictures, billboards, radio, television, cable, telephones, fax machines, and the Internet. Because each form of communication entails special problems, each needs a different degree of protection.

The Mails

More than 80 years ago, Justice Oliver Wendell Holmes Jr. wrote in dissent, "The United States may give up the Post Office when it sees fit, but while it carries it on, the use of the mails is almost as much a part of free speech as is the right to use our tongues."[63] In 1965, the Court adopted Holmes's view by striking down an act that had directed the postmaster general to detain foreign mailings of "communist political propaganda" and to deliver these materials only upon the addressee's request.[64] The Court has also set aside federal laws authorizing postal authorities to exclude from the mails materials they consider obscene.

Although government censorship of mail is unconstitutional, household censorship is not. The Court has sustained a law giving householders the right to ask the postmaster to order mailers to delete their names from certain mailing lists and to refrain from sending any advertisements that they believe to be "erotically arousing or sexually provocative."[65] Moreover, Congress may forbid—and has forbidden—the use of mailboxes for any materials except those sent through the United States mails.

Handbills, Sound Trucks, and Billboards

Religious and political pamphlets, leaflets, and handbills have been historic weapons in the defense of liberty, and their distribution is constitutionally protected. So, too, is the use of their contemporary counterparts, sound trucks and billboards. A state cannot restrain the distribution of leaflets merely to keep its streets clean,[66] but it may impose reasonable restrictions on their distribution so long as they are neutrally enforced, without regard to the content.

Motion Pictures and Plays

Prior censorship of films to prevent the showing of obscenity is not necessarily unconstitutional; however, laws calling for submission of films to a government review board are constitutional only if there is a prompt judicial hearing. The burden is on the government to prove to the court that the particular film in question is obscene. Prior censorship of films by review boards was once common, but no longer. Live performances, such as plays and revues, are also entitled to constitutional protection.[67]

At a press conference, Howard Stern defends his use of raunchy language and subject matter that led to the FCC fining the Infinity Broadcasting network.

Broadcast and Cable Communications

Television remains an important means of distributing news and appealing for votes, though the Internet has gained popularity. Yet of all the mass media, broadcasting receives the least First Amendment protection. Congress has established a system of commercial broadcasting, supplemented by the Corporation for Public Broadcasting, which provides funds for public radio and television. The Federal Communications Commission (FCC) regulates the entire system by granting licenses and making regulations for their use.

The First Amendment would prevent censorship if the FCC tried to impose it. The First Amendment does not, however, prevent the FCC from imposing sanctions on stations that broadcast indecent or filthy words, even if they are not legally obscene.[68] The FCC did precisely that when it fined Infinity Broadcasting for indecent remarks by "shock jock" Howard Stern. Nor does the First Amendment prevent the FCC from refusing to renew a license if, in its opinion, a broadcaster does not serve the public interest.

The Supreme Court allows more governmental regulation of broadcasters than of newspaper and magazine publishers because space on the airwaves was limited. However, technological advances such as cable television, videotapes, and satellite broadcasting have opened up new means of communication and brought competition to the electronic media. Recognizing these changes, Congress passed the Telecommunications Act of 1996, allowing telephone companies, broadcasters, and cable TV stations to compete with one another. In adopting the act, Congress did not abandon all government regulation of the airways. On the contrary, the act calls for many new regulations—for example, requiring that all new television sets sold in the United States be equipped with V-chips that allow viewers to block programs containing violent or sexual material.

The Court has upheld a congressional requirement that cable television stations must carry the signals of local broadcast television stations.[69] The Court has also held that Congress may authorize cable operators to refuse access to leased channels for "patently offensive" programs. The Court, however, struck down congressional requirements that if a cable operator allows such offensive programming, it must be blocked and unscrambled through special devices. In *United States* v. *Playboy Entertainment Group* (2000), the Court underscored the greater protection for cable than for broadcast television. Whereas broadcast television may be required to provide programming for children and not air violence at certain times, the Court held that such rules do not apply to cable television because unwanted programming can be blocked by homeowners.[70]

Telecommunications and the Internet

Millions of Americans log on to the Internet to buy books, clothing, jewelry, airplane tickets, stocks, and bonds. Because the Internet has become a commercial marketplace and a major channel for communication, Congress is struggling with issues raised by cyberspace communication. Although Congress has imposed a moratorium on state taxation of commercial transactions on the Internet, debate continues over whether the national government should preempt state taxation. How do existing laws against copyright piracy apply to the World Wide Web? Should there be national regulation of junk e-mail, or can state laws take care of the problem? In what ways may Congress regulate indecent and obscene communications on the Web? Should Congress try to protect the privacy of those who use the Web? (For more information about privacy and developments on the Web, go to the Electronic Privacy Information Center at www.epic.org.)

As Congress and the state legislatures begin to deal with these and other new problems, legislators and judges will have to apply traditional constitutional principles to new technologies and means of communication. The Court distinguishes between a limited ban on indecent messages on radio and broadcast television and those on telephones, cable television, and the Internet. Radio and broadcast messages are readily available to children and can intrude into the privacy of the home without prior warning. By contrast, telephone messages may be blocked, and access by minors is more readily restricted.[71] In

Regulating Decency on the Internet

The Communications Decency Act of 1996 made it a federal crime to use the Internet to knowingly transmit obscene or indecent and "patently offensive" words or pictures to minors. The constitutionality of the law was immediately challenged by the American Civil Liberties Union (ACLU), which contended that "the government cannot reduce the adult population to reading or viewing only what is appropriate for children." In defending the law, the Department of Justice countered, "The Internet threatens to give every child a free pass into the equivalent of every adult bookstore and every adult video store in the country."

In *Reno* v. *ACLU* (1997), the Supreme Court struck down the provisions against transmission of indecent communications and agreed with a lower court that the Internet, "as the most participatory form of mass speech yet developed, deserves the highest protection from government intrusion."* Cyberspace, the Supreme Court concluded, is a unique medium that should receive broad First Amendment protection like books and magazines. The Internet, unlike broadcasting, is not a scarce commodity and should not be subject to the same kind of regulation as the broadcast industry. Moreover, the Internet is not as invasive as radio and television and should be given the same constitutional protection as the print media.

In 1996, Congress also enacted the Child Pornography Prevention Act, making it a federal crime to create or distribute "virtual child pornography" generated by computer images of young adults rather than actual children. When that law was challenged, the Supreme

Court struck it down as unconstitutionally broad. The law went beyond punishing child pornography, which is a crime because actual children are involved, the Court ruled, and had the potential to chill clear artistic and literary expression.†

In response to *Reno* v. *ACLU,* Congress passed the Child Online Protection Act of 1998 (COPA), which made it a crime for a commercial Web site to knowingly make available to anyone under the age of 17 sexually explicit material considered "harmful to minors" based on "community standards." That law was challenged on the grounds that it would give conservative communities a veto over sexual content on the Web. The Supreme Court disagreed but held that the law may not go into effect until lower courts have addressed other questions about COPA's impact on free speech.‡

In 2002, a federal appellate court also invalidated the Children's Internet Protection Act of 2000, which required public schools and libraries to use electronic filters on computers to block access to pornographic Web sites. The court found that the technology inadvertently blocked access to legitimate sites and hence violated the First Amendment.§

*Reno v. ACLU, 521 U.S. 844 (1997).

†*Ashcroft v. Free Speech Coalition,* 122 S.Ct. 1389 (2002).

‡*Ashcroft v. ACLU,* 122 S.Ct. 1389 (2002).

§Robert O'Harrow, "Internet Filtering Overruled, "*Washington Post,* June 1, 2002, A1.

its first ruling on First Amendment protection for the Internet, *Reno* v. *American Civil Liberties Union* (1997), the Court struck down provisions of the Communications Decency Act of 1996 that had made it a crime to send obscene or indecent messages to anyone under 18 years of age. In doing so, the Court emphasized the unique character of the Internet, holding that it is less intrusive than radio and broadcast television.[72]

Freedom of Assembly

In the fall of 1998, Khallid Abdul Muhammad, a known racist and anti-Semite, organized the "Million Youth March" in New York City. Mayor Rudolph Giuliani denied a permit for the march on grounds that it would be a "hate march." A federal appeals court upheld a lower court ruling that denial of the permit was unconstitutional; however, the three-judge panel placed restrictions on the event, limiting its duration to four hours and scaling it back to a six-block area. The march proceeded, surrounded by police in riot gear who broke up the demonstration after Muhammad delivered a vitriolic speech against police, Jews, and city officials.[73]

It took judicial authorities to defend the rights of these unpopular speakers and marchers, but it is not always the "bad guys" whose rights have to be protected by the courts. It also took judicial intervention in the 1960s to preserve for Martin Luther King Jr. and those who marched with him the right to demonstrate in the streets of southern cities on behalf of civil rights for African Americans.

Such incidents present a classic free speech problem. It is almost always easier, and certainly politically more prudent, to maintain order by curbing public demonstrations by unpopular groups. However, if police did not have the right to order groups to disperse, public order would be at the mercy of those who resort to street demonstrations to create tensions and provoke street battles.

Free Speech on the Steps of the U.S. Capitol

In June 2002, a federal appellate court struck down a 30-year-old ban on protests and demonstrations on the sidewalks and entrances on the east side of the U.S. Capitol. Although the case

Protests held on the steps of the U.S. Capitol, like this large demonstration against the war in Vietnam and neighboring countries, were prohibited by law for 30 years until June 2002, when a federal appellate court struck down the ban as a violation of the right to freedom of speech.

originated before the terrorist attacks of the preceding September, the government contended that increased security concerns justified the prohibition. Attorneys for the Department of Justice argued that "if this country has learned anything at all from September 11, we learned that the unthinkable can happen, the unimaginable, in fact, can be imagined by someone, and a terrible toll that can stab the heart of our nation can be exacted by a small group of people."

The appellate court rejected the government's argument that increased security needs outweigh the value of free speech. The case originated when an artist, Robert Lederman, was arrested on the steps of the Capitol in 1997 for handing out leaflets protesting restrictions on sidewalk artists in New York City.

The U.S. Capitol, said the appellate court, is "a centerpiece of democracy," in rejecting "the proposition that demonstrations of any stripe pose a greater security risk to the Capitol building and its occupants than do pedestrians, who may come and go anonymously, travel in groups of any size, carry any number of bags and boxes, and linger as long as they please." The government may regulate the size and manner of protests in public places, but an absolute ban is a "serious loss to speech," concluded the court, "for a disproportionately small government gain."

Source: Neely Tucker, "Capitol Ban on Protests Nullified," *Washington Post,* June 1, 2002, p. A1.

A current controversy surrounds Attorney General John Ashcroft's decision in 2002 to allow law enforcement agents to go undercover to monitor activities and assemblies in any public place—including mosques, churches, and chat rooms on the Internet—in combating international terrorism. He thereby abandoned the Department of Justice's guidelines adopted in 1976 after Congress discovered that FBI agents were conducting surveillance and had infiltrated the civil rights movement and other groups engaged in lawful activities, as well as closely monitored King and other leaders. In response to criticisms that the new guidelines infringed on the freedoms of assembly and association, Ashcroft stressed that FBI agents would be limited to investigating terrorist activities.

Public Forums and Time, Place, and Manner Regulations

The Constitution protects the right to speak, but it does not give people the right to communicate their views to everyone, in every place, at every time they wish. No one has the right to block traffic or to hold parades or make speeches in public streets or on public sidewalks whenever he or she wishes. Governments may not censor what can be said, but they can make "reasonable" *time, place,* and *manner* regulations for protests or parades. The Supreme Court has divided public property into three categories: public forums, limited public forums, and nonpublic forums. The extent to which governments may limit access depends on the kind of forum involved.

Public forums are public places historically associated with the free exercise of expressive activities, such as streets, sidewalks, and parks. Courts look closely at time, place, and manner regulations that apply to these traditional public forums to ensure that they are being applied evenhandedly and that action is not taken because of what is being said rather than how and where or by whom it is being said.[74]

Other kinds of public property, such as rooms in a city hall or in a school after hours, may be designated as *limited public forums,* available for assembly and speech for

New York City police in riot gear formed a human wall in front of the Million Youth March and charged the stage after Khallid Abdul Muhammad, organizer of the rally, urged the audience to riot and kill.

Security Versus Civil Liberties

Judge Richard A. Posner.

In the aftermath of the terrorist attacks of September 11, 2001, Congress enacted the USA Patriot Act and President George W. Bush and Attorney General John Ashcroft issued new guidelines giving law enforcement expanded powers. Some people of Middle Eastern and Asian descent, along with civil libertarians, counter that the government is going too far in curbing basic freedoms in waging war against international terrorism. In an insightful yet provocative essay, Judge Richard A. Posner places the need for balancing security and civil liberties into legal and historical perspective.

In the wake of the September 11 terrorist attacks have come many proposals for tightening security; some measures to that end have already been taken. Civil libertarians are troubled. They fear that concerns about national security will lead to an erosion of civil liberties. They offer historical examples of supposed overreactions to threats to national security. They treat our existing civil liberties—freedom of the press, protections of privacy and of the rights of criminal suspects, and the rest—as sacrosanct, insisting that the battle against international terrorism accommodate itself to them.

I consider this a profoundly mistaken approach to the question of balancing liberty and security. The basic mistake is the prioritizing of liberty. It is a mistake about law and a mistake about history. Let me begin with law. What we take to be our civil liberties—for example, immunity from arrest except upon probable cause to believe we've committed a crime, and from prosecution for violating a criminal statute enacted after we committed the act that violates it—were made legal rights by the Constitution and other enactments. The other enactments can be changed relatively easily, by amendatory legislation. Amending the Constitution is much more difficult. In recognition of this the Framers left most of the constitutional provisions that confer rights pretty vague. The courts have made them definite.

Concretely, the scope of these rights has been determined, through an interaction of constitutional text and subsequent judicial interpretation, by a weighing of competing interests. I'll call them the public-safety interest and the liberty interest. Neither, in my view, has priority. They are both important, and their relative importance changes from time to time and from situation to situation. The safer the nation feels, the more weight judges will be willing to give to the liberty interest. The greater the threat that an activity poses to the nation's safety, the stronger will the grounds seem for seeking to repress that activity, even at some cost to liberty. This fluid approach is only common sense. . . .

It will be argued that the lesson of history is that officials habitually exaggerate dangers to the nation's security. But the lesson of history is the opposite. It is because officials have repeatedly and disastrously underestimated these dangers that our history is as violent as it is. Consider such underestimated dangers as that of secession, which led to the Civil War; of a Japanese attack on the United States, which led to the disaster at Pearl Harbor; of Soviet espionage in the 1940s, which accelerated the Soviet Union's acquisition of nuclear weapons and emboldened Stalin to encourage North Korea's invasion of South Korea; of the installation of Soviet missiles in Cuba, which precipitated the Cuban missile crisis; of political assassinations and outbreaks of urban violence in the 1960s; of the Tet Offensive of 1968; of the Iranian revolution of 1979 and the subsequent taking of American diplomats as hostages; and, for that matter, of the events of September 11.

It is true that when we are surprised and hurt, we tend to overreact—but only with the benefit of hindsight can a reaction be separated into its proper and excess layers. In hindsight we know that interning Japanese-Americans did not shorten World War II. But was this known at the time? If not, shouldn't the Army have erred on the side of caution, as it did? Even today we cannot say with any assurance that Abraham Lincoln was wrong to suspend *habeas corpus* during the Civil War, as he did on several occasions, even though the Constitution is clear that only Congress can suspend this right. (Another of Lincoln's wartime measures, the Emancipation Proclamation, may also have been unconstitutional.) . . .

Lincoln's unconstitutional acts during the Civil War show that even legality must sometimes be sacrificed for other values. We are a nation under law, but first we are a nation. I want to emphasize something else, however: the malleability of law, its pragmatic rather than dogmatic character. The law is not absolute, and the slogan *"Fiat iustitia ruat caelum"* ("Let justice be done though the heavens fall") is dangerous nonsense. The law is a human creation rather than a divine gift, a tool of government rather than a mandarin mystery. It is an instrument for promoting social welfare, and as the conditions essential to that welfare change, so must it change.

Judge Richard A. Posner was appointed by President Ronald Reagan to the U.S. Court of Appeals for the Seventh Circuit. He clerked for liberal Justice William J. Brennan before teaching at the University of Chicago School of Law.

SOURCE: Reprinted from Richard A. Posner, "Security Versus Civil Liberties," *Atlantic Monthly,* December 2001, pp. 46–48.

limited purposes, for a limited amount of time, and even for a limited class of speakers (such as only students, only teachers, or only employees), provided the distinctions between the people allowed access and those excluded are not biased.

Nonpublic forums include public facilities such as libraries, courthouses, prisons, schools, swimming pools, and government offices that are open to the public but are not public forums. As long as people use such facilities within the normal bounds of conduct, they may not be constitutionally restrained from doing so. However, people may be excluded from such places as a government office or a school if they engage in activities for which the facilities were not created. They have no right to interfere with programs or try to take over a building—especially facilities such as a university president's office—in order to stage a political protest.

Does the right of peaceful assembly include the right to violate a law nonviolently but deliberately? We have no precise answer, but in general, **civil disobedience**, even if peaceful, is not a protected right. When Martin Luther King Jr. and his followers refused to comply with a state court's injunction forbidding them to parade in Birmingham without first securing a permit, the Supreme Court sustained their conviction, even though there was serious doubt about the constitutionality of the injunction and the ordinance on which it was based.[75]

More recently, the First Amendment right of antiabortion protesters to picket in front of abortion clinics has come into conflict with a woman's right to go to an abortion clinic. Protesters have often massed in front of clinics, shouting at employees and patrons and blocking entrances to the clinic. The Supreme Court has struck down provisions that prohibit protesters from expressing their views. But the Court has upheld injunctions that keep antiabortion protesters outside of a buffer zone around abortion clinics and also upheld injunctions that were issued because of prior unlawful conduct by the protesters. The proper constitutional test for such injunctions is "whether the challenged provisions . . . burden no more speech than necessary to serve a significant government interest," such as public safety or the right of women to go into such a clinic.[76]

The combination of First Amendment guarantees for rights and freedoms and their judicial enforcement is one of the basic features of our government and political system. As Supreme Court Justice Robert H. Jackson wrote:

> The very purpose of [the] Bill of Rights was to withdraw certain subjects from the vicissitudes of political controversy, to place them beyond the reach of majorities and officials and to establish them as legal principles to be applied by the courts. One's right to life, liberty, and property, to free speech, a free press, freedom of worship and assembly, and other fundamental rights may not be submitted to vote: they depend on the outcome of no elections.[77]

The connection between constitutional limitations and judicial enforcement is an example of the "auxiliary precautions" James Madison believed were necessary to prevent arbitrary governmental action. Citizens in other free nations rely on elections and political checks to protect their rights; in the United States, we also appeal to judges when we fear our freedoms are in danger.

civil disobedience
Deliberate refusal to obey a law or comply with the orders of public officials as a means of expressing opposition.

CIVIL LIBERTIES: THE GREAT BALANCING ACT

The war against international terrorism has highlighted the politics of rights in balancing freedom and security. In this simulation, you judge the constitutionality of state and local policies affecting civil rights and civil liberties and find out the political implications as well as how liberals, conservatives, and centrists would decide.

Go to PoliSim "Civil Liberties: The Great Balancing Act."

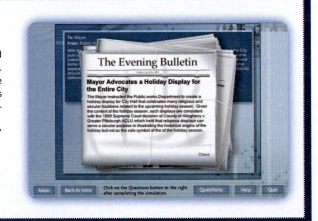

Summary

1. The Constitution protects our right to seek a writ of habeas corpus and forbids *ex post facto* laws and bills of attainder.

2. First Amendment freedoms—freedom of religion, of speech, of the press, and of assembly and association—are at the heart of a healthy constitutional democracy.

3. Since World War I, the Supreme Court has become the primary branch of government for giving meaning to these constitutional restraints. And since 1925, these constitutional limits have been applied not only to Congress but to all governmental agencies—national, state, and local.

4. The First Amendment forbids the establishment of religion and also guarantees the free exercise of religion. These two freedoms, however, are often in conflict with each other and represent conflicting notions of what is in the public interest.

5. The Supreme Court holds that there are only four categories of nonprotected speech—libel, obscenity, fighting words, and commercial speech. All other speech is protected under the First Amendment, and government may regulate that speech only when it has a compelling reason and does so in a content-neutral way.

6. Over the years, the Supreme Court has taken a pragmatic approach to First Amendment freedoms. It has refused to make them absolute rights above any kind of governmental regulation, direct or indirect, or to say that they must be preserved at whatever price. But the justices have recognized that a constitutional democracy tampers with these freedoms at great peril. They have insisted on compelling justification before permitting these rights to be limited. How compelling the justification is, in a free society, will always remain an open question, but is especially difficult during times of war.

Key Terms

writ of habeas corpus	establishment clause	preferred position doctrine	fighting words
ex post facto law	vouchers	nonprotected speech	commercial speech
bill of attainder	free exercise clause	libel	prior restraint
due process clause	bad tendency test	sedition	civil disobedience
selective incorporation	clear and present danger test	obscenity	

Further Reading

STUART BIEGEL, *Beyond Our Control? Confronting the Limits of Our Legal System in the Age of Cyberspace* (MIT Press, 2001).

LEE BOLLINGER AND GEOFFREY R. STONE, EDS., *Eternally Vigilant: Free Speech in the Modern Age* (University of Chicago Press, 2002).

JAMES MACGREGOR BURNS AND STEWART BURNS, *A People's Charter: The Pursuit of Rights in America* (Knopf, 1991).

JESSE CHOPER, *Securing Religious Liberty: Principles for Judicial Interpretation of Religion Clauses* (University of Chicago Press, 1995).

STEPHEN M. FELDMAN, ED., *Law and Religion: A Critical Anthology* (New York University Press, 2000).

MIKE GODWIN, *Cyber Rights: Defending Free Speech in the Digital Age* (Times Books, 1998).

ROBERT JUSTIN GOLDSTEIN, *Flag Burning and Free Speech: The Case of Texas v. Johnson* (University Press of Kansas, 2002).

NAT HENTOFF, *Living the Bill of Rights: How to Be an Authentic American* (HarperCollins, 1998).

LAWRENCE LESSIG, *Code and Other Laws of Cyberspace* (Basic Books, 1999).

LEONARD W. LEVY, *Emergence of a Free Press* (Oxford University Press, 1985).

LEONARD W. LEVY, *The Establishment Clause: Religion and the First Amendment* (Macmillan, 1986).

ANTHONY LEWIS, *Make No Law: The Sullivan Case and the First Amendment* (Random House, 1991).

CATHARINE A. MACKINNON, *Only Words* (Harvard University Press, 1993).

ALEXANDER MEIKLEJOHN, *Political Freedom: The Constitutional Powers of the People* (Harper & Row, 1965).

JOHN STUART MILL, *Essay on Liberty,* in *The English Philosophers from Bacon to Mill,* ed. Arthur Burtt (Random House, 1939), pp. 949–1041.

JOHN T. NOONAN JR., *The Lustre of Our Country: The American Experience of Religious Freedom* (University of California Press, 1998).

DAVID M. O'BRIEN, *Constitutional Law and Politics: Civil Rights and Civil Liberties,* 5th ed. (Norton, 2003).

SHAWN FRANCIS PETERS, *Judging Jehovah's Witnesses: Religious Persecution and the Dawn of the Rights Revolution* (University Press of Kansas, 2002).

J. W. PELTASON AND SUE DAVIS, *Understanding the Constitution,* 15th ed. (Harcourt, 2000).

FRANK S. RAVITCH, *School Prayer and Discrimination: The Civil Rights of Religious Minorities and Dissenters* (Northwestern University Press, 1999).

NADINE STROSSEN, *Defending Pornography: Free Speech, Sex, and the Fight for Women's Rights* (Scribner, 1995).

First Amendment Freedoms Questions

VOCABULARY

1. Explain the "clear and present danger test" as it applies to free speech.

2. Define "fighting words."

3. The authors say the Supreme Court has taken a "pragmatic approach" to First Amendment freedoms. What does pragmatic mean?

COMPREHENSION AND ANALYSIS

4. List the five freedoms guaranteed in the First Amendment.

5. Since World War I, which branch of government has assumed primary responsibility for interpreting the First Amendment?

6. The authors say the selective incorporation of most provisions of the Bill of Rights, including freedom of speech and press, into the Fourteenth Amendment is probably the "most significant constitutional development since the writing of the Constitution." Please explain why they believe that to be true.

7. Describe the controversy surrounding school vouchers and state aid as they relate to the separation of religion (church) and government (state).

8. What are the four narrow categories of nonprotected speech? Why are they nonprotected?

9. Does the right to "peaceful assembly" include the right to deliberately and nonviolently violate a law?

REFLECT AND CONNECT

10. The enactment of the USA Patriot Act has intensified concerns that our desire for national security will erode our individual civil liberties. In his essay on page 123, Judge Richard A. Posner says that in his view neither the "public-safety interest" or the "liberty interest" has priority. "They are both important, and their relative importance changes from time to time and situation to situation." In what ways do you agree with and/or disagree with Posner's view that "this fluid approach is only common sense"?

5 Tests of Your Freedoms

USA WEEKEND, THE FIRST AMENDMENT CENTER, AND LEE C. BOLLINGER

USA WEEKEND is a division of the Gannett Company. The First Amendment Center works to preserve First Amendment freedoms through information and education. Based at Vanderbilt University in Nashville, Tennessee, it is an operating program of the Freedom Forum. Mr. Bollinger is one of the nation's leading

First Amendment experts, president of Columbia University, and the author of The Tolerant Society *and* Eternally Vigilant: Free Speech in the Modern Era.

This survey was conducted April 21–28, 2003. A total of 517 surveys were completed online by adults age 18 or older. The margin of error is +/−4%.

VOCABULARY

hypothetical scenarios (¶1): situations that are made up to serve a particular purpose
landmark case (¶5): in legal circles, a court case that sets a precedent
in the abstract (¶10): in theory; in a theoretical situation
latent problems (¶10): hidden, unforeseen problems
abridgment (¶20): infringement, violation
partisan use (¶21): biased

AN IDEA TO THINK ABOUT

Speech. Religion. Press. Assembly. Petition. You learned about all those First Amendment rights in basic civics class. But how well do you really understand them? *As you read,* compare your answers to those of the expert.

5 TESTS OF YOUR FREEDOMS

USA WEEKEND, *the First Amendment Center, and Lee C. Bollinger*

[1]The USA, the first nation to be founded on principles of liberty and justice, is fueled by freedom, particularly the rights guaranteed in the First Amendment to the Constitution. But how well do we understand these basic rights? To find out, *USA WEEKEND* Magazine and the First Amendment Center commissioned a scientific online poll consisting of a series of hypothetical scenarios. Each was designed to challenge one of the five freedoms set out in the First Amendment: freedom of speech, press and religion, and the right to assemble and to petition government for constructive change.

[2]The poll results clearly show some serious confusion among Americans about their First Amendment protections and how they apply to a diverse and sometimes divided society.

[3]Take the poll yourself and test your own answers against the survey respondents'—and those of our expert, Lee C. Bollinger.

#1 A high school student wears a T-shirt to public school with the words "International Criminal" framing President Bush's picture on the front. The principal tells the student to put on a different shirt, turn the shirt inside out or go home. If those requests are refused, the student will face immediate suspension.

Does the principal have the right to ban the T-shirt?

America says: Yes 62%   No 38%

[4]**The expert says:** The majority has it wrong. Most people may want to ban the offending T-shirt, but they can't in this case. The First Amendment protects the right of "speech" even when it's symbolic, as when the message is in the form of an image on a piece of clothing. And although many may think the constitutional right of freedom of speech does not reach minors, the Supreme Court has held otherwise.

[5]The landmark case on this point (from the 1960s) recognized the free-speech rights of a 13-year-old to wear a black armband in class in protest against the war in Vietnam. As a society, we have staked our future on a robust right of freedom of expression (even for neo-Nazis and the Ku Klux Klan), and it is inconsistent with that commitment, the court has said, to make it available only when you turn 18 or 21.

[6]Still, nothing in life is absolute, and, contrary to what even a few Supreme Court justices have said, that is true of the First Amendment as well. If a principal can show significant "disruption" as a result of the speech, courts will give more leeway to restrict the speech. The mere fact that other students take offense would not be enough, but spontaneous fighting or outbursts making class discipline impossible very well might be.

[7]A final note: The First Amendment applies only to "state action" and hence to public schools. A principal in a private school can set whatever limits on speech he or she wishes.

#2 A town strapped for funds enters an agreement with the community's largest church by which the church will operate the town's failing convention center. The church agrees to raise the money itself to run the center and promises it will not discriminate against any religious, political, racial or other groups that might want to rent it for a fee.

Do you think such an arrangement is allowed under the First Amendment?

America says: Yes   70%   No   30%

[8]**The expert says:** The answer is no. This is not a good idea for the town, the public, the church or the First Amendment. The amendment's guarantees of religious freedom and free speech prevent the government from favoring one religion over another, so the choice itself may have involved improper bias against other groups who also sought to operate the center. Beyond that, appearances matter enormously here. Just imagine if Central Park were leased to a particular church to "operate." The First Amendment long has required the state to make available certain public property—most notably, streets and parks—for citizens to exercise their right of free speech. Although reasonable restrictions can be imposed (for instance, the time, place and manner of expression), the state cannot favor particular speakers or points of view over others.

[9]Furthermore, under the Establishment Clause, the Supreme Court has refused to permit relationships between church and state where there is the appearance of religious endorsement and where the prospects of "entanglement" are great. In this case, despite the church's assurances that it will not discriminate among speakers, we would have to expect an endless series of conflicts and disagreements over whether the church has administered this "public forum" with a religious bias.

[10]What can seem perfectly reasonable in the abstract, as it does to 70% of the respondents, can be filled with latent constitutional problems.

#3 A recent decision by the city council to reduce trash pickup from twice weekly to once a week upset one citizen so much that he has posted comments on a local Internet site, using the alias "Angry Citizen." In his comments, the citizen accuses one council member of being a "lying communist." When the councilman learns the identity of the writer, he contacts "Angry Citizen," who quickly offers to post another comment apologizing for his remark. ("Angry Citizen" says he was just upset at that moment.) Dissatisfied, the accused councilman threatens to sue him for libel.

Does the First Amendment protect "Angry Citizen" if the councilman files the lawsuit?

America says: Yes   60%   No   40%

[11]**The expert says:** The majority got it right this time. The First Amendment's guarantee of a free press does not apply only to professional journalists—it protects every citizen.

[12]It is exceedingly difficult for a public official to force a citizen to pay damages for a libelous statement. Under the Supreme Court's verdict in *The New York Times* v. *Sullivan,* the council member would have to show that the statement is false (maybe he is a "lying communist"), that the statement was one of fact rather than "opinion" (would the reasonable reader assume this accusation was just the speaker's interpretation of generally known facts, or perhaps just hyperbole?), that the false statement actually injured the council member's reputation, and that the injurious statement was made with knowledge of its falsity or with "reckless disregard of the truth" (i.e., with "actual malice").

[13]Those criteria are nearly insurmountable barriers to a successful lawsuit for defamation. Is this justified? The court's rationale is not a lack of concern for the reputations of public servants, nor a high regard for falsehoods. Rather, the idea is that, because we are committed to living in a democracy where the citizens are sovereign, we need to provide ample space for citizens to engage in public debate without being intimidated about speaking their minds by the prospect of having to defend themselves against lawsuits.

[14]In an imperfect world, someone's rights or interests often have to give way. Here it's the reputation of public officials.

[15]Neither the fact that this statement was made on the Internet nor the fact that it was made anonymously changes the outcome. Generally speaking, the rules in this area of First Amendment protections do not change, whether you are communicating with millions or speaking across the fence to a neighbor.

#4 County officials recently have been hounded and harassed at commission meetings by a small number of activists who oppose a county tax increase. In response, the officials have established new rules governing all public appearances before the county commission. Specifically, citizens wishing to speak at commission meetings now must apply seven days in advance for permission to do so and must limit their comments to two minutes.

Do county officials have the right to establish these new rules?

America says: Yes 56%   No 44%

[16]**The expert says:** Yes, the new rules appear to be fine on their face. Certainly, the county can require speakers to sign up in advance and impose a time limit on each speaker. Nothing in the First Amendment's right to petition for a redress of grievances or freedom of speech prohibits the state from bringing some order to a forum.

[17]What are prohibited, however, are regulations that discriminate against speakers because of the content of their messages. This is where I have concerns. We are not told what the "activists" did that "hounded and harassed" the officials, nor are we told why and how the new rules are a response to that behavior.

[18]So here's the caution: If the activists only criticized the county officials, even if harshly, and if the officials believe that they can use the new rules to treat the "activists" differently because of their criticisms, then we have a very real problem under the First Amendment. The officials may (constitutionally, at least) hope the activists won't have the foresight to apply and to limit their critiques to two minutes at a time—and thereby give county officials the right to prohibit them from speaking at commission meetings. But they must pursue these wishes in a content-neutral way, applying the same rules to everyone, not just the activists.

> #5 A citizen who participates in a neighborhood anti-war march learns that the local police department has secretly videotaped the rally and created a file with the names of everyone who participated. Police officials defend their actions by citing the increased possibility of terrorist threats and the needs of national security.

Do you think the police department has the right to videotape the marchers and keep files on them?

America says: Yes 54%   No 46%

[19]**The expert says:** Yes, it is permissible under the First Amendment's rights of free speech and assembly. As citizens, we have the right to march and to express our views—however sound, however outrageous. But the government may watch and keep information on us, for good or for bad reasons.

[20]That's not to say doing so under any and all circumstances is a good idea. There is much, in fact, to be said against it, not least because it may have a chilling effect on the exercise of constitutional liberties. But not all government actions that chill speech are unconstitutional, and thus far, at least, the Supreme Court has not declared keeping files on marchers to be an abridgment of the First Amendment.

[21]Everything depends on how the government uses the files. A systematic campaign to discredit its opponents through the partisan use of videos and other information selectively gathered, accompanied by baseless intimations of terrorist connections, could raise an interesting new case under the First Amendment. Certainly, it would be a violation of the spirit of democracy.

5 Tests of Your Freedoms Questions

VOCABULARY

1. Bollinger says, ". . . we have staked our future on a robust right of freedom of expression." (¶5) Explain the use of the word *robust*.

2. Bollinger says, ". . . appearances matter enormously here." (¶8) Please explain what he means.

3. Bollinger says the "new rules appear to be fine on their face." (¶16) Please explain what he means.

4. Define *baseless intimations*. (¶21)

COMPREHENSION AND ANALYSIS

5. In Scenario #1, under what circumstances could a public school principal make a case for requiring the student remove the T-shirt? Under what circumstances could a private school principal make the student remove the T-shirt? Why is there a difference in the rules for public school and private school principals?

6. There does not appear to be any immediate problem in Scenario #2, but Bollinger believes having the church run the city's convention center would be a bad idea. Please explain his reasoning.

7. Scenario #3 deals with an accusation of libel. In general, why is it so difficult to collect damages for libelous statements/defamation?

8. In Scenario #4, county officials are "technically" allowed to establish new rules governing how and when people can speak during their meetings. So, why does Bollinger have some concerns?

9. It is clear in Scenario #5 that a police department has the right to videotape protesters and keep files on them. However, under what circumstances might a police department's files on an individual's activities violate the "spirit of democracy"?

REFLECT AND CONNECT

10. Were you surprised, either pleasantly or unpleasantly, about how much the respondents knew about our First Amendment freedoms? In which scenario was Bollinger's answer most surprising to you? Please explain your answers.

State of the First Amendment 2003

KENNETH A. PAULSON

Mr. Paulson is executive director of the Freedom Forum's First Amendment Center. A veteran newspaper editor and lawyer, he hosts the weekly television series Speaking Freely *and writes and speaks on U.S. Supreme Court decisions, media and journalism, free speech and press, free expression in the arts, and other First Amendment issues. The Freedom Forum is a nonpartisan, international foundation based at Vanderbilt University in Nashville, Tennessee. This is the foreword to the 2003 Report.*

A State of the First Amendment survey is conducted annually by the First Amendment Center in partnership with American Journalism Review *magazine. Although the First Amendment encompasses five specific rights, the 2003 survey targeted freedom of speech, press, and religion for intensive study. The study pays extra attention to the tensions placed on these rights by government initiatives in the current war on terrorism and the war in Iraq.*

The survey results are from telephone interviews conducted with 1,000 adults, ages 18 or older, between June 3 and June 15, 2003, by the University of Connecticut's Center for Survey Research and Analysis. The sampling error is ± 3.1% at the 95% level of confidence. To read the complete 2003 report and more recent reports, go to www.firstamendmentcenter.org/sofa_reports/index.aspx.

AN IDEA TO THINK ABOUT

How would you describe the state of the First Amendment? For example, do you think the press has too much freedom? *As you read,* find out how a sampling of the American people felt about our First Amendment freedoms in 2003.

STATE OF THE FIRST AMENDMENT 2003

Kenneth A. Paulson

[1]Two years after the terrorist attacks in New York and Washington, D.C., our nation appears to have caught its breath—and regained some perspective.

[2]Those horrific assaults took a tremendous toll, in lives as well as on our collective psyche. How could we prevent this kind of attack from happening again? Did we need to limit liberties in the interest of security? Were we too free to be truly safe?

[3]That sense of freedom as an obstacle to the war on terrorism was reflected last year [2002] in our annual survey gauging public support for First Amendment freedoms. For the first time in our polling, 49% of respondents said they believed the First Amendment gives us too much freedom.

[4]While reaction to fear is largely reflexive, the passage of time allows us to be reflective. The 2003 State of the First Amendment survey—conducted in collaboration with *American Journalism Review*—suggested that public support for First Amendment freedoms may be returning to pre-9/11 levels. About 61% of respondents indicated overall support for First Amendment freedoms, while 34% said First Amendment freedoms go too far.

The First Amendment became part of the U.S. Constitution more than 200 years ago. This is what it says: "Congress shall make no law respecting an establishment or religion, or prohibiting the free exercise thereof; or abridging the freedom of speech, or of the press; or the right of the people peaceably to assemble, and to petit on the Government for a redress or grievances." Based on your own feelings about the First Amendment, please tell me whether you agree or disagree with the following statements: The First Amendment goes too far in the rights it guarantees.

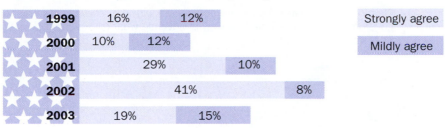

FIGURE 1

[5]While First Amendment advocates certainly can't regard it as a victory that one-third of Americans have misgivings about these fundamental freedoms, there are other signs that most Americans continue to embrace freedom of speech and religion. While respondents displayed less enthusiasm for freedom of the press, they did give high marks to the news media for their work during the war in Iraq.

Among the key findings:

- [6]The least popular First Amendment right continued to be freedom of the press—46% said the press in America has too much freedom to do what it wants, up from 42% last year.

Overall, do you think the press in America has too much freedom to do what it wants, to little freedom to do what it wants, or is the amount of freedom the press has about right?

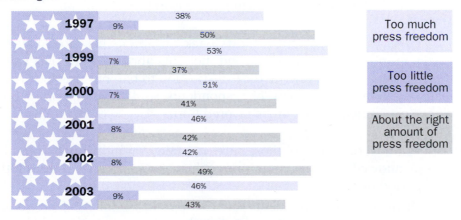

FIGURE 2

- [7]Sixty-five percent of those surveyed said they favor the policy of embedding U.S. journalists in individual combat units, and 68% said the news media did an excellent or good job in covering the war.

- [8]Despite the positive perception of war coverage, more than two out of three surveyed said the government should be able to review in advance journalists' reports directly from military combat zones.

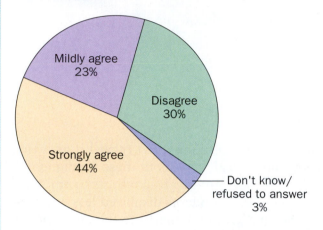

Please tell me whether you agree or disagree with the following statements: "The government should be able to review in advance what journalists report directly from military combat zones."

Mildly agree
23%

Disagree
30%

Strongly agree
44%

Don't know/
refused to answer
3%

FIGURE 3

- [9]Americans indicated a hunger for more information about the war on terrorism. Forty-eight percent of those surveyed said they believed that Americans have too little information about the federal government's efforts to combat terrorism.
- [10]When asked whether they believe the media has too much freedom to publish or whether there's too much government censorship, response was split: 43% said there's too much media freedom, and 38% said there's too much government censorship.

[11]The war in Iraq put protests back on newspaper front pages and gave a number of Americans second thoughts about dissent. The war also fueled a new effort to rewrite the Constitution to ban burning of the American flag. While a majority of respondents said they supported protest rights, a significant percentage favored limits:

- [12]Almost one-third of those surveyed said that individuals should not be allowed to protest in public against an American war during the period of active combat.
- [13]One in three respondents said that public school officials should be allowed to prohibit high school students from expressing their opinions about the war on school property. And roughly one in two said public schools should be allowed to ban armbands or other symbolic opposition to the war during a period of combat.
- [14]Perhaps echoing public sentiment concerning comments by the Dixie Chicks, 39% of those surveyed said they would be less likely to

buy a CD from a musician who has made controversial political remarks in public that differ from their own views.

- [15]About 55% of those surveyed opposed a constitutional amendment to ban flag-burning, up from 51% in 2002.

[16]Last year, a three-judge panel of the 9th U.S. Circuit Court of Appeals ruled that the recitation in public schools of the phrase "one nation under God" during the Pledge of Allegiance violated the U.S. Constitution. The outcry was immediate and angry. The 2003 State of the First Amendment survey found that most respondents were not concerned about the separation of church and state. In fact, a majority seemed comfortable with intermingling religious references with government business:

- [17]Almost seven in 10 said that the public school recitation of the phrase "one nation under God" in the Pledge of Allegiance does not violate the separation of church and state.

- [18]About 62% of those surveyed said government officials should be allowed to post the Ten Commandments inside government buildings. Almost eight in 10 said the government's use of the phrase "In God We Trust" on U.S. money does not violate the principle of the separation of church and state.

- [19]About 60% said they favored allowing the government to give money to religious institutions to help run drug-abuse prevention programs, even if the institutions included a religious message in their program.

[20]Do these responses reflect a trust in government not to go beyond symbolic references to faith? Or do the results reflect a majority who are receptive to seeing their own beliefs cited on government walls and in ceremonial references?

[21]The answers may lie in how Americans view God in the context of government activities. Most of those surveyed regarded government references to God as civic rather than spiritual.

[22]About 73% of those surveyed said the phrase "one nation under God" was "primarily a statement related to the American political tradition." Fewer than 20% said they thought this reference to God was "primarily a religious statement."

[23]Another area spurring fierce debate over the last year has been the Federal Communications Commission's move to loosen media-ownership restrictions.

[24]The public's unease with extensive media ownership by large corporations and conglomerates was reflected in the survey. The majority of respondents said the quality of news reporting has deteriorated and opposed the removal of limits on how many media outlets may be owned by a single company:

- [25]Fifty-two percent of those surveyed said media ownership by fewer corporations has meant a decreased number of viewpoints available to the public. Fifty-three percent said the quality of information also has suffered.

In your opinion, to what extent do corporate owners influence news organizations' decisions about which stories to cover or emphasize?

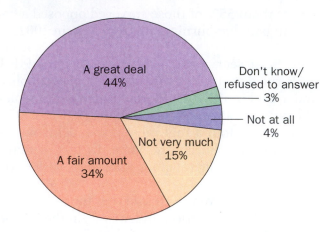

A great deal
44%

Don't know/
refused to answer
3%

Not at all
4%

Not very much
15%

A fair amount
34%

FIGURE 4

- [26]Fifty-four percent said they favor maintaining federal limits on how many radio, television and newspaper outlets may be owned by a single company, but one in two said they opposed any increased regulation.

- [27]Almost eight Americans in 10 said owners exert substantial influence over news organizations' newsgathering and reporting decisions. Only 4% said they believed there is no tampering with story selection or play.

[28]Overall, the 2003 State of the First Amendment survey results suggest some challenges for America's news media.

[29]While most respondents gave the press high marks for Iraq war coverage and said they count on the news media to provide more information about the war on terrorism, they also said the press has too much freedom and indicated suspicion of those who own the nation's newspapers and broadcast stations.

[30]Fortunately, Americans also recognize responsible and responsive news coverage when they see it. For all of the skepticism about news media ownership and excesses, the nation's journalists remain uniquely positioned to win support for a free press—and the First Amendment as a whole—by living up to the watchdog role envisioned by the founding fathers.

[31]At a time when many remain tempted to roll back civil liberties in the name of security, a free press plays a crucial role.

[32]The nation's news media truly honor the First Amendment when they ask the tough questions, fight to keep the public's business public and provide the kind of thorough and balanced reporting that is the lifeblood of a democracy.

State of the First Amendment 2003 Questions

VOCABULARY

1. Explain what Paulson means when he says, "While reaction to fear is largely reflexive, the passage of time allows us to be reflective." (¶4)

2. Paulson says, "the nation's journalists remain uniquely positioned to win support for a free press—and the First Amendment as a whole—by living up to the watchdog role envisioned by the founding fathers." (¶30) What is the "watchdog role" and how can a journalist fulfill that role?

COMPREHENSION AND ANALYSIS

For questions 3, 4, and 5, indicate whether the statement is true or false. If the statement is false, rewrite it to make it true.

3. More than half of the respondents for the 2003 poll indicated overall support for First Amendment freedoms.

4. The least popular First Amendment right continued to be freedom of speech.

5. A majority of the respondents for the 2003 poll seemed uncomfortable with intermingling religious references with government business.

6. What information does Figure 1 provide that is not in the text?

7. What percentage of Americans believes owners exert substantial influence over news organizations' newsgathering and reporting decisions? Do you believe media owners influence what is printed and broadcast? Please explain.

8. What is the relationship of paragraphs 12 to 15 to paragraph 11?

9. Which of the survey results surprised you the most? Please explain.

REFLECT AND CONNECT

10. Does the data in Figure 1 appear to support or contradict Judge Posner's view (in his essay on page 123) that while "public-safety" and "liberty" interests are both important, their relative importance changes from time to time and situation to situation. Please explain.

How Much Religious Freedom Is Too Much?

CHARLES HAYNES

Charles Haynes is a senior scholar and director of education programs at the First Amendment Center. An educator for more than 20 years, he writes and speaks on religious liberty in public schools, religion and values in American public life, and First Amendment issues in education. He is the author or co-author of six books, including Finding Common Ground: A First Amendment Guide to Religious Liberty in Public Schools. *He wrote this article in July 2003.*

AN IDEA TO THINK ABOUT

A Muslim woman asks to wear her veil for her driver's license photo. Why would some people want her to be able to wear the veil? Why would some people not want her to wear the veil? *As you read,* find out if the state can ever override a claim of religious conscience.

HOW MUCH RELIGIOUS FREEDOM IS TOO MUCH?

Charles Haynes

[1]Sultaana Freeman's refusal to remove her veil for a driver's license photo touched a nerve. Talk-show exchanges and letters to the editor are filled with exasperation—even outrage—over the Muslim woman's lawsuit against the state of Florida. If she doesn't want to show her face, fumes one annoyed citizen, "let her take a bus or hire a chauffeur."

[2]Americans are all for religious freedom—but often lose patience when someone dares to practice it. Then again, sometimes a compelling public interest makes certain restrictions necessary.

[3]The Florida fight isn't an isolated incident. As America's religious diversity explodes, a growing number of conflicts between religious conscience and government regulations are breaking out across the nation. Two other cases in the news illustrate the challenge:

- [4]Seventh-day Adventist students in Oregon sued to get the Oregon School Activities Association to alter the statewide basketball tournament schedule. As it stands, the students are barred from participating because the consolation round takes place on their Sabbath.

- [5]Two Amish farmers in rural Pennsylvania asked their township to exempt them from a town ordinance that bans horses. Since as a matter of faith they can't drive cars, the farmers need horses to pull their buggies.

[6]Annoying legal sideshows that clog the courts? Or vital issues of religious liberty?

[7]The answer depends on how seriously we take the First Amendment—and not on what we think of the religious claims themselves. If religious freedom was easy—or confined to religious practices that are popular and simple to accommodate—then it would mean little. We're supposed to be a nation that protects "free exercise of religion" for everyone—including the smallest minorities and least popular communities.

[8]Why? Because 200 years ago people like James Madison believed that every person has an "unalienable right" to follow the dictates of conscience. By definition, a person of deep religious commitment looks to a higher authority than the state. "This duty is precedent," argued Madison, "both in order of time and in degree of obligation, to the claims of Civil Society."

[9]Of course, Madison and other framers of the Constitution understood that religious freedom must have some limits. But they tried to invent a nation that would—for the first time in history—protect individual conscience in matters of faith as far as possible.

[10]But how much freedom is too much? In these current cases, you might be tempted to draw the line quickly and narrowly (unless you happen to be Muslim, Seventh-day Adventist or Amish). But here's the rub. Where the state has the power to draw the line for some, it has the power to draw

the line for all. Today a law or regulation may burden someone else's religious practice, but tomorrow it could burden mine or yours. And then it might be too late to argue for a robust application of the First Amendment.

[11]Does this mean religious conviction should always trump the law? Of course not. Sometimes the state (acting for the common good) has a compelling interest in overriding a claim of religious conscience—and no less-restrictive way to accomplish that interest.

[12]That's exactly why Sultaana Freeman lost in court. The state of Florida demonstrated a compelling interest in promoting public safety, including the ability of police officers to quickly and accurately determine someone's identity. In post-9/11 America, this case was a slam dunk for the state.

[13]Whether or not you agree with the outcome (and I do), the Florida judge asked the right questions. A sincere religious belief should be taken seriously. But if the government has a compelling interest at stake, and if there is no other way to meet that interest except by uniformly enforcing the regulation, then the religious claim for exemption can and should be denied.

[14]But the state's interest isn't always that compelling. Take the Oregon case involving the Seventh-day Adventist kids. Earlier this month a state appeals court ruled that a school activities association should make a reasonable effort to accommodate the religious beliefs of the students. Why not a change in game time? Or allowing a forfeit? Or some other reasonable accommodation? The court sent the case back—telling the state to look for a solution that allows these students to play basketball without violating their religious faith.

[15]As for the Amish farmers, they're supposed to get rid of their horses or start paying $100 per day in fines. If they file a suit, can the Amish win in court? They have a good shot.

[16]Although the Supreme Court no longer requires governments to show a compelling state interest in many "free exercise" cases, Pennsylvania (like Florida and a number of other states) has a new religious-freedom law that may well apply. And Congress passed a law a few years ago requiring local governments to apply the "compelling interest" test in zoning cases. So give the farmers a fighting chance to keep their horses.

[17]All of this makes life more complicated for the government, but where would you rather live? In a nation where state interests routinely override individual conscience—or in a nation where claims of conscience get a day in court? It may be messy, but what a glorious mess.

How Much Religious Freedom Is Too Much? Questions

VOCABULARY

1. Define a "compelling public interest." ([2] and [11])

2. Haynes says Madison believed "every person has an 'unalienable right' to follow the dictates of conscience." ([8]) Please explain what that means.

3. What does Haynes mean when he says, "Where the state has the power to draw the line for some, it has the power to draw the line for all"? ([10]) Why could that power be a problem for you or me?

4. Haynes asks if "religious conviction should always trump the law." (¶11) Explain what the term *trump* means. Where do you think the term originated?

COMPREHENSION AND ANALYSIS

5. State Haynes's thesis.

6. Why did Sultaana Freeman lose her bid to wear her veil for her driver's license? Why does Haynes think the Amish can win in court?

7. What do you think would be a "reasonable accommodation" for the Seventh-day Adventist kids in Oregon?

8. In paragraph 13, Haynes clearly states that he agrees with the Florida court's decision. Without that statement, could you have determined his view of the decision? Please give an example to support your answer.

9. In the last paragraph, Haynes says, "It may be messy, but what a glorious mess." What does *It* refer to? Why does Haynes think it creates a "glorious" mess? Do you think it creates a 'glorious mess'? Please explain.

REFLECT AND CONNECT

10. In paragraph 10, Haynes asks, "How much [religious] freedom is too much?" How do you think he would answer the question? How do you answer the question?

'Free' and Other 4-Letter Words

KENNETH A. PAULSON

Mr. Paulson is executive director of the Freedom Forum's First Amendment Center. A veteran newspaper editor and lawyer, he hosts the weekly television series Speaking Freely *and writes and speaks on U.S. Supreme Court decisions, media and journalism, free speech and press, free expression in the arts, and other First Amendment issues. The Freedom Forum is a nonpartisan, international foundation based at Vanderbilt University.*

AN IDEA TO THINK ABOUT

You're enjoying an outing with family and friends at your local park when a group of folks wearing "F—You" T-shirts claim the picnic table next to you. Your six-year-old niece loudly demonstrates her reading ability and then asks, "What does that mean?"—creating an uncomfortable situation for many in the group. Can park security make them remove the T-shirts or leave the park? *As you read,* find out why it's almost impossible for government to constitutionally designate some words as acceptable and others as unacceptable.

'FREE' AND OTHER 4-LETTER WORDS

Kenneth A. Paulson

[1]No matter how much you support free expression, there's always something that can challenge your beliefs.

[2]Some are unsettled by violence on television; others have second thoughts about sexist or racist Web sites. Others question liberties taken in provocative books or art.

[3]I can defend any banned book or controversial painting, but somehow the sight of a guy wearing a "F—You" T-shirt at a county fair or football game gets under my skin.

[4]You've seen him. Apparently unable to afford the "If I Only Had a Brain" T-shirt, he wears America's most overused phrase with pride.

[5]The tacky T-shirt puts parents in a tough spot. They try to steer their kids in another direction, determined to avoid an embarrassing moment or question. Why doesn't somebody do something about this rude behavior? Shouldn't government be able to stop public vulgarity of this sort?

[6]Of course, that's when I come to my senses. Public profanity isn't pretty, but it's almost impossible for government to constitutionally designate some words as acceptable and others as inappropriate. The truth is that public profanity can violate our sensibilities, but generally doesn't violate the law.

[7]The Idaho Supreme Court made that point a few weeks ago in overturning the misdemeanor conviction of a man who cursed at a police officer in a 1998 incident.

[8]Patrick Sheldon Suiter had gone to the Canyon County Courthouse to speak to an officer about a fraudulent-check case in which a friend was victimized. The officer refused to file a complaint without some verification that Suiter was authorized to act on behalf of the victim. Suiter became angry and critical of the police department. After being told by the detective to calm down, Suiter said, "Hey, f—off," and began to leave. He was then arrested by two officers and accused of disturbing the peace.

[9]Police said Suiter wasn't arrested for what he said, just how he said it. The U.S. Supreme Court concluded long ago that a profane expression cannot be the sole grounds for prosecution. In a landmark case in 1971, the high court dismissed a charge of disturbing the peace against a man whose jacket bore the message: "F—the draft." In finding that "one man's vulgarity is another's lyric," the court essentially barred the future prosecution of vulgar written messages, including bumper stickers and T-shirts.

[10]Suiter's profanity was spoken, not written, but the Idaho Supreme Court cited that profane protest of the draft in concluding that Suiter's insulting remark to the police officer was indeed speech protected by the First Amendment.

[11]The court noted that abusive and highly provocative epithets directed toward ordinary citizens can be banned as so-called "fighting words." But in this case, the comment was addressed to a police officer, a public servant with a duty not to be provoked to violence by mere words.

In addition, a total of just six people heard the remark, none of whom characterized it as yelling, shouting or screaming. It was an uncomfortable moment, but not a highly disruptive one.

[12]Courts face an extraordinary challenge in addressing these issues. Words that were once shocking to polite society are now staples on both cable and broadcast television. Rather than try to legislate language, government can realistically only prosecute the disruptive behavior that sometimes accompanies profane language.

[13]Profane words may be constitutionally protected, but that doesn't give us a license to say whatever we want, wherever we want, and most important, however we want. In other words, "fire" is not the only word you can't shout in a crowded theater.

'Free' and Other 4-Letter Words Questions

VOCABULARY

1. In 1971, the U.S. Supreme Court found that "one man's vulgarity is another's lyric." (¶9) Explain what the Court means.

2. The Court also found that "abusive and highly provocative epithets directed toward ordinary citizens can be banned." (¶11) Explain what *abusive and highly provocative epithets* are and give an example.

3. Paulson says, "Words that were once shocking to polite society are now staples on both cable and broadcast television." (¶12) What does the word *staples* mean in this context? Give an example of a word that was once shocking to polite society and is now a staple on television.

COMPREHENSION AND ANALYSIS

4. State Paulson's thesis.

5. What is the tone of paragraph 4? Please explain your answer.

6. Can profane written messages be prohibited? If they can, under what circumstances?

7. Can abusive, vulgar, provocative speech be prohibited? If it can, under what circumstances?

8. Why did the Idaho Supreme Court overturn the conviction of the citizen who cursed at a police officer?

9. In the final sentence of paragraph 13, Paulson says, "In other words, 'fire' is not the only word you can't shout in a crowded theater." Please explain what he means.

REFLECT AND CONNECT

10. In the "First Amendment Freedoms" text chapter that opens the theme, Burns and colleagues say, "Americans overwhelmingly support the principle of freedom of expression in general. Yet some who say they

believe in free speech draw the line at ideas they consider dangerous or when speech attacks them or is critical of their race, religion, or ethnic origins." They then ask, "But what is a dangerous idea? Who decides?" How would you answer their two very difficult questions?

Dilbert Cartoon

SCOTT ADAMS

Mr. Adams received his bachelor's degree in economics in 1979 from Hartwick College, Oneonta, New York, and his MBA from the University of California at Berkeley. He says from 1979 to 1986 he worked in a number of "humiliating and low paying jobs," and from 1986 until 1995 he worked a variety of day jobs that "defy description but all involve technology and finances" while doing the Dilbert *comic strip mornings, evenings, and weekends. Adams says Dilbert is a composite of his coworkers over the years. Dogbert was created so Dilbert would have someone to talk to.*

AN IDEA TO THINK ABOUT

If the college theatre arts department announced it was planning to produce a play with content you found personally objectionable, what would you do? Ask them to remove the play from the schedule? Ask that the objectionable passages be edited out? Ask that a program note be included about the objectionable material? Stage a peaceful protest? Just not attend the performance? *As you read,* decide how Adams feels about censorship.

(DILBERT reprinted by permission of United Features Syndicate, Inc.)

Dilbert Cartoon Questions

1. What is the topic/issue?

2. What is Adams's point of view?

3. What does Adams want the reader to do or think about after reading this cartoon?

Well, Would You Rather Have an Unfree Press?

BILL THOMPSON

Mr. Thompson is a columnist for the Fort Worth Star-Telegram. *This column appeared in July 1999.*

AN IDEA TO THINK ABOUT

Do you think the news media should be free to investigate and report all the "news"? If not, who do you think should set the limits? *As you read,* find out if Thompson thinks there should be limits on the press's freedom.

WELL, WOULD YOU RATHER HAVE AN UNFREE PRESS?

Bill Thompson

[1]Let's talk about the First Amendment.

[2]You've heard about it. It's the first item in the Bill of Rights, which is the term we use to describe the first 10 amendments to the Constitution of the United States. These amendments guarantee various fundamental rights and freedoms: the right to bear arms, the right to a fair trial, freedom from unreasonable search and seizure, freedom against self-incrimination. . . .

[3]The founders of this country went out of their way to make sure there would be no confusion about the importance of such constitutional rights in the new American republic.

[4]Most constitutional scholars agree that the numerical order of the first 10 amendments was not intended to prioritize them or rank their significance in any way. But there is no denying that the First Amendment set the tone for the Bill of Rights and helped set the direction that the new nation would take.

[5]The freedoms guaranteed by the First Amendment are crucial to the success of any democracy. To violate or abridge these rights is to undermine the essence of a democratic society.

[6]For those of us who have never committed the First Amendment to memory, here's what it says:

[7]Congress shall make no law respecting an establishment of religion, or prohibiting the free exercise thereof; or abridging the freedom of speech, or of the press, or the right of the people peaceably to assemble, and to petition the Government for a redress of grievances.

[8]It's short and to the point. Freedom of religion. Free speech. Freedom of the press. The right to protest.

[9]Those guys had a way with words.

[10]I don't mean to ramble. But as the American people look toward a new century, there is reason to fear for the future of those rights.

[11]The First Amendment, especially, is under attack as never before. The results of a new poll reported in *USA Today* suggest that freedom of the press, in particular, has fallen into disfavor with the public. The poll was commissioned by the Freedom Forum, a pro-First Amendment foundation.

[12]According to the newspaper, 53 percent of those who responded to the poll said that the press in America has too much freedom—an increase of 15 percent from a similar poll conducted two years ago.

[13]Tony Mauro of *USA Today* reported that the poll indicated "nearly two-thirds of the public thinks the press should not be allowed to probe the private lives of public officials. And shrinking numbers of respondents think the news media should be allowed to endorse political candidates, report government secrets or use hidden cameras."

[14]Mauro quoted a media lawyer/author named Bruce Sanford: "The public is so angry at the media these days that we are beginning to blind ourselves to the biggest threat, which is not the media but government regulation."

[15]Boy, is that the truth.

[16]It's understandable that the public gets disgusted with what seems to be the media's overemphasis on scandal, on violence, on "negative" news of every description. Even the media folks who serve up this stuff on a daily basis get disgusted with it.

[17]But the fact is, people are watching and reading all this news that they claim to hate. If they weren't, the media wouldn't be quite so eager to report it.

[18]But even if you happen to be one of those rare consumers who only reads the good news, who scrupulously avoids the bad and the ugly, you surely wouldn't want the government to decide what news can be printed and broadcast.

[19]Would you?

[20]The free press makes mistakes, just as any institution does, but the alternative is an unfree press. The sort of press, for example, that operates under the thumb of Yugoslav President Slobodan Milosevic. The sort of press that covers up Milosevic's crimes against humanity and refuses to tell the people of Yugoslavia why most of Western civilization has turned against their leaders and waged war against their country.

[21]We can't have it both ways. There is no such thing as a partly free press.

[22]We can accept the First Amendment and put up with occasional abuses of the freedom it guarantees. Or we can surrender this right that the founders considered so important that they placed it first on their list of most important rights.

[23]It's a clear-cut choice. There is nothing in between.

Well, Would You Rather Have An Unfree Press? Questions

VOCABULARY

1. Explain what Thompson means in paragraph 5 when he says, "To violate or abridge these rights is to undermine the essence of a democratic society."

Rephrase the underlined passages using your own words.

2. ". . . freedom of the press, in particular, <u>has fallen into disfavor with the public</u>." (¶11)

3. ". . . who <u>scrupulously avoids</u> the bad and the ugly, . . . (¶18)

COMPREHENSION AND ANALYSIS

For questions 4 to 6, indicate whether the statement is true or false. If the statement is false, rewrite it to make it true.

4. The poll Thompson refers to indicated that an increasing number of Americans felt the press has too much freedom.

5. If people didn't watch and read all the bad and disgusting news they claim to hate, the media probably wouldn't be so eager to report it.

6. There is no such thing as a partly free press.

7. State Thompson's thesis.

8. What does media lawyer/author Bruce Sanford believe is our "biggest threat"? Explain what that means.

9. Fifty-three percent of those responding to the 1999 State of the First Amendment poll Thompson refers to in paragraph 12 said that the press in America had too much freedom. How does that compare to the responses to the same question in the 2003 State of the First Amendment poll? What do you think might account for any differences?

REFLECT AND CONNECT

10. In the "First Amendment Freedoms" text chapter that opens the theme, Burns, and colleagues point out that when the First Amendment was written, freedom of "the press" referred to leaflets, newspapers, and books. However, today, the amendment protects a broad array of media. List five of the new media protected under the First Amendment. Which one(s) do you think present the most problems for consumers and government regulators.

The Right to Petition

ADAM NEWTON

Mr. Newton is counsel in the legal division at Procter & Gamble headquarters in Cincinnati. His interest in the interplay between media freedoms and legal regulation began while working in middle and high school for the Indianapolis Star. *He later studied journalism as a Wells Scholar at Indiana University and graduated with first honors from Vanderbilt Law School, where he cofounded and served as executive editor for the* Vanderbilt Journal of Entertainment Law & Practice. *After law school, Newton clerked for the Hon. Gilbert S. Merritt of the 6th U.S. Circuit Court of Appeals and was an associate in the law firm of Frost, Brown, Todd. He wrote this article for The First Amendment Center.*

VOCABULARY

minutiae (¶11): smallest details
nascent (¶12): budding, young and inexperienced
abject despotism (¶16): horrible tyranny, horrifying authoritarian rule
eclipsed (¶20): overshadowed, replaced

AN IDEA TO THINK ABOUT

The campus computer lab is increasingly plagued by hardware problems. As a result, you and your classmates must often wait a couple of hours to use a computer to complete your required homework. What would be a good way to make your college president aware of how many students are affected by the problem? *As you read,* trace the history of our right to petition and how its uses have changed through the years.

THE RIGHT TO PETITION

Adam Newton

[1]The petition clause concludes the First Amendment's ringing enumeration of expressive rights and, in many ways, supports them all. Petition is the right to ask government at any level to right a wrong or correct a problem.

[2]Although a petition is only as meaningful as its response, the petitioning right allows blocs of public interests to form, harnessing voting power in ways that effect change. The right to petition allows citizens to focus government attention on unresolved ills; provide information to elected leaders about unpopular policies; expose misconduct, waste, corruption, and incompetence; and vent popular frustrations without endangering the public order.

[3]Yet the petition clause seems to strike most courts and legal commentators as obvious and uninteresting. Citizens and litigants invoke the First Amendment to secure Internet freedom, undisturbed worship, or a robust press, but petitioning rights don't seem to attract much notice. The right to complain is hardly something that starts wars—or is it?

Some History

[4]On July 4, 1776, the country's founders adopted a famous statement of principles and list of grievances, declaring that:

[5]"In every state of these Oppressions We have Petitioned for Redress in the most humble terms: Our repeated Petitions have been answered only by repeated injury. A Prince, whose character is thus marked by every act which may define a Tyrant, is unfit to be the ruler of a free people."

[6]King George III's crowning wrong, in the end, was his indifference: Those who revolted felt they had no other recourse. In building a new democracy, the Founders avoided the king's mistake by guaranteeing political receptiveness to public concerns.

[7]The amendments that would become the Bill of Rights initially listed the rights of assembly and petition separately from free-speech protections. As the early House and Senate debated "the people's right to instruct their Representatives," their deliberations echoed the momentous accommodation between King John and his barons at Runnymede more than 500 years earlier. In 1215, King John signed the Magna Carta, which recognized the right of the barons to petition the crown. From this contract grew the tradition allowing British subjects to submit their grievances to the King's council and, with the ascendancy of Parliament, to the House of Commons.

[8]These early petitions usually stated personal grievances and individual requests for relief. With its overlapping executive, judicial and legislative functions, Parliament referred most of these to internal committees, appointed auditors or deferred to royal counselors. Wary that open airing of grievances would spark popular dissent, Parliament at times punished particularly severe complaints and prohibited petitions bearing more than 20 signatures. After the Glorious Revolution, however, the 1689 Declaration of Rights recognized that "it is the right of the subjects to petition the king, and all commitments and prosecutions for such petitioning is illegal."

[9]Transplanted from this tradition of petitioning, which William Blackstone described as "appertaining to every individual," the first American colonists viewed their local assemblies as royal surrogates for the lodging of complaints. In 1641, the Massachusetts Body of Liberties became the first royal charter to protect this right expressly, recognizing that "[e]very man whether Inhabitant or foreigner, free or not free shall have libertie to come to any publique Court, Councel or town meeting, and either by speech or writing to move any lawfull, seasonable, and materiall question, or to present any necessary motion, complaint, petition, Bill or information."

[10]Records of the colonial assemblies reveal that this was not a right reserved for the land-owning elite. Women, Native Americans, and even slaves sought—and, in some cases, obtained—relief from the authorities on questions of taxes, tribal lands, emancipation and public corruption.

[11]The breadth of participation was matched only by the minutiae of detail: debt actions, property settlements, estate contests, divorce judgments, criminal appeals, commercial disputes, road construction requests, charges of breaking the Sabbath, and a host of other public and private claims came before the assemblies, which enacted, interpreted and enforced the laws.

[12]Petitioning was a form of public dialogue in a time before mass media and national political parties. The nascent assemblies solicited the views and complaints of the colonists as a barometer of the popular mood and as justification for their measures. The intimacy between colonist and assembly meant that petitions essentially drove the legislative agenda, and so the early laws developed in a patchwork of special interests and personal appeals.

[13]With the commercial and geographic expansion of the colonies, however, many assemblies imposed internal rules to quell the tide of petitions, which had increased both in volume and complexity. Connecticut,

for example, raised the fees for submitting petitions, increased the jurisdictional amounts in controversy, introduced conditions of admissibility, and threatened contempt proceedings against grievances that proved to be false.

[14]In theory, disgruntled colonists could take their appeal to the royal governors, and, if still unsatisfied, to the King in England. Starting in the 1770s, an increasingly vocal and coordinated group of petitioners sought relief from England for a series of intolerable acts relating to restraints on trade, the quartering of troops, taxation, restrictions on westward expansion and numerous other limits on self-government. Denied redress, the petitioners became revolutionaries and, in 1776, leaders of a new nation.

[15]Inflamed by the royal stonewalling of their appeals, the Founders embedded the right to petition into their blueprint for a new democracy. The First Amendment prohibits Congress from abridging "the right of the people peaceably to assemble, and to petition the Government for a redress of grievances." The first test of this guarantee arose over the issue of slavery in the District of Columbia. Abolitionists in the 1830s sought to end slavery in the nation's capital for symbolic and practical reasons: Congress, as lawmaker for the District, could abolish slavery without trampling on states' rights.

[16]Abolitionists organized a massive petitioning campaign that flooded Congress with letters and special appeals. Besieged by paper, the House of Representatives adopted a "gag rule" that summarily tabled all such petitions without debate or acknowledgment. Former president John Quincy Adams articulated the outrage of the Northern antislavery position by decrying that only "the most abject despotism" could "deprive the citizen of the right to supplicate for a boon, or pray for mercy."

[17]Though the gag rule was repealed in 1844, this episode illustrates how far the nation had evolved and how the strategic goals of petitioning had changed. The first recorded act of Connecticut's general assembly in 1650 was consideration of a petition against a farmer who had "traded a peece [firearm] with the Indians for corne."

[18]Two hundred years later, however, petitioning was an instrument of mass politics, designed to make a point, not a plea. As with the divisive issue of slavery, petitioning was a means of uniting popular groups and overwhelming political opponents. As one modern commentator put it, petitions "were the sound bites of the early nineteenth century."

[19]Though some individual appeals persisted, public petitioning lost its local character and its immediacy, becoming instead a political ultimatum enforced at the ballot box. The authors and signers of mass petitions did not intend to convey a personal appeal. Nor did they seriously expect a personalized response. Instead, they were giving their representatives a preview of election day by showing the depth and extent of public sentiment on issues such as slavery, women's suffrage and the admission of new states into the Union.

[20]As the young nation matured, its democratic visions broadened the franchise, established political parties, fostered a national press and, after the shock of the Civil War, expanded the federal government. The United States had entered the industrial age of modern politics and markets that eclipsed strictly local loyalties.

[21]Patrick Henry, firebrand patriot of the founding generation, had seemed to predict this atomizing of citizenry and centralizing of authority when he protested constitutionalism:

[22]The act, called the Bill of Rights, comes here into view. What is it but a bargain, which the parts of government made with each other to divide powers, profits and privileges? You shall have so much, and I will have the rest; and with respect to the nation, you shall have the right of petitioning.

[23]But the 200 years since belie Henry's mocking denigration of the petition clause.

Petition Today

[24]"Petitioning" has come to signify any nonviolent, legal means of encouraging or disapproving government action, whether directed to the judicial, executive or legislative branch. Lobbying, letter-writing, e-mail campaigns, testifying before tribunals, filing lawsuits, supporting referenda, collecting signatures for ballot initiatives, peaceful protests and picketing: all public articulation of issues, complaints and interests designed to spur government action qualifies under the petition clause, even if the activities partake of other First Amendment freedoms.

[25]The U.S. Supreme Court has affirmed that the right to engage in such activity is a fundamental liberty, protected against encroachment by federal, state and local governments.

[26]For the breadth of activism it protects, however, the right to petition is surprisingly shallow in judicial consideration and academic analysis. The Supreme Court has exalted the right as "among the most precious liberties safeguarded by the Bill of Rights" and implicit in "the very idea of government."

[27]Yet the Court rarely considers the petition clause apart from the other guarantees of the First Amendment, collapsing it with protections for associational interests and political speech. Though the Court has recognized the constitutional significance of peaceful public activism generally, it has invoked the petition clause only peripherally, if at all, in the following areas:

- [28]Lobbying. Restrictions such as registration and disclosure requirements are constitutional because they do not effectively prevent exercise of the right of petition. Yet the Court has not affirmatively recognized lobbying as a constitutionally protected activity anchored in the petition clause. Whether a lobbyist, as a paid agent, stands in the same position as a citizen requesting government consideration is unclear. The Court has recognized the right to freely associate and take collective action as inherent in lobbying, but it has not highlighted the unique role petitioning plays in such activities.

- [29]Right to file suit. The right to petition the government for redress of grievances includes a right to file suit in a court of law. Again, the Court has collapsed the distinct right to petition with other protections for group speech. . . .

- [30]SLAPP suits. Strategic Lawsuits Against Public Participation, as they are called, are sometimes filed against citizens for speaking out about a range of public matters before city councils, county commissions, school boards and other agencies. From a First Amendment standpoint, SLAPPs are a disturbing attempt to use the law to suppress and punish citizens' exercise of their right to petition government regarding matters of public concern. Such lawsuits, fortunately, can be readily combatted.

- [31]Other immunities. In *McDonald* v. *Smith* (1985), a petitioner claimed absolute immunity from a private libel action based on two letters he sent to President Ronald Reagan. Writing against the appointment of a former state court judge to the position of U.S. Attorney in North Carolina, the petitioner accused the candidate of civil rights violations, fraud, conspiracy, blackmail and other illegal and unethical acts.

    [32]Alleging that these letters ruined his reputation and his prospects for appointment, the candidate sued the petitioner for libel, who invoked the petition clause as the basis for his immunity claim. Noting that the right to petition is "cut from the same cloth" as other First Amendment protections, the Supreme Court held that the petitioner was entitled only to the same qualified immunity as the other expressive freedoms under the "actual malice" standard of *New York Times* v. *Sullivan*.

    [33]In *McDonald,* the Court concluded that the petition clause "was inspired by the same ideals of liberty and democracy that gave us the freedoms to speak, publish, and assemble," and so was unwilling to afford petitioning "special First Amendment status." For this reason, the incidental activities of petitioning—gathering signatures, circulating fliers, rallying public support—are likewise subject to neutral time, place and manner restrictions consistent with public safety and order.

How Petition Has Changed

[34]The direct appeal and individualized response that once marked petitioning belong to a more organic past when leaders knew petitioners by name. No branch of the government today is equipped to provide such personal attention. As the Supreme Court has observed, the right to petition requires only that the state receive complaints and grievances, not respond to them. Historical practice aside, the Court has explained that "[N]othing in the First Amendment or in this Court's case law interpreting it suggests that the rights to speak, associate, and petition require government policymakers to listen or respond to individuals' communications on public issues."

[35]Even if the "redress" dimension of the petition clause merely expresses the hope of government response, the very act of channeling popular opinion for public officials serves important societal goals. It creates an information flow from the public to the government, and serves as a safety valve for public passions.

[36]Yet despite its social benefits, the First Amendment right of petition has not been developed as a doctrine or championed as a cause. Few scholars or courts have fully appreciated the historical and present right to petition—let alone its future.

[37]Perhaps the right of petition has escaped their attention precisely because it continues to work so well. The petition clause is the tacit

assumption in constitutional analysis, the primordial right from which other expressive freedoms arise. Why speak, why publish, why assemble against the government at all if such complaints will only be silenced?

[38]As Justice John Paul Stevens once pointed out, "The First Amendment was intended to secure something more than an exercise in futility." The petition clause ensures that our leaders hear, even if they don't listen to, the electorate. Though public officials may be indifferent, contrary, or silent participants in democratic discourse, at least the First Amendment commands their audience.

Notes

1. 620 F.2d 1301 (8th Cir., 1980)
2. 664 F.2d 891 (2nd Cir., 1981)

The Right to Petition Questions

VOCABULARY

1. Explain what Newton means when he says, "Denied redress, the petitioners became revolutionaries." (¶14)

2. Explain what the commentator meant when he said petitions "were the sound bites of the early nineteenth century." (¶18)

3. Explain what Newton means when he says, "But the 200 years since belie Henry's mocking denigration of the petition clause." (¶23)

COMPREHENSION AND ANALYSIS

4. How is the Magna Carta, signed by King John in 1215, related to our right to petition?

5. Describe the "first test" of the First Amendment's guarantee that people have the right to petition the government for a redress of grievances.

6. Why did the House of Representatives adopt a "gag rule"? Why was it repealed in 1844?

7. Describe how the primary use of the right to petition has changed through the years.

8. List two reasons Newton feels that the First Amendment right of petition is one of our most significant freedoms.

9. State Newton's thesis.

REFLECT AND CONNECT

10. Today, the right to petition is used for a variety of reasons and causes. Describe one situation you know about or have read about when the right to petition was used. Do you think it was used effectively?

LOG ON TO THE WEB

Our First Amendment freedoms impact us in many ways. Therefore, you can find a great amount of information about the freedoms on Websites such as the following:

- The Freedom Forum *http://www.freedomforum.org/* is an excellent starting point for research into all first amendment rights. The site contains a comprehensive archive of news, legal materials, and links to speech, religion, press, and assembly sites.

- *http://www.esquilax.com/flag/* details one of the more controversial forms of expression: flag burning. It contains extensive coverage of the issue, including a history of flag burning and details on the legal activity currently underway.

- Produced from the materials of Ralph E. McCoy, the dean emeritus of Library Affairs at Southern Illinois University, *http://www.lib.siu.edu/cni/homepage.html* is an exhaustive reference guide to freedom of the press materials.

Log on to one of these sites or use a search engine to locate another site with information about some aspect of our First Amendment freedoms. Read one section or story about First Amendment freedoms. Write down

1. the complete Web address
2. the name of the person or company who sponsors and maintains the site
3. the name of the person who wrote the information
4. what you know about the writer
5. one important thing you learned about First Amendment freedoms

REFLECT AND CONNECT

A. To protest the University of Colorado's softening of its policy on selling T-shirts produced in third-world sweatshops, a 20-year-old college student jumped onto the auditorium stage and shoved a blueberry pie into the face of the CU chancellor. After the police charged the student with third-degree assault, newspaper columnist Clint Talbot wrote: ". . . her [the student's] act, though criminal, was a political statement. Like other forms of protest, it reflects the values of the First Amendment."

   Do you share Talbot's feelings that such a protest reflects the values of the First Amendment, or do you disagree with him? Please explain.

B. In Nevada, an angry parent got into a pushing and shoving match with his daughter's basketball coach. The parent was charged in the incident. The local newspaper ran an article when the parent pleaded guilty to a misdemeanor battery charge and agreed to undergo an anger-management evaluation. It ran a photograph of the parent with the article. The parent complained that the photograph "made him look like a criminal."

Following the incident, a Nevada lawmaker asked for legislation to be drafted that would "restrict the use by newspapers of photographs of persons under certain circumstances."

According to Nevada Press Association executive director Kent Lauer, the proposal "should be dead on arrival at the Legislature because it's a blatant violation of the First Amendment. It's government censorship, plain and simple."

Do you feel such legislation is a good idea or agree with Lauer that it would be a violation of the First Amendment? Please explain.

C. A Boston bar owner put up a supposedly racist African-themed display allegedly mocking Black History month and Martin Luther King Jr.'s birthday. The Massachusetts Commission Against Discrimination said it's illegal for businesses to say things that "ridicule or create a racial stereotype and make certain people feel unwelcome" and thus create a "hostile public accommodations environment." Therefore, the Commission is investigating if the bar owner did this and should be punished.

Do you think the First Amendment protects his right to express his opinions—good, bad and ugly—or should he be punished? Please explain.

FURTHER READING

Michelangelo Delfino and Mary E. Day, *Be Careful Who You SLAPP* (MoBeta Publishing, 2003).

Terry Eastland (Editor), *Freedom of Expression in the Supreme Court* (Rowman & Littlefield Publishing, 2000).

Daniel A. Farber, *The First Amendment* (Foundation Press, 2002).

Anthony Lewis, *Make No Law: The Sullivan Case and the First Amendment* (Vintage Books, 1992).

Geoffrey R. Stone (Editor), Pamela S. Karlan, and Louis M. Seidman, *The First Amendment* (Aspen Publishers, 2003).

Today's Workplace

Futurists, business consultants, and management experts advise that to survive and thrive in today's workplace, you need an exceptional combination of skills, knowledge, confidence, and flexibility. Predictions like these abound:

In her book *Dictionary of the Future,* futurist Faith Popcorn defines some 50 possible job titles of the future. Most of the jobs she identifies involve services, about a quarter of which are related to health care. "More than half of us will be working at jobs that don't exist yet," Popcorn argues, "and many that exist now will vanish." She cites business analyst Tom Peter's forecast that 90% of white-collar jobs will be either "destroyed or altered beyond recognition in 10 to 15 years."

These days, blue collar still means manufacturing, but technology and globalization have transformed it dramatically. Gone are traditional assembly jobs that required little skill and less education. . . . Today's blue-collar workers are more involved in customizing manufacturing, coming up with solutions to a particular customer's needs rather than churning out standardized parts and commodities. (Clare Ansberry, *Wall Street Journal* reporter)

Emerging careers and job opportunities over the next 10–25 years include: artificial intelligence technician, aquaculturist, bionic medical technician, cryonics technician, information broker, leisure consultant, myotherapist, retirement counselor, and underwater archaeologist. (S. Norman Feingold and Norma R. Miller, career experts and World Future Society members)

The fastest-growing labor classification in the IT industry is the so-called contingent workforce: the army of free-lancers, consultants, contractors, free agents, and part-timers who fill the trenches, at least occasionally and very often regularly, in virtually every high-tech enterprise. (John Kador, *InfoWorld* reporter)

People should learn to live with the fact that job security is a thing of the past. As more companies adopt the tenets of reengineering, a growing number of people will need to reshape their careers to ensure they remain competitive in a flexible and increasingly knowledge-dependent job market. (Barbara Moses, author)

People entering the workforce today will have something like seven careers throughout their life instead of the one or two careers that most people in the Bob Hope generation could expect. (Harry Dent, Jr., economic forecaster and business consultant)

The nation's workforce is hitting middle age, and along with the wrinkles comes a crisis: the threat of a long-term labor shortage. . . . The first boomers will hit 65 in 2011, and if all of them retire between now and 2030, there won't be nearly enough new workers to take their places. (Michele Himmelberg, journalist)

The traditional march through education, work and retirement will become a more integrated process in which all three overlap. It will become normal for 50-year-olds to go back to school and for 70-year-olds to start new careers. (Ken Dychtwald, gerontologist and authority on aging)

Workers will look for different rewards from their careers, shifting their focus from achievement to personal satisfaction. (Thomas Grass, consultant with Watson Wyatt Worldwide, benefits consulting firm)

The selections in this theme provide a more in-depth look at some of the predictions. The theme opens with the U.S. Department of Labor's Bureau of Labor Statistics' snapshot of "Tomorrow's Jobs." Next, Brad McMillan's editorial cartoon gives us a clear picture of how he thinks underprepared workers are affecting business and industry.

The text chapter by professors Griffin and Ebert provides a comprehensive look at "Managing Human Resources and Labor Relations." Among the issues they examine are how managers plan for personnel needs, hire new employees, and enhance the quality and performance of workers.

Kim Clark's "Judgment Day," from *U.S. News and World Report,* looks at the changes in and impact of new trends in performance appraisals. In "Stop Stereotyping: Overcoming Your Worst Diversity Enemy," Sondra Thiederman at Monster.com urges us to let go of our stereotypes and strive to understand and value our coworkers.

Then, in an article adapted from his best-selling book of the same title, Po Bronson suggests that if we truly want to thrive in the workplace, it's time to stop asking, Where's the opportunity? and ask, "What Should I Do With My Life?"

"Money and Motivation," an excerpt from Thomas Petzinger's best-selling book *The New Pioneers: The Men and Women Who Are Transforming the Workplace and the Marketplace,* closes the theme with proof that money is not the only thing that motivates.

Tomorrow's Jobs

U.S. DEPARTMENT OF LABOR, BUREAU OF LABOR STATISTICS

Reprinted from the Occupational Outlook Handbook, 2002–03, February 2002 Bulletin 2540–1.

IDEAS TO THINK ABOUT

Are you preparing for a career in an occupation that is expanding or shrinking? If you haven't selected a career, what are some of the factors you should consider as you make your decision? *As you read,* connect the projections of the labor force and occupational and industry employment to your career plans.

TOMORROW'S JOBS

U.S. Department of Labor, Bureau of Labor Statistics

[1]Making informed career decisions requires reliable information about opportunities in the future. Opportunities result from the relationships between the population, labor force, and the demand for goods and services.

[2]Population ultimately limits the size of the labor force—individuals working or looking for work—which constrains how much can be produced. Demand for various goods and services determines employment in the industries providing them. Occupational employment opportunities, in turn, result from skills needed within specific industries. Opportunities for computer engineers and other computer-related occupations, for example, have surged in response to rapid growth in demand for computer services.

[3]Examining the past and projecting changes in these relationships is the foundation of the Occupational Outlook Program. This article presents highlights of Bureau of Labor Statistics projections of the labor force and occupational and industry employment that can help guide your career plans.

POPULATION

[4]Population trends affect employment opportunities in a number of ways. Changes in population influence the demand for goods and services. For example, a growing and aging population has increased the demand for health services. Equally important, population changes produce corresponding changes in the size and demographic composition of the labor force.

[5]The U.S. population is expected to increase by 24 million over the 2000–10 period, at a slightly faster rate of growth than during the 1990–2000 period but slower than over the 1980–90 period (chart 1).

[6]Continued growth will mean more consumers of goods and services, spurring demand for workers in a wide range of occupations and industries. The effects of population growth on various occupations will differ. The differences are partially accounted for by the age distribution of the future population. The youth population, aged 16 to 24, will grow more rapidly than the overall population, a turn-around that began in the mid-1990s. As the baby boomers continue to age, the group aged 55 to 64 will increase by 11 million persons over the 2000–10 period—more than any

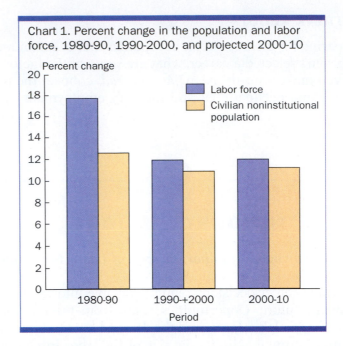

Chart 1. Percent change in the population and labor force, 1980-90, 1990-2000, and projected 2000-10

other group. Those aged 35 to 44 will be the only group to decrease in size, reflecting the birth dearth following the baby boom.

[7]Minorities and immigrants will constitute a larger share of the U.S. population in 2010 than they do today. Minority groups that have grown the fastest in the recent past—Hispanics and Asians and others—are projected to continue to grow much faster than white, non-Hispanics.

LABOR FORCE

[8]Population is the single most important factor in determining the size and composition of the labor force—comprising people who are either working or looking for work. The civilian labor force is projected to increase by 17 million, or 12 percent, to 158 million over the 2000–10 period.

[9]The U.S. workforce will become more diverse by 2010. White, non-Hispanic persons will continue to make up a decreasing share of the labor force, falling from 73.1 percent in 2000 to 69.2 percent in 2010 (chart 2).

[10]However, despite relatively slow growth, white, non-Hispanics will have the largest numerical growth in the labor force between 2000 and 2010, reflecting the large size of this group. Hispanics, non-Hispanic blacks, and Asian and other ethnic groups are projected to account for an increasing share of the labor force by 2010, growing from 10.9 to 13.3 percent, 11.8 to 12.7 percent, and 4.7 to 6.1 percent, respectively. By 2010, for the first time Hispanics will constitute a greater share of the labor force than will blacks. Asians and others continue to have the fastest growth rates, but still are expected to remain the smallest of the four labor force groups.

[11]The numbers of men and women in the labor force will grow, but the number of men will grow at a slower rate than the number of women. The male labor force is projected to grow by 9.3 percent from 2000 to 2010, compared with 15.1 percent for women. As a result, men's share of the labor force is expected to decrease from 53.4 to 52.1 percent, while women's share is expected to increase from 46.6 to 47.9 percent.

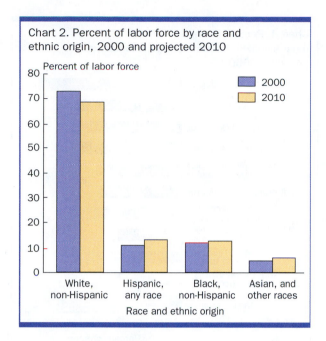

Chart 2. Percent of labor force by race and ethnic origin, 2000 and projected 2010

[12]The youth labor force, aged 16 to 24, is expected to increase its share of the labor force to 16.5 percent by 2010, growing more rapidly than the overall labor force. The large group 25 to 54 years old, who made up 71 percent of the labor force in 2000, is projected to decline to 66.6 percent of the labor force by 2010. Workers 55 and older, on the other hand, are projected to increase from 12.9 percent to 16.9 percent of the labor force between 2000 and 2010, due to the aging of the baby-boom generation (chart 3)

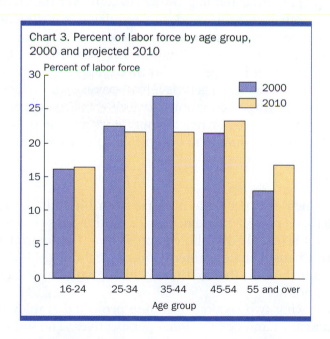

Chart 3. Percent of labor force by age group, 2000 and projected 2010

EDUCATION AND TRAINING

[13]Projected job growth varies widely by education and training requirements. All seven of the education and training categories projected to have faster than average employment growth require a postsecondary vocational or academic award (chart 4).

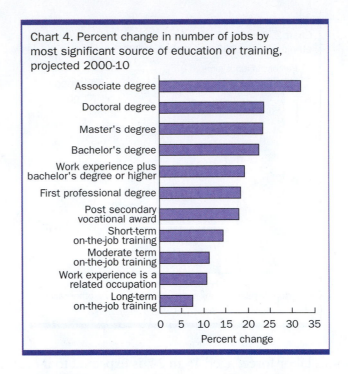

Chart 4. Percent change in number of jobs by most significant source of education or training, projected 2000-10

[14]These seven categories will account for two-fifths of all employment growth over the 2000–10 period.

[16]Employment in occupations requiring at least a bachelor's degree is expected to grow 21.6 percent and account for five out of the six fastest growing education or training categories. Two categories—jobs requiring an associate degree, projected to grow 32 percent over the 2000–10 period, faster than any other category, and jobs requiring a postsecondary vocational award—together will grow 24.1 percent. The four categories of occupations requiring work-related training are projected to increase 12.4 percent, compared with 15.2 percent for all occupations combined.

[16]Education is essential in getting a high-paying job. In fact, all but two of the 50 highest paying occupations require a college degree. Air traffic controllers and nuclear power reactor operators are the only occupations of the 50 highest paying that do not require a college degree.

EMPLOYMENT

[17]Total employment is expected to increase from 146 million in 2000 to 168 million in 2010, or by 15.2 percent. The 22 million jobs that will be added by 2010 will not be evenly distributed across major industrial and occupational groups. Changes in consumer demand, technology, and many other factors will contribute to the continually changing employment structure in the U.S. economy.

[18]The following two sections examine projected employment change from both industrial and occupational perspectives. The industrial profile is discussed in terms of primary wage and salary employment. Primary employment excludes secondary jobs for those who hold multiple jobs. The exception is employment in agriculture, which includes self-employed and unpaid family workers in addition to wage and salary workers. The occupational profile is viewed in terms of total employment—including

primary and secondary jobs for wage and salary, self-employed, and unpaid family workers. Of the nearly 146 million jobs in the U.S. economy in 2000, wage and salary workers accounted for 134 million; self-employed workers accounted for 11.5 million; and unpaid family workers accounted for about 169,000. Secondary employment accounted for 1.8 million of all jobs. Self-employed workers held 9 out of 10 secondary jobs; wage and salary workers held most of the remainder.

INDUSTRY

[19]The long-term shift from goods-producing to service-producing employment is expected to continue (chart 5).

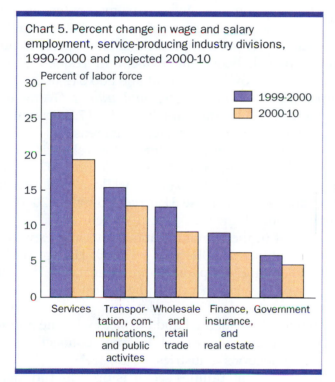

Chart 5. Percent change in wage and salary employment, service-producing industry divisions, 1990-2000 and projected 2000-10

[20]**Service-producing industries**—including finance, insurance, and real estate; government; services; transportation, communications, and utilities; and wholesale and retail trade—are expected to account for approximately 20.2 million of the 22.0 million new wage and salary jobs generated over the 2000–10 period. The services and four retail trade industry divisions will account for nearly three-fourths of total wage and salary job growth, a continuation of the employment growth pattern of the 1990–2000 period.

[21]*Services.* This is the largest and fastest growing major industry group and is expected to add 13.7 million new jobs by 2010, accounting for three out of every five new jobs created in the U.S. economy. Over two-thirds of this projected job growth is concentrated in three sectors of services industries—business, health, and social services.

[22]Business services—including personnel supply services and computer and data processing services, among other detailed industries—will add 5.1 million jobs. The personnel supply services industry, consisting

of employment agencies and temporary staffing services, is projected to be the largest source of numerical employment growth in the economy, adding 1.9 million new jobs. However, employment in computer and data processing services—which provides prepackaged and specialized software, data and computer systems design and management, and computer-related consulting services—is projected to grow by 86 percent between 2000 and 2010, ranking as the fastest growing industry in the economy.

[23]Health services—including home healthcare services, hospitals, and offices of health practitioners—will add 2.8 million new jobs as demand for healthcare increases because of an aging population and longer life expectancies.

[24]Social services—including child daycare and residential care services—will add 1.2 million jobs. As more women enter the labor force, demand for childcare services is expected to grow, leading to the creation of 300,000 jobs. An elderly population seeking alternatives to nursing homes and hospital care will boost employment in residential care services, which is projected to grow 63.5 percent and add 512,000 jobs by 2010.

[25]*Transportation, communications, and utilities.* Overall employment is expected to increase by 1.3 million jobs, or by 17.9 percent. Employment in the transportation sector is expected to increase by 20.7 percent, from 4.5 million to 5.5 million jobs. Trucking and warehousing will provide the most new jobs in the transportation sector, adding 407,000 jobs by 2010. Due to population growth and urban sprawl, local and interurban passenger transit is expected to increase 31 percent over the 2000–10 period, the fastest growth among all the transportation sectors.

[26]Employment in the communications sector is expected to increase by 16.9 percent, adding 277,000 jobs by 2010. Half of these new jobs—139,000—will be in the telephone communications industry; however, cable and other pay television will be the fastest growing segment of the sector over the next decade, with employment expanding by 50.6 percent. Increased demand for residential and business wireline and wireless services, cable service, and high-speed Internet connections will fuel the growth in communications industries.

[27]Employment in the utilities sector is projected to increase by only 4.9 percent through 2010. Despite increased output, employment in electric services, gas production and distribution, and combination utility services is expected to decline through 2010 due to improved technology that increases worker productivity. The growth in the utilities sector will be driven by water supply and sanitary services, in which employment is expected to increase 45.1 percent by 2010. Jobs are not easily eliminated by technological gains in this industry because water treatment and waste disposal are very labor-intensive activities.

[28]*Wholesale and retail trade.* Employment is expected to increase by 11.1 percent and 13.3 percent, respectively, growing from 7 million to 7.8 million in wholesale trade and from 23.3 million to 26.4 million in retail trade. Increases in population, personal income, and leisure time will contribute to employment growth in these industries as consumers demand more goods. With the addition of 1.5 million jobs, the eating and drinking places segment of the retail trade industry is projected to have the largest numerical increase in employment within the trade industry group.

[29]*Finance, insurance, and real estate.* Overall employment is expected to increase by 687,000 jobs, or 9.1 percent, by 2010. The finance sector of the industry—including depository and nondepository institutions and securities and commodity brokers—will account for one-third of these jobs. Security and commodity brokers and dealers are expected to grow the fastest among the finance segments; the projected 20.3-percent employment increase by 2010 reflects the increased number of baby boomers in their peak savings years, the growth of tax-favorable retirement plans, and the globalization of the securities markets. However, employment in depository institutions should continue to decline due to an increase in the use of Internet banking, ATM machines, and debit cards.

[30]The insurance sector—including insurance carriers and insurance agents and brokers—is expected to add 152,000 new jobs by 2010. The majority of job growth in the insurance carriers segment will be attributable to medical service and health insurance, in which employment is projected to increase by 16 percent. The number of jobs with insurance agents and brokers is expected to grow about 14.3 percent by 2010, as many insurance carriers downsize their sales staffs and as agents set up their own businesses.

[31]The real estate sector is expected to add the most jobs out of the three sectors, 272,000 by 2010. As the population grows, demand for housing also will grow.

[32]*Government.* Between 2000 and 2010, government employment, excluding public education and hospitals, is expected to increase by 6.9 percent, from 10.2 million to 10.9 million jobs. Growth in government employment will be fueled by growth at the state and local levels, in which the number of jobs will increase by 12.2 and 11.2 percent, respectively, through 2010. Growth at these levels is due mainly to an increased demand for services and the shift of responsibilities from the federal government to the state and local governments. Federal government employment is expected to decline by 7.6 percent as the federal government continues to contract out many government jobs to private companies.

[33]Employment in the **goods-producing industries** has been relatively stagnant since the early 1980s. Overall, this sector is expected to grow 6.3 percent over the 2000–10 period. Although employment is expected to increase more slowly than in the service-producing industries, projected growth within the goods-producing sector varies considerably (chart 6).

[34]*Construction.* Employment in construction is expected to increase by 12.3 percent, from 6.7 million to 7.5 million. Demand for new housing and an increase in road, bridge, and tunnel construction will account for the bulk of job growth in this industry.

[35]*Agriculture, forestry, and fishing.* Overall employment in agriculture, forestry, and fishing is expected to increase by 19.3 percent, from 2.2 million to 2.6 million. Three-fourths of this growth will come from veterinary services and landscape and horticultural services, which will add 96,000 and 229,000 jobs, respectively. Employment in crops, livestock, and livestock products is expected to continue to decline due to advancements in technology. The numbers of jobs in forestry and in fishing, hunting, and trapping are expected to grow only 1.9 percent by 2010.

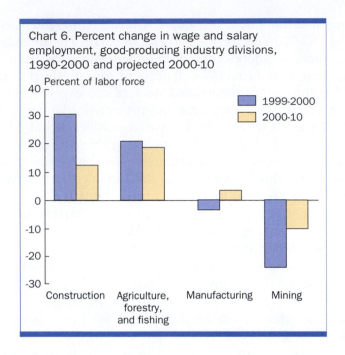

Chart 6. Percent change in wage and salary employment, good-producing industry divisions, 1990-2000 and projected 2000-10

³⁶*Manufacturing.* Rebounding from the 1990–2000 decline of 607,000 manufacturing jobs, employment in this sector is expected to grow modestly, by 3.1 percent, by 2010, adding 577,000 jobs. The projected employment growth is attributable mainly to the industries that manufacture durable goods. Durable goods manufacturing is expected to grow 5.7 percent, to 11.8 million jobs, over the next decade. Despite gains in productivity, the growing demand for computers, electronic components, motor vehicles, and communications equipment will contribute to this employment growth.

³⁷Nondurable manufacturing, on the other hand, is expected to decline by less than 1 percent, shedding 64,000 jobs overall. The majority of employment declines are expected to be in apparel and other textile products and leather and leather products industries, which together are expected to shed 131,000 jobs by 2010 because of increased job automation and international competition. On the other hand, drug manufacturing is expected to grow 23.8 percent due to an aging population and increasing life expectancies.

³⁸*Mining.* Employment in mining is expected to decrease 10.1 percent, or by some 55,000 jobs, by 2010. The majority of the decline will come from coal mining, in which employment is expected to decrease by 30 percent. The numbers of jobs in metal mining and nonmetallic mineral mining also are expected to decline by 13.8 and 3.2 percent, respectively. Employment decreases in these industries are attributable mainly to technology gains that boost worker productivity, growing international competition, restricted access to federal lands, and strict environmental regulations that require cleaning of burning fuels.

³⁹Oil and gas field services is the only mining industry in which employment is projected to grow, by 3.7 percent, through 2010. Employment growth is due chiefly to the downsizing of the crude petroleum, natural gas, and gas liquids industry, which contracts out production and extraction jobs to companies in oil and gas field services.

OCCUPATION

[40]Expansion of the service-producing sector is expected to continue, creating demand for many occupations. However, projected job growth varies among major occupational groups (chart 7).

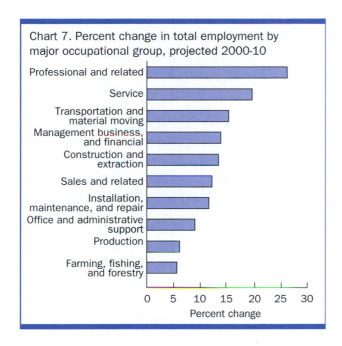

Chart 7. Percent change in total employment by major occupational group, projected 2000-10

[41]*Professional and related occupations.* Professional and related occupations will grow the fastest and add more new jobs than any other major occupational group. Over the 2000–10 period, a 26-percent increase in the number of professional and related jobs is projected, a gain of 6.9 million. Professional and related workers perform a wide variety of duties and are employed throughout private industry and government. Nearly three-quarters of the job growth will come from three groups of professional occupations—computer and mathematical occupations, healthcare practitioners and technical occupations, and education, training, and library occupations—which will add 5.2 million jobs combined.

[42]*Service occupations.* Service workers perform services for the public. Employment in service occupations is projected to increase by 5.1 million, or 19.5 percent, the second largest numerical gain and second highest rate of growth among the major occupational groups. Food preparation and serving-related occupations are expected to add the most jobs among the service occupations, 1.6 million by 2010. However, healthcare support occupations are expected to grow the fastest, 33.4 percent, adding 1.1 million new jobs.

[43]*Transportation and material moving occupations.* Transportation and material moving workers transport and transfer people and materials by land, sea, or air. These occupations should grow 15.2 percent and add 1.5 million jobs by 2010. Among transportation occupations, motor vehicle operators will add the most jobs, 745,000. Rail transportation occupations are the only group in which employment is projected to decline, by

18.6 percent, through 2010. Material moving occupations will grow 14 percent and will add 681,000 jobs.

[44]*Management, business, and financial occupations.* Workers in management, business, and financial occupations plan and direct the activities of business, government, and other organizations. Employment is expected to increase by 2.1 million, or 13.6 percent, by 2010. Among managers, the numbers of computer and information systems managers and of public relations managers will grow the fastest, by 47.9 and 36.3 percent, respectively.

[45]General and operations managers will add the most new jobs, 363,000 by 2010. Agricultural managers and purchasing managers are the only workers in this group whose numbers are expected to decline, losing 325,000 jobs combined. Among business and financial occupations, accountants and auditors and management analysts will add the most jobs, 326,000 combined. Management analysts also will be one of the fastest growing occupations in this group, along with personal financial advisors, with job increases of 28.9 and 34 percent, respectively.

[46]*Construction and extraction occupations.* Construction and extraction workers construct new residential and commercial buildings, and also work in mines, quarries, and oil and gas fields. Employment of these workers is expected to grow 13.3 percent, adding 989,000 new jobs. Construction trades and related workers will account for the majority of these new jobs, 862,000 by 2010. Most extraction jobs will decline, reflecting overall employment losses in the mining and oil and gas extraction industries.

[47]*Sales and related occupations.* Sales and related workers transfer goods and services among businesses and consumers. Sales and related occupations are expected to add 1.9 million new jobs by 2010, growing by 11.9 percent. The majority of these jobs will be among retail salespersons and cashiers, occupations that will add almost 1 million jobs combined.

[48]*Installation, maintenance, and repair occupations.* Workers in installation, maintenance, and repair occupations install new equipment and maintain and repair older equipment. These occupations will add 662,000 jobs by 2010, growing by 11.4 percent. Automotive service technicians and general maintenance and repair workers will account for three in 10 new installation, maintenance, and repair jobs. The fastest growth rate will be among telecommunications line installers and repairers, an occupation that is expected to grow 27.6 percent over the 2000–10 period.

[49]*Office and administrative support occupations.* Office and administrative support workers perform the day-to-day activities of the office, such as preparing and filing documents, dealing with the public, and distributing information. Employment in these occupations is expected to grow by 9.1 percent, adding 2.2 million new jobs by 2010. Customer service representatives will add the most new jobs, 631,000. Desktop publishers will be among the fastest growing occupations, growing 66.7 percent over the decade. Order clerks, tellers, and insurance claims and policy processing clerks will be among the jobs with the largest employment losses.

[50]*Production occupations.* Production workers are employed mainly in manufacturing, assembling goods and operating plants. Production occupations will grow 5.8 percent and add 750,000 jobs by 2010. Metal and

plastics workers and assemblers and fabricators will add the most production jobs, 249,000 and 171,000, respectively. Textile, apparel, and furnishings occupations will account for much of the job losses among production occupations.

[51]*Farming, fishing, and forestry occupations.* Farming, fishing, and forestry workers cultivate plants, breed and raise livestock, and catch animals. These occupations will have the slowest job growth among the major occupational groups, 5.3 percent, adding 74,000 new jobs by 2010. Farmworkers account for nearly three out of four new jobs in this group. The numbers of both fishing and logging workers are expected to decline, by 12.2 and 3.5 percent, respectively.

[52]Computer occupations are expected to grow the fastest over the projection period (chart 8). In fact, these jobs account for eight out of the 20 fastest growing occupations in the economy. In addition to high growth rates, these eight occupations combined will add more than 1.9 million new jobs to the economy. Health occupations comprise most of the remaining fastest growing occupations. High growth rates among computer and health occupations reflect projected faster-than-average growth in the computer and data processing and health services industries.

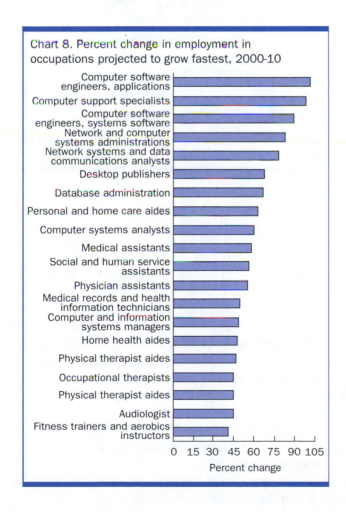

Chart 8. Percent change in employment in occupations projected to grow fastest, 2000-10

[53]The 20 occupations listed in chart 9 will account for over one-third of all new jobs, 8 million combined, over the 2000–10 period.

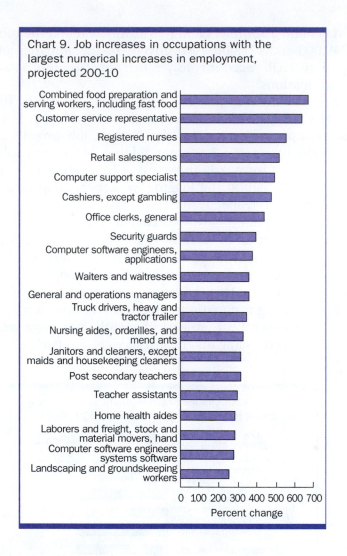

Chart 9. Job increases in occupations with the largest numerical increases in employment, projected 200-10

⁵⁴The occupations with the largest numerical increases cover a wider range of occupational categories than those occupations with the fastest growth rates. Computer and health occupations will account for some of these increases in employment, as well as occupations in education, sales, transportation, office and administrative support, and food service. Many of these occupations are very large, and will create more new jobs than those with high growth rates. Only four out of the 20 fastest growing occupations—computer software engineers, applications; computer software engineers, systems software; computer support specialists; and home health aides—also are projected to be among the 20 occupations with the largest numerical increases in employment.

⁵⁵Table 1 lists occupations projected to grow the fastest and to generate the largest numbers of new jobs over the 2000–10 period, by level of education or training required.

⁵⁶Declining occupational employment stems from declining industry employment, technological advancements, changes in business practices, and other factors. For example, increased productivity and farm consolidations are expected to result in a decline of 328,000 farmers over the 2000–10 period (chart 10).

TABLE 1.   Fastest growing occupations and occupations projected to have the largest numerical increases in employment between 2000 and 2010, by level of education or training

Fastest growing occupations	Occupations having the largest numerical increases in employment
First-professional degree	
Veterinarians	Lawyers
Pharmacists	Physicians and surgeons
Chiropractors	Pharmacists
Optometrists	Clergy
Lawyers	Veterinarians
Doctoral degree	
Computer and information scientists, research	Postsecondary teachers
Medical scientists	Biological scientists
Postsecondary teachers	Computer and information scientists, research
Biological scientists	Medical scientists
Astronomers and physicists	Astronomers and physicists
Master's degree	
Audiologists	Educational, vocational, and school counselors
Speech-language pathologists	Physical therapists
Mental health and substance abuse social workers	Speech-language pathologists
Substance abuse and behavioral disorder counselors	Psychologists
Physical therapists	Mental health and substance abuse social workers
Bachelor's or higher degree, plus work experience	
Computer and information systems managers	General and operations managers
Public relations managers	Computer and information systems managers
Advertising and promotion managers	Management analysts
Sales managers	Financial managers
Medical and health services managers	Sales managers
Bachelor's degree	
Computer software engineers, applications	Computer software engineers, applications
Computer software engineers, systems software	Computer software engineers, systems software
Network and computer systems administrators	Computer systems analysts
Network systems and data communications analysis	Elementary schoolteachers except special education
Database administrators	Network and computer systems administrators
Associate degree	
Computer support specialists	Registered nurses
Medical records and health information technicians	Computer support specialists
Physical therapist assistants	Medical records and health information technicians
Occupational therapist assistants	Paralegals and legal assistants
Veterinary technologists and technicians	Dental hygienists
Postsecondary vocational award	
Desktop publishers	Automotive service technicians and mechanics
Fitness trainers and aerobics instructors	Licensed practical and licensed vocational nurses
Surgical technologists	Welders, cutters, solderers, and brazers
Respiratory therapy technicians	Hair dressers, hairstylists, and cosmetologists
Gaming dealers	Fitness trainers and aerobics instructors
Work experience in a related occupation	
First-line supervisors/managers of correctional officers	First-line supervisors/managers of retail sales workers
Aircraft cargo handling supervisors	First-line supervisors/managers of construction trades and extraction workers
First-line supervisors/managers of protective service workers except police, fire and corrections	First-line supervisors/managers of office and administrative support workers
Private detectives and investigators	First-line supervisors/managers of food preparation and serving workers
Transportation, storage and distribution managers	First-line supervisors/managers of mechanics installers, and repairers

(continued)

TABLE 1. Fastest growing occupations and occupations projected to have the largest numerical increases in employment between 2000 and 2010, by level of education or training (*continued*)

Fastest growing occupations	Occupations having the largest numerical increases in employment
Long-term on-the-job training (more than 12 months)	
Telecommunications installers and repairers	Cooks restaurant
Actors	Police and sheriff's patrol officers
Recreational vehicle service technicians	Electricians
Interpreters and translators	Carpenters
Police and sheriff's patrol officers	Maintenance and repair workers general
Moderate-term on-the-job training (1 to 12 months)	
Medical assistants	Customer service representatives
Social and human service assistants	Truckdrivers, heavy and tractor-trailer
Dental assistants	Medical assistants
Pharmacy technicians	Executive secretaries and administrative assistants
Ambulance drivers and attendants, except emergency medical technicians	Social and human service assistants
Short-term on-the-job training (0 to 1 months)	
Personal and home care aides	Combined food preparation and serving workers, including fast food
Home health aides	Retail salespersons
Physical therapist aides	Cashiers, except gaming
Occupational therapist aides	Office clerks general
Veterinary assistants and laboratory animal caretakers	Security guards

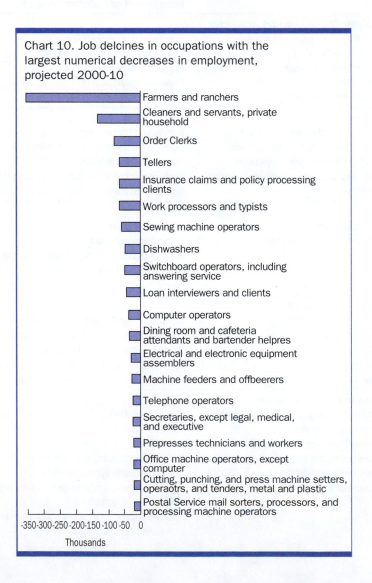

Chart 10. Job delcines in occupations with the largest numerical decreases in employment, projected 2000-10

Farmers and ranchers
Cleaners and servants, private household
Order Clerks
Tellers
Insurance claims and policy processing clients
Work processors and typists
Sewing machine operators
Dishwashers
Switchboard operators, including answering service
Loan interviewers and clients
Computer operators
Dining room and cafeteria attendants and bartender helpres
Electrical and electronic equipment assemblers
Machine feeders and offbeerers
Telephone operators
Secretaries, except legal, medical, and executive
Prepresses technicians and workers
Office machine operators, except computer
Cutting, punching, and press machine setters, operaotrs, and tenders, metal and plastic
Postal Service mail sorters, processors, and processing machine operators

-350 -300 -250 -200 -150 -100 -50 0

Thousands

[57]The majority of the 20 occupations with the largest numerical decreases are office and administrative support and production occupations, which are affected by increasing automation and the implementation of office technology that reduces the needs for these workers. For example, the increased use of ATM machines and Internet banking will reduce the number of tellers.

[58]*Total Job Openings.* Job openings stem from both employment growth and replacement needs (chart 11). Replacement needs arise as workers

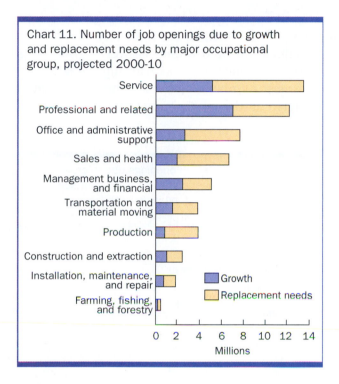

Chart 11. Number of job openings due to growth and replacement needs by major occupational group, projected 2000-10

leave occupations. Some transfer to other occupations while others retire, return to school, or quit to assume household responsibilities. Replacement needs are projected to account for 60 percent of the approximately 58 million job openings between 2000 and 2010. Thus, even occupations with little or no change in employment still may offer many job openings.

[59]Professional and related occupations are projected to grow faster and add more jobs than any other major occupational group, with 7 million new jobs by 2010. Three-fourths of this job growth is expected among computer and mathematical occupations; healthcare practitioners and technical occupations; and education, training, and library occupations. With 5.2 million job openings due to replacement needs, professional and related occupations are the only major group projected to generate more openings from job growth than from replacement needs.

[60]Due to high replacement needs, service occupations are projected to have the largest number of total job openings, 13.5 million. A large number of replacements are expected to arise as young workers leave food preparation and service occupations. Replacement needs generally are greatest in the largest occupations and in those with relatively low pay or limited training requirements.

[61]Office automation will significantly affect many individual office and administrative support occupations. Overall, these occupations are

projected to grow more slowly than the average, while some are projected to decline. Office and administrative support occupations are projected to create 7.7 million job openings over the 2000–10 period, ranking third behind service and professional and related occupations.

[62]Agriculture, forestry, and fishing occupations are projected to have the fewest job openings, approximately 500,000. Because job growth is expected to be slow, and levels of retirement and job turnover high, more than 80 percent of these projected job openings are due to replacement needs.

[63]Employment in occupations requiring an associate degree is projected to increase 32 percent, faster than any other occupational group categorized by education or training. However, this category ranks only eighth among the 11 education and training categories in terms of job openings. The largest number of job openings will be among occupations requiring short-term on-the-job training (chart 12).

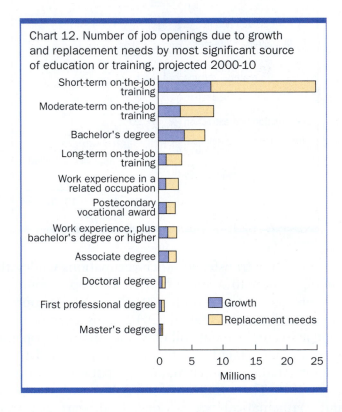

Chart 12. Number of job openings due to growth and replacement needs by most significant source of education or training, projected 2000-10

[64]Almost two-thirds of the projected job openings over the 2000–2010 period will be in occupations that require on-the-job training, and arise mostly from replacement needs. These jobs will account for 37.3 million of the projected 57.9 million total job openings through 2010. However, many of these jobs typically offer low pay and benefits; this is more true of jobs requiring only short-term on-the-job training, which will account for 24.8 million openings, than of the occupations in any other education or training category.

[65]Jobs requiring a bachelor's degree, and which usually offer higher pay and benefits, will account for about 7.3 million job openings through 2010. Most of these openings will result from job growth.

Tomorrow's Jobs Questions

VOCABULARY

1. Define *labor force*.

2. "The projected employment growth is attributable mainly to the industries that manufacture *durable goods*." (¶36) "*Nondurable [goods]* manufacturing, on the other hand, is expected to decline by less than 1 percent." (¶37) Define *durable goods* and *nondurable goods* and give an example of each.

COMPREHENSION AND ANALYSIS

For questions 3 to 5, indicate whether the statement is true or false. If the statement is false, rewrite it to make it true.

3. The U.S. workforce will become less diverse by 2010.

4. Education is essential in getting a high-paying job.

5. The long-term shift from goods-producing to service-producing employment is expected to continue.

6. Describe two ways population trends affect employment opportunities.

7. Describe the projected population changes over the 2000–10 period for each of these age groups: a. 16-24, b. 35-44, c. 55-64.

8. Over two-thirds of the projected job growth between 2000–10 is concentrated in three sectors of services industries. List the three sectors and give one example of the service jobs in each of the sectors.

9. Which occupation is projected to have the largest numerical decrease in employment between 2000–10? What are two factors that will contribute to the decrease?

REFLECT AND CONNECT

10. Are you preparing for a career in an occupation that is expanding or shrinking? What are some of the factors that are expected to impact your career field in the next five years? If you haven't selected a career, what are some of the factors you should consider as you make your decision?

McMillan Editorial Cartoon

BRAD MCMILLAN

Mr. McMillan began his art career in the early 1970s in Memphis, Tennessee, drawing cartoons and illustrations for alternative and underground publications. In 1981, he opened a gallery in downtown Memphis, devoted to his work and the work of other area cartoonists and illustrators, and in 1983 he became staff illustrator and editorial cartoonist for the Memphis Business Journal. *Now based in Dallas, Texas, McMillan has exhibited his paintings and drawings, freelanced, and done editorial cartoons and cartoon illustrations for many publications, including the* Dallas Morning News, *the* Dallas Business Journal, *and* Texas Catholic. *He has won numerous awards, including first place for editorial cartoon from the Society of Professional Journalists.*

AN IDEA TO THINK ABOUT

What are some of the ways your workplace would be impacted if you were working with a person who had difficulty reading and writing? *As you read,* find out how McMillan thinks illiterate workers are affecting the workplace.

© 1989 Brad McMillan/www.CartoonStock.com

McMillan Editorial Cartoon Questions

1. What is the topic/issue?

2. What is McMillan's point of view?

3. What does McMillan want the reader to do or think about after reading this cartoon?

Managing Human Resources and Labor Relations

RICKY W. GRIFFIN AND RONALD J. EBERT

Dr. Griffin is professor of business and director of the Center for Human Resource Management at Texas A&M University. He is the author or co-author of five books and more than 40 journal articles and book chapters. Dr. Griffin's research interests include leadership, workplace violence, and international management, and he has done consulting in the areas of task design, employee motivation, and quality circles.

Dr. Ebert is professor of management at the University of Missouri-Columbia. A member of and active participant in numerous professional organizations, Dr. Ebert has served as the editor of the Journal of Operations Management *and as chair of the Production and Operations Management Division of the Academy of Management. He is the co-author of three books:* Organizational Decision Processes, Production and Operations Management *(published in English, Spanish, and Chinese), and* Management.

This selection is Chapter 8 from their best-selling text Business, *seventh edition.*

VOCABULARY

Key terms are in boldface type in the text. Terms are defined in context and in marginal annotations.

AN IDEA TO THINK ABOUT

List the tasks you think a human resources manager has to consider and complete before a company can advertise a job opening. *As you read,* try to picture yourself on both sides of the HR desk—as a manager looking for good workers and as a worker looking for a good company.

CHAPTER

Managing Human Resources and Labor Relations

After reading this chapter, you should be able to:

1. Define *human resource management* and explain how managers plan for human resources.

2. Identify the tasks in *staffing* a company and discuss ways in which organizations *select, develop,* and *appraise* employee performance.

3. Describe the main components of a *compensation system*.

4. Describe some of the key legal issues involved in hiring, compensating, and managing workers in today's workplace.

5. Discuss *workforce diversity,* the management of *knowledge workers,* and the use of a *contingent workforce* as important changes in the contemporary workplace.

6. Explain why workers organize and what *labor unions* do for their members.

7. Explain the *collective bargaining* process and its possible outcomes.

From Hard Bargains to Hard Times

During the economic boom times of just a few years ago, workers had the advantage in the employment equation. A general labor shortage combined with an acute shortage of knowledge and other skilled workers to make the labor market a seller's market. Top college graduates had multiple offers, and skilled technical workers could take their pick of jobs. Moreover, businesses began rolling out new benefits, perquisites, and incentives to attract and retain the best and the brightest.

SAS Institute <www.sas.com>, a North Carolina software firm, offered employees unlimited sick days, on-site childcare, flexible work schedules, and free beverages. In Houston, BMC Software <www.bmc.com> greeted employees each morning with a pianist in the lobby and provided fresh vegetables for lunch from the firm's own garden. Other employers offered concierges, laundry pickup and delivery, and even on-site pet care. Some companies offered cash or new cars as signing bonuses.

But as the economy slowed in 2001 and into 2002, the advantage shifted to employers. Throughout the 1990s, as it turns out, companies had relied on technological advances ranging from robotics to the Internet to reduce costs in areas as diverse as advertising, production, and purchasing. When the economy turned sour, they realized that they had cut as many costs as possible from most areas of their operations, and not surprisingly, many turned to their labor forces for the next round of cuts.

Many firms have reduced or stopped hiring, and the hardest hit have even started layoffs. (Many of the dot-coms, among the most aggressive employers in terms of new and innovative benefits, have disappeared altogether.) This trend stems in part from the realization that workers have fewer options, either in finding or leaving jobs. One of the first areas hit was perquisites, or "perks." Among the lost amenities: the employee bowling alley at an Austin-based high-tech firm and Xerox's "Plant Caretaker" (employees must now water their own plants). But don't be fooled into thinking that these are trivial issues. "There is a huge dent in morale when you take anything away from employees, no matter how miniscule it may look," says workplace consultant Sharon Jordan-Evans.

Next in line have been more traditional benefits. Many firms have either reduced contributions to benefits programs or eliminated them altogether. Ford Motors and Lucent Technologies are just two of the many organizations that now pay less for health insurance or retirement plans. Bonuses, sick leave, and vacation time are also being squeezed. As a last resort, some firms are even asking workers to accept pay cuts. Pay at Agilent Technology has dropped 10 percent, and Disney has cut some pay rates by 30 percent.

Our opening story is continued on page 241.

"There is a huge dent in morale when you take anything away from employees, no matter how miniscule it may look."

~Sharon Jordan-Evans
Workplace Consultant

The Foundations of Human Resource Management

human resource management (HRM)

Set of organizational activities directed at attracting, developing, and maintaining an effective workforce

Human resource management (HRM) is the set of organizational activities directed at attracting, developing, and maintaining an effective workforce. Human resource management takes place within a complex and ever-changing environmental context and is increasingly being recognized for its strategic importance.[1]

The Strategic Importance of HRM

Human resources are critical for effective organizational functioning. HRM (or *personnel*, as it is sometimes called) was once relegated to second-class status in many organizations, but its importance has grown dramatically in the last several years. This new importance stems from increased legal complexities, the recognition that human resources are a valuable means for improving productivity, and the awareness today of the costs associated with poor human resource management.

Indeed, managers now realize that the effectiveness of their HR function has a substantial impact on a firm's bottom-line performance. Poor human resource planning can result in spurts of hiring followed by layoffs—costly in terms of unemployment compensation payments, training expenses, and morale. Haphazard compensation systems do not attract, keep, and motivate good employees, and outmoded recruitment practices can expose the firm to expensive and embarrassing legal action. Consequently, the chief human resource executive of most large businesses is a vice president directly accountable to the CEO, and many firms are developing strategic HR plans that are integrated with other strategic planning activities.

Human Resource Planning

As you can see in Figure 8.1, the starting point in attracting qualified human resources is planning. In turn, HR planning involves job analysis and forecasting the demand for and supply of labor.

job analysis

Systematic analysis of jobs within an organization

Job Analysis   **Job analysis** is a systematic analysis of jobs within an organization.[2] A job analysis results in two things:

job description

Outline of the duties of a job, working conditions, and the tools, materials, and equipment used to perform it

■   The **job description** lists the duties and responsibilities of a job; its working conditions; and the tools, materials, equipment, and information used to perform it.

job specification

Description of the skills, abilities, and other credentials required by a job

■   The **job specification** lists the skills, abilities, and other credentials and qualifications needed to perform the job effectively.

Job analysis information is used in many HR activities. For instance, knowing about job content and job requirements is necessary to develop appropriate selection methods and job-relevant performance appraisal systems and to set equitable compensation rates.

Forecasting HR Demand and Supply   After managers fully understand the jobs to be performed within an organization, they can start planning for the organization's future HR needs. The manager starts by assessing trends in past HR usage, future organizational plans, and general economic trends. A good sales forecast is often the foundation, especially for smaller organizations. Historical ratios can then be used to predict demand for types of employees, such as operating employees and sales representatives. Large organizations use much more complicated models to predict HR needs.

Forecasting the supply of labor is really two tasks:

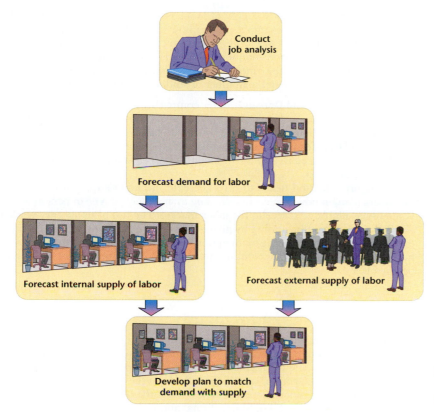

■ **FIGURE 8.1**

The Human Resource Planning Process

■ Forecasting *internal supply*—the number and type of employees who will be in the firm at some future date.

■ Forecasting *external supply*—the number and type of people who will be available for hiring from the labor market at large.

The simplest approach merely adjusts present staffing levels for anticipated turnover and promotions. Again, however, large organizations use extremely sophisticated models to make these forecasts.

Replacement Charts   At higher levels of the organization, managers plan for specific people and positions. The technique most commonly used is the **replacement chart,** which lists each important managerial position, who occupies it, how long that person will probably stay in it before moving on, and who (by name) is now qualified or soon will be qualified to move into it. This technique allows ample time to plan developmental experiences for people identified as potential successors to critical managerial jobs.[3] Charles Knight, the former CEO of Emerson Electric Co. <www.emersonelectric.com>, maintained an entire room for posting the credentials of his top 700 executives.

Skills Inventories   To facilitate both planning and identifying people for transfer or promotion, some organizations also have **employee information systems,** or **skills inventories.** These systems are usually computerized and contain information on each employee's education, skills, work experience, and career aspirations. Such a system can quickly locate every employee who is qualified to fill a position requiring, for example, a degree in chemical engineering, three years of experience in an oil refinery, and fluency in Spanish.

replacement chart

List of each management position, who occupies it, how long that person will likely stay in the job, and who is qualified as a replacement

employee information system (skills inventory)

Computerized system containing information on each employee's education, skills, work experience, and career aspirations

Forecasting the external supply of labor is a different problem altogether. How does a manager, for example, predict how many electrical engineers will be seeking work in California or Florida three years from now? To get an idea of the future availability of labor, planners must rely on information from outside sources, such as state employment commissions, government reports, and figures supplied by colleges on the number of students in major fields.

Matching HR Supply and Demand   After comparing future demand and internal supply, managers can make plans to manage predicted shortfalls or overstaffing. If a shortfall is predicted, new employees can be hired, present employees can be retrained and transferred into understaffed areas, individuals approaching retirement can be convinced to stay on, or labor-saving or productivity-enhancing systems can be installed.

If the organization needs to hire, the external labor-supply forecast helps managers plan on how to recruit according to whether the type of person needed is readily available or scarce in the labor market. The use of temporary workers also helps managers in staffing by giving them extra flexibility. If overstaffing is expected to be a problem, the main options are transferring the extra employees, not replacing individuals who quit, encouraging early retirement, and laying people off.[4]

Staffing the Organization

When managers have determined that new employees are needed, they must then turn their attention to recruiting and hiring the right mix of people. Staffing the organization is one of the most complex and important tasks of good HR management. In this section, we will describe both the process of acquiring staff from outside the company (*external staffing*) and the process of promoting staff from within (*internal staffing*). Both external and internal staffing, however, start with effective *recruiting*.

Recruiting Human Resources   Once an organization has an idea of its future HR needs, the next phase is usually recruiting new employees. **Recruiting** is the process of attracting qualified persons to apply for the jobs that are open. Where do recruits come from? Some recruits are found internally, while others come from outside of the organization.

Internal Recruiting   Internal recruiting means considering present employees as candidates for openings. Promotion from within can help build morale and keep high-quality employees from leaving. In unionized firms, the procedures for notifying employees of internal job-change opportunities are usually spelled out in the union contract. For higher-level positions, a skills inventory system may be used to identify internal candidates, or managers may be asked to recommend individuals who should be considered.

External Recruiting   External recruiting involves attracting people outside of the organization to apply for jobs. External recruiting methods include advertising, campus interviews, employment agencies or executive search firms, union hiring halls, referrals by present employees, and hiring "walk-ins" or "gate-hires" (people who show up without being solicited). A manager must select the most appropriate method for each job. The manager might, for instance, use the state employment service to find a maintenance worker but not a nuclear physicist. Private employment agencies can be a good source of clerical and technical employees, and executive search firms specialize in locating top-management talent. Newspaper ads are often used because they reach a wide audience and thus allow minorities equal opportunity to find out about and apply for job openings.

---

recruiting

Process of attracting qualified persons to apply for jobs an organization is seeking to fill

internal recruiting

Considering present employees as candidates for openings

external recruiting

Attracting persons outside of the organization to apply for jobs

As we noted at the beginning of this chapter, during the late 1990s, recruiters faced a difficult job as unemployment plummeted. By early 1998, for example, unemployment had dropped to a 23-year low of 4.6 percent. As a result, recruiters at firms such as Sprint, PeopleSoft, and Cognex had to stress how much "fun" it was to work for them, reinforcing this message with ice cream socials, karaoke contests, softball leagues, and free-movie nights. By 2001, however, the situation had begun to change. Unemployment began to creep back up, many larger employers (such as AT&T and Hewlett-Packard) announced major job cutbacks, and recruiters were again able to attract highly qualified employees. While most companies have tried to maintain the innovative benefits programs that they had inaugurated in the 1990s, they were also able to avoid costly new programs and could afford to be more selective in the employees they chose to hire.[5]

Selecting Human Resources

Once the recruiting process has attracted a pool of applicants, the next step is to select someone to hire. The intent of the selection process is to gather from applicants information that will predict their job success and then to hire the candidates likely to be most successful. Of course, the organization can only gather information about factors that can be used to predict future performance. The process of determining the predictive value of information is called **validation**.[6]

Application Forms   The first step in selection is usually asking the candidate to fill out an application. An application form is an efficient method of gathering information about the applicant's previous work history, educational background, and other job-related demographic data. It should not contain questions about areas unrelated to the job such as gender, religion, or national origin. Application form data are generally used informally to decide whether a candidate merits further evaluation, and interviewers use application forms to familiarize themselves with candidates before interviewing them.

Tests   Tests of ability, skill, aptitude, or knowledge that is relevant to a particular job are usually the best predictors of job success, although tests of general intelligence or personality are occasionally useful as well. In addition to being

validation

Process of determining the predictive value of a selection technique

Employees of Cingular Wireless <www.cingular.com>, a specialist in mobile voice and data communications, gather at the hometown Atlanta Zoo. Cingular markets itself as a company that "enhances the customer experience," and it wants to send a comparable message when communicating to employees and potential employees. "We want customers to use the wireless device as a tool to express themselves," says a vice president for human resources, "and we want to give our employees the opportunity to be just as expressive." The point, of course, is to foster productivity and loyalty in an era of impermanence in employer-employee relations.

validated, tests should be administered and scored consistently. All candidates should be given the same directions, allowed the same amount of time, and offered the same testing environment (temperature, lighting, distractions).[7]

Interviews   Although a popular selection device, the interview is sometimes a poor predictor of job success. For example, biases inherent in the way people perceive and judge others on first meeting affect subsequent evaluations. Interview validity can be improved by training interviewers to be aware of potential biases and by tightening the structure of the interview. In a structured interview, questions are written in advance and all interviewers follow the same question list with each candidate. Such structure introduces consistency into the interview procedure and allows the organization to validate the content of the questions. For interviewing managerial or professional candidates, a somewhat less structured approach can be used. Although question areas and information-gathering objectives are still planned in advance, specific questions vary with the candidates' backgrounds.

Other Techniques   Organizations also use other selection techniques that vary with circumstances. Polygraph tests, once popular, are declining in popularity. On the other hand, organizations occasionally require applicants to take physical exams (being careful that their practices are consistent with the Americans with Disabilities Act). More organizations are using drug tests, especially in situations in which drug-related performance problems could create serious safety hazards. Applicants at a nuclear power plant, for example, will probably be tested for drugs. Some organizations also run credit checks on prospective employees.

Developing the Workforce

After a company has hired new employees, it must acquaint them with the firm and their new jobs. Managers also take steps to train employees and to further develop necessary job skills. In addition, every firm has some system for performance appraisal and feedback. Unfortunately, the results of these assessments sometimes require procedures for demoting or terminating employees.

Self-Check Questions 1–3

You should now be able to answer Self-Check Questions 1–3*

1. **TRUE/FALSE** A *job analysis* is used to determine how much someone should be paid to perform a particular job.

2. **MULTIPLE CHOICE** Which of the following is a useful technique for planning for managerial positions? [select one] **(a)** skills inventory; **(b)** replacement chart; **(c)** job description; **(d)** job specification; **(e)** application blank.

3. **MULTIPLE CHOICE** Which of the following is **not** a common *selection tool*? [select one] **(a)** test; **(b)** interview; **(c)** polygraph exam; **(d)** interview; **(e)** drug test.

*Answers to Self-Check Questions 1–3 can be found on p. AN-5.

Training

As its name suggests, **on-the-job training** occurs while the employee is at work. Much of this training is informal, as when one employee shows another how to use the photocopier. In other cases, it is quite formal. For example, a trainer may teach secretaries how to operate a new e-mail system from their workstations.

Off-the-job training takes place at locations away from the work site. This approach offers a controlled environment and allows focused study without interruptions. For example, the petroleum equipment manufacturer Baker-Hughes uses classroom-based programs to teach new methods of quality control. Chaparral Steel's training program includes four hours a week of general education classroom training in areas such as basic math and grammar.

Other firms use **vestibule training** in simulated work environments to make off-the-job training more realistic. American Airlines, for example, trains flight attendants through vestibule training, and AT&T uses it to train telephone operators. Finally, many organizations today are increasingly using computerized and/or Web-based training.[8]

on-the-job training

Training, sometimes informal, conducted while an employee is at work

off-the-job training

Training conducted in a controlled environment away from the work site

vestibule training

Off-the-job training conducted in a simulated environment

Performance Appraisal

In some small companies, **performance appraisal** takes place when the owner tells an employee, "You're doing a good job." In larger firms, performance appraisals are designed to show more precisely how well workers are doing their jobs. Typically, the appraisal process involves a written assessment issued on a regular basis. As a rule, however, the written evaluation is only one part of a multistep process.

The appraisal process begins when a manager defines performance standards for an employee. The manager then observes the employee's performance. If the standards are clear, the manager should have little difficulty comparing expectations with performance. For some jobs, a rating scale like the abbreviated one in Figure 8.2 is useful in providing a basis for comparisons. In addition to scales for initiative, punctuality, and cleanliness, a complete form will include several other scales directly related to performance. Comparisons drawn from such scales form the basis for written appraisals and for decisions about raises, promotions, demotions, and firings. The process is completed when the manager and employee meet to discuss the appraisal.[9]

performance appraisal

Evaluation of an employee's job performance in order to determine the degree to which the employee is performing effectively

Compensation and Benefits

Most workers today also expect certain benefits from their employers. Indeed, a major factor in retaining skilled workers is a company's **compensation system**— the total package of rewards that it offers employees in return for their labor.[10]

Although wages and salaries are key parts of all compensation systems, most also include *incentives* and *employee benefits programs*. We discuss these and other types of employee benefits in this section. Remember, however, that finding the right combination of compensation elements is always complicated by the need to make employees feel valued while holding down company costs. Thus, compensation systems differ widely, depending on the nature of the industry, the company, and the types of workers involved.

compensation system

Set of rewards that organizations provide to individuals in return for their willingness to perform various jobs and tasks within the organization

Wages and Salaries

Wages and salaries are the dollar amounts paid to employees for their labor. **Wages** are paid for time worked. For example, workers who are paid by the hour receive wages. A **salary** is paid for discharging the responsibilities of a job. A salaried executive earning $100,000 per year is paid to achieve results even if that

wages

Compensation in the form of money paid for time worked

salary

Compensation in the form of money paid for discharging the responsibilities of a job

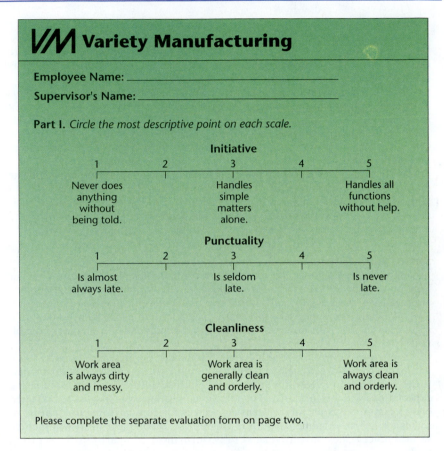

■ **FIGURE 8.2**
Performance Rating Scale

means working 5 hours one day and 15 the next. Salaries are usually expressed as an amount paid per year or per month.

In setting wage and salary levels, a company may start by looking at its competitors' levels. A firm that pays less than its rivals knows that it runs the risk of losing valuable personnel. Conversely, to attract top employees, some companies pay more than their rivals. M&M/Mars, for example, pays managerial salaries about 10 percent above the average in the candy and snack food industry.

A firm must also decide how its internal wage and salary levels will compare for different jobs. For example, Sears must determine the relative salaries of store managers, buyers, and advertising managers. In turn, managers must decide how much to pay individual workers within the company's wage and salary structure. Although two employees may do exactly the same job, the employee with more experience may earn more. Moreover, some union contracts specify differential wages based on experience.

Incentive Programs

Naturally, employees feel better about their companies when they believe that they are being fairly compensated; however, studies and experience have shown that beyond a certain point, more money will not produce better performance. Indeed, neither across-the-board nor cost-of-living wage increases cause people

"What was once a smushy, subjective effort by finger-in-the wind managers is hitting new levels of scientific precision."
—BUSINESS WEEK, ON THE ROLE OF TECHNOLOGY IN ASSESSING WORKER PERFORMANCE

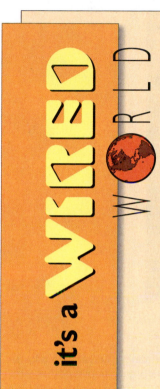

From the Smushy to the Scientific

Advances in technology permit companies to gather, analyze, report, and apply information in ways that would have been impossible a decade ago. One area that has long cried out for better use of information is worker performance measurement. "[W]hat was once a smushy, subjective effort by finger-in-the-wind managers is hitting new levels of scientific precision," reports *Business Week*.

Consider the technology revolution in performance measurement at household goods retailer Pier 1 Imports <www.pier1.com>. In the past, because daily sales reports could be calculated only at the end of the day, employees didn't know how well they were doing until it was too late to do anything about it. Now, Pier 1 uses technology to tabulate sales continuously. In cities where Pier 1 has multiple stores, the same technology pits one store against the others by allowing employees to see not only their own results, but also results from other stores. Employees check performance regularly, and use improvement goals to increase their bonuses.

At British Airways <www.britishairways.com>, software monitors employees to ensure that coffee breaks and personal phone calls don't get charged to the company. Progress toward corporate goals, such as ticket sales and complaint resolutions, is also tracked. Workers have instant access to performance scores and can see the impact of incentive compensation on their daily pay. Other firms, however, are using even more intrusive technologies, such as entry card data (to determine what time workers arrive and leave) and security cameras (sometimes without notification to the employees) that are placed in cubicles, hallways, and even restrooms. Software also allows managers to receive reports of every Web site accessed and can even record workers' every keystroke on company PCs. Many workers see the benefits of accurate and objective performance measurement, but some, not surprisingly, claim that technology is invading their privacy. As technology continues to progress, the debate is sure to continue.

---

to work harder. Money motivates employees only if it is tied directly to performance. The most common method of establishing this link is the use of **incentive programs**—special pay programs designed to motivate high performance. Some programs are available to individuals, whereas others are distributed on a companywide basis.[11]

Individual Incentives A sales bonus is a typical incentive. Employees receive **bonuses**—special payments above their salaries—when they sell a certain number or certain dollar amount of goods for the year. Employees who fail to reach this goal earn no bonuses. **Merit salary systems** link raises to performance levels in nonsales jobs.[12] For example, many baseball players have contract clauses that pay them bonuses for hitting over .300, making the All-Star team, or being named Most Valuable Player.

Executives commonly receive stock options as incentives. Disney CEO Michael Eisner, for example, can buy several thousand shares of company stock each year at a predetermined price.[13] If his managerial talent leads to higher profits and stock prices, he can buy the stock at a price lower than the market value for which, in theory, he is largely responsible. He is then free to sell the stocks at market price, keeping the profits for himself. Executive stock options have, unfortunately, been at the center of some of the recent accounting scandals plaguing some businesses today. In a nutshell, firms have chosen to not treat them as expenses at the time they were granted, contrary to what accountants suggest. In response to growing criticism, some companies, such

incentive program

Special compensation program designed to motivate high performance

bonus

Individual performance incentive in the form of a special payment made over and above the employee's salary

merit salary system

Individual incentive linking compensation to performance in nonsales jobs

Discovery Communications Inc. <www.discovery.com> faced a morale problem because its fixed-pay system meant that people doing a job in one division did not receive raises even when the pay scale for the same job description went up in another division. Employees saw the system as unfair, and so Discovery, which runs 33 cable networks out of its headquarters in Bethesda, Maryland, switched to a pay-for-performance compensation system that allows for healthy bonuses based on supervisors' evaluations and overall corporate performance.

pay for performance
(or variable pay)

Individual incentive that rewards a manager for especially productive output

profit-sharing plan

Incentive plan for distributing bonuses to employees when company profits rise above a certain level

gainsharing plan

Incentive plan that rewards groups for productivity improvements

pay-for-knowledge plan

Incentive plan to encourage employees to learn new skills or become proficient at different jobs

benefits

Compensation other than wages and salaries

workers' compensation insurance

Legally required insurance for compensating workers injured on the job

as Coca-Cola, have announced plans to change how they account for stock options.

A newer incentive plan is called **pay for performance,** or **variable pay.** In essence, middle managers are rewarded for especially productive output—for producing earnings that significantly exceed the cost of bonuses. Such incentives have long been common among top-level executives and factory workers, but variable pay goes to middle managers on the basis of companywide performance, business unit performance, personal record, or all three factors.

The number of variable pay programs in the United States has been growing consistently for the last decade, and most experts predict that they will continue to grow in popularity. Eligible managers must often forgo merit or entitlement raises (increases for staying on and reporting to work every day), but many firms say that variable pay is a better motivator because the range between generous and mediocre merit raises is usually quite small anyway. Merit raises also increase fixed costs: They are added to base pay and increase the base pay used to determine the retirement benefits that the company must pay out.

Companywide Incentives   Some incentive programs apply to all the employees in a firm.[14] Under **profit-sharing plans,** for example, profits earned above a certain level are distributed to employees. Conversely, **gainsharing plans** distribute bonuses to employees when a company's costs are reduced through greater work efficiency. **Pay-for-knowledge plans** encourage workers to learn new skills and to become proficient at different jobs. They receive additional pay for each new skill or job that they master.

Benefits Programs

A growing part of nearly every firm's compensation system is its benefits program. **Benefits**—compensation other than wages and salaries offered by a firm to its workers—comprise a large percentage of most compensation budgets. Most companies are required by law to provide social security retirement benefits and **workers' compensation insurance** (insurance for compensating workers injured on the job). Most businesses also voluntarily provide health, life, and disability insurance. Many also allow employees to use payroll deductions to buy stock at discounted prices. Another common benefit is paid time-off for vacations and holidays. Counseling services for employees with alcohol, drug, or emotional problems are also becoming more common. On-site child-care centers are also becoming popular.[15]

Retirement Plans   Retirement plans are also an important—and sometimes controversial—benefit that is available to many employees. Most company-sponsored retirement plans are set up to pay pensions to workers when they retire. In some cases, the company contributes all the money to the pension fund. In others, contributions are made by both the company and employees. Currently, about 60 percent of U.S. workers are covered by pension plans of some kind.

Containing the Costs of Benefits   As the range of benefits has grown, so has concern about containing their costs. Many companies are experimenting with cost-cutting plans under which they can still attract and retain valuable employees. One approach is the **cafeteria benefits plan.** A certain dollar amount of benefits per employee is set aside so that each employee can choose from a variety of alternatives.

    Another area of increasing concern is health-care costs. Medical procedures that once cost several hundred dollars now cost several thousand dollars. Medical expenses have increased insurance premiums, which in turn have increased the cost to employers of maintaining benefits plans.

    Many employers are looking for new ways to cut those costs. One increasingly popular approach is for organizations to create their own networks of health-care providers. These providers agree to charge lower fees for services rendered to employees of member organizations. In return, they enjoy established relationships with large employers and thus more clients and patients. Because they must make lower reimbursement payments, insurers also charge less to cover the employees of network members.

cafeteria benefit plan

Benefit plan that sets limits on benefits per employee, each of whom may choose from a variety of alternative benefits

The Legal Context of HR Management

As much or more than any area of business, HR management is heavily influenced by federal law and judicial review. In this section, we summarize some of the most important and far-reaching areas of HR regulation.

Equal Employment Opportunity

The basic goal of all **equal employment opportunity** regulation is to protect people from unfair or inappropriate discrimination in the workplace.[16] Let's begin by noting that discrimination in itself is not illegal. Whenever one person is given a pay raise and another is not, for example, the organization has made a decision to distinguish one person from another. As long as the basis for this discrimination is purely job related (made, for instance, on the basis of performance or seniority) and is applied objectively and consistently, the action is legal and appropriate.

    Problems arise when distinctions among people are not job related. In such cases, the resulting discrimination is illegal. Various court decisions, coupled with interpretations of the language of various laws, suggest that illegal discrimination actions by an organization or its managers cause members of a "protected class" to be unfairly differentiated from other members of the organization.

equal employment opportunity

Legally mandated nondiscrimination in employment on the basis of race, creed, sex, or national origin

Protected Classes in the Workplace   Illegal discrimination is based on a stereotype, belief, or prejudice about classes of individuals. At one time, for example, common stereotypes regarded black employees as less dependable than white

Mid-Chapter Internet Field Trip

"One of the 100 Best"

In this chapter, we've discussed some of the challenges that companies face in hiring, evaluating, and compensating employees, as well as some of the legal and safety issues that arise in the course of managing human resources.

Many companies manage these functions very well, maintaining safe workplaces where qualified employees are appraised and compensated fairly. Still other companies manage human resources *exceptionally* well, earning reputations as "the best places to work." Continental Airlines is one of these employers. Let's take a closer look at some of Continental's HR challenges and see how it meets them by exploring the airline's Web site at <www.continental.com>. From the home page go immediately to **About Continental,**

where you will find pages on several topics, including:

- Career Opportunities
- Global Alliances
- Investor Relations
- News Releases
- Company Profile
- Company History

From the list at **About Continental,** click on **Career Opportunities** and then select **Benefits and Incentives:**

❶ What are some of the benefits of working at Continental Airlines?

❷ Which of these listed benefits are also incentives designed to help motivate employee performance?

Return to **About Continental** and select **Company Profile.** Now click on **Diversity:**

❸ How does Continental use the diversity of its workforce to its best advantage?

Return to **Company Profile** and select **Awards:**

❹ How do other organizations judge Continental as a place to work?

Go back again to **About Continental** and select **Career Opportunities** once more. This time, chose either **Airport and Reservations Positions** or **Corporate Positions.** Select a job and read the description:

❺ How does Continental use its Web site as a staffing tool?

To continue your Internet Field Trip, click on www.prenhall.com/griffin

---

protected class

Set of individuals who by nature of one or more common characteristics are protected under the law from discrimination on the basis of that characteristic

Equal Employment Opportunity Commission (EEOC)

Federal agency enforcing several discrimination-related laws

---

employees, women as less suited to certain types of work than men, and disabled individuals as unproductive employees.

Based on these stereotypes, some organizations routinely discriminated against blacks, women, and the disabled. To combat discrimination, laws have been passed to protect various classes of individuals. A **protected class** consists of all individuals who share one or more common characteristics as indicated by a given law. The most common criteria for defining protected classes include race, color, religion, gender, age, national origin, disability status, and status as a military veteran.[17]

Enforcing Equal Employment Opportunity The enforcement of equal opportunity legislation is handled by two agencies. The **Equal Employment Opportunity Commission,** or **EEOC** <www.eeoc.gov>, is a division of the Department of Justice. It was created by Title VII of the 1964 Civil Rights Act and has specific responsibility for enforcing Title VII, the Equal Pay Act, and the Americans with Disabilities Act.

The other agency charged with monitoring equal employment opportunity legislation is the Office of Federal Contract Compliance Programs, or OFCCP <www.dol.gov/dol/esa/public/of_org.htm>. The OFCCP is responsible for enforcing executive orders that apply to companies doing business with the federal government. A business with government contracts must have on file a written **affirmative action plan**—that is, a written statement of how the organization intends to actively recruit, hire, and develop members of relevant protected classes.

Legal Issues in Compensation As we noted earlier, most employment regulations are designed to provide equal employment opportunity. Some legislation,

---

affirmative action plan

Practice of recruiting qualified employees belonging to racial, gender, or ethnic groups who are underrepresented in an organization

"I see by your résumé that you're a woman."

however, goes beyond equal employment opportunity and really deals more substantively with other issues. One such area is legislation covering compensation.

Contemporary Legal Issues in HR Management

In addition to these established areas of HR legal regulation, there are several emerging legal issues that will likely become more and more important with the passage of time. These include employee safety and health, various emerging areas of discrimination law, employee rights, and employment-at-will.

Employee Safety and Health   The **Occupational Safety and Health Act of 1970,** or **OSHA** <www.osha.gov>, is the single most comprehensive piece of legislation ever passed regarding worker safety and health. OSHA holds that every employer has an obligation to furnish each employee with a place of employment that is free from hazards that cause or are likely to cause death or physical harm. It is generally enforced through inspections of the workplace by OSHA inspectors. If an OSHA compliance officer believes that a violation has occurred, a citation is issued. Nonserious violations may result in fines of up to $1,000 for each incident. Serious or willful and repeated violations may incur fines of up to $10,000 per incident.

Emerging Areas of Discrimination Law   There are also several emerging areas of discrimination law that managers must also be familiar with. In this section, we will discuss some of the most important.

AIDS in the Workplace   Although AIDS is considered a disability under the Americans with Disabilities Act of 1990, the AIDS situation itself is sufficiently severe enough that it warrants special attention. Employers cannot legally require an AIDS or any other medical examination as a condition for making an offer of employment. Organizations must treat AIDS like any other disease covered by law. They must maintain the confidentiality of all medical records. They cannot discriminate against a person with AIDS, and they should try to educate coworkers about AIDS. They cannot discriminate against AIDS victims in training or in consideration for promotion, and they must accommodate or make a good-faith effort to accommodate AIDS victims.

Occupational Safety and Health Act of 1970 (OSHA)

Federal law setting and enforcing guidelines for protecting workers from unsafe conditions and potential health hazards in the workplace

sexual harassment

Practice or instance of making unwelcome sexual advances in the workplace

quid pro quo harassment

Form of sexual harassment in which sexual favors are requested in return for job-related benefits

hostile work environment

Form of sexual harassment deriving from off-color jokes, lewd comments, and so forth

employment-at-will

Principle, increasingly modified by legislation and judicial decision, that organizations should be able to retain or dismiss employees at their discretion

workforce diversity

Range of workers' attitudes, values, beliefs, and behaviors that differ by gender, race, and ethnicity

Sexual Harassment   Sexual harassment has been a problem in organizations for a long time and is a violation of Title VII of the Civil Rights Act of 1964. **Sexual harassment** is defined by the EEOC as unwelcome sexual advances in the work environment. If the conduct is indeed unwelcome and occurs with sufficient frequency to create an abusive work environment, the employer is responsible for changing the environment by warning, reprimanding, or perhaps firing the harasser.[18]

The courts have ruled and defined that there are two types of sexual harassment:

■   In cases of **quid pro quo harassment,** the harasser offers to exchange something of value for sexual favors. A male supervisor, for example, might tell or suggest to a female subordinate that he will recommend her for promotion or give her a raise in exchange for sexual favors.

■   The creation of a **hostile work environment** is a subtler form of sexual harassment. A group of male employees who continually make off-color jokes and lewd comments and perhaps decorate the work environment with inappropriate photographs may create a hostile work environment for a female colleague, who becomes uncomfortable working in that environment. As we noted earlier, it is the organization's responsibility for dealing with this sort of problem.

Regardless of the pattern, the same bottom-line rules apply: Sexual harassment is illegal, and the organization is responsible for controlling it.

Employment-at-Will   The concept of **employment-at-will** holds that both employer and employee have the mutual right to terminate an employment relationship anytime for any reason and with or without advance notice to the other. Specifically, it holds that an organization employs an individual at its own will and can, therefore, terminate that employee at any time for any reason. Over the last two decades, however, terminated employees have challenged the employment-at-will doctrine by filing lawsuits against former employers on the grounds of wrongful discharge.

In the last several years, such suits have put limits on employment-at-will provisions in certain circumstances. In the past, for example, organizations were guilty of firing employees who filed workers' compensation claims or took excessive time off to serve on jury duty. More recently, however, the courts have ruled that employees may not be fired for exercising rights protected by law.

New Challenges in the Changing Workplace

As we have seen throughout this chapter, human resource managers face several ongoing challenges in their efforts to keep their organizations staffed with effective workforces. To complicate matters, new challenges arise as the economic and social environments of business change. In the following sections, we take a look at several of the most important human resource management issues facing business today.

Managing Workforce Diversity

One extremely important set of human resource challenges centers on **workforce diversity**—the range of workers' attitudes, values, beliefs, and behaviors that differ by gender, race, age, ethnicity, physical ability, and other relevant characteristics. In the past, organizations tended to work toward homogenizing their workforces, getting everyone to think and behave in similar ways. Partly as a result of affirmative action efforts, however, many U.S. organizations are now creating more

Self-Check Questions 4–6

You should now be able to answer Self-Check Questions 4–6*

4. MULTIPLE CHOICE Which of the following is a common training method today? [select one] **(a)** on-the-job training; **(b)** off-the-job training; **(c)** vestibule training; **(d)** Web-based training; **(e)** all of these.

5. MULTIPLE CHOICE Both Jason Giambi of the New York Yankees and Sheryl Swoopes of the Houston Comets have contract clauses that pay them extra if they are voted Most Valuable Player of their respective leagues. This clause is an example of which of the following? [select one] **(a)** individual incentive; **(b)** profit-sharing plan; **(c)** gainsharing plan; **(d)** pay-for-knowledge plan; **(e)** cafeteria benefit.

6. TRUE/FALSE As long as hiring rules are applied uniformly, an employer can choose to not hire members of a protected class.

*ANSWERS TO SELF-CHECK QUESTIONS 4–6 CAN BE FOUND ON P. AN-5.

diverse workforces, embracing more women, ethnic minorities, and foreign-born employees than ever before.

Figure 8.3 helps put the changing U.S. workforce into perspective by illustrating changes in the percentages of different groups of workers—males and females, whites, African Americans, Hispanics, Asians, and others—in the total workforce in the years 1986, 1996, and (as projected) 2006. The picture is clearly one of increasing diversity. By 2006, say experts, almost half of all workers in the labor force will be women and almost one-third will be blacks, Hispanics, Asian Americans, and others.

Today, organizations are recognizing not only that they should treat everyone equitably, but also that they should acknowledge the individuality of each person they employ. They are also recognizing that diversity can be a competitive advantage.[19] For example, by hiring the best people available from every single group rather than hiring from just one or a few groups, a firm can develop a higher quality labor force. Similarly, a diverse workforce can bring a wider array of information to bear on problems and can provide insights on marketing products to a wider range of consumers. Says the head of workforce diversity at IBM, "We think it is important for our customers to look inside and see people like them. If they can't . . . the prospect of them becoming or staying our customers declines."

Managing Knowledge Workers

Traditionally, employees added value to organizations because of what they did or because of their experience. In the Information Age, however, many employees add value because of what they know.[20]

The Nature of Knowledge Work   These employees are usually called **knowledge workers,** and the skill with which they are managed is a major factor in determining which firms will be successful in the future. Knowledge workers, including computer scientists, engineers, and physical scientists, provide special challenges for the HR manager. They tend to work in high-technology firms and are

> **"We think it is important for our customers to look inside and see people like them. If they can't, the prospect of them becoming or staying our customers declines."**
>
> ~Head of workforce diversity at IBM

knowledge workers

Employees who are of value because of the knowledge they possess

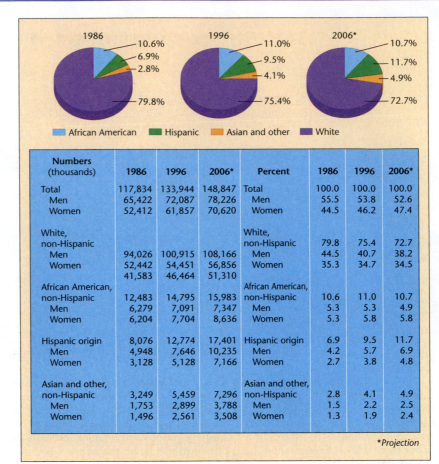

■ FIGURE 8.3

Changing Composition of the U.S. Workforce

Numbers (thousands)	1986	1996	2006*	Percent	1986	1996	2006*
Total	117,834	133,944	148,847	Total	100.0	100.0	100.0
Men	65,422	72,087	78,226	Men	55.5	53.8	52.6
Women	52,412	61,857	70,620	Women	44.5	46.2	47.4
White, non-Hispanic				White, non-Hispanic	79.8	75.4	72.7
Men	94,026	100,915	108,166	Men	44.5	40.7	38.2
Women	52,442	54,451	56,856	Women	35.3	34.7	34.5
	41,583	46,464	51,310				
African American, non-Hispanic	12,483	14,795	15,983	African American, non-Hispanic	10.6	11.0	10.7
Men	6,279	7,091	7,347	Men	5.3	5.3	4.9
Women	6,204	7,704	8,636	Women	5.3	5.8	5.8
Hispanic origin	8,076	12,774	17,401	Hispanic origin	6.9	9.5	11.7
Men	4,948	7,646	10,235	Men	4.2	5.7	6.9
Women	3,128	5,128	7,166	Women	2.7	3.8	4.8
Asian and other, non-Hispanic	3,249	5,459	7,296	Asian and other, non-Hispanic	2.8	4.1	4.9
Men	1,753	2,899	3,788	Men	1.5	2.2	2.5
Women	1,496	2,561	3,508	Women	1.3	1.9	2.4

*Projection

usually experts in some abstract knowledge base. They often like to work independently and tend to identify more strongly with their professions than with any organization—even to the extent of defining performance in terms recognized by other members of their professions.

As the importance of information-driven jobs grows, the need for knowledge workers continues to grow as well. But these employees require extensive and highly specialized training, and not every organization is willing to make the human capital investments necessary to take advantage of these jobs. In fact, even after knowledge workers are on the job, retraining and training updates are critical to prevent their skills from becoming obsolete. It has been suggested, for example, that the half-life of a technical education in engineering is about three years. The failure to update such skills will not only result in the loss of competitive advantage but will also increase the likelihood that the knowledge worker will go to another firm that is more committed to updating the worker's skills.

Knowledge Worker Management and Labor Markets   In recent years, the demand for knowledge workers has grown at a dramatic rate. Even the economic downturn in 2000 only slowed the demand for highly skilled knowledge workers. As a result, organizations that need these workers must introduce regular market

Say what you mean

TOP-DOWN SENSITIVITY

By definition, global companies must communicate with employees in many different countries and cultures, and a firm's success in communicating with local workers can mean success or failure in an overseas operation. The most successful global companies know how to talk to the people who work for them.

In some countries, the gap between managers and workers is quite wide, and managers are used to bridging it with orders that are simply to be followed. In many Asian cultures, for example, you simply don't question the boss' decisions or the policies of the company. In the United States, by contrast, people are often encouraged to provide feedback and to say what they think. The gap is relatively narrow, and communication channels tend to be informal and wide open.

The same arrangements usually apply when it comes to dealing with workplace disputes. In some countries, such as Germany and Sweden, there's a formal system for ensuring that everyone involved gets a say in resolving workplace disputes. In these countries, although communication channels are always open, they're also highly structured.

But being culturally sensitive to local employees means much more than just knowing how to settle workplace disputes. As a rule, companies also need to convey a sense of good "citizenship" through their behavior in the host country. This means respecting the social and cultural values of employees and communicating to them the fact that the company cares about the things that they care about.

adjustments (upward) in order to pay them enough to keep them. This is especially critical in areas in which demand is still growing, since even entry-level salaries for these employees are continuing to escalate. Once an employee accepts a job with a firm, the employer faces yet another dilemma. Once hired, workers are more subject to the company's internal labor market, which is not likely to be growing as quickly as the external market for knowledge workers as a whole. Consequently, the longer employees remain with a firm, the further behind the market their pay falls—unless it is regularly adjusted upward.

The continuing demand for these workers has inspired some fairly extreme measures for attracting them in the first place.[21] High starting salaries and sign-on bonuses are common. British Petroleum Exploration <www.bpamoco.com> was recently paying starting petroleum engineers with undersea platform-drilling knowledge—not experience, just knowledge—salaries in the six figures, plus sign-on bonuses of over $50,000 and immediate profit sharing. Even with these incentives, HR managers complain that in the Gulf Coast region, they cannot retain specialists because young engineers soon leave to accept even more attractive jobs with competitors. Laments one HR executive, "We wind up six months after we hire an engineer having to fight off offers for that same engineer for more money."[22]

Contingent and Temporary Workers

A final contemporary HR issue of note involves the use of contingent and temporary workers. Indeed, recent years have seen an explosion in the use of such workers by organizations.

Trends in Contingent and Temporary Employment   In recent years, the number of contingent workers in the workforce has increased dramatically. A **contingent**

> "We wind up six months after we hire an engineer having to fight off offers for that same engineer for more money."
>
> ~Eric Campbell,
> **HR EXECUTIVE AT DOCENT INC.**

contingent worker

Employee hired on something other than a full-time basis to supplement an organization's permanent workforce

worker is a person who works for an organization on something other than a permanent or full-time basis. Categories of contingent workers include independent contractors, on-call workers, temporary employees (usually hired through outside agencies), and contract and leased employees. Another category is part-time workers. The financial services giant Citigroup <www.citigroup.com>, for example, makes extensive use of part-time sales agents to pursue new clients. About 10 percent of the U.S. workforce currently uses one of these alternative forms of employment relationships. Experts suggest, however, that this percentage is increasing at a consistent pace.

Managing Contingent and Temporary Workers   Given the widespread use of contingent and temporary workers, HR managers must understand how to use such employees most effectively. That is, they need to understand how to manage contingent and temporary workers.

One key is careful planning. Even though one of the presumed benefits of using contingent workers is flexibility, it still is important to integrate such workers in a coordinated fashion. Rather than having to call in workers sporadically and with no prior notice, organizations try to bring in specified numbers of workers for well-defined periods of time. The ability to do so comes from careful planning.

A second key is understanding contingent workers and acknowledging their advantages and disadvantages. That is, the organization must recognize what it can and can't achieve from the use of contingent and temporary workers. Expecting too much from such workers, for example, is a mistake that managers should avoid.

Third, managers must carefully assess the real cost of using contingent workers. We noted previously that many firms adopt this course of action to save labor costs. The organization should be able to document precisely its labor-cost savings. How much would it be paying people in wages and benefits if they were on permanent staff? How does this cost compare with the amount spent on contingent workers? This difference, however, could be misleading. We also noted, for instance, that contingent workers might be less effective performers than permanent and full-time employees. Comparing employee for employee on a direct-cost basis, therefore, is not necessarily valid. Organizations must learn to adjust the direct differences in labor costs to account for differences in productivity and performance.

Finally, managers must fully understand their own strategies and decide in advance how they intend to manage temporary workers, specifically focusing on how to integrate them into the organization. On a very simplistic level, for example, an organization with a large contingent workforce must make some decisions about the treatment of contingent workers relative to the treatment of permanent full-time workers. Should contingent workers be invited to the company holiday party? Should they have the same access to such employee benefits as counseling services and child care? There are no right or wrong answers to such questions. Managers must understand that they need to develop a strategy for integrating contingent workers according to some sound logic and then follow that strategy consistently over time.[23]

labor union

Group of individuals working together to achieve shared job-related goals, such as higher pay, shorter working hours, more job security, greater benefits, or better working conditions

labor relations

Process of dealing with employees who are represented by a union

Dealing with Organized Labor

A **labor union** is a group of individuals working together to achieve shared job-related goals, such as higher pay, shorter working hours, more job security, greater benefits, or better working conditions.[24] **Labor relations** describes the process of dealing with employees who are represented by a union.

Labor unions grew in popularity in the United States in the nineteenth and early twentieth centuries. The labor movement was born with the Industrial

Revolution, which also gave birth to a factory-based production system that carried with it enormous economic benefits. Job specialization and mass production allowed businesses to create ever greater quantities of goods at ever lower costs.

But there was also a dark side to this era. Workers became more dependent on their factory jobs. Eager for greater profits, some owners treated their workers like other raw materials: resources to be deployed with little or no regard for the individual worker's well-being. Many businesses forced employees to work long hours—60-hour weeks were common, and some workers were routinely forced to work 12 to 16 hours a day. With no minimum-wage laws or other controls, pay was also minimal and safety standards virtually nonexistent. Workers enjoyed no job security and received few benefits. Many companies, especially textile mills, employed large numbers of children at poverty wages. If people complained, nothing prevented employers from firing and replacing them at will.

Unions appeared and ultimately prospered because they constituted a solution to the worker's most serious problem: They forced management to listen to the complaints of all their workers rather than to just the few who were brave (or foolish) enough to speak out. The power of unions, then, comes from collective action. **Collective bargaining** (which we discuss more fully later in this chapter) is the process by which union leaders and managers negotiate common terms and conditions of employment for the workers represented by unions. Although collective bargaining does not often occur in small businesses, many midsize and larger businesses must engage in the process.

collective bargaining

Process by which labor and management negotiate conditions of employment for union-represented workers

Unionism Today

Although understanding the historical context of labor unions is important, so too is appreciating the role of unionism today, especially trends in union membership, union–management relations, and bargaining perspectives. We discuss these topics in the sections that follow.

Trends in Union Membership Since the mid-1950s, U.S. labor unions have experienced increasing difficulties in attracting new members. As a result, although millions of workers still belong to labor unions, union membership *as a percentage of the total workforce* has continued to decline at a very steady rate. In 1980, for example, nearly 25 percent of U.S. wage and salary employees belonged to labor unions. Today, that figure is about 14 percent. Figure 8.4(a) traces the decades-long decline in union membership. Moreover, if public employees are excluded from consideration, then only around 11 percent of all private industry wage and salary employees currently belong to labor unions. Figure 8.4(b) illustrates the different trends in membership for public employees versus private nonfarm employees.

Furthermore, just as union membership has continued to decline, so has the percentage of successful union-organizing campaigns. In the years immediately following World War II and continuing through the mid-1960s, most unions routinely won certification elections. In recent years, however, labor unions have been winning certification fewer than 50 percent of the time in which workers are called upon to vote. By the same token, of course, unions still do win. Meat cutters at a Florida Wal-Mart

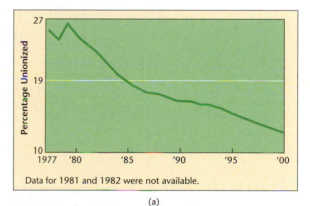

Data for 1981 and 1982 were not available.

(a)

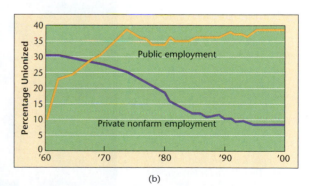

(b)

■ **FIGURE 8.4**

Trends in Union Membership

store recently voted to unionize—the first-ever successful organizing campaign against the retailing giant. "You'll see a lot more attention to Wal-Mart now," exulted one AFL-CIO official. "It's not like Wal-Mart stands out as some unattainable goal."[25]

From most indications, however, the power and significance of U.S. labor unions, while still quite formidable, are also measurably lower than they were just a few decades ago.

Trends in Union–Management Relations   The gradual decline in unionization in the United States has been accompanied by some significant trends in union–management relations. In some sectors of the economy, perhaps most notably the automobile and steel industries, labor unions still remain quite strong. In these areas, unions have large memberships and considerable power in negotiating with management. The United Auto Workers (UAW), for example, is still one of the strongest unions in the United States.

In most sectors, however, unions are clearly in a weakened position, and as a result, many have taken much more conciliatory stances in their relations with management. This situation contrasts sharply with the more adversarial relationship that once dominated labor relations in this country. Increasingly, for instance, unions recognize that they don't have as much power as they once held and that it is in their own best interests, as well as in those of the workers that they represent, to work with management instead of working against it. Ironically, then, union–management relations are in many ways better today than they have been in many years. Admittedly, the improvement is attributable in large part to the weakened power of unions. Even so, however, most experts agree that improved union–management relations have benefited both sides.

Trends in Bargaining Perspectives   Given the trends described in the two previous sections, we should not be surprised to find changes in bargaining perspectives as well. In the past, most union–management bargaining situations were characterized by union demands for dramatic increases in wages and salaries. A secondary issue was usually increased benefits for members. Now, however, unions often bargain for different benefits, such as job security. Of particular interest in this area is the trend toward relocating jobs to take advantage of lower labor costs in other countries. Unions, of course, want to restrict job movement,

Members of the Hotel Employees and Restaurant Employees union (HERE) at a rally in California. What's the issue? As is often the case, it's saving jobs, but this time the problem is unusually severe for both hotel owners and hotel employees. Since 9/11, no less than 40 percent of the union's 175,000 North American members have been laid off, and another 20 percent are working short weeks. Because laid-off workers don't pay dues, HERE is strapped for cash, and union president John Wilhelm has cut his own salary by 20 percent.

whereas companies want to save money by moving facilities—and jobs—to other countries.

As a result of organizational downsizing and several years of relatively low inflation in this country, many unions today find themselves fighting against wage cuts rather than striving for wage *increases*. Similarly, as organizations are more likely to seek lower health care and other benefits, a common goal of union strategy is to preserve what's already been won. Unions also place greater emphasis on improved job security. A trend that has become especially important in recent years is the effort to improve pension programs for employees.

Unions have also begun increasingly to set their sights on preserving jobs for workers in the United States in the face of business efforts to relocate production in some sectors to countries where labor costs are lower. For example, the AFL-CIO has been an outspoken opponent of efforts to normalize trade relations with China, fearing that more businesses might be tempted to move jobs there. General Electric <www.ge.com> has been targeted for union protests recently because of its strategy to move many of its own jobs—and those of key suppliers—to Mexico.[26]

The Future of Unions Despite declining membership and some loss of power, labor unions remain a major factor in the U.S. business world. The 86 labor organizations in the AFL-CIO, as well as independent major unions such as the Teamsters and the National Education Association (NEA), still play a major role in U.S. business. Moreover, some unions still wield considerable power, especially in the traditional strongholds of goods-producing industries. Labor and management in some industries, notably airlines and steel, are beginning to favor contracts that establish formal mechanisms for greater worker input into management decisions. Inland Steel <www.inland.com>, for instance, recently granted its major union the right to name a member to the board of directors. Union officers can also attend executive meetings.

Collective Bargaining

When a union has been legally certified, it assumes the role of official bargaining agent for the workers whom it represents. Collective bargaining is an ongoing process involving both the drafting and the administering of the terms of a labor contract.[27]

Reaching Agreement on Contract Terms

The collective bargaining process begins when the union is recognized as the exclusive negotiator for its members. The bargaining cycle itself begins when union leaders meet with management representatives to agree on a contract. By law, both parties must sit down at the bargaining table and negotiate in good faith.

When each side has presented its demands, sessions focus on identifying the *bargaining zone*. The process is shown in Figure 8.5. For example, although an employer may initially offer no pay raise, it may expect to grant a raise of up to 6 percent. Likewise, the union may initially *demand* a 10-percent pay raise while *expecting* to accept a raise as low as 4 percent. The bargaining zone, then, is a raise between 4 and 6 percent. Ideally, some compromise is reached between these levels, and then the new agreement is submitted for a ratification vote by union membership.

Sometimes this process goes quite smoothly. At other times, however, the two sides cannot—or will not—agree. The speed and ease with which such an

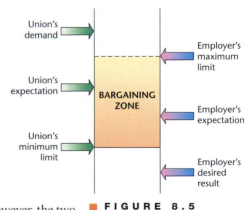

■ **FIGURE 8.5**

The Bargaining Zone

impasse is resolved depend in part on the nature of the contract issues, the willingness of each side to use certain tactics, and the prospects for mediation or arbitration.[28]

Contract Issues

The labor contract itself can address an array of different issues. Most of these concern demands that unions make on behalf of their members. In this section, we will survey the categories of issues that are typically most important to union negotiators: *compensation, benefits,* and *job security.* Although few issues covered in a labor contract are company sponsored, we will also describe the kinds of management rights that are negotiated in most bargaining agreements.

Compensation   The most common issue is compensation. One aspect of compensation is current wages. Obviously, unions want their employees to earn higher wages and try to convince management to raise hourly wages for all or some employees.

Of equal concern to unions is future compensation: wage rates to be paid during subsequent years of the contract. One common tool for securing wage increases is a **cost-of-living adjustment (COLA).** Most COLA clauses tie future raises to the *Consumer Price Index (CPI),* a government statistic that reflects changes in consumer purchasing power. The premise is that as the CPI increases by a specified amount during a given period of time, wages will automatically be increased. Almost half of all labor contracts today include COLA clauses.

Wage reopener clauses are now included in almost 10 percent of all labor contracts. Such a clause allows wage rates to be renegotiated at preset times during the life of the contract. For example, a union might be uncomfortable with a long-term contract based solely on COLA wage increases. A long-term agreement might be more acceptable, however, if management agrees to renegotiate wages every two years.

Benefits   Employee benefits are also an important component in most labor contracts. Unions typically want employers to pay all or most of the costs of insurance for employees. Other benefits commonly addressed during negotiations include retirement benefits, paid holidays, and working conditions.

Job Security   Nevertheless, the UAW's top priority in its most recent negotiations with U.S. automakers has been job security, an increasingly important agenda item in many bargaining sessions today. In some cases, demands for job security entail the promise that a company not move to another location. In others, the contract may dictate that if the workforce is reduced, seniority will be used to determine which employees keep their jobs.

Other Union Issues   Other possible issues might include such things as working hours, overtime policies, rest period arrangements, differential pay plans for shift employees, the use of temporary workers, grievance procedures, and allowable union activities (dues collection, union bulletin boards, and so forth).

Management Rights   Management wants as much control as possible over hiring policies, work assignments, and so forth. Unions, meanwhile, often try to limit management rights by specifying hiring, assignment, and other policies. At a DaimlerChrysler plant in Detroit, for example, the contract stipulates that three workers are needed to change fuses in robots: a machinist to open the robot, an electrician to change the fuse, and a supervisor to oversee the process. As in this case, contracts often bar workers in one job category from performing work that

---

cost-of-living adjustment (COLA)

Labor contract clause tying future raises to changes in consumer purchasing power

wage reopener clause

Clause allowing wage rates to be renegotiated during the life of a labor contract falls in the domain of another. Unions try to secure jobs by defining as many different categories as possible (the DaimlerChrysler plant has over 100). Of course, management resists the practice, which limits flexibility and makes it difficult to reassign workers.

When Bargaining Fails

An impasse occurs when, after a series of bargaining sessions, management and labor have failed to agree on a new contract or a contract to replace an agreement that is about to expire. Although it is generally agreed that both parties suffer when an impasse is reached and some action by one part, against the other is taken, each side can use several tactics to support its cause until the impasse is resolved.[29]

Union Tactics   When their demands are not met, unions may bring a variety of tactics to the bargaining table. Chief among these are the *strike*, which may be supported by *pickets* and *boycotts,* and the *slowdown.*

The Strike   A **strike** occurs when employees temporarily walk off the job and refuse to work. Most strikes in the United States are **economic strikes,** triggered by stalemates over mandatory bargaining items, including such noneconomic issues as working hours. For example, the Teamsters union struck United Parcel Service (UPS) a few years ago over several noneconomic issues. Specifically, the union wanted the firm to transform many of its temporary and part-time jobs into permanent and full-time jobs. Strikers returned to work only when UPS agreed to create 10,000 new jobs. More recently, the same union struck Union Pacific Corp. <www.up.com> in January 2000 over wages and new jobs. In April 2000, machinists at a Lockheed-Martin <www.lmco.com> plant in Fort Worth, Texas, staged a two-week strike. Reflected the president of the union local, "I think our people gained a lot of respect for taking a stand. We had a good strike."

Still, there arc far fewer strikes today than there were in previous years. For example, there were 222 strikes in the United States in 1960 involving a total of 896,000 workers. In 1970, 2,468,000 workers took part in 381 strikes. But in 1990, there were only 44 strikes involving 185,000 workers. Since 1990, the annual number of strikes has ranged from a high of 45 (in 1994) to a low of 29 (in 1997).[30]

Not all strikes are legal. **Sympathy strikes** (also called **secondary strikes**), which occur when one union strikes in sympathy with action initiated by another, may violate the sympathetic union's contract. **Wildcat strikes**—strikes unauthorized by the union that occur during the life of a contract—deprive strikers of their status as employees and thus of the protection of national labor law.

Other Labor Actions   To support a strike, a union faced with an impasse has recourse to additional legal activities:

■   In **picketing,** workers march at the entrance to the employer's facility with signs explaining their reasons for striking.

■   A **boycott** occurs when union members agree not to buy the products of a targeted employer. Workers may also urge consumers to boycott the firm's products.

■   Another alternative to striking is a work **slowdown.** Instead of striking, workers perform their jobs at a much slower pace than normal. A variation is the *sickout,* during which large numbers of workers call in sick. Pilots at American Airlines engaged in a massive sickout in early 1999, causing the airline to cancel thousands of flights before a judge ordered them back into the cockpit.

---

strike

Labor action in which employees temporarily walk off the job and refuse to work

economic strike

Strike usually triggered by stalemate over one or more mandatory bargaining items

sympathy strike (or **secondary strike**)

Strike in which one union strikes to support action initiated by another

wildcat strike

Strike that is unauthorized by the strikers' union

picketing

Labor action in which workers publicize their grievances at the entrance to an employer's facility

boycott

Labor action in which workers refuse to buy the products of a targeted employer

slowdown

Labor action in which workers perform jobs at a slower than normal pace

Management Tactics   Like workers, management can respond forcefully to an impasse:

■   **Lockouts** occur when employers deny employees access to the workplace. Lockouts are illegal if they are used as offensive weapons to give management a bargaining advantage. However, they are legal if management has a legitimate business need (for instance, avoiding a buildup of perishable inventory). Although rare today, ABC <www.abc.go.com> locked out its off-camera employees in 1998 because they staged an unannounced one-day strike during a critical broadcasting period. Likewise, almost half of the 1998–1999 NBA season was lost when team owners <www.nba.com> locked out their players over contract issues.

■   A firm can also hire temporary or permanent replacements called **strikebreakers.** However, the law forbids the permanent replacement of workers who strike because of unfair practices. In some cases, an employer can also obtain legal injunctions that either prohibit workers from striking or prohibit a union from interfering with its efforts to use replacement workers.

Mediation and Arbitration   Rather than wield these often unpleasant weapons against one another, labor and management can agree to call in a third party to help resolve the dispute:

■   In **mediation,** the neutral third party (the mediator) can suggest but cannot impose a settlement on the other parties.

■   In **voluntary arbitration,** the neutral third party (the arbitrator) dictates a settlement between the two sides, which have agreed to submit to outside judgment.

■   In some cases, arbitration is legally required to settle bargaining disputes. **Compulsory arbitration** is used to settle disputes between the government and public employees such as firefighters and police officers.

---

lockout

Management tactic whereby workers are denied access to the employer's workplace

strikebreaker

Worker hired as permanent or temporary replacement for a striking employee

mediation

Method of resolving a labor dispute in which a third party suggests, but does not impose, a settlement

voluntary arbitration

Method of resolving a labor dispute in which both parties agree to submit to the judgment of a neutral party

compulsory arbitration

Method of resolving a labor dispute in which both parties are legally required to accept the judgment of a neutral party

---

Self-Check Questions 7–9

You should now be able to answer Self-Check Questions 7–9*

7. **Multiple Choice**   In general, which of the following is **true** about workforce diversity? [select one] **(a)** It is decreasing. **(b)** It is increasing. **(c)** It remains constant. **(d)** It is becoming less important to business. **(e)** none of these.

8. **Multiple Choice**   Which of the following is **true** about union membership in recent years? [select one] **(a)** It has generally remained constant. **(b)** It has generally become more diverse. **(c)** Generally, it has steadily increased. **(d)** Generally, it has steadily declined. **(e)** It has generally changed in unknown ways because of new privacy laws.

9. **True/False**   In recent years, the number of contingent workers has sharply increased.

*Answers to Self-Check Questions 7–9 can be found on p. AN-6.

Continued from page 217

Time Out on the Labor Front

As we explained at the beginning of this chapter, many firms have reduced or frozen hiring, and some are reducing or eliminating benefits and perquisites. These firms are seeking ways to lower costs, and they've found that current economic conditions give them more flexibility than they had just a few years ago. But while these actions may lower costs and protect profits in the short term, firms that follow this path may face problems when the economy rebounds. In particular, they may find that they've tarnished their reputations as employers and find it more difficult to attract workers when they need them again.

The repercussions may include low morale, reduced productivity, or worse. When the Indiana Social Services Administration left job vacancies unfilled in 1990, the state soon led the country in welfare fraud cases. And the effects can be long-lasting. Says one executive whose company instituted pay cuts, "People are lying low, but when the economy improves, they'll be out of here." Workers complain that they shouldn't bear a disproportionate share of the cost cutting burden, and studies verify that median CEO compensation rose seven percent in 2001 and worker pay just three percent. Company profits fell 35 percent.

The good news for struggling firms is that there are still effective incentives. The most powerful, and least expensive, perk can be time off. Experts suggest, for example, that up to 20 percent of workers would be willing to work fewer hours for lower pay. Siemens, a German electronics firm, is offering workers a year-long "time-out," with reduced pay and a guaranteed job when they return. "It's a possibility for us not to lose good workers despite bad times," says Siemens' spokesperson Axel Heim. Firms are also finding that technology workers and professionals, who need to stay on the leading edge of their fields, want more training and increased job responsibilities. Many people, warns Patti Wilson, founder of a high-tech career-management firm, "will jump jobs to learn more or stay if they feel that they're being challenged."

Questions for Discussion

1. What are the basic human resource issues reflected in labor force reductions and other HR cutbacks?
2. What benefits seem to be the most valuable to employees, and what benefits seem trivial and/or extravagant?
3. Aside from laying off workers, what other costs might be cut in managing an organization's labor force?
4. What other incentives besides benefits might a company be able to offer its best workers in order to retain them?
5. How might current employment trends affect unionization? Why?

> **"It's a possibility for us not to lose good workers despite bad times."**
>
> ~Siemens executive
> ON THE COMPANY'S POLICY OF OFFERING EMPLOYEES
> A YEAR-LONG "TIME-OUT"

Summary of Learning Objectives

1. *Define* **human resource management,** *and explain how managers plan for human resources.*

Human resource management (HRM) is the set of organizational activities directed at attracting, developing, and maintaining an effective workforce. Because of the importance of HRM, many firms integrate strategic HR plans with other strategic planning activities.

HR planning involves two tasks: (1) *Job analysis:* **Job analysis** is a systematic analysis of jobs within an organization. It has two parts: (i) The **job description** lists the duties of a job, working conditions, and needed tools, materials, and equipment; (ii) the **job specification** lists the skills, abilities, and other credentials needed to do a job. Job analysis includes developing selection methods, performance appraisal systems, and compensation rates.

(2) *Forecasting HR demand and supply*: Managers must plan for future HR needs by assessing past trends, future plans, and general economic trends. Forecasting labor supply is really two tasks: (i) Forecasting *internal supply*—the number and type of employees who will be in the firm at some future date; (ii) forecasting *external supply*—the number and type of people who will be available from the labor market at large.

Large organizations use sophisticated models to make forecasts, including the following: (i) **Replacement charts** list such items as important managerial positions, who occupies them, and who is or will be qualified to move into them. (ii) **Employee information systems,** or **skills inventories,** are computerized systems which contain information on each employee and which can locate any employee who is qualified to fill a position.

The next step in HR planning is *matching HR supply and demand*—dealing with predicted shortfalls or overstaffing. If a shortfall is predicted, new employees can be hired. The external labor forecast helps managers recruit on the basis of which type of workers are available or scarce.

2. Identify tasks in staffing *a company and discuss ways in which organizations* select, develop, *and* appraise *employee performance.*

Staffing an organization means recruiting and hiring the right mix of people. **Recruiting** is the process of attracting qualified persons to apply for open jobs. **Internal recruiting** means considering present employees as candidates—a policy that helps build morale and keep high-quality employees. **External recruiting** involves attracting people from outside the organization. Methods include advertising, campus interviews, employment agencies or executive search firms, union hiring halls, and referrals by present employees.

The next step is the *selection* process—gathering information that will predict applicants' job success and then hiring the most promising candidates. The process of analyzing gathered information is called **validation.** The first step in selection is asking the candidate to fill out an *application form* (to find out work history, educational background, and so forth). Next, recruiters may give *tests* of ability, aptitude, or knowledge relevant to a particular job. Finally, in a structured *interview*, questions are written in advance, and all interviewers follow the same format. Some organizations also use such selection techniques as polygraphs and drug tests.

New employees must be trained and allowed to develop job skills. **On-the-job training** occurs while the employee is at work. **Off-the-job training** takes place at off site locations where controlled environments allow focused study. Some firms use **vestibule training**—off-the-job training in simulated work environments.

In larger firms, **performance appraisals** show how well workers are doing their jobs. Typically, appraisal involves a regular written assessment as part of a multistep process that begins when a manager defines performance standards for an employee. The manager then observes the employee, and the process ends when manager and employee meet to discuss the appraisal.

3. Describe the main components of a compensation system.

A **compensation system** is the total package that a firm offers employees in return for their labor. The right combination of compensation elements will make employees feel valued while holding down company costs. Systems differ widely, but the dollar amounts paid to employees are key parts of all systems. **Wages** are paid for time worked (for example, by the hour). A **salary** is paid for discharging the responsibilities of a job. In setting levels, companies look at competitors' levels and also decide how internal levels should compare for different jobs.

Beyond a certain point, money motivates employees only when tied directly to performance. One way to establish this link is the use of **incentive programs**—special pay programs designed to motivate high performance. They may be applied on two different levels: (1) *Individual incentives*: Employees receive sales **bonuses**—special payments above their salaries—when they sell a certain number or certain dollar amount of goods. **Merit salary systems** link raises to performance levels in nonsales jobs. Under **pay for performance,** or **variable pay,** plans, middle managers are rewarded for especially productive output. (2) *Companywide incentives* apply to all of a firm's employees. Under **profit-sharing plans,** profits above a certain level go to employees. **Gainsharing plans** give out bonuses when costs are reduced through greater work efficiency. **Pay-for-knowledge plans** give additional pay to workers who learn new skills or different jobs.

Benefits—compensation other than wages and salaries—comprise a large percentage of most compensation budgets. The law requires most companies to provide social security retirement benefits and **workers' compensation insurance** (insurance for compensating workers injured on the job). Most companies provide health, life, and disability insurance; *retirement plans* pay pensions to workers when they retire. Sometimes, the company puts all the money in the pension fund; sometimes, it comes from both company and employees. Many companies are experimenting with cost-cutting plans, such as the **cafeteria benefit plan,** in which a certain dollar amount of benefits per employee is set aside so that each employee can choose from a variety of alternatives.

4. Describe some of the key legal issues involved in hiring, compensating, and managing workers in today's workplace.

HR management is heavily influenced by the law. One area of HR regulation is **equal employment opportunity**—regulation to protect people from unfair or inappropriate discrimination in the workplace. Discrimination in the workplace is illegal when distinctions among people are not job related. Because illegal discrimination is based on a prejudice about classes of individuals, laws protect various classes. A **protected class** consists of all individuals who share one or more common characteristics as indicated by a given law (such as race, color, religion, gender, age, national origin, and so forth). Enforcement of equal opportunity legislation is handled by the **Equal Employment Opportunity Commission,** or **EEOC,** which is responsible for federal regulations, and the Office of Federal Contract Compliance Programs, or OFCCP, which is responsible for executive orders applying to companies doing business with the government. Such a business must file an **affirmative action plan**—a written statement of how it intends to recruit, hire, and develop members of protected classes.

Other legislation deals with emerging legal issues, including the following: (1) *Employee safety and health*: The **Occupational Safety and Health Act of 1970,** or **OSHA,** guarantees that places of employment are free from hazard and is enforced by OSHA inspectors. (2) *Emerging areas of discrimination law*: There are three such areas: (i) *AIDS in the workplace*: Employers can't require an AIDS exam as a condition of employment and must treat AIDS like any other disease. (ii) *Sexual harassment:* **Sexual harassment** is defined as unwelcome sexual advances in the work environment. Employers will be held responsible for changing an environment by warning or perhaps firing harassers. The courts recognize two types of sexual harassment: (a) In cases of **quid pro quo harassment,** the harasser offers to exchange something of value for sexual favors. (b) A **hostile work environment** may develop, for example, when a group of male employees makes the work environment uncomfortable for a female colleague. (iii) *Employment-at-will*: Under the concept of **employment-at-will,** an organization employs an individual at its own will and can terminate employment at any time for any reason. Lawsuits, however, have limited employment-at-will provisions in certain circumstances.

5. *Discuss* **workforce diversity,** *the management of* **knowledge workers,** *and the use of a* **contingent workforce** *as important changes in the contemporary workplace.*

Three of the most important issues in HR management are the following: (1) **Workforce diversity** refers to the range of workers' attitudes, values, beliefs, and behaviors that differ by gender, race, age, ethnicity, physical ability, and other relevant characteristics. Many U.S. organizations regard diversity as a competitive advantage. (2) Employees who add value because of what they know are usually called **knowledge workers,** and managing them skillfully helps to determine which firms will be successful in the future. Knowledge workers generally require extensive specialized training.

(3) **Contingent workers,** including independent contractors, on-call workers, temporary employees, contract and leased employees, and part time employees, work for organizations on something other than a permanent or full-time basis. Managers must integrate such workers in a coordinated fashion, and they must carefully assess the real cost of using contingent workers, learning to adjust the direct differences in labor costs to account for differences in performance.

6. *Explain why workers organize and what* **labor unions** *do for their members.*

A **labor union** is a group of individuals working together to achieve shared job-related goals (higher pay, more job security, and so forth). **Labor relations** describes the process of dealing with employees represented by a union. Unions appeared and prospered because they forced management to listen to the complaints of all their workers rather than to just the few who were brave (or foolish) enough to speak out. Their power comes from collective action, such as **collective bargaining**—

the process by which union leaders and company managers negotiate conditions of employment for unionized workers. Although millions of workers still belong to unions, membership *as a percentage of the total workforce* has declined at a steady rate since the mid-1950s. Thus union power is much lower than it was just a few decades ago, and this decline has led to some significant trends in union–management relations.

In the past, most bargaining situations featured union demands for increases in wages and salaries. Now, however, unions often bargain for different benefits, such as job security. Another recent trend is union emphasis on improved pension programs. Unions now negotiate to preserve jobs for American workers in the face of business efforts to relocate to countries with lower labor costs.

7. *Explain the* **collective bargaining** *process and its possible outcomes.*

The collective bargaining process begins when the union is recognized as the negotiator for its members. The bargaining cycle begins when union leaders and management meet to agree on a contract. By law, both parties must bargain in good faith. Each presents its demands, and then the two sides focus on identifying the *bargaining zone*. When a compromise is reached, the new agreement is submitted to a vote by union membership.

Among issues that are important to union negotiators are the following: (1) *Compensation*: Unions try to convince management to raise current hourly wages and to secure good future compensation—wage rates to be paid during subsequent years of the contract. One tool for getting increases is a **cost-of-living adjustment (COLA)**—a contract clause tying future raises to changes in consumer purchasing power. **Wage reopener clauses** allow wage rates to be renegotiated at preset times during the life of a contract. (2) *Benefits*: Unions want employers to pay all or most of the costs of employees' insurance and also work to secure such benefits as retirement programs, paid holidays, and better working conditions. (3) *Job security*: Job security is an increasingly important issue. Unions may want employers to promise not to move or to reduce the workforce, but if they do, to use seniority to determine which employees keep their jobs.

An impasse occurs when management and labor fail to agree on a contract. Each side can use several tactics to support its cause until the impasse is resolved. The most important union tactic is the **strike,** which occurs when employees temporarily walk off the job and refuse to work. Most strikes are **economic strikes** resulting from stalemates over both economic and noneconomic issues (such as working hours). Illegal **sympathy strikes** (also called **secondary strikes**) occur when one union strikes in support of another. **Wildcat strikes**—strikes unauthorized by the union that occur during the life of a contract—deprive strikers of the protection of national labor law. Unions may also use **picketing,** in which workers march at an employer's facility to explain their reasons for striking. Under a **boycott,** union members agree not to buy the products of a targeted employer. During a work **slowdown,** workers perform their jobs at a much slower pace than normal. During a *sickout,* large numbers of workers call in sick.

Management may resort to **lockouts**—denying employees access to the workplace. A firm can also hire temporary or permanent replacements called **strikebreakers,** but the law forbids the permanent replacement of workers who strike because of unfair practices. An employer might also get a legal injunction to prohibit workers from striking or to prohibit a union from interfering with replacement workers.

Rather than use these tactics, labor and management can call in a third party to help resolve the dispute. In **mediation,** the neutral third party (the mediator) can suggest but can't impose a settlement. In **voluntary arbitration,** the third party (the arbitrator) dictates a settlement between the two sides, which have agreed to submit to outside judgment. **Compulsory arbitration,** which may be legally required, settles disputes between the government and public employees such as firefighters and police officers.

KEY TERMS

human resource management (HRM) (p. 218)
job analysis (p. 218)
job description (p. 218)
job specification (p. 218)
replacement chart (p. 219)
employee information system (skills inventory) (p. 219)
recruiting (p. 220)
internal recruiting (p. 220)
external recruiting (p. 220)
validation (p. 221)
on-the-job training (p. 223)
off-the-job training (p. 223)
vestibule training (p. 223)
performance appraisal (p. 223)
compensation system (p. 223)
wages (p. 223)
salary (p. 223)
incentive program (p. 225)
bonus (p. 225)
merit salary system (p. 225)

pay for performance (or variable pay) (p. 226)
profit-sharing plan (p. 226)
gainsharing plan (p. 226)
pay-for-knowledge plan (p. 226)
benefits (p. 226)
workers' compensation insurance (p. 226)
cafeteria benefit plan (p. 227)
equal employment opportunity (p. 227)
protected class (p. 228)
Equal Employment Opportunity Commission (EEOC) (p. 228)
affirmative action plan (p. 228)
Occupational Safety and Health Act of 1970 (OSHA) (p. 229)
sexual harassment (p. 230)
quid pro quo harassment (p. 230)
hostile work environment (p. 230)
employment-at-will (p. 230)
workforce diversity (p. 230)

knowledge workers (p. 231)
contingent worker (p. 233)
labor union (p. 234)
labor relations (p. 234)
collective bargaining (p. 235)
cost-of-living adjustment (COLA) (p. 238)
wage reopener clause (p. 238)
strike (p. 239)
economic strike (p. 239)
sympathy strike (or secondary strike) (p. 239)
wildcat strike (p. 239)
picketing (p. 239)
boycott (p. 239)
slowdown (p. 239)
lockout (p. 240)
strikebreaker (p. 240)
mediation (p. 240)
voluntary arbitration (p. 240)
compulsory arbitration (p. 240)

QUESTIONS AND EXERCISES

Questions for Review

1. What are the advantages and disadvantages of internal and external recruiting? Under what circumstances is each more appropriate?

2. Why is the formal training of workers so important to most employers? Why don't employers simply let people learn about their jobs as they perform them?

3. What different forms of compensation do firms typically use to attract and keep productive workers?

4. Why do workers in some companies unionize whereas workers in others do not?

Questions for Analysis

5. What are your views on drug testing in the workplace? What would you do if your employer asked you to submit to a drug test?

6. Workers at Ford, GM, and DaimlerChrysler are represented by the UAW. However, the UAW has been unsuccessful in its attempts to unionize U.S. workers employed at Toyota, Nissan, and Honda plants in the United States. Why do you think this is so?

7. What training do you think you are most likely to need when you finish school and start your career?

Managing Human Resources and Labor Relations Questions

VOCABULARY

1. Define *human resource (HR) management*.

2. Define *knowledge workers*. Describe how they differ from traditional workers in past eras.

3. Define *contingent workers*. Describe one advantage and one disadvantage of hiring contingent workers and one advantage and one disadvantage of being a contingent worker.

COMPREHENSION AND ANALYSIS

For questions 4 to 7, indicate whether the statement is true or false. If the statement is false, rewrite it to make it true.

4. The effectiveness of an HR department has a substantial impact on a company's bottom-line performance.

5. A company's compensation system has little impact on retaining skilled workers.

6. The basic goal of all equal employment opportunity regulation is to protect people from unfair or inappropriate discrimination in the workplace.

7. Because of declining membership, labor unions are no longer a major factor in the U.S. business world.

8. Describe how the unemployment rate affects the job of HR recruiters.

9. List and explain the three major components of a compensation system.

10. Griffin and Ebert list and explain several emerging legal issues that will likely become increasingly important in HR management. Describe one of these issues and tell why you think it is likely to become more important in the coming years.

11. Explain why workers organize and what labor unions do for their members. How might current employment trends affect unionization?

REFLECT AND CONNECT

12. Describe three things, in addition to the wage/salary, you would investigate before accepting a job.

Judgment Day

KIM CLARK

Ms. Clark is a senior staff writer at U. S. News & World Report, *where this article appeared in January 2003.*

VOCABULARY

eke out (¶2): make a little go a long way, stretch
allege (¶3): claim, contend

AN IDEA TO THINK ABOUT

The last time your boss (or instructor) evaluated your performance, did you think it was a fair appraisal of your work? If you could have changed one aspect of the evaluation, what would you have changed? *As you read,* look for the advantages and disadvantages of the various new approaches to performance appraisals.

JUDGMENT DAY

Kim Clark

[1]Of all the nerve-racking, stomach-churning days of the work year, only one is scheduled in advance: performance review day. The consolation used to be that it didn't matter much. If your boss checked "exceeds expectations," you might get a 6 percent raise. "Needs improvement" might get you just 2 percent. No big deal.

[2]Grab your antacid: It's a big deal now. Companies, desperate to eke out ever more returns on their human capital, are using computers to turn every day into rating day. And they are turning every customer, subordinate, and peer into a rater. Most important, the companies have raised the stakes in a go-slow economy. Increasingly, top ratings are rewarded with eye-opening goodies like 30 percent bonuses. And in nearly two-thirds of all companies, a subpar rating can mean a pink slip.

BIASED?

[3]These changes are turning what was once a mild annoyance into one of the hottest workplace controversies. Some researchers and disillusioned executives say some of the newest appraisal methods aren't returning the promised profits. And some workers claim the new systems are biased. A corporate Who's Who—including Ford, Goodyear, General Electric, and Capital One—have been sued for adopting tough new systems that, workers allege, are designed to weed out workers of a specific race, age, or gender rather than just poor performers.

[4]But the controversy isn't likely to curb the trend toward new and different appraisal systems. If anything, companies will tinker even more, says University of Wisconsin management Prof. Ken De Meuse. "When times were good, companies could retain fat more than they can today," he says.

[5]One of the biggest and most controversial trends: changing who does the ratings. The traditional method of having only a boss rate an employee has been criticized for almost 2,000 years. A third-century Chinese

philosopher complained that one civil service evaluator "seldom rates men according to their merits but always according to his likes and dislikes." And modern-day research confirms what every employee knows: A boss who happens to be in a bad mood gives employees harsher ratings. Studies also show that managers' subconscious stereotypes about race, age, physical attractiveness, and other characteristics affect their ratings.

[6]In an attempt at greater fairness, companies began trying out "360-degree" appraisals in the 1990s. Today, one-fifth of all employers build such well-rounded appraisals with comments from customers, subordinates, and peers as well as bosses. Michael Lieberman, vice president of marketing for Synygy, a Philadelphia-area firm that sells rating systems to other companies, likes what 360-degree appraisals do for his firm. At previous employers, he noticed lots of office politics as workers tried to ingratiate themselves with the one or two managers who controlled their careers. "But there is very little politicking here," he says, "You had better treat people with respect," because anyone can submit a rating on any employee.

[7]Despite their logic and rising popularity, 360s have drawn plenty of flak. A 2002 study by the Watson Wyatt consulting firm found that companies using 360s returned, on average, 10.6 percent less to shareholders than did companies using more-traditional reviews. Watson Wyatt theorized that while the 360 idea is sound, it's time consuming, and too many companies stint on training needed to make sure raters give constructive criticism. De Meuse says anyone who watched the *Survivor* TV show knows the problems of badly run 360s. "One way to make me look better is to make you look bad," he says. "And people make alliances."

[8]Companies are also changing how frequently they rate workers. The old once-a-year rating often really only covered the previous three months, since studies have found most people tend to forget events further back in time. But now, using computer programs similar to those that track telephone operators' minute-to-minute performance, companies are reviewing performance of all kinds of workers much more frequently. Health insurers and retailers are experimenting with monitoring systems that can appraise claims processors' and salespeople's daily performance, and hand out bonuses or warnings as often as every month. And Seagate Technology last year started requiring high-level executives and engineers to fill out computer forms reporting on their progress toward company goals each week.

TOP TO BOTTOM.

[9]The most controversial change, though, dates to when Jack Welch took over as CEO of General Electric in 1981. Welch was intent on breaking up GE's legendary bureaucracy. His idea: Instead of following a traditional system, in which bosses could—and often did—rate all their employees as "above average," Welch had executives identify the top 20 percent of managers and mark them for advancement. They also had to identify the bottom 10 percent, who would then either have to improve or leave. As GE's profits soared, legions of executives copied that "forced ranking" system.

[10]Today, one-third of all employers use such rankings on at least some of their staff, more than double the 1997 level. And fully two-thirds of all

U.S. companies use performance as at least one factor when deciding whom to lay off. Dick Grote, a former GE executive who has helped dozens of companies install forced ranking systems, says executives like them because they are the fairest and easiest way to downsize. "The alternative is retaining people who are less competent" and promoting people who aren't stars, he says.

[11]But in a slew of class action lawsuits, workers who have been given low ranks say that it is the companies that deserve the flunking grade in meritocracy. Until 2001, Jack McGilvrey, 59, got good ratings throughout his 36 years as a chemist for Goodyear. Then, executives at the Akron, Ohio, tire company said they would try to boost profits by insisting that 10 percent of the staff be rated as "A performers" and tagged for promotion, and 10 percent rated C and tagged for improvement or eventual dismissal.

[12]In a complaint filed in federal court last fall, McGilvrey and seven other workers say that it was older employees like them and not the poor performers who got the C's. After McGilvrey received a second C rating in May of 2002, he says he was terminated. Just a few days after he was forced out, he received a patent for a new kind of aircraft tire. "It is very unfair to start out with the assumption that a certain percentage of your employees are unsatisfactory," McGilvrey says. "It was very subjective and designed to weed out the older people."

[13]Goodyear, which scrapped the forced ranking system shortly before McGilvrey's lawsuit was filed, is fighting the case, saying the appraisals weren't biased. Forced rankings "worked wonderfully for GE," says Goodyear spokesman Keith Price. But internal confusion over what the letter grades meant was distracting Goodyear employees from the goal of improving company performance, he says. Goodyear is now pinning its hopes on a revamped appraisal system. Managers are taking a one-day training course on how to give ratings such as "exceeds expectations" based on progress toward clearly stated and pragmatic company goals such as meeting delivery deadlines.

[14]The flurry of lawsuits is prompting many other companies to make similar changes. After settling an age discrimination suit of its own, Ford last year also scrapped rankings. And a growing number of other employers are newly unhappy with the GE system. In a fall 2002 survey by DDI, only 39 percent of companies using forced rankings found them to be even "moderately effective." The lawsuits aren't slowing down the rate of change, however. Instead, employers are making more changes to jury-proof their appraisals by backing up ratings with evidence and objective data. "The use of data really helps avoid litigation," says Linda Martin, a Seattle-based appraisal expert for Towers, Perrin. She says clients are increasingly asking for help "calibrating" ratings across departments so that employees who might be rated A in one department aren't given C's in another. These kinds of changes not only prevent lawsuits but also make appraisals fairer and more accurate, she says. Nobody likes litigation, of course. But the result, in this case, could be a little more fairness and a little less stress in the workplace.

Judgment Day Questions

VOCABULARY

1. Explain what De Meuse means when he says, "When times were good, companies could retain fat more than they can today." (¶4)

2. Explain what Wyatt means when he says, ". . . while the 360 idea is sound. . . too many companies stint on training needed to make sure raters give constructive criticism." (¶7)

COMPREHENSION AND ANALYSIS

For questions 3 to 5, indicate whether the statement is true or false. If the statement is false, rewrite it to make it true.

3. Most companies hope that improving the effectiveness of performance appraisals will increase profits.

4. We will likely see companies doing even more experimenting with new and different appraisal systems.

5. Everyone agrees that the "forced ranking" system is the fairest way to downsize.

6. In a traditional appraisal system, who rates the employee? List one disadvantage of the traditional method.

7. In a 360-degree appraisal system, who rates the employee? List one advantage and one disadvantage of the 360-degree method.

8. Explain the forced ranking system (also called the GE system) and why it is controversial.

9. Describe two changes employers are making to prevent lawsuits and also make appraisals fairer and more accurate. Does Clark believe the changes will be effective?

REFLECT AND CONNECT

10. If you could choose which performance appraisal method your boss was going to use, would you select a traditional, 360-degree, or forced ranking system? Please explain your selection. Would you choose that same method if you were selecting an appraisal system to use on people working for you? Please explain.

Stop Stereotyping: Overcome Your Worst Diversity Enemy

SONDRA THIEDERMAN

Dr. Thiederman is a contributing writer for Monster.com.

AN IDEA TO THINK ABOUT

Has anyone ever "assumed" you would or would not do something, react in a particular way, or enjoy or not enjoy a specific activity because of a personal characteristic such as your sex, hair color, or race? What kinds of problems did it create? *As you read,* find out why it's important for us to avoid stereotypical thinking.

STOP STEREOTYPING: OVERCOME YOUR WORST DIVERSITY ENEMY

Sondra Thiederman

[1]Perceiving individuals accurately is an important skill for anyone who wants to get hired and be successful once on the job. And while most people strive to understand those who are different, the tendency to stereotype can skew perceptions. Still, it's important to comprehend the difference between a stereotype and a reasonable generality about a group of people.

[2]The thing that distinguishes a stereotype from other types of generalities is that stereotypes are inflexible. When we generalize, for example, that all men may like sports, that women tend to be nurturing or that people from parts of Asia generally value saving face, we are making working generalities. These are flexible, and we clearly recognize they do not apply to all members of those groups.

[3]Stereotypes are different from working generalities in that they are applied inflexibly to all members of a group. It is one thing to say, "Some gay men are artistic," and another to declare with certainty that, "All gay men are artistic." The latter statement, and ones like it, are just plain inaccurate. In fact, anthropologists have established there are more differences within groups than between them. For those of us who like life and relationships to be simple, this is bad news and might make us a bit uncomfortable, but the brutal reality is that inflexible stereotypes will always be wrong.

[4]Given that stereotypes are so wrong, it is odd how quickly they are learned. Our family, friends, coworkers and the media all easily implant these inflexible categories on our impressionable minds and hearts. The most powerful source of stereotypes, however, is our own negative experiences.

[5]The reason negative experiences are more apt to create stereotypes is that we want so much to keep from repeating them. A child touches a hot stove and feels pain. From that experience, he generalizes all hot stoves will cause pain. This learning mechanism works great with hot stoves but is less effective with people and human behavior. Just because one man is sexist, it does not mean all are. Just because one disabled person takes advantage of status does not mean they all will. Just because one white person is racist does not mean all are.

[6]Even the most enlightened among us resist giving up the stereotypes that make us feel more secure and in control. Here's how to let go:

- *Identify Stereotypes.* [7]One challenge to ridding ourselves of stereotypes is the fact that we are unaware of what they are. Identifying your stereotypes is easier than you think. It is a matter of monitoring your thoughts when you hear an ethnic last name, see a skin color, hear an accent, see a disability, learn that a person is gay, etc.

- *Look for Consistency.* [8]Do you have the same reaction to members of a given group each time you encounter them? Ask yourself: "Do I have these reactions before or after I have a chance to know the individual?" If the answer is before, these are your stereotypes. Practice labeling these automatic responses as stereotypes and reminding yourself that they have little validity as accurate indicators of an individual's character, skills or personality.

- *Push Stereotypes Aside.* [9]After you have identified your stereotypes, learn to shove them aside long enough to see individuals for who they are. Stereotyping is a habit. Just as it is learned through repetition, it can be unlearned through practice. Each time a thought you have identified as a stereotype appears, push it aside. Do not judge yourself harshly; after all, it is just a thought and not an action.

[10]Without stereotypes blocking your view, you will be able to see individuals accurately, not as mere reflections of your preconception. The more you do this, the more experiences you will have with individuals who do not conform to your stereotypes and, in turn, the less credibility those stereotypes will have.

Stop Stereotyping: Overcome Your Worst Diversity Enemy Questions

VOCABULARY

1. Define *stereotype*.

2. Explain what Thiederman means when she says, ". . . the tendency to stereotype can skew perceptions." (¶1)

COMPREHENSION AND ANALYSIS

For questions 3 to 5, indicate whether the statement is true or false. If the statement is false, rewrite it to make it true.

3. Anthropologists have established there are more differences within groups than between them.

4. Stereotyping is a habit that, with practice, can be unlearned.

5. Stereotyping will always be wrong.

6. What distinguishes a stereotype from other types of generalities?

7. Predict one problem that stereotyping could cause in your workplace or classroom.

8. List and explain two actions a person can use to start letting go of his or her stereotypes.

9. State Thiederman's thesis.

REFLECT AND CONNECT

10. Describe a situation in which you stereotyped someone. Indicate the kinds of problems it caused and some steps you can take to rid yourself of the habit.

What Should I Do with My Life?

PO BRONSON

Mr. Bronson is the author of three best-selling books. This article from Fast Company *is adapted from his newest book,* What Should I Do with My Life? The True Story of People Who Answered the Ultimate Question *(Random House, January 2003).*

AN IDEA TO THINK ABOUT

Do you and your classmates ask questions like, "What will be the hottest new jobs?" "What jobs will pay the most?" "What company will put me on a fast track for promotions?" *As you read,* find out why Bronson thinks it's time for us to start asking, and answering, a very different question.

WHAT SHOULD I DO WITH MY LIFE?

Po Bronson

¹It's time to define the new era. Our faith has been shaken. We've lost confidence in our leaders and in our institutions. Our beliefs have been tested. We've discredited the notion that the Internet would change everything (and the stock market would buy us an exit strategy from the grind). Our expectations have been dashed. We've abandoned the idea that work should be a 24-hour-a-day rush and that careers should be a wild adventure. Yet we're still holding on.

²We're seduced by the idea that picking up the pieces and simply tweaking the formula will get the party started again. In spite of our best thinking and most searing experience, our ideas about growth and success are mired in a boom-bust mentality. Just as LBOs gave way to IPOs, the market is primed for the next engine of wealth creation. Just as we traded in the pinstripes and monster bonuses of the Wall Street era for T-shirts and a piece of the action during the startup revolution, we're waiting to latch on to the new trappings of success. (I understand the inclination. I've surfed from one boom to the next for most of my working life—from my early days as a bond trader to my most recent career as a writer tracking the migration of my generation from Wall Street to Silicon Valley.)

[3]There's a way out. Instead of focusing on what's *next,* let's get back to what's *first.* The previous era of business was defined by the question, Where's the opportunity? I'm convinced that business success in the future starts with the question, What should I do with my life? Yes, that's right. The most obvious and universal question on our plates as human beings is the most urgent and pragmatic approach to sustainable success in our organizations. People don't succeed by migrating to a "hot" industry (one word: dotcom) or by adopting a particular career-guiding mantra (remember "horizontal careers"?). They thrive by focusing on the question of who they really are—and connecting that to work that they truly love (and, in so doing, unleashing a productive and creative power that they never imagined). Companies don't grow because they represent a particular sector or adopt the latest management approach. They win because they engage the hearts and minds of individuals who are dedicated to answering that life question.

[4]This is not a new idea. But it may be the most powerfully pressing one ever to be disrespected by the corporate world. There are far too many smart, educated, talented people operating at quarter speed, unsure of their place in the world, contributing far too little to the productive engine of modern civilization. There are far too many people who look like they have their act together but have yet to make an impact. You know who you are. It comes down to a simple gut check: You either love what you do or you don't. Period.

[5]Those who are lit by that passion are the object of envy among their peers and the subject of intense curiosity. They are the source of good ideas. They make the extra effort. They demonstrate the commitment. They are the ones who, day by day, will rescue this drifting ship. And they will be rewarded. With money, sure, and responsibility, undoubtedly. But with something even better too: the kind of satisfaction that comes with knowing your place in the world. We are sitting on a huge potential boom in productivity—if we could just get the square pegs out of the round holes.

[6]Of course, addressing the question, What should I do with my life? isn't just a productivity issue: It's a moral imperative. It's how we hold ourselves accountable to the opportunity we're given. Most of us are blessed with the ultimate privilege: We get to be true to our individual nature. Our economy is so vast that we don't have to grind it out forever at jobs we hate. For the most part, we get to choose. That choice isn't about a career search so much as an identity quest. Asking The Question aspires to end the conflict between who you are and what you do. There is nothing more brave than filtering out the chatter that tells you to be someone you're not. There is nothing more genuine than breaking away from the chorus to learn the sound of your own voice. Asking The Question is nothing short of an act of courage: It requires a level of commitment and clarity that is almost foreign to our working lives.

[7]During the past two years, I have listened to the life stories of more than 900 people who have dared to be honest with themselves. Of those, I chose 70 to spend considerable time with in order to learn how they did it. Complete strangers opened their lives and their homes to me. I slept on their couches. We went running together. They cried in my arms. We traded secrets. I met their families. I went to one's wedding. I witnessed many critical turning points.

[8]These are ordinary people. People of all ages, classes, and professions—from a catfish farmer in Mississippi to a toxic-waste inspector in the oil fields of Texas, from a police officer in East Los Angeles to a long-haul trucker in Pennsylvania, from a financier in Hong Kong to a minister at a church on the Oregon coast. These people don't have any resources or character traits that give them an edge in pursuing their dream. Some have succeeded; many have not. Only two have what accountants call "financial independence." Only two are so smart that they would succeed at anything they chose (though having more choices makes answering The Question that much harder). Only one, to me, is saintly. They're just people who faced up to it, armed with only their weaknesses, equipped with only their fears.

[9]What I learned from them was far more powerful than what I had expected or assumed. The first assumption to get busted was the notion that certain jobs are inherently cool and that others are uncool. That was a big shift for me. Throughout the 1990s, my basic philosophy was this: Work = Boring, *but* Work + Speed + Risk = Cool. Speed and risk transformed the experience into something so stimulating, so exciting, so intense, that we began to believe that those qualities defined "good work." Now, betrayed by the reality of economic uncertainty and global instability, we're casting about for what really matters when it comes to work.

[10]On my journey, I met people in bureaucratic organizations and bland industries who were absolutely committed to their work. That commitment sustained them through slow stretches and setbacks. They never watched the clock, never dreaded Mondays, never worried about the years passing by. They didn't wonder where they belonged in life. They were phenomenally productive and confident in their value. In places unusual and unexpected, they had found their calling, and those callings were as idiosyncratic as each individual.

[11]And this is where the second big insight came in: Your calling isn't something you inherently "know," some kind of destiny. Far from it. Almost all of the people I interviewed found their calling after great difficulty. They had made mistakes before getting it right. For instance, the catfish farmer used to be an investment banker, the truck driver had been an entertainment lawyer, a chef had been an academic, and the police officer was a Harvard MBA. Everyone discovered latent talents that weren't in their skill sets at age 25.

[12]Most of us don't get epiphanies. We only get a whisper—a faint urge. That's it. That's the call. It's up to you to do the work of discovery, to connect it to an answer. Of course, there's never a single right answer. At some point, it feels right enough that you choose, and the energy formerly spent casting about is now devoted to making your choice fruitful.

[13]This lesson in late, hard-fought discovery is good news. What it means is that today's confused can be tomorrow's dedicated. The current difficult climate serves as a form of reckoning. The tougher the times, the more clarity you gain about the difference between what really matters and what you only pretend to care about. The funny thing is that most people have good instincts about where they belong but make poor choices and waste productive years on the wrong work. Why we do this cuts to the heart of the question, What should I do with my life? These wrong turns hinge on a small number of basic assumptions that have ruled our working lives, career choices, and ambitions for the better part

of two decades. I found hardly any consistencies in how the people I interviewed discovered what they love to do—the human soul resists taxonomy—*except* when it came to four misconceptions (about money, smarts, place, and attitude) that have calcified into hobbling fears. These are stumbling blocks that we need to uproot before we can find our way to where we really belong.

MONEY DOESN'T FUND DREAMS

[14]Shouldn't I make money first—to fund my dream? The notion that there's an order to your working life is an almost classic assumption: Pay your dues, and then tend to your dream. I expected to find numerous examples of the truth of this path. But I didn't find any.

[15]Sure, I found tons of rich guys who were now giving a lot away to charity or who had bought an island. I found plenty of people who had found something meaningful and original to do after making their money. But that's not what I'm talking about. I'm talking about the garden-variety fantasy: Put your calling in a lockbox, go out and make a ton of money, and then come back to the lockbox to pick up your calling where you left it.

[16]It turns out that having the financial independence to walk away rarely triggers people to do just that. The reality is, making money is such hard work that it changes you. It takes twice as long as anyone plans for. It requires more sacrifices than anyone expects. You become so emotionally invested in that world—and psychologically adapted to it—that you don't really want to ditch it.

[17]I met many people who had left the money behind. But having "enough" didn't trigger the change. It had to get personal: Something had to happen such as divorce, the death of a parent, or the recognition that the long hours were hurting one's children. (One man, Don Linn, left investment banking after he came home from a business trip and his two-year-old son *didn't recognize him*.)

[18]The ruling assumption is that money is the *shortest* route to freedom. Absurdly, that strategy is cast as the "practical approach." But in truth, the opposite is true. The shortest route to the good life involves building the confidence that you can live happily within your means (whatever the means provided by the choices that are truly acceptable to you turn out to be). It's scary to imagine living on less. But embracing your dreams is surprisingly liberating. Instilled with a sense of purpose, your spending habits naturally reorganize, because you discover that you *need* less.

[19]This is an extremely threatening conclusion. It suggests that the vast majority of us aren't just putting our dreams on ice—we're killing them. Joe Olchefske almost lost his forever. Joe started out in life with an interest in government. In the early 1980s, he made what seemed like a minor compromise: When he graduated from Harvard's Kennedy School of Government, he went into public finance. He wouldn't work *in* government, he'd work *with* government.

[20]Joe went on to run Piper Jaffray in Seattle. By the mid-1990s, he realized that one little compromise had defined his life. "I didn't want to be a high-priced midwife," he said. "I wanted to be a mother. It was never *my* deal. It was my clients' deal. They were taking the risk. They were building hospitals and bridges and freeways, not me. I envied them for that."

[21]One night, riding up the elevator of his apartment building, Joe met newly hired Seattle schools superintendent John Stanford. Soon after, Stanford offered Olchefske a job as his CFO—and partner in turning the troubled school system around. Olchefske accepted. Stanford rallied the city around school reform and earned the nickname Prophet of Hope. Meanwhile, Olchefske slashed millions from the budget and bloodlessly fired principals, never allowing his passions to interfere with his decisions. People called him Prophet of Doom.

[22]Then Stanford died suddenly of leukemia. It was one of the great crises in the city's history. Who could fill this void? Certainly not the green-eyeshade CFO. But Stanford's death transformed Olchefske. It broke him open, and he discovered in himself a new ability to connect with people emotionally, not just rationally. As the new superintendent, he draws on that gift more than on his private-sector skills. He puts up with a lot of bureaucrap, but he says that avoiding crap shouldn't be the objective in finding the right work. The right question is, How can I find something that moves my heart, so that the inevitable crap storm is bearable?

SMARTS CAN'T ANSWER THE QUESTION

[23]If the lockbox fantasy is a universal and eternal stumbling block when it comes to answering The Question, the idea that smarts and intensity are the essential building blocks of success and satisfaction is a product of the past decade. A set of twin misconceptions took root during the celebration of risk and speed that was the 90s startup revolution. The first is the idea that a smart, motivated individual with a great idea can accomplish *anything*. The corollary is that work should be fun, a thrill ride full of constant challenge and change.

[24]Those assumptions are getting people into trouble. So what if your destiny doesn't stalk you like a lion? Can you *think* your way to the answer? That's what Lori Gottlieb thought. She considered her years as a rising television executive in Hollywood to be a big mistake. She became successful but felt like a fraud. So she quit and gave herself three years to analyze which profession would engage her brain the most. She literally attacked the question. She dug out her diaries from childhood. She took classes in photography and figure drawing. She interviewed others who had left Hollywood. She broke down every job by skill set and laid that over a grid of her innate talents. She filled out every exercise in *What Color Is Your Parachute?*

[25]Eventually, she arrived at the following logic: Her big brain loved puzzles. Who solves puzzles? Doctors solve health puzzles. Therefore, become a doctor. She enrolled in premed classes at Pepperdine. Her med-school applications were so persuasive that every school wanted her. And then—can you see where this is headed?—Lori dropped out of Stanford Medical School after only two and a half months. Why? She realized that she didn't like hanging around sick people all day.

[26]The point is, being smarter doesn't make answering The Question easier. Using the brain to solve this problem usually only leads to answers that make the brain happy and jobs that provide what I call "brain candy." Intense mental stimulation. But it's just that: *candy*. A synthetic substitute for other types of gratification that can be ultimately more rewarding and

enduring. As the cop in East L.A. said of his years in management at Rockwell, "It was like cheap wood that burns too fast."

[27]I struggled with this myself, but not until I had listened to hundreds of others did the pattern make itself shockingly clear. What am I good at? is the wrong starting point. People who attempt to *deduce* an answer usually end up mistaking intensity for passion. To the heart, they are vastly different. Intensity comes across as a pale *busyness,* while passion is meaningful and fulfilling. A simple test: Is your choice something that will stimulate you for a year or something that you can be passionate about for 10 years?

[28]This test is tougher than it seems on paper. In the past decade, the work world has become a battleground for the struggle between the boring and the stimulating. The emphasis on intensity has seeped into our value system. We still cling to the idea that work should not only be challenging and meaningful—but also invigorating and entertaining. But really, work should be like life: sometimes fun, sometimes moving, often frustrating, and defined by meaningful events. Those who have found their place don't talk about how exciting and challenging and stimulating their work is. Their language invokes a different troika: meaningful, significant, fulfilling. And they rarely ever talk about work without weaving in their personal history.

PLACE DEFINES YOU

[29]Every industry has a culture. And every culture is driven by a value system. In Hollywood, where praise is given too easily and thus has been devalued, the only honest metric is box-office receipts. So box-office receipts are all-important. In Washington, DC, some very powerful politicians are paid middling salaries, so power and money are not equal. Power is measured by the size of your staff and by how many people you can influence. In police work, you learn to be suspicious of ordinary people driving cars and walking down the street.

[30]One of the most common mistakes is not recognizing how these value systems will shape you. People think that they can insulate themselves, that they're different. They're not. The relevant question in looking at a job is not *What will I do?* but *Who will I become?* What belief system will you adopt, and what will take on heightened importance in your life? Because once you're rooted in a particular system—whether it's medicine, New York City, Microsoft, or a startup—it's often agonizingly difficult to unravel yourself from its values, practices, and rewards. Your money is good anywhere, but respect and status are only a local currency. They get heavily discounted when taken elsewhere. If you're successful at the wrong thing, the mix of praise and opportunity can lock you in forever.

[31]Don Linn, the investment banker who took over the catfish farm in Mississippi, learned this lesson the hard way. After years as a star at PaineWebber and First Boston, he dropped out when he could no longer bring himself to push deals on his clients that he knew wouldn't work. His life change smacked of foolish originality: 5.5 million catfish on 1,500 water acres. His first day, he had to clip the wings of a flock of geese. Covered in goose shit and blood, he wondered what he had gotten himself into. But he figured it out and grew his business into a $16 million operation with five side businesses. More important, the work reset his

moral compass. In farming, success doesn't come at another farmer's expense. You learn to cooperate, sharing processing plants, feed mills, and pesticide-flying services.

³²Like Don, you'll be a lot happier if you aren't fighting the value system around you. Find one that enforces a set of beliefs that you can really get behind. There's a powerful transformative effect when you surround yourself with like-minded people. Peer pressure is a great thing when it helps you accomplish your goals instead of distracting you from them.

³³Carl Kurlander wrote the movie *St. Elmo's Fire* when he was 24. For years afterward, he lived in Beverly Hills. He wanted to move back to Pittsburgh, where he grew up, to write books, but he was always stopped by the doubt, Would it really make any difference to write from Pittsburgh instead of from Beverly Hills? His books went unwritten. Last year, when a looming Hollywood writers' strike coincided with a job opening in the creative-writing department at Pitt, he finally summoned the courage to move. He says that being in academia is like "bathing in altruism." Under its influence, he wrote his first book, a biography of the comic Louie Anderson.

ATTITUDE IS THE BIGGEST OBSTACLE

³⁴Environment matters, but in the end, when it comes to tackling the question, What should I do with my life? it really is all in your head. The first psychological stumbling block that keeps people from finding themselves is that they feel guilty for simply taking the quest seriously. They think that it's a self-indulgent privilege of the educated upper class. Working-class people manage to be happy without trying to "find themselves," or so the myth goes.

³⁵But I found that just about anybody can find this question important. It's not just for free agents, knowledge workers, and serial entrepreneurs. I met many working-class people who found this question essential. They might have fewer choices, but they still care. Take Bart Handford. He went from working the graveyard shift at a Kimberley-Clark baby-wipes plant in Arkansas to running the Department of Agriculture's rural-development program. He didn't do this by just pulling up his bootstraps. His breakthrough came when his car was hit by a train, and he spent six months in bed exploring The Question.

³⁶Probably the most debilitating obstacle to taking on The Question is the fear that making a choice is a one-way ride, that starting down a path means closing a door forever.

³⁷"Keeping your doors open" is a trap. It's an excuse to stay uninvolved. I call the people who have the hardest time closing doors Phi Beta Slackers. They hop between esteemed grad schools, fat corporate gigs, and prestigious fellowships, looking as if they have their act together but still feeling like observers, feeling as if they haven't come close to living up to their potential.

³⁸Leela de Souza almost got lost in that trap. At age 15, Leela knew exactly what she wanted to be when she grew up: a dancer. She pursued that dream, supplementing her meager dancer's pay with work as a runway model. But she soon began to feel that she had left her intellect behind. So, in her early twenties, with several good years left on her legs, she took the SATs and applied to college. She paid for a $100,000 education at the

University of Chicago with the money that she had earned from modeling and during the next seven years made a series of seemingly smart decisions: a year in Spain, Harvard Business School, McKinsey & Co., a White House Fellowship, high-tech PR. But she never got any closer to making a real choice.

[39]Like most Phi Beta Slackers, she was cursed with tremendous ability and infinite choices. Figuring out what to do with her life was constantly on her mind. But then she figured something else out: Her need to look brilliant was what was keeping her from truly answering The Question. When she let go of that, she was able to shift gears from asking "What do I do next?" to making strides toward answering "To what can I devote my life?"

[40]Asking What Should I Do With My Life? is the modern, secular version of the great timeless questions about our identity. Asking The Question aspires to end the conflict between who you are and what you do. Answering The Question is the way to protect yourself from being lathed into someone you're not. What is freedom for if not the chance to define for yourself who you are?

[41]I have spent the better part of the past two years in the company of people who have dared to confront where they belong. They didn't always find an ultimate answer, but taking the question seriously helped get them closer. We are all writing the story of our own life. It's not a story of conquest. It's a story of discovery. Through trial and error, we learn what gifts we have to offer the world and are pushed to greater recognition about what we really need. The Big Bold Leap turns out to be only the first step.

What Should I Do with My Life? Questions

VOCABULARY

1. Explain what Bronson means when he says, "Most of us don't get epiphanies. We only get a whisper—a faint urge." (¶12)

2. Explain what Bronson means when he says, "Every industry has a culture. And every culture is driven by a value system." (¶29)

COMPREHENSION AND ANALYSIS

3. Describe the process Bronson used to arrive at his conclusions.

4. What is The Question?

5. What does it take for people to survive and thrive?

6. What are two characteristics of people who love what they do?

7. Explain why Bronson believes that addressing The Question is a moral imperative.

8. Describe the two big "insights" Bronson gained from his journey.

9. Bronson said he found hardly any consistencies in how the people he interviewed discovered what they love to do except when it came to four topics. List the four topics people have misconceptions about that create stumbling blocks.

10. Why does Bronson feel that asking, What am I good at? is the wrong starting point?

11. State Bronson's thesis.

REFLECT AND CONNECT

12. Bronson says, "We are all writing the story of our own life. It's not a story of conquest. It's a story of discovery. Through trial and error, we learn what gifts we have to offer the world and are pushed to greater recognition about what we really need." Describe some of the "gifts you have to offer the world" and some of the "things you really need."

Money and Motivation

THOMAS PETZINGER, JR

Mr. Petzinger has spent 21 years at The Wall Street Journal *as a beat reporter, investigative reporter, bureau chief, and Washington ecomomics editor, and weekly columnist. He is the author of three books. This selection is excerpted from Chapter 8 of his best-selling book* The New Pioneers: The Men and Women Who Are Transforming the Workplace and the Marketplace.

VOCABULARY

> *ethos (¶10):* culture and philosophy
> *anthropomorphic (¶18):* giving human characteristics to an animal or object
> *incredulous (¶25):* disbelieving, skeptical

AN IDEA TO THINK ABOUT

Is there any job you would *not* do, no matter how much money someone offered you? Is there any job you would do even if the salary was low? *As you read,* find out what motivates people besides money.

MONEY AND MOTIVATION

Thomas Petzinger, Jr

¹In the spring of 1997 outfielder Al Martin of the Pittsburgh Pirates made professional sports history: He left money on the table.

²Not chicken scratch, either. Though already handsomely paid at about $2 million a year, his contract was up for renewal and he was free to talk to another team. He could easily have locked in additional millions elsewhere. Everyone in the league was positive he could double his salary. Yet with hardly a thought he signed a new contract committing him to the

Pirates until the year 2000, with a modest salary increase. Sports agents cringed. The players' union was aghast. It seemed almost un-American. It was definitely un-baseball. What kind of elite athlete walks away from money?

[3]Martin grew up in a working-class neighborhood near Los Angeles surrounded by great athletes. He watched an uncle build a long and rewarding career as a defensive back with the Oakland Raiders of football. Then he watched a brother wind up with much less after jumping among the Raiders, Pittsburgh Steelers, and Buffalo Bills of football. So when Al Martin left USC for professional baseball he resolved to start and end his career in a single city, wherever he happened to reach the major leagues first. After seven years and 963 games in the minors, that turned out to be Pittsburgh. He was a .300 hitter with a reliable glove in left field, and his salary climbed steadily.

[4]Pittsburgh happens to be where I live these days. And although I have never been much of a baseball fan, you can't live here without recognizing that Pittsburgh has very demanding and moody fans. This was especially so after the 1994 players' strike. Diamond-studded ballplayers go over poorly in a lunch-pail town like Pittsburgh. So despite a solid playoff record and the presence of many league-leading players, the Pirates were losing favor with their fans. Attendance at the Sovietesque Three Rivers Stadium, never a sellout to begin with, plunged further.

[5]Then, in 1996, some new nickel-biting owners came in, offering to release every high-priced player from his contract in order to rebuild the team with cheap recruits. Freed to sign richer deals elsewhere, every big-name player immediately bolted, except Al Martin.

[6]A short time later Martin showed up at 1997 spring training to find himself surrounded by a bunch of minor-leaguers, many from as far down as single-A. It was like something out of *The Bad News Bears*. They were barely shaving! Many earned the major-league minimum of $150,000 a year. The entire Pirate roster, in fact, made barely $10 million a year, less than the Chicago White Sox paid a single player, Albert Belle. By baseball standards the Pirates were so working class they clipped grocery coupons and treated their clubhouse supper as a feast. "On most teams guys will take a few bites and go home or go out to eat," Martin said. "On this ball club we have guys loading up two and three plates and then wrapping some up for leftovers. I'm not kidding. You see guys carrying food out of here."[1]

[7]The competition laughed, the fans rolled their eyes, and the pundits roundly predicted a hundred losses for the season. There wasn't a soul who followed baseball predicting the Pirates would wind up anywhere but dead last in their division. Even the new owners, stifling their delight at fielding the cheapest team in baseball, could promise no more than a "rebuilding" year.

[8]Looking around him at camp, Martin realized that if leadership were to come from anywhere it would be from him. At barely thirty years old he was the granddaddy of this team, and the only one, it would appear, with the chance of a league-leading performance. So he built a culture of hard work. "This," he told people, "is how we will do business." When everybody else was still eating Egg McMuffins, Martin was already in the batting cage. He was the first to break a sweat, the first to leap to his feet, the first to greet a player returning to the dugout after a big play. "He leads by

example," the first baseman Kevin Young told me later in the Pirates club-house. "It's something the younger players feed off of."

[9]The youth and low pay of his teammates strengthened his leadership. "If you bring in veterans from other places, they bring in their own baggage," he explained on one occasion. "With young guys, it's kind of like putty. You can mold them and build something that's mainstream throughout the organization. 'This is how we go about our business. This is the way we play. If you don't agree with it, you're not going to be here.' You can't do that with a bunch of veterans that make a lot of money."[2]

[10]In an ingenious (if unwitting) display of systems thinking, the Pirates' marketing people picked up on the team's work ethic and realized how smoothly it would harmonize with the ethos of the hometown crowd. They created a new logo for the team: a lunch pail. They rolled out a new marketing slogan: "Let's go to work." And they filmed brazenly cheap-looking TV spots that featured various ballplayers moonlighting in unlikely jobs: one as a lifeguard, another as a crossing guard. Al Martin was shown in uniform turning a wrench under the hood of a car, an air wrench wheezing in the background. "Come see the team that works as hard as you do," the announcer said.

[11]The season opened, and to the astonishment of everyone, the Pirates were winning ballgames, barely more than half, to be sure, but, in a weak division, enough to propel them to the top. They made as many spectacular plays as they did spectacular mistakes because every player was at full throttle on practically every play. It seemed they either lost big or won narrowly. No single player dominated; on the contrary, their individual statistics were rather mediocre except in the categories that reflected sheer hustle and sacrifice: triples, steals, and even in getting hit by pitches.

[12]Remember the cycle of action, feedback, and synthesis? Sports is full of it. A dedicated player inspires dedication in others, bringing back the fans, which inspires the players even further, which brings in more fans. Attendance climbed 15 percent despite the worst spring weather in years, including snow in the bleachers. One Saturday the Pirates sold out Three Rivers for the first time in twenty years (not counting opening days). Bursting with pride, Martin hauled the entire team one unseasonably blustery evening down to the gates, where the fans were arriving under umbrellas and stocking caps. Martin told each player to introduce himself to the arriving fans and shake every hand he could. The event was totally spontaneous; the players were as stunned and as thrilled as the fans. Through the determined play of their rookies and the leadership of their veteran, the Pirates were mending their ties with their hometown.

[13]It was in the midst of this Cinderella year that Martin's contract came up for renewal. The Pirates offered to extend him for roughly $3 million a year, a figure he could have easily doubled elsewhere. But why? "I'm comfortable enough," he told people. "What am I going to do? Buy a million-dollar car?" Making a couple million dollars is awful nice—no fooling anyone about that. But there isn't much a family man could do with a second million that he couldn't accomplish with the first—except run up his point total on the scoreboard of bragging rights. Al Martin preferred keeping score on the field. Indeed, as he watched his son's sheer delight in playing Little League, Martin began to see images of himself in the midst of the improbable '97 season. "For the first time in my life as a professional," he later told me, "I realized I'm having as much fun as he is."

[14]In fact, Martin feared that making too much money might penalize his team play. At such elite levels of performance, athletes can easily calibrate between maximum individual achievement and maximum team achievement, and Martin knew that the pressure of additional millions would put any human on the defensive. The owners of baseball, still afflicted with linear mind-sets, figured that any increase in salary could only make for better play, when in fact after a certain point it might well have the reverse effect. At the very least, Martin feared that such high stakes would cause him to feel the chill of self-awareness in the batter's box. "I'd rather be a bargain than overpaid any day," he said.

[15]It was days after Martin re-upped with the Pirates that disaster struck. In the space of a week, injuries felled the team's top run producer, its best defensive player, its clutch reliever—and the top hitter, Al Martin, sidelined with a hand injury. In came more bottom-scale minor-leaguers. Yet the team roared on, the culture of hustle surviving those who had created it. The amazing thing about leadership is how it persists in the absence of the leaders themselves.

[16]Martin made it back into play after a few weeks. The Pirates had fallen a few games out of first place and spent the rest of the season mightily struggling to regain the lead. It came down to the last few days of September. It was close, but not meant to be. But the narrow second-place finish took nothing away from the astonishment over what a bunch of kids and Al Martin had accomplished. One small exercise in arithmetic by the Associated Press, conducted in the middle of the season, said it all: On average, the Cincinnati Reds paid their roster $1.78 million per victory. The Yankees paid $1.64 million. The Florida Marlins paid $1.25 million. The Pirates paid $284,000.[3] There isn't a compensation model in the world that can account for numbers like that, except perhaps the model that says all compensation models are worthless.

[17]Things went a bit differently in the 1998 season. Facing eye surgery, Al Martin slipped into a hitting slump. The team owners began dropping hints of a trade, despite Martin's history of loyalty to the franchise. But the memory persisted of that magical season in which the team had defied all the odds—a season in which money mattered not a whit. . . .

[18]I won't pretend that the Al Martin story signals an end to salary inflation, least of all in the corporate world. Al "Chainsaw" Dunlap pulled down $100 million in his final year as chairman of Scott Paper; a fact that delighted him less for the riches it created than for the bragging rights it bestowed. "I'm a superstar in my field," he explained, "much like Michael Jordan in basketball and Bruce Springsteen in rock 'n' roll."[4] At nearly every other level of work life, compensation remains structured as if it were the only source of motivation. Psychologists call this the Law of Effect—"do this and you get that"—an axiom lifted straight from Newtonian cause-and-effect logic. Behavioral scientists legitimized the pay-for-performance mind-set by using rewards to make lab mammals do just about anything of which a mammal was capable (causing the historian Arthur Koestler to accuse psychologists of replacing the anthropomorphic view of the rat with the "rattomorphic view of man.")[5]

[19]There's no point in denying that money is supremely motivating to people who have little or none of it. An extra penny per seam will cause faster sewing when it means the difference between one cabbage and two. But for the preponderance of people for whom the extra penny does not

spell such a difference, the "rattomorphic" view falls apart. The reason is that each additional dollar in anyone's possession is less valuable than the one that preceded it. James Baldwin once quipped that money was exactly like sex: "You thought of nothing else if you didn't have it and thought of other things if you did." [6]

[20]Willie Sutton was famous for saying he robbed banks because "that's where the money is." Yet in his autobiography he told a slightly different story. "I was more alive when I was inside a bank robbing it than at any other time in my life," he wrote. If money is not the whole story, then what's the rest of it? Consider to begin with the concept that made the late Abraham Maslow one of the most important thinkers of the modern age.

[21]To a little-known degree, Maslow helped spark the revolution in work and economy that this book is about. A professor at Brooklyn College (later Brandeis) who once scored the second-highest IQ ever tested, he resisted both of the psychological schools that held sway in the prewar years: the darkness of Freudianism and the bleakness of behaviorism. Instead of studying sick minds, Maslow thought it might be interesting to study healthy ones for a change—the whole person within the whole society. In keeping with the retreat from Newtonianism then accelerating in the physical sciences, Maslow began to grasp the relativity of the human condition: the notion that what someone aspired to depended on what he already had. It was a radical approach to human motivation.

[22]It is quite true," he wrote in the early 1940s, "that man lives by bread alone—where there is no bread. But what happens to man's desires when there is plenty of bread?" The answer was that "higher needs emerge. . . . And when these in turn are satisfied, again new (and still 'higher') needs emerge, and so on." People, in other words, are motivated by the needs they haven't satisfied. The first $1 million meant a lot to Al Martin, but no additional millions could inspire him more than his love of the Pirates organization. By the 1950s Maslow had popularized his famous "hierarchy of needs," a stairstep of aspirations pursued in succession by humans. First they fulfill physiological needs, for food and water; then physical security, such as shelter. With these needs met, humans seek love, through affection and belonging, followed by esteem, through social approval. Having accomplished all this, man finally yearns for what Maslow called "self actualization," or self-fulfillment, of which he said, "What a man can be, he must be."[8]

[23]Maslow attained celebrity for his work. It helped to launch a broad interest in the study of "peak experiences" in sports and the arts. It deeply influenced early feminist writers, establishing much of the intellectual foundation for what became the "women's liberation" movement. And to return to the subject of money and motivation, Maslow's hierarchy convinced a small group of managers that after a certain point, money alone ceased to motivate their workers. Once they had provided for their lower-rung needs, people in the workplace needed to belong. They needed to be loved. And in the best cases, they needed jobs to help them become everything of which they were capable. As Maslow wrote, "The only happy people I know are the ones who are working well at something they consider important."[9]

[24]Though scarcely known for management theory, Maslow also spent a sabbatical at a company near San Diego called (appropriately enough) Non-Linear Systems, which made voltmeters for the aerospace industry in an old blimp hangar. The owner of the business, Andy Kay, had immersed

himself in Maslow's writings in the late 1950s—ideas that helped him understand the mystery of why workers at the end of the assembly line were invariably the most productive. It was there, Kay finally realized, that people could feel the fulfillment that comes from completing the job, conducting the last few tasks standing between a long chain of work and the customer's use of a valued product. Andy Kay took this realization and broke his workforce into small groups, each responsible for an entire product, a clear precursor to the kind of self-directed teams that Charlene Pedrolie would one day introduce at Rowe Furniture.

[25]A representative from *Reader's Digest* visited the plant in 1963 and published an incredulous report: "When Non-Linear discarded its assembly line it kept all its people—some with only a grammar school education—but divided them into small teams of fewer than a dozen people. Each team runs its own little business. Each has its own rooms, for which it decides the decors. . . . There are no time clocks. . . . Anyone can get coffee whenever he feels like it."[10] Notably, workers signed their names on the equipment they built and fielded queries from the individual customers who used their machines, extending the employees' feeling of belonging into the heart of the marketplace itself. This was radical stuff for a time when the American Management Association published a popular guidebook called *Tough-Minded Management*.

[26]At Kay's invitation and expense, Maslow spent the summer of 1962 roaming the corridors of Non-Linear Systems, marveling at what he saw and dictating his impressions into an early model hand-held tape recorder. Each day Kay's secretary typed Maslow's comments, which he later compiled into a mimeographed volume he called *Summer Notes*. It was an extraordinary piece of work. In it Maslow coined the phrase "enlightened management." He took an obscure term from anthropology, "synergy," and applied it for perhaps the first time to business to describe how cooperation creates wealth. "The more influence and power you give to someone else in the team situation," he noted, "the more you have yourself." He discussed "continual improvement" as an operating concept before anyone in the West had heard of the Japanese *kaizen*.

[27]But Maslow's main interest was fulfillment as a source of motivation on the shop floor. "Highly evolved individuals," he said in his notes, "assimilate their work into the identity, into the self. Work actually becomes part of the self, part of the worker's definition of himself. . . . You participate in the glory, the pleasure, and the pride of the place." In part, this attitude reflected the growing affluence of society, which, even in 1962, was causing workers to rank the quality of their work ahead of the quantity of the financial reward. "Money," Maslow insisted, "is no longer a very important motivation."[11]

[28]Alas, the Non-Linear story had an unhappy ending for all concerned. The company slipped into a steep tailspin in the aerospace downturn of the early 1970s, and although Kay's innovative practices helped to slow the decline, critics used the company's failure as proof that the new-fangled management methods were all wet. *Business Week* published an account under the headline, "Where Being Nice to Workers Didn't Work."[12] Maslow's *Summer Notes*, meanwhile, was published commercially under the ghastly title of *Eupsychian Management*, based on Maslow's coinage ("eupsychia") for the ideal society. Instead of becoming the management equivalent of *The Jungle* or *Silent Spring*—a book that by itself might have

ignited a revolution in its field, holding a light against the dark vision of *The Organization Man*—Maslow's book instead slipped into obscurity.

[29]Maslow's summer at Non-Linear Systems did have important secondary effects, however. His notes deeply influenced such eminent management and leadership gurus as Peter Drucker, Warren Bennis, Douglas McGregor, and Peter Senge. I wrote a column on the book that rekindled publisher interest in it, and a new volume was scheduled for publication. By then, of course, Maslow's observations could only reinforce changes that were already well under way.

[30]In my view Maslow's most brilliant insight was that people try to give their best when they can see the widest known effects of their actions. They want to reach to the greatest distance possible. Self-actualized people listen for the "echoes" of their work, he said. "It's like the holistic way of thinking, not so much in chains of causes and effects, but rather in terms of concentric circles or rings of waves spreading out from the center."[13]

NOTES

1. Quoted in "What a Steal," by Tom Verducci, *Sports Illustrated*, June 16, 1997.
2. Quoted in "Pirates' Martin Finds Happiness for Less Money," Scripps Howard News Service, May 17, 1997.
3. "Low-Paid Pirates Getting Most for Their Money," Associated Press, June 14, 1997. Figures are based on the first sixty-nine games of the season.
4. Dunlap, *Mean Business*, page 21.
5. Quoted in Kohn, *Punished by Rewards*, page 3.
6. James Baldwin, *Nobody Knows My Name* (Vintage, 1961), page 222.
7. Willie Sutton with Edward Linn, *Where the Money Was*, cited in Flannery et al., *People, Performance & Pay*.
8. Quoted in Hoffman, *The Right to Be Human*, page 155.
9. Maslow, *Eupsychian Management*, page 5.
10. "A Chance for Everyone to Grow," by Vance Packard, *Reader's Digest*, November, 1963.
11. Maslow, *Eupsychian Management*, page 188.
12. *Business Week*, January 20, 1973.
13. Maslow, *Eupsychian Management*, page 208–209.

Money and Motivation Questions

VOCABULARY

1. Explain what Petzinger means when he says, "Diamond-studded ballplayers go over poorly in a lunch-pail town like Pittsburgh." (¶4)

2. Explain what Petzinger means when he says, ". . . the Pirates' marketing people picked up on the team's work ethic and realized how smoothly it would harmonize with the ethos of the hometown crowd." (¶10)

COMPREHENSION AND ANALYSIS

For questions 3 to 5, indicate whether the statement is true or false. If the statement is false, rewrite it to make it true.

3. In most work settings, compensation is structured as if it is the only source of motivation.

4. Money is always the primary factor that motivates people.

5. Maslow proposed the idea that what someone aspires to depends on what he already has.

6. What did Al Martin do that surprised everyone? Why does Petzinger include Martin's story?

7. How did Maslow help spark a revolution in work and economy?

8. Why and how did Andy Kay at Non-Linear Systems change the way his assembly line operated? Was it a good idea?

9. State Petzinger's thesis.

10. Maslow wrote, "The only happy people I know are the ones who are working well at something they consider important." Do you think Petzinger agrees or disagrees with Maslow? Please explain.

11. Petzinger says he believes Maslow's "most brilliant insight was that people try to give their best when they can see the widest known effects of their actions." Describe two jobs where you think people can see the "wide effects" of their work.

REFLECT AND CONNECT

12. Assume you have been offered a job by two top companies. The first job offers extremely high pay, a standard benefits package, and work you think would probably be routine. The second job offers standard pay, a generous benefits package and challenging work. What factors do you consider as you struggle to make your decision. Do you think the factors would change over time?

LOG ON TO THE WEB

Conduct research on one or two occupations you are interested in on these two sites:

1. To learn more about occupations, see the *Occupational Outlook Handbook* at *http://www.bls.gov/oco*. The *Occupational Outlook Handbook* is a nationally recognized source of career information, designed to provide valuable assistance to individuals making decisions about their future work lives. Revised every two years, the *Handbook* includes descriptions for hundreds of occupations, describes what workers do on the job, working conditions, the training and education needed, earnings, and expected job prospects in a wide range of occupations.

2. The *Occupational Employment Statistics* program produces employment and wage estimates for over 700 occupations. These are estimates of the number of people employed in certain occupations, and estimates of the wages paid to them (*http://www.bls.gov/oes*). Self-employed persons are not included in the estimates. These estimates are available for the nation as a whole, for individual states, and for metropolitan areas; national occupational estimates for specific industries are also available.

Write down (1) the description of the occupation(s), (2) what you as a worker would do, (3) the training and education needed for the occupation, (4) the estimate of the number of people currently employed in the occupation—nationally and in your metropolitan area, and (5) the wage estimate—nationally and in your metropolitan area.

REFLECT AND CONNECT

A. A new business has moved into your community and hired a large number of college students and recent graduates. Their management team pays a group of students from your college to help them understand the needs and motivations of their new workers. Explain what you believe your group's top three suggestions would be for "keeping talented workers." Include a list of "alternative compensation" ideas.

B. Ask yourself how you can distinguish yourself from the competition. Make a list of the skills, knowledge and experience that you have to offer. Identify the businesses or work areas that would be interested in you, and develop a strategy to penetrate that marketplace.

C. What career planning advice would you give an eighth-grader? a high school senior? your 35-year-old brother? your 50-year-old aunt? Please explain your reasoning.

FURTHER READING

Richard Nelson Bolles, *What Color Is Your Parachute 2004: A Practical Manual for Job-Hunters and Career* (Ten Speed Press, 2003).

Marcus Buckingham and Donald O. Clifton, *Now, Discover Your Strengths* (Free Press, 2001).

John Gray, *Mars and Venus in the Workplace: A Practical Guide for Improving Communication and Getting Results at Work* (HarperCollins, 2001).

Nicholas Lore, *The PATHFINDER: How to Choose or Change Your Career for a Lifetime of Satisfaction and Success* (Fireside, 1998).

Stephen C. Lundin (Editor), Harry Paul, John Christensen, and Philip Strand, *Fish! Tales: Real-Life Stories to Help You Transform Your Workplace and Your Life* (Hyperion, 2002).

Violence and Crime

Being on either end of a violent situation, whether you seem to have come out with the upper hand or whether you don't seem to, it doesn't resolve anything. It escalates the problem. Hatred leads to more hatred. Violence leads to more violence.

—Adam Yauch of the Beastie Boys

During the economic boom of the 1990s, crime rates declined. However, according to the FBI's *Uniform Crime Reports,* there was a 2 percent increase in serious crime between 2000 and 2002 and the upward trend continues.

"Crime," says Stephen S. Ware, editor-in-chief of the *Crime Beat Gazette* "is an equal opportunity offender that transcends a person's educational level or economic status. It is likely that you know someone—friend or foe—who has been assaulted, burglarized, raped, robbed, swindled or even murdered."

On average, it is estimated that in the United States:

- Every 15 seconds a woman is battered,
- Every 35 seconds a person is the victim of an aggravated assault,
- Every minute six children are reported abused and neglected,
- Every 70 seconds a person is robbed,
- Every 6 minutes a person is raped,
- Every 34 minutes a person is murdered,
- Every day more than 100,000 children take a gun to school,
- Every day 160,000 students skip school because of concerns about bullying situations,
- Every year about 3 million crimes occur in schools,
- Every year there are 600 cases of mothers killing their children,
- Every year one in 25 elderly persons is victimized, and that number is growing.

We have a never-ending list of explanations for the roots of violence: poverty, unemployment, substance abuse, prejudice, inadequate health care, disregard for children, breakdown of families, the media, and more. Unfortunately, no consensus exists on the solutions.

The authors in this theme confront the issue of violence in our society. They discuss violence in our homes, schools, media, sports, and society to give insight into what Delaware Senator Joseph R. Biden has called "the most dangerous country in the world."

Opening the theme is an excerpt from Dr. James Garbarino's book, *Lost Boys: Why Our Sons Turn Violent and How We Can Save Them*. In "The Moral Circle," Dr. Garbarino proposes that we all have a *moral circle* when it comes to violence; but the boundaries of the circle vary.

In the chapter "Crime and Violence," from their *Social Problems* text, professors Kornblum and Julian look at the nature of crime, types of crimes and criminals, gangs, guns and violent death, conditions and causes of crime, controlling crime, and controlling violence.

Editorial cartoonist Don Wright suggests that schools now have "Four R's." Then, in an excerpt from his book *Guns, Crime, and the Second Amendment*, Justin Fernandez asks us to explore "A Well-Regulated Controversy."

Jack Levin describes the perils associated with studying a phenomenon that makes people feel uncomfortable, if not personally threatened, in his essay "Hatred: Too Close for Comfort."

Charles Gordon talks about censorship and violence in "Much Ado About Violence," and in "Why Rocky III?" from *Sex, Violence, and Power in Sports: Rethinking Masculinity*, sociologist Mike Messner looks at a type of violence that we reward with celebrity status and money.

The theme concludes with an excerpt from Greg Lichtenberg's memoir *Playing Catch with My Mother*. In "Prologue: New Year's Eve," he recalls the cruel realities of harsh words and physical blows.

The Moral Circle

JAMES GARBARINO

Dr. Garbarino is Codirector of the Family and Life Development Center, professor of human development at Cornell University, and the author of many books. This selection is from his book, Lost Boys: Why Our Sons Turn Violent and How We Can Save Them.

VOCABULARY

> *qualms* (¶3): doubts, misgivings, reservations
> *carnivorousness* (¶3): the characteristic of being a meat eater
> *marshal our resources* (¶4): gather our forces in a unified effort

AN IDEA TO THINK ABOUT

When do you believe violence is justified? When do you believe it is morally wrong? *As you read,* try to understand why others may have different views of when violence is justifiable and when it is not.

THE MORAL CIRCLE

James Garbarino

[1]All of us have a *moral circle* when it comes to violence; some acts are inside the circle of moral justification while other acts are outside that circle. Would you kill an intruder in your home? Would you kill a terminally ill relative? Would you abort a third-trimester pregnancy? Would you agree to the assassination of Saddam Hussein? Would you kill a relative if he were sexually abusing your child? Would you kill a raccoon that bit your son? What if there was a remote possibility the animal had rabies and killing it was the only way to find out for sure? Would you kill it? Killing a raccoon is not the same as killing a human being. Nor is killing Saddam Hussein the same as killing Martin Luther King. Stabbing an abuser is different from stabbing a stranger. Where does one draw the line, and how does one determine which killings make moral sense and which do not?

[2]Cultures and societies set different standards for the morality of killing. Watching the film *Seven Years in Tibet* about the youthful Dalai Lama, many of us were amused to watch the lengths to which Tibetan Buddhists went to avoid killing worms while digging the foundation for a new building. Their reverence for life extends their moral circle very widely. Most of us would put worms outside our moral circle when it comes to killing. Does that make us immoral, or does it make much of the killing we do amoral (in the sense that few Americans can relate to the killing of worms as a *moral* issue at all)? Yet any four-year-old Tibetan Buddhist child knows the wrongness of killing any living being, worms included. How many Christian, Jewish, or Muslim children appreciate *this* moral distinction? Are worms inside the moral circle of these children?

[3]What about dogs and cats? Most of us would put dogs and cats inside the circle, particularly if they are household pets (less so if they are strays). Thus, most Americans would have moral qualms about killing a dog or a cat but not a cow, a pig, or a chicken. How and where do we draw these lines? Is vegetarianism more moral than carnivorousness? Is cannibalism absolutely different from the killing and eating of our fellow mammals? Let us start by keeping these complicated moral distinctions in mind as we look deeper into the stories of young people who commit murder. Let's walk a bit in the lost boys' shoes before we judge them.

[4]Most of us can morally justify some form of killing when it seems necessary. Most of us legitimize violence when we see no moral alternatives and denounce it when we believe alternatives are available. In this sense, necessity is the moral mother of murder. And that is the key to understanding boys who kill and their legitimization of violence. At the moment of crisis they don't see positive alternatives, because of who they are and their emotional history, and where they come from and how they see the world. They do what they have to do—*as they see it*. Understanding this horrible reality is very difficult; it requires a kind of open-heartedness and open-mindedness that is hard for anyone to achieve, particularly in

today's political and emotional climate. But achieve it we must if we are to understand the motivations and experiences that drive boys to commit acts of lethal violence and then marshal our resources to prevent this from happening with other troubled boys.

The Moral Circle Questions

COMPREHENSION AND ANALYSIS

1. What is a *moral circle* when it comes to violence?

2. According to Garbarino, when do most of us believe violence is justifiable? When do we condemn it?

3. Who are the "lost boys"?

4. According to Garbarino, what is the key to understanding the lost boys? Why does he believe it is important to understand them?

5. State Garbarino's thesis.

REFLECT AND CONNECT

6. Garbarino urges us to "walk a bit in the lost boys' shoes before we judge them." Assume your sociology professor has asked your work group to develop a simulation in which you "walk in the shoes" of another person in order to better understand his or her point of view. What person or people would you choose? Please explain.

Crime and Violence

WILLIAM KORNBLUM AND JOSEPH JULIAN

Dr. Kornblum is a professor of sociology in the Graduate School and University Center at the City University of New York. Dr. Julian is a professor of sociology at San Francisco State University. This selection is Chapter 5 from their text Social Problems, *eleventh edition.*

VOCABULARY

Key vocabulary terms are in boldface type and are defined in context.

AN IDEA TO THINK ABOUT

If you were to make a list of the five most serious social problems confronting America today, such as health care and the economy, where would you rank crime and violence compared to other problems? Do you think your perception about the seriousness of crime and violence in America has changed over the last two years? *As you read,* think about how closely your perception of crime and violence matches the data.

5

Crime and Violence

FACTS ABOUT CRIME AND VIOLENCE

- In 2000 about 11.6 million violent and property crimes were committed in the United States.

- Crimes reported to the police make up about a third of actual offenses and about half of violent crimes.

- When weapons are involved, guns account for about 60 percent of murders.

- People under 25 account for about 59 percent of all arrests for property crimes.

- Women make up 16 percent of the total prison population in the United States.

Americans consistently rank crime among the most serious social problems in the United States. Depending on their concerns about such issues as health care or the state of the economy, they may rank these as more serious problems at a given moment. But for many decades crime has been ranked at or very near the top of the list of major social problems. During the past few years some crime rates have decreased. The public's perception of crime as a serious social problem has similarly abated, although it remains high on any survey list. But at the same time, as we will see in this chapter, governments at all levels continue to invest heavily in crime control. As a result, the prison population in the United States has reached record proportions.

It is important to realize that at least some crime has existed in almost all societies. As the French sociologist Émile Durkheim (1895/1950) pointed out, wherever there are people and laws, there are crime and criminals:

> Crime is present . . . in all societies of all types. There is no society that is not confronted with the problem of criminality. Its form changes; the acts thus characterized are not the same everywhere; but, everywhere and always, there have been men who have behaved in such a way as to draw upon themselves penal repression. . . . What is normal, simply, is the existence of criminality. (p. 65)

According to the *Uniform Crime Reports (UCR)* of the Federal Bureau of Investigation (FBI), between 2000 and 2001 there was a 2 percent increase in serious crime. This finding reverses a downward trend in crime during the economic boom years of the 1990s. Between 1997 and 1998, for example, there was a 6 percent drop in serious crimes, and the 1998 rate was 14 percent below the rate for 1994 and 20 percent below the rate for 1989 (*UCR*, 2002). The encouraging decline in crime seems to have been associated with good economic times, and the recessionary economy, rising unemployment rates, and uncertainty due to the threat of terrorism may all have contributed to recent rises in some types of serious crime. While violent crimes have not increased significantly, property crimes have, providing further evidence that economic factors (rather than drugs or gangs, for example) account for the increases in crime rates.

In this chapter we examine these and other trends in crime and violence more fully. We will see that there is a good deal of argument among experts about whether these trends are likely to continue. Another problem is that these statistics are based on reports provided by local police departments, which often contain errors of various kinds.

One reason for the disagreement is that it is extremely difficult to measure actual rates of crime. An annual survey of American households by the U.S. Department of Justice asks respondents detailed questions about their experiences with crime. This survey, known as the National Crime Victimization Survey of the Bureau of Justice Statistics, reveals that the actual rates of violent personal and property crime are several times higher than the official rates presented in the Federal Bureau of Investigation's *Uniform Crime Reports,* which are based on crimes reported to the police. Many victims do not report crimes because they believe that nothing can be done or that the crime was unimportant. Sample surveys of Americans indicate that crimes reported to the police account for about 33 percent of actual offenses and about 50 percent of violent crimes (Bureau of Justice Statistics, 1996; Reid, 1991).

Even with a large proportion of unreported crimes, statistics showed a rapid increase in crime in the early 1970s. The crime rate continued to increase in the late 1970s, but in the early 1980s it leveled off. Beginning in 1985 there was a steady increase in the absolute number of serious crimes and in the rate of crime per 100,000 inhabitants, which controls for any increase in population size that alone might result in more crime. These trends continued until the early 1990s, when, as just mentioned, the rate of serious crime began to decrease. The number of serious crime offenses reported to the police in 2001 was approximately 11,800,000, of which almost 60 percent were larceny or theft. Violent crimes, including murder, forcible rape, robbery, and aggravated assault, accounted for 12.2 percent of all known crimes in 2001 (*UCR,* 2002). (See Figures 5–1, 5–2, 5–3, and 5–4.)

According to the National Crime Victimization Survey, the violent crime rate fell 15 percent and the property crime rate 10 percent between 1999 and 2000. But we saw earlier that the FBI's *Uniform Crime Reports* indicate that the rate of property crimes began rising again between 2000 and 2001. Comparable data from the victimization survey were not available at this writing.

Sociologists believe that the recent decline in crime rates is a result of the rapid increase in the number of prison inmates, the waning of the crack epidemic in the largest metropolitan centers, and increases in police forces throughout the nation (Krauss, 1996). Nevertheless, although the deceleration of crime rates since the 1970s is most welcome, the rates remain higher than those in European nations.

The extent of the nation's crime problem is measured by the **crime index,** developed in the 1930s by the Committee on Uniform Crime Records of the International Association of Chiefs of Police. The crime index collects data on the most serious and

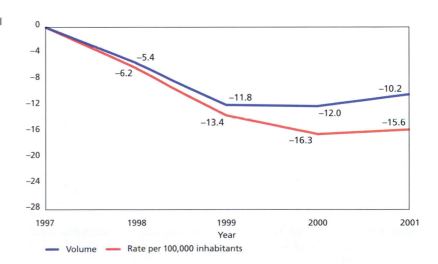

FIGURE 5–1 Crime Index Total (Percent Change from 1996)

Source: Federal Bureau of Investigation, *Uniform Crime Reports,* 2002.

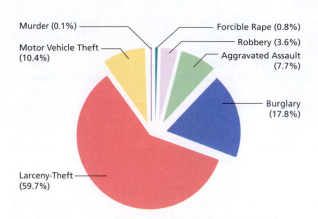

Murder (0.1%)
Motor Vehicle Theft (10.4%)
Forcible Rape (0.8%)
Robbery (3.6%)
Aggravated Assault (7.7%)
Burglary (17.8%)
Larceny-Theft (59.7%)

FIGURE 5-2 Crime Index Offenses, 2001 (Percent Distribution)*

*Percentages do not add up due to rounding.

Source: Federal Bureau of Investigation, *Uniform Crime Reports,* 2002.

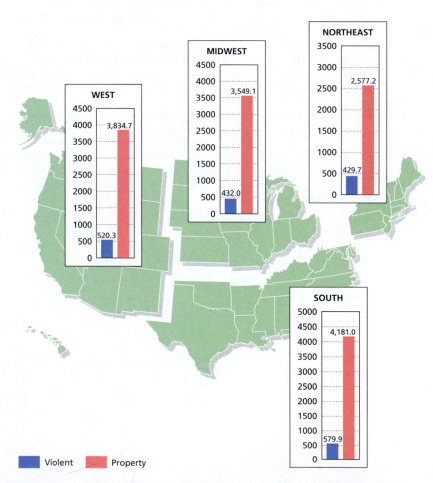

FIGURE 5-3 Regional Violent and Property Crime Rates, 2001 (per 100,000 Inhabitants)

Source: Federal Bureau of Investigation, *Uniform Crime Reports,* 2002.

132 CHAPTER 5

FIGURE 5-4 The Crime Clock, 2001

The Crime Clock should be viewed with care. Being the most aggregate representation of *UCR* data, it is designed to convey the annual reported crime experience by showing the relative frequency of occurrence of the index offenses. This mode of display should not be taken to imply a regularity in the commission of offenses; rather, it represents the annual ratio of crime to fixed time intervals.

Source: Federal Bureau of Investigation, *Uniform Crime Reports,* 2002.

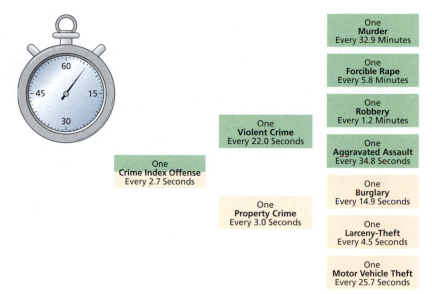

One
Murder
Every 32.9 Minutes

One
Forcible Rape
Every 5.8 Minutes

One
Robbery
Every 1.2 Minutes

One
Violent Crime
Every 22.0 Seconds

One
Aggravated Assault
Every 34.8 Seconds

One
Crime Index Offense
Every 2.7 Seconds

One
Burglary
Every 14.9 Seconds

One
Property Crime
Every 3.0 Seconds

One
Larceny-Theft
Every 4.5 Seconds

One
Motor Vehicle Theft
Every 25.7 Seconds

most frequently occurring crimes—those that are most likely to come to the attention of the police. These include murder and nonnegligent manslaughter, forcible rape, robbery, aggravated assault, burglary, larceny-theft, motor vehicle theft, and arson. The statistics reported throughout this chapter are taken from the crime index.

Official statistics, of course, do not tell the whole story. It has never been easy, for example, to assess accurately the extent of organized and occupational (white-collar) crime. Exposures of scandals in government and business show that these types of crimes are far more widespread and pervasive than is generally realized. Not only is the rate of crime itself extremely high, but fear of crime, especially in large cities, significantly affects the lives of many people. Large numbers of Americans feel unsafe in their homes, neighborhoods, or workplaces. Many have stopped going to areas they used to go to at night, and fear of violent crime is widespread.

Sociologists who study the effects of media coverage of crime report that attitudes about safety in one's neighborhood and about going out at night in the city in which one resides vary directly with the rate of index crimes in that city; however, reports of crimes in other cities make people feel safe in comparison. The reports that are most closely correlated with fear of crime are those describing sensational murders in one's own city, that is, murders that are reported on the front pages of newspapers and on television. Less sensational murders, even in one's own city, do not have a measurable impact (Liska & Baccaglini, 1990; Schmalleger, 2000). Of course, the crimes that are most likely to generate fear are those that directly affect one's family and friends, even if they are relatively minor.

The Nature of Crime

There is no single, universally agreed-upon definition of crime. In the words of one of the world's foremost historians of crime, the late Sir Leon Radzinowicz, crime

is something that threatens serious harm to the community, or something generally believed to do so, or something committed with evil intent, or something forbidden in the interests of the most powerful sections of society. But there are crimes that elude each of these definitions and there are forms of behavior under each of them that escape the label of crime. The argument that crime is anything forbidden, or punishable, under the criminal law is open to the objection that it is circular. But at least it is clear cut, it refers not to what ought to be but to what is, and it is an essential starting point. (Radzinowicz & King, 1977, p. 17)

According to this argument, a **crime** is any act or omission of an act for which the state can apply sanctions. This is the most frequently used definition of crime and the one we will use in this chapter. However, it should be kept in mind that definitions of crime are subject to changing values and public sentiments; moreover, as we will see shortly, factors like police discretion play a major role in the interpretation of particular behaviors as crimes.

The **criminal law** in any society prohibits certain acts and prescribes the punishments to be meted out to violators. Confusion frequently arises because although the criminal law prescribes certain rules for living in society, not all violations of social rules are violations of criminal laws. A swimmer's failure to come to the aid of a drowning stranger, for example, would not constitute a criminal act, although it might be considered morally wrong not to have done whatever was possible to save the victim, short of risking one's own life.

Many acts that are regarded as immoral are ignored in criminal law but are considered civil offenses. Under **civil law**—laws that deal with noncriminal acts in which one individual injures another—the state arbitrates between the aggrieved party and the offender. For example, civil law is involved when a person whose car was destroyed in an accident sues the driver responsible for the accident to recover the cost of the car. The driver at fault is not considered a criminal unless he or she can be shown to have broken a criminal law, for instance, to have been driving while intoxicated. Further confusion results from changes in social attitudes, which usually precede changes in criminal law. In some states, for example, old laws that are still on the books continue to define as criminal some acts that are no longer considered wrong by society, such as certain forms of sexual behavior between consenting adults.

Police Discretion

In addition to problems of definition, such as ambiguity about whether loitering is a crime, certain other factors contribute to the difficulty of knowing what crimes are committed in a particular society. A significant factor is the role of police discretion. In practice, the definition of criminality changes according to what the police believe criminal behavior to be. Given the thousands of laws on the books, police officers have considerable discretion about which laws to ignore, which laws to enforce, and how strongly to enforce them. This discretionary power, in turn, gives them many opportunities to exercise their own concept of lawful behavior in decisions about what complaints merit attention, whom they should arrest, and who should be released (deLint, 2000).

In an important study of police discretion, Michael K. Brown (1988) compared police activities in two Los Angeles Police Department (LAPD) districts and three suburban towns in the Los Angeles metropolitan region. On the basis of interviews with patrol officers and their supervisors, he concluded that "a police bureaucracy has a significant impact on the behavior of patrolmen. . . . Patrolmen in the two divisions of the LAPD are formalistic and more willing to make an arrest in a variety of incidents than patrolmen in small departments, who are consistently more lenient and less willing to invoke the force of the law in the same circumstances" (p. 275). When asked whether they would normally arrest disorderly juveniles on their beat, for example, 28 percent of veteran police officers with five years or more experience in the smaller departments said that they would not arrest the offenders, whereas 65 percent of the LAPD veteran officers said that they would arrest disorderly juveniles.

Police discretion has become a controversial issue in Los Angeles and other major cities. In Los Angeles, where there are more street gangs than in any other U.S. city, the police have developed a policy of issuing what are known as "gang injunctions." These local policy orders target specific gangs and their members. They order people wearing gang colors off the street, and they ban driving or congregating with other

134   CHAPTER 5

Unintended Consequences

IS THERE A CASE FOR DISCRETION?

Since at least 1986, many state and federal regulations severely restrict the discretion of judges in individual sentencing decisions. Perhaps the most controversial of these mandatory sentencing rules is California's "three strikes, you're out" law, under which offenders convicted of their third felony must be sentenced to life imprisonment. Many such laws are in effect throughout the nation, reflecting a more punitive public attitude toward offenders.

On one hand, it appears that mandatory sentencing has the desired effect of making it clear to criminals what the penalties for their actions will be. Criminologists James Q. Wilson and John

Dilulio argue that this clarity is partly responsible for the recent decreases in some categories of crime. On the other hand, the majority of the million or more people incarcerated in federal and state prisons are there for drug-related crimes, often as a result of mandatory sentencing. As we saw in Chapter 4, those convicted of selling crack cocaine have received far stiffer sentences than those convicted of selling powdered cocaine. According to the chief federal drug official, Lee Brown, this disparity in mandatory sentencing reflects class and racial bias, since crack is used mainly in poor inner-city neighborhoods. Also controversial are reports that in Florida and other states violent offenders who are serving terms for rape or armed robbery, but not under mandatory sentences, have been released to make

room in crowded prisons for drug offenders who are serving mandatory sentences.

Chief Justice William Rehnquist has called mandatory minimum sentences "a good example of the law of unintended consequences" (quoted in Brennan, 1995, p. 18). The California Supreme Court has decided that judges in lower courts have the right to disregard the three strikes rule if they believe that the mandatory sentence would represent "cruel and unusual punishment." So, although there is strong public support for clarity in sentencing requirements and attention to the injuries suffered by victims, there is growing support among professionals and citizens alike for restoring some of the judicial discretion eliminated by mandatory sentencing rules.

known gang members. This is a response to demands for action to prevent gang crimes. But the wide use of gang injunctions has drawn the criticism of citizens who are concerned about the curtailment of personal liberties and civil rights. The Supreme Court has so far refused to rule on the use of gang injunctions, but the controversy further demonstrates how police discretion can account for important differences in the enforcement of laws from one community to another (Lipsky, 1980; Shoop, 1998). (See the Unintended Consequences box above.)

In a classic study of two groups of adolescents in the same high school, William Chambliss (1973) examined how the biases of the local police affected their treatment of middle- and lower-class delinquents. A group of middle-class boys (the Saints) had been truant almost every day of the two-year period during which they were studied. They drove recklessly, drank excessively, and openly cheated on exams. Yet only twice were members of the Saints stopped by police officers; even then, nothing appeared on their school records. The members of the other group (the Roughnecks) all came from lower-class families. Unlike the Saints, who had cars and could "sow their wild oats" in parts of town where they were not known, the Roughnecks were confined to an area where they could be easily recognized; they therefore developed a reputation for being delinquent.

The demeanor of the two groups of boys differed markedly when they were apprehended by the police. The Saints, who were apologetic, penitent, and generally respectful of middle-class values, were treated as harmless pranksters. The Roughnecks, who were openly hostile and disdainful toward the police, were labeled deviant. These results demonstrate that factors such as low income, unemployment, or minority status are not the only ones that have a bearing on the commission of juvenile crimes. Although these factors did account for a higher rate of detection and punishment, the rates of actual misbehavior in Chambliss's study were virtually the same for both groups. Differences in the official records of the two groups reflect the discretionary power of the police. Chambliss's experience with the empirical facts of police discretion and unequal application of state power has made him one of the nation's foremost critical criminologists (Chambliss, 2000).

Problems of Accuracy

Another factor that contributes to the problem of determining the level of crime in a society is that police statistics depend on police reports, which in turn depend on the level and quality of police personnel in a given area. Since police are assigned to lower-income communities in greater numbers, there is a tendency for police records to show higher crime rates for those communities and lower rates for more affluent areas.

If official data on crime are less than fully accurate on a limited scale, it is possible that similar problems undermine the accuracy of national crime statistics. The standard index of criminal activity in the United States is the *Uniform Crime Reports (UCR)*, which supplies racial and economic profiles of people arrested for such crimes as murder, rape, assault, and robbery. Recent data support the long-held assumption that minority group members are more likely than nonminority individuals to be involved in crimes. Yet it must be remembered that *UCR* statistics cite only individuals who are apprehended. If, like the Saints in the Chambliss (1973) study, adult offenders in middle- and upper-class groups are rarely caught or punished, *UCR*-based data become inaccurate. Because it does not profile those who successfully evade apprehension and prosecution, the *UCR* fails to reveal the entire range of criminal activity in the United States.

Acting on this hypothesis, researchers have attempted to devise more reliable ways of tracking criminal activity. Self-report studies, which ask respondents to report their own criminal involvement through an anonymous questionnaire, have provided alternative data. Whereas minority groups have higher crime rates when judged by official data (such as juvenile or criminal court records or the *UCR* index), self-reporting techniques indicate that whites and nonwhites have similar rates of criminal activity. Thus, on one hand, the idea that race is a factor in criminality is called into question when different standards of measurement are used. On the other hand, some criminologists argue that although self-report studies question the distribution of crime in the population, they do not show significant differences in levels of crime from those shown in the *UCR* (Maltz, 1999).

Another attempt to supplement *UCR* data has led to the development of **victimization reports.** These surveys, conducted by the Census Bureau, collect information from a representative sample of crime victims. Comparisons of *UCR* and victimization indexes reveal discrepancies in the data, and depending on which standard is used, different conclusions can be drawn about the correlation between crime and socioeconomic status (Reid, 1993). The *UCR* data reflect only crimes that are reported, yet many victims—through fear, ignorance, or alienation—do not file reports. Victimization surveys indicate that this is particularly true in low-income, high-crime areas. Certain crimes—especially sex-related crimes such as rape and child molestation—are underreported, and the statistics are distorted as a result.

In sum, it appears that the poor, the undereducated, and minority groups have become the victims of selective law enforcement, stereotyping, and misleading statistics. The rich and powerful, in contrast, have been insulated from these problems; they are so seldom sent to prison that when one of them is finally jailed for fraud, embezzlement, or tax evasion, it makes headlines. Some sociologists, noting the difficulty of obtaining accurate information on the incidence of these crimes, have contended that the upper classes may actually have a higher rate of crime than the lower classes (Pepinsky & Quinney, 1991; Reckless, 1973). The discovery of criminal dealings by high officials of U.S. corporations in 2002 reinforces this hypothesis. It will be helpful to keep these contrasts in mind as we discuss the various types of crimes, including corporate crime.

Types of Crimes and Criminals

In this section we review ten major types of crimes and criminals (Siegel, 1999). Seven of them have been classified by sociologists according to how large a part criminal activity plays in people's lives; that is, whether or not people see themselves as criminals and the extent to which they commit themselves to a life of crime. To these we add an eighth category, juvenile delinquency, and a ninth, corporate crimes. Two forms of illegal activity—occupational and organized crime—receive more extensive treatment here because their social costs probably exceed those of all the others combined. Hate crimes, a tenth category, are not accorded official status in all states, but the increase in such crimes is an important exception to the recent decline in U.S. crime rates and a subject of much current debate.

Violent Personal Crimes

Violent personal crimes include assault, robbery, and various types of homicide—acts in which physical injury is inflicted or threatened. Although robbery occurs most often between strangers, murders are very often a result of violent disputes between friends or relatives. In 2001, 42 out of every 100 murder victims were related to or acquainted with their assailants, and murders initiated by arguments (as opposed to premeditated murders) accounted for 28 percent of all murders committed during that year. Murders and aggravated assaults, therefore, are usually considered unpremeditated acts. The offenders are portrayed in the media as normally law-abiding individuals who are not likely to engage in other criminal activities. Some murders may be contract murders, which are committed by hired killers and are often linked to organized crime. When weapons are involved, guns account for about 70 percent of murders (*UCR*, 2002).

Despite signs of progress, the level of deadly violence remains higher in the United States than in any other urban industrial nation. Although rates of interpersonal violence may be higher in a few poorer nations, no major industrialized nation has homicide rates as high as those in the United States. For black men in the United States, the chances of living beyond age 40 are worse than in the poorest nations of the world, mainly because of the toll taken by violence. The widespread availability of guns and the contribution of drugs to violence are important factors in this situation, but those who study the problem also point to the pervasiveness of violence in our culture. Increasingly frequent incidents of aggressive driving, often referred to as "road rage," increases in fights at sports events and school outings, rising rates of family violence, and outbreaks of deadly violence in workplaces such as post offices have drawn attention to the underlying levels of interpersonal violence that result in spectacular and grisly headlines (Elvin, 1999).

Much violent action throughout the world is not recognized as such. This is particularly true of violence associated with the rise or expansion of a political party or social movement; most groups try to forget, justify, or disguise their use of violence for these purposes. Whereas extralegal violent acts like murder, rape, or gang wars elicit public condemnation, other forms of violence are accepted or even praised, for example, those that occur in war. Similarly, in troubled times and in frontier areas, vigilante activities are often approved by the local community as the only available means of maintaining order. In general, violence by or on behalf of the state is less likely to be condemned than violent personal crimes.

Despite the relative stability of its institutions, the United States has witnessed more violent behavior than other Western industrial nations. According to official statistics, approximately 15,980 murders were committed in 2001, as well as 90,491 rapes, 907,219 aggravated assaults, and 422,921 robberies (*UCR*, 2002). (See Figure 5–5.) The significance of violence and the need to find means to control and prevent it are apparent.

Criminal Homicide. Criminal homicide takes two forms: **Murder** is defined as the unlawful killing of a human being with malice aforethought; **manslaughter** is unlawful homicide without malice aforethought. In practice, it is often difficult to distinguish between them. Someone may attack another person without intending to kill, but the

Although we think of ourselves as a peace-loving people, we continually resort to violence in defense of what we consider our vital interests. The American Civil War was among the bloodiest in world history. (Scala/Art Resource, NY. Currier and Ives (sec. XIX) Battaglia di Sharpsburg 17 Settembre 1862. Museum of the City of New York, New York, U.S.A.)

attack may result in death. Depending on the circumstances, one case might be judged to be murder and another to be manslaughter. Often the deciding factor is the extent to which the victim is believed to have provoked the assailant.

Paradoxically, most murderers do not have a criminal record. Of course, there are those who use actual or threatened violence as tools in a criminal career, but these are exceptions. As a rule, professional criminals try to keep violence—especially killing—to a "necessary" minimum because of the "heat" it would bring from the law. Most murderers do not see themselves as real criminals, and until the murder occurs, neither does society. Murderers do not conform to any criminal stereotype, and murder does not usually form part of a career of criminal behavior.

Murder does, however, follow certain social and geographic patterns. Reported murders occur most often in large cities. The murder rate for large metropolitan areas

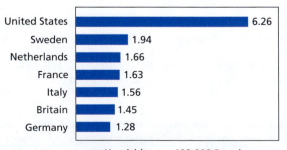

Homicides per 100,000 People
(average per year, 1997–1999)

FIGURE 5-5 Murders in Europe and the United States
Source: British Home Office.

is 6.1 per 100,000 people, compared to 3.7 per 100,000 in rural counties and 3.5 per 100,000 in cities outside metropolitan areas (*UCR*, 2002). The incidence of murder is unevenly distributed within cities; as Donald T. Lunde (1975) has pointed out, "Most city neighborhoods are just as safe as the suburbs" (p. 38). There are also regional differences; for example, murder is more likely to occur in the South, even though it is one of the more rural parts of the country. This seems to be a result of the culture of the region, which tends to legitimize personal violence and the use of weapons.

Most murderers are men, who generally are socialized to be more violent than women and to use guns for recreation or for military purposes; guns are the most common murder weapon. Many murderers are young; in 2001, 45 percent of those arrested for murder were between the ages of 17 and 34. The victims are young too; in 2001, 54 percent were between the ages of 17 and 34 (*UCR*, 2002). More than half of all murder victims are members of minority groups. Most of the time, the killer and the victim are of the same race. In 2001, 85 percent of white murder victims were slain by white offenders, and 94 percent of black victims were slain by black offenders (*UCR*, 2002).

More significant than the demographic characteristics of murderers and their victims is the relationship between them. Several studies have indicated that this relationship is generally close; often the murderer is a member of the victim's family or an intimate friend. A high proportion of murderers are relatives of their victim, often the spouse. Victim studies suggest that there is a great deal of unreported domestic violence and that the majority of violent crimes are committed by family members, friends, or acquaintances (Reid, 1991). One study found that

> more than 40 percent of murder victims are killed in residences. . . . More women die in their own bedrooms than anywhere else. One in every five murder victims is a woman who has been killed there by her spouse or lover. Husbands are most vulnerable in the kitchen; that's where wives are apt to pick up knives to finish family arguments.
>
> The other half of murders involving close relatives include parents killing children, children killing parents, or other close relatives killing each other. These victims usually die in the living room from gunshot wounds. Another 6 percent of murders [are] between more distant relatives. (Lunde, 1975, pp. 35–36)

Most murders occur during a quarrel between two people who know each other well. Both the murderer and the victim may have been drinking, perhaps together, before the event. Even though many homicides occur during the commission of other crimes, these killings, too, are usually unpremeditated—a thief surprised by a security officer, a bank robber confronted by an armed guard, and so on. In addition, some homicides involve police officers, many of whom are killed in the line of duty. In 1960, 48 law enforcement officials were killed in the states and territories of the United States. This number reached a peak of 134 in 1975 and stood at 70 in 2001 (*UCR*, 2002).

The mentally ill commit murder at the same rate as the general population, but serial killers are almost always psychotic—either paranoid or sexual sadists (Nocera, 1999). These murderers may hear voices commanding them to kill, think they are superhuman or chosen for a special mission, or kill to avert imagined persecution. Sadists may torture before killing and/or mutilate their victims afterwards. Unlike most murderers, psychotic killers are seldom acquainted with their victims, who are often representatives of a type or class—rich businessmen, for example, or young middle-class women.

Mass Murders. There is some evidence that mass murders (in which four or more people are killed by the same person in a short time) are becoming more frequent. Although the number fluctuates from year to year, some of the worst cases have occurred since 1980.

On July 18, 1984, James Oliver Huberty, a recently fired security guard, opened fire in a McDonald's restaurant, killing 21 people and injuring 20 others. Before the 1995

Oklahoma City bombing, this was the worst massacre by a single person in a single day in U.S. history. In 1989, Theodore ("Ted") Bundy, an articulate and rather charming drifter, was executed for the murder of numerous children and teenagers throughout the United States. These two cases, one a psychotic who murdered in a fit of rage, the other a cool but also psychotic individual who organized a series of killings (and therefore is known as a serial killer), illustrate quite well the types of people who commit mass murders. Generally, a mass murderer like Huberty kills in a fit of spontaneous rage, whereas a serial killer is highly organized and seeks to perfect a murder technique that will prevent detection and apprehension. Most serial killers have deep emotional problems concerning sexuality and describe the act of violence itself as thrilling and compelling (Holmes & DeBurger, 1987; Levin & Fox, 1985; Reid, 1991).

Workplaces like post offices, banks, and factories are increasingly frequent scenes of mass murders or outbreaks of lethal violence, apparently because of a buildup of rage in a person who fits the profile of a potential mass murderer. Unfortunately, it is extremely difficult to know beforehand whether a person fits that profile. There is a need, therefore, for greater vigilance and more open lines of communication in the workplace (Nigro & Waugh, 1996).

Occasional Property Crimes

Occasional property crimes include vandalism, check forgery, shoplifting, and some kinds of automobile theft. These crimes are usually unsophisticated, and the offenders lack the skills of the professional criminal. Because occasional offenders commit their crimes at irregular intervals, they are not likely to associate with habitual lawbreakers. Nonprofessional shoplifters, for example, view themselves as respectable law-abiders who steal articles from stores only for their own use. They excuse their behavior on the grounds that what they steal has relatively little value and the "victim" is usually a large, impersonal organization that can easily replace the stolen article (Schmalleger, 2000; Siegel, 1999).

Neither nonprofessional shoplifters nor nonprofessional check forgers are likely to have a criminal record. Like vandals and car thieves, they usually work alone and are not part of a criminal subculture; they do not seek to earn a living from crime.

Occupational (White-Collar) Crimes

The phenomenon of occupational crime was defined and popularized by sociologist Edwin H. Sutherland, first in a 1940 article and then in his 1961 book *White Collar Crime.* Sutherland analyzed the behavior of people who break the law as part of their normal business activity: corporate directors who use their inside knowledge to sell

Shoplifting or "boosting" is one of the most common forms of juvenile crime.

large blocks of stock at tremendous profits; accountants who juggle books to conceal the hundreds of dollars of company funds that they have pocketed; firms that make false statements about their profits to avoid paying taxes. Such acts tend to be ignored by society. They rarely come to the criminal courts, and even then they are rarely judged as severely as other kinds of criminal activities. Since Sutherland first described it, the category of occupational crime has also come to include such acts as false advertising, violations of labor laws, price-fixing, antitrust violations, and black-market activities.

The occupational offender is far removed from the popular stereotype of a criminal. Few people imagine that a lawyer or stockbroker is likely to engage in illegal activities. Because of their respectable appearance, it is difficult to think of these offenders as criminals. In fact, occupational offenders often consider themselves respectable citizens and do everything possible to avoid being labeled as lawbreakers—even by themselves.

Sutherland's theory of **differential association** asserts that occupational criminality, like other forms of systematic criminal behavior, is learned through frequent direct or indirect association with people who are already engaging in such behavior. (We discuss this theory later in the chapter.) Thus, people who become occupational criminals may do so simply by going into businesses or occupations in which their colleagues regard certain kinds of crime as the standard way of conducting business.

A good example of occupational crime is the insider trading that frequently occurs in the securities industry. Some stockbrokers and major shareholders may be privy to inside information about an impending corporate merger or a change in the financial condition of a company that will affect the price of its stock. Brokers who possess such information are prohibited from either profiting from it themselves or selling it to others who may be able to profit from it. Nevertheless, in the 1980s the senior partners of several large brokerage houses were convicted of using inside information to make hundreds of illegal stock transactions worth many millions of dollars (Auletta, 1987).

Embezzlement. Embezzlement, or theft from one's employer, is usually committed by otherwise law-abiding people during the course of their employment. Embezzlement occurs at all levels of business, from a clerk who is stealing petty cash to a vice-president who is stealing large investment sums. Most cases are not detected, and companies are often unwilling to prosecute for fear of bad publicity. In the United States more than 13,000 people a year are arrested for embezzlement (*UCR,* 2002).

Donald Cressey's (1953) book, *Other People's Money,* is a classic study of embezzlers. On the basis of interviews with convicted embezzlers, Cressey concluded that three basic conditions are necessary before people will turn to embezzlement. First, they must have a financial problem that they do not want other people to know about. Second, they must have an opportunity to steal. Third, they must be able to find a formula to rationalize the fact that they are committing a criminal act—such as "I'm just borrowing it to tide me over."

Fraud. Fraud, or obtaining money or property under false pretenses, can occur at any level of business and in any type of business relationship. A citizen defrauds the government by evading the payment of income taxes; workers defraud their employers by using company property or services for their personal benefit; an industry defrauds the public when its members agree to keep prices artificially high. The cost of fraud may run from a few cents to millions of dollars, and the methods may be as crude as the butcher's thumb on the scale or as sophisticated as the coordinated efforts of dozens of lawyers, executives, and government officials. More than 200,000 people are arrested for fraud each year in the United States (*UCR,* 2002).

Within this category, the incidence of crimes committed through computer technology has increased dramatically. Computer crimes are quite diverse, ranging from data diddling, or changing the data stored in a computer system, to superzapping, or making unauthorized use of specialized programs to gain access to data stored in a computer system. In 1999 the first conviction for creation of a computer virus (the Melissa virus) was handed down. No doubt many more will follow. And along with the boom in electronic commerce has come a rash of online fraud, which was estimated to have risen by 600 percent in 1999 (Mollman, 1999).

Corporate Crimes

Corporate crimes include, but are not limited to, environmental crimes, illegal credit card manipulations, insider trading in financial institutions, intimidation of competitors and employees, illegal labor practices, defrauding of pension plans, falsification of company records, bribery of public officials, and computer crimes. Because it is so often undetected or unpunished, there are no reliable estimates of the cost of corporate crime to the public (Sherrill, 1997; Weston, 1987).

Disclosures of corporate crime in the tobacco and food industries have commanded large headlines and been the subject of movies like *The Insider*. But measured in terms of loss of public and private funds, the single worst example of corporate crime in American history occurred toward the end of the 1980s (Sherrill, 1997). It is known as the savings and loan scandal, and in the early 1990s it was estimated that it would cost taxpayers up to $500 billion, not to mention the large amounts of unprotected savings lost by individuals. In fact, the seizure and sale of properties involved in the scandal eventually reduced the overall financial damage (Foust, 1993). However, to assess the impact of this crime one needs to realize that the total value of property reported stolen in other kinds of crimes each year amounts to about $15.4 billion.

The spectacle of high-level corporate officials testifying before Congress or paraded before law enforcement officials and television cameras during the "corporate crime wave" of 2002 brought the subject of corporate crimes to the attention of a world audience. Authorities charged executives of Enron, Tyco, Arthur Andersen, WorldCom, and many other firms, some of them among the largest and most powerful companies in the United States, with fraud and other criminal activities. Millions of Americans lost funds invested in the securities (stocks and bonds) of these companies, while key executives sold their shares at high prices and reaped millions of dollars in personal gains, knowing that very shortly the shares' value would drop sharply. Not only was this "insider trading" illegal, but the values of the stocks themselves had in many cases been illegally inflated, and accountants and company executives often colluded to hide the way they were "cooking the books"—that is, reporting false profit statements in order to keep the value of the firm's securities high (Colvin, 2002).

Companies involved in corporate crime after the bursting of the high-technology investment "bubble" after 2000 were often shielded from careful scrutiny by their close relationships with public officials. The Enron Corporation, which has been charged not only with stock manipulation and accounting fraud but also with illegally causing the rise of electricity prices in California in 2001, had extremely close ties to numerous members of the Bush administration, including Vice President Cheney and President Bush himself. Although it does not appear that either political leader colluded with Enron in its illegal dealings, their ties to Enron executives helped create an aura of great power and respectability around the corporation that helped mask its criminal activities from the public (Dunham & Walczak, 2002).

Public-Order Crimes

In terms of sheer numbers, public-order offenders constitute the largest category of criminals; their activities far exceed reported crimes of any other type. Public-order offenses include prostitution, gambling, use of illegal substances, drunkenness, vagrancy, disorderly conduct, and traffic violations. These are often called *victimless crimes* because they cause no harm to anyone but the offenders themselves. Society considers them crimes because they violate the order or customs of the community, but some of them, such as gambling and prostitution, are granted a certain amount of tolerance.

142 CHAPTER 5

Public-order offenders rarely consider themselves criminals or view their actions as crimes. The behavior and activities of prostitutes and drug users, however, tend to isolate and segregate them from other members of society, and these individuals may find themselves drawn into criminal roles.

Prostitution is a particularly relevant example of public-order crime because of the way women (and young men or adolescents) are exploited by older adults in the sex trade, both in the United States and, increasingly, in third world nations with thriving "sex tourism" industries (Wonders & Michalowski, 2001). Prostitution is illegal everywhere in the United States except in some counties of Nevada. Although there is little pressure on other states to follow Nevada's example, many arguments have been offered in support of legalization. It is claimed that prostitution will continue to exist regardless of the law and that recognizing this fact would bring many benefits: Legalization would make prostitutes' incomes taxable; it could eliminate or reduce the frequent connection of prostitution with crime and government corruption; and health regulations for prostitutes could be enacted and enforced, reducing the incidence of venereal disease. It has been suggested that legalization of brothels would result in a reduction of streetwalking and public solicitation, which disturb residents of the neighborhoods where they occur.

Many advocates of legalization point to class differences in the enforcement of the laws. Unless they are very indiscreet, call girls and their upper-middle-class customers are seldom targets of police action. It is the lower-class prostitutes, with their lower-class customers, who bear the brunt of antisolicitation laws.

It has also been pointed out that prostitution is usually a victimless crime, since the customer participates willingly and generally has few complaints. Because most laws against prostitution and solicitation require specific evidence of an offer to exchange sexual favors for money, a major means of curbing prostitution is entrapment by plainclothes officers posing as customers. This method is objected to as unjust in that it singles out only one partner in the crime; if a prostitute commits a crime, so does the customer. A few states and cities now have laws (rarely enforced effectively) under which a man can be jailed for as much as a year and fined up to $1,000 for offering to pay for sexual services.

In Thailand, Cambodia, and other Asian nations, tourism motivated by the desire to engage in sex with juveniles or to engage in unprotected sex, or simply to enjoy low-cost sexual favors from highly exploited sex workers, has set off a crusade against such sex tourism, as this sign in a Thai hotel indicates.

Entrapment of participants of either sex is protested by civil libertarians, who argue that it is a violation of the right to privacy. They favor legalization on the ground that sex for a fee is a private matter between consenting adults. Supporters of legalization argue that it is harmful to the social order to have laws on the books that are routinely flouted; since laws against prostitution are not enforced effectively, it would be better not to have them at all.

Still another argument for legalizing prostitution is that prostitutes would no longer be viewed as lawbreakers. This change in status might go a long way toward reducing the tension and stress experienced by most prostitutes. Legally at least, they would no longer have to define themselves negatively; moreover, they would no longer be constantly in fear of arrest, even though by other norms prostitution would still be regarded as a social problem.

Some experts continue to argue against legalization. They believe that society is the ultimate victim of prostitution and that legalization would not necessarily remove the prostitute from exploitation by pimps or organized crime figures. Moreover, it might encourage more young women to enter "the life." They therefore question whether any benefits would accrue from legalization (Williamson & Cluse-Tolar, 2002).

Conventional Crimes

Conventional offenders tend to be young adults who commit robbery, larceny, burglary, and gang theft as a way of life. They usually begin their criminal career in adolescence as members of juvenile gangs, joining other truants from school to vandalize property and fight in the streets. As juvenile offenders, they are not organized or skillful enough to avoid arrest and conviction, and by young adulthood they have compiled a police record and may have spent time in prison.

Conventional offenders could be described as semiprofessional, since their techniques are not as sophisticated as those of organized and professional criminals, and they move into a criminal life only by degrees. For this reason, their self-concept as criminals develops gradually. By the time they have built up a criminal record, they have usually identified fairly strongly with criminality. The criminal record itself is society's way of defining these offenders as criminals. Once they have been so defined, it is almost impossible for them to reenter the mainstream of society.

Since only a small percentage of conventional crimes results in arrest, most offenders in this category are convinced that crime does pay. Moreover, the life of a successful criminal has a certain excitement, and many criminals are seduced into a life of crime by the excitement they experience in the criminal act itself (Siegel, 1999). Not only the sudden windfall of money but also the thrill of getting away with an illegal act and the release of tension after it has been committed can become part of the reward system (Katz, 1988). Because offenders associate mostly with other criminals, they develop a shared outlook that scorns the benefits of law-abiding behavior.

Organized Crime

Organized crime is a term that includes many types of criminal organizations, from large global crime syndicates that originated in Sicily and Italy (the Mafia), and more recently in Russia, to smaller local organizations whose membership may be more transient. Based on research in England, British sociologist Dick Hobb makes this observation:

> Contemporary serious crime groups possess the ability to splinter, dissolve, mutate, self-destruct, or simply decompose. For instance, I found that a group dealing in amphetamines splintered into both legal and illegal enterprise when a key member was arrested for a crime totally unconnected with their business. They were not bonded by some mysterious brotherhood of villainy, their collaboration was temporary and sealed with money. (Hobb, 1997, p. 57)

The groups that we usually think of as representing organized crime tend to be large and diversified regional or national units. They may organize initially to carry on a particular crime, such as drug trafficking, extortion, prostitution, or gambling. Later they may seek to control this activity in a given city or neighborhood, destroying or absorbing the competition. Eventually they may expand into other types of crime, protecting their members from arrest through intimidation or bribery of public officials.

Unlike other types of crime, organized crime is a system in which illegal activities are carried out as part of a rational plan devised by a large, often global organization that is attempting to maximize its overall profit. To operate most efficiently, organized crime relies on the division of labor in the performance of numerous diverse roles. Within a typical organized crime syndicate in a large metropolitan area, there will be groups in the stolen car and parts business, others in gambling, and still others in labor rackets. In each of these and other businesses there will be specific occupations like enforcer, driver, accountant, lawyer, and so on. Another major feature of organized crime is that the crime syndicate supplies goods and services that a large segment of the public wants but cannot obtain legally. Without the public's desire for gambling or drugs, for example, organized crime's basic means of existence would collapse.

In recent years the American FBI has investigated large and well-organized crime syndicates on the Mexican border that deal in international drug smuggling, as well as a growing number of Russian crime syndicates that have been caught moving large amounts of illegally gained money through U.S. and European banks (Shaw, 1999). These large, globally organized crime organizations derive huge profits from supplying illegal goods and services to the public. Their major source of profit is illegal gambling in the form of lotteries, numbers games, off-track betting, illegal casinos, and dice games. Much illegal gambling is controlled by organized crime syndicates that operate through elaborate hierarchies. Money is transferred up the hierarchy from the small operator, who takes the customer's bet, through several other levels until it finally reaches the syndicate's headquarters. This complex system protects the leaders, whose identities remain concealed from those below them. The centralized organization of gambling also increases efficiency, enlarges markets, and provides a systematic way of paying graft to public officials.

In Sicily, where the Mafia retain a powerful grip over community leaders, social activists use photos of Mafia killings to stimulate local and international protest. (© Franco Zecchin.)

Closely related to gambling and a major source of revenue for organized crime is *loan sharking,* or lending money at interest rates above the legal limit. These rates can be as high as 150 percent a week, and rates of more than 20 percent are common. Profits from gambling operations provide organized crime syndicates with large amounts of cash to lend, and they can ensure repayment by threatening violence. Most of the loans are made to gamblers who need to repay debts, to drug users, and to small businesses that are unable to obtain credit from legitimate sources.

Drug trafficking is organized crime's third major source of revenue. Its direct dealings in narcotics tend to be limited to imports from abroad and wholesale distribution. Lower-level operations are considered too risky and unprofitable and are left to others.

Organized Crime and Corruption. Organized crime could not flourish without bribery. By corrupting officials of public and private agencies, the syndicate tries to ensure that laws that would hamper its operations are not passed, or at least not enforced.

Corruption occurs at all levels of government, from police officers to high elected and appointed officials. It is especially effective with individuals in more powerful positions, since they can prevent lower-level personnel from enforcing laws against organized crime activities. If the cooperation of the police chief can be obtained, for example, a police officer who tries to arrest gamblers may be shifted to another assignment or denied a raise or promotion. Other officers will quickly learn from this example.

Professional Crimes

Professional criminals are the ones we read about in detective novels or see on television: the expert safecracker with sensitive fingers; the disarming con artist; the customer in a jewelry store who switches diamonds so quickly that the clerk does not notice; the counterfeiters who work under bright lights in the basement of a respectable shop. This class of criminals also includes the less glamorous pickpockets, full-time shoplifters and check forgers, truck hijackers, sellers of stolen goods, and blackmailers.

Professional criminals are dedicated to a life of crime; they live by it and pride themselves on their accomplishments. These criminals are seldom caught, and even if they are, they can usually manage to have the charges dropped or a sentence reduced. Meyer Lansky, a particularly successful thief who was a top figure in a national crime syndicate, spent only 3 months and 16 days in jail out of a criminal career that spanned over 50 years (Plate, 1975). These are the cleverest of all criminals, with the most sophisticated working methods.

Professional criminals tend to come from higher social strata than most people who are arrested for criminal activities. They frequently begin as employees in offices, hotels, and restaurants, with criminal life as a sideline. Eventually their criminal careers develop to the point at which they can make a living almost entirely from criminal activities. This phase usually starts at the same age at which conventional criminals are likely to give up crime. As criminologist E. M. Lemert put it, "Unemployment occasioned by old age does not seem to be a problem of con men; age ripens their skills, insights, and wit, and it also increases the confidence they inspire in their victims" (quoted in Quinney, 1979, p. 245). Most professional criminals enjoy long, uninterrupted careers because experience improves their skill at avoiding arrest. They often justify their activities by claiming that they are simply capitalizing on the fact that all people are dishonest and would probably be full-time criminals themselves if they had the ability and opportunity. Many are employed in operations carried on by organized crime syndicates.

Juvenile Delinquency

Historically, children have been presumed to lack the criminal intent to commit willful crimes; hence, juvenile law is designed primarily to protect and redirect young offenders rather than to punish them. There is a separate family court system for dealing with juvenile offenders, and their sentencing is limited. Within those limits, however, judges have wide discretion in dealing with youthful offenders and can choose the approach that they feel will be most effective.

In recent years there has been increasing dissatisfaction with the workings of juvenile law (Jacobs, 1990). Some critics contend that law-enforcement authorities have too much latitude in interpreting juvenile behavior and that standards differ too much from one community to another (Bennett, DiIulio, & Walters, 1996; Traub, 1996). The epidemic of violent youth crime—especially the violence that broke out in some U.S. schools in the late 1990s and the extremely violent gang warfare that coincided with the crack epidemic—created a public perception that young people were becoming especially prone to violence and crime. In fact, however, the long-term aging of the American and European populations and the waning of the crack epidemic have tended to help reduce youth crime and violence (*The Economist*, 2002). The Critical Research box below discusses this issue further.

As noted in the preceding chapter, many young people become involved in drug commerce at the retail level, especially because as juveniles they often run somewhat less risk of incarceration than people over 18 years of age. Involvement in petty sales and other aspects of drug commerce puts juveniles at risk of addiction and,

Critical Research

CRISIS OF YOUTH VIOLENCE OR ADULT PANIC?

Sensational and drastic acts of violence, such as the shootings and suicides at Columbine and other high schools, result in copycat violence, calls for urgent legislation, sermons about wayward youths, and a host of other immediate reactions. Critical sociologists, however, warn about overreaction. They warn that tragic violence can distort realities. Panic can stifle more constructive responses and worsen the underlying problems by denying students' rights and gagging their voices. Harvard research fellow Wendy Kaminer and University of California sociologist Mike Males exemplify this critical view. Here is how Kaminer (1999) applies her critical viewpoint on youth, school, and violence:

Fearful of violence and drugs, intolerant of dissent or simple nonconformity, public school officials are on the rampage. They're suspending and expelling even grade school students for making what might be considered, at worst, inappropriate remarks, dressing

oddly, or simply expressing political opinions. Efforts to strip students of rights are hardly new, but they have been greatly accelerated in recent months by hysteria about school violence and "terroristic" threats.

In Ohio a third-grader was suspended after writing a fortune cookie message, "You will die an honorable death," which he submitted for a school project. (A terroristic threat? Or an innocent, well-intentioned remark by a child who watches martial-arts videos?) Eleven high school students in Ohio were suspended for contributing to a gothic-themed web site. In Virginia a 10th-grader was suspended for dying his hair blue. In Missouri, high school junior Dustin Mitchell was suspended and required to perform 42 days of community service with the local police department for offering a flippant opinion on school violence in an Internet chat room (when asked if a tragedy like the Littleton shootings could happen in his school, Mitchell responded "yes").

Those students who dare to use their speech rights to protest such draconian restrictions on speech are

In the aftermath of school violence, young people who choose to dress and act in nonconforming ways often face hostility from more conforming adults and peers.

increasingly, of violent death. As the demand for cocaine and crack abates while law-enforcement pressure continues, there is an escalation of violence, often involving automatic weapons, among drug dealers and their associates. Thus, in some large American cities the homicide rate among juvenile males has reached record levels.

Teenagers who are arrested on minor sales or possession charges often begin a career in and out of detention centers and jails, where they are initiated into the world of professional crime (Sullivan, 1989). Young women who become involved in the drug world and associated illegal hustling often trade sexual services for drugs and thus are recruited into the culture of prostitution. Although prostitution may not be considered a serious crime, it places young women at serious risk of violent death or injury and of sterility or death from sexually transmitted diseases.

Status offenses, such as running away and vagrancy, are a very common reason for arrests of juveniles. In 2001 about 91,000 juvenile runaways were arrested in the United States, of whom 59 percent were females (*UCR,* 2002). This is one of the few types of arrest in which the usual gender distribution is reversed. The reason so many girls are runaways is that they are far more likely than boys to be abused, both sexually and otherwise, in their homes.

---

liable to be punished severely. In Texas, 17-year-old high school student Jennifer Boccia was suspended for wearing a black armband to school to protest restraints on free speech that followed the shootings in Littleton. Boccia was also reprimanded by her school principal, Ira Sparks, for daring to tell her story to the media; she was told that if she wanted to clear her record, she should refrain from speaking to the media before discussing her remarks with school officials. Boccia made a federal case of it and won a settlement from her school vindicating her First Amendment rights. The landmark 1969 Supreme Court decision *Tinker* v. *Des Moines Independent Community School District* upholding the right to wear a black armband to school to protest the Vietnam War has not been overruled, but its assertion that students do not leave their First Amendment rights at the schoolhouse door has not been honored either. (p. 11)

Kaminer and Males both point out that despite sensational juvenile violent acts, the trends in youth violence have actually been quite favorable in recent years. Males (1998) observes,

The sharp increase in teenage murder and violent crime from 1984 to 1992 occurred only among inner-city populations stressed by poverty, job loss, isolation, and growth in warring gangs. States which separate statistics by ethnicity, such as California, show that violence and homicide among white (non-Latino) teenagers actually declined over the last two decades. A white California teenager is only one-fifth as likely to be murdered as a black fifty-year-old. So concentrated is youth homicide that two or three Los Angeles zip codes account for more than the entire state of Minnesota. (p. 22)

The most frightening myth, Males believes, is "that kids today are more murderous and that the nation faces rising

hordes of 'adolescent super-predators.'" Magazine covers and "experts," Males argues, "trumpet that teenagers everywhere are slaughtering in record bloodlust. Not true" (p. 22).

Do these critical sociological viewpoints suggest that school violence is not a social problem? On the contrary. They simply warn that demonizing youth in response to sensational episodes of violence is not justified by the facts. Depriving students of their liberties, they assert, will further alienate many young people who expect to be able to voice criticisms of society in their schools. We have seen that the American public is genuinely worried about school violence and that the facts about its prevalence support their concern, especially if it is directed at violence in disadvantaged communities. The role of critical sociology, however, is to channel that concern away from panic and toward policies based on genuine conditions.

Arrests in the War on Drugs often lead to felony convictions for youthful offenders. As a consequence of efforts to lengthen prison terms for people with multiple felony convictions, these early episodes could greatly increase the risk of eventual life imprisonment.

Hate Crimes

It is perhaps appropriate to follow juvenile crimes with a discussion of hate crimes. Many of the most sensational recent crimes that were motivated by deep hatreds for people of other groups were committed by teenagers and young adults. The killings at Columbine High School in Colorado and those of James Byrd, Jr., in Texas and Matthew Shepard in Wyoming are hate crimes that most readers will remember vividly. Even when they do not result in murder and mayhem, these criminal acts reveal hatreds and violent propensities that go far beyond what we usually categorize as juvenile crime. Hatred of gays or people of other races and religions is widespread in all societies, but the propensity to express it through violent acts tends to be a

Bias Motivation	Offenses	Percent[a]	Bias Motivation	Offenses	Percent[a]
TABLE 5-1 — HATE CRIMES, 1999					
Total	9,384	100.0	Anti-Islamic	34	2.2
Race, total	5,293	56.4	Anti-other religious group	173	11.2
Anti-White	981	18.5	Anti-multireligious group	35	2.3
Anti-Black	3,574	67.5	Anti-atheism, agnosticism, etc.	5	0.3
Anti-American Indian/Alaskan native	50	0.9	Sexual orientation, total	1,492	15.9
Anti-Asian/Pacific Islander	369	7.0	Anti-male homosexual	1,030	69.0
Anti-multiracial group	319	6.0	Anti-female homosexual	215	14.4
Ethnicity/national origin, total	1,026	11.0	Anti-homosexual	206	13.8
Anti-Hispanic	588	58.7	Anti-heterosexual	16	1.1
Anti-other ethnicity/national origin	438	41.3	Anti-bisexual	25	1.7
Religion, total	1,539	10.9	Disability, total	22	0.2
Anti-Jewish	1,119	72.7	Anti-physical	11	50.0
Anti-Catholic	41	2.7	Anti-mental	11	50.0
Anti-Protestant	52	3.4	Multiple bias	12	0.1

[a]Percentages may not total 100 because of rounding.

Source: Statistical Abstract, 2001.

phenomenon of youth and young adulthood. Yet the emotions that motivate the deeds are taken from the adults who socialize young people. Throughout the world—in Kosovo, Rwanda, Northern Ireland, Israel, Pakistan, Russia, the United States, and elsewhere—adult hatreds spawn violence, which is often carried out by the young.

In an exhaustive study of hate crimes, the FBI concluded that 61 percent of such incidents were based on race, 13 percent on sexual orientation, and another 10 percent on ethnicity or national origin. Intimidation, the single most frequently reported hate crime offense, accounts for 41 percent of the total; damage, destruction, or vandalism of property for 23 percent; simple assault for 18 percent; and aggravated assault for 13 percent (Gondles, 1999). Table 5–1 shows that the most common hate crimes are those involving racial hatred, but crimes against people of other religions and against people who are or appear to be gay are major categories of hate crime as well.

The 1994 Crime Act defines a hate crime as "a crime in which the defendant intentionally selects a victim, or in the case of a property crime, the property that is the object of the crime, because of the actual or perceived race, color, national origin, ethnicity, gender, disability, or sexual orientation of any person." Thirty-seven states have statutes addressing hate crime, and others have pending legislation in this area. But the major controversy surrounding the issue of hate crimes is whether the federal government needs a stronger law that sets greater penalties for crimes motivated by hatred against specific social groups.

Gangs, Guns, and Violent Death

Why has the homicide rate in the United States reached levels as much as 20 times those found in other industrialized nations? (See Figure 5–5.) There is no one answer, but important explanations may be found in an analysis of changing patterns of juvenile violence, the increased firepower available to violent people, and the inability of American society to agree on appropriate controls on lethal weapons.

In many sensational headlines, one reads of brutal violence by juvenile gangs in large cities. In Los Angeles, the Crips and Bloods are said to be especially violent gangs engaged in the distribution of crack cocaine. In Chicago and elsewhere, violence is attributed to the activities of armed gangs of various kinds. Residents of public housing projects routinely must negotiate with gang leaders to ensure the safety of their buildings and grounds and prevent gang members from killing children (Vankatesh, 2000). In the depressed manufacturing city of Paterson, New Jersey, rumors of a pending violent act by local gangs caused parents to keep their children home from school (Hanley, 2002).

In the 1980s and early 1990s there was an upsurge of gang activity and gang-related violence in smaller cities and suburban areas, most often associated with drug dealing. More recently, skinheads and other groups of teenagers and young adults have committed hate crimes, often involving violent attacks on homosexuals, Jews, and Asian immigrants (Males, 1998). Today much lethal gang violence is still associated with the sale and use of crack cocaine or other illicit rugs, especially in some smaller cities and towns and in specific inner-city communities.

Between 1960 and 1990 the rate of offenses involving dangerous weapons, especially handguns, increased from less than 50 per 100,000 people to well over 100. Although the rate has decreased recently, largely because of a decline in gang-related shootings, Figure 5–6 shows that weapons offenses vary greatly by state; the highest rates are found in the South and Southwest and in urban areas in the Northeast. Figure 5–7 shows that the rate of death due to firearms is from three to six times the rate in Western nations with comparable levels of industrial and urban development. Although gun possession and deaths from guns are problems that extend well beyond the phenomenon of youth gangs, early involvement in crime, gangs, and weapons possession among teenagers, of whom the large majority come from poverty-stricken and socially isolated neighborhoods, is a strong signal that creative programs to combat poverty and neglect are urgently needed in communities throughout the nation.

150   CHAPTER 5

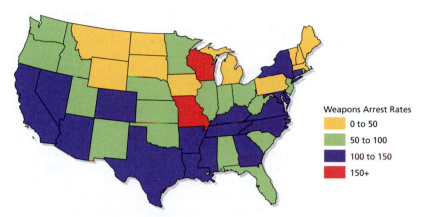

Weapons Offense Arrest Rates per 100,000 Population, by State

State	Rate	State	Rate	State	Rate
District of Columbia	301	Michigan	107	Alabama	67
Missouri	199	Kentucky	106	Minnesota	61
Wisconsin	165	Maryland	104	Rhode Island	60
Georgia	149	New York	102	Hawaii	60
Louisiana	142	Ohio	97	Indiana	59
Nevada	141	New Jersey	94	Idaho	52
Colorado	140	Kansas	94	Pennsylvania	49
Texas	139	Oklahoma	91	South Dakota	41
Mississippi	135	Utah	85	Massachusetts	35
California	135	Oregon	81	Wyoming	31
North Carolina	132	Nebraska	78	Delaware	30
Tennessee	131	West Virginia	77	Iowa	30
Virginia	129	South Carolina	77	North Dakota	25
Arkansas	126	Washington	75	Maine	23
Connecticut	116	Illinois	75	New Hampshire	16
Arizona	114	New Mexico	71	Montana	12
Alaska	107	Florida	68	Vermont	1

FIGURE 5-6 Weapons Offense Rates by State

Source: Greenfield & Zawetz, 1995.

Gangs range from the peer groups that hang out on street corners to the well-organized, hierarchical gangs of crime syndicates. The latter often include contract killers, professional murderers who kill for money. But killings related to organized crime account for only a small percentage of all murders. Do deaths caused by other types of gangs account for the remainder? This does not seem to be the case.

Juvenile and young-adult gangs often begin as street corner cliques and become incorporated into a larger gang confederation. These organizations are often located

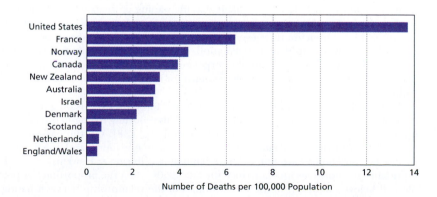

FIGURE 5-7 Death Rates from Firearms, Selected Countries (Average Annual Deaths per 100,000 Population)

Source: Data from *Statistical Abstract*, 1999.

in poor, segregated communities, where much of their activity is dedicated to the defense of local territory, or turf (Venkatesh, 2000). But experts on the sociology of gangs are quick to point out that there are many types of juvenile gang structures and many different types of gang activity, not all of which are violent or criminal.

In a thorough study of gang confederations in Milwaukee, John M. Hagedorn (1988; Hagedorn, Torres, & Giglio, 1998) found that while gangs in large cities like Los Angeles, Chicago, and New York have been present more or less continuously for generations, in smaller cities and suburban areas gangs may be a new phenomenon. And simply because a community does not have recognizable gangs does not mean that gangs may not form in the near future. Much depends on relations between teenagers and the police, on the drug trade and its control, and on how young people perceive the need (or lack of it) to defend their turf from other teenagers. Thus, in Milwaukee, although there is some fighting, especially as young men strive to gain prestige within the gangs, there is relatively little gang warfare or homicide attributable to gang warfare. In Chicago, in contrast, there seems to be far more gang-related homicide, especially among Hispanic gangs.

A large majority of the gang members Hagedorn (1988) interviewed admitted owning at least one handgun. He concludes that the problem of violence and homicide is related more to the increasing availability of guns and the involvement of some gangs in the illegal drug industry than to inherent features of the gangs themselves; this conclusion is shared by most students of gang behavior. Martin Sanchez-Jankowsky (1991), one of the nation's foremost authorities on violent gangs, notes that contrary to what some members of the public—and some sociologists—think, gang members typically do not like violence and the risks to personal safety that it entails. But most gang members believe that "if you do not attack, you will be attacked." This worldview implies that much gang violence is premeditated with the goal of taking the opponent by surprise. In addition, Sanchez-Jankowski notes, "the injuries incurred as a result of organizational violence [in the gang] become the social cement that creates group bonds in a deviant individualist setting." Overall, he concludes, gang violence "is understood to be the instrument used to achieve objectives that are not achievable in other ways" (p. 177).

Another study of gang activity and involvement in drug dealing supports Hagedorn's conclusions and reinforces the idea that high rates of lethal violence are attributable more to the widespread use of guns than to the presence of gangs themselves. Terry Williams (1989) spent three years following the activities of a mobile drug "crew" in New York. This small and highly entrepreneurial gang was in the retail crack business. Its success depended on discipline—on ensuring that members did not become too high to function in their jobs or so careless that they became victims of violent robberies. Williams, like Hagedorn, documents the widespread and routine possession of handguns, but he also notes the increasing availability of more powerful automatic weapons and submachine guns.

As noted earlier, rates of gun violence, homicide, and aggravated assault reached their peaks in the early 1990s. It is likely that the waning of the crack epidemic is part of the reason for the recent declines in those rates. But the United States had extremely high homicide rates even before the advent of crack; drugs alone, therefore, do not provide a sufficient explanation. The availability of easily concealed handguns, together with the traditions of interpersonal violence that date from the frontier period of American history, probably accounts for much of the deadly violence in the United States.

Franklin E. Zimring (1985), one of the nation's foremost experts on guns and gun control, states that the "proportion of all households reporting handgun ownership has increased substantially over a twenty-year period" (p. 138). On the basis of survey research, Zimring and associates estimate that between one-fourth and one-third of all American households have one or more handguns (Zimring & Hawkins, 1997). This represents an enormous increase since the late 1950s, when the proportion was probably well below one in ten households. Studies of the relationship between handgun

152   CHAPTER 5

possession and homicide find that when people arm themselves out of fear and a desire for protection, there is also an increased risk of fatalities from accidents involving guns, as well as homicides caused by mistaken recourse to fatal force—as in the tragic case of a Japanese exchange student in New Orleans who was killed when he approached the wrong house in search of a party to which he had been invited (Reiss & Roth, 1993).

Conditions and Causes of Crime and Violence

In this section we consider several explanations for crime, beginning with nonsociological ones and continuing with various sociological approaches based on the theoretical perspectives described in Chapter 1.

Biological Explanations of Crime

A medieval law stated that "if two persons fell under suspicion of crime the uglier or more deformed was to be regarded as more probably guilty" (Ellis, 1914; quoted in Wilson & Herrnstein, 1985, p. 71). This law and others like it illustrate the age-old and deep-seated belief that criminality can be explained in terms of certain physical characteristics of the criminal. An example of this point of view is the theory of crime advanced by an Italian physician, Cesare Lombroso, in the late nineteenth century.

Lombroso was convinced that there is a "criminal man" (or woman), a type of human being who is physically distinct from ordinary human beings. In the course of his examinations of convicts both before and after their deaths, he developed the concept of *criminal atavism*—the notion that criminality is associated with physical characteristics that resemble those of primitive humans and lower primates: a sloping forehead, long arms, a primitive brain, and the like. Lombroso believed, in short, that there was such a thing as a "born criminal." Although this explanation was wrong, it served to initiate scientific inquiry into the causes of crime.

In the twentieth century, Lombroso's theory and other biologically based explanations of crime have been discredited and supplanted by sociological theories. However, some theorists (e.g., Wilson & Herrnstein, 1985) defend the identification of biological characteristics that appear to be predisposing factors in criminal behavior rather than full explanations of it. They believe that certain inherited traits, such as an extra Y chromosome or a particularly athletic physique, may be correlated with a greater than average tendency to engage in criminal behavior.

Research on the possibility of a link between criminality and an extra Y chromosome has consistently found that no such relationship can be demonstrated. Nevertheless, biologists, medical researchers, and some behavioral scientists continue to search for possible genetic causes of crime. Efforts by the National Academy of Sciences and other prestigious scientific organizations to study the possible biological basis of crime have generated heated controversy and scientific debate, in part because biological research on crime usually fails, as sociologist Joan McCord points out, "to look at the social and psychological variables." McCord herself analyzed data from a long-term study of pairs of brothers in the Boston area between 1926 and 1933, comparing their criminal histories with each other and with those of subjects from similar backgrounds; she found no evidence of a genetic contribution to criminality (cited in Horgan, 1993). Although new efforts to establish genetic or other biological origins of criminality are also likely to fail, most sociologists agree with Troy Duster, who argues that such studies can help, because if they properly account for social variables such as racism and class inequality, they will counteract the notion of a biological basis for crime in the lower classes or among some racial groups (cited in Horgan, 1993).

Biology, Violence, and Criminality

Of course, not all crimes involve interpersonal violence, but those we fear most—murder, rape, assault, and robbery (mugging)—definitely do. But violence is hardly limited to violent criminals. Homo sapiens, self-proclaimed to represent the pinnacle of evolution, is in fact the earth's most dangerous living species. Between 1820 and 1945, human beings killed 59 million other human beings—one every 68 seconds—in wars, murders, quarrels, and skirmishes (Boelkins & Heiser, 1970). Violence is also commonplace in many American homes. In recent years the volume of reports of child abuse and complaints to the police of domestic violence has been high enough to prompt Congress to hold numerous hearings on the subject (Berry, 1995; Gelles, 1996). Even before the sensational trial of O. J. Simpson brought family violence and spouse abuse to national attention, professionals who work with families in distress were warning that violence is an everyday occurrence in far too many families.

Is violence simply part of human nature? Since it is such a common occurrence, some social scientists have argued that human aggressive tendencies are inherent or instinctual. According to this view, only social organization keeps violent tendencies under control. Other experts argue that aggression is natural but violence is not. In an exhaustive review of research on the causes of interpersonal violence, a panel of experts convened by the National Academy of Sciences concluded that there is no solid evidence to support neurological or biological explanations of violent behavior. The panel did note, however, that findings from studies of animals and humans point to several features of the nervous system as possible sources of such explanations and recommended continued research (Reiss & Roth, 1993). Given the weight of evidence in favor of social and psychological explanations of violent behavior, this recommendation drew considerable criticism from social scientists (Kornblum, 1993).

In her response to the report, Dorothy Nelkin (1995), a well-known evaluator of scientific panels, argued that "biology is not destiny" and "it is not necessary to explain through biology why a child exposed to poverty and racism might become violent." The real source of violence, she believes, can be found in the growing inequality in the United States and other societies. This is an important sociological viewpoint, to which we will return in later chapters.

Gender and Crime

Since nations began collecting systematic statistics on crime, analysts have realized that men are far more likely than women to commit crimes. Indeed, gender is one of the most obvious correlates of criminality. Although there are significant variations from one society to another, numerous studies of crime in different countries demonstrate that the gender gap is universal. Males are 5 to 50 times as likely to be arrested as females (Steffensmeier & Allan, 1996). As women have gained greater social equality with men in industrialized countries, however, the ratio of male to female arrests has decreased, although men still lead in most categories of crime. (See Figure 5–8.)

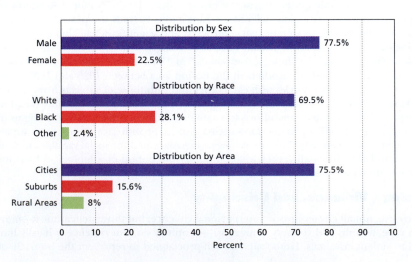

FIGURE 5–8 Total Arrests by Sex, Race, and Area, 2001

Source: Data from Federal Bureau of Investigation, *Uniform Crime Reports,* 2002.

The different arrest rates for men and women seem to be a result of different patterns of socialization. In our society men have traditionally been raised to be more aggressive than women, and they have therefore been more likely to commit certain kinds of crimes. Women generally have been regarded more protectively by the police and the courts; therefore, they have been less likely to be arrested and, if arrested, less likely to be punished severely, especially if they are wives or mothers. Despite the persistent differences in arrest rates of women and men, with men more than eight times more likely to appear in official crime statistics, rates of crime by women increased rapidly in the second half of the twentieth century. As more women are socialized under conditions of deprivation and abuse, we can expect that larger numbers will be recruited into street hustling, prostitution, and shoplifting, which in turn will account for increasing numbers of arrests (Friedman, 1993; Miller, 1986). Indeed, today women make up 16 percent of the total prison population in the United States, compared to only 7.7 percent in 1997 (Greenfield & Snell, 1999).

Age and Crime

Criminologists have found age to be more strongly correlated with criminal behavior than any other factor (McKeown, Jackson, & Valois, 1998). The age of the offender is closely related not only to crime rates but also to the types of crimes committed. Data from several nations, including England, Wales, and France, provide evidence that the correlation between age and crime holds across geographic boundaries (Gottfredson & Hirschi, 1995; Hirschi & Gottfredson, 1983).

Teenagers and young adults accounted for 45.9 percent of arrests in the United States in 2001, and 31.4 percent of all arrests were of people under the age of 21. A solid majority of arrests for property crimes—58.3 percent—were of people under 25 (*UCR*, 2002). Although young people may be arrested more than older offenders because the young are less experienced, it is clear that many teenagers and young adults, especially those who become involved in gang activities, are enticed by opportunities to commit various kinds of thefts. Automobile and bicycle thefts and vandalism are among the major juvenile crimes, although they are by no means limited to the young.

Violent Youth Crime. The rate of violent felonies committed by children aged 10 to 17 has increased for most of the past ten years, a trend that runs counter to the decrease in violence among adults in the United States (Belluck, 1996). Figure 5–9 shows the rate of arrests for violent crimes per 100,000 boys and girls aged 10 to 17. The graph clearly shows that violent youth crime peaked in 1994 and then began to decline quite

FIGURE 5-9 Arrests of Youths, 1980–1999

Source: U.S. Surgeon General, 2001.

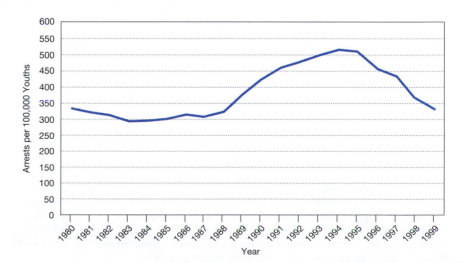

Census 2000: Implications for the Future

CHANGING YOUTH COHORTS

One of the fascinating mysteries of the crime situation in the United States is why youth crime has not diminished more than it did during the past two decades. Since the proportion of young people between the ages of 15 and 30 in the population declined rather dramatically, many social scientists believed that youth and young-adult crime would also drop quickly as well. But the number of arrests of young people on criminal charges and the number of people under 30 in the nation's prisons did not follow the expected trend.

In this box we examine this situation more closely. First we look at what the 2000 census reveals about the number of young people in the U.S. population. Then we apply social-scientific analysis to explain why the expected trend did not occur.

The following table presents data on the number of young people in the U.S. population:

PEOPLE UNDER AGE 30 IN THE UNITED STATES, 1980–2000

	1980	1990	2000
% 15–19	9.3	7.2	7.2
% 20–24	9.4	7.7	6.6
% 24–29	8.6	8.6	8.7
# 18–24 (millions)	30	27	26
Median age	30.0	32.8	35.5

Source: U.S. Census Bureau, 2002.

The 2000 census revealed that the U.S. population is aging quite rapidly. In 1980 the median age of Americans was about 30, and by 2000 it was over 35. The median age measures the age at which half the population is over that age and half under it. As the median age creeps upward, fewer people are in the younger age cohorts and more are in the elderly ones. We will see in Chapter 9 that these changes are of extreme importance in any society, and that the aging of the U.S. population carries with it many vital policy issues. But if we look for a moment at the declining proportional size of the youthful population, the census figures reveal that between 1980 and 2000 the number of people between 18 and 24 fell by about 6 million. This change led many criminologists and sociologists to support the hypothesis that as the youthful population declined, there would be a decline in crimes committed by youth—a decline that could be measured in a number of ways, including the number of young people arrested and the number incarcerated.

It appears that the combined effects of increased arrests and imprisonment for drug possession and sales, greater use of mandatory sentencing for drug and other felony arrests, longer prison sentences, and increased capacities of state prisons throughout much of the nation have all contributed to rising prison populations, despite demographic changes that would otherwise contribute to decreases in crime and incarceration (Marvell & Moody, 1997). From 1980 to 2001 the number of people arrested on drug charges increased from about 581,000 to more than 1.5 million. The prison population (all levels) of those convicted and sentenced on drug charges went from 40,000 to 453,000 in the same period. Fifty-eight percent of those sentenced to prison under federal mandatory sentencing guidelines were not engaged in criminal violence, and four out of five were either black or Hispanic. These facts help explain why, as we see in Figure 5–9, the rate of arrests of young people can decrease while the number of those incarcerated can continue to rise (Barlow & Kauzlarich, 2002; King & Maurer, 2002; Wacquant, 2001).

Harsh critics of the U.S. justice system, such as Loïc Wacquant (2002), argue that high rates of arrest and prison sentencing, predominantly of teenagers and young adults, in impoverished minority communities are a new way for the powerful to exercise their control over poor people of color and to sustain the deep inequalities that separate the races. In the states with the greatest racial disparities in sentencing, blacks are ten times more likely to be imprisoned than whites, and with over 800,000 black men behind bars, Wacquant argues, the United States has created a drastically unjust new form of ghettoization. The U.S. Department of Justice counters such claims by attempting to show that the rate of incarceration of African Americans and Hispanics is declining as a proportion of those imprisoned, but for many critics the continuing disparities in prison populations speak for themselves.

sharply. This positive shift is not due to any one factor, but as we see in Census 2000: Implications for the Future above, part of the explanation simply has to do with the longer-term trend toward an older population and a relative decline in the size of the youth cohorts. Another explanation is that in many cities and towns the crack epidemic has waned, and with it the tendency for youth gangs to resort to violence—although, as noted earlier, youth violence and gangs continue to plague many communities. Experience in gangs and socialization into the adult world of crime (either by older gang members or by professional criminals) often carries young people into lives of crime, but most young people who have engaged in juvenile delinquency do not become career criminals. Moreover, young adults who have been involved in crime often seek more constructive and less risky alternatives as they grow older.

156 CHAPTER 5

It is fortunate for society that some criminals give up crime in their late 20s or early 30s, for reasons that are not clear to criminologists (Gottfredson & Hirschi, 1995). Perhaps they marry and find their family life more rewarding than crime. For these individuals, family responsibilities seem to be a more powerful inhibitor of criminal behavior than rehabilitation or coercion. This "maturing out" is a subject of great interest to sociologists. In a study of the criminal careers of juvenile males in three urban communities of whites, African Americans, and Latinos respectively, Mercer Sullivan (1989) found that as the boys grew older there was an increasingly marked convergence in their tendency to reduce their criminal activity in favor of increased income from legitimate sources. Sullivan attributes this change to their greater maturity, their recognition that sanctions were becoming more severe, and their perception that their opportunities to hold real jobs were better than they had been when they were younger.

Sociological Explanations of Crime

Demographic factors do not offer a complete explanation of crime. They do not, for example, explain why some juveniles and young adults drift into long-term criminal careers or why some young people never commit crimes. Nor do they tell us why some individuals, such as white-collar criminals, begin breaking laws during adulthood and middle age (Barlow & Kauzlarich, 2002). Thus, in addition to demographic analyses of crime, sociologists have proposed at least four theoretical approaches to explain why some people become criminals and others do not.

The first theoretical approach discussed here has evolved from conflict theory; it claims that most crime is either a form of rebellion by members of lower social classes or a form of illegal exploitation by the rich and powerful. A second approach, derived from the functionalist perspective, holds that crime stems from the uncertainty about norms of proper conduct that accompanies rapid social change and social disorganization. A third major explanation applies the interactionist perspective to the study of how people drift toward criminal subcultures and become socialized for criminal careers.

Conflict Approaches to the Study of Crime. Conflict theorists identify inequalities of wealth, status, and power as the underlying conditions that produce criminal behavior. Groups in society that are more disadvantaged than other groups, such as the poor and racial minorities who experience discrimination, are thought to be likely to rebel against their situation. Criminality, in this view, is one way in which disadvantaged individuals act out their rebellion against society (Quinney, 1979).

Inequality and Crime. As noted earlier in the chapter, official statistics show a high incidence of crime among members of the lower socioeconomic classes. Those statistics have fueled a sociological debate over the relationship between social class and criminality. For much of the twentieth century many sociologists believed that people in lower socioeconomic classes were more likely than those in higher classes to commit crimes. In 1978 criminologists Charles R. Tittle, Wayne J. Villemez, and Douglas A. Smith (1978) analyzed existing studies of crime and class status to determine whether the inverse relationship between class status and the commission of crime always held. When they examined data from arrest records, they found evidence to support the prevailing view. But when they reviewed data from self-report studies, they found no link between class and crime. On the basis of these results, the investigators concluded that "it is time to shift away from class-based theories to those emphasizing more generic processes" (p. 654).

Cross-cultural research on crime suggests that rapid increases in inequality, rather than long-standing patterns of poverty and wealth (e.g., as in India), tend to produce increases in crime (Bunnell, 1995). For example, in the nations of the former Soviet Union there have been rapid increases in poverty and in the number of wealthy individuals, many of whom have made their fortunes in connection with organized crime or other criminal activity. This rapid social change, in which it is no longer clear what the rules of behavior are or whether laws will be enforced, tends to produce lawlessness and crime.

As the total U.S. prison population has grown to record levels, the conflict perspective on crime has gained new adherents. Joseph Califano (1998), former secretary of Health and Human Services, is an example. Califano is highly critical of theories of crime that suggest that only punishment can deter people from committing crimes. He sees the failure of U.S. drug policy and the failure to provide adequate rehabilitation as major causes of the boom in prison populations—which, he believes, only increases the chances that people in prison will become criminal recidivists later in their lives. In other words, in Califano's view it is conflicts in American society over how to deal with drug and alcohol abuse that result in some types of crime and, more important, in the dramatic increases in the prison population. More critical theorists, however, still view major differences in income in a society as the most important contributor to crime (Anderson, 1992, 1999; Methwin, 1997).

Race and Crime. Every study of crime based on official data shows that blacks are overrepresented among those who are arrested, convicted, and imprisoned for street crimes. According to official statistics, blacks are arrested at higher rates than whites on charges of murder, rape, robbery, and other index crimes.

In any society one can find differences in crime rates among various racial and ethnic groups. Chinese and Japanese Americans have lower crime rates than other Americans; Hungarian immigrants to Sweden have higher crime rates than native Swedes; Scandinavian immigrants to the United States get into less trouble with the police than do Americans of Anglo-Saxon descent (Reckless, 1973). In the case of black Americans, however, the differences are pronounced; for example, "If blacks were arrested for robbery at the same rate as are whites, there would be half as many robbers arrested in the United States" (Wilson & Herrnstein, 1985, pp. 461–462).

It is possible that the overrepresentation of blacks in official crime statistics is due to greater surveillance of black communities by the police and to the greater likelihood that blacks who commit crimes will be arrested and imprisoned. One expert has calculated that about 80 percent of the disproportion in the rates of imprisonment can be attributed to the disproportion in arrest rates (Blumstein, 1982). However, victimization surveys show that police and court bias cannot be the sole cause. Blacks are far more likely than whites to be victims of crime, and it is unlikely that these higher victimization rates are caused by whites who enter black neighborhoods to commit crimes (Wilson & Herrnstein, 1985). (See the Critical Research box on page 158.)

A more plausible explanation is the disproportionately high percentage of blacks in the lower classes, which, as we saw earlier, are associated with higher crime rates. But economic disadvantage alone cannot fully account for the racial disparity in crime rates. The higher arrest rates for blacks persist even when socioeconomic status is taken into consideration. Moreover, offenders who commit numerous crimes begin to exhibit delinquent behavior early in life, before their outlook has been affected by such factors as inability to find a good job (Adler, Mueller, & Laufer, 1995).

Research by William Julius Wilson (1996a) points to the growing isolation of some black communities from sources of jobs and income. This trend is especially marked in and around cities that have lost large numbers of manufacturing jobs, which once provided a relatively decent livelihood for African American and other minority workers. In communities where legal employment is in short supply, people often turn to illegal activities.

The Functionalist View: Anomie Theory. Anomie theory, also known as the goals-and-opportunities approach, is favored by many scholars who seek explanations of crime. Robert K. Merton (1968) argues that a society has both approved goals and approved ways of attaining them. When some members of the society accept the goals (e.g., home ownership) but do not have access to the approved means of attaining them (e.g., earned income), their adherence to the approved norms is likely to be weakened, and they may try to attain the goals by other, socially unacceptable means (e.g.,

158 CHAPTER 5

RACIAL PROFILING

David Cole and Kathryn Russell are two of the leading critical criminologists in the United States. Both have been documenting patterns of racial unfairness and discrimination in the criminal justice system. Cole's (2000) newest study, *No Equal Justice,* is a compendium of facts about racial injustice in arrest procedures, court proceedings, prison sentencing, and much more. Cole also suggests some timely policy changes that would begin to balance the scales of justice, which he shows are heavily weighted against non-white Americans.

Why, for example, do California blacks, who make up only 7 percent of the state's population, account for over 40 percent of the "third-strike" defendants sent to state prisons? Even when one accounts for greater poverty and higher crime rates among African Americans, these differences are way out of line. What happens, Cole demonstrates, is that patterns of racial profiling in arrests bring more minorities into the justice system. Lack of access to better legal services, along with patterns of bias in jury selection, help account for much higher conviction rates among people of color. Unequal sentencing accounts for longer prison terms for minority group members and thus for higher proportions in prison. These patterns of racial injustice are examples of what is known as *institutional racism.* They are discriminatory practices engaged in by the institutions of law, not acts of personal prejudice or racial bigotry. But their effects, according to Cole, are a major threat to American democracy.

Cole is particularly critical of the use of racial profiling in federal, state, and municipal police forces. This term refers to the tendency to view members of certain minority groups as more likely to commit crimes than the general population, and to use that assumption in making decisions about such procedures as traffic stops, personal searches, and customs investigations. The subject of racial profiling has become extremely controversial in many states in the past few years. Russell (1999) also conducts research on profiling and its racial bias. As she puts it, "The high number of blacks arrested are partially the result of police targeting them in the first place" (p. 12).

Are black Americans more likely to commit crimes, or are their higher arrest rates a function of discriminatory police profiling? The National Household Survey of Substance and Drug Abuse finds that roughly the same proportion of blacks and whites—12 to 13 percent—say that they use illegal substances. Yet 37 percent of those arrested for drug-related crimes such as trafficking or possession are black (Russell, 1999).

In many minority communities, feelings against racial profiling are profound and bitter. The phrase "driving while black" sums up much of the attitude; it seems as if merely being an African American driver is a crime. Cole (2000) has gathered large amounts of data to support this perception. His data show that wherever police have broad discretion, they disproportionately stop and search minorities. The following are among the many examples he cites:

■ Reviewing police videotapes, the *Orlando Sentinel* found that in 1992 in Volusia County, Florida, on a road where approximately 5 percent of the drivers are identifiably black or Hispanic, 70 percent of those stopped and 80 percent of those searched were black or Hispanic.

■ Analyzing some 16 million driving records, the *Houston Chronicle* found that in 1995 blacks who traveled in white enclaves of Houston were twice as likely as whites to be ticketed for traffic offenses.

■ In 1998 the American Civil Liberties Union reported that during a nearly three-year period 70 percent of the drivers stopped and searched on Interstate 95 in Maryland were African American, whereas only 17.5 percent of the drivers and speeders on that road were black.

■ A 1998 analysis of police records found that in Philadelphia African Americans were subject to both car stops and pedestrian stops at rates that were disproportionate to their representation in the population.

■ According to the New Jersey attorney general, 77 percent of the motorists stopped and searched by New Jersey state troopers are black or Hispanic, even though only 13.5 percent of the drivers on New Jersey highways are black or Hispanic.

■ A 1999 ACLU analysis of Illinois traffic data found that Hispanics account for less than 8 percent of the state's population but for 27 percent of those stopped and searched by drug-interdiction units.

This evidence suggests that racial profiling is a nationwide problem (Cole, 2000).

fraud). In other words, criminal behavior occurs when socially approved means are not available for the realization of highly desired goals.

Anomie, the feeling of being adrift that arises from the disparity between goals and means, may vary with nationality, ethnic background, bias, religion, and other social characteristics. Some societies emphasize strict adherence to behavioral norms—the case in Japan, for example—and for them the degree of anomie may be fairly low.

Others place relatively more emphasis on the attainment of goals and less on their being attained in socially approved ways. Merton (1968) maintains that the United States is such a society. Identifying anomie as a basic characteristic of American society, he lists several kinds of common adaptations. One of these, innovation, consists of rejecting approved practices while retaining the desired goals. This seems to characterize the behavior of certain lower-class gang members, who have adopted socially approved goals but abandoned socially approved methods of attaining them.

This rejection of approved practices occurs widely in groups with the greatest disjuncture among goals, norms, and opportunities. In this country it is most often found among those who have the greatest difficulty in obtaining a good education or training for high-paying jobs, particularly members of disadvantaged minority groups. Higher crime rates among such groups are not automatic, but they can be expected when the goals that people internalize are dictated to them by a society that at the same time erects barriers to the attainment of those goals by approved means. If more attainable goals were set for people in lower socioeconomic classes, presumably there would be less disjuncture between goals and means and hence less anomie. For example, if low-cost rental housing were more widely available as a goal, more poor people could see how even low-wage jobs would improve their lives. When only luxury homes are available (and shown as models on television), the poor sense the futility of conventional jobs or other approved means.

Since the initial formulation of the anomie approach, research seems to have provided at least some support for its basic premise, although there are types of crimes that it fails to explain adequately, such as assault for purposes other than monetary gain. This omission is related to the question that is most frequently raised about Merton's theory: Are financial success and material possessions only middle-class goals? Do members of the lower classes have different values and aspirations? Many sociologists believe that people in the lower classes tend to hold two sets of beliefs simultaneously. That is, they share the norms and values of the larger society but are forced to develop standards and expectations of their own so that they can deal realistically with their particular circumstances. For example, people in the lower classes share with the affluent the view that crime is bad, but they lack conventional means to attain such goals as secure jobs. They may consider illegal "hustles" as an alternative means to some goals, especially when these crimes seem justified by the behavior of others outside their communities whom they observe buying drugs or sex or other illicit goods and services. It is not surprising, therefore, that studies have supported Merton's view that anomie, rather than poverty itself, is a major cause of crime and delinquency.

Interactionist Approaches: Differential Association and Delinquent Subcultures. Interactionist explanations of criminal behavior focus on the processes by which individuals actually internalize the norms that encourage criminality. This internalization results from the everyday interaction that occurs in social groups. Interactionist theories differ in this respect from anomie theory, which sees criminal behavior as the result of certain aspects of social structure. Two examples of interactionist theories of criminality are Edwin Sutherland's theory of differential association and the subcultural approach to the study of juvenile delinquency.

Differential Association. Introduced by Sutherland in 1939, the approach known as *differential association,* with some later modifications, still seems to explain the widest range of criminal acts. According to this theory, criminal behavior is a result of a learning process that occurs chiefly within small, intimate groups—family, friends, neighborhood peer groups, and the like. The lessons learned include both the techniques for committing crimes and, more important, the motives for criminal behavior. The law is defined not as a set of rules to be followed but as a hindrance to be avoided or overcome.

Briefly stated, the basic principle of differential association is that "a person becomes delinquent because of the excess of definitions favorable to violation of law

160 CHAPTER 5

over definitions unfavorable to violation of law" (Sutherland & Cressey, 1960, p. 28). People internalize the values of the surrounding culture, and when their environment includes frequent contact with criminal elements and relative isolation from noncriminal elements, they are likely to become delinquent or criminal. The boy whose most admired model is another member of his gang or a successful neighborhood pimp will try to emulate that model and will receive encouragement and approval when he does so successfully.

Although a child usually encounters both criminal and noncriminal behavior patterns, these encounters vary in frequency, duration, priority, and intensity. The concepts of frequency and duration are self-explanatory. *Priority* means that attitudes learned early in life, whether lawful or criminal, tend to persist in later life, although this tendency has not been fully demonstrated. *Intensity* refers to the prestige of the model and the strength of the child's emotional ties to that person.

Delinquent Subcultures and Conflicting Values. The legal definition of crime ignores the effect of social values in determining which laws are enforced. Although judges and prosecutors use criminal law to determine the criminality of certain acts, the process of applying the law involves class interest and political power: One group imposes its will on another by enforcing its definition of illegality. For example, authorities are not nearly as anxious to enforce laws against consumer fraud as they are to enforce laws against the use of certain drugs. Consumer fraud is often perpetrated by powerful business interests with strong political influence. The drug user, on the other hand, usually lacks power and public support.

The issue of class interests is especially relevant to the study of delinquent subcultures. Albert K. Cohen (1971), for example, viewed the formation of delinquent gangs as an effort to alleviate the difficulties gang members encounter at the bottom of the status ladder. Gang members typically come from working-class homes and find themselves measured, as Cohen put it, with a "middle-class measuring rod" by those who control access to the larger society, including teachers, businesspeople, the police, and public officials. Untrained in such "middle-class virtues" as ambition, ability to defer gratification, self-discipline, and academic skills, and therefore poorly prepared to compete in a middle-class world, they form a subculture whose standards they can meet. This delinquent subculture, which Cohen described as nonutilitarian, malicious, and negativistic, "takes its norms from the larger culture, but turns them upside down. The delinquents consider something right, by the standards of their subculture, precisely because it is wrong by the norms of the larger culture" (p. 28).

Other sociologists do not believe that the formation of delinquent subcultures is a frustrated reaction to exclusion by the dominant culture. Instead, they see delinquency as a product of lower-class culture. A study of street gangs by Walter Miller (1958), for example, identified six "focal concerns" of lower-class culture that often lead to the violation of middle-class social and legal norms:

1. *Trouble.* Trouble is important to the individual's status in the community, whether it is seen as something to be kept out of or as something to be gotten into. Usually there is less worry about legal or moral questions than about difficulties that result from the involvement of police, welfare investigators, and other agents of the larger society.

2. *Toughness.* Toughness comprises an emphasis on masculinity, physical strength, and the ability to "take it," coupled with a rejection of art, literature, and anything else that is considered feminine. This is partly a reaction to female-dominated households and the lack of male role models both at home and in school.

3. *Smartness.* In the street sense of the term, *smartness* denotes the ability to outwit, dupe, or "con" someone. A successful pimp, for example, would be considered smarter than a bank clerk.

4. *Excitement.* To relieve the crushing boredom of ghetto life, residents of lower-class communities often seek out situations of danger or excitement, such as gambling or high-speed joyrides in stolen automobiles.

5. *Fate.* Fate is a major concern because lower-class citizens frequently feel that important events in life are beyond their control. They often resort to semimagical resources such as "readers and advisers" as a way to change their luck.

6. *Autonomy.* Members of this group are likely to express strong resentment toward any external controls or exercise of coercive authority over their behavior. At the same time, however, they frequently seem to seek out restrictive environments, perhaps even engineering their own committal to mental hospitals or prisons.

Research by Gerald Suttles (1970) and Elijah Anderson (1992, 1999) on the street corner culture of delinquents and other groups provides evidence of continuity in these values. Anderson, for example, writes that lower-class life has an internal coherence that is seldom appreciated by the casual observer. Both show that teenagers and young adults in lower-class street corner groups make careful distinctions based on trust and confidence. They may be labeled street people by the larger society, but among themselves they continually rank each other according to notions of respect and trust derived from their life on the street.

Controlling Crime

Efforts by the police, courts, and other agencies to control crime need to be understood as part of society's much larger system of social control (Wouters, 1999). In its broadest sociological sense, **social control** is the capacity of a social group, which could be an entire society, to regulate itself according to a set of "higher moral principles beyond those of self-interest" (Janowitz, 1978, p. 3). The Ten Commandments are a good example of what is meant by such values as they are translated into norms of everyday life. All of a society's ways of teaching the young to conform to its values and norms (i.e., *socialization*), together with the ways in which people in a society reward one another for desired behaviors, contribute to social control. But every society also includes members who deviate from its norms, even strongly held norms like the prohibition against murder or thievery. Viewed in terms of the problems created by such deviance, social control can be defined somewhat more narrowly as "all the processes by which people define and respond to deviant behavior" (Black, 1984, p. xi).

Techniques of social control range from informal processes such as gossip, ridicule, advice, and shunning to the formal processes embodied in the actions of the police, courts, corrections officers, and others who work in the criminal-justice system and in related systems like the mental-health and juvenile-justice systems. These formal systems of social control, established by government, are so important and complex and subject to so much study and debate that in this chapter we focus on them more than on the informal processes. Nevertheless, it is important to recognize that without the great array of informal controls that exist in every community and society, none of the formal systems would be of much use. If the police and the courts and other formal institutions of social control are at all effective, it is because most people are law-abiding and these institutions need deal only with a relatively small minority (which may still be a very large number in absolute terms).

Most formal systems of social control rely on coercion rather than on reward. Surely this is true of courts and prisons. But it is not true by definition. In a prison or other correctional facility a person can be rewarded for behavior that is defined as positive and as having favorable consequences for the individual and for society. The fact that coercion and punishment often far outweigh persuasion and reward reflects the different goals society has incorporated into its institutions of criminal law, that is, police, prosecution, and corrections. As we examine how these formal institutions of social control operate (and sometimes fail to operate), we need to remember that formal efforts to control crime can be classified under four headings: retribution-deterrence, rehabilitation, prevention, and reforms in the criminal-justice system. The last category includes efforts to improve society's ability to deal with all kinds of crime; it is discussed in the Social Policy section of the chapter.

Retribution-Deterrence

Retribution and deterrence—"paying back" the guilty for their misdeeds and discouraging them and others from committing similar acts in the future—have historically been the primary focus of efforts to control crime. Only relatively recently has rehabilitation of offenders—attempts to give them the ability and motivation to live in a law-abiding and socially approved manner—gained wide acceptance. The correctional system, however, is still largely punitive. Although retribution no longer follows the "eye for an eye, tooth for a tooth" formula (in which slanderers had their tongues cut out, thieves had their hands amputated, and rapists were castrated), the retributive orientation can be seen in public demands for longer sentences for such crimes as murder.

The punishments meted out to murderers, forgers, and other offenders are meant to serve several purposes. Besides the often-cited goals of preventing crime and rehabilitating offenders, punishment serves to sustain the morale of those who conform to society's rules. In other words, law-abiding members of society demand that offenders be punished partly to reinforce their own ambivalent feelings about conformity. They believe that if they must make sacrifices to obey the law, someone who does not make such sacrifices should not be allowed to "get away with it." Even those who view criminals as sick rather than evil, and who call for the "treatment" of offenders to correct an organic or psychological disorder, are essentially demanding retribution (Barlow & Kauzlarich, 2002).

In recent years the public's desire for more retribution has resulted in pressure in many states to restore capital punishment and to restore more punitive, as opposed to rehabilitative, forms of correction. In 1995, for example, Alabama reinstituted the penal practices of chain gangs and rock breaking, practices that were far more common in southern prisons a century ago than they are today.

Some criminologists, such as James Q. Wilson (1977, 1993), have suggested that society needs the firm moral authority derived from stigmatizing and punishing crime. Although Wilson grants that prisoners must "pay their debts" without being deprived of their civil rights after release from prison and without suffering the continued indignities of parole supervision and unemployment, he stresses the moral value of stigmatizing crime and those who commit it: "To destigmatize crime would be to lift from it the weight of moral judgment and to make crime simply a particular occupation or avocation which society has chosen to reward less (or perhaps more) than other pursuits. If there is no stigma attached to an activity, then society has no business making it a crime" (1977, p. 230).

Laws that establish penalties for crimes are enacted by the states and by the federal government. But concern for the rights of citizens faced with the power of the state to enforce laws and inflict punishment is a prominent feature of the United States Constitution. The Fourth Amendment guarantees protection against "unreasonable searches and seizures"; the Fifth Amendment guarantees that citizens shall not be compelled to testify against themselves or be tried more than once for the same crime (double jeopardy) or be deprived of due process of law; the Sixth Amendment guarantees the right to a public trial by an impartial jury, the right to subpoena and confront witnesses, and the right to legal counsel; the Eighth Amendment prohibits "cruel and unusual punishment" and "excessive" bail or fines.

It is important to note these points because they are at the heart of conflicts about how fairly laws are enforced and how impartially justice is meted out. In the controversy over capital punishment, for example, opponents argue that it has become a form of cruel and unusual punishment. Others argue that because those who are condemned are often unable to afford adequate counsel, they have been deprived of their rights under the Sixth Amendment. Whatever one believes about such controversies, it is clear that the Constitution establishes the basis for protection of individual rights but also leaves much discretion to citizens and lawmakers to establish the ground rules for how justice is to be carried out.

The trend toward "hard time" incarceration for both teenage and adult offenders is becoming popular throughout the United States. It has yet to be determined whether these measures actually reduce recidivism.

The role of the sociologist in these debates is to help establish a scientific basis for decision making. Empirical data collected by social scientists and government statisticians can be used to compare homicide rates in states that have the death penalty and states that do not. When this is done, as in Figure 5–10, the results provide dramatic support for the contention that the death penalty does not deter murderers. As a form of retribution, it allows victims' family members to feel that justice has been done, but the data show that murder rates in states like Texas and Louisiana, where the death penalty is legal and executions routine, remain higher than average despite capital punishment.

Many social scientists also cite the negative effects of the severe anti-drug-dealing and anti-gun-possession laws put into effect in New York during the 1970s. In the years since these laws were passed, there have been significant increases in rates of drug dealing and arrests on drug and gun possession charges, despite much higher penalties for these offenses (Califano, 1998). Critics of such findings point out that very often criminals ask themselves before committing a crime, "Will I be punished if I am caught, and how severe will the punishment be?"

Research on the deterrent effects of punishment for crimes other than murder is made extremely difficult by the fact that very few perpetrators of these crimes are actually caught and sentenced. For many decades researchers have been able to show that whatever the punishment, a high likelihood of arrest is the greatest deterrent to crime. However, the arrest rate for property crimes is only 16.7 percent, and for all index felonies it is only 20.5 percent (*UCR*, 2001). These rates are based on crimes reported to the police. Since far more crimes are committed than are known to the police, the actual rates are even lower.

Rehabilitation

The idea of rehabilitating offenders, which has developed only during the past century and a half, rests on the concept of crime as a social aberration and the offender as a social misfit whose aberrant behavior can be modified to conform to society's norms—in other words, "cured." As yet there are no clear guidelines concerning the

164 CHAPTER 5

FIGURE 5-10 Homicide Rates in Death Penalty and Non-Death Penalty States

Source: Data from *Uniform Crime Reports,* 2001.

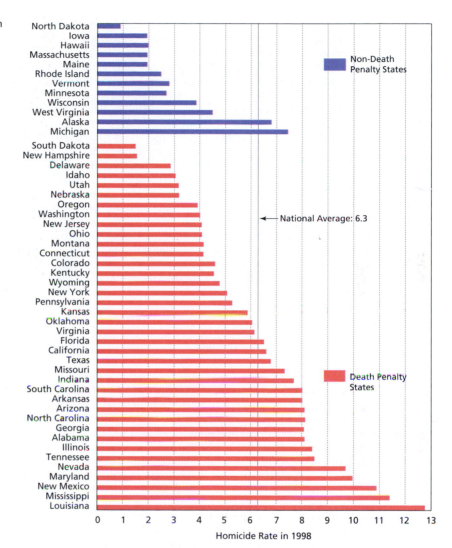

form of rehabilitation that will be most effective with a particular kind of offender. Rehabilitation usually includes varying amounts of counseling, educational and training programs, and work experience. In the past the programs that have had the most success have been those that prepare criminals to enter the world of legitimate work and help them actually secure and hold jobs after incarceration. However, such ambitious programs are unlikely to be implemented on a large scale.

By the 1990s both the ideal and the practice of rehabilitation in prisons and among paroled offenders had reached a low point in what has historically been a cyclical process. Efforts to institute rehabilitation programs often follow efforts to increase the severity of sentencing. When it is shown that longer sentences and harsher punishment do not prevent crime or repeated offenses, society tends to shift toward efforts to rehabilitate criminals (Adler, Mueller, & Laufer, 1995; Friedman, 1993).

Studies of **recidivism**—the probability that a former inmate will break the law after release and be arrested again—have found no conclusive evidence that various approaches to rehabilitation, such as prison counseling programs or outright discharge, are more effective in reducing recidivism rates than more punitive alternatives. All that can be said is that some of the rehabilitation experiments undertaken to date—in particular, those that include extensive job training and job placement—have been more successful than others.

In an in-depth study of the juvenile-justice system and rehabilitation, sociologist Mark Jacobs (1990) found that professionals in the system—court officials, parole officers, psychologists, correctional administrators, and others—often believe that they must "screw the system" to make it rehabilitate rather than do further harm to juvenile offenders and young "persons in need of supervision." (The latter is a court-designated category of juveniles who are judged by their parents and others to be highly at risk of falling into a criminal subculture; courts can order these children to be placed in foster homes or residential care facilities even if they have committed no crimes.)

Jacobs's (1990) study showed that rehabilitation is hampered by a maze of organizations and regulations. Juveniles are shuttled from one jurisdiction or program to another and are often the victims of inadequately funded training programs and haphazard supervision by overburdened caseworkers. Given the extreme splintering of the system—family courts, juvenile courts, schools, parents, parole officers, correctional officers, psychologists, and many more—the young offender is often deprived of the rehabilitation to which he or she is entitled. And no coherent set of laws holds anyone in the system accountable for the youth's rehabilitation; that is, no single institution, group, or person can be said to be at fault. In such a no-fault society, Jacobs argues, rehabilitation will remain a distant ideal.

The nature of the prison system itself is a major hindrance to rehabilitative efforts. Prisons remove offenders from virtually all contact with society and its norms and subject them to almost continual contact with people who have committed crimes ranging from murder and petty larceny to homosexual rape and fraud. Often inmates are abused by their guards. A notorious case, probably indicative of more widespread patterns of abuse, was revealed in a 1992 court ruling against 119 former officials and guards at a Georgia prison for women; inmates were able to prove that they had been subjected to sexual abuse and rape over a period of several years (Applebome, 1992).

Within prison walls, offenders are punished by being deprived of liberty, autonomy, heterosexual contacts, goods and services, and the security that is normally obtained from participation in ordinary social institutions. At the same time, prisoners create a social order of their own. Adherence to the norms of prison life, which may be necessary for both mental and physical well-being, further separates inmates' goals and motivations from those of the larger society and makes it more difficult for them to benefit from whatever rehabilitative measures are available.

The most common type of rehabilitation program consists of work training. However, prison work is generally menial and unsatisfying, involving such jobs as kitchen helper or janitor. The difficulty of rehabilitating offenders in prison has led to various attempts to reform them outside prison walls. This approach seems to have several benefits. Treating offenders without exposing them to all the deficiencies of the prison system not only reduces the antisocial effects of prolonged exposure to a criminal society but also reduces the cost of custodial facilities and personnel. This makes treatment resources more available to those who seem to have the best prospects for rehabilitation. Perhaps the oldest and most widely used system of this kind is the *work release* program, in which prisoners are allowed to leave the institution for part of the day or week to work at an outside job. Although this type of program was first authorized in Wisconsin in 1913, it has become widely used only since the mid-1950s. Today many states and the federal government have authorized various kinds of work release programs.

The idea of releasing convicted felons into society, even for limited periods, has met with considerable opposition, but in general such programs seem to work well. Besides removing convicts from the criminal society in the prison, work release programs reimburse the state for some of the costs of supporting them and also allow the prisoners to support their dependents, thereby helping them stay off the welfare rolls. In addition, a work release program is a practical step toward reintegrating offenders into society, since many of those who successfully complete the program retain their jobs after release. In fact, in a classic study Martinson (1972) found that the most effective single factor in rehabilitating offenders is a program of training for work following release; work during the prison term itself; and above all, job placement and training during probation.

At present there are two competing tendencies in corrections in the United States with regard to work and occupational training. On one hand, state prison systems are seeking to put prisoners to work, usually at unskilled jobs, on contracts with private businesses that will reduce soaring prison costs. On the other hand, there has been a decrease in the number of job training programs that prepare inmates for productive work after incarceration (Califano, 1998; Gondles, 1999b).

The controversy over youthful offenders raises further questions about what kinds of corrections are most appropriate for this segment of the criminal population. So far it does not appear that more punitive programs, or "boot camps," are more effective than others. In addition, it is extremely costly to keep teenagers in prison or detention; the costs range from $20,000 to $90,000 per year, depending on the state and the particular form of incarceration (Belluck, 1996). Many states, therefore, are experimenting with programs in which youthful offenders can attend school or job training while in prison or in lieu of prison (Barlow & Kauzlarich, 2002).

Programs like these are controversial because violent offenders are expected to do "hard time." In consequence, a few states (New Jersey, Texas, Florida, and California) have created residential training schools for juvenile offenders. This is an old concept that is being modified with new techniques for supervision, mentoring, and training. Although such programs may not work for the most violent or hardened young criminals, many penologists believe that when young inmates can be released to their communities with new skills and education, more positive options are open to them and they are less likely to drift back into a criminal lifestyle (Sadd & Grinc, 1996). But many young offenders return to extremely troubled families and peer groups. The more contact they have with professionals who can help them find alternatives to a violent home or neighborhood group, the better their chances—and society's—of avoiding crime and violence (Belluck, 1996).

Prevention

The idea of preventing crime and delinquency before they occur is an attractive one, but like rehabilitation, it is difficult to implement. Aside from the deterrent effect of punishment, crime prevention is customarily defined in three different ways: (1) the sum total of all influences and activities that contribute to the development of a non-deviant personality; (2) attempts to deal with conditions in a person's environment that are believed to lead to crime and delinquency; and (3) specific services or programs designed to prevent further crime and delinquency.

Programs based on the first definition include measures designed to improve the social environment, such as improved housing and job opportunities for ghetto dwellers. Although one of their goals may be the reduction of crime and delinquency in the target area, this is rarely their primary goal. Moreover, studies of youths involved in antipoverty programs have not demonstrated a positive correlation between such participation and reduced delinquency rates. The most positive results are found in evaluations of Job Corps and other education, job-training, and social-skills programs in which young people at risk are given a chance to leave their neighborhood peer groups.

The second definition includes efforts based on Sutherland's theory of differential association (Sutherland & Cressey, 1960), such as efforts to reduce children's exposure to the antisocial and/or illegal activities of people around them, to improve their family life, and to create a viable and conforming social order in the community itself. Several projects of this sort have been attempted; some, like the Chicago Area Project (discussed shortly), have had notable success.

Most crime prevention programs attempt to work within the third definition—prevention of further delinquency and crime. They include well-established approaches such as parole, probation, and training schools, as well as more experimental programs. It is difficult to compare these approaches with those attempted under the other two definitions, since they deal with quite different sets of circumstances.

An early prevention program, the Chicago Area Project, was established in the mid-1930s in the Chicago slums, where immigrant families were no longer able to control their children because of a weakening social order. The project sought to develop youth welfare programs that would be viable after the project leaders had left. It was assumed that local youths would have more success than outside workers in establishing recreation programs (including summer camping), community improvement campaigns, and programs devoted to teaching and assisting delinquent youths and even some adults who were returning to the community after release from prison. The project not only demonstrated the feasibility of using untrained local youths to establish welfare programs but also indicated a possible decrease in the delinquency rate (Kobrin, 1959). This model has been used successfully in many communities to diminish gang violence.

It is difficult to prove the effectiveness of preventive measures. Although they seem to fail at least as often as they succeed, the difficulty may lie more in the specific kinds of services offered than in the concept of prevention itself. When delinquency prevention seems to fail, there are often signs that there were some beneficial effects, even if they were not of the desired magnitude. It should be kept in mind that most of the programs described here are experimental and have not been attempted on a large scale. Delinquency prevention needs further research and more government funding (Hagedorn, 1988; Williams & Kornblum, 1994).

According to Charles Silberman (1980), one of the major problems with programs designed to control juvenile delinquency is that they place too much emphasis on methods of policing, more efficient courts, and improved correctional programs, and too little emphasis on community programs that give families the support they need to deal with delinquency:

> If a community development program is to have any chance of success, those in charge must understand that the controls that lead to reduced crime cannot be imposed from the outside; they must emerge from changes in the community itself and in the people who compose it. Hence the emphasis must be on enabling poor people to take charge of their own lives—on helping them gain a sense of competence and worth, a sense of being somebody who matters. (p. 430)

In their efforts to reduce crime, governments at all levels experience more frustration than success. In a few short periods, such as the present period of relative and sustained affluence in the United States, crime rates have fallen, or at least the rates of some crimes have, but such lulls have been temporary. As crime historian Lawrence M. Friedman (1993) points out, crime is far too complicated and diverse and too firmly embedded in American culture to be controlled and eliminated. Whenever one kind of crime is reduced, criminals invent others. And social change is constantly at work on the criminal-justice system, producing a recurrent pattern of criminalizing, decriminalizing, and recriminalizing certain behaviors.

The fact that important decreases in some categories of violent crimes were announced in recent years also calmed public fear of crime somewhat. For the first time in recent memory, in fact, the public rated educational quality above crime and drugs as the foremost issue facing the nation in coming years. Crime remains a major concern of Americans, especially the elderly and residents of central cities, but according to the National Opinion Research Center (NORC), citizens are beginning to question such policies as mandatory sentences, the "three-strikes" policy, and some aspects of the War on Drugs, which have resulted in large increases in the prison population (NORC, 1999).

Social policies to control crime or punish criminals are not formulated only at the federal level. States and municipalities often take the lead in promoting new approaches and policies. Examples include the reinstitution of capital punishment and chain gangs in some states and new rehabilitative programs in others. In this review of social policy we discuss trends and reforms in policies aimed at conventional, occupational, and organized criminals, and then examine proposed changes in the juvenile-justice system and gun control.

Conventional Crimes

In 2001 about 11.8 million violent and property crimes were committed in the United States. Of these, only 19.6 percent were cleared by arrests, and even fewer ended in convictions, making crime an attractive pursuit for many people (*UCR*, 2002). Even the relatively small number of people apprehended presents an almost insurmountable burden for existing correctional systems. Court calendars and prison cells are so overloaded that there is continual pressure to find ways to reduce sentences or to create new forms of corrections. One of the most controversial yet widespread strategies is **plea bargaining,** in which the offender agrees to plead guilty to a lesser charge and free the courts from the need to conduct a jury trial. By this means most of those who are convicted of serious crimes receive shortened sentences. Plea bargaining has been criticized for allowing dangerous criminals to receive mild sentences. It has been estimated, however, that if the plea-bargaining process were reduced to even 80 percent of serious crimes, the number of trials would double and put an enormous strain on the court system (Reid, 1993).

The prison system is also experiencing severe strains. By 2000, because of the increase in drug arrests in many parts of the United States, prison populations had reached record levels (see Figure 5–11). The U.S. rate of imprisonment of 460 people per 100,000 is higher than that of any other nation (Califano, 1998).

More than 100,000 juveniles are incarcerated on any given day, even though they make up a smaller proportion of the total population than they did in the 1970s. Adult prison populations have also reached extremely high levels. However, of the 6 million people in custody in all U.S. correctional systems, only about 20 percent are in prisons. The majority are under community supervision through probation or parole. (**Probation** is supervision of offenders who have not been sentenced to jail or prison;

FIGURE 5-11 Adult Correctional Populations, 1980–2001

Source: King & Maurer, 2002. Reprinted by permission of Bureau of Justice Statistics.

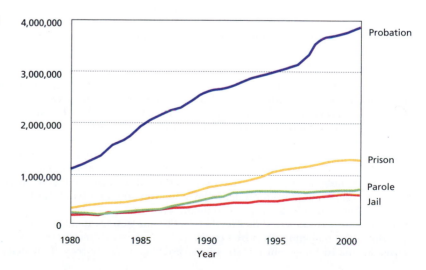

parole is supervision of people who have been released from prison.) And although both probation and parole were originally intended for nonviolent offenders, they are increasingly being used for those who have committed felonies because of the costs of incarceration and the problems of overcrowded prisons.

Recidivism rates are quite high among felons who are placed on probation. Research indicates that from half to two-thirds are rearrested, a situation that indicates the continuing need to develop a greater array of sentencing options and rehabilitation strategies while ensuring public safety (Adler, Mueller, & Laufer, 1995; Jenson & Howard, 1998). Faced with these problems, many states have been seeking alternatives to conventional incarceration and parole. Community corrections, in which the offender provides a service to social-welfare agencies or neighborhood associations, is one approach. Another is house arrest and monitoring by electronic devices.

Occupational and Corporate Crimes

A variety of legal reforms have been proposed to curb occupational and corporate crimes. One approach would be to increase the penalties for such crimes. Frequently a company with a net worth of hundreds of millions of dollars faces a fine of only $50,000, and its executives may be fined only $5,000, upon conviction for fraud or price-fixing. Large corporations can regard such penalties as an acceptable risk. One way to increase fines is simply to raise the dollar amount of the penalty; another is to make the penalty a fixed percentage of the company's profits. It is widely believed that the ten-year prison sentence received by junk bond dealer and stock manipulator Michael Milken in 1990 was a signal to other white-collar criminals that the era of light sentences had ended.

Another aspect of legal reform involves changing laws to make them less easy to break. For example, complicated tax laws full of alternatives and loopholes may invite cheating. Streamlining the laws might both discourage cheating and make it easier to detect when it does occur. The law could also be reformed to make accomplices in occupational crimes vulnerable to court action, so that for each crime many more corporate employees would face punishment.

Obviously, stronger enforcement must accompany legal reform if it is to be meaningful, and this means more money and personnel for enforcement agencies. To detect more income tax cheating, for example, the IRS must hire more auditors. To detect more white-collar crime, the FBI must devote more resources to investigations in this area. Similarly, once a case against occupational offenders has been won in court, the judge must be willing to invoke the full penalty allowed under the law.

These two approaches—legal reform (particularly tougher penalties) and stronger enforcement—would probably deter much occupational crime. More than most other types of crimes, occupational crimes involve calculation, planning, and the weighing of gains against costs. Increasing the costs of crime as well as the risk of detection might lead occupational criminals to conclude that honesty is more profitable.

Organized Crime

It is particularly hard to fight organized crime, for several reasons. A major one is the difficulty of obtaining proof of syndicate activities that will be accepted in court. Witnesses rarely come forward; either they fear retaliation or they themselves are too deeply implicated. Since the top levels of the syndicate's hierarchy are so well insulated from those below them, witnesses are rarely able to testify against them. Documentary evidence is equally rare, since the transactions of organized crime are seldom written down. Finally, corruption hinders effective prosecution of organized crime.

Despite these obstacles, in recent decades the FBI has made immense progress in its battle against organized crime; today numerous reputed syndicate leaders are under indictment or in jail. Experts credit this breakthrough to a number of factors, of which the most prominent is the fact that the FBI now devotes about one-quarter of its personnel to combating organized crime. Other important factors are using undercover agents in long-term investigations, pooling the resources of agencies that formerly competed with one another, and giving the FBI jurisdiction in narcotics cases. Especially significant has been the use of sophisticated surveillance techniques and computer technology. The witness protection program, in which witnesses are offered new identities, support, and protection in moving away from their organized-crime contacts, has also proven successful in a number of instances. An example is the successful arrest and conviction of mob boss John Gotti and his son, both major organized-crime figures who were notorious for flouting the law.

Public-Order and Juvenile-Justice Reforms

Many criminologists and legal authorities agree that there are too many laws that make certain behaviors (such as truancy) illegal only for children, as well as too many laws that address nonviolent victimless crimes like adultery, homosexuality, prostitution, and drunkenness. Offenders in both categories account for 40 percent of the caseload in both juvenile and adult courts. In addition, abuse at home often causes juveniles to become runaways. When they are apprehended for this offense, they spend even more time in juvenile detention. The large number of arrests of juvenile runaways has led experts such as Edwin M. Schur (1973) to advocate a thorough reform of the concept of juvenile justice that would tolerate a broader range of behaviors and define as crimes only specific antisocial acts. Similarly, many citizens advocate lessening of penalties for possession of drugs like marijuana. The conservative mood of the nation makes such reforms unlikely, however.

By the early 1990s rates of juvenile crimes and the number of juveniles in criminal detention had risen dramatically. These trends, combined with the impact of some highly sensational juvenile crimes, have tended to blur the distinction between juvenile and adult offenders. In 1996, for example, a 12-year-old boy became the youngest inmate of a high-security prison. He and his 13-year-old accomplice had been convicted of dropping a small child from a 14-story building in Chicago. The sentencing itself, carried out under a new Illinois law, was an example of the trend toward judging serious juvenile crimes on the same basis as adult crimes.

Fears of an increase in juvenile crimes are supported by statistical evidence, and victims of these crimes are calling for tougher penalties (Gest, 1996). But the trend toward greater punitiveness has its critics, who believe that putting young offenders in prison will simply produce more super-predators (Males, 1996).

In addition to proposals directed at law-enforcement agencies, some small-scale community-based approaches have been attempted. An example is the House of Umoja in Philadelphia. This program, which combines surrogate family relationships with job opportunities and placement counseling for youths, has virtually eliminated street violence in a ghetto neighborhood. A similar program in Ponce, Puerto Rico, provides a wide range of services to an entire community; one of its achievements has been to cut the delinquency rate in half despite a rapidly growing teenage population (Kornblum & Boggs, 1984). Maryland, New York, and other states are also experimenting with programs that provide intensive home surveillance and counseling for delinquents from high-crime and poor neighborhoods.

Despite these and other measures, many experts agree that the problem remains far from a solution. None of the approaches taken so far has been shown to be successful (Reid, 1993). As a result, public policy toward serious juvenile crime is in a state of considerable confusion, and opinions on what can be done vary widely. As the rate of juvenile violence rises throughout the nation, policymakers are debating the causes and the possible remedies. The Department of Justice's position is that the problem is caused by the breakdown of family and community controls and that until these are strengthened there is little that federal funds can accomplish. However, members of the Congressional Select Committee on Children argue that the rate of poverty among children has increased to 20 percent at the same time that there have been immense cuts in child welfare services (32 percent), juvenile delinquency prevention programs (55 percent), and drug and mental-health treatment programs (30 percent). Most law-enforcement officials believe that without more resources to address joblessness, lack of education, and lack of housing and recreational facilities and to provide drug treatment on demand, there will be little overall improvement in the juvenile crime situation (Diesenhouse, 1990; Males, 1996).

Gun Control

In recent decades there has been increasing demand for stricter federal supervision of the purchase and sale of firearms, particularly the cheap handguns that are readily available in many areas. However, opponents of gun control legislation, represented primarily by the National Rifle Association (NRA), constitute one of the most powerful interest groups in the nation. The NRA draws much of its strength from areas of the nation where hunting is popular and there is a strong feeling that people need to be able to protect themselves and their families. Members of the NRA claim that gun control measures would violate the "right to bear arms" that is contained in the Second Amendment to the United States Constitution. This is a strong position and one that most political leaders are unwilling to challenge directly.

Opponents of gun control claim that the decision to commit murder has nothing to do with possession of a gun; a killer can stab, strangle, poison, or batter a victim to death. Gun control, therefore, would make little difference. Although this argument sounds logical, it ignores the lethal potential of guns, which are about five times more likely to kill than knives, the next most commonly used murder weapon. And since most murders are spontaneous results of passion rather than carefully planned acts, it follows that the easy availability of guns is likely to increase the death rate in criminal assaults. In most cases murders are a result of three factors: impulse, the lethal capacity of the weapon, and the availability of the weapon. Strict gun control would eliminate or at least reduce the latter two factors.

Record levels of gun violence in 1999 seemed likely to turn public opinion firmly against supporters of the free market in firearms. Columbine (15 dead, 23 wounded), the Wedgwood Baptist Church in Fort Worth (8 dead, 7 wounded), the North Valley Jewish Community Center near Los Angeles (5 wounded), Atlanta (9 dead, 13 wounded), Honolulu (7 dead), and Seattle (2 dead, 2 wounded) received intensive media coverage. But even as political leaders and the majority of the public joined the outcry against widespread availability of heavy firepower, the National Rifle Association experienced its largest jump in membership ever. And in fact, public opinion on the basic issues of gun control was altered, but not dramatically (Birnbaum, 1999).

A significant majority of the American public has long favored tighter controls over firearms that stop short of a complete ban on handguns. This support for gun control correlates most closely with the nation's murder rate. Throughout the1980s and 1990s the murder rate varied between about 8 and 10 per 100,000. Table 5–2 demonstrates that high poll numbers favoring gun control in the early part of the period correlate to a high murder rate (associated with the crack cocaine epidemic, among other factors). The lower figures in the mid-1980s correlate with a lower murder rate. When the murder rate increased in the early 1990s, support for gun control moved upward again. Most likely, the low figures reported before the Columbine incident reflect the recent substantial drop in the murder rate to under 7 per 100,000 (Gillespie & Lynch, 1999; Kleck, 1999).

In 1993, in response to what had come to be perceived as a national epidemic of gunshot injuries and deaths, as well as the earlier shooting of President Reagan and his press secretary Matthew Brady, Congress finally passed the Brady Act and other legislation to limit the access of felons to handguns and assault weapons. In 1996 Congress attempted to repeal the ban on assault weapons, but the repeal was vetoed by President Clinton. This veto became an important issue in the 1996 presidential election because many voters, especially women, strongly favored gun control. In the campaigns leading up to the 2000 presidential election, gun control figured as a major issue as the Democrats attempted to capitalize on their efforts to close loopholes in the Brady Act, especially those concerning sales of weapons at gun shows and auctions; the Republicans attempted to maintain the support of gun advocates while not seeming to be influenced by the NRA and thereby alienating the majority that favors gun control.

TABLE 5–2	RESPONSES TO GALLUP POLL ON GUN CONTROL

In general, do you feel that the laws covering the sale of handguns should be made more strict, less strict, or kept as they are now?

Date	More Strict	Less Strict	Kept as Now	No Opinion
1999	68%	6%	25%	1%
1993	72	5	22	1
1988	64	6	27	3
1986	60	8	30	2
1981	65	3	30	2
1980	59	3	30	2
1975	69	3	24	4

Source: The Gallup Poll, Statistical Assessment Service, 1999.

Not all antigun, antiviolence policy is made at the federal level. Many states and municipalities have recognized that the alarming increase in the number of youths aged 10 to 17 who are arrested for violent crimes demands more creative approaches than simply trying them in adult courts and locking them up with adult prisoners. In the wake of the rash of killings in 1999, California passed both a ban on assault weapons and a "gun a month" law that limits handgun purchases to one every 30 days.

Laws that limit product liability lawsuits are particularly troubling for gun control advocates because this is the newest and, from their perspective, most promising strategy in the battle to limit the use of firearms. At the national level, the Department of Housing and Urban Development (HUD) has taken up lawsuits against gun manufactures in the name of residents of public housing projects who have suffered inordinate numbers of shootings because of the failure of gun manufacturers to limit the lethal firepower of the weapons they put on the market. In California the state supreme court has granted municipalities the right to bring suits against gun makers. This opens the way for court battles against gun makers similar to the strategies used successfully by the states against tobacco companies.

But as can be seen from the pro-gun laws passed by some states, the power of gun advocates remains strong in many parts of the nation. In many congressional and legislative districts, especially in the South and West, there are lawmakers who are in office because the NRA mobilized pro-gun voters on election day. With 3 million dedicated members and an annual budget of $137 million, the NRA is one of the nation's largest and wealthiest cause-oriented groups (Birnbaum, 1999). But activists on both sides of the issue agree that the NRA is fighting at best a holding action against the rising tide of public opinion in favor of more gun control.

While the political debate has continued, there have been quite successful efforts to decrease the number of available guns in high-risk communities—that is, places where there have been recent histories of high murder rates and deaths of bystanders. Since 1991, Congress and the Justice Department have cooperated in instituting experimental programs to decrease the number of guns carried in "high-risk places at high-risk times" (Sherman, Shaw, & Rogan, 1995). Perhaps the most important of these is the Kansas City Gun Experiment, part of the Justice Department's Weed and Seed program in which local authorities were given wide latitude in planning strategies to reduce gun violence. The Kansas City experiment attempted to show a relationship between seizures of guns and reduced crimes committed with guns. A target police beat, covering a neighborhood where homicides were 20 times above the national average, was selected. The beat was patrolled by officers with special training in detecting people who were carrying weapons. On another beat, similar in demographic and crime characteristics, the police continued to use their traditional methods. After 29 weeks of operations, statistics showed that gun crimes had dropped significantly on the beat with the special patrols. Drive-by shootings also decreased, as did homicides of all kinds. In patrolling the beat, the police concentrated on likely gun carriers in special hot spots, where crimes had often been committed in the past. Since the focus was on crimes committed with guns, it is not surprising that there was little difference between the two beats in other violent crimes or in property crimes.

From a policy standpoint, the most important conclusion of the experiment is that "the police can increase the number of guns seized in high crime areas at relatively modest cost" (Sherman, Shaw, & Rogan, 1995, p. 9). Specially trained patrols seize about three times as many guns over a similar period as do traditional police patrols. Similar programs of community policing and gun interdiction (funded by private foundations as well as by the federal government) are likely to become a major area of antiviolence policy in high-crime communities throughout the nation.

An important issue related to gun control is the extent to which women who are heads of households will choose to arm themselves with handguns for protection. Since the number of female-headed households is rising rapidly, any increase in the propensity of women to arm themselves could raise the overall level of handgun ownership to 50 million in the next decade. But research shows that women are still far more reluctant than men to purchase handguns; female-headed households are half as likely to have handguns as male-headed households (Zimring, 1985). This suggests that the outcome of the political battle over handguns may eventually depend on how both sides manage to appeal to female voters.

BEYOND LEFT and RIGHT

There are many differences among people on the liberal left and the conservative right concerning crime and its control. Liberals believe that crime is caused by social-structural factors, such as poverty, and recommend rehabilitative strategies for offenders. Conservatives stress personal responsibility and the rights of crime victims. Are there no areas of common ground? Yes, there are. Sociology offers some important ones, especially if one thinks globally.

Indeed, on the global level the differences between left and right diminish, at least when confronted by the threat of organized criminal attacks on the rule of law. If a society like Russia or Italy or even, in some specific cases, the United States cannot protect its citizens against criminal victimization and organized crime, it can no longer claim to be the legitimate representative of its people, nor can it guarantee order within its borders or contribute to world peace. These are fundamental issues of human existence. Without the rule of law, the distinctions between left and right are absurd. A sociological analysis of global crime shows us that policies to address the threat of criminal victimization are vital to economic and social well-being at all levels of society.

SUMMARY

- The criminal law prohibits certain acts and prescribes punishments to be meted out to offenders. In practice, the definition of criminality changes according to what law enforcement authorities perceive as criminal behavior.

- Researchers have attempted to find more reliable ways of tracking criminal activity. Self-report studies and victimization surveys provide useful data; both are used to supplement the FBI's *Uniform Crime Reports*.

- Violent personal crimes include assault, robbery, and the various forms of homicide. Robbery usually occurs between strangers, murder between friends or relatives.

- Occasional property crimes include vandalism, check forgery, shoplifting, and so on. Offenders are usually unsophisticated and unlikely to have a criminal record.

- Occupational, or white-collar, crimes are committed by people who break the law as part of their normal

174 CHAPTER 5

business activity. They include such acts as embezzlement, fraud (including computer crimes), and insider trading in the securities industry. Occupational offenders have a respectable appearance and often consider themselves to be respectable citizens.

■ Corporate crimes include a variety of illegal practices of private corporations, including environmental crimes, insider trading, illegal labor practices, defrauding of pension plans, and the like. Such crimes are extremely difficult to control.

■ Public-order offenses include prostitution, drunkenness, vagrancy, and the like. They are often called victimless crimes because they cause harm only to the offender.

■ Conventional criminals commit robbery, burglary, and other crimes as a way of life, usually beginning their criminal careers as members of juvenile gangs.

■ Organized crime is a system in which illegal activities are carried out as part of a rational plan devised by a large organization for profit. The profits come largely from supplying illegal goods and services to the public.

■ Professional criminals are dedicated to a life of crime and are seldom caught. They include safecrackers, check forgers, and blackmailers.

■ Teenagers and young adults account for almost half of all arrests in the United States. The majority of arrests for property crimes are of people under 25 years of age. In addition, many young people become involved in drug commerce at the retail level. Status offenses like running away and vagrancy are another common reason for arrests of juveniles, especially young women.

■ Hate crimes are crimes in which the defendant intentionally selects a victim, or in the case of a property crime, the property that is the object of the crime, because of the actual or perceived race, color, national origin, ethnicity, gender, disability, or sexual orientation of any person. They are often carried out by young people, acting on emotions taken from the adults who socialize them.

■ The much higher rate of homicide in the United States than in other urban industrial nations is sometimes attributed to violence by juvenile gang members, but the available evidence indicates that it is not the presence of gangs per se but the ready availability of guns that accounts for the prevalence of lethal violence in American cities.

■ Various explanations of the causes and prevalence of crime have been suggested. They include biological explanations; demographic factors (including gender and age); and sociological explanations based on conflict theory, functionalism, and interactionism.

■ Conflict approaches to the study of crime see inequalities of wealth, status, and power as the underlying conditions that produce criminal behavior. These inequalities are thought to explain the overrepresentation of blacks in official crime statistics.

■ The functionalist explanation of crime is based on anomie theory, in which crime is considered to be the result of a disparity between approved goals and the means of achieving them.

■ Interactionist explanations include differential association, in which criminal behavior is said to be learned from family and peers, and theories about the origin and character of delinquent subcultures.

■ Efforts to control crime take four forms: retribution-deterrence, rehabilitation, prevention, and reform of the criminal-justice system. Retribution-deterrence focuses on punishing the criminal and attempting to deter others from committing similar crimes. The idea of rehabilitating offenders rests on the concept of cure; the most successful form of rehabilitation is work release. Programs to prevent crime and delinquency include parole, probation, training schools, and more experimental programs.

■ Proposals for reform of the criminal- and juvenile-justice systems include imposing harsher and more specific penalties for conventional crimes, increasing the penalties for occupational and corporate crimes and improving law enforcement in this area, repealing laws dealing with status and public-order offenses, and passing more stringent gun control legislation. Recently there has been increased emphasis on punishment and incapacitation as opposed to rehabilitation. However, higher rates of imprisonment have resulted in severe overcrowding of the prison system, leading to proposals like community corrections and house arrest.

KEY TERMS

SOCIAL PROBLEMS ONLINE

The Internet offers a plethora of resources on crime and the criminal justice system. Starting with the FBI at **http://www.fbi.gov/**, one can locate several sources of information about current and historical investigations. Clicking on Ten Most Wanted Fugitives brings up the Internet's version of the "wanted" poster. On the FBI's home page are links to monographs about the agency's most famous cases, including the capture of John Dillinger, investigations of Nazi saboteurs, and the Lindberg kidnapping. Press releases, hotlines on current unsolved crimes, congressional testimony, and downloadable files that contain statistics from the *Uniform Crime Reports* are available.

The U.S. Department of Justice, at **http://www .usdoj.gov/**, has a regularly updated home page with links to various agencies and projects. The Violence Against Women Office has a Web site at **http://www.usdoj.gov/vawo/** with information on the National Domestic Violence Hotline, copies of federal legislation and regulations, ongoing research reports and studies, and a Domestic Violence Awareness Manual targeted to federal employees but applicable to almost anyone. The Bureau of Justice Statistics, at **http://www.ojp. usdof.gov/bjs/welcome.html**, provides statistics, most in downloadable format, about crimes and their victims, drugs and crime, and the criminal-justice system. It also has links to other sources of data on crime.

The Federal Bureau of Prisons site can be accessed at **http://www.bop.gov/**. It provides statistics on the federal prison population (inmates and staff) broken down by age, ethnicity, race, sentences, types of offenses, and other variables. The bureau's Program Statements can be accessed, as can links to other pages, such as those of the Federal Prison Industries and the National Institute of Corrections. Research documents pertaining to the prison system are available, and most can be downloaded.

For a view from inside the jailhouse, there is a lively and innovative journal written for, by, and about inmates. The Journal of Prisoners on Prison at **http://www. synapse.net/~arrakis/jpp/jpp.html** is an academically oriented journal published since 1988 by prisoners whose purpose is "to bring the knowledge and experience of the incarcerated to bear upon more academic arguments and concerns." This remarkable publication offers insight and analysis from people for whom imprisonment is or has been the reality of their daily existence. Articles have appeared on Native Americans in the prison system, prison education, attitude and behavior modification, the death penalty, and other topics. Back issues are available online.

INTERNET EXERCISE

The Web destinations for Chapter 5 are related to different aspects of crime and criminals. To begin your explorations, go to the Prentice Hall Companion Web site: **http://prenhall.com/kornblum**. Then choose **Chapter 5** (Crime and Violence). Next, select **destinations** from the menu on the left side of the screen. There are a variety of sites to investigate. We suggest that you begin with **Racial Profiling in America.** This site is sponsored by the American Civil Liberties Union. The *Critical Research* box in this chapter deals with the problems associated with this extremely controversial practice. After you reach the opening page of the ACLU site, click on **Tales of DWB** (Driving While Black). Here you will be able to read about *actual cases* involving racial profiling and associated acts of discrimination. If you have time, there are various "news stories" accessible from this site that highlight this debatable procedure. You may wish to take a look at a few of them. After you have explored the Racial Profiling site, answer the following questions:

■ What are your reactions to the practice of racial profiling? Do you think that this procedure violates people's rights? Why or why not?

■ Do you think that the benefits of racial profiling outweigh the costs? Why or why not?

Crime and Violence Questions

VOCABULARY

1. Define and give an example of the following:
    a. violent personal crimes
    b. property crimes
    c. white-collar crimes
    d. corporate crimes
    e. "victimless" crimes

COMPREHENSION AND ANALYSIS

For questions 2, 3, and 4, indicate whether the statement is true or false. If the statement is false, rewrite it to make it true.

2. Crime rate statistics are extremely accurate.

3. Teenagers and young adults account for almost half of all arrests in the United States.

4. There is no single, universally agreed-upon definition of crime.

5. Describe the apparent relationship between the rise and fall of the crime rate and the economy.

6. What does the evidence indicate is the primary reason the homicide rate is higher in the United States than in other urban industrialized nations?

7. There are various explanations of the causes and prevalence of crime. Explain the difference in views among the three primary sociological explanations: conflict theory, functionalism, and interactionism.

8. Efforts to control crime take four forms. List and describe them.

9. List the two proposals for reform of the criminal- and juvenile-justice systems that you think are most likely to work. Explain your choices.

REFLECT AND CONNECT

10. Assume your city council is looking for ways to reduce street violence. You have an opportunity to suggest programs that would interest and educate young teens. What kinds of activities would you suggest? Please explain.

Editorial Cartoon: The Four R's

DON WRIGHT

Mr. Wright is a political cartoonist for the Palm Beach Post. *He gave up an award-winning career as a photographer and photo editor and began his career as an editorial cartoonist in 1963. In addition to winning two Pulitzer prizes and two Reuben awards, he is the recipient of the Robert F. Kennedy Memorial Journalism Award for outstanding coverage of the problems of the disadvantaged and the David Brinkley Award for Excellence in Communication. Wright's work is on permanent display at Syracuse University in New York and has been featured in numerous national shows. He is the author of three books:* Wright On!, Wright Side Up, *and* Gang of Eight.

AN IDEA TO THINK ABOUT

What are the traditional 3 R's in school? *As you read,* consider why Wright has added a fourth R.

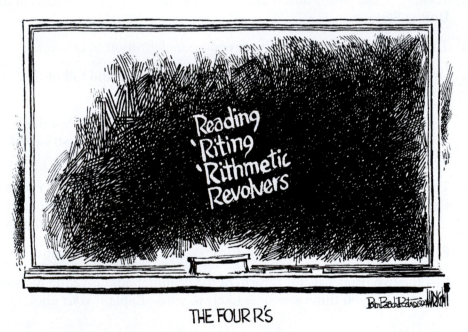

THE FOUR R'S

(© Tribune Media Services, Inc. All Rights Reserved. Reprinted with permission.)

The Four R's Questions

1. What is the topic/issue?

2. What is Wright's point of view?

3. What does Wright want the reader to do or think about after reading this cartoon?

A Well-Regulated Controversy

JUSTIN FERNANDEZ

Mr. Fernandez is a licensed attorney in Ohio, a former law clerk for the Ohio Court of Appeals, Second Appellate District, and the author of several books, including High Crimes and Misdemeanors: The Impeachment Process. *This is the first chapter in his book* Guns, Crime and the Second Amendment.

AN IDEA TO THINK ABOUT

What is your position on gun control? How did you reach your position? *As you read,* try to summarize the views on both sides of the issue.

A WELL-REGULATED CONTROVERSY

Justin Fernandez

[1]Outside the Washington Hilton Hotel, under gray skies and a chill typical for an early spring day in the nation's capital, a small crowd gathered around President Ronald Reagan's parked motorcade. It was March 30, 1981. The new president had just finished his second month in office. Reaganomics, the fall of the Berlin Wall, and the end of the cold war— each part of Reagan's popular legacy as president—lay ahead. Inside, the president was finishing his speech to a large audience at the AFL-CIO convention. Cameramen positioned equipment behind the rope cordoning off the security zone where officers from the Secret Service and the District of Columbia police force roamed. A woman in the crowd yelled something as the president emerged with his entourage. Reagan, striding toward his car, smiled and gave a big wave in her direction. Cameras clicked and more onlookers shouted, trying to get the president's attention.

[2]Suddenly someone in the crowd began firing a gun. Shots ricocheted off concrete and brick, causing momentary confusion for everyone but Secret Service agent Timothy McCarthy, who jumped in front of the president at the sound of the gun and took a bullet in the abdomen. The bullets fired at the president were "exploding head Devastators" designed to spread on impact into twisty shards to shred a maximum amount of flesh and create a massive injury.

[3]Cameras kept rolling and bystanders ran, dove, or stood frozen in astonishment or fear. Reagan, hit in the left chest but still standing, was pushed inside the car and rushed to the hospital. On the sidewalk, critically wounded, lay the president's press secretary, James Brady, and police officer Thomas Delahanty. Brady had sustained a massive gunshot wound to the head; Delahanty had been shot in the neck.

[4]Months before, in a pawnshop in Dallas, Texas, the shooter had filled out a federal form in order to purchase a handgun. John Hinckley Jr.

hadn't been entirely truthful in filling out that form, but without any fact verification, a waiting period, or a detailed background check, the pawn-shop owner had quickly sold him the gun.

[5]Hinckley, who first bought a handgun in August 1979, soon built a small firearms collection. Meanwhile, he was apparently experiencing mental problems; he reportedly played Russian roulette in November and December of 1979. In 1980 Hinckley began taking prescription antidepressants and tranquilizers.

[6]After seeing the movie *Taxi Driver*, in which Jodie Foster played a young prostitute, Hinckley became obsessed with the actress. When he read, in the May 1980 issue of *People* magazine, that Foster would be attending Yale University in the fall, Hinckley decided to enroll in a writing course at Yale. He left letters and poems in Foster's mailbox and called her twice, hoping to establish a relationship with the film star. To his dismay, however, no relationship developed.

[7]Hinckley's obsession with Foster led to a more dangerous fixation. Like a character in *Taxi Driver*, he decided to assassinate a politician. Through this "historic deed," he would later write, he hoped to win Foster's "respect and love." Hinckley chose President Jimmy Carter as his target. For weeks he crisscrossed the country on the president's trail, but he never got the chance to shoot at Carter. Once, at an airport, security guards found guns in his bags. The weapons were confiscated and Hinckley had to pay a fine, but he was easily able to buy replacements for the firearms. In the November presidential election, Ronald Reagan defeated Carter.

[8]On March 29, 1981, Hinckley checked into the Park Central Hotel in Washington, D.C. The following day he wrote Jodie Foster a letter informing her of his undying love and his plan to shoot the president. Then he took his handgun to the Washington Hilton and awaited Reagan's appearance.

[9]The assassination attempt on Ronald Reagan marked the beginning of a new era in the interpretation of the Second Amendment of the United States Constitution, which reads:

> A well-regulated Militia, being necessary to the security of a free State, the right of the people to keep and bear Arms, shall not be infringed.

[10]The essential question in the gun controversy is whether the Second Amendment provides an individual right to own or carry guns. Interpretations of the Second Amendment by scholars, commentators, and courts generally fall into one of two categories: individualist or collectivist.

[11]Collectivists, mostly gun control advocates, oppose reading an individual right into the Second Amendment. Attorney and law review author Roy G. Weatherup makes the case for the collectivist view as follows:

> [12]Delegates to the Constitutional Convention had no intention of establishing any personal right to keep and bear arms. Therefore the "individualist" view of the Second Amendment must be rejected in favor of the "collectivist" interpretation, which is supported by history and a handful of Supreme Court decisions on the issue. . . . The nature of the Second Amendment does not provide a right that could be interpreted as being incorporated into the Fourteenth Amendment. It was designed solely to protect the states against the [federal] government, not to create a personal right which either state or federal authorities are

bound to respect. The contemporary meaning of the Second Amendment is the same as it was at the time of its adoption. The federal government may regulate the National Guard, but may not disarm it against the will of state legislatures. Nothing in the Second Amendment, however, precludes Congress or the states from requiring licensing and registration of firearms; in fact, there is nothing to stop an outright congressional ban on private ownership of all handguns and all rifles.

[13]Supporters of the "individualist" reading of the Second Amendment, mostly gun rights advocates, argue that an individual right to bear arms is explicitly granted in the Second Amendment and fully supported by the history of gun rights in England and the American colonies as well as the history of the actual drafting of the Bill of Rights. The history of the drafting of the Second Amendment shows that while an individual right for everyone to "bear Arms" was not inherited from the English common law—the law upon which most American law was patterned during colonial times—the right of self-defense was considered fundamental by the Framers of the Constitution, all of whom had lived through the experience of having a "well-regulated" militia resist disarmament by the British. The Framers—living at a time when many people had to hunt wild animals for food, defend against armed attack by Native Americans, and survive in cities and towns that lacked police—appeared to believe that there was an individual right, derived from the need for self-defense and militia preparedness, to bear arms.

[14]Individualists sometimes claim that the attempt to avoid an individualist reading of the Second Amendment is dishonest—that certain rights, including the grant of the right to bear arms, are at the mercy of a cultural elite whenever convenient. Robert Dowlut, an attorney for the National Rifle Association, observed:

> [15]History teaches us the unfortunate lesson that cultural values supplant constitutional rights whenever the cultural elite consider a right too burdensome to suit the needs of the moment. The outlandish pronouncement in Dred Scott "that the Negro might justly and lawfully be reduced to slavery for his benefit," the shameful court-approved internment of Japanese-Americans during World War II, and the separate but equal doctrine that officially existed until 1954 are all examples of the evils that result when cultural values are given more weight than constitutional rights.

[16]Dowlut also argues that "the Framers considered the right to keep and bear arms peculiarly important and also uniquely vulnerable to infringement," protecting individuals "against even popular conceptions of the public good."

[17]Commentator Vernon Gray also believes that the gun prohibition movement intends to dishonestly discredit the Second Amendment in its applicability to individuals, weaken the concept and acceptability of self-defense, and "change our traditions as they relate to firearms."

[18]Behind the debate over how to properly read and apply the Second Amendment lies genuine concern for the public good. Gun control advocates argue that too many people in a heavily armed society become victims to otherwise preventable gun violence. The statistics support the

notion that gun violence is expensive, tragic, and often linked to the easy availability of weapons.

[19]For example, the *Journal of Trauma* reported that taxpayers pay more than 80 percent of the medical costs for treatment of firearm-related injuries. According to the National Center for Health Statistics, 14 children in the United States are killed each day by gun violence. A study by the Harvard School of Public Health found that 59 percent of all children in grades 6 to 12 knew where to get a gun if they wanted one, and two-thirds of those students claimed that they could acquire a firearm within 24 hours.

[20]But the problem of gun violence as it relates to gun availability is complex. Statistics can be interpreted in different ways. Handgun availability is often a focus of gun control supporters who claim that the easy purchase of a handgun fuels crimes of passion, opportunity, and violence. According to the U.S. Justice Department, 78 percent of all murders of law enforcement officers involved handguns. From 1977 to 1996, according to the Bureau of Alcohol, Tobacco and Firearms, the U.S. firearm industry produced 39,024,786 handguns. But another 50 million rifles and shotguns were manufactured during the same period. While gun control legislation in the 1990s made it more difficult for people with criminal records to buy handguns from licensed gun shops, guns remain available from shows or private sales, including so-called swap-meets. This displeases gun control advocates who say that the easy availability of handguns and assault-style weapons leads to unnecessary deaths.

[21]However, a mid-1980s survey of convicted felons in 12 state prisons found that fewer than 1 percent obtained guns at gun shows. A 1997 Justice Department survey put the figure at only 2 percent.

[22]For some gun control supporters, even 2 percent is too much. But many criminologists believe that even fairly restrictive gun control legislation, including background checks at gun shows, wouldn't prevent such tragedies as the mass shootings at Columbine High School in Littleton, Colorado.

[23]Gun rights advocates argue that depriving citizens of the right to bear arms leaves citizens more vulnerable to criminal attack. Citing statistics tending to show that citizens experience less violent crime in states where laws allow for the carrying of concealed firearms, gun rights advocates argue that attempts to disarm otherwise law-abiding citizens aren't good for public safety. Gun rights advocates also cite studies showing that guns are used about five times more often to stop crimes than to commit them.

[24]Public opinion favors both sides of the gun control debate. Most voters continue to believe strongly that the Constitution protects the right of individuals to bear arms, including handguns, according to a *Washington Post*-ABC News poll published on September 9, 1999. But 63 percent of the public supports moderate gun control measures. The survey found suburban residents are as likely as urban residents to support a range of gun control measures. More than 8 of 10 surveyed supported the requirement that guns be sold with trigger locks and favored background checks at gun shows. In rural areas, such support is significantly lower. However, about two-thirds oppose a nationwide ban on the sale of handguns. And voters are evenly split on whether there should be a national ban on carrying concealed weapons.

[25]The Hinckley assassination attempt permanently disabled James Brady, whose brain injuries were so severe that he was not expected to live through surgery, and Officer Delahanty, whose left arm paralysis forced him to take early retirement from police work. Outraged at how easy it was for criminals and other high-risk individuals to obtain guns and ammunition, James Brady's wife and a group of citizens that included the survivors of other gun violence tragedies began lobbying for new legislation. In 1993, after years of acrimonious debate and intense pressure on Congress from both well-financed sides of the gun control issue, the legislation named after Sarah Brady's husband was passed by Congress and signed into law by President Bill Clinton.

[26]Many gun rights advocates were outraged at the passage of the Brady Act. Gun control advocates, on the other hand, criticized loopholes in the bill and urged the adoption of stronger measures aimed at preventing the sale of guns to anyone with a history of criminality or mental instability.

[27]The gun debate continues to escalate. While statistics showed a 21 percent drop in gun deaths from 1993 to 1997 and diminishing firearms injuries and gun crime since the passage of the Brady Act, gun violence is still much higher than it was in the 1960s. The United States remains the annual leader in gun violence. In 1995, for example, handguns were used to kill 2 people in New Zealand, 15 in Japan, 30 in Great Britain, 106 in Canada, 213 in Germany, and 9,390 in the United States.

A Well-Regulated Controversy Questions

VOCABULARY

1. Explain what Weatherup means when he says, "The contemporary meaning of the Second Amendment is the same as it was at the time of its adoption." (¶12)

2. Explain what Dowlut means when he says, ". . . cultural values supplant constitutional rights whenever the cultural elite consider a right too burdensome to suit the needs of the moment." (¶15)

COMPREHENSION AND ANALYSIS

For questions 3, 4, and 5, indicate whether the statement is true or false. If the statement is false, rewrite it to make it true.

3. Behind the debate over how to properly read and apply the Second Amendment lies genuine concern for the public good.

4. The problem of gun violence as it relates to gun availability is complex.

5. Passage of the Brady Act pleased both sides of the gun control debate.

6. Why do you think Fernandez believes "the assassination attempt on Ronald Reagan marked the beginning of a new era in the interpretation of the Second Amendment of the United States Constitution"?

7. What does Fernandez believe is the "essential question in the gun controversy"?

8. Interpretations of the Second Amendment by scholars, commentators, and courts generally fall into one of two categories. List and explain the two opposing views.

9. Does Fernandez think the gun debate is likely to be resolved soon? Please explain.

REFLECT AND CONNECT

10. Would you describe your interpretation of the Second Amendment more as an individualist or collectivist? Please explain how you reached your position.

Hatred: Too Close for Comfort

JACK LEVIN

Dr. Levin is the Irving and Betty Brudnick Professor of Sociology and Criminology at Northeastern University in Boston. Originally prepared for the St. Petersburg Times, *this is from his book with James Alan Fox,* Dead Lines: Essays in Murder and Mayhem *(Allyn & Bacon, 2001). Their other books include* Mass Murder: America's Growing Menace; Killer on Campus; *and* The Will to Kill: Making Sense of Senseless Murder. *A nationally recognized authority on homicide, Levin frequently provides expert commentary for print and electronic media, and he lectures widely on topics related to violent crime in America.*

AN IDEA TO THINK ABOUT:

How would you define a hate crime? Do you know anyone who has been a victim of a hate crime? *As you read,* find out why Levin has come to believe people are more "comfortable" hearing about serial murders than hate crimes.

HATRED: TOO CLOSE FOR COMFORT

Jack Levin

[1]For the past decade, I have studied serial and mass killers. In the course of conducting research, I have interviewed them, consulted with their attorneys, talked with their wives and mothers, and written about them.

[2]During this entire period, my ideas about murder were generally well received. In fact, many people apparently found them fascinating; so fascinating that the book I co-authored a few years ago, *Mass Murder: America's Growing Menace,* sold more than 50,000 copies and got me on national television talk shows from *Geraldo* to *Oprah,* from *48 Hours* to *Unsolved Mysteries.* Even *Saturday Night Live,* in a skit about Jeffrey Dahmer's trial, alluded to my work. In all candor, I began to feel like a celebrity.

³Sure, there was an occasional death threat (for example, from a fan of Charlie Manson) and a few nasty phone calls. But the overwhelming response was quite positive. Even the serial killers didn't seem to mind. One Canadian killer I got to know used to call me from his prison cell every Tuesday (collect, of course) and was very cooperative in responding to my students' letters to him about serial murder. He must have been flattered by the attention.

⁴Then, a couple of years ago, I began to notice that racial conflagrations in the major cities of the United States were becoming more commonplace. Believing that a national crisis was at hand, I began to research the rising tide of bigotry in America in the form of hate crimes—offenses committed against individuals because of their race, religion, national origin, or sexual orientation. In my talks and lectures to students, I pointed out that only 5 percent of such crimes are perpetrated by members of organized groups like the Klan or the White Aryan Resistance. Most are committed by otherwise ordinary citizens—teenagers down the block, the guy at the next desk at work, or the neighbors next door. I emphasized also that I was not talking about first amendment, free speech issues such as whether or not it is legal to insult someone with a racial slur. Actually, half of all hate crimes reported to the police are nothing less than assaults, often brutal attacks that put their victims in the hospital. I noted that African-Americans are most often victimized, but that gay men are most likely to suffer severe injuries as a result of an attack against them.

⁵All of a sudden, I was no longer regarded as fascinating. On the contrary, people seemed uncomfortable, upset, even angered, by what I had to say. I got the strong feeling that I was perceived as a personal threat, as someone who stirs up trouble and delves into matters better left unsaid. In response to a talk I had given on campus, for example, a student wrote an angry letter to the editor of the school newspaper, in which he defended the most racist ideas and referred to me as a "left-wing fascist." I later determined that he had not even attended my lecture, but had used the topic of my speech as an excuse to vent his anger.

⁶The pattern was now obvious. By shifting my attention from serial killers to the perpetrators of hate crimes, I had turned away from *them* and toward *us*. Serial murder is so extraordinary that, for the average American, it might as well be fiction. The topic of hate crimes, by contrast, is real; it simply hits too close to home.

⁷The particularly enlightened host of a local radio talk show in Boston recently asked me to be on her show. For more than an hour, I was scolded, reprimanded, and castigated in phone calls from her listeners. First, I talked with an outraged German-American man who claimed that recent acts of violence against immigrants in German cities had been grossly exaggerated. He blamed the "media." I agreed with him that relatively few radical skinheads had been directly responsible for the violence in Germany, but I also pointed out that 15 percent of German youths said that they now consider Adolph Hitler to be a great man and up to 40 percent of all German citizens express some sympathy for issues of "racial purity" and "Germany for Germans." I also emphasized that violence against foreigners was not a German predicament exclusively, but a worldwide problem. The next caller was a Rush Limbaugh fan who was furious because I had criticized his conservative idol for belittling gay activists and for referring to women as "FemiNazis." I tried to explain that Rush

was probably a very nice guy, but that his name-calling may be misinterpreted by naive youngsters looking to justify their bashings of women and gays. Next, I heard from a Jewish man from Framingham, Massachusetts, who was angry because I hadn't mentioned black anti-Semitism. I suggested to him that hatred can be found on all sides of the race issue, but that vulnerable people everywhere—blacks, Jews, Latinos, Asians, gays, and the disabled—should put aside their differences to form a powerful coalition against bigotry. He wasn't convinced. My final call was from a white supremacist in New Hampshire who claimed that Jews control the government, the banks, and the media and that black-Americans would be better off if they all went back to Africa. I should have calmly retorted that Jews probably do control the delis in New York City but that they are vastly underrepresented among bank executives. Or, I should have pointed out that the average income of Irish-Americans is almost identical to that of Jews, yet Irish-Americans are never accused of controlling anything except the bars and the local police force (a stereotype no less absurd). I should have told the white supremacist that the ancestors of most black Americans have probably been in this country longer than any of his relatives. . . . Maybe he should be the one to pack his bags. Before I could respond, however, the white racist had hung up and the program was over. The experience left me totally depressed.

⁸Hardly a day passes without some grotesque hate crime being reported in the local newspapers; and I am convinced more than ever that our nation is in serious trouble, that we could easily be torn apart in the next few years by the growing presence of hatred. Coming to grips with bigotry and violence might well be central to our survival as a free society into the next century. Yet Americans don't seem to be willing to address the problem, even if it is spiraling out of control. Perhaps they prefer watching escapist fare like *The Silence of the Lambs* or *The Texas Chainsaw Massacre*. Maybe I should go back to studying something safer . . . like serial killers.

Hatred: Too Close for Comfort Questions

VOCABULARY

1. Define *hate crime*.

2. Explain what Levin means when he says, "Serial murder is so extraordinary that, for the average American, it might as well be fiction." (¶6)

3. Explain what Levin means when he says he tried to point out that "his name-calling may be misinterpreted by naive youngsters looking to justify their [actions]." (¶7)

COMPREHENSION AND ANALYSIS

4. What type of crimes and criminals did Levin originally study? How was his work received by the public?

5. What types of crimes and criminals has Levin studied more recently? Why did he change his area of study? How has this work been received by the public?

6. Why does Levin believe people are more uncomfortable with his more recent work?

7. Who or what type of person commits most hate crimes?

8. What does Levin believe "vulnerable people everywhere" should do?

9. State Levin's thesis.

REFLECT AND CONNECT

10. If you or one of your classmates found your car in the campus parking lot covered with "hate graffiti," how would you want college security/officials to handle the situation? Please explain.

Much Ado About Violence

CHARLES GORDON

Mr. Gordon is a columnist with the Ottawa Citizen. *He wrote this article for* Maclean's *in May, 1999.*

AN IDEA TO THINK ABOUT

Have you ever seen a movie or read a book or listened to music that you found so violent and offensive you wondered how it ever got published? Did you ever consider that it should be censored? *As you read,* find out if Gordon thinks censoring media would put an end to violence.

MUCH ADO ABOUT VIOLENCE

Charles Gordon

[1]In the first days after the horrible shootings at Littleton, [Colorado] and Taber, [Alberta, Canada], the experts spoke, the open-line shows and letters-to-the-editor pages were deluged, and the following emerged as the things to blame for the tragedies: parents; copycats; the media; the Internet; guns; the free-love generation; gun control; the bombing of Serbia; large schools; the movie *The Matrix;* permissiveness; conformity; the movie *The Basketball Diaries;* the loss of family values; education cutbacks; the rocker Marilyn Manson; violence on television; bullying in school; the rock group KMFDM; the improper storage of firearms; the 40,000 killings children will see on television and in the movies by the time they are 18; cults; loners; the lack of counsellors in schools; the movie *Natural Born Killers.*

[2]Not as many possible solutions were available, although some of them were creative, such as the repeated playing of a song called "Drop Your Guns" by the vintage Canadian rock group April Wine.

³Merely listing the putative causes shows how broad and inescapable are the influences to which kids (as well as adults) are subjected in this complicated and violent age. And merely reading the list should demonstrate that no single factor can be blamed. Various influences come together, either to twist a mind or to give an evil direction to a mind that is already twisted.

⁴So the question is: what are we doing to drive people crazy? And how do we stop?

⁵It is here that the question of censorship enters the discussion, sometimes raised by well-meaning citizens who fear the impact of strong lyrics, pornographic books and magazines, violent movies and TV programs, and sometimes raised by people who are simply uncomfortable with modern means of expression and will use any event as an excuse to roll back the clock.

⁶But with the multitude of potential influences at work, it should be clear that no single book, no single song, no single movie can be shown to have caused an evil act. The other factors that cause the madness have to be present, too. Merely taking away the book, movie, or song will not solve anything.

⁷The censors are barking up the wrong tree. Sometimes, in fact, the most violent works can be shown to have social value, because they help us to understand violence. That is not to say that they all have value. The anti-censorship forces sometimes blunder into a trap of their own making by treating something as great art merely because an attempt is being made to suppress it. They then wind up having to defend the indefensible rather than merely having to defend the principle.

⁸There were walkouts and cries of protest during a reading from Lynn Crosbie's novel *Paul's Case* at a recent gala fund-raiser for PEN Canada, an organization devoted to defending freedom of expression around the world. The novel takes the form of a woman's letters to the imprisoned Paul Bernardo, the letters improvising freely and often graphically on themes and details brought out in the trial of the sex murderer and multiple rapist. Writing in *The Globe* and *Mail*, Doug Saunders said that "true supporters of free speech, after all, must support most staunchly those works that they most detest." Most people accept that thought, which has been reflected in most of the big freedom of expression cases in recent memory. To defend freedom of expression, it has been necessary to defend Ernst Zundel and Larry Flynt.

⁹There's another thought that you don't hear often enough when the issue of freedom of expression arises. It is that those who defend freedom of expression have an obligation to promote quality of expression as well. Defending bad books may be necessary, but let's not, in the process, kid ourselves that they are good books. Larry Flynt may have every right to publish *Hustler*, but the world is not necessarily a better place because he does. Readers can refuse to buy it and writers can refuse to write for it without anyone's freedoms being compromised.

¹⁰Back at the PEN gala, *The Globe* and *Mail* writer speculated that "even the people who walked out would fully support Lynn Crosbie's right to publish and distribute her novel." There's no question about that. In a democracy, the right to publish and distribute is not seriously questioned and should be vigorously supported. But to assert that is not to say that

every novel deserves publication, every song deserves recording or every movie deserves distribution.

[11]Should *Natural Born Killers* have been suppressed? Of course not. Should it have been filmed in the first place? That's a better question. The question applies to quite a bit of mass culture at this time in history. You don't have to accept the argument that movies cause murders to agree that a lot of truly horrible movies are being made. The same goes for books and songs.

[12]The publishers and studios and those who create the products they market cannot pretend that what they put out has no impact. Those who defend freedom of expression should also demand the production of works that are worthy of being defended. The line is not an easy one to draw, nor should the power to draw it be concentrated in a few hands. All artists should have it, and use it.

Much Ado About Violence Questions

VOCABULARY

1. Explain what Gordon means when he says, "Merely listing the putative causes shows how broad and inescapable are the influences to which kids (as well as adults) are subjected in this complicated and violent age." (¶3)

2. Explain what Saunders meant when he said, ". . . true supporters of free speech, after all, must support most staunchly those works that they most detest." (¶8)

3. Explain what Gordon means when he says, "The line is not an easy one to draw, nor should the power to draw it be concentrated in a few hands." (12)

COMPREHENSION AND ANALYSIS

For questions 4 and 5, indicate whether the statement is true or false. If the statement is false, rewrite it to make it true.

4. Those who defend freedom of expression have an obligation to promote quality of expression as well.

5. Every novel deserves publication, every song deserves recording, and every movie deserves distribution.

6. Does Gordon believe censorship would eliminate violence? Give an example to support your answer.

7. Does Gordon believe anti-censorship forces are always "in the right"? Please explain.

8. Does Gordon believe any violent works can ever be shown to have social value? Please explain.

9. State Gordon's thesis.

REFLECT AND CONNECT

10. Assume you are interviewing for a great job with a company that creates video games. The interviewer's first question to you is, "How do you think violence in video games influences players?" How do you respond? How would you feel about creating a video game for children that you felt contained unnecessary violence?

Why Rocky III?

MIKE MESSNER

Dr. Messner is an associate professor in the Department of Sociology and the Program for the Study of Women and Men in Society at the University of Southern California in Los Angeles. He is a former athlete and the author of Power at Play. *This selection is from* Sex, Violence, and Power in Sports: Rethinking Masculinity, *which he wrote with Don Sabo.*

VOCABULARY

> *impertinence (¶11):* nerve, audacity
> *chastised (¶14):* scolded
> *egging them on (¶14):* inciting the fighters to fight

IDEAS TO THINK ABOUT

Do you enjoy watching boxing? What do you like and/or dislike about boxing? Do you get frustrated when neither of the boxers gets knocked out and the match is a draw? *As you read,* find out why Messner is rethinking his view of boxing.

WHY ROCKY III?

Mike Messner

¹I faithfully watched the first two. But I can't go see the third one. Not Rocky III. The Italian Stallion will have to go this final round without me.

²Lately, I've been thinking more about boxing and enjoying it less. While watching the sports news on TV recently, I saw a "promising young boxer" by the name of Dave Moore finishing off an opponent. I have never enjoyed watching a man being beaten into unconsciousness, but this particular instance was especially chilling. I felt as though I were seeing a ghost, for the fight brought back to me a song written by Bob Dylan in 1963 about a boxer of the same name, who was killed in the ring.* Dylan angrily asks several times through the song,

---

*In *Blood and Guts: Violence in Sports* (New York and London: Paddington Press, 1979; page 173), Don Atyeo tells the story of Davey Moore's last fight. In 1963, when Moore was featherweight champion, he was pounded in the ring by his opponent, Sugar Ramos. He died seventy-five hours later. A week after his death, three more boxers were killed in the ring, leading the Pope (among others) to call for the abolition of boxing.

Who killed Davey Moore?
Why did he die
And what's the reason for?

[3]This question has plagued me for some time. Just who is responsible when a man is seriously injured or loses his life in the boxing ring? This issue was raised following last year's highly promoted championship bout between Sugar Ray Leonard and Thomas Hearns. Nearing the end of the fight, when Hearns was ahead on points, Leonard stung him with what was described as a "vicious combination of lefts and rights to the head" that left Hearns "dazed and staggering." The referee, who concluded that Hearns was "out on his feet," called the fight and awarded Leonard a technical knockout. Although the fight was applauded as a great one, some people were not so happy with its finish. For instance, the next day a young man commented to me that "the ref shouldn't have called the fight—you've gotta go down in a championship fight."

[4]Indeed, boxing referees are caught in an extremely difficult bind. On the one hand, they are responsible for seeing that the fight ends before someone gets seriously injured. On the other hand, they face tremendous pressure from fans, promoters, television networks, and sometimes the fighters themselves to let the fight go on until there is a clear-cut victory—until someone "goes down."

Not I, said the referee,
Don't point your little finger at me.
Sure, I coulda stopped it in the eighth
And saved him from his terrible fate.
But the crowd would have booed, I'm sure,
At not getting their money's worth.
Too bad that he had to go,
But there was pressure on me, too, you know.
No, it wasn't me that made him fall,
You can't blame me at all.

[5]The need for a "clear decision" to end every boxing contest seems to be a growing problem. An earlier title fight between Leonard and Roberto Duran (the Animal, the Destroyer who had previously dethroned Leonard) was yet another example. After several hard-fought rounds, Duran was clearly being beaten. He was hurt, and was losing the ability to defend himself. Between rounds, he decided to quit, claiming that he had stomach cramps. He was soundly booed. The fans, who had paid large sums of money to witness what was promised to be a "monumental battle," were disappointed and angry. The criticism of Duran has not died down to this day. Some say he threw the fight. Most boxing fans agree that when the chips were down, he was a "gutless quitter."

[6]At about the same time that the Leonard-Duran fight was making news, I was following another story about the Welsh boxer Johnny Owen, who had been critically injured in a boxing match. "Owen Still in Coma" read the small blurbs—and, later, "Owen Dies." Like the mythological Rocky Balboa, Owen was a hard-working, ambitious young man from a

poor, working-class background. He had said that his goal was to "fight a few more times and then get out of it before I get hurt." Certainly he was not a "gutless" man. He stayed in the fight to the end, undoubtedly pleasing the fans.

> *Not I, said the angry crowd,*
> *Whose screams filled the arena loud*
> *Too bad that he died that night,*
> *But we just like to see a good fight*
> *You can't blame us for his death,*
> *We just like to see some sweat*
> *There ain't nothing wrong in that*
> *No, it wasn't us that made him fall,*
> *You can't blame us at all.*

[7]Why do we fans push boxers to their limits, always demanding a clear-cut victory? This phenomenon can be seen as a result of a social-psychological malaise in modern life. Increasing instability and uncertainty in daily life, brought on by high unemployment, rising living costs, and increasingly shaky international relations (the United States, no longer the undisputed heavyweight champ, has been pushed around by relative lightweights like Iran), as well as insecure family relations and challenges to the traditional bases of masculinity, all bring about a need for some arena where there are obvious "good guys and bad guys"—clear winners and losers. For many people, sports has provided that arena. The National Football League has in recent years instituted a "fifth quarter" to decide games that end in a tie during regulation time. For players and for fans, it seems that "a tie is as good as a loss—it's like kissing your sister," as one fan told me.

[8]Added to the fans' emotional investment is financial investment in boxing. Millions of dollars are bet on big matches. Fans pay hefty sums to watch the matches on cable television at home or on closed-circuit television in theaters. Like any other multimillion-dollar product on the market, boxing is heavily hyped by promoters and by the media. After all the hype and heavy betting preceding a match, a man can't just quit because he has stomach cramps. He's gotta go down.

> *Not I, says the boxing writer,*
> *Pounding the print on his old typewriter.*
> *Who says, boxing ain't to blame,*
> *There's just as much danger in a football game.*
> *Boxing is here to stay,*
> *It's just the old American way.*
> *No, you can't blame me at all,*
> *It wasn't me that made him fall.*

[9]But what about the boxers themselves? What is it that made Sugar Ray Leonard return to the ring and risk losing the sight in an injured eye? As many would argue, the fighters know what they're getting into—they know the dangers. Of course, they also want the glory and the money that

go with being on top. But those of us who watch boxing matches should ask some other questions. For instance, who are these men who risk life and limb for our entertainment? Most boxers are from poor, working-class backgrounds. Many are members of minority groups for whom boxing may seem to be one of the few ways out of the misery they were born into. According to Chris Dundee, a Miami boxing promoter, "Any man with a good trade isn't about to get knocked on his butt to make a dollar" (Atyeo 1979, 176–77). But an impoverished society (such as in many Latin American nations) or an economically depressed city (such as Detroit) is fertile ground for a flourishing boxing industry.

[10]So even though nobody forces young boxers to enter the ring, it would be foolish to suggest that most of them freely choose boxing from a number of attractive alternatives. (Although many of the elite may romanticize the strength, stamina, courage, and masculinity of a John Wayne, we don't see many of the Rockefellers or the Kennedys taking up careers as pugilists, duking it out in the ring.) In any society which restricts the opportunities of certain groups of people, one will be able to find a significant number of those people who will be willing to pursue very dangerous careers for the slim chance of "making it big." Boxers are modern-day equivalents of Roman gladiators—they are both our victims and our heroes—and we are increasingly giving them the "thumbs down."

[11]For every millionaire Ali and for every smiling Sugar Ray we see on our TV, there are hundreds of fighters who have never made enough money boxing even to live on. All they have received for their efforts are a few scattered cheers, some boos, and some permanent injuries. But to the fans they are mostly invisible—unless one of them has the impertinence to die in the ring. We just don't see the long-term damage a boxer takes from years of severe jolts to the internal organs and to the brain. According to J. A. N. Corsellis, a neurologist who has studied boxers and their injuries, "By the time a fighter has had even as few as 150 bouts, he is really, I think, very likely to have suffered brain damage" (Atyeo 1979, 182).

[12]Does it make us wonder when we hear Muhammad Ali's once poetic and lightning-quick tongue, which used to "float like a butterfly," now often sticking to the roof of his mouth, as though it had been stung by a bee? And do we think about what boxing does to the people who watch the spectacle of boxing? Do we wonder to what extent boxing may serve to legitimate violence in everyday life?

> *Who killed Davey Moore?*
> *Why did he die*
> *And what's the reason for?*

[13]Dylan's question still troubles me. I think we can begin to find the answer by examining our own complicity in turning a brutal tradition into a profitable sport. The boxing business both meets the needs of an alienated and frustrated populace and at the same time generates millions of dollars for promoters, the media, and big-time bettors. And part of the problem is in our society's conception of manhood. When the traditional bastions of masculinity are crumbling or being undermined by historical forces, few things are so affirming to the threatened male ego as a good boxing match. Boxing lets us feel our solidarity with other men as we vicariously express our repressed anger and violence.

[14]When I was in junior high school, my friend Ron asked me to meet him after school because he was going to fight another boy and wanted some moral support. I watched as they fought. Ron's opponent was bigger, quicker, and a better fighter. Before long, Ron was bleeding from the mouth. In a last-ditch effort, he let out a terrible scream and came at his opponent with a desperate and reckless windmill-like flailing of the arms. His pitiful attempt to take the offensive was answered with a stiff right to the nose that put him down on the ground, sobbing and humiliated. Two young men then showed up and broke up the fight. To my surprise, they did not say a thing to the two fighters, but, rather, they chastised those of us who had been watching and cheering the fighters on. "You're worse than those two," they told us. "Their fight would have ended before someone got hurt if you hadn't been here egging them on like you did. You should be ashamed of yourselves."

[15]. . . and what's the reason for?

REFERENCE

Atyeo, Don. 1979. *Blood and Guts: Violence in Sports*. New York and London: Paddington Press.

Why Rocky III? Questions

VOCABULARY

1. In paragraph 7, Messner says, "This phenomenon can be seen as a result of a social-psychological malaise in modern life." What is the "phenomenon" he is referring to? What does he think is causing the phenomenon?

2. In paragraph 13, Messner says, ". . . we can begin to find the answer by examining our own complicity in turning a brutal tradition into a profitable sport." What's the question? Where does he think we should start looking for the answer?

3. Messner says boxing lets men "vicariously express our repressed anger and violence." (¶13) Explain what he means.

COMPREHENSION AND ANALYSIS

4. Why weren't people happy with the finish of the Leonard-Hearns fight or the Leonard-Duran fight? In both fights, what outcome did people want?

5. List four reasons Messner gives for why Americans need an arena where there are obvious "good guys and bad guys." What other reasons would you add?

6. According to Messner, who typically becomes a boxer? Do you agree with his analysis? Why or why not?

7. Why does Messner use the lyrics from the Bob Dylan song throughout his essay? Do you think it is an effective device? Why or why not? How do the lyrics help to develop and support his thesis?

8. In paragraph 14, Messner recalls a personal experience of watching a fight. How does the story help to develop and support his thesis?

9. In the story Messner recalls from junior high school, why did the young men who broke up the fight yell at the spectators? Do you think blaming the spectators was appropriate? Why or why not?

10. How do you answer Messner's question ". . . to what extent does boxing serve to legitimize violence in everyday life?" How do you think Messner would answer this question?

11. State Messner's thesis.

REFLECT AND CONNECT

12. How do you answer Messner's question "Just who is responsible when a man is seriously injured or loses his life in the boxing ring?" How do you think Messner would answer this question?

Prologue: New Year's Eve

GREG LICHTENBERG

Mr. Lichtenberg's work has appeared in the New York Times Magazine, Fence, *and other publications. He has taught fiction and creative nonfiction writing for the Johns Hopkins University. This is the introductory chapter in his memoir,* Playing Catch with my Mother, *where he reflects on the ways gender roles and behaviors were defined by his family and society during his early life.*

IDEAS TO THINK ABOUT

What is your favorite memory from when you were about six or seven? What memory from that time makes you the most sad or confused? What "lesson" do you remember learning about that time? *As you read,* find out what lesson Lichtenberg learned.

PROLOGUE: NEW YEAR'S EVE

Greg Lichtenberg

¹If this is obsession—obsession, one could say, right down to the words, *boy, man, girl, woman*—then I've had it since I could speak. I've breathed it, no more conscious of it than of the bite of pollution in the New York City air. I went about my business like any other boy until someone brought it to my attention, as when my tall father bent down the branch of a young maple on our street in Greenwich Village to show me the brown-edged

holes in the green leaves. Invisible acid in the air had burned holes just big enough to peer through. When I looked, I saw my long-haired father, my cobblestone street, my upthrust city darkly framed as by a pinhole camera.

[2]On the first New Year's Eve I remember, when my parents brought my toddler sister and me to celebrate with family friends, I was not thinking that the air between men and women burned with angry confusion. I knew that my struggling parents had been fighting more, and more publicly, than before, but their fights were beyond me, facts of nature, forest fires. On the way to Princeton, I remember thinking of my good luck—we'd gotten to ride not just the subway but two real trains, the impressively long Trenton local and now, from the junction, the little "dinky," with its deep-voiced conductor and its door excitingly open to the air.

[3]When I tired of the train, I thought about the toy airplane in our overnight bag. I'd made it in my kindergarten's first-ever turn in wood shop, with a scrap of two-by-two for a body, and for wings a flat narrow board the shop teacher held while I painstakingly hammered. The wheels were wooden buttons that really spun, and across the wings and to each side of the nose, where model planes showed military insignia, I'd inked the numbers of the coming year with indelible purple Magic Marker: 1972!

[4]We got to our friends' house as the evening sky deepened. The trees beyond their living room windows had turned black. Peter's mother lit candles by the stereo, on the side tables, and in the dining room. Firelight flickered off glass tabletops and chrome tubing and bright black leather. The whole downstairs filled with a fireplace glow, cozy and unreal.

[5]Soon the dads, long-haired and bearded, were sitting on the couch, talking in important-sounding dad sentences, and the moms were standing in the kitchen, chopping salad vegetables on wooden boards. The kitchen had doorways but no doors, so what the moms said could be heard in the living room even over the music: sharp laughter, criticisms long pent up.

[6]My friend Peter and I went upstairs to his room, to push toy cars and trucks and to play—fly my New Year's plane. The comforter on his bed was good to sit on, but bumpy for Matchbox vehicles and wooden wheels. In time, Peter's sister came to the door, and a familiar dispute began. Peter argued from strict principle—older brothers with older brothers, younger sisters with younger sisters—and his sister countered with a plea for reason and flexibility: Amanda downstairs, just two, was too young for games. Peter relented. The three of us were playing together when I felt the tremor of my parents' argument on the stairs.

[7]My father's step was heavy, his voice distorted; it was hard to recognize him. My mother's voice made a flat, distancing drone, a sound that said *not you, not what you say, never, nothing, no*. This was a bad one. I felt I should step into the hallway and show myself, to remind them where we were, that this was supposed to be a holiday.

[8]Peter was driving a dump truck up the side of his bed, and his sister was asking how it kept from crashing when the mountain was so steep; to them, adult voices on the stairs were nothing to notice. I wished then that I didn't have this ear always listening for out-of-tune conversations.

[9]My father's voice rose and my mother's followed. She yelled his name, and something thumped dully down the stairs. Peter and Amy

looked up. My father's fast steps pounded toward us, shaking the floor, then veered into Amy's room, one wall away. We heard a crack, and rapid distant tinkling—wind chimes in a gale. Then came a sound I'd never heard before, like the ripping of heavy fabric, but deeper. We heard my father cross the hall again, then the slam of a door and the snap of the bathroom lock.

¹⁰In the silence, I pulled open Peter's door, and all three of us edged out into the hall. At first we saw no one, only the stairway railing and the shelf of books built into the wall. The air was strangely cold. Downstairs, I could hear my sister crying and Peter's father asking my mother if she was all right.

¹¹We leaned into the room where the strange noises had come from, saw the holes my father had punched in the glass window and the wall. Until then I hadn't thought of the wall of a house as something a man's fist could break. Night air, cold and oily, snaked past the shards of the broken windowpane.

¹²Peter's mother ran up the stairs to shepherd us into the safety of her office, a room with midnight blue walls where we weren't usually allowed. In that grown-up place there was nothing to do but listen. We heard her knock on the locked bathroom door and speak soothingly to my father, as though to a child who had been ill and now would be put to bed. He unlocked the door and went downstairs.

¹³No one seemed to know what had happened or what to do about it. In time I think we were led to the dinner table for spaghetti. I don't remember if we ate. My mother lay stretched out on the couch, wincing at the pain in her ribs. My father sat apart, staring out the darkened windows. Peter's mother spoke to him again.

¹⁴"I'd like you to leave," she said.

¹⁵Peter's father stood up and moved beside his wife, his jaw set hard beneath the thick red-brown of his beard. My father had barely spoken since he'd come downstairs.

¹⁶"I want you out of my house," she said. She spoke in a controlled, formal voice put on for the occasion. I didn't recognize her in it, as I hadn't recognized my father in his screaming.

¹⁷My mother lay wounded on the couch while my father—suddenly, now, my not-kind, not-brave, not-right father—collected his things in a brown paper shopping bag. Everyone was quiet, waiting for him to leave.

¹⁸With just quick kisses on the head for my sister and me, and an awful jerky nod to my mother, he followed Peter's father out the door. I watched from the window seat, kneeling by little panes closing up with frost as he walked past the porch light into the darkness. A slow draft crept up from around my knees, and I tilted my head so my breath on the glass wouldn't fog my view of him. I could see him in the passenger seat with his paper bag on his lap, staring at nothing.

¹⁹As the car's red taillights dwindled down the driveway, my sister ran stiff-legged to my mother on the couch. She clung tight and burrowed her head into my mother's uninjured side. Peter's mother joined them, and over my shoulder I watched hungrily, imagining how good Amanda must feel in that gathering of reassurance and warmth. My mother held out an arm to me, offering a hug and a sad smile. I wanted to run to her, to be comforted and to let her know I was with her, but I hesitated. Peter and Amy had been sent upstairs; I was the only boy in the room now.

²⁰I stood alone, learning to feel like a traitor. It was as though some-thing dug into me then, setting barbs, never meaning to let me go. Knotted to those barbs were ropes, one tied to my mother's outstretched hand, one pulling from the fender of my father's retreating car. It's hard for me to say how long I waited by that window. Perhaps it was fifteen years.

²¹The next day in our little apartment, my mother talked to me on the brown corduroy couch. I sat with my back against a cushion, my legs sticking straight out in front, wishing I'd distracted my parents before the fight got so bad. I kept my eyes on the floor, away from the bare wooden beams of their empty loft bed rising up near the ceiling.

²²My mother told me that my father would not be coming back unless he learned to control himself and to treat us right. She would call a lock-smith to change the locks, she explained, and then we would be safe. On this unthinkable day, she knew what had to be done. I felt gratitude, so much gratitude it knocked the wind out of me.

²³She told me that sometimes when parents have fights, kids think it's their fault. I stared up at her, amazed at what she knew—just hearing her say so made me feel a little better. I pulled my legs in close where I could hug them, and I looked at her, the sincerity in her dark brown eyes, the upbeat gestures she made when she gave explanations.

²⁴She said that in the past, when my father had screamed and hit, she'd thought it was her fault. She'd thought she made him angry by being a bad wife. But now, thanks to her women's group, she understood that he had a problem. His screaming and hitting and smashing were wrong, she said. It was very important that she realize, and I realize, and even baby Amanda realize that he had this problem. It was his problem. His alone.

²⁵When she glanced down to see if I understood, I studied the blue valleys on the denim-patched tops of my knees. I knew she was waiting for me to say something, but I sat silent, lost. In my silence, she repeated her idea slowly and carefully, as if it was hard to understand. It was not. Nearly every day in school, kids pushed other kids. They punched and wrestled and screamed and smacked until a teacher stopped them. Mostly, those kids were boys. Boys broke things that didn't even belong to them. Boys gave scratches and bloody noses. Boys made other kids cry. I'd done these things myself sometimes. Everyone knew it was bad.

²⁶My mother didn't try to explain to her five-year-old all she had learned in her women's group, but I got the message. My father had a problem. His problem was being a boy.

Prologue: New Year's Eve Questions

VOCABULARY

1. Explain what Lichtenberg means in paragraph 2 when he says, ". . . their fights were beyond me, facts of nature, forest fires."

2. Explain what Lichtenberg means in this first part of paragraph 20: "I stood alone, learning to feel like a traitor. It was as though something dug into me then, setting barbs, never meaning to let me go. Knotted to those barbs were ropes, one tied to my mother's outstretched hand, one pulling from the fender of my father's retreating car."

COMPREHENSION AND ANALYSIS

3. What did Lichtenberg's mother want him to understand?

4. What did Lichtenberg "understand"? If you read the rest of the book, do you think you would find that his understanding changed over the years? Please explain.

5. Although there could be many reasons, why do you think Lichtenberg opened his memoir with this recollection of "New Year's Eve"?

REFLECT AND CONNECT

6. After class, you often join a group of students for coffee in the cafeteria. Over the last couple of weeks, someone in the group, a woman in her late twenties, has tried to hide a variety of bruises on her face and arms. Today she has a broken arm. She talks with you and describes an abusive relationship. She asks for your advice. What do you tell her?

LOG ON TO THE WEB

As Kornblum and Julian noted in the "Social Problems Online" section at the end of their text chapter, the Internet offers a large variety of resources on violence, crime, and the criminal justice system. For this Web exercise,

1. Select a topic or issue related to violence, crime, and the criminal justice system that you would like to know more about, such as hate crimes, racial profiling, reforming the criminal justice system, death penalty, recidivism rates, explanations of crime, the influence of media on crime and violence.

2. Write two questions about the topic that you want to answer. For example, if your topic is hate crimes your questions might be, What type of hate crime has increased the most in the last year (in my city or state or nationally)? In what ways are people who perpetrate violent hate crimes similar to or different than perpetrators of other violent crimes? Do all states have statutes addressing hate crimes? If not, why not? What are two good ideas for teaching tolerance?

3. Use your favorite search engine to locate at least four Web sites with information about your topic (visit more sites if you haven't yet found the answers to your questions). For each site, write down the complete URL and the sponsor and/or creator of the site.

4. Write down the answers to your two questions and note which Web sites were most useful in your research.

REFLECT AND CONNECT

A. A local elementary school principal asks your college president if a group of students would create a presentation and accompanying booklet to help children understand that there is never a reason to abuse or be abused. You are part of the six-person team selected. What approach do you recommend—serious, funny, dramatic, scary? Why? What one idea or concept would you like all students to leave your presentation thinking about?

B. Three months ago your next-door neighbor's father moved in with him. During the first few weeks, you saw the elderly father walking or sitting outside. However, for the last three weeks, you haven't seen him and have heard your neighbor's loud voice issuing threats and insults. What, if anything, do you do? Please explain.

C. Describe the type of violence/crime that you believe is most prevalent in and harmful to your community. Discuss why you think that type of violence/crime is flourishing in your community and what citizens, law enforcement, and legislators could do to reduce it.

FURTHER READING

Aaron T. Beck, *Prisoners of Hate: The Cognitive Basis of Anger, Hostility, and Violence* (Perennial Press, 2000).

Thomas F. Homer-Dixon, *Environment, Scarcity, and Violence* (Princeton University Press, 2001).

Valerie Polakow (Editor) and Jonathan Kozol, *The Public Assault on America's Children: Poverty, Violence, and Juvenile Injustice* (Teachers College Press, 2001).

Diane Ravitch and Joseph P. Viteritti (Editors), *Kid Stuff: Marketing Sex and Violence to America's Children* (Johns Hopkins University Press, 2003).

Susan Sontag, *Regarding the Pain of Others* (Farrar Straus & Giroux, 2002).

Biodiversity

Many scientists believe humankind faces three great threats. The first is nuclear war. The second is global warming. The third "is the rapid loss of the earth's rich biodiversity, its variety of life—the only living things known to exist in the universe.

—Lawrence Pringle in *Living Treasure—*
Saving Earth's Threatened Biodiversity

Time it takes to grow 1 inch of soil	1,000 years
Time it has taken to erode and wash away one-third of the topsoil in the United States	40 years
Number of black rhinos in Africa in the 1960s	100,000
Number of black rhinos in Africa now	2,500
Number of pieces of live coral broken off from reefs (which are habitat to 1 million species) and purchased by Americans each year	350,000
Number of pieces purchased by the rest of the world each year	90,000
Number of Boeing 747 airplanes that could fit on the ground in New York's Yankee Stadium	2
Number of Boeing 747s that could fit inside the largest size of trawl net used to catch ocean fish by commercial "factory ships"	12

Source: "Biodiversity 911: Saving Life on Earth," a traveling exhibit of the World Wildlife Fund and Worldwatch Institute.

Every person on the planet relies on biodiversity—for the air we breath, the water we drink, the food we eat, the medicines we use, the way we live— every day.

According to Fred Powledge in "Biodiversity at the Crossroads," *Bio-Science,* May 1998, "In 1986 a group of prominent scientists gathered in Washington, DC, to report on a new way of looking at the planet and the people who use it. The staff of the National Research Council, which cosponsored the conference with the Smithsonian Institution, came up with a new term to describe the subject of inquiry: biodiversity.

"The word (spelled Bio Diversity and sometimes BioDiversity in documents at the time) was short for 'biological diversity,' nine syllables that refer, in the words of Harvard entomologist E. O. Wilson, to the 'variation in the entirety of life on the planet.'"

The ultimate measure of biodiversity is the total number of species in existence. About 1.8 million species of organisms have been described and named, but those are thought to be a small part of the total. However, there is no agreement on how many species have existed at any given time or do exist now.

If the earth is home to 10 million species, wrote biologist Thomas Lovejoy of the Smithsonian Institution, "they then represent 10 million successful sets of solutions to a series of biological problems, any one of which could be immensely valuable to us."

But are all species equally valuable?

While it's true that some of those organisms may have little significance in their community and no economic value to people, we know so little about the species that are being lost that, as Lawrence Pringle says in *Living Treasure—Saving Earth's Threatened Biodiversity,* "The one-millionth species of beetle *might* be a 'keystone' species—one that plays a key role in the workings of the habitat where it lives."

We also don't know how fast species are disappearing. Although extinction is natural and some kinds of plants and animals become extinct each century, some biologists estimate that within the next century nearly half of the earth's plants, animals, and microorganisms may become extinct.

Is that a loss worth worrying about? Is it really abnormally high?

In 1850, Earth was home to about 1 billion people. Today, it has 6 billion and there is general agreement that our increased human activity is the major threat to biodiversity. As author Bill Bryson says in his recent book, *A Short History of Nearly Everything,* "we don't know what we are doing right now or how our present actions will affect the future. What we do know is that there is only one planet to do it on, and only one species of being capable of making a considerable difference."

"The planet is at a crucial crossroads," conclude the authors of the 2002 report of the UN Environment Programme. The choices made today are "critical to the forests, oceans, rivers, mountains, wildlife and other life support systems upon which current and future generations depend." However, is altering human activities by prohibiting hunting, restricting logging, or curbing mining activity worth the economic and social costs? Can we balance the needs of people who worry about needing to eat and needing to work with those concerned about the life of our planet?

The authors in this theme tackle those questions and related issues.

Chris Howes opens the theme with the introduction from his thought-provoking book, *The Spice of Life—Biodiversity and the Extinction Crisis.*

In Chapter 14 from their engaging new text *Biology: Science for Life,* Professors Belk and Borden explore the primary question, "Is Earth Experiencing a Biodiversity Crisis?" Then, Julie Majeres discusses "The Politics of Biodiversity."

The next two selections deal with endangered species. First, editorial cartoonist Steve Greenberg tells us a not-so-pleasant bedtime story, and then Todd Wilkinson takes us to Yellowstone Nation Park and "A Grizzly Future."

The final two articles discuss the fragile link between agriculture and biodiversity: Kevin Parris discusses how "Sustainable Agriculture Depends on Biodiversity," and Paul Richards and Louise Sperling look at "The Silent Casualties of War."

Imagine

CHRIS HOWES

After obtaining a degree in zoology and teaching biology for many years, Mr. Howes now works as a freelance author and photographer specializing in the natural world, conservation, and outdoor sports. Based in Cardiff, England, he is a Fellow of the Royal Photographic Society, has written several books on photography, and is the editor of the caving magazine Descent. *This selection is the introduction to his thought-provoking book,* The Spice of Life—Biodiversity and the Extinction Crisis, *a study of how life began, what affects its species, and where it is heading.*

VOCABULARY

wanly (¶1)*:* faintly, palely
altruistic (¶3)*:* unselfish

AN IDEA TO THINK ABOUT

How many species do you estimate are on this planet today? How many species would you estimate have gone out of existence during your lifetime? How many would you estimate will become extinct in the next twenty-four hours? *As you read,* see if Howes thinks we can answer such questions.

IMAGINE

Chris Howes

¹Imagine a darkened, brown room. Heavy drapes are held each side of a north-facing window, sunlight wanly peering in from a cobbled street. There is a slightly musty smell, as if the room requires airing more often. The slow tock, tick, tock of a grandfather clock paces the minutes. A large, oak table, perfectly polished, dominates the carpet, while walls bear a writing bureau, books bound in calf and cloth, and a series of wooden cabinets. A preserved owl, a few small bones neatly numbered, snail shells, racks of insects pinned to cork in serried rows. The tools of the trade lie to one side: a butterfly net, pins, killing jar, a microscope near the window. This is a room of the nineteenth century, dedicated to natural history: a collector's room.

²How precise is this stereotyped image, fostered by Hollywood? There certainly were Victorian collectors who ranked elements of the natural world one above the other and performed endless, minute comparisons

of beetles and moths, grasses and flowers. Why? What drove them to such dedication? What did these often amateur naturalists hope to achieve?

[3]The answer is not as altruistic as might be first assumed; there were sometimes other motives in force than simply a search for knowledge and science, such as entertainment. Neither is this Victorian world the start of the search for and recording of biological diversity: biodiversity. That story starts far earlier.

[4]There is an immense catalogue of data in existence which covers all the known species of earth, with more being continually added. This is the arena of biological specialists: ask any museum or specialist for a list of all known insects and you will receive a blank look. Try for the latest species' names, some of which have changed once, twice, and more times in recent years, and the same response is likely. Yes, more species are continually added as collections are made, differences are noted, and the catalogue changes—but there are so many niches for study that it is impossible to follow every minute addition. It is no longer possible for any one person to keep up with all the literature (there are now 500,000 scientific journal titles listed by UNESCO), any more than a doctor can read every medical journal and know details of every new drug. New species are being discovered daily; yet more life to name and file. While the rare and unexpected discovery of a large mammal new to science causes waves of surprise around the world, more microbes, worms and beetles are ten a penny.

[5]The cycle of life is never ending: leaves take in sunlight and grow on the forest floor, nourishing the plant until it dies, to decay under the forces of fungi and decomposers, leaving its nutrients available for the next generation.

[6]A true and complete catalogue of life? There is no such thing. There is only a feeling that we have been through the forests and oceans of earth and catalogued what we have found, however poorly. So how do we know how many species there are on this planet? We don't—we can only make estimates, just as we are restricted to estimating the numbers of living, individual organisms. Some estimates are more accurate than others, of course, and we find interesting facts: the largest single group of organisms is that of the insects, with over three-quarters of a million species described. As a group, this means that insects outnumber mammalian species at something approaching 200:1, and all plants by about 3:1. Through all time, insects have been the most successful of all life-forms.

[7]It goes further. Choose a number for the extinction rate of animals and plants: how many species wink out of existence, to join the world of fossils, for all the good their genes brought them? Is it ten a year, ten a week, ten a day? How about the staggering estimate of four every hour, day and night, year in year out, a rate of extinction that far outstrips all others throughout the millennia. Fossils themselves represent a fixed record of life that was; why did the organisms die, what caused the loss of their species? How many animals and plants have existed in the distant past, to go the way of the dinosaurs? What of evolution and the production of all this life? How does it work?

[8]It's a numbers game to form arguments like this, serving only to fuel the statistician's pen. Biodiversity is a wider concept, a word which represents the array of living things, known and unknown. There is a real world of nature out there, one which numbers try to quantify. Biodiversity

struggles to exist with or without that expression; it is a blind lottery of chance which controls the progression. You are reading this volume, so you already, presumably, have an interest in this living world, a curiosity of passing importance or driving force. Others—friends, neighbours, "foreigners," businessmen, media presenters, politicians—may feel differently.

[9]It comes down to this: why does life exist on our earth, yet other planets remain barren? What is life; how did it form, how does it die? How do we know how many living organisms and species there are? Of even more importance, how do we estimate the numbers yet to be found, identified and catalogued? How do we know where to direct our energies into the study of biodiversity and, once we begin to find answers, what do we do with them? We have knowledge of these life-forms, this biodiversity. We, the species supposedly at the pinnacle of an evolutionary procession, can count, we can measure. We question.

[10]Does it stagger you that 99 percent of all species which have ever existed are now extinct? That some hundred or so species now follow them into oblivion every day? Does it matter? So what? Who cares?

Imagine Questions

VOCABULARY

1. Explain what Howes means when he says, "While the rare and unexpected discovery of a large mammal new to science causes waves of surprise around the world, more microbes, worms and beetles are ten a penny." ([4])

2. Explain what Howes means when he says, "It's a numbers game to form arguments like this, serving only to fuel the statistician's pen." ([8])

COMPREHENSION AND ANALYSIS

For questions 3, 4, and 5, indicate whether the statement is true or false. If the statement is false, rewrite it to make it true.

3. Any listing of how many species there are on this planet is only an estimate.

4. Mammals have been the most successful of all life-forms.

5. New species are discovered every day; some species become extinct every day.

6. What does paragraph 1 describe? What is the purpose of paragraph 1?

7. Why is there no "true and complete catalogue of life"?

8. How does Howes define biodiversity? How important are numbers to his concept of biodiversity? Please explain.

9. State Howes's thesis.

REFLECT AND CONNECT

10. How do you answer the series of questions Howes asks in the last paragraph: "Does it stagger you that 99 per cent of all species which have ever existed are now extinct? That some hundred or so species now follow them into oblivion every day? Does it matter? So what? Who cares?"

Is Earth Experiencing a Biodiversity Crisis?

COLLEEN BELK AND VIRGINIA BORDEN

Dr. Belk and Dr. Borden have collaborated on teaching the nonmajors biology course at the University of Minnesota-Duluth for over a decade. Their collaboration led them to develop Biology: Science for Life *in which each chapter is structured around a compelling story involving the integral role of biology. In Chapter 14, "Is Earth Experiencing a Biodiversity Crisis?" we meet the farmers of the Klamath Basin as they struggle to understand the "price" of preserving biodiversity.*

VOCABULARY

Key terms appear in boldface type in the text and are defined in context.

AN IDEA TO THINK ABOUT

Do you think every species should be protected and preserved? If not, which species should we allow to vanish? *As you read,* determine some of the factors that should be considered to balance the costs and benefits of protecting endangered species.

CHAPTER 14

Is Earth Experiencing a Biodiversity Crisis?

Ecology and Conservation Biology

The Lost River sucker is endangered . . .

. . . and these farmers are angry.

Who has the right to use this lake for their survival—the farmers or the fish?

In June and July of 2001, angry farmers in the Klamath Basin of Oregon and California repeatedly occupied and disrupted a Bureau of Reclamation facility. The farmers used diamond-bladed chainsaws, pry bars, and blowtorches to open the head gate of an irrigation canal designed to bring water from Upper Klamath Lake to the agricultural fields of the basin. The water the irrigation canal delivers is crucial to the success of crops grown in the high desert of southern Oregon and northern California, and farmers in the Klamath Basin had been able to count on receiving this life-giving water since the early 1900s. The water source was suddenly and completely cut off in April 2001, when the U.S. Fish and Wildlife Service determined that a severe drought and the resulting loss of water from Upper Klamath Lake was decreasing the survival of several species of threatened and endangered fish—including the shortnose and Lost River suckers.

Many residents of the Klamath Basin are outraged that their homes and livelihoods are threatened by an attempt to preserve some dull-colored and economically unimportant fish. Ty Kliewer, a senior at Oregon State University whose family farms in the Basin, told his senator that he had learned the

Why should we care about the fate of such a controversial endangered species—or any endangered species?

357

importance of balancing mathematical and chemical equations in school. "It appears to me that the people who run the Bureau of Reclamation and the U.S. Fish and Wildlife Service slept through those classes," Kliewer said. "The solution lacks balance and we've been left out of the equation." His comment is echoed by thousands of people all over the United States whose jobs have been threatened or eliminated by the government's attempts to protect endangered species.

Why is the federal government so concerned with threatened and endangered species that they are willing to take actions that cause the disruption and displacement of ordinary Americans, such as the Klamath Basin farmers? Why are such drastic measures necessary to save imperiled organisms?

14.1 The Sixth Extinction

The government agencies that stopped water delivery to the Klamath Basin farmers were acting under the authority of the **Endangered Species Act (ESA)**, a law passed in 1973 with the express purpose of protecting and encouraging the population growth of threatened and endangered species. The Lost River and shortnose suckers were once among the most abundant fish in Upper Klamath Lake—at one time they were harvested and canned for human consumption. Now, with populations of fewer than 500 and little reproduction, these fish are in danger of **extinction**—the complete loss of the species. Critically imperiled species such as the Lost River and shortnose suckers are exactly the type of organisms legislators had in mind when they enacted the ESA.

The ESA was passed as a result of the public's concern about the continuing erosion of **biological diversity**, the entire variety of living organisms. Passage of the ESA was prompted in part by the fate of the whooping crane, one of only two cranes native to North America and among the most majestic of all birds. Biologists estimate that there were more than 1,000 whooping cranes alive in the mid-1860s. By 1938—due to the loss of nesting areas and because of human hunting—the bird had disappeared from much of the continent and only two small flocks existed. By 1942, only 16 birds remained in the wild.

Increasing the number of whooping cranes has proven a challenge, because these birds reproduce slowly and require "teachers" to help them learn migratory routes. To bolster the recovery of this species, the Fish and Wildlife Service and other agencies began the laborious process of hand-rearing cranes, teaching them to behave like cranes, training them to follow traditional migration paths (Figure 14.1), and reintroducing the population to its native range. Thanks to these intensive and costly efforts, the population of whooping cranes in the wild now numbers over 300. Congress passed the ESA to stave off the potential for other species to reach the same precarious position once held by whooping cranes.

Unfortunately, the near-extinction of the whooping crane was not a unique event. Bald eagles, peregrine falcons, gray wolves, and woodland caribou—once abundant species—are or recently were critically endangered. One of the most numerous bird species on the planet, the passenger pigeon (Figure 14.2), was driven to extinction in North America a little over 100 years ago.

The extinction of the passenger pigeon was primarily the result of human activity. The conversion of North American forests to agricultural land reduced the nesting and feeding areas of these birds, and unregulated commercial hunting dealt the final blow. The dramatic population declines of eagles, falcons, wolves, caribou, and the Lost River and shortnose suckers have also been caused by humans. The ESA was drafted because humans appeared to be initiating an

Figure 14.1   Saving endangered species. These whooping cranes are following an ultralight airplane, which is leading them from their summer range in Wisconsin to their wintering grounds in Florida. Since there are no longer any wild whoopers that follow this traditional migration route, humans must teach it to these young cranes.

unprecedented rapid rate of species loss. (See Essay 14.1 for a discussion of possibly human-caused extinctions beginning about 15,000 years ago.)

Critics of the ESA argue that the goal of saving all species from extinction is unrealistic. After all, extinction is a natural process—the species living today constitute less than 1% of the species that ever existed—and trying to save rare species, as we have seen in the Klamath Basin, can be detrimental to humans. The next section explores the scientific questions ESA critics seem to pose: How does the rate of extinction today compare to the rate in the past? Is the ESA just postponing the inevitable, natural process of extinction?

Measuring Extinction Rates

If ESA critics are correct that the current rate of species extinctions is "natural," then extinction rates today should be roughly equal to rates in previous eras. The rate of extinction in the past can be estimated by examining the *fossil record*, the physical evidence left by organisms that existed in the past.

Figure 14.2   An extinct species. Passenger pigeons were once the most common bird in North America, but they were driven to extinction by human activity.

360   Chapter 14   Is Earth Experiencing a Biodiversity Crisis?

Figure 14.3   Estimating the life span of a species. The ages of these fossil shells are estimated from the age of the rocks they are embedded in via radiometric dating (Chapter 8). Fossils of the same species are arranged on a timeline from oldest to youngest. The difference in age between the oldest and youngest fossil of a species is an estimate of life span.

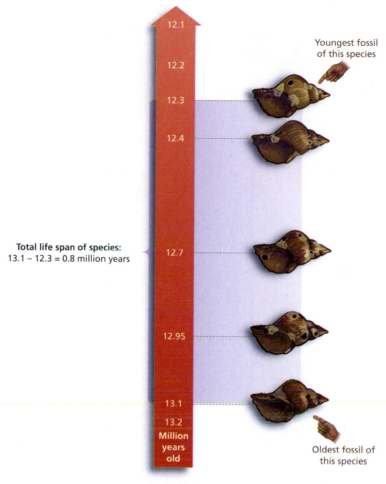

Total life span of species:
13.1 – 12.3 = 0.8 million years

The span of geologic time in which fossils of an individual species are found represents the life of that species (Figure 14.3). Biologists have thus estimated that the "average" life span of a species is around 1 million years (although there is tremendous variation), and that the overall rate of extinction is about one species per million per year, or about 0.0001% per year. Some scientists have argued that these estimates are too low, since they are based on observations of the fossil record, a record that may be biased toward long-lived species. However, most biologists agree that the estimates are currently the best approximation of background extinction rates—that is, the constant rate of species loss.

Current rates of extinction are calculated from actual recorded extinctions. This is harder to do than it seems, because extinctions are surprisingly difficult to document. The only way to conclude that a species no longer exists is to exhaustively search all areas where it is likely to have survived. In the absence of a complete search, most conservation organizations have adopted the standard that, to be considered extinct, no individuals of a species must have been seen in the wild for 50 years.

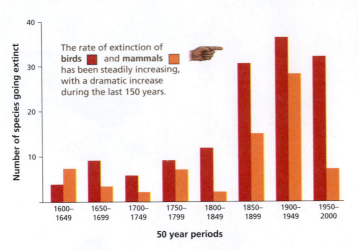

The rate of extinction of **birds** ■ and **mammals** ■ has been steadily increasing, with a dramatic increase during the last 150 years.

50 year periods

Figure 14.4   Rate of extinction. This graph illustrates the number of species of mammals and birds known to have become extinct since 1600. Note that the rate of extinction in both groups has been generally increasing, with the most dramatic increase occurring within the last 150 years.

A few searches for species of concern give a hint of the recent extinction rate. In peninsular Malaysia, a 4-year search for 266 known species of freshwater fish turned up only 122. In Africa's Lake Victoria, 200 of 300 native fish species have not been seen for years. On the Hawaiian island of Oahu, half of 41 native tree snail species were not found; and in the Tennessee River, 44 of the 68 shallow-water mussel species are missing. However, few of the missing species in any of these searches is officially considered extinct.

The most complete records of documented extinction occur in groups of highly visible organisms, primarily birds and mammals. Since A.D. 1600, 83 mammal species out of an approximate 4,500 identified have become extinct, while 113 of approximately 9,000 known bird species have disappeared. The known extinctions of mammals and birds correspond to a rate of 0.005% per year spread out over the 400 years of these records. Compared to the background rate of extinctions calculated from the fossil record, the current rate of extinction is 50 times higher. If we examine the past 400 years more closely, we see that the extinction rate has actually risen since the start of this historical record (Figure 14.4)—to about 0.01% per year, making the current rate 100 times higher than the calculated background rate.

In addition, there are reasons to expect that the current elevated rate of extinction will continue into the future. The World Conservation Union (known by its French acronym, IUCN), a highly respected global organization made up of and funded by states, government agencies, and nongovernmental organizations from over 140 countries, collects and coordinates data on threats to biodiversity. According to the IUCN's most recent assessment, 11% of all plants, 12% of all bird species, and 24% of all mammal species (the three best-studied groups of organisms) are in danger of extinction, and human activities on the planet pose the greatest threat to most of these species.

Nowhere to Live: Human Causes of Extinction

The dramatic reduction in the numbers of shortnose and Lost River suckers in Upper Klamath Lake is almost entirely the result of human modification of their **habitat**, the place where they live. At one time, 350,000 acres of wetlands protected the quality and regulated the amount of water entering the lake. Most of these wetlands have been drained and converted to irrigated agricultural

Essay 14.1 The Pleistocene Extinctions

During the last great Ice Age, approximately 100,000 to 10,000 years ago, a widespread extinction of large mammals occurred on Earth. Dozens of mammal species in 27 genera were lost, and eight of these genera were in North America—including the wooly mammoth, mastodon, sabertooth cat, and giant ground sloth (Figure E14.1). The majority of extinctions in North America took place at the end of the Pleistocene period, 13,000–10,000 years ago. Curiously, no other group of animals suffered this level of extinction; plants and small animals were largely unaffected.

Wooly mammoth   Giant ground sloth   Sabertooth cat   Mastodon

Figure E14.1   Large animals of the Pleistocene.

fields. Alterations of the natural water flow in and out of the lake have reduced the number of offspring produced by suckers by as much as 95%. In addition to the loss of breeding habitat, accumulations of fertilizer from water draining off nearby farms have resulted in massive fish kills in Upper Klamath Lake.

Most other endangered species are in this vulnerable state for similar reasons. The primary cause of species loss is **habitat destruction**—principally, the modification and degradation of natural forests, grasslands, wetlands, and waterways by people during agricultural, industrial, and residential development. An IUCN review of the risks faced by endangered species indicates that 83% of endangered mammals, 89% of endangered birds, and 91% of endangered plants are directly threatened by habitat destruction. As the amount of a *natural landscape* (one that is not strongly modified by humans) declines, the number of species supported by the habitats in these landscapes also falls.

The relationship between the size of a natural area and the number of species it can support follows a general pattern called a **species–area curve**. A species–area curve for reptiles and amphibians on a West Indian archipelago is illustrated in Figure 14.5a. Similar graphs have been generated by studies of different groups of organisms in a variety of habitats, although the actual relationship between habitat area and number of species depends on the type of species that is of interest. The general pattern is that the number of species in an area increases rapidly as the size of the area increases, but the rate of increase slows as the area becomes very large. This "rule of thumb," an approximation derived from the studies, is shown in Figure 14.5b. From the graph, we can estimate that a 10-fold decrease in landscape area will cut the number of species living in the remaining area in half.

The cause of Pleistocene extinctions is the focus of intense research and is a subject of great debate among scientists. The leading hypotheses include overhunting by humans (also called "overkill") and rapid climate change.

The timing of large mammal extinctions in different geographic regions supports the overkill hypothesis. Human populations that were presumably experienced big-game hunters are believed to have crossed the Bering Strait on the land bridge joining Asia to North America approximately 15,000 to 12,000 years ago. This migration shortly precedes the majority of large-mammal extinctions that occurred in North America. Similar patterns are apparent in South America, Australia, and northern Eurasia where mass extinctions occurred shortly after humans moved into each area.

Additional support for the overkill hypothesis is found in the archeological record of these early hunters—spear points have been discovered in association with large-mammal remains at many sites. Large kill sites in ravines and at the bottom of cliffs of wooly mammoths, mastodons, and bison have been identified in several North American locales, indicating that the hunting techniques employed by early humans resulted in the slaughter of thousands of individual animals. The loss of these large grazing animals probably caused the subsequent extinction of other species, including large predators such as the sabertooth cat.

Critics of the overkill hypothesis argue that humans were not numerous enough to drive these abundant animals to extinction in such a short period of time, nor could they have achieved such an effective hunting style.

These critics point out that bison remained a mainstay of the Native American diet until European settlement and were incredibly numerous until both the widespread conversion of prairie into agricultural land and indiscriminate sport hunting. These scientists argue that a much more powerful force than humans led to these extinctions—the change in climate that occurred after the retreat of the continental glaciers.

The real challenge of climatic change for large grazers was the subsequent change in vegetation. Records of pollen grains in lake sediments indicate that warmer temperatures at the end of the Ice Age resulted in an increase in forest cover and a decrease in grassland. Supporters of the climate-change hypothesis also argue that the survivors should possess traits that increase their survival in warmer, wetter environments. It is true that the modern descendants of Ice Age survivors (such as bison and beaver) are smaller, as is expected of animals in warmer environments. Perhaps extinct wooly mammoths and mastodons simply did not have genetic traits that would enable their populations to adapt to the new climate conditions. Finally, the fossil record shows that larger animals are always more significantly affected by climate change than smaller animals, which may explain the pattern of loss affecting only the largest mammal species.

It is likely that both climate change and overkill played roles in the extinction of large mammals at the end of the Pleistocene. It also appears that many large animals that survived, but that were negatively affected by climate change, could have been pushed over the brink by human activity.

www

Media Activity 14.1 Species–Area Curve

(a) Species diversity increases with area.

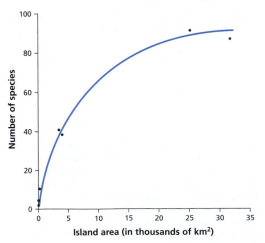

(b) Habitat reduction is predicted to result in loss of species.

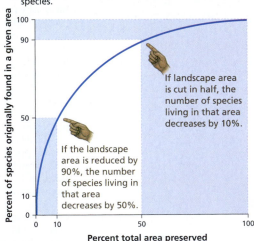

Figure 14.5 Predicting extinction resulting from habitat destruction. (a) This curve demonstrates the relationship between the size of an island in the West Indies and the number of reptiles and amphibians that live there. (b) We use a generalized species–area curve to roughly predict the number of extinctions in an area experiencing habitat loss.

Applying species–area curves to estimate extinction rates requires that we calculate the amount of natural landscape that has been lost in recent decades—a difficult task. Most studies have focused on tropical rainforests, which cover a broad swath of land roughly 20 degrees north and south of the equator. Tropical rainforests contain, by far, the greatest number of species of any *biome*, or major habitat type, on Earth. An early estimate of the rate of habitat destruction in the rainforest was made by biologist Edward O. Wilson, who calculated that about 1% of the tropical rainforest is converted to agricultural use every year. Conservatively estimating the number of species in the rain forest at 5 million, Wilson applied the generalized species–area curve and projected that nearly 20,000 to 30,000 species are lost each year due to rainforest destruction.

More modern studies using images from satellites (Figure 14.6a) indicate that approximately 20,000 square kilometers (about 7,722 square miles, an area the size of the state of Massachusetts) of rainforest in South America's Amazon River basin is cut each year. This is a rate of 2% per year, or twice the rate Wilson estimated. At this rate of habitat destruction, tropical rainforests will be reduced to 10% of their original size within about 35 years. If we apply the species–area curve, the habitat loss translates into the extinction of about 50% of the species that call Amazonian rainforests home. The extinct species in the rainforest would include about 50,000 of all the known 250,000 species of plants, about 1,800 of the known 9,000 species of birds, and about 900 of the 4,500 kinds of mammals in the world.

Of course, habitat destruction is not limited to tropical rainforests. When all of Earth's biomes are evaluated, freshwater lakes and streams, grasslands, and temperate forests are also experiencing high levels of modification. According to the IUCN, if habitat destruction around the world continues at present rates, nearly $\frac{1}{4}$ of *all* living species will be lost within the next 50 years.

Some critics have argued that these estimates of future extinction are too high, because not all groups of species are as sensitive to habitat area as the curve in Figure 14.5b suggests, and many species may still survive and even thrive in human-modified landscapes. Other biologists counter that there are also other threats to species, therefore the rate of species loss should be even higher than these estimates.

Other threats to biodiversity by humans include habitat fragmentation, the introduction of exotic species, overexploitation, and pollution (Figure 14.6b–e). **Habitat fragmentation** occurs when large areas of intact natural habitat are subdivided by human activities. The species remaining in the habitat fragments are more susceptible to extinction because it is more difficult for individuals to move across modified landscapes than across natural landscapes. Habitat fragmentation thus makes it impossible for species to move from an area that is becoming unsuitable because of natural environmental changes to areas that are suitable. Individual organisms within habitat fragments are also more susceptible to being killed or disrupted by humans and human-adapted species (such as domestic cats), because they are in closer proximity to these threats than individuals in unfragmented habitats. For example, grizzly bears need from 200–2,000 square kilometers of habitat to survive a Canadian winter, but the Canadian wilderness is increasingly bisected by roads built for tree harvesting. Every interaction between grizzly bears and humans represents a greater danger to the bears than to humans—for example, of the 136 grizzlies that died in Canada's national parks between 1970 and 1995, 119 were killed by humans. **Exotic species** include domestic cats and organisms introduced by human activity to a region where they had never been found. Exotic species are often dangerous to native species because they have not evolved together—for instance, many birds on oceanic islands such as Hawaii and New Zealand are unable to defend themselves from introduced ground hunters, such as rats. **Overexploitation** encompasses overhunting and overharvesting and occurs when the rate of human destruction or use of a species outpaces its

(a) Habitat destruction

Humans are rapidly destroying tropical rainforests. This 1999 satellite photo illustrates the extent of destruction in an area of Brazilian rainforest, that, until 30 years ago, contained no agricultural lands. The lighter parts of the photo are agricultural fields; the darker regions are intact forest.

(b) Habitat fragmentation

This "island" of tropical forest was created when the surrounding forest was logged. Scientists have documented hundreds of localized extinctions within fragments such as this.

(c) Introduction of exotic species

The introduced brown tree snake is responsible for the extinction of dozens of native bird species on the Pacific island of Guam.

(d) Overexploitation of species

These tiger skins represent a small fraction of the illegal harvest of tigers in Asia, primarily for the Chinese market.

(e) Pollution

Pollution from herbicides appears to be responsible for the increase of deformities in frogs in the midwestern United States and may partially explain the worldwide decline in frog species.

Figure 14.6   The causes of extinction.

366   **Chapter 14**   Is Earth Experiencing a Biodiversity Crisis?

ability to reproduce. Humans overexploited passenger pigeons to the point of extinction and decimated populations of gray wolves, sea turtles, and many whale species as well. **Pollution**, the release of poisons, excess nutrients, and other wastes into the environment, poses an additional threat to biodiversity. The massive fish kills in Upper Klamath Lake were caused by fertilizer pollution, and as we discuss in Essay 14.2, global climate change caused by pollution may be the most serious threat to biodiversity yet.

All of these threats indicate that ESA critics who describe modern species extinction rates as "natural" are most likely incorrect. Over the past 400 years, humans have caused the extinction of species at a rate that appears to far exceed past rates, and it is clear that human activities continue to threaten thousands of additional species around the world. In fact, many scientists argue that the Earth is on the brink of a **mass extinction**—a loss of species that is global in scale, affects large numbers of species, and is dramatic in its impact. Earth has experienced five episodes of mass extinction, in which 50–90% of all living species were lost over the course of a few thousand to a few hundred-thousand years (Figure 14.7). Past mass extinctions were probably caused by massive global changes—for instance, changes in sea level brought about by climate fluctuations, or changes in ocean and landform caused by movements of Earth's *tectonic plates*. Many scientists argue that we are now seeing biodiversity's sixth great mass extinction—and the pervasive global change causing this extinction is human activity.

After previous mass extinctions, biological diversity did not reach pre-extinction levels for 5–10 million years. The species that replaced those lost in the mass extinction were also very different. We cannot predict what biodiversity will look like after another mass extinction. Many people who feel a moral responsibility to minimize the human impact on other species and preserve the majority of biological diversity for future generations continue to support actions that preserve species, despite the cost. However, in addition to supporting the ideals of rights for nonhuman species and preservation for the sake of our children and grandchildren, there is a practical reason to prevent the sixth extinction from occurring—the loss of nonhuman species can cause human suffering as well.

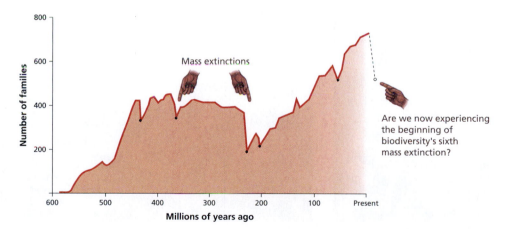

Figure 14.7   Mass extinction. This graph illustrates the general rise in biodiversity over the past 600 million years, as indicated by an increase in the number of marine families present in the fossil record. However, this rise has been punctuated by five mass extinctions, marked with black dots, which resulted in a global decline in biodiversity. The number of species lost during these mass extinction events appears to be even greater than the number of families lost, because families containing many species died out.

14.2   The Consequences of Extinction

Concern over the loss of biological diversity is not simply a matter of ethics or a theoretical issue. The human species and our societies and cultures have evolved with and among the variety of species that exist on our planet, and the loss of these species often results in negative consequences for us.

Loss of Resources

The Lost River and shortnose suckers were once numerous enough to support a fishing and canning industry on the shores of Upper Klamath Lake. Even before the arrival of European settlers, the native people of the area relied heavily upon these fish, which are referred to as "c'wam" and "qapdo" in the Klamath language, as a mainstay of their diet. The loss of these species represents a tremendous impoverishment of wild food sources. The list of species that are harvested directly from natural areas is large and diverse—for example, wood for fuel, shellfish for protein, plants for local medicines, and flowers for perfume. The loss of any of these species affects human populations economically—one estimate places the economic value of wild species in the United States at $87 billion a year, or about 4% of the gross domestic product. Some of the thousands of valuable species known to humans are described in Chapter 3.

Wild relatives of plants and animals that have been domesticated by humans (such as agricultural crops and cattle) are also valuable resources for humans (Figure 14.8). Genes and gene variants that have been "bred out" of domesticated species are often still found in their wild relatives. These genetic resources represent a reservoir of traits that could be reintroduced into agricultural species by breeding or genetic engineering (see Chapter 7). Often, traits that seem unimportant in agricultural crops later prove to be useful, or in fact critical, to the species when it is exposed to new diseases or pests. Agricultural scientists who are attempting to produce better strains of wheat, rice,

(a) Teosinte, ancestor of modern corn

(b) Aurochs, ancestor of modern cattle

Figure 14.8   Wild relatives of domesticated crops and animals. (a) Teosinte is the ancestor of modern corn, which was first cultivated in Central America. This species, *Zea diploperennis*, was discovered in a remote Mexican site in 1978. (b) An aurochs, the wild ancestor of modern cattle species, disappeared from its original range in Northern Europe in the 1500s. This modern aurochs was produced after many generations of cross-breeding domesticated cattle and is probably very similar to the extinct wild aurochs.

Essay 14.2 Global Climate Change

Carbon dioxide, a gas produced by burning fossil fuels such as oil, coal, and natural gas, has been steadily accumulating in the atmosphere over the past 150 years (Figure E14.2a). At current rates of production, levels of carbon dioxide in the atmosphere are expected to double by the year 2075.

Scientists who study climate agree that such a large and rapid change in carbon dioxide levels influences weather patterns on Earth. Atmospheric carbon dioxide contributes to the *greenhouse effect*, which keeps Earth relatively warm by preventing the heat generated by the sun shining on its surface from escaping into space (Figure E14.2b). Given this effect, an increase in carbon dioxide in the atmosphere should result in an increase in global temperature. In fact, most computer models of Earth's climate predict that average global temperatures will increase between 3° and 8° F (1.5–4.5° C) by 2075 as a result of increasing carbon dioxide emissions. These models also predict that the warming will not be uniform. Certain areas of the globe, such as at the North and South poles, will warm faster and to a greater degree than other areas, and some regions may even cool slightly. Accompanying this temperature shift will be a change in rain and snowfall—again, a change that varies from region to region. Models predict the future long-term effect of warming on Earth, but there is plenty of evidence that our planet is already warming—from the retreat of alpine glaciers to the gradual upward creep in average yearly temperatures over the past several decades.

Long-term temperature records, such as the data shown in Figure E14.2c that were inferred from ice cores taken from Antarctica, indicate that global temperatures have always fluctuated. However, as you can see on the graph, the concentration of carbon dioxide in the atmosphere is much higher now than at any time in the past 400,000 years. If the change in the level of greenhouse gases is followed by the rapid development of higher global temperatures, species in many habitats will certainly suffer. Melting of glaciers and ice caps will

cause sea levels to rise, flooding low-lying coastal areas and some of the most unique and diverse habitats on the planet—tropical oceanic islands. Warmer winters and longer summers will allow some species of plant-eating insects to thrive, potentially causing severe damage to many different environments. Insects that carry disease may also thrive in a warmer climate, threatening the health of human and nonhuman populations alike. If the ice-core record of Figure E14.2c is any guide, it is possible that the current spike in temperature will be followed by rapid global cooling, another blow to the remaining species.

Global warming is already posing a threat to biodiversity. A review published in the journal *Nature* in March 2002 described various species and ecosystems that have been affected by climate change. Many of these species are temperature-sensitive and must move closer to the poles or higher in elevation to find regions with the proper climate. Responses to climate change have been documented—for instance, arctic fox are retreating northward and being replaced by the less cold-hardy red fox; Edith's checkerspot butterfly is now found 124 meters higher in elevation and 92 kilometers north of its range in 1900; and a wide variety of corals have experienced a dramatic increase in the frequency and extent of damage resulting from increased ocean temperatures.

Habitat destruction greatly interferes with a species' ability to respond to global warming. If climate change renders the current habitat of an organism unsuitable for its survival, its only hope of persisting is dispersal to a more appropriate habitat. If the species is slow to disperse, such as a long-lived tree species, or if it cannot cross human-modified landscapes, it may not be able to establish a new population in an appropriate habitat before it becomes extinct in its rapidly changing home. Global climate change is another uncertainty created by humans that threatens the survival of thousands of species on Earth.

and corn look to the wild relatives of these crops as sources of genes for pest resistance and for traits that improve yields in specific environmental conditions. The survival of these wild relatives is crucial for maintaining and expanding crop production. There is value in preserving wild relatives in their natural habitats as well—often the organisms in these communities provide the key to reducing pest damage and disease on the domestic crop. For example, the original habitat of the crop may be home to an insect that is an effective predator of the crop's insect pests.

Other species currently provide, or may provide, future direct benefits to humans for less obvious reasons. Nearly 25% of the drugs prescribed in the United States come from wild sources, and there are potentially thousands of other medically useful organisms that have not been investigated. Modern

(a) Carbon dioxide (CO_2) levels in the atmosphere are increasing

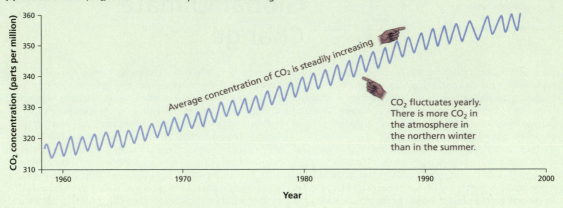

CO_2 fluctuates yearly. There is more CO_2 in the atmosphere in the northern winter than in the summer.

(b) Increased levels of CO_2 contribute to the greenhouse effect

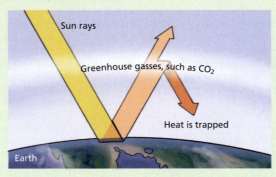

(c) Records of temperature and atmospheric carbon dioxide concentration from Antarctic ice cores

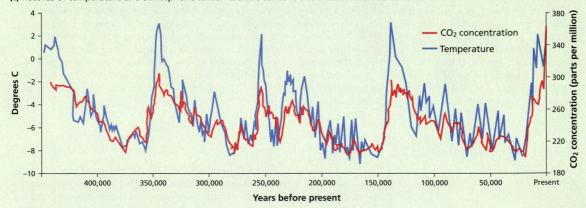

Figure E14.2   (a) The increase of carbon dioxide in the atmosphere near Mauna Loa, Hawaii. (b) The greenhouse effect. (c) Long-term temperature records.

370 Chapter 14 Is Earth Experiencing a Biodiversity Crisis?

Figure 14.9 The web of life. Species are connected to each other and to their environment in many and complex ways. This drawing shows some of the important relationships among organisms and their environments in a North American prairie. Black arrows represent feeding relationships; for example, thirteen-lined ground squirrels eat wheat grass and in turn are eaten by badgers.

organisms contain an enormous variety of biologically active chemicals; a few of these chemicals are directly useful against human disease. Many medicinal plants and other organisms are used by local cultures and provide crucial health benefits to these human populations. If we are unable to screen living species because they have become extinct, we will never know which ones might have provided compounds that would improve our lives.

Disrupting the Web of Life

Although humans receive a direct benefit from thousands of species, most threatened and endangered species are probably of little or no use to people. Even the Lost River and shortnose suckers, as valuable as they once were to the native people of the Klamath Basin, are not especially missed as a food source—no one has starved simply because these fish are less common.

In reality, most species are beneficial to humans because they are connected to other species and natural processes in an **ecosystem**, which is the sum total of organisms and natural features in a given area. The proper functioning of ecosystems, the natural world's **ecosystem services**, supports human life and our economy. The connection among organisms and natural processes in an ecosystem is often referred to as the "web of life" (Figure 14.9). As with a spider's web, any disruption in one strand of the web of life is felt by other portions of the web. Disruptions caused by the loss of seemingly insignificant species have the potential to cause great damage to human economies.

How Bees Feed the World   An interaction between two species that provides benefits to both is called a **mutualism**. Cleaner-fish that remove and consume parasites from the bodies of larger fish and ants that live in the thorns of acacia trees and defend the trees from other insects are examples of mutualists.

372   Chapter 14   Is Earth Experiencing a Biodiversity Crisis?

Figure 14.10   A mutualism. Honeybees transfer pollen, allowing one plant to "mate" with another plant some distance away.

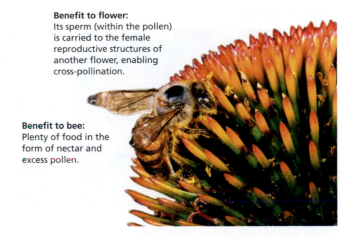

Benefit to flower:
Its sperm (within the pollen) is carried to the female reproductive structures of another flower, enabling cross-pollination.

Benefit to bee:
Plenty of food in the form of nectar and excess pollen.

However, perhaps the most often-described mutualistic interaction exists between plants and bees (Figure 14.10).

Bees are the primary *pollinators* of many species of flowering plants; that is, they transfer sperm, in the form of pollen grains, from one flower to the female reproductive structures of another flower. The flowering plant benefits from this relationship because insect pollination increases the number and vigor of seeds the plant produces. The bee benefits by collecting excess pollen and the nectar produced by the flower to feed itself and its relatives in the hive.

Wild bees pollinate at least 80% of the $10 billion of agricultural crops in the United States. Thus, populations of wild honeybees have a major and direct impact on approximately $8 billion of our agricultural production and many more billions of dollars of impact around the globe.

Unfortunately, bees have suffered dramatic declines in recent years. According to the U.S. Department of Agriculture, we are facing an "impending pollination crisis," because both wild and domesticated bees are disappearing at alarming rates. These dramatic declines are believed to be the result of *pesticides*, such as chemicals that kill insects, an increased level of bee **parasites** (infectious organisms that cause disease or drain energy from their hosts) caused by poor management of domestic bees, and habitat destruction. The endangerment and extinction of these inconspicuous mutualists of crop plants would be extremely costly to humans.

How Songbirds May Save Forests   Wood warblers are a family of North American bird species that are characterized by their small size, colorful summer plumage, and habit of catching and eating insects (Figure 14.11a). Their consumption of another species makes warblers **predators**, and it is in their role as insect predators that they potentially provide benefits to humans.

There are hundreds of millions of individual warblers in the forests of North America during the summer. They spend most of their waking hours catching insects for themselves and their quickly growing offspring; thus, warblers collectively remove literally tons of insects from forest trees and shrubs every year. Most of these insects are predators as well—on plants. By reducing the number of insects in forests, warblers reduce the damage the insects inflict on forest plants. The results of a study that excluded birds from white oak seedlings showed that the trees were about 15% smaller as a result of insect damage over two years when compared to trees where birds were not excluded. Other studies have shown less dramatic benefits.

(a) Black-throated blue warbler, predator of insects.

(b) Forests suffer when insects are unchecked by predators.

Figure 14.11   Birds and forests. (a) The black-throated blue warbler is one of many warbler species native to North American forests. These colorful birds are among the most active predators of plant-eating insects in these forests. (b) Insects can kill many trees, as seen in this photo of a spruce budworm infestation. Warblers and other insect-eating birds probably reduce the number and severity of such insect outbreaks.

Although scientists still disagree about exactly how important warblers and other insect-eating birds are to the survival of trees, most agree that reducing the number of forest pests increases the growth rate of the trees. Harvesting forest trees for paper and lumber production fuels an industry worth over $200 billion dollars in the United States alone. At least some of the wood harvested by the timber industry was produced only because warblers were controlling insects in forests (Figure 14.11b).

Many species of forest-inhabiting warblers appear to be experiencing declines in abundance. The loss of warbler species has several causes, including habitat destruction in their summer and winter habitats and increased predation by human-associated animals such as raccoons and house cats. Although other, less vulnerable birds may increase in number when warblers decline, it is unlikely that warblers' effects on insect pest populations can be completely replaced by less insect-dependent birds. If smaller warbler populations correspond to lower forest growth rates and higher levels of forest disease, these tiny, beautiful birds definitely have an important effect on the human economy.

How an Infected Chicken Could Save a Life   When two species of organisms both require the same resources for life, they will be in **competition** for the resources within a habitat. We may imagine lions and hyenas fighting over a freshly killed antelope as a typical example of competition, but most competitive interactions are invisible.

In general, competition limits the size of competing populations. To determine whether two species are in competition, we remove one from an environment; if the population of the other species increases, the two species are competitors. One of the least visible forms of competition occurs among microorganisms. Competitive interactions among microbes may be the most essential factors for maintaining the health of people and ecosystems.

Salmonella enteritidis is a leading (and growing) cause of food-borne illness in the United States—between 2 million and 4 million people in this country will be infected by this bacterium in the coming year, experiencing fever, intestinal cramps, and diarrhea as a result. In about 10% of cases, the infection spreads to the bloodstream—if it is not treated promptly, individuals in whom this happens may die. Nearly 2,000 Americans die as a result of *S. enteritidis* infections every year.

Most *S. enteritidis* infections result from the consumption of raw or improperly cooked poultry products, especially eggs. The U.S. Centers for Disease Control estimate that as many as one in 50 consumers are exposed to eggs contaminated with *S. enteritidis* every year. Most of these eggs have had their shells disinfected and do not look damaged in any way—the bacteria were deposited in the egg by the hen when the egg was forming inside her. Thus, the only way to prevent *S. enteritidis* from contaminating eggs is to keep it out of hens in the first place.

A common way to control *S. enteritidis* is to feed hens *antibiotics*, chemicals that kill bacteria. However, antibiotic use is costly and, like most microbes, *S. enteritidis* strains evolve to become resistant to the effects of the antibiotic. (The evolution of drug resistance is discussed in detail in Chapter 9.) Another way to reduce infections in poultry is to reduce the space available for the bacteria's growth. Most *S. enteritidis* infections originate in an animal's digestive system. If another bacterial species is well-established in a hen's digestive system, *S. enteritidis* has trouble colonizing it. Some poultry producers now establish harmless bacteria in hens' digestive systems, a practice called *competitive exclusion*, to reduce *S. enteritidis* levels in their flocks. This technique involves feeding cultures of bacteria from the intestinal tract of healthy adult chickens to 1-day-old birds to prevent subsequent *S. enteritidis* colonization (Figure 14.12). There is evidence that this practice is working; infections in chickens have dropped nearly 50% in the United Kingdom, where competitive exclusion in poultry is common practice.

The competitive exclusion of *S. enteritidis* from hens' guts by less harmful bacteria mirrors the role of some human-associated bacteria, such as those that normally live in our intestines and genital tracts. For instance, many women who take antibiotics for a bacterial infection develop vaginal yeast infections because the antibiotic kills noninfectious bacteria as well, including species in the genital tract that normally compete with yeast. Competitive exclusion in hen's intestines also mirrors the role of native soil bacteria in maintaining the health and function of soil by balancing all the different species of bacteria that are required for recycling the nutrients within ecosystems. However, the widespread use (and misuse) of antibiotics, the use of pesticides in agricultural settings, and ironically, a "too-clean" environment may reduce the populations of these beneficial bacteria on a local or even global scale. Biologists are a long way from identifying all of the species of bacteria, let alone knowing which are vulnerable to human-caused extinction or identifying their part in maintaining ecosystem health. However, the role of bacteria in preventing *S. enteritidis* poisoning indicates that preserving these competitive interactions is worthwhile.

Biophilia

Species provide benefits to humans directly and as members of functioning ecosystems on which humans rely. In addition, some scientists argue, the diversity of living organisms sustains humans by satisfying a deep psychological need. One of the most prominent scientists to promote this idea is Edward O. Wilson, who calls this instinctive desire to commune with nature *biophilia*.

Wilson contends that people seek natural landscapes because our distant ancestors evolved within such landscapes (Figure 14.13). According to this hypothesis, ancient humans who had a genetic predisposition that drove them to find diverse natural landscapes were more successful than those without this disposition, since more diverse areas provide a wider variety of food, shelter, and tool sources. Wilson claims that we, the modern descendants of successful early humans, have inherited the genetic imprint of our pre-agricultural past.

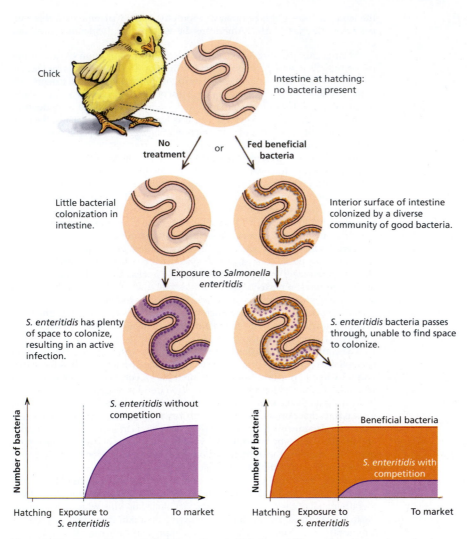

Figure 14.12   Competitors exclude *Salmonella enteritidis* from chickens. If poultry producers feed very young chicks non-disease-causing bacteria, the bacteria take up the space and nutrients in the intestine that would be used by *S. enteritidis*; thus, they will have no site to colonize and increase their population.

While there is as yet no evidence of a "gene" for *biophilia* (in fact, there is considerable debate over whether *any* complex human behavior has a strong genetic component), there is evidence that our experience with nature does have powerful psychological effects. For instance, studies in hospitals indicate that blood pressure drops 10 to 15 points when patients are exposed to serene landscape paintings; and when patients can see trees and other natural scenes from their windows, they need fewer painkillers and recover from illnesses more quickly than patients who are confined to rooms that overlook buildings. Other studies indicate that office workers who have desks facing windows with a view of a natural setting are less stressed and take fewer sick days. While these

Figure 14.13 Is our appreciation of nature innate? Humans evolved in a landscape much like this one in East Africa. Some scientists argue that we have an instinctive need to immerse ourselves in the natural world.

studies are certainly not conclusive, they are intriguing, for they suggest that the continued loss of biological diversity could make human society a less pleasant place to live.

14.3 Saving Species

In the previous sections of this chapter, we have established the potential for a modern mass extinction and described the possibly serious costs of this loss of biodiversity to human populations. Since current elevated extinction rates are largely a result of human activity, reversing the trend of species loss requires political and economic, rather than scientific, decisions. But what can science tell us about how to stop the rapid erosion of biological diversity?

How to Stop a Mass Extinction

In the absence of knowing exactly which species are closest to extinction and where they are located, the most effective way to prevent loss of species is to preserve many habitats. The same species–area curve that Wilson used to estimate

the future rate of extinction also gives us hope for reducing this number. Recall that according to the curve in Figure 14.5b, species diversity declines rather slowly as habitat area declines. Thus, in theory, we can lose 50% of a habitat but still retain 90% of its species. However, this estimate is somewhat optimistic because habitat destruction is not the only threat to biodiversity. In any case, the species–area curve does tell us that if the rate of habitat destruction is slowed or stopped, extinction rates will slow as well.

Given the growing human population (discussed in detail in Chapter 15), it is difficult to imagine completely halting habitat destruction. However, biologist Norman Myers and his collaborators have concluded that 30–50% of all plant, amphibian, reptile, bird, and mammal species are found in just 25 biodiversity "hotspots" that make up less than 2% of Earth's ice-free land area (Figure 14.14). Thus, stopping habitat destruction in the hotspots could greatly reduce the global extinction rate. By focusing immediate conservation efforts on hotspot areas at the greatest risk of losing much of their natural landscape, humans can very quickly prevent the loss of a large number of species. Of course, even preserving these biodiversity hotspots is no easy task—it requires the concerted actions of a diverse community of nations and people, some of whom must also address the immediate concerns of poverty, hunger,

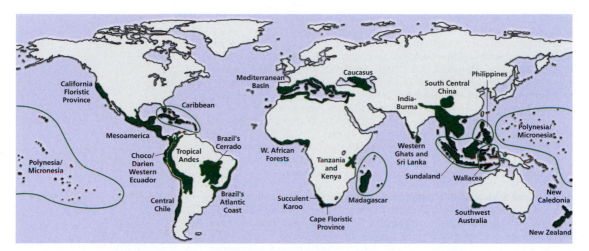

Figure 14.14 Diversity hotspots. This map shows the locations of 25 hotspots that have been identified. Note their uneven distribution around Earth.

www

Media Activity 14.2 Conserving Global Biodiversity Hotspots

and disease. It is likely that even with habitat protection, many of the species in these hotspots will become extinct anyway because so little habitat is left for them. In the long term, we must devise ways to preserve biological diversity that include human activity in the landscape. Strategically preserving relatively small amounts of land today may prevent our descendants from identifying this period as the sixth mass extinction.

There are other things everyone can do to reduce the rate of habitat destruction. Reducing the consumption of goods that cause habitat destruction is primary among these. Conversion of land to agricultural production is a major cause of habitat destruction, so reducing our consumption of meat and dairy products (domestic animals require large amounts of crops for feed) is one of the most effective actions we can take. We will explore the effect of agriculture on biodiversity and other aspects of our environment in Chapter 15. Increasing financial support to developing countries, enabling them to take advantage of advances in technology that reduce their use of wood for heating and cooking, may also help slow the rate of habitat destruction. Strategies that can slow the rate of human population growth are another way to avoid a mass extinction.

Although protecting habitat from destruction can reduce extinction rates, for species on the brink of extinction like the shortnose and Lost River suckers, preserving habitat is not enough. These species may only have tiny fragments of suitable habitat remaining, and many have very small populations as well. To save these species, humans must concentrate on their individual needs and causes of endangerment.

www

Media Activity 14.3 Biodiversity Inventories for Conservation and Economic Development

One Species at a Time

Habitat destruction is a leading cause of endangerment and extinction, and it follows that the primary requirement for species recovery is restoration of habitat. The ESA requires the Department of Interior to designate *critical habitats* for endangered species, the areas in need of protection for the survival of the species. The amount of critical habitat that is designated depends upon political as well as biological factors. Federal designation of a critical habitat results in restriction of the human activities that can take place there—thus, landowners are usually interested in keeping their lands out of this designation. If landowners are politically powerful, they can exert their influence on elected officials and have profound effects on the *recovery plan* for a particular endangered species.

The biological part of a critical habitat designation includes a study of the habitat requirements of the endangered species and setting a *population goal* for it. The Department of Interior's critical habitat designation has to include enough area to support the recovery population. The designation of critical habitat has an extra benefit as well—protection of this habitat can protect dozens of other less well-known species that may be approaching endangerment.

The recovery plans for both the Lost River and the shortnose suckers sets a short-term goal of one stable population made up of at least 500 individuals for each unique stock of suckers. To understand why at least this many individuals of a species are required to protect the species from extinction, we need to review some of the special problems of small populations.

Growth and Catastrophe in Small Populations   A species' *growth rate* is influenced by how long the species takes to reproduce, how often it reproduces, the number of offspring produced each time, and the death rate of individuals under ideal conditions. (Calculation of growth rate is discussed in Chapter 15.) For instance, species that reproduce slowly take longer to grow in number than species that reproduce quickly. Thus the growth rate of an endangered species influences how rapidly it can attain a target population size. Shortnose and Lost River suckers have relatively high growth rates and will meet their population goals quickly if the environment is ideal (Figure 14.15a). For more slow-growing species, such as the California condor (Figure 14.15b), populations may take decades to

(a) Lost River sucker

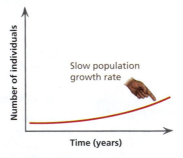

(b) California condor

Figure 14.15   The effect of growth rate on species recovery. (a) This graph illustrates the rapid growth of a hypothetical population of quickly reproducing Lost River suckers. (b) The slow growth rate of the California condor has made the recovery of this species a long process. Today, nearly 30 years after recovery efforts began, the population of wild condors is still only in the dozens. Two wild populations of 150 condors each must be established for the bird to be removed from endangered status.

380 Chapter 14 Is Earth Experiencing a Biodiversity Crisis?

Figure 14.16 A victim of small population size. The heath hen was once abundant throughout the eastern United States. Although it was protected when its population was nearly 50 individuals, a series of unexpected disasters caused its extinction. (© Steven Holt/VIREO)

recover. The rate of a species' recovery is important because the longer a population remains small, the more it is at risk of experiencing a catastrophic environmental event that could eliminate it entirely. The story of the heath hen is a classic example of the dangers facing small populations.

The heath hen was a small relative of the prairie chicken that lived on the East Coast of the United States (Figure 14.16) and was a favorite game bird of early European settlers. Prior to the American Revolution, the heath hen was found from Maine to Virginia. Increased settlement resulted in loss of habitat and increased hunting, noticeably lowering heath hen populations by the time of the Revolutionary War. In the 1870s, the only heath hens that were left occupied a tiny island called Martha's Vineyard off the coast of Cape Cod in Massachusetts. Human development on the island further reduced the suitable habitat for heath hen breeding, and in 1907 there were only 50 heath hens left on Martha's Vineyard. A 1,600-acre sanctuary was established for their protection the following year.

The sanctuary seemed to be successful—the original 50 heath hens reproduced rapidly and there were 2,000 individuals on Martha's Vineyard by 1915. Unexpectedly, a fire in 1916 wiped out much of the habitat that the birds used for breeding. In addition, the next winter was unusually harsh and food was scarce, and an influx of goshawks, predatory birds that preyed on the heath hens, reduced the population further. Finally, many of the remaining heath hens fell victim to a poultry disease brought to the island by domestic turkeys. There were only 14 heath hens left by 1927, and most of them were males. The last living heath hen was seen on March 11, 1932. He died that year.

Why did the heath hen become extinct? The last birds were wiped out by a series of relatively common and entirely natural events: fire, starvation, predation, and disease. The heath hen's continued existence as a species would not have been so vulnerable to these occurrences if the population size had not been severely reduced by habitat loss and overhunting. A small population is very vulnerable to normal fluctuations in its numbers, which are the consequence of disease and disasters. A population of 1,000 individuals can survive a population drop of 100; the same fluctuation dooms a population that starts with only 100 individuals. In the case of the heath hen, even when hunting and habitat destruction were halted, the species' survival was still extremely precarious.

The population goal of 500 individuals for both species of suckers in Upper Klamath Lake is still quite small, but in the short term it will help these fish avoid the same fate as the heath hen.

Genetic Variability and Survival   Small populations of endangered species can still be protected from the fate that befell the heath hen. Having additional populations of the species at sites other than Martha's Vineyard would have nearly eliminated the risk that *all* members of the population would be exposed to the same series of environmental disasters. This is the rationale behind placing captive populations of endangered species at several different sites. For instance, the captive whooping crane population is located at the U.S. National Biological Service's Patuxent Wildlife Research Center in Maryland, the International Crane Foundation in Wisconsin, the Calgary Zoo in Canada, and the Audubon Center for Endangered Species Research in New Orleans. However, if endangered species populations remain small in number, they are subject to a subtler but potentially equally damaging disaster—the loss of genetic variability.

A species' **genetic variability** is the sum of all of the *alleles* and their distribution within the species. Differences among alleles produce the variety of traits within a population. For example, the gene that determines your blood type comes in three different forms, and the combination of alleles that you possess determines whether your blood type is O, A, B, or AB. Thus, a population containing all three blood-type alleles contains more genetic variability (for this gene) than a population that contains only two alleles.

The loss of genetic variability in a population is a problem for two reasons: (1) On an individual level, low genetic variability leads to low fitness; and (2) on a population level, rapid loss of genetic variability may lead to extinction.

Individual Genetic Variability   As we discussed in Chapter 9, *fitness* refers to an individual's ability to survive and reproduce in a given set of environmental conditions. There are two reasons that high genetic variability on an individual level increases fitness. We will use an analogy to illustrate the costs of low genetic variability in individuals. First, imagine that you could own only two sets of footwear (Figure 14.17a). If both pairs are dressy shoes, you might be prepared to meet a potential employer, but if you had to walk across campus to your job interview

(a) Heterozygote has higher fitness than either homozygote.

Homozygote: Relatively low fitness

Homozygote: Relatively low fitness

Heterozygote: Relatively high fitness

(b) Heterozygote masks the deleterious allele.

Homozygote: Relatively high fitness

Homozygote: Relatively low fitness

Heterozygote: Relatively high fitness

Figure 14.17   The benefits of heterozygosity. In this analogy, each pair of shoes represents an allele. (a) Heterozygotes may better prepared for a diversity of life experiences than homozygotes. (b) Heterozygotes may have higher fitness than some homozygotes because certain alleles are deleterious and recessive. In this case, homozygotes for the normal allele also have higher fitness than homozygotes for the recessive allele.

382 **Chapter 14** Is Earth Experiencing a Biodiversity Crisis?

in a snowstorm, you would be pretty uncomfortable. If you own two sets of winter boots, your feet will always be protected from the cold, but you would look pretty silly at a dinner party. However, if you own both dress shoes and winter boots, you are ready for slush and snow as well as a nice date. In a way, individuals experience the same advantages when they carry two different alleles for a gene—that is, when they are *heterozygous*. If a protein produced by each allele works best in different environments, heterozygous individuals are able to function efficiently over a wider range of conditions.

The second reason that high individual genetic variability increases fitness is that, in many cases, one allele for a gene is deleterious—that is, it produces a protein that is not very functional. In our shoe analogy, this might be sneakers with blown-out toes. If you have these sneakers and dress shoes, at least you have one pair of shoes that covers your feet (Figure 14.17b). In the case of a deleterious allele, a heterozygous individual still carries one functional copy of the gene. Genetic variability can help mask the effects of deleterious alleles, because the functional allele is *dominant*—that is, it tends to drown out the deleterious allele (see Chapter 4). An individual who is *homozygous* (carries two identical copies of a gene) for the deleterious allele will have low fitness—in our analogy, two pairs of blown-out sneakers and nothing else. When individuals are heterozygous for many genes, the cumulative effect is often greater fitness relative to individuals who are homozygous for many genes.

In a small population, where mates are more likely to be related to each other than in a very large population simply because there are fewer mates to choose from, heterozygosity declines. When related individuals mate—known as **inbreeding**—the chance that their offspring will be homozygous for any allele (one that both parents inherited from a shared ancestor) is relatively high. The negative effect of homozygosity on fitness is known as **inbreeding depression**. This is seen in humans as well as other species—numerous studies consistently show that the children of first cousins have higher mortality rates (thus, lower fitness) than children of unrelated parents. In a population of an endangered species, the low rates of survival and reproduction associated with high rates of inbreeding can seriously hamper its ability to recover from endangerment.

We should note that in some populations, inbreeding does not lead to lower fitness. This appears to be the case in populations in which inbreeding has been historically common. Here, deleterious alleles have been "purged" from the population because inbreeding exposes these alleles to natural selection (that is, allows them to be expressed in homozygotes). Because these homozygotes have low fitness, the alleles they carry are rarer in subsequent generations and are lost over time. However, this appears to be a relatively rare occurrence—in an examination of 25 captive mammal species, only one showed clear evidence that deleterious alleles had been purged. For most species, inbreeding seems to be a significant threat to survival.

Genetic Variability in Populations Small populations also lose genetic variability as a result of **genetic drift**, a change in the frequency of an allele in a population occurring simply by chance. Genetic drift was discussed as a process for causing evolutionary change in Chapter 10. However, genetic drift in a small population can have detrimental consequences.

Imagine a population in which the frequency of blood-type allele A is 1%—that is, only one out of every 100 blood-type genes in the population is the A form (we use the symbol I^A). In a population of 20,000 individuals, we calculate the total number of I^A alleles as follows:

$$\text{total number of blood-type alleles in population} =$$
$$\text{total population} \times 2 \text{ alleles/person}$$

$$20{,}000 \times 2 = 40{,}000$$

total number of I^A alleles =
total number of alleles in population $\times$ frequency of allele I^A

$40,000 \times 1\% = 40,000 \times 0.01$

$= 400.$

If a few of the individuals who carry the I^A allele die accidentally before they reproduce, the number of copies of the allele drops slightly in the next generation of 20,000 people, say to 385 out of 40,000 alleles. The chance occurrences that led to this drop result in a new allele frequency:

frequency of I^A alleles in population =
total number of I^A alleles / total number of blood-type alleles in population

$\frac{385}{40,000} = 0.0096$

$= 0.96\%.$

The change in frequency from 1% to 0.96% is the result of genetic drift.

A change in allele frequency of 0.04% is relatively minor. There will still be hundreds of individuals who carry the I^A allele. It is not unlikely that in a subsequent generation, a few individuals carrying allele I^A will have an unusually large number of offspring, thus increasing the allele's frequency in the next generation.

Now imagine the effects of genetic drift on a small population. In a population of only 200 individuals and with an I^A frequency at 1%, only four of the individuals in the population carry the allele. If two of these individuals fail to pass it on, the frequency will drop to 0.5%. Another chance occurrence in the following generation could completely eliminate the two remaining I^A alleles from the population. Thus, genetic drift occurs more rapidly in small populations and is much more likely to result in the complete loss of alleles (Figure 14.18). Typically, the alleles that are lost via genetic drift have little current effect on fitness—after all, if the protein produced by the allele significantly

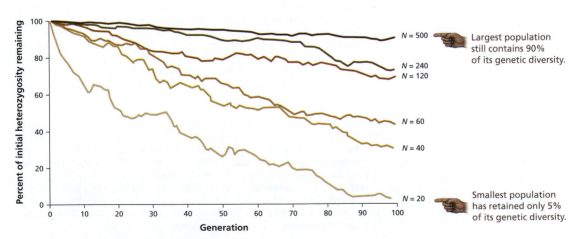

Figure 14.18   Genetic drift affects small populations more than large populations. In this graph, each line represents the average of 25 computer simulations of genetic drift for a given population size. After 100 generations, a population of 500 individuals still contains 90% of its genetic variability. In contrast, a population of 20 individuals has less than 5% of its original variability.

384 Chapter 14 Is Earth Experiencing a Biodiversity Crisis?

increased fitness, natural selection should result in the allele increasing in the population. However, many alleles that appear to be neutral with respect to fitness in one environment may have positive fitness in another environment. For example, there is some evidence that individuals with type A blood are more resistant to cholera and bubonic plague than people with blood-type O or B. Therefore, possessing the I^A allele may be neutral relative to other blood-type alleles in areas where these diseases are rare, but it could be an advantage where the diseases are common.

Populations with low levels of genetic variability have an insecure future for two reasons. First, when alleles are lost, the level of inbreeding depression in a population increases, which means lower reproduction and higher death rates, leading to smaller populations that are susceptible to all of the other problems of small populations. Second, populations with low genetic variability may be at risk of extinction because they cannot respond to changes in the environment. When few alleles are available for any given gene, it is possible that no individuals in a population possess a trait that allows them to survive an environmental challenge. For example, if blood-type A really does protect against some infectious diseases, a population with no individuals carrying the I^A allele could have no survivors after exposure to bubonic plague.

As always, there are some exceptions to the "rule" described above. For example, widespread hunting of northern elephant seals in the 1890s reduced the population to 20 individuals—this probably wiped out much of the genetic variation in the species. However, elephant seal populations have rebounded to include about 150,000 individuals today. Although genetic variability is quite low in this species today, elephant seals continue to thrive, but there are many more examples of the costs of low genetic variability. The Irish potato is perhaps the most dramatic example of this cost.

Potatoes were a staple crop of rural Irish populations until the 1850s—a healthy adult man consumed about 10 potatoes, or 14 pounds, each day. Although the population of Irish potatoes was high, it had remarkably low genetic variability for two reasons. First, potatoes are not native to Ireland (in fact, they originated in South America), meaning the crop was limited to few varieties that were originally imported—and the majority of potatoes grown on the island were of a single variety, called Lumper for its bumpy shape. Second, new potato plants are grown from potatoes produced by the previous year's plants, and thus are genetically identical to their parents. This agricultural practice ensured that all of the potatoes in a given plot had identical alleles for every gene. All of the available evidence indicates that the genetic variability of potatoes grown in Ireland during the nineteenth century was extremely low.

When the organism that causes potato blight arrived in Ireland in September 1845, nearly all of the planted potatoes became infected and rotted in the fields. The few potatoes that had escaped the initial infection were used to plant the following year's crops. Some varieties of potatoes in South America carry alleles that allow them to resist potato blight and escape an infestation unaffected. However, apparently very few or no Irish potatoes carried these alleles, and in 1846 the entire Irish potato crop failed. As a result of this failure and another in 1848, along with harsh policies instituted by the ruling British government in Ireland, nearly 1.5 million Irish peasants died of starvation and disease and another 1 million left home for North America.

Irish potatoes descended from a small group of plants that were missing the allele for blight resistance, so even an enormous population of these plants could not escape the catastrophe caused by this disease. Similarly, since small populations lose genetic variability rapidly via genetic drift, keeping endangered species from declining to very small population levels may be critical for avoiding a similar genetic disaster. This is why preserving adequate numbers of Lost River and shortnose suckers, even at the expense of crop production in the Klamath Basin, is such a high priority if we wish to save the species from extinction.

Fish versus Humans?

Saving the Lost River and shortnose suckers from extinction requires totally protecting the remaining fish and dramatic action to restore the habitat they need for reproduction. These actions cause economic and emotional suffering for humans who make their living in the Klamath Basin. In fact, many of the actions necessary to save endangered species usually result in some immediate problems for people. As the Oregon State University student we quoted in our introduction inquired, what can we do to balance the costs and benefits of preserving endangered species?

The Endangered Species Act contains a provision that allows members of a committee to weigh the relative costs and benefits of actions taken to protect endangered species. This Endangered Species Committee, a group of Cabinet-level political appointees—including the secretaries of Agriculture and the Interior, and the chairman of the Council of Economic Advisors—has been convened a number of times for just this purpose. This so-called "God Squad" decides if they should overrule a federal action meant to save an endangered species to protect the economic benefits of the people involved. Farmers in the Klamath Basin have advocated for a God-Squad ruling on the diversion of water from Upper Klamath Lake, but history suggests that the decision is not likely to be in their favor. The Endangered Species Committee convened four times from 1973 through 2001; however, only once did concern for human needs outweigh the decision to protect a species—and that ruling was subsequently overturned in court.

If the debate in the Klamath Basin follows the pattern set by other ESA controversies, a political decision that causes some economic hardship while ensuring at least the immediate survival of the fish will prevail. Biologists working on the problem agree that the recovery goal for the shortnose and Lost River suckers is high enough to ensure short-term survival (50 years), but it is not high enough to ensure both species' long-term survival (500 years). Their assessment is based on computer models that take into account population fluctuations and predicted environmental changes. The recovery population size is large enough to withstand these threats in the short term but in the long term, continued loss of genetic variability and uncertainty about future environmental change results in the extinction of most of the "recovered" populations in their models. The risk to the long-term survival of the fish helps balance the cost to the farmers of the Klamath Basin. The cost to farmers will be immediately alleviated when they receive federal disaster assistance from fellow American taxpayers to help them adjust to the loss of lake-derived irrigation water. Some farmers will use the money to drill wells and provide groundwater to their thirsty crops, while others will use it to establish new income-producing occupations. The federal government will also purchase farmland from willing sellers in the Basin at fair market prices to protect and restore the fishes' habitat. The Fish and Wildlife Service hopes that this long-term solution will help provide habitat for many more than 500 individuals of both shortnose and Lost River suckers.

The ESA has been a successful tool for bringing species such as the peregrine falcon, bald eagle, and gray wolf back from the brink of extinction, but all of these successes have come with some cost to citizens and taxpayers. If the solution to these and other endangered species controversies is any guide, most Americans will feel that the price of saving the shortnose and Lost River suckers ultimately enriches the United States by restoring our natural heritage (Figure 14.19).

386   **Chapter 14**   Is Earth Experiencing a Biodiversity Crisis?

Figure 14.19   Protecting our natural heritage. Snow geese alight on a pond in the Lower Klamath Wildlife Refuge. A solution to the water crisis on the Klamath must balance the needs of people and wildlife.

CHAPTER REVIEW

Summary

- The loss of biological diversity through species extinction is apparently exceeding historical rates by 50 to 100 times.

- Species–area curves help us predict how many species will become extinct due to human destruction of natural habitat.

- The additional threats of habitat fragmentation, introduction of exotic species, overexploitation, and pollution also contribute to species extinction.

- Species may be important to us as resources, either directly as consumed products or indirectly as organisms used to provide potential medicines or genetic resources.

- Species are members of ecosystems; their loss as mutualists, predators, and competitors may change an ecosystem such that it is less valuable or even harmful to humans.

- Biological diversity may fulfill a human need to experience natural landscapes.

- If habitat protection is focused upon a few well-defined biodiversity hotspots, the rate of extinction can be markedly reduced.

- When species are already endangered, restoring larger populations is critical for preventing extinction.

- Small populations are at higher risk of extinction due to environmental catastrophes.

- Small populations are at risk when individuals have low fitness due to inbreeding and are thus less able to rapidly increase population size.

- Small populations lose genetic variability as a result of genetic drift, the loss of alleles from a population due to chance events, and thus may have a reduced ability to evolve in response to environmental change.

- The political process enables people to craft plans that help endangered species recover from the brink of extinction while minimizing the negative affects of these actions on people.

Key Terms

biological diversity p. 358
competition p. 373
ecosystem p. 371
ecosystem services p. 371
Endangered Species Act
   (ESA) p. 358

exotic species p. 364
extinction p. 358
genetic drift p. 382
genetic variability p. 381
habitat p. 361
habitat destruction p. 362

habitat fragmentation p. 364
inbreeding p. 382
inbreeding depression p. 382
mass extinction p. 366
mutualism p. 371

overexploitation p. 364
parasite p. 372
pollution p. 366
predator p. 372
species–area curve p. 362

Learning the Basics

1. How is the estimate of historical rates of extinction generated? What are the criticisms of these estimates?

2. Describe how habitat fragmentation endangers certain species. Which types of species do you think are most threatened by habitat fragmentation?

3. Compare and contrast the species interactions of mutualism, predation, and competition.

4. Why is genetic drift a more serious problem for small populations than large populations?

5. What is inbreeding depression and why does it occur in small populations?

6. Current rates of species extinction appear to be approximately _____ historical rates of extinction.

   a. equal to

   b. 10 times lower than

   c. 10 times higher than

   d. 50–100 times higher than

   e. 1,000–10,000 times higher than

7. The relationship between the size of a natural habitat and the number of species the habitat supports is described by a

   _____.

   a. habitat fragmentation measure

   b. inbreeding depression matrix

   c. species–area curve

   d. overexploitation scale

   e. ecosystem services cost

8. According to the generalized species–area curve in Figure 14.5b, when 50% of a habitat area is lost, approximately _____ of species originally found there will become extinct.

   a. 90%

   b. 75%

   c. 50%

   d. 10%

   e. 0%

9. Loss of habitat is a primary cause of the extinction and endangerment of biodiversity. Other human-induced causes of extinction and endangerment include _____.

   a. habitat fragmentation

   b. introduction of exotic species

   c. overexploitation

   d. pollution

   e. all of the above

10. A mass extinction _____.

    a. is global in scale

    b. affects many different groups of organisms

    c. is only caused by human activity

    d. a and b are correct

    e. a, b, and c are correct

11. The web of life refers to the _____.

    a. evolutionary relationships among living organisms

    b. connections between species in an ecosystem

    c. complicated nature of genetic variability

    d. flow of information from parent to child

    e. predatory effect of humans on the rest of the natural world

12. According to many scientists, the most effective way to reduce the rate of extinction is to _____.

    a. preserve habitat, especially in highly diverse areas

    b. focus on a single species at a time

    c. eliminate the risk of genetic drift

    d. produce less trash by recycling more

    e. encourage people to rely more on agricultural products and less on wild products

13. The risks faced by small populations include _____.

    a. erosion of genetic variability through genetic drift

    b. decreased fitness of individuals as a result of inbreeding

    c. increased risk of experiencing natural disasters

    d. a and b are correct

    e. a, b, and c are correct

388 Chapter 14 Is Earth Experiencing a Biodiversity Crisis?

14. One advantage of preserving more than one population and more than one location of an endangered species is _____.

   a. lower risk of extinction of the entire species if a catastrophe strikes one location
   b. higher levels of inbreeding in each population
   c. higher rates of genetic drift in each population
   d. lower numbers of heterozygotes in each population
   e. higher rates of habitat fragmentation in the different locations

15. Recovery plans for endangered species crafted under the Endangered Species Act ideally represent a balance between _____.

   a. long-term survival of the species and short-term survival of the species
   b. the costs to people in the species' habitat and the risks for these people's future survival
   c. long-term survival of the species and short-term disruption and hardship of people in the species' habitat
   d. the financial benefits provided by the endangered species and the costs of their protection
   e. saving species and allowing them to go extinct

Analyzing and Applying the Basics

1. Review Figure 14.5a. The graph depicts the relationship between island size and number of amphibian and reptile species found on an island chain in the West Indies. How many species of reptiles and amphibians would you expect to find on an island that is 15,000 square kilometers in area? Imagine that humans colonize this island and dramatically modify 10,000 square kilometers of the natural habitat. What percentage of the species that were originally found on the island would you expect to go extinct?

2. Examine the web of relationships among organisms depicted in Figure 14.9. Which of the following species pairs are likely competitors? In each case, describe what they compete for.

   a. badger, jackrabbit
   b. bison, coyote
   c. rattlesnake, badger
   d. ground squirrel, deer mouse
   e. jackrabbit, prairie dog

   How could you test your hypothesis that these animals are in competition?

3. Widespread use of the pesticide DDT caused a reduction in the populations of many species, including songbirds such as the American robin and raptors such as the bald eagle. Once this effect was recognized, DDT use was banned and these bird populations began to recover. However, only the bald eagle, and not the American robin, was ever considered endangered as a result of DDT use. Use your understanding of the effects of a species' growth rate on its recovery and the problems of small populations to explain why the eagles were more at risk of extinction than the robins.

4. What could have been done with the potato crop in Ireland to reduce the risk of widespread crop failure from potato blight? Today, the number of varieties of crop plants (that is, different genetic strains) in the United States is much lower than it was in the early 1900s. What are the risks of this change to our food supply?

5. The piping plover is a small shorebird that nests on beaches in North America. The plover population in the Great Lakes is endangered and consists of only around 30 breeding pairs. Imagine that you have been charged with developing a recovery plan for the piping plover in the Great Lakes. What sort of information about the bird and the risks to it would help you determine the population goal for this species as well as the method of reaching this goal?

Is Earth Experiencing a Biodiversity Crisis? Questions

VOCABULARY

1. In the opening scenario, Ty Kliewer says, "It appears to me that the people who run the Bureau of Reclamation and the U.S. Fish and Wildlife Service slept through those classes. The solution lacks balance and we've been left out of the equation." Explain what he means.

2. Define *ecosystem*.

COMPREHENSION AND ANALYSIS

3. The species living today constitute _____ percent of all the species that ever existed?

   a. 10 percent   c. 1 percent
   b. 5 percent   d. less than 1 percent

4. Current rates of species extinction appear to be approximately _____ historical rates of extinction.

   a. 10 times less than   c. 10 times higher than
   b. equal to   d. 50 to 100 times higher than

5. What was/is the purpose of the Endangered Species Act?

6. Describe the concept of the web of life.

7. Define *habitat*. What is habitat destruction? What is habitat fragmentation? What usually results from habitat destruction and/or fragmentation?

8. Since we don't know exactly which species are closest to extinction and where they are located, what do Belk and Borden say is the most effective way to prevent the loss of species?

9. List three reasons small populations of a species are at higher risk of extinction.

REFLECT AND CONNECT

10. Many of the actions required to save endangered species result in some immediate problems for people. What advice would you offer the Endangered Species Committee on how to balance the costs and benefits of actions needed to save the Lost River and shortnose suckers from extinction?

The Politics of Biodiversity

JULIE MAJERES

Ms. Majeres is marketing and public affairs coordinator at the Pacific Research Institute in San Francisco where she helps to organize media relations activities and grassroots/community outreach and works on environmental policy. Prior to joining PRI, she worked in information technology for several major companies, including Hewlett-Packard and MCI Worldcom. This article appeared in World and I, *December 2002.*

AN IDEA TO THINK ABOUT:

How many of your family and friends take medicines that have been developed through research on biochemicals found in wild plants and animals? What could have happened if the plant or animal used in that research had become extinct before it was discovered? *As you read,* find out if Ms. Majeres is optimistic or pessimistic about our chances of improving our ability to preserve Earth's biodiversity.

THE POLITICS OF BIODIVERSITY

Julie Majeres

[1]For many of the more than 190,000 women who will be diagnosed with breast cancer this year, the drug Taxol could be what saves their lives. The active ingredient in Taxol, termed one of the "miracle drugs" of the past 10 years, was originally isolated from the Pacific yew tree.

[2]"Thanks in large part to medicines developed in the past decade, cancer deaths are on the decline," said Alan Holmer, president of Pharmaceutical Research and Manufacturers of America (PhRMA). Still, one out of every four Americans will die from cancer, which remains the second leading cause of death by disease.

[3]The No. 1 weapon against cancer today has come to be pharmaceuticals, which are often developed through research on biochemicals found in wild plants and animals. The industry had revenues of $359 billion in 2000, as much as $180 billion of which came from products developed from living things. According to a recent study by the UN Environment Program (UNEP), however, one potentially lifesaving drug is lost every two years as a result of plant extinction.

[4]Thus, biodiversity loss could have a big impact on medicine, bioengineering, and health care in the United States and other Western countries, promising to make it one of the more serious environmental—and ultimately political—issues of this century. Why? Because wealthy nations want access to potentially drug-rich biodiversity, and the greatest diversity of organisms is found in an equatorial belt of relatively poor countries in which poverty, war, and corruption are apparently contributing to the extinction of plant and animal species. A hopeful recent trend is the emergence of a movement by private-sector philanthropic groups to aggressively conserve targeted tropical areas.

[5]The problem of biodiversity loss is illustrated in Brazil, where vast stretches of rain forest teeming with plants and animals, many as yet unknown to science, are being cleared by poverty-stricken homesteaders, who farm for a few years and then abandon the exhausted soil. Another example is Liberia, in which the West African tropical forest has shrunk before an onslaught of illegal lumbering that has financed the barbarous

Revolutionary United Front rebel group in next-door Sierra Leone. In the United States, government and corporations have improved air and water quality and greatly reduced the concentration of toxins in the environment, but efforts to protect endangered species have been less successful.

[6]With the human population rising worldwide, the battle promises to get worse before it gets better. Still, there are reasons for optimism. One is a proposal to spend $30 billion to purchase and protect a slew of rain-forest tracts that contain the world's greatest biodiversity concentrations.

WHY WE SHOULD CARE

[7]Some might reasonably ask why we should worry about the loss of species as a result of human activity, especially when more than 99 percent of all species that have ever come into existence have become extinct. What is the point of trying to prevent what may be inevitable?

[8]Scientists and environmentalists contend that we should care because all species—in addition to their potential medical value—provide scientific, economic, and recreational benefits. Harrison Ford, a longtime Conservation International board member, tells us we should worry because "plants and animals provide food and medicine, clean our air and water, and keep our planet alive."

[9]As a PhRMA report, *The Value of Medicines,* indicates, drugs "help people—and the health care system—avoid disability, surgery, hospitalization, and nursing home care, often decreasing the total cost of caring for an illness." In addition, according to the U.S. Department of Agriculture, finding new plants is crucial for improving farming, because they can be bred with existing domesticated varieties to make crops "more productive, nutritious, durable, or simply better tasting."

[10]Many environmentalists and scientists contend that these benefits provided by Mother Nature are but a few reasons for concern over the loss of biodiversity. It's a concern that will only increase as the human population continues to grow, peaking at an expected 9–10 billion people in the late twenty-first century.

[11]But biologists sharply disagree over the severity of the biodiversity-loss problem. The most extreme warn that 20 percent of all tropical species will go extinct by 2022 and 50 percent by 2042. Others predict a much smaller figure—less than 1 percent by 2050. They expect the extinction rate to decline as human population growth decelerates and biodiversity protection becomes more affordable and successful. However, some scientists predict a sixth mass worldwide extinction, similar to what occurred when the dinosaurs disappeared 65 million years ago.

[12]All previous mass extinctions resulted from climate change or some global catastrophe, such as a huge meteor striking Earth. Although biodiversity has actually increased throughout the planet's history, it would be well for the human community to do all it can to avert a sixth catastrophic event, which would drastically affect the growing human population through species loss. If we are to avert disaster, what exactly should we save, and how do we achieve success with limited capital?

WHAT HAS BEEN DONE

[13]The current approach in the United States and around the world is simply to make lists of threatened animals and plants and then try to protect them. U.S. policy is embodied in the controversial Endangered Species Act (ESA). Unlike the Clean Air and Clean Water Acts, the ESA does little more than maintain lists while establishing modest policy—while provoking hardworking landowners whose private property all too often comes under the statute's regulations.

[14]Of the 1,259 threatened and endangered species listed for the United States, only 13 have been delisted because they recovered, while 7 apparently became extinct. These poor results have added fuel to the fires of accusation and outrage. They stand as evidence of the urgent need to establish better methods of assessing and monitoring biodiversity. They also show that little can be done unless private landowners—environmental stewards of roughly 80 percent of American land—are given proper incentives to protect species.

[15]The rest of the world has fared only slightly better. The global list used by the United Nations is the World Conservation Union's Red List, which has completely assessed the world's mammals and birds but only a fraction of the plants, invertebrates, fish, reptiles, and amphibians. The 2000 Red List reported 11,046 species threatened with extinction. Though this number represents only 0.6 percent of all known species, it includes 24 percent of all mammals and 12 percent of birds.

[16]The Red List goes a step further than the ESA, identifying the ways in which critical habitats are threatened, such as habitat loss, exploitation, or natural disasters. The data show that the primary threat to biodiversity is habitat degradation. This knowledge is spurring a shift in public conservation policy from protection of individual species to conservation of entire ecosystems.

[17]To date, however, there has been no worldwide or even U.S. consensus on which system is best—not even agreement on what scale should be used (global or local). To illustrate the difficulty of whether to use a global or local approach to species conservation, take the example of the grizzly bear. It once roamed as far south as Texas but has become locally extinct in many states; nonetheless, it is far from extinct globally.

[18]The United Nations states in its *Global Environment Outlook-3* report, "Much of the relevant information on the status of species is qualitative or anecdotal, and it is therefore difficult to develop a quantitative overview of global trends." It is precisely this lack of agreement on any verifiable data that makes biodiversity so contentious an issue, because the true costs of species extinction are difficult to estimate in proportion to other important social goals.

PRIVATE SECTOR TO THE RESCUE

[19]The shift in policy toward ecosystem conservation has added weight to some new ideas. In his latest book, *The Future of Life*, biologist Edward Wilson makes a dozen policy recommendations, one of which has received considerable public attention. Wilson asks conservationists to rescue 25 special ecosystems, called "hot spots," that cover 1.4 percent

of the world's land surface and contain the largest concentration of biodiversity.

[20]He estimates the price tag for such an endeavor to be $30 billion. This may seem like chump change compared to the gross world product of about $30 trillion, but measured against the annual budgets of the U.S. Department of the Interior ($13 billion) or UNEP ($3.9 million), the number is formidable. Because governments have done so little on this issue, the private sector has become by comparison quite prominent. Along the way, the task of raising the money and protecting the hot spots has developed some unexpected relationships.

[21]These ties are so strange that ABC's Robert Krulwich expressed surprise that Conservation International (CI) is "run by the cement king of Mexico; the head of British Petroleum, a giant oil company; the chief of a Filipino power conglomerate; a computer billionaire from California," and actor Harrison Ford. The Gordon and Betty Moore Foundation (Gordon Moore is chairman of CI's board and founder of Intel Corporation) gave the organization a quarter of a billion dollars to jump-start the hot spots conservation effort.

[22]CI is not alone in its efforts. The Nature Conservancy (TNC), the revenues of which last year topped all environmental organizations at $546 million, has started a "One Billion Dollar Campaign," the largest private conservation campaign ever undertaken, to conserve 200 spots. In addition, all the top environmental organizations work in some way to conserve biodiversity.

[23]Private conservation efforts have long taken the lead in forging partnerships at the community level and protecting biodiversity on an international scale. These efforts initiated the shift toward ecosystem protection long before governments prompted such policy changes. TNC alone boasts having almost 13 million acres privately protected in the United States and more than 80 million acres abroad.

[24]Private entities are also a step ahead of government in fostering incentives for landowners to protect endangered species and habitat. They are achieving successes that would be too costly for government bureaucracies. The task is accomplished one local problem at a time, working with farmers, ranchers, governments, and industry. Take, for example, the gray wolf compensation program started by Hank Fischer of Defenders of Wildlife.

[25]The number of wolves in Yellowstone National Park and Idaho has grown from zero to more than 400 since 1995. It could not have been accomplished without the $175,000 that Defenders paid ranchers to compensate for livestock losses. Before, ranchers would have implemented the "shoot, shovel, and shut up" method of ridding their land of wolves. As former National Park Service director William Penn Mott states, "It's economics that makes ranchers hate wolves. Pay them for their losses, and the controversy will subside." The program has been so successful that Defenders has started a similar grizzly bear compensation program.

A UNITED EFFORT

[26]Although biodiversity remains a controversial issue, there is reason for hope as corporations, individuals, and organizations are uniting in an effort to transcend conflict.

[27]Can humans and other species continue to coexist and flourish together? Majority opinion tends to be cautiously optimistic. Advances in science and technology are the only means to ensure that humanity will reach its population peak with continued declines in poverty and hunger, steady increases in wealth across the globe, and sustained biodiversity protection.

[28]To protect animal and plant diversity, we need to know how many organisms there actually are on Earth. After all, we can't know if we are succeeding in protecting, say, a particular plant unless we know that it exists and whether it's threatened by human encroachment. So we need to accelerate the cataloging of organisms the world over—especially in the tropical regions, where there is the greatest biodiversity. Today's computer information systems make it possible to map all habitat, ecosystem, and species locations and analyze them as never before.

[29]Once the complete "endangered" list is in place, then scientific expertise and private-sector conservation organizations can come into play, perhaps leading to the day when humankind will "subdue" the Earth by husbanding it wisely and well.

How Many Species Are Going?

[1]Most scientists agree that the actual number of species taxonomically identified on Earth today is 1.75 million. They also agree that this number is woefully imprecise, as they have only tallied the more obvious species, including most of the mammals and birds, while sharply undercounting the numbers of other species, such as many insects and fungi. The disagreement begins over estimates of the planet's total number of species, which range from 3.6 million to 100 million.

[2]Ranging further, the dispute is carried into questions about the background extinction rate—reflected in the number of species lost before humans arrived. These estimates range from 3 species lost for every 10 million species per year (0.00003 percent) to biologist Edward Wilson's overly simple number of 1 extinction for every 1 million species per year (0.0001 percent).

[3]The most consistently strident debate pertains to the estimated number of species dying above the background rate as a result of human activity. The estimates of some biologists and the United Nations range between 0.1 and 1 percent of species lost every 50 years. Wilson comes in at the high end with an estimate of 0.5 percent decline per year for every 1.8 percent of tropical forest habitat lost.

[4]Assuming that his figure is correct on a global scale, that means at least 8,750 species will be lost per year if the actual number of species is 1.75 million. That figure soars to 500,000 per year if the actual number of species is 100 million.

[5]Now let's take a look at some concrete numbers. As reported in *Global Biodiversity Outlook*, published by the United Nations Environment Program, 816 species are believed to have become extinct in the last 500 years. That is about 1.6 species per year—higher than the background rate, but far from 8,750 and even further from 500,000

The Politics of Biodiversity Questions

VOCABULARY

1. Explain what Majeres means when she says, "These poor results have added fuel to the fires of accusation and outrage." (¶14)

2. The United Nation's report states, "Much of the relevant information on the status of species is qualitative or anecdotal, and it is therefore difficult to develop a quantitative overview of global trends." (¶18) Please explain *qualitative, anecdotal,* and *quantitative* and the meaning of the sentence.

COMPREHENSION AND ANALYSIS

For questions 3, 4, and 5, indicate whether the statement is true or false. If the statement is false, rewrite it to make it true.

3. According to a recent study by the UN Environment Program, one potentially lifesaving drug is lost every two years as a result of plant extinction.

4. As human population grows, we should be able to become less concerned with preserving biodiversity.

5. The data from the World Conservation Union shows that the primary threat to biodiversity is habitat degradation.

6. What areas of the world have the greatest diversity of organisms? Give an example of the problems accelerating the loss of biodiversity in those areas?

7. Why does actor Harrison Ford believe we should be concerned about preserving Earth's biodiversity?

8. Majeres says, "Private conservation efforts have long taken the lead in forging partnerships at the community level and protecting biodiversity on an international scale." Describe one example of a private conservation effort.

9. State Majeres's thesis.

REFLECT AND CONNECT

10. Since more than 99 percent of all species that have ever come into existence have become extinct, how do you answer people who ask, "What is the point of trying to prevent what may be inevitable?"

Editorial Cartoon

STEVE GREENBERG

Mr. Greenberg is currently an editorial cartoonist and graphic artist for the Ventura County Star *in Southern California. His cartoons have won numerous awards, and his originals have been exhibited in cities around the world, including the International Museum of Cartoon Art. He has written for Disney comic books and is a sometimes cartoonist/writer contributor to* Mad *magazine. He has a BFA in art from California State University Long Beach and is a member of the Association of American Editorial Cartoonists, the National Cartoonists Society, the Comic Art Professional Society of Los Angeles, and Cartoonists Northwest.*

AN IDEA TO THINK ABOUT

Can you think of any animals that were alive when your great grandparents were young that are now extinct? Can you think of any animals that are nearing extinction today and will be gone in another couple of generations? *As you read,* see what legacy Greenberg is predicting?

Greenberg Cartoon Questions

1. What is the topic/issue?

2. What is Greenberg's point of view?

3. What does Greenberg want the reader to do or think about after reading this cartoon?

A Grizzly Future

TODD WILKINSON

Mr. Wilkinson, who lives at the foot of the Bridger Mountains in Bozeman, Montana, has written about art and nature for a wide variety of international publications. He is the author of ten books, including the critically acclaimed work, Science Under Siege: The Politician's War on Nature and Truth. *He is a regular contributor to* National Parks *magazine, where this article appeared in the Fall of 2002.*

AN IDEA TO THINK ABOUT

Have you ever seen a grizzly bear or a picture of one? The grizzly is often considered a symbol of the American wilderness and one of the nation's most beautiful and imposing creatures. According to the World Wildlife Federation, at one time 50,000 grizzlies ranged throughout the American West. Today, only 800 to 1,000 grizzlies remain, mostly concentrated in Yellowstone National Park and the surrounding national forest lands of Wyoming and Montana. *As you read,* find out what some scientists predict the future holds for the grizzlies.

A GRIZZLY FUTURE

Todd Wilkinson

[1]Early one morning, an 11-year-old grizzly bear mother known as Bear #264 wanders the steamy, geothermal flanks of Roaring Mountain with her two cubs. As Kerry Gunther, Yellowstone National Park's lead grizzly biologist looks on, her main challenge is holding back the eager tourists piling out of their cars and rushing forward for a closer look. "You can't blame people for getting excited about grizzlies," Gunther says. "We're just here to make sure that folks give them enough space to live without being harassed."

[2]That space is critical for the survival of this, the world's most famous bruin population. Even in an ecosystem as vast as Greater Yellowstone, which encompasses thousands of square miles and is home to between 400 and 600 grizzlies, the loss of only a few breeding females can mean the difference between a growing population and one in decline.

[3]The good news is that in recent years, grizzly numbers have been steadily ascending. Today, these big brown bears are recolonizing corners of the ecosystem where they haven't been seen in years—not since hunters, poachers, and ranchers eradicated them in the mid-20th century. Sightings of mothers with cubs, a key barometer of the status of the population, are also up.

[4]Only a quarter-century ago, Yellowstone's grizzlies were on a fast slide toward possible extinction, prompting the federal government in 1975 to declare the population "threatened" under the federal Endangered Species Act (ESA).

[5]"The present stability of Yellowstone grizzlies is a major success that wildlife biologists and bear supporters can take great credit for," says Tony Jewett, National Parks and Conservation Association's (NPCA) senior director of the Northern Rockies region. "However, no one should be lulled into complacency because the threats to the bear are extensive, and we're entering a dangerous period."

[6]The primary immediate danger is political. With bear numbers appearing to grow, Wyoming, Montana, and Idaho are pressing the U.S. Fish and Wildlife Service to remove grizzlies from the Endangered Species Act and turn management authority for them over to the states as early as 2005. Ultimately, the Fish and Wildlife Service will decide whether these states have crafted management plans that convincingly demonstrate they are up to the task.

[7]Anti-grizzly sentiment has boiled up recently among lawmakers in Wyoming and Idaho, at least partly because the Greater Yellowstone region is one of the fastest growing rural areas in the West. Already, Wyoming, Idaho, and Montana are planning to resurrect a trophy hunt of grizzlies. Politicians have also signaled resource extraction industries, like energy developers, that they support increased exploration in bear-occupied habitat. Critics of the Endangered Species Act, including high-ranking administration officials, say the act is too cumbersome for developers.

[8]The states' delisting proposal has met with concern from conservationists who believe the Endangered Species Act has been a pivotal tool in protecting habitat. It has controlled invasive land uses, ranging from oil and gas drilling and livestock grazing to logging and off-road vehicle use on public lands outside Yellowstone where many bears live.

[9]"But for Endangered Species Act protections, the great bear in the Lower 48 would have gone the way of the passenger pigeon by now," says Louisa Willcox, a Montana activist involved with grizzly bear conservation for three decades.

[10]Not long ago, U.S. Geological Survey bear researcher David Mattson and independent biologist Troy Merrill devised a formula for calculating the efficacy of the ESA with regard to bears. Their findings, published in the scientific journal *Conservation Biology*, concluded that, without the ESA, the chances of Yellowstone grizzlies being as abundant today would be about one in a quadrillion.

[11]"The value of the Endangered Species Act is that it changed human behavior," Mattson says. "It made us less lethal in how we as humans interact with bears, and in greater Yellowstone it prevented us from repeating destructive patterns that led to grizzlies being eliminated from most of the West."

[12]Even with those gains, the 1,100 or so grizzlies inhabiting the Lower 48 today represent just 1 percent of historic numbers and occupy less than 2 percent of their original homelands. Although five different clusters live south of Canada, only the isolated concentrations in greater Yellowstone (the southernmost population) and the Northern Continental

Divide Ecosystem (around Glacier National Park and the Bob Marshall Wilderness to the north) hang on in any sizable number. "In some ways, the fact that we still have grizzlies in Yellowstone is a miracle, but it's a miracle that the American people made happen, and they deserve praise for it," says Charles Schwartz, head of the Yellowstone Grizzly Bear Study Team, a division of the U.S. Geological Survey and the most renowned bear research unit in the world.

[13]However, conservation biologists say ensuring the Yellowstone grizzly's genetic viability over the long term requires a population twice as large. It should also be connected to other populations via a navigable corridor of wildlands because isolated populations are more vulnerable to extinction than those with wide distribution.

[14]Under provisions of the ESA, grizzlies have received management priority inside a 9,200-square-mile zone known as the Primary Conservation Area that includes Yellowstone and adjacent federal wilderness in national forests. As the growing bear population has filled up all available habitat in the park, bears have established new territories outside the area. At present, between one-third and one-half of the Yellowstone grizzly population resides outside of the national park, Schwartz notes.

[15]Just as states are pushing to eliminate federal protection, several biological indicators suggest more trouble ahead. Once-abundant natural foods long associated with rising bear numbers in and around Yellowstone are either declining or face an uncertain future. Whitebark pine, whose seeds are a crucial source of nutrition for grizzlies, are rapidly disappearing from the West, although the Yellowstone population is currently doing well. The loss is the result of an outbreak of an arboreal plague called blister rust. Populations of cutthroat trout, another important nutrient-rich food source, have been affected by predation by non-native lake trout. Grizzlies also feast on army cutworm moths, whose future is uncertain in an age of global climate change, and bison, which are threatened by livestock industry proposals to reduce the park's herd to help control brucellosis, which the animals are known to carry.

[16]Although grizzlies could eat earthworms, ants, hornets, and mushrooms, when "you stack them up against what we are likely to lose . . . there is a net loss of nutritional value for bears," says Mattson. Among the possible outcomes: a smaller bear population, smaller cub litter sizes, bears having to roam farther beyond Yellowstone, and bears foraging for these alternative foods in places located near people.

[17]Conservationists say now is the time, before the bear population is removed from federal protection, for grizzly scientists to learn more about the effects of losing key natural foods, expanding human development, and more human-bear conflicts. Yet the Bush administration's recently proposed budget for the Interior Department reflected substantial cuts to science, which could force the cancellation of annual bear counts crucial to assessing the health of the Yellowstone population. NPCA has been among a cadre of vocal groups reminding Congress that scientific research is the guiding light to making informed decisions about imperiled public wildlife.

[18]Beyond science, however, the bear's future may depend on the outcome of a struggle between the public and special interests. After all,

NPCA's Jewett notes, grizzlies belong to the American people, and citizens have taken great pride in showing the world they are willing to make a place for these great bears on public lands.

[19]"Wyoming and Idaho have yet to engage a realistic discussion on this issue, and haven't established the necessary cultural parameters to accept the grizzly as a part of who they are as a state," he says. "It's largely political obstacles and entrenched special interests, because the people of Wyoming want the grizzly there by a huge majority. Unfortunately, it's exactly these powerful interests that control the decision making and politics, and ultimately pose the greatest threat to the grizzly in those states."

[20]Not long ago, as Bear # 264 wandered into the tourist development at Yellowstone's Mammoth Hot Springs, grizzly ranger Kerry Gunther shooed her back into the wild with care. A couple of generations ago, the bear might have been killed by managers or shipped to a zoo. Today, every bear counts, Gunther says. The only proof you need is to drive through Yellowstone when a grizzly appears along the roadside and watch people who have come from around the world to catch a glimpse of one of these rare animals. It's a sight they cherish the rest of their lives.

A Grizzly Future Questions

VOCABULARY

1. Explain what NPCA's Jewett means when he says, ". . .no one should be lulled into complacency." (¶5)

2. In paragraph 8, Wilkinson says, ". . . conservationists believe the Endangered Species Act has been a pivotal tool in protecting [grizzly] habitat." Explain what he means.

COMPREHENSION AND ANALYSIS

3. According to U.S. Geological Survey bear researcher David Mattson, what is the real value of the Endangered Species Act? Please explain.

4. In paragraph 9, Willcox says that without the Endangered Species Act protections, "the great bear in the Lower 48 would have gone the way of the passenger pigeon by now." What are the Lower 48? What does she mean, ". . . would have gone the way of the passenger pigeon"?

5. Does the research of Mattson and Merrill support or contradict Willcox's assertion (that without the Endangered Species Act protections, the great bear in the Lower 48 would have gone the way of the passenger pigeon by now)? Please explain.

6. According to Wilkinson, what is the "primary immediate danger" for the grizzly? Please explain.

7. What is one reason "anti-grizzly sentiment has boiled up recently among lawmakers in Wyoming and Idaho"?

8. Mattson predicts the decrease of their natural, nutrient-rich food sources will greatly affect the grizzlies. List three of his predicted outcomes.

9. Do you categorize the tone and viewpoint of Wilkinson's article to be primarily pro-grizzly, objective (presenting pro- and anti-grizzly views equally), or anti-grizzly? Please explain. What people and publications might present a different viewpoint?

REFLECT AND CONNECT

10. As you discovered in Belk and Borden's text chapter, there is a continual struggle to balance the costs and benefits of actions needed to protect endangered species. What advice would you give to the Endangered Species Committee on how to balance the costs and benefits of actions needed to save grizzly from extinction? Is your advice on how to save the grizzly the same as or different than your advice on how to save the Lost River and shortnose suckers? Please explain your reasoning.

Sustainable Agriculture Depends on Biodiversity

Food production relies on biodiversity. Yet farming can weaken it. Increasing food production will mean finding ways of expanding agriculture without upsetting our planet's biological interdependence.

KEVIN PARRIS

Mr. Parris is with the Organisation for Economic Cooperation and Development (OECD) Agriculture Directorate. Wilfrid Legg, Ken Ash, and Laetitia Reille also contributed to this article, which appeared in the OECD Observer *in August 2002.*

VOCABULARY

motley collection (¶1): group of unrelated objects
emperilled (imperiled) (¶2): put in danger, at risk
feral (¶5): wild, not domesticated

AN IDEA TO THINK ABOUT

In their text chapter, Belk and Borden discuss the *web of life.* What are some ways agriculture fits into that web—some living things that farming depends on and some living things that depend on farming? *As you read,* find out how agriculture depends on biodiversity yet often weakens it.

SUSTAINABLE AGRICULTURE DEPENDS ON BIODIVERSITY

Kevin Parris

[1]Earthworms, bees, Ethiopian wild barley, peregrine falcons, orchids, mangrove swamps and tropical rainforest: on the face of it, these might seem a motley collection, but they are all symbols of both the diversity and the fragility of the linkages between agriculture and nature.

[2]Biodiversity is the term commonly used by scientists and policymakers to capture nature's richness and diversity, but also its biological interdependence. In fact, all species on earth may to a greater or lesser extent be dependent on one another; each species that disappears may weaken the survival chances of another. On a broad scale, tropical forests, for instance, digest carbon dioxide from the atmosphere and produce oxygen. So, without them, our future could be seriously emperilled. And because farming occupies more land than any other human activity in most countries, it should be no surprise to learn that agriculture and biodiversity are interdependent too.

[3]While biodiversity "richness" differs according to climate, terrain, farming practices and so on, farms based on multiple crops and livestock with natural pasture are richer in biodiversity than monocultural farms. But most systems, by seeking to maximise the yield of a limited number of plant and animal species, inevitably weaken and reduce competition from unwanted species.

[4]Farming can affect the worms and soil micro-organisms that play a critical part in maintaining soil fertility, or the bees that provide an important eco-service as pollinators for agricultural crops. The parasitic mite, varroa, in bee populations in North America and Europe has, for example, reduced yields for some crops in affected areas. But in some cases farmers are in a constant battle to control invasive species like weeds and pests that can harm their stock and threaten crop production.

[5]Take the southern maize leaf blight in the early 1970s that led to a 15% fall in US maize yields and an estimated loss to producers and consumers of more than US $2 billion. The crop recovered thanks to help from a Mexican maize variety, but it shows that biological interdependence is not just about preserving wild birds or flowers, but about hard, sustainable, economics. In Australia feral populations of mammals, such as rabbits, dogs and foxes, have inflicted economic losses on farmers through damage to crops, the spread of disease to livestock and the destruction of native wild species.

[6]Farming develops crop species and livestock breeds, as the genetic raw material providing the basis for food production and agricultural raw materials, like cotton. Breeding commercial crop species with wild relatives has also played a vital role in combating pests and diseases. For example, a gene from an Ethiopian wild barley variety has provided protection for the farmed barley crop in North America.

[7]But while farming depends on biodiversity, it is also considered a major contributor to its loss. The intensification of farm production across OECD countries has been associated with the decline in certain wild species, both fauna, such as the peregrine falcon in Europe, and flora such as orchids. In some regions the spread of agriculture has led to the loss of valued wildlife habitats, such as mangrove swamps in the United States and tropical rainforests in Australia. At the same time, farming can enrich society through maintaining and enhancing a variety of wild plant and animal species and habitats, all of which have not just economic or scientific value, but also recreational, even aesthetic advantages, too, such as alpine pastures and water meadows.

[8]One complication is that biodiversity can suffer from invasion of introduced species. These can be beneficial, as in the Mexican maize example, but can be damaging too, whether it be wild mink attacking poultry in Denmark or wire grass spreading in Greece. A US government study estimated economic losses from non-indigenous fauna and flora in the US over the 20th century at US $97 billion. The question of invasion has a new urgency these days, with the development of genetically modified crops and our need to understand their potential effects on local species.

[9]The underlying challenge is how to expand and improve agricultural production—especially given the projected need to increase global food production by over 20% by 2020—while securing our planet's biodiversity. Up to now, the main focus of policy in the area of biodiversity has been to protect and conserve endangered species and habitats, but a number of countries are beginning to move toward a more holistic policy approach by developing national biodiversity plans that include agriculture. These plans often reflect the commitments countries have made under the international Convention on Biological Diversity, agreed in 1992, which aims at the conservation of biodiversity, including genetic resources, wild species and habitats.

[10]Part of the task is to quantify the linkages between human activities and biodiversity. As Harvard University specialist, E. O. Wilson, comments, "New indicators of progress are needed to monitor the economy, wherein the natural world and human well-being, not just economic production, are awarded full measure." In a similar vein the Nobel prize winning economist, Kenneth Arrow, observes, "It would be especially useful to develop better data quantifying the losses of natural capital we currently are experiencing."

[11]This is not an easy task. Few countries have systematic monitoring systems in place that track trends in biodiversity. In addition, there are formidable scientific difficulties in linking changes in biodiversity associated with agriculture to specific policy measures. To overcome some of these deficiencies the OECD is developing a set of agri-biodiversity indicators.

[12]The first step has been to establish a common agri-biodiversity framework or tool that helps simplify the complexity of agri-biodiversity linkages and identifies suitable indicators to track trends. The framework depicts agriculture in terms of a three-tier, hierarchical structure. The first and basic layer refers to farmland itself, to see if it is expanding or contracting or affecting nearby ecosystems, like forests. The extent of crop and livestock production species—the genetic resources of farming—are

also covered in this layer, as is the effect of support species, like earth worms, on soil quality.

[13]The second layer focuses more on structural elements that may affect the ability of a farm to support a varied biodiversity, such as the variability in cropping patterns, field size, and the distribution and extent of uncultivated areas such as ditches, ponds and trees usually associated with a greater biodiversity. This layer also checks for the impact of different farming practices on biodiversity: organic, extensive, intensive and so on.

[14]The final layer assesses the quality of the farming system by finding out how many wild species use it for breeding, feeding and other needs. The richer the biodiversity, the higher the farming quality will be. That means actually counting species, a job for which some governments already earmark budgets.

[15]Perhaps not a spectacular framework, but it should help us answer several key questions. What are the impacts of alternative farming systems, such as organic farming, on sustainable food production capacity? What are the impacts on biodiversity of current farm policies, and in the future, of reducing subsidies to agriculture? And are international interests in biodiversity and trade liberalisation complementary, or in conflict?

[16]Further work will also be necessary to explain and monitor these complex, two-way, dynamic relationships. Still, it is the only way to identify alternative ways to achieve sometimes competing public objectives while not upsetting Earth's fragile biological system.

REFERENCES

OECD (2001), Environmental Indicators for Agriculture Volume 3: Methods and Results, *OECD*, Paris.

OECD (2001), Agri-biodiversity Indicators, Proceedings from an experts' meeting, 5–8 November, 2001, Zurich, Switzerland, available at: *http://www1.oecd.org/agr/biodiversity/ index.htm.*

Sustainable Agriculture Depends on Biodiversity Questions

VOCABULARY

1. Explain and give an example of what Parris means by *biological interdependence*. (¶2) What phrase do text authors Belk and Borden use to describe this concept?

2. A U.S. government study estimates economic losses in the twentieth century from "non-indigenous fauna and flora" to be about $97 billion. (¶8) Define *non-indigenous fauna and flora*.

COMPREHENSION AND ANALYSIS

For questions 3, 4, and 5, indicate whether the statement is true or false. If the statement is false, rewrite it to make it true.

3. In most countries farming occupies more land than any other human activity.

4. Crossbreeding commercial crop species with wild species always creates problems.

5. Although farming depends on biodiversity, it is a major contributor to its loss.

6. Give one example of how farming depends on biodiversity. Give one example of how farming has contributed to the loss of biodiversity.

7. Explain what Parris feels is "the underlying challenge."

8. Parris says the "main focus of policy in the area of biodiversity has been to protect and conserve endangered species and habitats." Describe how that policy is changing is some countries and why.

9. State Parris's thesis.

REFLECT AND CONNECT

10. As with endangered animals, agricultural experts are looking for ways to achieve "competing objectives"—to balance the costs and benefits of actions. What is one way you believe U.S. farmers could expand and improve agricultural production without diminishing Earth's biodiversity?

The Silent Casualties of War

PAUL RICHARDS AND LOUISE SPERLING

Dr. Richards is with the Technology and Agricultural Development Group, Wageningen Agricultural University, The Netherlands. Dr. Sperling is a senior scientist at the International Centre for Tropical Agriculture, The Hague, The Netherlands. This article is from the UNESCO Courier.

AN IDEA TO THINK ABOUT

When you think of war-torn countries like Iraq, Bosnia, Liberia, and Sierra Leone, who and what are some of the "casualties" that come to mind? What are some ways the United States and others have tried to help the survivors? *As you read,* find out how one of our efforts to "help" often causes unintended problems.

THE SILENT CASUALTIES
OF WAR

Paul Richards and Louise Sperling

[1]Moved by the human tragedy of war, we often overlook one of the other major casualties—the environment and, more specifically, agriculture. Globally, the number of armed conflicts has been rising steadily since 1945, reaching an estimated 30 major and 80 to 100 minor conflicts today.

[2]Unlike high-tech wars involving well-armed industrial countries, many of these conflicts are low-intensity insurrections in rural areas, where farmers are the victims. Here, directly or indirectly, local seed systems may come under stress or even collapse. Apart from jeopardizing immediate food needs, the very sustainability of local agriculture can be threatened, with potentially serious consequences for the variety of genetic resources.

[3]Biodiversity is often assessed in terms of the number of existing species. But, at least for crop plants, the genetic variation within species is equally important. Although there are half a million flowering plant species (only half of which have been named and described), 95 percent of human calorie and protein requirements come from a mere 30 of the 7,000 edible plant species that humans plant or collect. And more than half the global energy intake comes from just three major crops—rice, wheat and maize. Genetic variation enables farmers and agricultural scientists to continue to adapt these key crops to changing circumstances—critical for our long-term survival. According to the Food and Agriculture Organization of the United Nations (FAO), there are as many as 100,000 distinct varieties of Asian rice (Oryza sativa) alone.

[4]But what happens to seed systems when they are repeatedly disrupted by war? Farmers use several kinds of seed from different sources. They are mainly varieties taken from their previous harvests, adapted to local conditions and managed over many generations, or seeds from other regions obtained through small local markets or by exchange. Farmers also use varieties developed by research in national or multinational centres and purchased annually through formal supply networks.

VULNERABLE LOCAL SEED VARIETIES

[5]Conflict affects the supply of these kinds of seeds in different ways—and with different long-term consequences for biodiversity. For the formal (non-local) varieties, the supply of seed may dry up in times of conflict, for example because transport routes are disrupted, or because the pesticides and fertilizers needed to grow these varieties have become unavailable. This is what happened in Rwanda, when the formal potato system stopped functioning countrywide around 1991–1992—although direct combat only spread two years later.

[6]Usually, when peace returns, these formal varieties become available once again and there are few new varietal concerns. The war in Bosnia caused a breakdown in the supply of crops. But it now appears that there were relatively few adverse genetic consequences. This is because farmers were using registered varieties supplied through formal channels. Registered seeds are likely to be backed up in collections in a number of countries. A multinational seed business caught in a war zone simply withdraws for the time being and continues its business elsewhere, with its seed collections intact.

[7]More vulnerable in the long term are the local varieties. These may be ancient varieties, often unrecorded and at the heart of complex social interactions. Local or farmer-managed seed systems tend to be decentralized and small scale. The seeds can be obtained from small open markets, or as the currency of gift-giving, loans, and exchange among people with firm social bonds.

[8]In many African countries, up to 90 percent of the seeds planted in any normal year comes from informal sources. Even where purchase (for example, from local merchants) is an important part of an informal seed system, it is rarely backed up by the kind of specialist seed research facilities found in more developed economies. In war-affected Sierra Leone, for example, a recent study showed that the informal system was responsible in normal years for about 80 per cent of seed supply for the main staple, rice. Most informal transactions were farmer-to-farmer, in the form of gifts, purchases, and loans. In Rwanda, Burundi and Zaire, before their respective wars, over 95 percent of bean seeds, their main protein source, came from informal seed systems.

[9]When rural communities are forced to flee, the fine web of mutual seed support is wrecked. Refugee farmers no longer have the means to repay at harvest the seeds they borrowed from fellow-farmers in the planting season, so the system breaks down. Without the security of peace, rural communities cannot hold the markets to buy and sell seed. And farmers no longer know that what they plant can indeed be harvested in four, nine or 18 months' time (the cycles of beans, potatoes and cassava, respectively). Seed may be totally lacking, or farmers may be unable to access it, because social ties are ruptured, or because they are just too poor. In some cases, farmers under fire may have stored appropriate seed, but simply cannot plant it. Alternatively, seed may be available, but of poor quality.

[10]Genetic loss, then, is most likely when conflict is concentrated in remote rural areas, where it is fairly widespread geographically, and when it lasts for several years in succession. This was the case in Angola and Mozambique, where isolated and vulnerable rural populations lost many planting seasons. War affected fourteen African countries during the 1990s, with rural populations most heavily dependent on locally adapted seeds being the major casualties.

[11]Some countries are especially rich in local varieties and the wild relatives of crop species. The breakdown of local seed systems in these countries can cause irreversible damage to the global genetic resources of food crops. For example, major wars in Guinea Bissau, Liberia and Sierra Leone, along with lesser insurrections in Casamance (Senegal) and Guinea have affected every country in the West African coastal zone of

ancient rice agriculture. This region is a key centre for genetic diversity in African rice (Oryza glaberrima), which, as a result of recent technological advances, can now be cross-bred with Asian rice, one of the world's key food crops. It will be of global significance if this under-collected and little-studied African crop is a casualty of the regional warfare and massive displacement of rural civilians.

¹²So what can be done to offset this kind of genetic disaster? During the Tigrean conflicts in the northern highlands of Ethiopia, that lasted on and off for two decades, community elders organized emergency seed banks of maize, sorghum, wheat, barley, finger millet, and teff—an annual grass grown for its grain. This was mostly to improve the deteriorating seed quality, rather than because of short supply. In Ethiopia, a country with rich local varieties, plant scientists have invested in crop genetic resource conservation and in understanding the impact of war and drought on seed supply.

¹³Ironically, humanitarian agencies often make the situation worse, by responding to seed system breakdown by supplying farmers with seed from outside the country: Giving "seed and tools" is the standard second relief response after food. Seed aid is usually "exotic," not tested or suited to local conditions and is alien to the cultural management practices of farmers.

¹⁴In some countries there are national efforts to restore crop diversity lost due to war. International Agricultural Research Centres have been restoring bean and sorghum genetic material to gene banks in war-torn Rwanda and Burundi, local varieties of barley, durum wheat and bread wheat to Eritrea and rice seeds to institutes in the trouble-spots of Liberia and Guinea Bissau—and even Cambodia. All these countries lost their centralized gene bank stocks, although it is not known if there was any loss of diversity at farm level.

¹⁵To reinforce this kind of work, some regions, such as the West African zone of ancient rice cultivation, will need specialist missions to rescue and conserve endangered local varieties. This will mean gathering information on cultural and farming practices, too. War threatens not only seeds but also the knowledge that farming populations possess about how, where, and when to use locally adapted local varieties.

¹⁶It is difficult to estimate the true scale of crop biodiversity loss in war-torn regions. For several decades, small farmers have given oral accounts of significant variety loss. It is only now, with the development of biotechnologies, that plant scientists have the tools to measure genetic losses precisely.

The Silent Casualties of War Questions

VOCABULARY

1. Richards and Sperling say, "Ironically, humanitarian agencies often make the situation worse." (¶13) What is ironic about the situation?

2. In paragraph 9, Richards and Sperling say, "When rural communities are forced to flee, the fine web of mutual seed support is wrecked." Explain what they mean.

COMPREHENSION AND ANALYSIS

3. Ninety-five percent of human calorie and protein requirements come from _____ of the 7,000 edible plant species that humans plant or collect.

a.	1,000	**c.**	50
b.	300	**d.**	30

4. More than half the human calorie and protein intake comes from what three major crops?

5. Why is the genetic variation within species important to farmers and agricultural scientists?

6. Describe the three primary seed systems farmers use—the kinds of seeds farmers use and their sources. Where do farmers in the areas continually disrupted by war, like many African countries, most often get their seeds?

7. Why are local seed varieties obtained through local or farmer-managed seed systems most vulnerable in the long term? Why is that a problem?

8. How does giving "seed and tools" to farmers in war-torn countries often make the situation worse?

9. All of the countries mentioned in this article are very distant from the United States. Why should what happens to agriculture in those countries be of concern to us?

REFLECT AND CONNECT

10. Since giving "seed and tools" is not always a helpful response, how would you suggest humanitarian groups help to restore crops?

LOG ON TO THE WEB

The Internet offers a large variety of resources on topics related to biodiversity. For this Web exercise,

1. Select a topic/issue related to biodiversity that you would like to know more about, such as the Endangered Species Act, grizzly populations, habitat destruction and fragmentation, mass extinction, mutualism, pollution, global warming, or sustainable agriculture.

2. Write two questions about the topic that you want to answer. For example, if your topic is grizzly populations your questions might be, What are the primary causes of grizzly deaths today? What is happening in the push to delist the grizzly from the ESA? or, What seem to be the major "costs" of protecting the grizzly?

3. Use your favorite search engine to locate at least four Web sites with information about your topic/issue (visit more sites if you haven't yet found the answers to your questions). For each site, write down the complete URL and the sponsor or creator of the site.

4. Write down the answers to your two questions and note which Web sites were most useful in your research.

REFLECT AND CONNECT

A. There are costs and benefits of protecting any endangered species. At this time, do you think all species are worth saving, regardless of the costs? If not, what criteria would you use to determine whether or not a species should be saved?

B. One of the most controversial of all endangered species recovery programs is that of the gray wolf. The wolf was once common over much of North America and northern Mexico, but was almost completely eliminated from the continental United States by a systematic extermination program in the nineteenth and early twentieth centuries because the wolf directly competes with humans for prey, including wild deer and domestic animals such as cattle, sheep, and turkeys. The gray wolf came under the protection of the Endangered Species Act in 1974 and has since expanded in numbers and range in several regions of the country. (For example, as Majeres pointed out, the number of wolves in Yellowstone National Park and Idaho has grown from zero to more than 400 since 1995.) As the number of wolves increases and they increasingly prey on livestock and other domestic animals, there is increased debate over whether the wolf should be protected by the ESA.

Do you think wolves should be allowed to recolonize areas where they will come into contact with humans, or are the costs of returning the wolf to its former range too great relative to its benefits? Explain your reasoning.

C. Is earth experiencing a biodiversity crisis? Please explain your reasoning.

FURTHER READING

Bill McKibben, *Hope, Human and Wild: True Stories of Living Lightly on the Earth* (Ruminator Books, 1997).

Gaylord Nelson, Susan Campbell, Robert F. Kennedy, Jr., and Paul Wozniak, *Beyond Earth Day: Fulfilling the Promise* (University of Wisconsin Press, 2002).

J. F. Rischard, *High Noon: Twenty Global Problems, Twenty Years to Solve Them* (Basic Books, 2002).

Ian Swingland (Editor), *Capturing Carbon and Conserving Biodiversity: The Market Approach* (Earthscan Publications, Ltd., 2003).

Edward Osborne Wilson, *The Future of Life* (Knopf, 2002).

Appendices

STRATEGIES FOR TAKING CONTROL OF YOUR TIME

USING TEXTBOOK DESIGN CLUES

STRATEGIES FOR TAKING CONTROL OF YOUR TIME

Spending time, like spending money, is a personal matter. Unlike money, however, you can't get a "time raise" or "save some hours" for a busy day. We all have to live on 168 hours each week. Successful students—like other successful people—budget time according to their priorities to ensure they spend it effectively.

IDENTIFY YOUR GOALS AND PRIORITIES

The first step in learning to manage your time and taking control of your life is to identify your goals and priorities. For example, is learning—getting an education—high on your priority list? How about your current job? Your family?

ANALYZE HOW YOU USE YOUR TIME

For the next seven days, keep a detailed log of everything you do. Account for all activities: class attendance, study, work, eating, commuting, recreation, exercise, sleep, and so on. Also note when (during what hours) you do these activities.

During the week, how much time did you spend

in classes?	_____ hours
studying for classes?	_____ hours
working?	_____ hours
meeting the needs of others?	_____ hours
exercising?	_____ hours
relaxing?	_____ hours
sleeping?	_____ hours
_____?	_____ hours
_____?	_____ hours

MATCH HOW YOU'RE USING TIME WITH YOUR PRIORITIES

No one can judge your use of time as efficient or inefficient—not even you—unless you do it in relation to your priorities. In addition to looking at how much time you spend on each activity, consider if you are spending quality time on your priorities. For example, if learning is high on your priority list, do you study during your prime energy hours or only after everything else is done for the day?

DEVELOP A PLAN TO SPEND QUALITY TIME ON YOUR PRIORITIES

If you found some time blocks that are not in line with what you want to be doing to reach your goals, begin to systematically change your life by taking control of your time. Start by building a realistic schedule that gives time to the activities that fit with your priorities and will help you reach your goals. And, work at sticking to your time schedule. Some flexibility is necessary, of course, to take care of unexpected demands. But, if you spend too much time on nonpriority tasks, you will not meet your goals.

LIVE SMART

- *Keep a "Things To Do" list with the items in priority order.* Most people tend to do low-ranking, little things first and never get around to the important tasks.
- *Eliminate tasks when possible.* Carefully evaluate each task you do and, when possible, don't spend valuable hours on time-consuming routine tasks like washing the car weekly or dusting.
- *Delegate or negotiate tasks.* Ask yourself, "Who else can do this task?" (maybe not as well as you would do it, but acceptably). Ask, "What tasks can I trade or share with someone?" Learn to ask for help.
- *Consolidate tasks.* Whenever possible, do more than one thing at a time—except thinking! If you're running errands, make your trip count. If you're going to the library to prepare your biology report, also work on your research paper and look up that reference you need for literature.
- *Evaluate your habits.* Why do you do routine tasks in a certain way? Is your way the most efficient way to accomplish these tasks? Could you save time by changing your routine actions? Could getting up fifteen minutes earlier be helpful?
- *Be prepared to lower your standards.* Given the heavy demands on your time, it is doubtful that everything you do can be perfect. Based on your priorities, decide which tasks you want to be "A" quality and which can be "B" quality.
- *Learn to say no.* We rarely have time to do everything we want to do. Learn to do those things that move you toward your goals and say no to those that do not.
- *Be flexible, but remain in control.* Expect interruptions, as they are bound to occur. If you are doing things in priority order—not leaving big things to the last—you and your schedule will easily survive.

STUDY SMART

- *Use your prime working times wisely.* There really are "morning people" and "night owls." Determine the time of day when you're at your best and use those hours wisely.

- *Schedule time for the many tasks of studying and use it.* The best way to ensure that you'll have enough study time to meet your goals in each course is to plan for it. Schedule time to read and review material in preparation for class; complete homework; and regularly review class notes, text assignments, and supplementary material.

- *Understand assignments and write them down.* Keep all assignments in one place to avoid forgetting something.

- *Break major assignments down into manageable chunks.* We often avoid big projects because we have limited time or we don't know where to begin. Break major projects into small pieces and tackle them one at a time.

- *Begin each study session with goal setting.* Predict specifically what you want to accomplish and then work to meet your goals.

- *Be an active learner.* Vary your activities within a study session—read, write, recite, research—to stay interested and alert. Try studying for 45 minutes and taking a 10-minute exercise break.

- *Use all of your available time.* Even small bits of time—for example, while waiting for the dentist—can be put to use. Don't be caught without something to read or study.

USING TEXTBOOK DESIGN CLUES

The various styles of type and design used in a textbook aren't just decorations to make it visually appealing. These devices are selected to give the reader clues about the relative importance of the ideas. Using these clues can help you accurately and efficiently gather information.

TITLES AND HEADINGS

Although every textbook has its own way of displaying information, within a text there is a consistent visual pattern. This means you can use the size, style and placement of the titles and headings to identify different levels of information. Typical techniques include:

- *using different type fonts* —such as using a sans serif type font for one level of heading and a serif type font for another level;
- *varying the sizes of type* —such as using a large type size for the most important or broadest idea (such as the chapter title) and using smaller type sizes as headings become more specific;
- *using different type styles* —such as color, bold, italic, all capital letters, and underlining;
- *varying the amount of indentation from the margin* —such as putting the title of a chapter close to the left margin and using more indentation (white space) from the left margin as a heading becomes more specific, similar to an outlining technique.

Analyze the levels of headings in this example from *Government by the People* by Burns, Peltason, Cronin, Magleby, O'Brien, and Light. What is the organization scheme in your textbooks?

WHAT PARTIES DO FOR DEMOCRACY
Party Functions

Political parties are organizations that seek political power by electing people to office so that their positions and philosophy become public policy. American political parties serve a variety of political and social functions, some obvious and some not so obvious. They perform some functions well and others not so well, and how they perform them differs from place to place and time to time.

Organize the Competition One of the most important functions of parties is to organize the competition by designating candidates to run under their label. For some races, parties recruit and nominate candidates for office; they register and activate voters; and they help candidates by training them, raising money for them, providing them with research and voter lists, and enlisting volunteers to work for them. For more visible contests, especially ones where there is a real chance of winning multiple candidates often compete with each other for the nomination, often without party efforts to recruit them. Recently, campaign consultants rather than party officials have taken over some of these responsibilities; we explore this topic at some length in Chapter 10^3.

BODY TEXT

Authors use different type styles within paragraphs to direct you to important words and ideas. And, although putting words in boldface or italic type or underlining them are the most common styles used for emphasis, authors can use a vast array of clues. So again, your job is to analyze each of your textbooks, discover the patterns, and use those clues to help you understand the information you need.

Consider how Macionis's use of bold and italic type point out important terms and their definitions in this example from *Sociology,* ninth edition.

> Once measurements are made, investigators can pursue the real payoff; seeing how variables are related. The scientific ideal is **cause and effect,** *a relationship in which change in one variable causes change in another.* Cause-and-effect relationships occur around us every day, as when studying for an exam results in a high grade. *The variable that causes the change* (in this case, studying) is called the **independent variable.** *The variable that changes* (the exam grade) is called the **dependent variable.** In other words, the value of one variable depends on the value of another. Why is linking variables in terms of cause and effect important? Because this kind of relationship allows us to *predict* how one pattern of behavior will produce another.

WHITE SPACE

White space on a page isn't accidental. White space is built into the design for a purpose such as directing the reader's eye to information or providing a rest stop. For example, authors can use white space to help a reader identify a new paragraph by indenting the first line of a paragraph or by leaving extra space between each paragraph.

Analyze how the authors of your texts use white space.

GRAPHIC ELEMENTS

Authors can also use a variety of graphic elements such as boxes, bullets, and color-tinted boxes as cues to a specific kind or level of information. Often, they combine several design elements to more clearly communicate their message. See how Griffin and Ebert combine white space, color bullets, and italic type to cue important information in this example from *Business,* eleventh edition.

> The first step in developing the structure of any business, large or small, involves two activities:
>
> ■ *Specialization:* determining who will do what
> ■ *Departmentalization:* determining how people performing certain tasks can best be grouped together
>
> These two activities are the building blocks of all business organizations.[3]

OTHER FACTORS

Line length: Long lines of type are difficult to follow and may cause you to lose your place in the text. Although you cannot physically change the length of the lines of type in the books you read, you can reduce problems. To keep your place and encourage your eyes to move ahead, try sliding an index card over the line you have just finished.

Capital letters: Most people read by the shapes of words, not letter by letter. We use ascenders (the portions of letters that extend above a line of print in letters like b, d, t, and h) and descenders (the portions of letters that extend below a line of print in letters like y, p, g, and j) to help us quickly identify the shape of a word. Text printed in all capital letters—with no ascenders or descenders—forms uniform blockish shapes that make word identification difficult. You need to slow down when you have to read text in all capitals.

GLOSSARY

advocate a supporter or defender of a particular position or point of view; advocates attempt to prove their view or position is right

analyze examine a topic by separating it into its basic parts or elements; separate the parts—thesis and evidence—and see how they fit together

annotate, annotation an active strategy for interacting with and marking readings; a way to highlight and organize main ideas and details by writing brief, useful information in the margins

antonym a word that means the opposite of another word

argument, argumentation the descriptive term for an essay or article that has the intent of persuading readers to believe or act in a certain way; an argument consists of a writer's thesis (also called position, proposition, or conclusion) and the reasons (also called premises; the emotional appeals and logical evidence) used to support it

assumption an idea we believe to be true; something we take for granted

authority an individual cited as an expert; one with special skill, knowledge, or mastery of a particular subject

bias, biases a personal and sometimes unreasoned judgment; prejudice

caption a brief description of the contents of a graphic

cause and effect reasoning that assumes one event, action, or condition can bring about another

clarify make clear; explain

cliché an expression or idea that has been so overused it no longer has any meaning

column vertical lines of data in a table

compare; comparison looking at two or more objects, places, events, people, or ideas to see how they are similar; the similarities or degree of similarity between things of comparable nature

comprehension monitoring strategies tactics to make certain that the reader's understanding is satisfactory for his or her purpose

connotation; connotative the implied meaning of a word triggered by the feelings and emotions it creates

context how words are used with the other words in a sentence and surrounding sentences—how they are used in conjunction with other words; the meaning of words taken from their surrounding words or phrases

context clue information an author provides within the sentence or paragraph to help the reader understand important words

contrast looking at two or more objects, places, events, people, or ideas to see how they are different; the differences or degree of difference between things of comparable nature

controlling thought what the author wants the reader to know or understand about the topic; the most important point the author makes about that topic

credibility the reader's belief that the writer is trustworthy

critical reader one who comprehends, questions, clarifies, and analyzes in order to reach objective, reasoned judgments; being willing and able to objectively evaluate what you read; reaching reasoned judgments on the basis of the evidence presented rather than accepting or rejecting information based on emotion and anecdote

denotation; denotative a word's literal, dictionary meaning

description; descriptive text that paints a picture using words

diagram a general term that refers to any type of drawing an author uses to help the reader understand ideas, objects, plans, processes, or sequences

directly stated main idea the topic and controlling thought of a paragraph stated in a sentence; often called a topic sentence

Do the second phase of the Plan→Do→Review cycle; requires active physical and mental involvement

evidence any information a writer uses, such as details, facts, examples, opinions, and reasoned judgments, to support and develop a thesis or argument

expert an authority, a specialist; experts work to uncover the accuracy and exactness of a view or position

exposition; expository writing that explains, sets forth, or makes clear facts, events, or ideas; a more or less neutral reporting of information

fact objective information that can be verified by observation or experimentation; a fact can change over time as new discoveries are made; also called empirical evidence, because the interpretation does not change because of the view of the interpreter

fallacy   an error in reasoning because of faulty evidence or an incorrect inference

figurative language   words used in an imaginative way to help the reader comprehend the message more clearly by forming a mental image of what an author is talking about; figurative expressions often compare something the author thinks the reader knows about to what he or she wants the reader to understand

flowchart   a type of diagram that uses boxes, rectangles, diamonds, or circles with connecting lines or arrows to show the step-by-step procedure of a complicated process

generalize   form a sensible, rational inference based on a limited sample; reach a conclusion about what is not known or has not happened on the basis of what is known or has happened

graph   a type of graphic that uses bars, lines, or pictures of objects to show the relationships between or among quantities

graphic   any visual an author uses to highlight, clarify, or illustrate (often through an example), summarize, or add to the text information

graphic organizer   a graphic, such as an informal outline or information map, that you create to show the basic structure of a selection

implied main idea   when the author doesn't directly state the main idea and leaves it up to the reader to piece together the information from all the sentences and infer the main idea

imply   often confused with *infer*, the two words are not interchangeable; imply means to suggest or hint; infer means to reach a reasoned conclusion based on the information given; writers imply, readers infer

infer   arrive at a logical conclusion from information

inference   a sensible, reasoned conclusion about what we do not know based on the information we do know; some people call an inference an educated guess

information map   a type of graphic organizer for main ideas and details that uses different sized boxes or circles and different sized writing to create a picture of the relationships among the ideas

irrelevant information   information that is interesting, and sometimes important, but does not support or develop the main idea is called *irrelevant* to the paragraph

irony; ironic   text that states the opposite of what the author really means

jargon   a unique language developed and understood by a specific group, such as football fans or computer users; when used outside its specific group, jargon is usually meaningless or confusing

key; legend   a reference center on a graphic that defines codes being used

literal meaning   dictionary definition

main idea   the umbrella idea that unifies, or holds together, all the sentences of one paragraph; the primary thought the writer wants you to understand in a paragraph

major supporting detail   a specific piece of information that directly supports and explains the main idea

map   a diagram that depicts all or part of the earth's three-dimensional surface on a two-dimensional flat surface

metaphor   a type of figurative language that uses an implied comparison

minor supporting detail   a very specific piece of information that supports and explains a major detail

multiparagraph selection   a group of related paragraphs—such as an essay or text chapter—each with a main idea that supports and explains one thesis, or overall main idea

narration; narrative   text that tells a story

objectively analyze   impartial examination of the author's ideas and information separate from the reader's personal opinions and biases

opinion   a subjective statement that expresses a person's thoughts, feelings, beliefs, and attitudes, which cannot be proved true or false; an opinion is not right or wrong, or good or bad, but depending on the amount and type of evidence the author considered before forming the opinion, it can be valid or invalid.

outline   a type of graphic organizer that uses different amounts of indentation to create a picture of the relationships among the ideas

paragraph   a group of sentences that fit together to support and explain one main idea

paraphrase   an active strategy that requires you to think about and understand what the author is saying and express it in your own words; a *substantially* different sentence structure and vocabulary than the original—one that is typical of your writing style; paraphrase when you need a total, accurate restatement of short segments, such as a thesis or main idea

persuasion; persuasive   text that influences the reader by engaging his or her emotions or by presenting logical arguments to make the reader believe or feel a certain way or take a particular action

pie chart; circle graph   a type of graphic that illustrates the ratio of the values of a category to the total; the whole pie or circle represents 100 percent, and various segments, or pieces of the pie, show relative magnitude or frequencies

Plan   the first phase of a Plan→Do→Review cycle; developing a plan is based on a reading assignment's two critical factors: (1) the purpose for reading the assignment, and (2) how difficult the material is for the reader

Plan→Do→Review cycle   an approach that encourages the reader to become more successful at reading for learning; the reader plans before beginning, does the reading actively, reviews what has been read, and continues to plan, do, and review until comprehension goals are met

planning strategies   techniques such as setting a purpose, previewing, activating your prior knowledge, and estimating the difficulty level of the material that help you become an active reader and give you a head start on good comprehension; they set you up to be successful

point of view   fundamental attitude, position, or opinion about a topic or issue

prereading strategies   tactics that prime the reader's brain and give him or her a head start on good comprehension

prefix   a word part added to the beginning of a root word to change its meaning

prejudice   a preconceived judgment or opinion; a negative opinion that is formed without evidence or before sufficient knowledge is gathered

premise   the parts of an argument that support and develop the thesis

preview   to survey, or examine, reading material in an orderly way *before* you begin to read; gives you an overall picture of what you are going to read and gives you the chance to make connections between what you know and what you are going to read

prior knowledge   what you know about a topic before you begin reading about it; you should take time to think about a subject before you begin reading about it

prose   writing other than poetry

purpose for reading   specific reasons for reading based on what you need to know when you finish reading

purpose for writing   an author's reason for writing

reasoned judgment   thoughtful, coherent evaluations that informed individuals make from the available evidence; my label for critical thinkers' opinions

relevant   has a clear supportive connection to the thesis

reliable   can be counted on to give a fair analysis of the issue; does not respond to undue influence from others; trustworthy and accurate

Review   the third phase of the Plan→Do→Review cycle; information is put into perspective and the reader begins working to remember it; without good review, spaced over time, the reader will probably forget as much as 80 percent of what was read

root word   the basic part of a word

row   horizontal lines of data in a table

satire; sarcasm   an ironic tone that uses ridicule, mockery, exaggeration, and understatement to poke fun at people and deride foolish or dishonest human behaviors

scale   a map element that shows the relationship between a length measured on a map and the corresponding distance on the ground

sentence   the basic unit of writing authors use to express their ideas

signal words   words or phrases or punctuation that point out a particular type of information or move you in a specific direction of thought; also called directional words or transitions

simile   a type of figurative language that makes direct comparisons using the words *like* or *as*

stance   point of view; a writer's or reader's position or opinion on a topic or issue

strategy   a tool or technique you consciously select in order to complete a task accurately and efficiently; strategies are means to an end

structural organizers   parts of an article or essay, such as titles and subtitles, that you read during preview to give you an overview of the content

subjective   based on one's personal perceptions

suffix   a word part added to the end of a root word to change its meaning or the way it can be used in a sentence

summary; summarize   a condensed version of the original; it begins with a paraphrase of the thesis and includes the main ideas in the same order and with the same emphasis as the original; summarize when you need the essence or gist of long segments, such as a complete essay

table   a graphic that provides several pieces of specific data, often numbers or statistics, arranged systematically in rows and columns; the information often compares qualities or quantities or shows how things change over time

text structures/rhetorical patterns   the organization an author uses to develop and support the thesis or main ideas; the structure he or she gives the information; six common methods of organizational structure are examples, comparison and/or contrast, cause and effect, sequence or process, classification, and definition; authors often combine two structures

thesis   the primary idea of a multiparagraph selection that combines the main ideas of all the paragraphs; the frame that holds the paragraphs of the essay or chapter together

tone   the emotional feeling or attitude created with words; the writer's attitude toward the reader and the topic determine the tone

topic   the who or what the author is writing about; the one general subject the whole paragraph is about

transition sentence   connects what you have just read with what you are about to read

transition words   see signal words

valid   reasoning and inferences that are relevant, meaningful, and logically correct

Venn diagram   a diagram that uses circles to help readers view interrelated and independent aspects of concepts; similar points appear in the areas where the circles overlap, and dissimilar points appear in the areas of the circles outside the overlap

word analysis   defining a word by defining its root and any prefixes and/or suffixes

INDEX